RETIREMENT PLACES RATED®

What You Need to Know to Plan the Retirement You Deserve

6th Edition

by
DAVID SAVAGEAU

Wiley Publishing, Inc.

Acknowledgments

This revision of *Retirement Places Rated* couldn't have begun without the criticisms of hundreds of readers. Nor would the book have been finished minus the generous advice from experts. Their affiliations and data are cited throughout.

Thanks to the people at **Wiley Publishing, Inc.,** especially to redoubtable nit-picking editors, **Michael Kelly, Doreen Russo, Donna Wright,** and **Kathleen Warnock.** Thanks also to capable researchers **Jon Dembling, Fred Evers,** and **Karyl Savageau;** to **Calvin Beale,** Washington, D.C.; **Alan Borne,** American Automobile Association; **Paul Gourhan,** PM Workshop, Inc.; **Don Larson,** Mapping Specialists, Ltd.; and **Bob Fulton** at Open Cellular.

Finally, special thanks to **Woods & Poole Economics, Inc.,** for population, income, and employment forecasts. The use of this information and the conclusions drawn from it are solely the author's responsibilities.

Publisher's Note

Published by:

Wiley Publishing, Inc.

111 River St.

Hoboken, NJ 07030-5774

ISBN 0-7645-4438-1

Interior design by Madhouse Studios and contributed to by Marie Kristine Parial-Leonardo
Icons designed by Rashell Smith

Editors: Michael Kelly and Kathleen Warnock
Production Editor: Donna Wright
Copy Editor: Doreen Russo
Cartographer: John Decamillis
Photo Editor: Richard Fox
Production by Wiley Indianapolis Composition Services

For information on our other products and services or to obtain technical support, please contact our Customer Care Department within the U.S. at 800/762-2974, outside the U.S. at 317/572-3993 or fax 317/572-4002.

Wiley also publishes its books in a variety of electronic formats. Some content that appears in print may not be available in electronic formats.

Manufactured in the United States of America

5 4 3 2 1

Contents

About the Author

David Savageau is the author of the best-selling *Places Rated Almanac.* Since 1982, he has traveled throughout the country visiting locations that attract older adults. He lives in Washington, D.C., and is a featured speaker at the U.S. Department of State's quarterly seminars on retirement.

PREFACE

Readers will see differences in the final rankings for retirement places profiled in both the fifth edition and in this one. There are four reasons for this:

New Geography. Nineteen new places have been introduced in this edition, and three locations profiled previously have been dropped.

The Interval Effect. Changes in geography necessarily change the ranks of the 184 retirement places common to both editions. The Outer Banks in North Carolina's Dare County, for example, has nearly the same climate rate as it had in the previous edition, yet its rank in this factor moved up from 110 to 103. The spot isn't getting more pleasant; it's just that a number of newly profiled places with slightly worse climatological figures have moved it to a higher ranking.

Time Series Data. Local population figures (for deriving the number of physicians per capita access to public golf courses, for example), prices (for gauging living costs), and personal incomes (for measuring how far Social Security benefits will stretch in a given place) have increased at varying rates since the previous edition was published.

New Scoring Methods. All the chapters show changes—some slight, others major—in scoring methods. Scores continue to be expressed in percentiles where 50 is average, 100 best, and 0 worst.

As a result of these changes, the rankings better reflect what each retirement place has to offer older adults.

America's Top 30 Retirement Places

RANK	RETIREMENT PLACE	MEAN SCORE
1.	Florence, OR	70.1
2.	Scottsdale, AZ	69.6
3.	Charleston, SC	69.3
4.	Melbourne–Palm Bay, FL	68.7
5.	North County San Diego, CA	68.6
6.	Tucson, AZ	68.5
7.	Medford–Ashland, OR	68.4
8.	Lake Winnipesaukee, NH	68.2
9.	Daytona Beach, FL	66.9
10.	Fayetteville, AR	65.8
11.	Bellingham, WA	65.8
12.	Santa Barbara, CA	65.6
13.	Sedona, AZ	65.1
14.	Lakeland–Winter Haven, FL	64.7
15.	Hanover, NH	64.6
16.	Laguna Beach–Dana Point, CA	64.4
17.	Fort Collins–Loveland, CO	64.3
18.	Largo, FL	64.2
19.	Mission–McAllen–Alamo, TX	63.6
20.	Asheville, NC	63.4
21.	Santa Rosa, CA	62.8
22.	Savannah, GA	62.7
23.	Wickenburg, AZ	62.2
24.	Sarasota, FL	61.9
25.	Traverse City, MI	61.3
26.	Mesa, AZ	61.0
27.	Grand Junction, CO	61.0
28.	New Port Richey, FL	60.9
29.	Pensacola, FL	60.8
30.	East End Long Island, NY	60.8

INTRODUCTION

Ah, to wear shorts throughout the year in laid-back Key West, or to sit on a bench in the evening and watch the locals stroll around the plaza in historic Santa Fe. Oh, for winter quiet and the smell of pinyon pine on the western slope of the Colorado Rockies. How about the ambiance of a New England college town, painted white Cape and saltbox houses behind drifting red and gold leaves on a Homecoming Weekend? If you could snap your fingers and find yourself living somewhere else, would you?

Let's put the question another way: What if there were someplace else in America that suited you better for retirement than where you're living now, and you knew nothing about it?

"The best place to retire," advises Dr. Robert Butler, former head of the National Institute on Aging, "is the neighborhood where you spent your life." True enough; most of us have more power, independence, and plain practical knowledge in the place where we're living than we may ever have in a distant, unfamiliar location. And the statistics bear this out. For all the hype about moving away, the number of older adults who actually settle each year in another state for retirement wouldn't crowd the route for the Cotton Bowl parade. Most of us choose to stay where we are.

There's more to this decision than convenience. The emotional connection that comes from raising children, working at a job, and paying off a mortgage in one place may be missed in a new one. When you move, you can take the philodendron, the oak blanket chest, the canoe, and the satellite dish, but you can't pack a deep sense of place.

Perhaps for you, relocation is unthinkable. You've known your neighbors for years; your doctor knows you and your medical history; you don't need to look up the bank's phone number, ask for directions to a discount hardware store, or scratch your head for the name of the one person in city hall who can get the sewer fixed. What you may ultimately want is R and R in familiar territory, not an agenda that takes high energy and risk to put down new roots.

If all this is true, stay right where you are and travel whenever and wherever you want instead. But possibly—just possibly—there is someplace in this country where you may prosper more than where you now live. And possibly, too, it is a lack of information that keeps you from taking a look.

Eighteen Regions

In addition to the retirement places in this guide, you'll find references to broadly defined regions where each of these places is grouped. None of the regions match the political boundaries shown in a road atlas. Two regions—the California Coast and the Florida Interior—are found within single states. Most embrace parts of more than one state, however, and some states are apportioned among more than one region. Yet each region contains spots that share a distinctive look and feel, geography, outlook, and manners. The Desert Southwest and the Rocky Mountains each take in 20 retirement places, the most of any region; the Heartland embraces a large area but it also has the fewest places, just four (except for Hawaii).

CALIFORNIA COAST

Carmel–Pebble Beach, CA
Laguna Beach–Dana Point, CA
Mendocino–Fort Bragg, CA
Morro Bay–Cambria, CA
North County San Diego, CA
Santa Barbara, CA

DESERT SOUTHWEST

Apache Junction, AZ
Bisbee, AZ
Bullhead City, AZ
Cottonwood–Verde Valley, AZ
Henderson, NV
Kingman, AZ
Lake Havasu City, AZ
Mesa, AZ
Pahrump Valley, NV
Palm Springs–Coachella Valley, CA
Payson, AZ
Prescott–Prescott Valley, AZ
St. George–Zion, UT
Scottsdale, AZ
Sedona, AZ
Silver City, NM
Tucson, AZ
Victorville–Apple Valley, CA
Wickenburg, AZ
Yuma, AZ

FLORIDA INTERIOR

Gainesville, FL
Inverness, FL
Kissimmee–St. Cloud, FL
Lakeland–Winter Haven, FL
Leesburg–Mount Dora, FL
Ocala, FL
Sebring–Avon Park, FL

GULF COAST

Apalachicola, FL
Bay St. Louis–Pass Christian, MS
Bradenton, FL
Fairhope–Gulf Shores, AL
Fort Myers–Cape Coral, FL
Largo, FL
Naples, FL
New Port Richey, FL
Panama City, FL
Pensacola, FL
Port Charlotte, FL
Rockport–Aransas Pass, TX
Sarasota, FL
Western St. Tammany Parish, LA

HAWAII

Kauai, HI
Maui, HI

HEARTLAND

Brown County, IN
Columbia, MO
Iowa City, IA
Madison, WI

INNER SOUTH

Aiken, SC
Athens, GA
Chapel Hill–Carrboro, NC
Eufaula, AL
Hattiesburg, MS
Murray–Kentucky Lake, KY
Natchitoches, LA
Oxford, MS
Southern Pines–Pinehurst, NC
Thomasville, GA

MID-ATLANTIC METRO BELT

Annapolis, MD
Berkeley Springs, WV
Charles Town–Shepherdstown, WV
Charlottesville, VA
Chestertown, MD
East End Long Island, NY
Easton–St. Michaels, MD
Fredericksburg–Spotsylvania, VA
Front Royal, VA
Lake Placid, NY
Lower Cape May, NJ
Northern Neck, VA
Ocean City, MD
Pike County, PA
Rehoboth Bay–Indian River Bay, DE
State College, PA
Toms River–Barnegat Bay, NJ
Virginia Beach, VA
Williamsburg, VA

NORTH WOODS

Door Peninsula, WI
Eagle River–Woodruff, WI
Leelanau Peninsula, MI
Oscoda–Huron Shore, MI
Petoskey–Harbor Springs, MI
Traverse City, MI

OZARKS & OUACHITAS

Branson, MO
Eureka Springs, AR
Fayetteville, AR
Hot Springs, AR
Lake of the Cherokees, OK
Lake of the Ozarks, MO
Norfork Lake, AR
Table Rock Lake, MO

PACIFIC NORTHWEST

Anacortes, WA
Bellingham, WA
Bend, OR
Brookings–Gold Beach, OR
Chewelah, WA
Florence, OR
Grants Pass, OR
Medford–Ashland, OR
Newport–Lincoln City, OR
Palmer–Wasilla, AK
Port Angeles–Sequim, WA
Port Townsend, WA
San Juan Islands, WA
Wenatchee, WA
Whidbey Island, WA

RIO GRANDE COUNTRY

Alamogordo, NM
Alpine–Big Bend, TX
Las Cruces, NM
Las Vegas, NM
Mission–McAllen–Alamo, TX
Rio Rancho, NM
Roswell, NM
Ruidoso, NM
Santa Fe, NM
Taos, NM

ROCKY MOUNTAINS

Bozeman, MT
Cedar City, UT
Coeur d'Alene, ID
Colorado Springs, CO
Delta County, CO
Durango, CO
Flagstaff, AZ
Fort Collins–Loveland, CO
Grand Junction, CO
Hamilton–Bitterroot Valley, MT
Jackson Hole, WY
Kalispell–Flathead Valley, MT
Ketchum–Sun Valley, ID
McCall, ID
Montrose, CO
Pagosa Springs, CO
Park City, UT
Polson–Mission Valley, MT
Salida, CO
Sandpoint–Lake Pend Oreille, ID

SOUTH ATLANTIC

Beaufort, SC
Beaufort–Bogue Banks, NC
Boca Raton, FL
Charleston, SC
Conway, SC
Dare Outer Banks, NC
Daytona Beach, FL
Edenton, NC
Hilton Head Island, SC
Key West, FL
Melbourne–Palm Bay, FL
Myrtle Beach, SC
New Bern, NC
St. Augustine, FL
St. Simons–Jekyll Islands, GA
Savannah, GA
Southport–Brunswick Islands, NC
Summerville, SC
Vero Beach, FL

SOUTHERN HIGHLANDS

Asheville, NC
Boone–Blowing Rock, NC
Brevard, NC
Crossville, TN
Hendersonville–East Flat Rock, NC
Maryville, TN
Pendleton District, SC
Rabun County, GA
Smith Mountain Lake, VA
Tryon, NC

TAHOE BASIN & SIERRAS

Amador County, CA
Carson City–Carson Valley, NV
Grass Valley–Nevada City, CA
Mariposa, CA
Oakhurst–Coarsegold, CA
Paradise–Magalia, CA
Reno–Sparks, NV
Santa Rosa, CA
Sonora–Twain Harte, CA

TEXAS INTERIOR

Boerne, TX
Cedar Creek Lake, TX
Fredericksburg, TX
Georgetown, TX
Kerrville, TX
Lake Conroe, TX
Marble Falls–Lake LBJ, TX
New Braunfels, TX
Trinity Peninsula, TX
Wimberley, TX

YANKEE BELT

Bar Harbor, ME
Burlington, VT
Camden, ME
Hanover, NH
Lake Winnipesaukee, NH
Litchfield Hills, CT
Martha's Vineyard, MA
Middle Cape Cod, MA
Monadnock Region, NH
Northampton–Amherst, MA
St. Jay–Northeast Kingdom, VT
Southern Berkshire County, MA
Woodstock, VT
York Beaches, ME

RETIREMENT PLACES RATED

Over a period of 20 years and five previous editions, *Retirement Places Rated* has profiled hundreds of retirement spots throughout the country. This new, sixth edition takes the same approach as all of its predecessors and has been thoroughly updated, revised, and expanded.

Retirement Places Rated is meant for those who are planning for retirement and are weighing the pros and cons of moving or staying where they are. This guide offers facts about 203 carefully chosen places that have attracted most of the retired persons who move between states.

It is more than a collection of interesting and useful information about places, however. It also rates these places on the basis of six factors influencing the quality of retirement life: ambiance, costs of living, climate, personal safety, services, and the economy.

Retirement Places Rated doesn't treat later life as a kind of autumn or a second career, turning point, third age, or transformation. It simply gives you the facts you need to start appraising other geographic locations where you may choose to settle.

After using this book, your hunch that you'll never find a better place than your own hometown may well be confirmed. On the other hand, given this country's geographic variety, what are the odds the place where you happen to live is the right one for you?

WHERE ARE THESE PLACES?

If you were asked, in a kind of geographic word-association test, to name the states that spring to mind when you hear the word retirement, you may well tick off the big ones in the Sun Belt: Arizona, California, Florida, Georgia, Nevada, New Mexico, North Carolina, South Carolina, and Texas.

You'd be right, of course. In the generations since the end of World War II, these states attracted most of the older adults who packed up and moved to a distant location.

But states well above the Sun Belt deserve a place in retirement geography, too. Oregon and Washington continue to attract thousands of equity-rich Californians. New Jersey's sandy Atlantic coastline from Cape May up to Monmouth owes a good part of its economic health to older newcomers moving in from New York and Philadelphia. And catalogs mailed out by coastal Maine real estate brokers to baby boomers planning their retirement are thick and slick.

It's no secret that places in every part of the country benefit from older adults moving into them. Roughly every tenth person over 60 is a newcomer in one out of eight of the country's 3,142 counties. If these locations were to be daubed in red on a blank map of the United States, the nation would look as if it had measles.

THE LAST MOVE?

An odd statistic from AT&T market researchers says that we change our address 11 times in a lifetime. The common reasons are job changes or job transfers, shifts out of rental housing into home ownership, moves up to bigger homes, and divorce.

Is retirement still another reason to move? Not at all. Each year, fewer than half a million persons between the ages of 55 and 65 pack up and relocate to another state. Another million and a half simply trade the big family house for a smaller place within the same city. Consider your own options. You may:

- Stay at your current address—47 out of 50 persons between 55 and 65 do.
- Stay close to town but sell or rent your home and move into an apartment, condominium, or smaller home—1 in 27 older adults take this route.
- Move out of town to another part of the state to occupy a vacation home year-round, perhaps—just 1 in 70 older adults does this.
- Move to another state—among 94 older adults, only 1 will take this course.
- Move abroad—the longest shot of all, just 1 of 432 retired persons does this, and most that do are returning to their native country.

Clearly, hometown turf beats the distant happy valley. Even if you're not thrilled with your current location, you still have to decide whether moving is the key to a more satisfying later life. The anecdotes of people who moved, became disillusioned, and later moved again or returned home are getting more common.

A basic rule for successful relocation says that the day-to-day attractions of a destination must be much, much stronger than the day-to-day attractions of home, and a corollary requires that hometown attractions be weakened by hometown faults.

To identify likely places from among the hundreds of possibilities, *Retirement Places Rated* uses several criteria:

- *The place should have a 2004 area population greater than 10,000.* A smaller population may signal a lower level of human services. Moreover, *the place should be growing.* In the 5 years between 2004 and 2009, the U.S. population is projected to grow by 6 percent. The retirement places profiled here will together grow 9 percent over the same period.
- *The place should be attractive to older adults.* In almost all of the retirement places in this book, the number of persons 60 to 65 years of age in residence today is much greater than the number of persons 50 to 55 years of age 10 years ago. This simple demographic exercise means that older newcomers have moved into the area over the previous decade.
- *The place should be relatively safe.* The U.S. annual average crime rate, for example, is 4,123 per 100,000 people. In eight out of ten of the places profiled here, the crime rate is less than the national average.
- *The place should be affordable.* The money it takes to live in nine out of ten of the places included in this book is much less than U.S. average estimated costs for a retired household.
- *The place should have natural endowments.* Most of the locations included here have at least one of the following: large areas of federal recreation land, state recreation land, large areas of inland water, or an ocean coastline. Several places are blessed with all four.

Based on repeated visits and recommendations from hundreds of older adults, *Retirement Places Rated* profiles 203 places. Of these, 104 are in the 9 Sun Belt states noted above. Retirement relocation is still a march to low-cost living and milder winters, that much is certain. Because there is a growing countermovement to attractive places outside the Sun Belt, 99 of these are profiled. In all, locations in 43 states—from the Florida Keys to Hawaii's island of Kauai and from the Down East Maine coast to southern California—are represented.

Although this selection of places does not by any means include every desirable destination, it does include many of the country's best, and it does represent the variety of choices many persons have for retirement living.

SOME WORDS ABOUT PLACE NAMES

None of the 203 places profiled here coincide with the corporate limits of towns or cities. For good reason, most of them are counties. Thanks to the car, the space you can cover on a typical day has expanded since the nostalgic era when Main Street truly was the noisy, exciting center of things. Now people likely live in one town, work in another, visit friends in still another, shop at a mall miles away, and escape to open country—all within an easy drive.

It is no different in retirement places. Metropolitan Colorado Springs, with a population of more than half a million, takes in the country's 54th biggest city. It also includes Black Forest, Cimarron Hills, Fountain, Manitou Springs, Palmer Lake, and other suburban places in surrounding El Paso County, some in the Rocky Mountain foothills, and others downslope at the beginning of the shortgrass prairie.

County names ring a bell with travelers. Hawaii's Maui, Wisconsin's Door County, and New Jersey's Cape May are three such places. Other counties—South Carolina's Aiken, Santa Fe in New Mexico, and Yuma in Arizona—have the same name as their well-known seats of government. In these instances, it's natural to call the retirement place by its county name.

But county names aren't usually tossed around in your basic where-to-retire scuttlebutt. Washington County, Arkansas, is one of 31 counties honoring the first president of the United States. The name draws a blank to Texans, Louisianans, Missourians, and Oklahomans (neighboring states that have their *own* Washington County). But everyone recognizes Fayetteville, the seat of Washington County and home of the University of Arkansas.

Another case is Barnstable County, Massachusetts, which includes all of Cape Cod from Buzzards Bay out old U.S. 6 on the famous sandy spit of land to Provincetown. Centuries ago, Cape Cod elbowed Barnstable County aside in popular New England usage.

Sometimes the name given a retirement place is that of the one or two biggest population centers. Thus North Carolina's Orange County becomes Chapel Hill–Carrboro, Florida's Charlotte County changes into Port Charlotte, and California's Nevada County turns into Grass Valley–Nevada City.

In other instances, the name of a town may be paired with a well-known natural feature. Alpine–Big Bend identifies the county seat and one of our finest national parks, all in sparsely peopled Brewster County, Texas. Murray–Kentucky Lake names the college town and one of the world's largest man-made lakes, both in Calloway County, Kentucky.

The following chart identifies the 203 places as they are used throughout *Retirement Places Rated* and details the geography—usually a county—that defines the place. Included in the chart are population figures for today and a reasonable projection of what they will be by the year 2009.

203 Retirement Places

RETIREMENT PLACE AND COUNTY	POPULATION 2004	POPULATION 2009	GROWTH 2004–09
Aiken, South Carolina Aiken County	149,759	159,605	7%
Alamogordo, New Mexico Otero County	62,547	65,399	5%
Alpine–Big Bend, Texas Brewster County	9,098	9,446	4%
Amador County, California Amador County	38,851	42,987	11%
Anacortes, Washington Skagit County	110,560	119,345	8%
Annapolis, Maryland Part of Anne Arundel County	520,771	558,663	7%
Apache Junction, Arizona Part of Pinal County	203,280	227,309	12%
Apalachicola, Florida Franklin County	11,570	12,209	6%
Asheville, North Carolina Buncombe County	218,470	233,645	7%
Athens, Georgia Clarke County	105,016	110,098	5%
Bar Harbor, Maine Hancock County	53,491	55,557	4%
Bay St. Louis–Pass Christian, Mississippi Part of Hancock and Harrison counties	46,438	50,473	9%
Beaufort, South Carolina Beaufort County	134,374	149,761	11%
Beaufort–Bogue Banks, North Carolina Carteret County	62,749	67,259	7%
Bellingham, Washington Whatcom County	179,205	193,034	8%
Bend, Oregon Deschutes County	133,663	153,253	15%
Berkeley Springs, West Virginia Morgan County	15,702	16,449	5%
Bisbee, Arizona Cochise County	124,961	134,473	8%
Boca Raton, Florida Part of Palm Beach County	1,251,087	1,395,423	12%
Boerne, Texas Kendall County	26,718	29,673	11%
Boone–Blowing Rock, North Carolina Watauga County	44,622	47,304	6%
Bozeman, Montana Gallatin County	74,469	82,740	11%
Bradenton, Florida Manatee County	298,769	339,909	14%
Branson, Missouri Taney County	45,891	55,112	20%

continued

203 Retirement Places (cont.)

RETIREMENT PLACE AND COUNTY	POPULATION 2004	POPULATION 2009	GROWTH 2004–09
Brevard, North Carolina Transylvania County	30,638	32,456	6%
Brookings–Gold Beach, Oregon Curry County	22,072	23,699	7%
Brown County, Indiana Brown County	15,871	17,042	7%
Bullhead City, Arizona Part of Mohave County	174,547	195,891	12%
Burlington, Vermont Chittenden County	152,038	159,505	5%
Camden, Maine Knox County	41,340	43,461	5%
Carmel–Pebble Beach, California Part of Monterey County	426,660	456,470	7%
Carson City–Carson Valley, Nevada Carson City and Douglas County	57,362	63,401	11%
Cedar City, Utah Iron County	37,687	42,832	14%
Cedar Creek Lake, Texas Henderson County	80,226	88,898	11%
Chapel Hill–Carrboro, North Carolina Orange County	128,363	141,982	11%
Charles Town-Shepherdstown, West Virginia Jefferson County	45,084	47,824	6%
Charleston, South Carolina Part of Charleston County	326,191	350,004	7%
Charlottesville, Virginia Albemarle County and Charlottesville city	130,309	139,232	7%
Chestertown, Maryland Kent County	19,810	20,306	3%
Chewelah, Washington Stevens County	42,337	45,084	6%
Coeur d'Alene, Idaho Kootenai County	121,671	137,305	13%
Colorado Springs, Colorado El Paso County	568,783	624,913	10%
Columbia, Missouri Boone County	143,724	155,019	8%
Conway, South Carolina Part of Horry County	216,672	240,420	11%
Cottonwood–Verde Valley, Arizona Yavapai County	194,709	226,655	16%
Crossville, Tennessee Cumberland County	50,740	55,074	9%
Dare Outer Banks, North Carolina Dare County	34,012	38,638	14%
Daytona Beach, Florida Volusia County	471,180	499,611	6%
Delta County, Colorado Delta County	29,853	32,100	8%
Door Peninsula, Wisconsin Door County	29,276	30,778	5%
Durango, Colorado La Plata County	48,776	54,583	12%
Eagle River–Woodruff, Wisconsin Vilas County	22,631	24,443	8%
East End Long Island, New York Part of Suffolk County	1,477,419	1,533,000	4%
Easton–St. Michaels, Maryland Talbot County	35,142	36,943	5%

RETIREMENT PLACE AND COUNTY	POPULATION 2004	POPULATION 2009	GROWTH 2004–09
Edenton, North Carolina Chowan County	14,799	15,166	2%
Eufaula, Alabama Barbour County	29,739	30,977	4%
Eureka Springs, Arkansas Carroll County	27,158	29,393	8%
Fairhope–Gulf Shores, Alabama Baldwin County	159,922	183,154	15%
Fayetteville, Arkansas Washington County	170,965	185,542	9%
Flagstaff, Arizona Coconino County	124,684	135,985	9%
Florence, Oregon Part of Lane County	338,185	361,323	7%
Fort Collins–Loveland, Colorado Larimer County	274,795	299,021	9%
Fort Myers–Cape Coral, Florida Lee County	495,701	552,161	11%
Fredericksburg, Texas Gillespie County	22,061	23,300	6%
Fredericksburg–Spotsylvania, Virginia Fredericksburg city and Spotsylvania County	126,751	141,402	12%
Front Royal, Virginia Warren County	33,693	35,861	6%
Gainesville, Florida Alachua County	225,962	238,429	6%
Georgetown, Texas Williamson County	318,303	384,348	21%
Grand Junction, Colorado Mesa County	125,285	134,733	8%
Grants Pass, Oregon Josephine County	80,987	87,408	8%
Grass Valley–Nevada City, California Nevada County	100,616	110,585	10%
Hamilton–Bitterroot Valley, Montana Ravalli County	39,998	44,384	11%
Hanover, New Hampshire Grafton County	84,775	89,016	5%
Hattiesburg, Mississippi Forrest County	74,104	76,102	3%
Henderson, Nevada Clark County	1,597,152	1,826,981	14%
Hendersonville–East Flat Rock, North Carolina Part of Henderson County	95,066	101,009	6%
Hilton Head Island, South Carolina Part of Beaufort County	134,374	149,761	11%
Hot Springs, Arkansas Garland County	93,793	100,525	7%
Inverness, Florida Citrus County	129,373	141,284	9%
Iowa City, Iowa Johnson County	116,658	125,127	7%
Jackson Hole, Wyoming Teton County	19,859	22,220	12%
Kalispell–Flathead Valley, Montana Flathead County	81,640	90,471	11%
Kauai, Hawaii Kauai County	61,127	64,076	5%
Kerrville, Texas Kerr County	46,243	48,877	6%

continued

203 Retirement Places (cont.)

RETIREMENT PLACE AND COUNTY	POPULATION 2004	POPULATION 2009	GROWTH 2004–09
Ketchum–Sun Valley, Idaho Blaine County	21,855	25,277	16%
Key West, Florida Monroe County	81,359	86,280	6%
Kingman, Arizona Part of Mohave County	174,547	195,891	12%
Kissimmee–St. Cloud, Florida Osceola County	199,664	229,960	15%
Laguna Beach–Dana Point, California Part of Orange County	3,025,986	3,237,654	7%
Lake Conroe, Texas Part of Montgomery County	349,487	405,120	16%
Lake Havasu City, Arizona Part of Mohave County	174,547	195,891	12%
Lake of the Cherokees, Oklahoma Delaware County	39,983	43,616	9%
Lake of the Ozarks, Missouri Camden County	40,624	45,506	12%
Lake Placid, New York Essex County	39,471	40,290	2%
Lake Winnipesaukee, New Hampshire Belknap and Carroll counties	61,058	65,514	7%
Lakeland–Winter Haven, Florida Polk County	513,322	548,613	7%
Largo, Florida Part of Pinellas County	939,479	968,662	3%
Las Cruces, New Mexico Dona Ana County	186,005	201,141	8%
Las Vegas, New Mexico San Miguel County	31,532	33,761	7%
Leelanau Peninsula, Michigan Leelanau County	22,740	24,671	8%
Leesburg–Mount Dora, Florida Lake County	238,628	257,630	8%
Litchfield Hills, Connecticut Part of Litchfield County	189,634	197,485	4%
Lower Cape May, New Jersey Part of Cape May County	105,191	109,425	4%
Madison, Wisconsin Dane County	451,769	483,315	7%
Marble Falls–Lake LBJ, Texas Burnet County	39,514	44,983	14%
Mariposa, California Mariposa County	17,799	18,758	5%
Martha's Vineyard, Massachusetts Dukes County	16,296	17,728	9%
Maryville, Tennessee Blount County	114,606	124,896	9%
Maui, Hawaii Maui County	140,616	154,860	10%
McCall, Idaho Valley County	8,214	9,084	11%
Medford–Ashland, Oregon Jackson County	199,373	223,231	12%
Melbourne–Palm Bay, Florida Brevard County	509,175	542,818	7%
Mendocino–Fort Bragg, California Mendocino County	89,454	93,384	4%
Mesa, Arizona Part of Maricopa County	3,440,341	3,849,239	12%

RETIREMENT PLACE AND COUNTY	POPULATION 2004	POPULATION 2009	GROWTH 2004–09
Middle Cape Cod, Massachusetts Part of Barnstable County	236,355	251,185	6%
Mission–McAllen–Alamo, Texas Hidalgo County	634,141	705,065	11%
Monadnock Region, New Hampshire Cheshire County	75,739	78,201	3%
Montrose, Colorado Montrose County	36,361	39,171	8%
Morro Bay–Cambria, California Part of San Luis Obispo County	266,825	292,319	10%
Murray–Kentucky Lake, Kentucky Calloway County	35,217	36,807	5%
Myrtle Beach, South Carolina Part of Horry County	216,672	240,420	11%
Naples, Florida Collier County	286,326	321,114	12%
Natchitoches, Louisiana Natchitoches Parish	38,784	39,100	1%
New Bern, North Carolina Craven County	94,501	99,450	5%
New Braunfels, Texas Comal County	88,732	98,743	11%
New Port Richey, Florida Pasco County	385,843	424,712	10%
Newport–Lincoln City, Oregon Lincoln County	45,802	48,326	6%
Norfork Lake, Arkansas Baxter County	40,519	43,639	8%
North County San Diego, California Part of San Diego County	3,009,357	3,240,261	8%
Northampton–Amherst, Massachusetts Hampshire County	156,082	160,616	3%
Northern Neck, Virginia Lancaster and Northumberland counties	11,831	12,291	4%
Oakhurst–Coarsegold, California Madera County	135,646	150,361	11%
Ocala, Florida Marion County	279,757	300,082	7%
Ocean City, Maryland Worcester County	49,583	52,084	5%
Oscoda–Huron Shore, Michigan Iosco County	27,839	28,932	4%
Oxford, Mississippi Lafayette County	40,793	44,038	8%
Pagosa Springs, Colorado Archuleta County	11,980	14,153	18%
Pahrump Valley, Nevada Part of Nye County	36,135	39,804	10%
Palm Springs–Coachella Valley, California Part of Riverside County	1,766,282	1,973,859	12%
Palmer–Wasilla, Alaska Part of Matanuska–Susitna Borough	57,824	66,295	15%
Panama City, Florida Bay County	157,810	170,614	8%
Paradise–Magalia, California Part of Butte County	214,749	228,568	6%
Park City, Utah Summit County	35,921	43,823	22%
Payson, Arizona Part of Gila County	55,273	61,734	12%

continued

203 Retirement Places (cont.)

RETIREMENT PLACE AND COUNTY	POPULATION 2004	POPULATION 2009	GROWTH 2004–09
Pendleton District, South Carolina Oconee County	68,857	71,310	4%
Pensacola, Florida Escambia County	298,694	309,425	4%
Petoskey–Harbor Springs, Michigan Emmet County	33,728	36,168	7%
Pike County, Pennsylvania Pike County	51,876	57,497	11%
Polson–Mission Valley, Montana Lake County	28,331	30,617	8%
Port Angeles–Sequim, Washington Clallam County	68,698	73,676	7%
Port Charlotte, Florida Charlotte County	161,866	187,135	16%
Port Townsend, Washington Jefferson County	28,938	32,829	13%
Prescott–Prescott Valley, Arizona Part of Yavapai County	194,709	226,655	16%
Rabun County, Georgia Rabun County	15,895	16,724	5%
Rehoboth Bay–Indian River Bay, Delaware Sussex County	169,623	183,331	8%
Reno–Sparks, Nevada Washoe County	369,849	399,762	8%
Rio Rancho, New Mexico Sandoval County	102,692	117,065	14%
Rockport–Aransas Pass, Texas Aransas County	23,629	25,057	6%
Roswell, New Mexico Eddy County	52,207	54,029	3%
Ruidoso, New Mexico Lincoln County	21,012	23,126	10%
St. Augustine, Florida St. Johns County	144,212	165,378	15%
St. George–Zion, Utah Washington County	108,689	129,628	19%
St. Jay–Northeast Kingdom, Vermont Caledonia County	30,432	31,494	3%
St. Simons–Jekyll Islands, Georgia Part of Glynn County	70,515	74,077	5%
Salida, Colorado Chaffee County	17,258	18,441	7%
San Juan Islands, Washington San Juan County	15,326	16,661	9%
Sandpoint–Lake Pend Oreille, Idaho Bonner County	40,041	44,299	11%
Santa Barbara, California Part of Santa Barbara County	410,330	426,681	4%
Santa Fe, New Mexico Santa Fe County	140,598	156,404	11%
Santa Rosa, California Part of Sonoma County	489,650	530,363	8%
Sarasota, Florida Sarasota County	354,805	387,623	9%
Savannah, Georgia Chatham County	237,265	244,999	3%
Scottsdale, Arizona Part of Maricopa County	3,440,341	3,849,239	12%
Sebring–Avon Park, Florida Highlands County	93,033	100,012	8%

RETIREMENT PLACE AND COUNTY	POPULATION 2004	POPULATION 2009	GROWTH 2004–09
Sedona, Arizona Part of Coconino County	124,684	135,985	9%
Silver City, New Mexico Grant County	31,655	33,174	5%
Smith Mountain Lake, Virginia Bedford and Franklin counties	112,435	121,017	8%
Sonora–Twain Harte, California Tuolumne County	57,987	61,840	7%
Southern Berkshire County, Massachusetts Part of Berkshire County	133,711	132,430	–1%
Southern Pines–Pinehurst, North Carolina Moore County	80,813	86,564	7%
Southport–Brunswick Islands, North Carolina Brunswick County	85,193	98,365	15%
State College, Pennsylvania Centre County	139,227	144,375	4%
Summerville, South Carolina Dorchester County	103,136	110,490	7%
Table Rock Lake, Missouri Stone County	31,157	34,759	12%
Taos, New Mexico Taos County	33,140	37,680	14%
Thomasville, Georgia Thomas County	43,671	44,660	2%
Toms River–Barnegat Bay, New Jersey Ocean County	552,423	591,837	7%
Traverse City, Michigan Grand Traverse County	85,587	94,291	10%
Trinity Peninsula, Texas Trinity County	14,388	15,139	5%
Tryon, North Carolina Polk County	19,767	21,410	8%
Tucson, Arizona Pima County	911,702	992,959	9%
Vero Beach, Florida Indian River County	124,178	137,167	10%
Victorville–Apple Valley, California Part of San Bernardino County	1,878,742	2,056,565	9%
Virginia Beach, Virginia Virginia Beach city	444,641	473,366	6%
Wenatchee, Washington Chelan County	69,332	72,877	5%
Western St. Tammany Parish, Louisiana Part of St. Tammany Parish	209,310	228,136	9%
Whidbey Island, Washington Island County	77,726	83,615	8%
Wickenburg, Arizona Part of Maricopa County	3,440,341	3,849,239	12%
Williamsburg, Virginia James City County and Williamsburg city	66,277	72,634	10%
Wimberley, Texas Hays County	114,857	130,667	14%
Woodstock, Vermont Windsor County	59,177	61,704	4%
York Beaches, Maine York County	196,927	204,564	4%
Yuma, Arizona Yuma County	194,949	212,019	9%

Source: Woods & Poole Economics, Inc., population forecasts; Places Rated Partnership estimates. All percentages are rounded.

203 Retirement Places

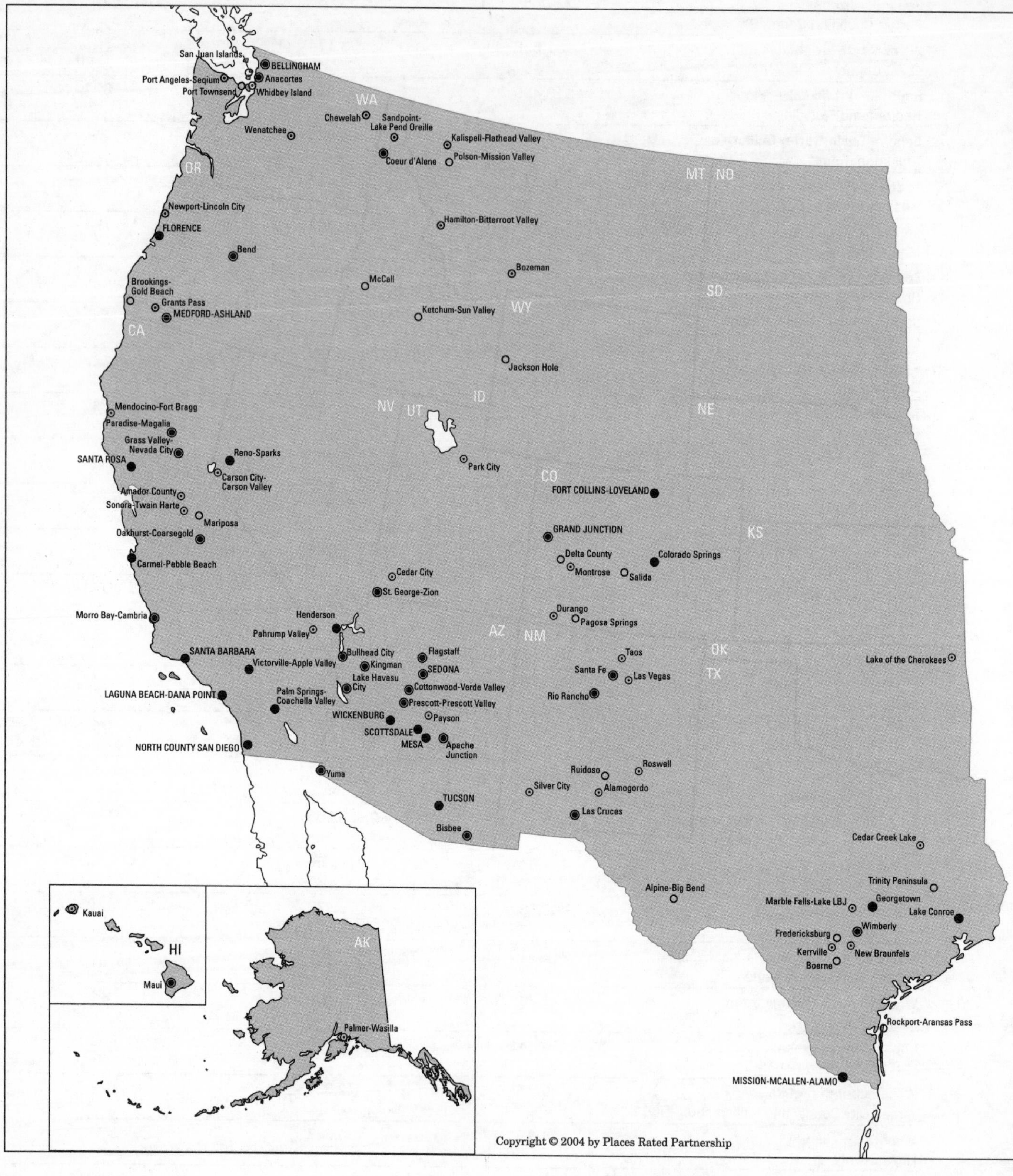

MN
WI
IA
IL
MO
IN
OH
MI
KY
WV
VA
TN
MS
AL
GA
AR
LA
FL
SC
NC
PA
NY
NJ
MD
DE
VT
NH
ME
MA
CT
RI
Eagle River-Woodruff
Door Peninsula
Leelanau Peninsula
Petoskey-Harbor Springs
TRAVERSE CITY
Oscoda-Huron Shore
Madison
Iowa City
Columbia
Lake of the Ozarks
Table Rock Lake
Branson
Eureka Springs
Norfolk Lake
FAYETTEVILLE
Hot Springs
Natchitoches
Brown County
Murray-Kentucky Lake
Crossville
Maryville
Oxford
Hattiesburg
Western St. Tammany Parish
Bay St. Louis-Pass Christian
Fairhope-Gulf Shores
PENSACOLA
Panama City
Apalachicola
Eufaula
Thomasville
Athens
Rabun County
Brevard
Pendleton District
ASHEVILLE
Hendersonville-East Flat Rock
Tryon
Boone-Blowing Rock
Smith Mountain Lake
Charlottesville
Northern Neck
Williamsburg
Virginia Beach
Edenton
Dare Outer Banks
Chapel Hill-Carrboro
New Bern
Beaufort-Bogue Banks
Southern Pines-Pinehurst
Southport-Brunswick Islands
Conway
Myrtle Beach
Aiken
Summerville
CHARLESTON
Beaufort
Hilton Head Island
SAVANNAH
St. Simons-Jekyll Islands
St. Augustine
Gainesville
Ocala
DAYTONA BEACH
Inverness
Leesburg-Mount Dora
Kissimmee-St. Cloud
LAKELAND-WINTER HAVEN
MELBOURNE-PALM BAY
NEW PORT RICHEY
LARGO
Sebring-Avon Park
Bradenton
Vero Beach
SARASOTA
Port Charlotte
Boca Raton
Fort Myers-Cape Coral
Naples
Key West
State College
Berkeley Springs
Charles Town-Shepherdstown
Annapolis
Front Royal
Fredericksburg-Spotsylvania
Chestertown
Lower Cape May
Rehoboth Bay-Indian River Bay
Easton-St. Michaels
Ocean City
Toms River-Barnegat Bay
Pike County
EAST END LONG ISLAND
Southern Berkshire County
Litchfield Hills
Martha's Vineyard
Middle Cape Cod
Northampton-Amherst
Monadnock Region
Woodstock
HANOVER
York Beaches
LAKE WINNIPESAUKEE
Lake Placid
Burlington
St. Jay-Northeast Kingdom
Camden
Bar Harbor
Population
250,000 and over
100,000 to 249,000
30,000 to 99,000
less than 29,999
BELLINGHAM = One of the top 30 retirement places

MAKING THE CHAPTERS WORK FOR YOU

When it comes to rating places for livability, there are three points of view. The first says that defining what's good for all people all the time isn't just unfair, it's impossible and shouldn't be attempted at all. "Livable for whom?" the argument goes. The artist who wants mountain vistas? The businessman who wants low taxes and no red tape? A new college graduate starting a career, a retired person looking for a healthful climate, or parents searching for good public schools?

The second view says that you *can* rate places but shouldn't, because measuring a prickly thing like livability makes places unwilling rivals of one another. When you claim your own turf is the most livable, you're implying others aren't. Look at the old jokes and occasional ill will between neighbors such as Dallas and Ft. Worth, Minneapolis and St. Paul, or San Francisco and Oakland. According to this view, rating places from best to worst is an unbecoming exercise. Every place is habitable; that's why people live in them.

The third point of view says nonsense to the first two. Of course you can measure livability. As long as you know who your audience is and make clear what your statistical yardsticks are and use them consistently, you'll be doing what's done all the time by Chambers of Commerce from Key West to Puget Sound and from West Quoddy Head to San Diego.

Although one can argue with confidence for viewpoints one and two, *Retirement Places Rated* takes sides with the third.

RATING PLACES: AN AMERICAN TRADITION

It may seem the height of effrontery, this business of judging places from best to worst with numbers. After all, how can intangible things such as friendliness and optimism be measured with statistics? Yet *numeracy* is almost as strong a national character trait as *literacy.* When it comes to choosing a new place to live, we've been digesting numbers for a long, long time.

- To sell colonists on settling in Maryland rather than in Virginia, 17th-century boosters assembled figures showing heavier livestock, more plentiful game, and lower mortality from summer diseases and Indian attacks.
- *California for Health, Wealth, and Residence,* just one volume in a library of post–Civil War guides touting the West's superior quality of life, gathered data to show the climate along the southern Pacific coast to be the world's best. Not so, countered the Union Pacific Railroad's land office in 1871; settlers will find the most "genial and healthy seasons" in western Kansas.
- In our own century, the statistical nets were flung even wider. "There are plenty of Americans who regard Kansas as almost barbaric," noted H.L. Mencken back in 1931, "just as there are other Americans who shudder whenever they think of Arkansas, Ohio, Indiana, Oklahoma, Texas, or California."

  Mencken wrote these words in his *American Mercury* magazine to introduce his formula for measuring the progress of civilization in each of the states. He mixed the number of Boy Scouts and *Atlantic Monthly* subscribers with lynchings and pellagra cases, added a dash of *Who's Who* listings along with rates for divorce and murder, threw in figures for rainfall and gasoline consumption, and found that, hands down, Mississippi was the worst American state. This surprised few since Mencken hated the South. Massachusetts, a state he liked, came out best.
- Decades later, in 1978, the Bay State was demoted when Chase Econometrics, an economic consulting firm, rated it the worst state for retirement. And the best state according to the Chase forecasters? Utah.
- Fast forwarding to 2003, *Kiplinger's* magazine elevated tiny Delaware to the "most retirement-friendly" of all the states, at least in the favorable tax treatment of retirement income and a lack of sales tax. And the worst state according to the Kiplinger analysts? Pennsylvania, right next door.

Rating Retirement Places: One Way

Retirement Places Rated is more useful than any system that just looks at states. When it comes to finding your own spot for retirement, you would do well to ignore the shopworn truisms about states and their track records in attracting older adults.

Thinking of Florida as a destination still means having to make a choice from among thousands of cities, towns, and unincorporated places that stretch from the Gulf beaches and farming backcountry in Escambia County in the western panhandle all the way some 900 miles down the peninsula to the causeway to subtropical Key West. People don't retire to states; they retire to specific places.

Moreover, statewide averages hide local realities. For some persons, there may be a world of difference between Laguna Beach and Palm Springs in California and these differences may be more important in retirement than the differences between California and Florida.

Certainly, this book is more objective than the hearsay that travelers share at an interstate highway rest stop or at an airport gate. Each of the 203 locations is rated by six factors that most persons planning for retirement consider highly important.

- **Ambiance** looks at historic preservation, water recreation, protected scenic and recreation areas, good restaurants, and the fine arts scene.
- **Costs of Living** measures typical expenses for the big items such as housing, utilities, food, transportation, and health care. The chapter also looks at the bite that various state personal income and sales taxes take from retirement income.
- **Climate** reviews winter discomfort factors such as wind chill and summer discomfort factors such as humidity and dampness. Psychological factors such as cloudiness, rain, darkness, and fog plus hazards such as snow, thunderstorms, and high wind also receive scrutiny.
- **Personal Safety** measures the annual rate of violent and property crime in each place and looks also at the latest 5-year trends: Up, down, or unchanged.
- **Services** evaluates physician specialists, the supply of hospital services, public library, and continuing education assets in each place.

- **The Economy** compares the prospects for jobs in three basic industries most promising to older adults: finance, insurance, and real estate; retail trade; and services. The chapter also scans how vulnerable a spot is to recessions and how competitive the part-time job market is.

You may fault *Retirement Places Rated*'s criteria. Admittedly, this book's measurements for health care, services, and ambiance favor big places over small ones. On the other hand, the ratings for crime and costs of living favor small places over big ones. The standards for climate mildness are certainly not everyone's. But they have nothing to do with population size.

Rating Retirement Places: Your Way

At the end of this book, in the chapter entitled "Putting It All Together," ambiance, costs of living, climate, crime, the local economy, and community services get equal weight to identify retirement places with across-the-board strengths.

You may not agree with this system. You may prefer year-round sunshine to an abundance of medical specialists. You may give more weight to personal safety than to good fishing spots. For you, a place where retirement income goes further might be more important than historic homes and good restaurants. To identify which factors are more important and which are less, you may want to take stock of your own preferences, using the following Preference Inventory.

YOUR PREFERENCE INVENTORY

The following Preference Inventory has 45 pairs of statements. For each pair, decide which statement is more important to you when judging a retirement place. Even if both statements are equally important or neither is important, select one anyway. If you can't decide quickly, pass up the item but return to it after you complete the rest of the inventory.

Don't worry about being consistent. The paired statements aren't repeated. There aren't any right or wrong answers, only those that are best for you. Although the inventory takes about 10 minutes to finish, there is no time limit. You may want to ask your spouse or a friend to use one of the extra preference profiles on the last page of this chapter. Comparing your own Preference Inventory with another person's is an interesting exercise.

FINDING YOUR WAY IN THE CHAPTERS

Each of the chapters in *Retirement Places Rated* has four parts:

- The **Introduction** gives basic information on the chapter's topic, peppered with facts and figures to help you evaluate places.
- The **Scoring** and **Ranking** sections explain how the places are rated.
- The **Place Profiles** are capsule comparisons, arranged alphabetically by place, covering all the elements used in the ratings. Here you can see differences among places at a glance.
- The **Et Cetera** section expands on topics mentioned in the introduction and also has essays on related subjects. These range all the way from state-by-state tax treatment of retirement income to tactics for avoiding property crime.

The last chapter, "Putting It All Together," averages the scores to identify America's best all-around retirement places and describes the strengths and weaknesses of each place.

PREFERENCE INVENTORY

Directions

For each numbered item, decide which of the two statements is *more important* to you when choosing a place to retire. Mark the box next to that statement. Be sure to make a choice for all of the items.

1. C. ❑ The duration of the winter.

D. ❑ The odds of being a crime victim.

2. A. ❑ Beaches, boating, hiking, and fishing.

B. ❑ Typical household incomes in an area.

3. E. ❑ Opportunities for taking college courses.

F. ❑ Opportunities for part-time work.

4. D. ❑ Local burglaries and holdups.

E. ❑ Medical specialists and accredited hospitals.

5. C. ❑ A mild, four-season climate.

A. ❑ Preserved historic buildings.

6. B. ❑ Typical household incomes in an area.

C. ❑ Elevation, humidity, and temperatures.

7. C. ❑ A mild, four-season climate.

E. ❑ Academic programs at local colleges.

8. D. ❑ The local crime rate.

F. ❑ Variety of seasonal job opportunities.

9. B. ❑ The bite state and local taxes might take.

F. ❑ Job opportunities in retail trade and real estate.

10. A. ❑ The local performing arts calendar.

D. ❑ The burglary and auto theft rate.

11. C. ❑ Annual temperature extremes.

F. ❑ Opportunities for work in the service sector.

12. B. ❑ Where the living is inexpensive.

D. ❑ The local odds of being burglarized.

13. F. ❑ The strength of the local economy.

A. ❑ Good restaurants and the performing arts scene.

14. B. ❑ State and local tax bites.

E. ❑ The variety of local college courses.

15. A. ❑ Nearby National Parks and Forests.

E. ❑ Medical specialists and good hospitals.

16. A. ❑ Boating and fishing.

D. ❑ Violent and property crime rates.

17. E. ❑ Accredited short-term, acute-care hospitals.

F. ❑ Outlook for part-time employment.

18. A. ❑ Historic neighborhoods and good restaurants.

B. ❑ State income and sales taxes.

19. D. ❑ The area's criminal activity.

E. ❑ Public transit alternatives to the car.

20. C. ❑ Temperature highs and lows throughout the year.

A. ❑ Performing arts and concert halls.

21. B. ❑ The local costs of living index.

C. ❑ The number of thunderstorms in a year.

22. C. ❑ Humidity, elevation, and wind speed.

E. ❑ Public library branches and collections.

23. D. ❑ Good restaurants, the symphony, and theater.

F. ❑ Forecasted employment growth in retail trade.

24. B. ❑ Where physician fees are low.

F. ❑ Opportunities for work in the finance sector.

25. C. ❑ Annual amounts of rain and snow.

F. ❑ Forecasted employment growth.

26. A. ❑ National Parks, Forests, and Wildlife Refuges.

D. ❑ Whether crime is a major problem.

27. B. ❑ Where a fixed income will stretch further.

D. ❑ Where criminal activity is least.

28. B. ❑ Making retirement income stretch further.

E. ❑ The area's supply of public transportation.

29. C. ❑ The area's number of foggy and rainy days.

D. ❑ Historic neighborhoods and good restaurants.

30. E. ❑ Specialized medical care.

F. ❑ Local potential for unemployment.

31. A. ❑ Beaches and boating.

F. ❑ A recession-proof local economy.

32. D. ❑ Crime-free neighborhoods.

E. ❑ Variety of local medical specialists.

33. B. ❑ The bills for heating and cooling a home.

C. ❑ January wind chill and July humidity.

34. A. ❑ Historic homes and buildings.

D. ❑ Crime-free neighborhoods.

35. C. ❑ The potential for cloudy days.

E. ❑ Public libraries and bus routes.

36. F. ❑ Seasonal jobs in the tourist season.

D. ❑ An area's crime rate.

37. B. ❑ Local tax breaks for older adults.

F. ❑ The area's unemployment ratF.

38. C. ❑ Elevation, windiness, and cloudiness.

A. ❑ Local performing arts.

39. C. ❑ How hot the summers are.

F. ❑ Competition for part-time or seasonal work.

40. B. ❑ The cost of food and utilities.

D. ❑ Crime-free neighborhoods.

41. A. ❑ Local performing arts calendar.

E. ❑ Continuing education opportunities.

42. B. ❑ The cost of food and utilities.

E. ❑ The supply of physician specialists.

43. A. ❑ Good restaurants and historic neighborhoods.

B. ❑ State income and sales taxes.

44. F. ❑ Launching a part-time business.

C. ❑ How hot the summers are.

45. D. ❑ The local robbery and burglary rate.

A. ❑ Historic neighborhoods and good bookstores.

Source: Adapted from "The Prospering Test," courtesy Thomas F. Bowman, Ph.D.; George Giuliani, Ph.D.; and M. Ronald Minge, Ph.D.

PLOTTING YOUR PREFERENCE PROFILE

It is important that you make a choice for each of the 45 items. Have you left any unchecked? If not, you're ready to draw your Preference Profile.

1. Count all the marks you've made in the boxes next to the letter A. Then enter the number of "A" statements on the line next to the words "Ambiance" on your Preference Profile. In the same way, count the number of statements for each of the other letters. Enter their totals in their respective places on your Preference Profile.
2. Now plot your totals on the blank chart. Place a dot on the appropriate line for each of the numbers and connect the dots to form a line graph of your results (see the Sample Preference Profile).

Analyzing Your Preference Profile

Each of the six factors in your Preference Profile—ambiance, costs of living, climate, crime, community services, and the economy—is not only a major concern when finding a likely place to retire; it also has a complete chapter in this book. The purpose of the Preference Inventory is to help you decide the relative importance of each of the chapters to you personally.

If your scores are high for one or two of these factors, you may want to give extra attention to the chapters covering them. Likewise, if your scores are low for any of the six, you may not need to give as much consideration to them as you would the ones with high scores. Bear in mind that the inventory orders your preferences in a hierarchy, that each of the factors has some importance to you, and that none should be entirely ignored.

SAMPLE PREFERENCE PROFILE

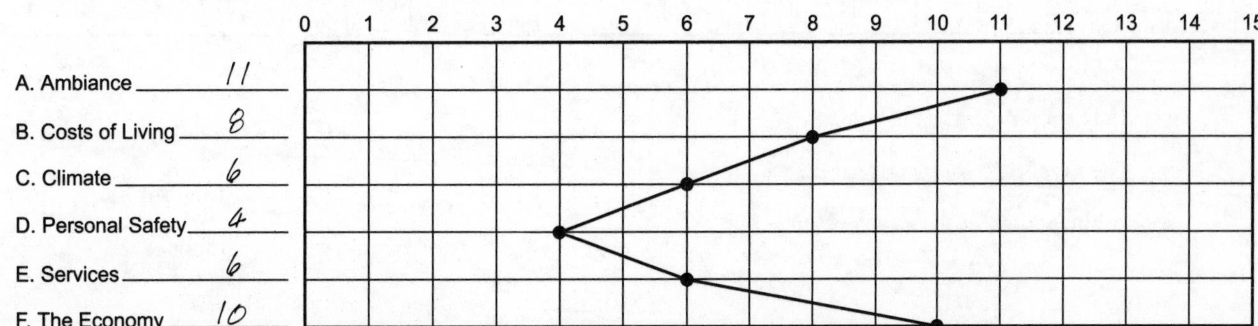

Your Preference Profiles

	0	1	2	3	4	5	6	7	8	9	10	11	12	13	14	15
A. Ambiance																
B. Costs of Living																
C. Climate																
D. Personal Safety																
E. Services																
F. The Economy																

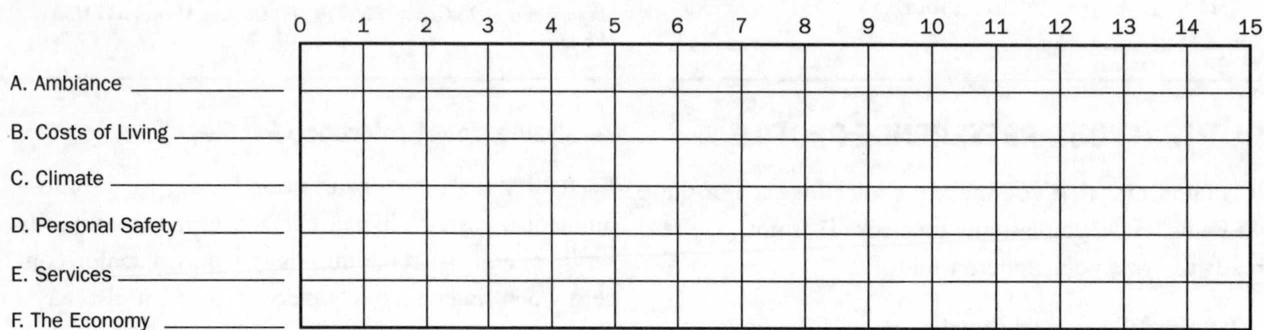

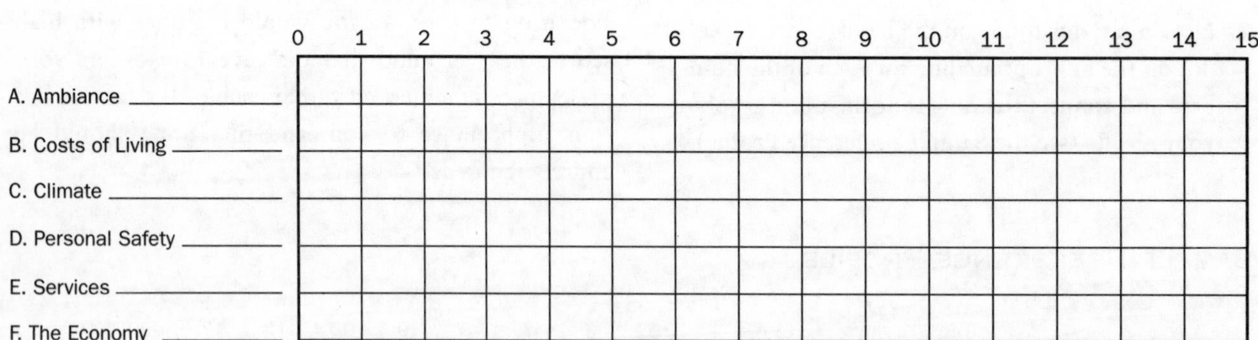

Ambiance

The hardest-to-define dimension of a place—harder than its costs of living, climate, crime, job opportunities, or the availability of health care and educational services—is its ambiance, its atmosphere, the way it feels, the way it may make you feel about living there. Is this location interesting, exciting, diverse, comfortable, relaxed? Does it have a history and a soul that you notice when you walk down the sidewalk, drive down the street, or simply stretch out in your backyard?

Along with an acceptable alternative spelling ("ambience"), there isn't one kind of ambiance, but many. Some people thrive on the hustle and bustle of Manhattan. Others can think of nothing more idyllic than a quiet spot by a rural lake. But a number of elements comprise that elusive feel—the people, the natural surroundings, the sense of history, the recreational opportunities, the food, the arts, the culture. For many older adults, the best places to retire boast an interesting mix of all these elements.

Like mild and dry climates, ambiance isn't distributed fairly. Chapel Hill–Carrboro, North Carolina, for example, has indoor blessings in good restaurants and a fine performing arts calendar, but few amenities outdoors in scenic or protected recreation land. Over in Rabun County, Georgia, hundreds of miles to the west, the situation is reversed: no lively arts but enviable riches in lakes and extensive natural areas. In still other places, such as Middle Cape Cod, Massachusetts, or Santa Barbara, California, free-time attractions are plentiful indoors and out. For many older adults, an ideal haven balances fun and games with culture and the arts, culture and the arts with the great outdoors, and all of it in an interesting setting.

OBSERVING A VISIBLE PAST

Stroll the cobblestone streets of Charleston, South Carolina, and you feel as if you've journeyed back in time to before the outbreak of the Civil War. Step into the central plaza of Santa Fe, New Mexico, and imagine the days when the city was an outpost of Spain. Travel a bit outside of the New Mexico capital, and you encounter the pueblos of Native Americans as they existed before the Europeans had any idea that there was a "New World."

Charleston is quite different from Santa Fe. But one of the reasons both cities are among the top-rated retirement places is the contribution that history makes to their ambiance. Santa Fe mandates the Spanish–Pueblo adobe-and-wood construction that recalls the city's 18th- and 19th-century past, for instance, and Charleston's zoning code protects even the most dilapidated antebellum "shotgun" shack from demolition. Their histories are different, but both have preserved a palpable sense of their pasts, and thus have created an enticing present.

The visible past is an important component of all places' ambiance. As Richard Moe, president of the National Trust for Historic Preservation, puts it, historical places are important, "not just as isolated bits of architecture and landscape, not just as lifeless monuments, but as environments where we can connect with the lives of the generations that came before us, places where we can build and maintain safe, rich, meaningful lives for ourselves and the generations that will come after us."

You don't have to live in an exceptional place like Charleston or Santa Fe to enjoy a sense of the past. Communities preserve their visible history by saving a school, a house, a hotel, or a department store that provides a link to the years gone by. And the preserved buildings don't have to be frozen as museum pieces, either. The school can become a restaurant, the house a bed-and-breakfast, the department store an apartment house, the hotel . . . well, it can still be a hotel.

Retirement Places Rated scores a community's visible past by counting the number of "contributing" residential buildings in historic districts listed on the National Register of Historic Places. The Register was established by the *National Historic Preservation Act of 1966*. It calls attention to "districts, sites, buildings, structures and objects that are significant in American history, architecture, archeology, engineering and culture." Contributing buildings are "unaltered, authentic historic structures" that are eligible for preservation tax credits.

TWENTY VISIBLE PASTS

Just one in three retirement places with significant collections of historic buildings are in the Sun Belt. But the ones that count—Savannah, Tucson, Key West, and Charleston—are among the best-known places in the U.S. for historic preservation. Below are 20 retirement places with the most contributing residential buildings in historic districts.

Annapolis, MD
Burlington, VT
Charles Town–Shepherdstown, WV
Charleston, SC
Charlottesville, VA
Daytona Beach, FL
East End Long Island, NY
Kalispell–Flathead Valley, MT
Key West, FL
Lakeland–Winter Haven, FL
Litchfield Hills, CT
Madison, WI
Medford–Ashland, OR
Middle Cape Cod, MA
Northampton–Amherst, MA
Rehoboth Bay–Indian River Bay, DE
Savannah, GA
Southern Berkshire County, MA
State College, PA
Tucson, AZ
Woodstock, VT

Source: Derived from the National Park Service, National Register of Historic Places.

SAMPLING THE LIVELY ARTS CALENDAR

How do you measure the cultural goings-on in another place? If you loved your hometown's symphony, will you, after surfacing somewhere else, have to settle for shaded seats at the annual outdoor Country Harmonica Blowoff?

Put it another way: if you exchange a big place for a smaller one, dirty air for clean, cold seasons for warm sun, the costly for the economical, do you also risk trading the lively arts for a cultural desert?

A catalog of culture can include, among many things, art and history museums, comedy clubs, live theater, bookstore readings, National Public Radio stations, street festivals, and charity auctions. *Retirement Places Rated* doesn't attempt such comprehensiveness. Instead, it focuses on three common crowd-pleasers that take place on the local campus or in civic auditoriums.

Touring Artists Bookings

Long before a touring pianist, European boys choir, or visiting New York contemporary dance troupe comes to town for a date at the local performing arts center, the guest performer is booked by a nonprofit college or community concert association.

Does this mean you'll find the performing arts only in a big city blessed with an expensive concert hall and a nonprofit community concert association bankrolled by philanthropists, managed by paid professionals, and attended by season member-subscribers? Not necessarily.

The attendance growth at fine arts concerts is due not to turning up the volume and variety of performances in big cities but to popular interest in smaller cities and towns. And a good part of the interest comes from older fans. Among the 203 places in this guide, 124 benefit from 287 college and community arts series that regularly book touring artists.

Resident Ensembles

Besides taking in the touring attractions, people in some places have the additional option of attending performances of resident ensembles.

Opera. The image of horned helmets, silvery shields, and unintelligible singing is a low-brow cliché. Fans boast that operatic stagecraft is the most demanding of the performing arts because of the unique commingling of instruments and voice with theater and dance; if you're introduced to a good production, they say, you'll be hooked for life. Among the 23 places in this book with live opera, Brevard, North Carolina; Madison, Wisconsin; and Santa Fe, New Mexico may have little else in common but they all belong to this group.

Symphony Orchestras. Orchestras are more common than opera companies; in fact, 63 places in this book have at least one. Their music is heard in woodsy state parks, high-school auditoriums, philharmonic halls, impressive new civic arts centers, and small-town bandboxes and pavilions.

CONSIDERING OUTDOOR RECREATION ASSETS

For many, the great outdoors is one of the most important factors behind a move in retirement. It takes in a wide range of possibilities. It might mean lying on a Gulf Coast beach, tramping the Appalachian Trail, fly-casting for Rocky Mountain rainbow trout, day-sailing on Chesapeake Bay, or just getting away from it all to a cabin on the edge of a Pacific Northwest wilderness area.

Well before the time comes for shedding job obligations, many people have already identified from past family vacations the places where, when they retire, their own ideal of the great outdoors will be right outside their door.

Enviable Touring Artist Bookings

What will $60 get you in Iowa City? Two tickets for any of the nearly 50 performance dates at the University of Iowa's Hancher Auditorium—all in Orchestra I, the best seats in the house, with parking thrown in. In New York or Chicago, that money won't cover dinner before the show.

Below, the Hancher's schedule for the 2003–04 season rebuts any notion that the lively arts aren't cultivated out on the Iowa prairie.

Stefon Harris Quartet—Sept 20
The Full Monty—Sept 23–28
Brentano String Quartet—Oct 8
Bill T. Jones/Arnie Zane Dance Company—Oct 11
Emmylou Harris—Oct 15
Academy of St. Martin in the Fields—Oct 18
Drummers of West Africa—Oct 19
Terence Blanchard—Oct 23
Estonian Philharmonic Chamber Choir—Oct 26
Cloud Gate Dance Theatre of Taiwan—Nov 12
Charlie Haden and Gonzalo Rubalcaba—Nov 15
Mamma Mia!—Dec 9–14
Urban Tap—Jan 24
SoVoSó—Jan 28
Moscow Festival Ballet: *Cinderella*—Jan 30
Cirque Éloize—Feb 6–8
Christopher O'Riley/UI Symphony—Feb 11
Aquila Theatre Company: *Othello*—Feb 17–18
New York Festival of Song—Feb 19
Kalichstein-Laredo-Robinson Trio—Feb 24
Bang on a Can All-Stars—Feb 28
Pilobolus Dance Theatre—Mar 5
Antares—Mar 25
Paul Taylor Dance Company—Apr 16–17

Source: The University of Iowa.

Lively Arts Calendars

Certainly for Tucson or San Diego's northern suburbs, the market for performing arts gets better with population size. Being the location for summer music festivals, as in Traverse City, Michigan's case, or home to a large university, as in Madison, Wisconsin's case, doesn't hurt either. The following table lists the places with the most active performing arts calendars during 2003:

PLACE	PERFORMANCE DATES
North County San Diego, CA	367
Boca Raton, FL	264
East End Long Island, NY	257
Sarasota, FL	255
Tucson, AZ	233
Traverse City, MI	215
Naples, FL	180
Palm Springs–Coachella Valley, CA	180
Lake Winnipesaukee, NH	175
Pensacola, FL	160
Chapel Hill–Carrboro, NC	157
Laguna Beach–Dana Point, CA	154
Madison, WI	137
Santa Barbara, CA	131
Fort Collins–Loveland, CO	127

Source: Primedia, Musical America: 2002 International Directory of the Performing Arts.

The Water Draw

Maryland watermen tell mainland tourists, many who come to Chesapeake Bay fishing villages for the oysters and soft-shell crabs, that the true length of estuarine shore reached by the bay's tide would total more than 8,000 miles if all the kinks and bends were flattened out.

They say in Michigan's Roscommon County that the locals tend to live away from Houghton Lake, the state's biggest inland body of water, while the transplanted retired folks who've migrated up from Detroit or Cleveland or Chicago unerringly light on the shore like loons there for the duration.

And Oklahomans vaunt the state's collection of Corps of Engineer lakes. If you could tip the state a bit to the south, they say, the water would flow out and flood Texas for a good while.

There's not much connection between the migration of retired people on the one hand and the sight of water on the other, however. Water didn't play nearly as great a part in attracting older adults during the 1980s as did a mild climate and resort development. In fact, certain Arizona, Nevada, and New Mexico counties that are desert-dry attracted retired people at a faster rate than wet counties in other parts of the country.

For all that, you'll spot lakes, ponds, and marine bays in 9 out of 10 of the 203 *Retirement Places Rated* locations. Aside from being a basic necessity for supporting life, water is regarded by most people as a scenic amenity; many regard it as a recreational amenity—as long as there is enough of it to fish in, boat on, or swim in without enduring snow-melt-cold temperatures. What's Petoskey, Michigan, without the Straits of Mackinac?

Or Cape Cod minus the Atlantic Ocean? Four out of five Americans today live within a hundred miles of a coastline; in another 10 years, the Department of the Interior predicts three out of four will live within 50 miles. Not surprisingly, 67 *Retirement Places Rated* havens have an ocean or Great Lakes coastline.

Counting Acres: The Public Lands

Of all the outdoor activities that older adults take to most frequently, the leading ones—pleasure driving, walking, picnicking, sightseeing, bird-watching, nature walking, and fishing—might arguably be more fun in the country's splendid system of federal- and state-run public recreation areas.

National Forests. "Clear-Cutting Turns Off Tourists" say the bumper stickers in northwest Arkansas. So do rumbling, 18-wheel logger's trucks. Although various parts of the national forests are classified as "wilderness," "primitive," "scenic," "historic," or "recreation" areas, the main purpose of the system is silviculture: growing wood, harvesting it carefully, and preserving naturally beautiful areas from the depredations of amateur chain saws, burger palaces, miniature golf, and time-share condos.

In rainy Deschutes National Forest near Bend, Oregon, the harvest is Douglas fir. Among the widespread components of Mark Twain National Forest in the southern Missouri Ozarks, the crop is local hardwoods of blackjack oak and hickory. Within Pisgah National Forest in western North Carolina (near Asheville), the trees are virgin oak, beech, and black walnut.

But also within the forest system are more than a quarter of a million miles of paved roads, built not just for logging crews but for everyone. They lead to a wide variety of recreation developments: some 400 privately operated resorts, marinas, and ski lodges, plus fishing lakes and streams, campgrounds, and hiking trails. In 92 places profiled in the following pages, more than 3½ million acres are national forest lands.

National Parks. Where multiple use is the philosophy behind national forests, the National Park Service preserves irreplaceable geographic and historic treasures for public recreation. This has been its mission ever since Congress created Yellowstone National Park back in 1872, in adjacent western corners of the old Montana and Wyoming territories, "as a public park or pleasuring ground for the benefit and enjoyment of the people."

The collection of national parks, preserves, monuments, memorials, battlefields, seashores, river ways, and trails makes up the oldest and largest national park system in the world. Eleven million of the National Park System's 79 million acres are found in *Retirement Places Rated* areas.

National Wildlife Refuges. Wildlife refuges protect native flora and fauna from people. This purpose hasn't changed since 1903, when Theodore Roosevelt created the first refuge, Pelican Island near Vero Beach, Florida, to save the mangrove-nesting egrets from poachers scrounging for plumage to adorn women's hats.

Most of the country's 498 refuges are open for wildlife activities, particularly photography and nature observation. In certain of the refuges and at irregular times, fishing and hunting are permitted, depending on the size of the refuge's wild populations. But you don't have to move to the sticks to be close to nature: one-third of the land area of Clark County, Nevada (where Las Vegas is the seat of government), is dedicated to wildlife refuges. Fort Myers–Cape Coral, Florida, has four refuges on 5,664 acres—Caloosahatchee, J.N. "Ding" Darling, Matlacha Pass, and Pine Island.

State Recreation Areas. The 10 million acres of state-run recreation areas are often equal in quality to the federal public lands, and in most states, older visitors get a break on entrance fees. They range from small day-use parks in wooded areas or on beaches, offering little more than picnic tables and restrooms; to large rugged parks and forests with developed hiking trails and campsites; to big-time destination resorts complete with golf courses, swimming pools, tennis courts, and full-time recreation staffs.

DIAMONDS AND STARS: FINDING GOOD RESTAURANTS

The most common service establishment in this country is the one where you walk in, sit down, and order something to eat. If you enjoy an occasional dinner splurge, you may as well go to a worthwhile eatery instead of a diner or a portion-controlled *Casa de la Maison House* where distantly prepared frozen packs of beef Wellington and veal cordon bleu are microwaved, dished out, and "menued" at 10 times what the chef paid for them.

To learn which places have restaurants more than just a cut or two above average, *Retirement Places Rated* consulted the *American Automobile Association (AAA) TourBooks* and the *Mobil Travel Guides,* which for decades have rated restaurants across the country.

The ratings come from two sources: customer comments and inspection reports of field representatives who dine anonymously at establishments throughout the year. Restaurants are judged by the quality of their food, service, and ambiance.

One AAA diamond or Mobil star indicates a simple, family or specialty meal in clean, pleasant, and informal surroundings. The food is basic and wholesome, and the service is casual or self-serve. *Contrary Mary's*, near Branson, Missouri, fits this description with its takeout and inexpensive family menu.

Las Cruces' reasonably priced *Hacienda* restaurant, serving New Mexico specialties, is an example of a two-diamond establishment. Eateries at this level offer a more extensive menu for family or adult dining. Service is attentive but informal, and the decor presents a unified theme that is either comfortable or trendy and upbeat.

Three-star or three-diamond restaurants present upscale adult or special family dining. There is a wine

list, and food is cooked to order and creatively prepared with quality ingredients. The wait staff is skilled and professional, and the ambiance is inviting and trendy or formal. Scottsdale, Arizona's *Windows on the Green*, specializing in American Southwest cuisine, illustrates this category.

Asheville, North Carolina, has two four-diamond establishments: *Gabrielle's* in the Richmond Hill Inn and *Horizon's* in the Grove Park Inn. As with four-star restaurants, the service is formally attired and sophisticated; the wine list extensive; the food complex and creatively presented.

The five-diamond and the five-star designation represents the ultimate and most memorable adult dining experiences, with "flawless" being a key word—in food preparation and presentation, in service, and in atmosphere.

Eating Out

Like Michelin with its three-star ratings, the *AAA TourBooks* are stingy with their five diamonds. Among the 2,884 AAA-rated establishments in the places profiled throughout this book, just eight earn that designation.

AAA FIVE-DIAMOND RESTAURANTS

The Dining Room at the Ritz-Carlton Laguna Niguel—Dana Point, CA

The Dining Room at the Ritz-Carlton Naples—Naples, FL

The Dining Room at Woodlands—Summerville, SC

Erna's Elderberry House—Oakhurst, CA

Fearrington House—Chapel Hill, NC

Marquesa—Scottsdale, AZ

Mary Elaine's—Scottsdale, AZ

White Barn Inn—Kennebunk (York Beaches), ME

SCORING: AMBIANCE

Even if we could all agree on the measurable things that contribute to a place's ambiance, ranking places, let's admit, can't be done fairly. There are simply too many likes and dislikes. A Florida bass fisherman, hauling out his smoky outboard motor for a tune-up, may care less about the announced dates of a local civic concert series. A Cape Cod couple lolling on the beach may never know the joys of rehabbing a Queen Anne house in Port Townsend, Washington, nor would they ever regret the loss.

There are too many differences in taste for a rating system to suit everyone. Yet it's still possible to measure the supply of specific amenities. Chamber of Commerce brochures and state tourism promotion kits do it all the time. Travelers make their own comparisons. Hearsay may hold that winter living in the northern Michigan flatwoods is as dull and lonesome today as it was for the natives who quit the area for the city generations ago, or that there's little historical feel to sun-baked Henderson, Nevada.

Retirement Places Rated tries a more objective approach. It neither judges the quality of music by local symphonies and opera companies nor pushes the scenic benefits of the desert over seashore or forest environs. It simply indicates the presence of things that most persons agree enhance retirement living.

Each place starts with a base score of zero, to which scores are added according to the following criteria.

VISIBLE PAST

Within each place, the number of residential buildings defined by the National Register of Historic Places as "contributing" to the authentic appearance of historic districts is totaled. The result is then scaled against a standard where the greatest number of contributing homes gets a score of 100, the average number produces a score of 50, and none yields a score of 0. Savannah, Georgia, with its collection of historic districts and homes gets 100. Santa Barbara, California, earns 50. Henderson, Nevada, a rapidly growing suburb of Las Vegas with no historic buildings, earns 0.

THE LIVELY ARTS CALENDAR

In the calendar year, the number of dates booked for touring fine arts groups to perform at campus and civic auditoriums is added to the number of performance dates for local opera and ballet companies and symphony orchestras. The result is then scaled against a standard where the greatest number of dates gets 100, the average number produces 50, and no dates yields 0. North County San Diego, California; Fredericksburg, Texas; and 75 locations from Amador County in the California Sierras to the York Beaches on Maine's Atlantic coast are respectively, among the best, average, and worst in the lively arts calendar.

OUTDOOR RECREATION ASSETS

In the United States, a total of 18.63 percent of the land area is classified as inland or coastal water, federal protected land, or state recreation area.

Each place's own area percentage for each of these four kinds of outdoor recreation assets is totaled. The result is then scaled against a standard where the highest figure gets 100, the average figure produces 50, and none yields 0. Of the 203 retirement places, Jackson Hole, Wyoming; Largo, Florida; and Athens, Georgia, are respectively among the best, average, and worst for outdoor assets.

GOOD RESTAURANTS

The number of quality diamonds and quality stars are added for restaurants rated by AAA and Mobil in each place. The result is then scaled against a standard where the highest figure gets 100, the average figure produces 50, and none yields 0. Out of 203 retirement places, Charleston, South Carolina; Hot Springs, Arkansas; and some 16 places with no restaurants rated by AAA or Mobil, are respectively among the best, average, and worst for good restaurants.

RANKINGS: AMBIANCE

Eight factors are used to rate a place's leisure-living assets: (1) **good restaurants;** (2) **campus and civic auditorium touring artist bookings;** (3) **resident ballet companies, opera companies, and symphony orchestras;** (4) **ocean and Great Lakes coastal water areas;** (5) **inland water areas;** (6) **federal protected lands;** (7) **state recreation areas;** and (8) **"contributing buildings" in the National Register of Historic Places.** Scores are rounded to one decimal place. Locations that are tied get the same rank and are listed alphabetically.

Retirement Places from First to Last

RANK	PLACE	SCORE
1.	Tucson, AZ	100.0
2.	Bellingham, WA	99.5
3.	Charleston, SC	99.0
4.	East End Long Island, NY	98.5
5.	Kalispell–Flathead Valley, MT	98.0
6.	Lake Winnipesaukee, NH	97.5
7.	Fort Collins–Loveland, CO	97.0
8.	North County San Diego, CA	96.5
9.	Savannah, GA	96.0
10.	Medford–Ashland, OR	95.5
11.	Key West, FL	95.0
12.	Durango, CO	94.5
13.	Middle Cape Cod, MA	94.0
14.	Flagstaff, AZ	93.5
15.	Daytona Beach, FL	93.0
16.	Santa Barbara, CA	92.5
17.	Bozeman, MT	91.5
17.	Toms River–Barnegat Bay, NJ	91.5
19.	Santa Fe, NM	91.0
20.	Cottonwood–Verde Valley, AZ	90.0
20.	Hanover, NH	90.0
22.	Melbourne–Palm Bay, FL	89.6
23.	Victorville–Apple Valley, CA	89.1
24.	Pensacola, FL	88.6
25.	Litchfield Hills, CT	88.1
26.	Williamsburg, VA	87.6
27.	Burlington, VT	87.1
28.	Taos, NM	86.6
29.	Charlottesville, VA	86.1
30.	Palm Springs–Coachella Valley, CA	85.6
31.	Southern Berkshire County, MA	85.1
32.	Florence, OR	84.6
33.	Fredericksburg–Spotsylvania, VA	84.1
34.	Woodstock, VT	83.6
35.	Lower Cape May, NJ	83.1
36.	Asheville, NC	82.1
36.	Naples, FL	82.1
38.	Bar Harbor, ME	81.6
39.	Madison, WI	81.1
40.	Northampton–Amherst, MA	80.6
41.	Brevard, NC	79.7
41.	Camden, ME	79.7
43.	Colorado Springs, CO	79.2
44.	Chestertown, MD	78.7
45.	Annapolis, MD	78.2
46.	Carson City–Carson Valley, NV	77.7
47.	Hot Springs, AR	77.2
48.	Fort Myers–Cape Coral, FL	76.7
49.	Wenatchee, WA	76.2
50.	St. George–Zion, UT	75.7
51.	Lakeland–Winter Haven, FL	75.2
52.	Ocala, FL	74.7
53.	Yuma, AZ	74.2
54.	Silver City, NM	73.7
55.	State College, PA	73.2
56.	Coeur d'Alene, ID	72.7
57.	Monadnock Region, NH	72.2
58.	Maryville, TN	71.7
59.	Mariposa, CA	71.2
60.	Rio Rancho, NM	70.7
61.	Easton–St. Michaels, MD	70.2
62.	Sandpoint–Lake Pend Oreille, ID	69.3
62.	Sarasota, FL	69.3
64.	Chapel Hill–Carrboro, NC	68.8
65.	Gainesville, FL	68.3
66.	Santa Rosa, CA	67.8
67.	Grand Junction, CO	67.3
68.	Door Peninsula, WI	66.8
69.	Petoskey–Harbor Springs, MI	66.3
70.	Carmel–Pebble Beach, CA	65.3
70.	Natchitoches, LA	65.3

continued

Retirement Places from First to Last (cont.)

RANK	PLACE	SCORE	RANK	PLACE	SCORE
72.	Reno–Sparks, NV	64.8	138.	Lake Placid, NY	32.1
73.	Western St. Tammany Parish, LA	64.3	139.	Fredericksburg, TX	31.6
74.	Charles Town–Shepherdstown, WV	63.8	140.	Rabun County, GA	31.1
75.	Martha's Vineyard, MA	63.3	141.	Alpine–Big Bend, TX	30.6
76.	St. Augustine, FL	62.8	142.	Brookings–Gold Beach, OR	30.1
77.	Las Vegas, NM	62.3	143.	Rehoboth Bay–Indian River Bay, DE	29.7
78.	Jackson Hole, WY	61.3	144.	Largo, FL	29.2
78.	Port Townsend, WA	61.3	145.	New Bern, NC	28.7
80.	Traverse City, MI	60.8	146.	Pike County, PA	28.2
81.	Ketchum–Sun Valley, ID	60.3	147.	Anacortes, WA	27.7
82.	Mesa, AZ	59.9	148.	Front Royal, VA	27.2
83.	Oxford, MS	59.4	149.	Leelanau Peninsula, MI	26.7
84.	Laguna Beach–Dana Point, CA	58.9	150.	Northern Neck, VA	26.2
85.	Grants Pass, OR	58.4	151.	Pagosa Springs, CO	25.7
86.	Prescott–Prescott Valley, AZ	57.4	152.	Rockport–Aransas Pass, TX	25.2
86.	Scottsdale, AZ	57.4	153.	New Port Richey, FL	24.2
88.	Fayetteville, AR	56.4	153.	Sebring–Avon Park, FL	24.2
88.	Hendersonville–East Flat Rock, NC	56.4	155.	Amador County, CA	23.7
90.	Apalachicola, FL	55.4	156.	Panama City, FL	23.2
90.	San Juan Islands, WA	55.4	157.	Whidbey Island, WA	22.7
92.	Port Angeles–Sequim, WA	54.9	158.	York Beaches, ME	22.2
93.	Beaufort, SC	54.4	159.	Myrtle Beach, SC	21.7
94.	Virginia Beach, VA	53.9	160.	Cedar City, UT	21.2
95.	Hilton Head Island, SC	53.4	161.	Oakhurst–Coarsegold, CA	20.7
96.	Maui, HI	52.9	162.	Smith Mountain Lake, VA	20.2
97.	Salida, CO	52.4	163.	Roswell, NM	19.8
98.	Beaufort–Bogue Banks, NC	50.9	164.	Bradenton, FL	19.3
98.	Port Charlotte, FL	50.9	165.	Polson–Mission Valley, MT	18.8
98.	Southern Pines–Pinehurst, NC	50.9	166.	Bullhead City, AZ	17.8
101.	Bay St. Louis–Pass Christian, MS	50.4	166.	Kingman, AZ	17.8
102.	Sedona, AZ	50.0	168.	Chewelah, WA	17.3
103.	Sonora–Twain Harte, CA	49.5	169.	Lake Havasu City, AZ	16.8
104.	Las Cruces, NM	48.5	170.	Murray–Kentucky Lake, KY	16.3
104.	Newport–Lincoln City, OR	48.5	171.	Montrose, CO	15.8
106.	Iowa City, IA	48.0	172.	Summerville, SC	15.3
107.	Thomasville, GA	47.5	173.	Delta County, CO	14.8
108.	Grass Valley–Nevada City, CA	46.0	174.	Alamogordo, NM	14.3
108.	Hattiesburg, MS	46.0	175.	Eufaula, AL	13.8
108.	Payson, AZ	46.0	176.	Lake Conroe, TX	13.3
111.	Bend, OR	45.5	177.	Brown County, IN	12.8
112.	Boca Raton, FL	45.0	178.	Apache Junction, AZ	12.3
113.	Aiken, SC	44.5	179.	Ocean City, MD	11.8
114.	Georgetown, TX	44.0	180.	Oscoda–Huron Shore, MI	11.3
115.	Ruidoso, NM	43.5	181.	Vero Beach, FL	10.8
116.	Mendocino–Fort Bragg, CA	43.0	182.	Norfork Lake, AR	10.3
117.	Columbia, MO	42.5	183.	Kissimmee–St. Cloud, FL	9.9
118.	St. Jay–Northeast Kingdom, VT	42.0	184.	Pahrump Valley, NV	9.4
119.	Fairhope–Gulf Shores, AL	41.5	185.	Branson, MO	8.9
120.	Palmer–Wasilla, AK	41.0	186.	Eureka Springs, AR	8.4
121.	Morro Bay–Cambria, CA	40.5	187.	Wimberley, TX	7.9
122.	McCall, ID	40.0	188.	Inverness, FL	7.4
123.	Athens, GA	39.6	189.	Tryon, NC	6.9
124.	Mission–McAllen–Alamo, TX	39.1	190.	Lake of the Ozarks, MO	6.4
125.	Pendleton District, SC	38.6	191.	Conway, SC	5.9
126.	Eagle River–Woodruff, WI	38.1	192.	Kauai, HI	5.4
127.	Dare Outer Banks, NC	37.6	193.	Trinity Peninsula, TX	4.9
128.	Leesburg–Mount Dora, FL	37.1	194.	Southport–Brunswick Islands, NC	4.4
129.	Crossville, TN	36.6	195.	Table Rock Lake, MO	3.9
130.	Park City, UT	36.1	196.	Wickenburg, AZ	3.4
131.	Berkeley Springs, WV	35.6	197.	Cedar Creek Lake, TX	2.9
132.	Bisbee, AZ	35.1	198.	Boerne, TX	2.4
133.	Paradise–Magalia, CA	34.6	199.	Marble Falls–Lake LBJ, TX	1.9
134.	Hamilton–Bitterroot Valley, MT	34.1	200.	Henderson, NV	1.4
135.	Boone–Blowing Rock, NC	33.6	201.	Lake of the Cherokees, OK	0.9
136.	Edenton, NC	33.1	202.	New Braunfels, TX	0.4
137.	St. Simons–Jekyll Islands, GA	32.6	203.	Kerrville, TX	0.0

PLACE PROFILES: AMBIANCE

The following capsule profiles are selective features that contribute interest, ambiance, and difference to the retirement places rated in this book. To the right of the bolded headings for each place, in parentheses, is a rating scaled to a standard where 100 is best, 50 average, and 0 worst.

The profiles begin with the category **Visible Past,** which counts the number of local "contributing buildings" in the National Register of Historic Places database, the year most of the area's housing was built (the older, the better), and units of the national and state park systems categorized as "historic/cultural." Listed below the Visible Past heading are designated Historic Districts that are residential—as opposed to commercial—neighborhoods, if any.

The next category, **Lively Arts Calendar,** identifies the place's major campus or civic auditorium in italics and counts the annual number of dates booked for touring arts groups as reported by *Musical America*'s most recent survey. The number of dates for resident ballet, opera, and symphony performances is also counted. If a place has no entry, then it has no established performing arts series or resident musical ensemble tracked by *Musical America.*

The next category, **Outdoor Recreation Assets,** counts the square miles of ocean or Great Lakes coastal water, the square miles of inland water, the national and state park acres categorized as "scenic" or "recreational," and National Forest and National Wildlife Refuges acres within each retirement place.

The figures for inland water include ponds and lakes if their surface areas are 40 acres or more. Streams, canals, and rivers are also counted if their width is ⅛ mile or more. The water area along irregular Great Lakes and ocean coastlines is counted, too, if the bays, inlets, and estuaries are between 1 and 10 miles in width.

A list of federal protected lands—units of the National Park Service, National Forests, and National Wildlife Refuges—is included as are each unit of the state's park system. In this section, the following abbreviations are used:

NF:	National Forest
NHP:	National Historic Park
NHS:	National Historic Site
NM:	National Monument
NMP:	National Military Park
NP:	National Park
NRA:	National Recreation Area
NS:	National Seashore
NWR:	National Wildlife Refuge
SB:	State Beach
SF:	State Forest
SHP:	State Historic Park
SHS:	State Historic Site
SNA:	State Natural Area
SP:	State Park
SR:	State Reserve or Refuge
SRA:	State Recreation Area
SVRA:	State Vehicular Recreation Area

The last category, **Good Restaurants,** takes into account weighted quality stars in the multi-volume *Mobil Travel Guides* and weighted quality diamonds in the *AAA TourBooks* awarded to local restaurants.

A place's final score equally weights the **Visible Past, Lively Arts Calendar, Outdoor Recreation Assets,** and **Good Restaurants** scores and scales the result against a standard where 100 is best, 50 average, and 0 worst. A star (★) preceding a place's name highlights it as one of the top 30 places for ambiance.

Information comes from these sources: ABC Leisure Magazines, *Musical America: 2002 International Directory of the Performing Arts*; American Automobile Association unpublished restaurant ratings, 2003; American Symphony Orchestra League, *Orchestra and Business Directory*, 2003; Globe Pequot Press, *Mobil Travel Guides*, 2003; Places Rated Partnership survey of state parks and recreation departments, 2003; U.S. Department of Agriculture, *Land Areas of the National Forest System*, 2003; U.S. Department of Commerce, Bureau of the Census, unpublished land and water area measurements, 2000; National Oceanic and Atmospheric Administration, *The Coastline of the United States*, 1975; U.S. Department of the Interior, Fish and Wildlife Service, *Annual Report*, 2003, and unpublished master deed listing, 2003; and National Park Service, *Index to the National Park System and Related Areas*, 2003, unpublished master deed listing, 2003, and unpublished National Register of Historic Places database, 2003.

Aiken, SC

Visible Past (75)
Aiken Winter Colony Historic District
Salley Historic District
Vaucluse Mill Village Historic District

Lively Arts Calendar (58)
Etherredge Center
Touring artists bookings: 14 dates

Outdoor Recreation Assets (4)
Inland water: 7.46 square miles
State recreation areas:
Aiken SP (1,067 acres)
Redcliffe SP (350 acres)

Good Restaurants (22)

Score: 44.5 **Rank: 113**

Alamogordo, NM

Visible Past (35)
La Luz Historic District
Tularosa Original Townsite District

Outdoor Recreation Assets (47)
Inland water: 0.90 square miles
Federal protected areas:
Lincoln NF (563,712 acres)
White Sands NM (90,955 acres)
State recreation area:
Oliver Lee Memorial SP (200 acres)

Good Restaurants (9)

Score: 14.3 **Rank: 174**

Alpine–Big Bend, TX

Visible Past (51)

Outdoor Recreation Assets (60)
Inland water: 0.18 square miles
Federal protected areas:
Big Bend NP (775,279 acres)
Rio Grande Wild and Scenic River
State recreation area:
Big Bend Ranch SNA (18,000 acres)

Good Restaurants (9)

Score: 30.6 **Rank: 141**

Amador County, CA

Visible Past (36)
Fiddletown
Jackson Downtown Historic District

Outdoor Recreation Assets (65)
Inland water: 11.70 square miles
Federal protected area:
Eldorado NF (77,955 acres)
State recreation area:
Indian Grinding Rock SHP (135 acres)

Good Restaurants (18)

Score: 23.7 **Rank: 155**

Anacortes, WA

Visible Past (17)

Outdoor Recreation Assets (89)
Pacific coastal water: 14.55 square miles
Inland water: 40.12 square miles
Federal protected areas:
Mt. Baker NF (368,690 acres)
North Cascades NP (156,114 acres)
Ross Lake NRA (8,791 acres)
San Juan Islands NWR (4 acres)
State recreation areas:
Bay View SP (25 acres)
Burrows Island SP (344 acres)
Cascade Island (37 acres)
Cone Island SP (10 acres)
Deception Pass SP (1,233 acres)
Everett Property (10 acres)
Heart Lake SP (436 acres)
Huckleberry Island SP (10 acres)
Larrabee SP (294 acres)
Northwest Region (1 acre)
O'Brien-Riggs SP (100 acres)
Rasar SP (669 acres)
Saddlebag Island SP (23 acres)
Skagit River SP (30 acres)

Good Restaurants (63)

Score: 27.7 **Rank: 147**

Annapolis, MD

Visible Past (88)
Colonial Annapolis Historic District

Lively Arts Calendar (78)
Maryland Hall for the Creative Arts
Touring artists bookings: 3 dates
Resident ensembles:
Annapolis Chamber Orchestra (8 dates)
Annapolis Opera (5 dates)
Annapolis Symphony Orchestra (14 dates)
Ballet Theatre of Annapolis (18 dates)

Outdoor Recreation Assets (28)
Chesapeake coastal water: 134.02 square miles
Inland water: 37.87 square miles
Federal protected area:
National Capital Parks (432 acres)
State recreation areas:
Patapsco Valley SP (986 acres)
Sandy Point SP (786 acres)

Good Restaurants (77)

Score: 78.2 **Rank: 45**

Apache Junction, AZ

Visible Past (1)
Florence Townsite Historic District

Lively Arts Calendar (55)
Touring artists bookings: 12 dates

Outdoor Recreation Assets (20)
Federal protected areas:
Casa Grande Ruins NM (473 acres)
Coronado NF (23,331 acres)
Hohokam Pima NM (1,690 acres)
Tonto NF (199,824 acres)
State recreation areas:
Boyce Thompson Southwestern Arboretum (35 acres)
Lost Dutchman SP (292 acres)
McFarland SHS (2 acres)
Oracle SP (4,000 acres)
Picacho Peak SP (3,440 acres)

Good Restaurants (18)

Score: 12.3 **Rank: 178**

★ = *one of the top 30 places for ambiance.*

Apalachicola, FL

Visible Past (74)

Apalachicola Historic District

Outdoor Recreation Assets (76)

Gulf coastal water: 199.00 square miles

Inland water: 32.00 square miles

Federal protected areas:

Apalachicola NF (21,816 acres)

St. Vincent NWR (12,445 acres)

State recreation areas:

Gorrie State Museum (1 acre)

St. George Island SP (1,963 acres)

Good Restaurants (9)

Score: 55.4 Rank: 90

Asheville, NC

Visible Past (95)

Chestnut Hill Historic District

Downtown Asheville Historic District

Grove Park Historic District

Montford Area Historic District

Lively Arts Calendar (77)

Thomas Wolfe Auditorium

Touring artists bookings: 35 dates

Resident ensemble:

Asheville Symphony Orchestra (10 dates)

Outdoor Recreation Assets (29)

Inland water: 3.77 square miles

Federal protected areas:

Blue Ridge Parkway (5,552 acres)

Pisgah NF (31,464 acres)

Good Restaurants (83)

Score: 82.1 Rank: 36

Athens, GA

Visible Past (74)

Bloomfield Street Historic District

Boulevard Historic District

Buena Vista Heights Historic District

Cobbham Historic District

Downtown Athens Historic District

West Hancock Avenue Historic District

Winterville Historic District

Lively Arts Calendar (54)

University Union

Touring artists bookings: 11 dates

Outdoor Recreation Assets (0)

Inland water: 0.46 square miles

Good Restaurants (18)

Score: 39.6 Rank: 123

Bar Harbor, ME

Visible Past (82)

Blue Hill Historic District

Castine Historic District

Somesville Historic District

West Street Historic District

Lively Arts Calendar (55)

Touring artists bookings: 12 dates

Outdoor Recreation Assets (61)

Atlantic coastal water: 166.00 square miles

Inland water: 299.01 square miles

Federal protected area:

Acadia NP (36,641 acres)

State recreation areas:

Duck Lake SNA (25,000 acres)

Four Ponds SNA (4,500 acres)

Holbrook Island Sanctuary SP (1,345 acres)

Lamoine SP (55 acres)

Scraggly Lake SNA (10,000 acres)

Good Restaurants (82)

Score: 81.6 Rank: 38

Bay St. Louis–Pass Christian, MS

Visible Past (82)

Beach Boulevard Historic District

Scenic Drive Historic District

Outdoor Recreation Assets (63)

Gulf coastal water: 386.96 square miles

Inland water: 23.16 square miles

Federal protected areas:

De Soto NF (62,516 acres)

Gulf Islands NS (19,997 acres)

State recreation area:

Buccaneer SP (393 acres)

Good Restaurants (39)

Score: 50.4 Rank: 101

Beaufort, SC

Visible Past (50)

Beaufort Historic District

Lively Arts Calendar (50)

McVey Performing Arts Center

Touring artists bookings: 9 dates

Outdoor Recreation Assets (48)

Atlantic coastal water: 55.81 square miles

Inland water: 109.66 square miles

Federal protected areas:

Ace Basin NWR (833 acres)

Pinckney Island NWR (1,325 acres)

State recreation area:

Hunting Island SP (5,000 acres)

Good Restaurants (68)

Score: 54.4 Rank: 93

Beaufort–Bogue Banks, NC

Visible Past (52)

Beaufort Historic District

Outdoor Recreation Assets (93)

Atlantic coastal water: 28.84 square miles

Inland water: 532.03 square miles

Federal protected areas:

Cape Lookout NS (25,174 acres)

Cedar Island NWR (14,482 acres)

Croatan NF (56,624 acres)

State recreation areas:

Fort Macon SP (389 acres)

Theodore Roosevelt SNA (265 acres)

Good Restaurants (48)

Score: 50.9 Rank: 98

★ Bellingham, WA

Visible Past (89)

Eldridge Avenue Historic District

Fairhaven Historic District

Sehome Hill Historic District

Lively Arts Calendar (74)

Mt. Baker Theatre

continued

★ = one of the top 30 places for ambiance.

★ **Bellingham, WA (cont.)**
Touring artists bookings: 30 dates
Resident ensemble:
Whatcom Symphony (6 dates)
Outdoor Recreation Assets (95)
Puget Sound coastal water: 328.16 square miles
Inland water: 55.43 square miles
Federal protected areas:
Mt. Baker NF (452,736 acres)
North Cascades NP (281,690 acres)
Ross Lake NRA (107,067 acres)
San Juan Islands NWR (3 acres)
State recreation areas:
Birch Bay SP (193 acres)
Larrabee SP (1,687 acres)
Peace Arch SP (20 acres)
Good Restaurants (67)
Score: 99.5 Rank: 2

Bend, OR
Visible Past (47)
Old Town Historic District
Outdoor Recreation Assets (93)
Inland water: 36.64 square miles
Federal protected area:
Deschutes NF (980,193 acres)
State recreation areas:
Cline Falls State Wayside (9 acres)
LaPine SP (2,333 acres)
Pilot Butte State Wayside (101 acres)
Robert Sawyer SP (1 acre)
Sisters SP (28 acres)
Smith Rock SP (624 acres)
Tumalo SP (330 acres)
Good Restaurants (46)
Score: 45.5 Rank: 111

Berkeley Springs, WV
Visible Past (64)
Outdoor Recreation Assets (54)
Inland water: 1.00 square mile
Federal protected area:
Chesapeake and Ohio Canal NHP (124 acres)
State recreation areas:
Berkeley Springs SP (4 acres)
Cacapon Resort SP (6,115 acres)
Good Restaurants (9)
Score: 35.6 Rank: 131

Bisbee, AZ
Visible Past (75)
Bisbee Historic District
Douglas Residential Historic District
Outdoor Recreation Assets (43)
Inland water: 49.00 square miles
Federal protected areas:
Chiricahua NM (11,982 acres)
Coronado NF (490,125 acres)
Coronado NM (4,743 acres)
Fort Bowie NHS (1,000 acres)
Leslie Canyon NWR (1,244 acres)
San Bernardino NWR (2,368 acres)
State recreation areas:
Kartchner Caverns SP (55 acres)
Tombstone Courthouse (1 acre)
Good Restaurants (43)
Score: 35.1 Rank: 132

Boca Raton, FL
Visible Past (3)
Lively Arts Calendar (100)
Florida Atlantic University Center
Touring artists bookings: 199 dates
Resident ensembles:
Piccolo Opera Company (25 dates)
Outdoor Recreation Assets (2)
Atlantic coastal water: 9.59 square miles
Inland water: 256.27 square miles
Federal protected area:
Loxahatchee NWR (2,550 acres)
State recreation area:
MacArthur Beach SP (225 acres)
Good Restaurants (96)
Score: 45 Rank: 112

Boerne, TX
Visible Past (31)
Comfort Historic District
Outdoor Recreation Assets (2)
Inland water: 1.12 square miles
State recreation area:
Guadalupe River SP (938 acres)
Score: 2.4 Rank: 198

Boone–Blowing Rock, NC
Visible Past (42)
Green Park Historic District
Lively Arts Calendar (59)
Farthing Auditorium
Touring artists bookings: 15 dates
Outdoor Recreation Assets (15)
Inland water: 0.20 square miles
Federal protected areas:
Blue Ridge Parkway (9,873 acres)
Pisgah NF (393 acres)
Good Restaurants (66)
Score: 33.6 Rank: 135

★ **Bozeman, MT**
Visible Past (69)
Bon Ton Historic District
Cooper Park Historic District
South Tracy–South Black Historic District
South Willson Historic District
Lively Arts Calendar (64)
MSU Wilson Auditorium
Touring artists bookings: 15 dates
Resident ensembles:
Bozeman Symphony Orchestra (10 dates)
Intermountain Opera (3 dates)
Outdoor Recreation Assets (88)
Inland water: 26.00 square miles

★ = *one of the top 30 places for ambiance.*

Federal protected areas:
Beaverhead NF (35 acres)
Gallatin NF (627,049 acres)
Yellowstone NP (64,237 acres)
Good Restaurants (75)
Score: 91.5 Rank: 17

Bradenton, FL
Visible Past (61)
Braden Castle Park Historic District
Palmetto Historic District
Outdoor Recreation Assets (28)
Gulf coastal water: 46.73 square miles
Inland water: 55.15 square miles
Federal protected areas:
De Soto National Memorial (25 acres)
Passage Key NWR (36 acres)
State recreation areas:
Benjamin Memorial SHS (17 acres)
Bickel Mound SHS (10 acres)
Lake Manatee SRA (556 acres)
Myakka River SP (10,150 acres)
Good Restaurants (53)
Score: 19.3 Rank: 164

Branson, MO
Visible Past (12)
Outdoor Recreation Assets (58)
Inland water: 19.12 square miles
Federal protected area:
Mark Twain NF (63,941 acres)
State recreation area:
Table Rock SP (294 acres)
Good Restaurants (74)
Score: 8.9 Rank: 185

Brevard, NC
Visible Past (24)
Lively Arts Calendar (86)
Touring artists bookings: 15 dates
Resident ensembles:
Brevard Chamber Orchestra (4 dates)
Brevard Music Center & Opera Workshop (58 dates)
Outdoor Recreation Assets (85)
Inland water: 2.21 square miles
Federal protected areas:
Blue Ridge Parkway (1,031 acres)
Nantahala NF (4,533 acres)
Pisgah NF (82,154 acres)
Good Restaurants (9)
Score: 79.7 Rank: 41

Brookings–Gold Beach, OR
Visible Past (18)
Outdoor Recreation Assets (92)
Pacific coastal water: 35.41 square miles
Inland water: 7.07 square miles
Federal protected areas:
Oregon Islands NWR (368 acres)
Siskiyou NF (617,356 acres)
State recreation areas:
Alfred Loeb SP (320 acres)
Azalea SP (36 acres)
Cape Blanco SP (1,880 acres)
Cape Sebastian Scenic Corridor (1,104 acres)
Floras Lake SNA (1,371 acres)
Harris Beach SP (173 acres)
Humbug Mountain SP (1,842 acres)
Pistol River State Wayside (440 acres)
Samuel Boardman Scenic Corridor (1,471 acres)
Good Restaurants (27)
Score: 30.1 Rank: 142

Brown County, IN
Visible Past (21)
Outdoor Recreation Assets (56)
Inland water: 3.96 square miles
Federal protected area:
Hoosier NF (17,749 acres)
State recreation area:
Brown County SP (15,692 acres)
Good Restaurants (34)
Score: 12.8 Rank: 177

Bullhead City, AZ
Visible Past (37)
Outdoor Recreation Assets (51)
Inland water: 158.08 square miles
Federal protected areas:
Grand Canyon NP (517,156 acres)
Havasu NWR (12,248 acres)
Kaibab NF (5,468 acres)
Lake Mead NRA (796,812 acres)
Pipe Spring NM (40 acres)
State recreation areas:
Cattail Cove SP (480 acres)
Lake Havasu SP (13,072 acres)
Good Restaurants (9)
Score: 17.8 Rank: 166

★ Burlington, VT
Visible Past (95)
Battery Street Historic District
Battery Street Historic District (Boundary Increase)
Buell Street–Bradley Street Historic District
Fort Ethan Allen Historic District
Jericho Village Historic District
Shelburne Village Historic District
South Union Street Historic District
South Willard Street Historic District
Lively Arts Calendar (75)
Memorial Auditorium
Touring artists bookings: 26 dates
Resident ensemble:
Vermont Symphony Orchestra (50 dates)
Outdoor Recreation Assets (41)
Inland water: 81.00 square miles
Good Restaurants (72)
Score: 87.1 Rank: 27

Camden, ME
Visible Past (81)
Chestnut Street Historic District
High Street Historic District
Rockland Residential Historic District
Rockport Historic District
Lively Arts Calendar (68)
Rockport Opera House
Touring artists bookings: 23 dates

continued

★ = *one of the top 30 places for ambiance.*

Camden, ME (cont.)

Outdoor Recreation Assets (47)
Atlantic coastal water: 159.36 square miles
Inland water: 74.51 square miles
Federal protected areas:
Acadia NP (4,144 acres)
Franklin Island NWR (12 acres)
Seal Island NWR (65 acres)
State recreation areas:
Camden Hills SP (5,474 acres)
Montpelier SHS (7 acres)
Rocky Lake SNA (8,800 acres)
Good Restaurants (66)
Score: 79.7 Rank: 41

Carmel–Pebble Beach, CA

Visible Past (39)
Lively Arts Calendar (85)
Sunset Theatre
Touring artists bookings: 15 dates
Resident ensembles:
Hidden Valley Opera Ensemble (25 dates)
Monterey Bay Chamber Orchestra (4 dates)
Monterey County Symphony Orchestra (27 dates)
Outdoor Recreation Assets (45)
Pacific coastal water: 132.49 square miles
Inland water: 12.72 square miles
Federal protected areas:
Los Padres NF (305,072 acres)
Pinnacles NM (1,283 acres)
Salinas River NWR (364 acres)
State recreation areas:
Andrew Molera SP (4,749 acres)
Asilomar Conference and SB (106 acres)
Carmel River SB (297 acres)
Fremont Peak SP (54 acres)
Garrapata SP (2,939 acres)
John Little SR (21 acres)
Julia Pfeiffer Burns SP (3,642 acres)
Marina SB (171 acres)
Moss Landing SB (60 acres)
Pfeiffer Big Sur SP (802 acres)
Point Lobos SR (1,325 acres)
Point Sur SHP (33 acres)
Salinas River SB (246 acres)
Zmudowski SB (156 acres)
Good Restaurants (92)
Score: 65.3 Rank: 70

Carson City–Carson Valley, NV

Visible Past (40)
Genoa Historic District
Lively Arts Calendar (78)
Carson City Community Center
Touring artists bookings: 42 dates
Resident ensemble:
Carson City Symphony (6 dates)
Outdoor Recreation Assets (75)
Inland water: 40.11 square miles
Federal protected areas:
Eldorado NF (53 acres)
Toiyabe NF (71,669 acres)
State recreation areas:
Lake Tahoe SP (3,690 acres)
Mormon Station SHS (2 acres)
Good Restaurants (62)
Score: 77.7 Rank: 46

Cedar City, UT

Visible Past (10)
Lively Arts Calendar (48)
Jones Performing Arts Center
Touring artists bookings: 10 dates
Outdoor Recreation Assets (39)
Inland water: 4.00 square miles
Federal protected areas:
Cedar Breaks NM (6,155 acres)
Dixie NF (241,151 acres)
Fishlake NF (2,297 acres)
Zion NP (2,851 acres)
State recreation area:
Iron Mission SP (11 acres)
Good Restaurants (27)
Score: 21.2 Rank: 160

Cedar Creek Lake, TX

Visible Past (2)
Outdoor Recreation Assets (35)
Inland water: 74.72 square miles
State recreation area:
Purtis Creek SRA (566 acres)
Good Restaurants (8)
Score: 2.9 Rank: 197

Chapel Hill–Carrboro, NC

Visible Past (78)
Cedar Grove Rural Crossroads Historic District
Chapel Hill Historic District
Gimghoul Neighborhood Historic District
Hillsborough Historic District
West Chapel Hill Historic District
Lively Arts Calendar (95)
UNC Memorial Hall
Touring artists bookings: 157 dates
Outdoor Recreation Assets (1)
Inland water: 1.36 square miles
Good Restaurants (85)
Score: 68.8 Rank: 64

Charles Town–Shepherdstown, WV

Visible Past (93)
Downtown Charles Town Historic District
Old Charles Town Historic District
Shepherdstown Historic District
Lively Arts Calendar (62)
Frank Creative Arts Center
Touring artists bookings: 14 dates
Resident ensemble:
Millbrook Orchestra (4 dates)
Outdoor Recreation Assets (11)
Inland water: 2.03 square miles
Federal protected areas:
Appalachian National Scenic Trail (1,050 acres)
Harpers Ferry NHP (1,024 acres)
Good Restaurants (34)
Score: 63.8 Rank: 74

★ = *one of the top 30 places for ambiance.*

★ **Charleston, SC**

Visible Past (97)

Ashley River Historic District
Hampton Park Terrace Historic District
McClellanville Historic District
Old Charleston Historic District

Lively Arts Calendar (90)

Gaillard Municipal Auditorium
Touring artists bookings: 8 dates
Resident ensemble:
Charleston Symphony Orchestra (90 dates)

Outdoor Recreation Assets (68)

Atlantic coastal water: 35.06 square miles
Inland water: 119.13 square miles
Federal protected areas:
Cape Romain NWR (34,049 acres)
Charles Pinckney NHS (29 acres)
Fort Sumter NM (28 acres)
Francis Marion NF (59,525 acres)
State recreation areas:
Charles Towne Landing SP (664 acres)
Drayton Hall SP (550 acres)
Hampton Plantation SP (322 acres)

Good Restaurants (100)

Score: 99 Rank: 3

★ **Charlottesville, VA**

Visible Past (100)

Charlottesville–Albemarle County Courthouse Historic District
Rugby Road–University Corner Historic District
Scottsville Historic District
Southwest Mountains Rural Historic District

Lively Arts Calendar (89)

Cabell Hall Auditorium
Touring artists bookings: 56 dates
Resident ensembles:
Ash Lawn–Highland Opera Company (28 dates)
Charlottesville & University Symphony Orchestra (10 dates)

Outdoor Recreation Assets (20)

Inland water: 3.49 square miles
Federal protected areas:
Appalachian National Scenic Trail (692 acres)
Shenandoah NP (14,861 acres)

Good Restaurants (74)

Score: 86.1 Rank: 29

Chestertown, MD

Visible Past (72)

Betterton Historic District
Chestertown Historic District

Lively Arts Calendar (40)

Tawes Theatre
Touring artists bookings: 5 dates

Outdoor Recreation Assets (82)

Chesapeake coastal water: 110.00 square miles
Inland water: 23.00 square miles
Federal protected area:
Eastern Neck NWR (2,286 acres)

Good Restaurants (18)

Score: 78.7 Rank: 44

Chewelah, WA

Visible Past (25)

Outdoor Recreation Assets (62)

Inland water: 62.00 square miles
Federal protected areas:
Colville NF (208,265 acres)
Kaniksu NF (11,774 acres)
Lake Roosevelt NRA (36,215 acres)
Little Pend Oreille NWR (39,979 acres)
State recreation area:
Crystal Falls SP (156 acres)

Score: 17.3 Rank: 168

Coeur d'Alene, ID

Visible Past (24)

Sherman Park Addition
Spirit Lake Historic District

Lively Arts Calendar (72)

Touring artists bookings: 28 dates

Outdoor Recreation Assets (83)

Inland water: 70.57 square miles
Federal protected area:
Idaho Panhandle NF (245,147 acres)
State recreation areas:
Farragut SP (2,688 acres)
Heyburn SP (7,838 acres)
Old Mission SP (114 acres)

Good Restaurants (50)

Score: 72.7 Rank: 56

Colorado Springs, CO

Visible Past (79)

Manitou Springs Historic District
North End Historic District
North Weber Street–Wahsatch Avenue Historic Residential District
Old Colorado City Historic Commercial District

Lively Arts Calendar (91)

Pikes Peak Center
Touring artists bookings: 22 dates
Resident ensembles:
Colorado Opera Festival (4 dates)
Colorado Springs Symphony (70 dates)
Pikes Peak Civic Orchestra (7 dates)

Outdoor Recreation Assets (24)

Inland water: 3.02 square miles
Federal protected area:
Pike NF (100,597 acres)

Good Restaurants (84)

Score: 79.2 Rank: 43

Columbia, MO

Visible Past (48)

East Campus Neighborhood Historic District
Rocheport Historic District

Lively Arts Calendar (76)

Missouri Theatre
Touring artists bookings: 20 dates
Resident ensemble:
Missouri Symphony Society (23 dates)

continued

★ = *one of the top 30 places for ambiance.*

Columbia, MO (cont.)

Outdoor Recreation Assets (9)

Inland water: 6.13 square miles
Federal protected area:
Mark Twain NF (3,762 acres)
State recreation areas:
Finger Lakes SP (1,132 acres)
Jewell Cemetery SHS (1 acre)
Rock Bridge Memorial SP (2,238 acres)

Good Restaurants (52)

Score: 42.5 Rank: 117

Conway, SC

Visible Past (13)

Conway Downtown Historic District
Galivants Ferry Historic District
Waccamaw River Warehouse Historic District

Lively Arts Calendar (20)

Touring artists bookings: 5 dates

Outdoor Recreation Assets (7)

Inland water: 11.78 square miles
State recreation area:
Myrtle Beach SP (312 acres)

Good Restaurants (93)

Score: 5.9 Rank: 191

★ Cottonwood–Verde Valley, AZ

Visible Past (88)

Clarkdale Historic District
Cottonwood Commercial Historic District

Lively Arts Calendar (45)

Touring artists bookings: 6 dates

Outdoor Recreation Assets (86)

Inland water: 4.79 square miles
Federal protected areas:
Coconino NF (427,107 acres)
Kaibab NF (25,119 acres)
Montezuma Castle NM (841 acres)
Prescott NF (1,194,459 acres)
Tonto NF (316,997 acres)
Tuzigoot NM (58 acres)
State recreation areas:
Dead Horse Ranch SP (320 acres)
Fort Verde SHS (11 acres)
Jerome SHS (3 acres)
Red Rock SP (286 acres)

Good Restaurants (87)

Score: 90 Rank: 20

Crossville, TN

Visible Past (77)

Cumberland Homesteads Historic District

Lively Arts Calendar (40)

Cumberland County Playhouse
Touring artists bookings: 5 dates

Outdoor Recreation Assets (4)

Inland water: 3.34 square miles
Federal protected area:
Obed Wild and Scenic River (50 acres)
State recreation area:
Cumberland Mountain SP (1,562 acres)

Score: 36.6 Rank: 129

Dare Outer Banks, NC

Visible Past (28)

Nags Head Beach Cottages Historic District

Outdoor Recreation Assets (98)

Atlantic coastal water: 31.23 square miles
Inland water: 867.65 square miles
Federal protected areas:
Alligator River NWR (124,353 acres)
Cape Hatteras NS (24,704 acres)
Fort Raleigh NHS (279 acres)
Pea Island NWR (5,823 acres)
Wright Brothers NM (425 acres)
State recreation area:
Jockey's Ridge SP (385 acres)

Good Restaurants (75)

Score: 37.6 Rank: 127

★ Daytona Beach, FL

Visible Past (85)

Coronado Historic District
Daytona Beach Surfside Historic District
New Smyrna Beach Historic District
Seabreeze Historic District
South Beach Street Historic District
South Pennisula Historic District
Southwest Daytona Beach Black Heritage District
West DeLand Residential District

Lively Arts Calendar (82)

Peabody Auditorium
Touring artists bookings: 57 dates
Resident ensemble:
Stetson University Orchestra (4 dates)

Outdoor Recreation Assets (58)

Atlantic coastal water: 16.77 square miles
Inland water: 158.97 square miles
Federal protected areas:
Canaveral NS (28,148 acres)
Lake Woodruff NWR (18,225 acres)
State recreation areas:
Addison Blockhouse SHS (5 acres)
Blue Spring SP (2,192 acres)
Bulow Creek SP (2,198 acres)
Green Mound SHS (6 acres)
Haw Creek SNA (1,756 acres)
Hontoon Island SP (1,051 acres)
North Peninsula SRA (442 acres)
Ponce De Leon Springs SP (401 acres)
Spruce Creek SRA (610 acres)
Tomoka SP (998 acres)

Good Restaurants (80)

Score: 93 Rank: 15

Delta County, CO

Visible Past (11)

Outdoor Recreation Assets (72)

Inland water: 6.40 square miles
Federal protected areas:
Grand Mesa NF (91,529 acres)
Gunnison NF (100,141 acres)
Uncompahgre NF (3 acres)

★ = *one of the top 30 places for ambiance.*

State recreation areas:
Crawford SRA (337 acres)
Sweitzer Lake SRA (73 acres)
Good Restaurants (15)
Score: 14.8 Rank: 173

Door Peninsula, WI

Visible Past (68)
Lively Arts Calendar (73)
Door Community Auditorium
Touring artists bookings: 30 dates
Outdoor Recreation Assets (29)
Great Lakes coastal water: 186.00 square miles
Inland water: 24.71 square miles
Federal protected areas:
Gravel Island NWR (27 acres)
Green Bay NWR (2 acres)
State recreation areas:
Ahnapee State Trail (156 acres)
Grand Traverse Island SP (12 acres)
Newport SP (2,368 acres)
Peninsula SP (3,763 acres)
Potawatomi SP (1,226 acres)
Rock Island SP (912 acres)
White Fish Dunes SP (863 acres)
Good Restaurants (71)
Score: 66.8 Rank: 68

★ Durango, CO

Visible Past (57)
East Third Avenue Historic Residential District
Main Avenue Historic District
Lively Arts Calendar (90)
Fort Lewis College Concert Hall
Touring artists bookings: 100 dates
Resident ensemble:
San Juan Symphony (4 dates)
Outdoor Recreation Assets (85)
Inland water: 7.74 square miles
Federal protected area:
San Juan NF (402,555 acres)
State recreation area:
Mancos Lake SRA (338 acres)
Good Restaurants (65)
Score: 94.5 Rank: 12

Eagle River–Woodruff, WI

Visible Past (20)
Lively Arts Calendar (40)
Northland Pines HS Auditorium
Touring artists bookings: 5 dates
Outdoor Recreation Assets (66)
Inland water: 145.12 square miles
Federal protected areas:
Chequamegon NF (6,459 acres)
Nicolet NF (48,010 acres)
Good Restaurants (60)
Score: 38.1 Rank: 126

★ East End Long Island, NY

Visible Past (98)
East Hampton Village Historic District (Boundary Increase)
Greenport Village Historic District
Sag Harbor Village District (Boundary Increase)
Sagaponack Historic District
Shelter Island Heights Historic District
Southampton Village Historic District
Southold Historic District
Lively Arts Calendar (99)
Touring artists bookings: 112 dates
Resident ensembles:
Ballet Long Island (100 dates)
Long Island Philharmonic (27 dates)
Sound Symphony (12 dates)
Stony Brook Symphony Orchestra (6 dates)
Outdoor Recreation Assets (56)
Atlantic coastal water: 838.45 square miles
Inland water: 248.41 square miles
Federal protected areas:
Amagansett NWR (36 acres)
Conscience Point NWR (60 acres)
Elizabeth A. Morton NWR (187 acres)
Fire Island NS (6,235 acres)
Lake Woodruff NWR (18,225 acres)
Seatuck NWR (183 acres)
Target Rock NWR (80 acres)
Wertheim NWR (2,398 acres)
State recreation areas:
Bayard Cutting Arboretum SP (690 acres)
Belmont Lake SP (459 acres)
Bethpage SP (1,475 acres)
Brookhaven SP (2,137 acres)
Caleb Smith SP (543 acres)
Camp Hero SP (415 acres)
Connetquot River SP (3,473 acres)
Captree SP (298 acres)
Caumsett SHP (1,486 acres)
Gilgo SP (1,223 acres)
Heckscher SP (1,657 acres)
Hither Hills SP (1,755 acres)
Montauk Downs SP (171 acres)
Montauk Point SP (861 acres)
Napeague SP (1,364 acres)
Orient Beach SP (363 acres)
Robert Moses SP (875 acres)
Sunken Meadow SP (1,266 acres)
Walt Whitman SHS (1 acre)
Wildwood SP (767 acres)
Good Restaurants (98)
Score: 98.5 Rank: 4

Easton–St. Michaels, MD

Visible Past (90)
Easton Historic District
Lively Arts Calendar (40)
Touring artists bookings: 5 dates
Outdoor Recreation Assets (46)
Chesapeake coastal water: 150.46 square miles
Inland water: 57.17 square miles
State recreation area:
Wye Oak SP (29 acres)
Good Restaurants (55)
Score: 70.2 Rank: 61

★ = *one of the top 30 places for ambiance.*

Edenton, NC

Visible Past (44)
Edenton Cotton Mill Historic District
Edenton Historic District
Outdoor Recreation Assets (71)
Inland water: 60.68 square miles
Good Restaurants (9)
Score: 33.1 Rank: 136

Eufaula, AL

Visible Past (71)
Lore, Seth and Irwinton Historic District
Outdoor Recreation Assets (10)
Inland water: 20.00 square miles
Federal protected area:
Eufaula NWR (24 acres)
State recreation areas:
Blue Springs SP (103 acres)
Lakepoint Resort SP (1,220 acres)
Score: 13.8 Rank: 175

Eureka Springs, AR

Visible Past (55)
Eureka Springs Historic District
Outdoor Recreation Assets (13)
Inland water: 9.00 square miles
State recreation areas:
Beaver Lake SP (619 acres)
Old Carrollton SP (3 acres)
Good Restaurants (60)
Score: 8.4 Rank: 186

Fairhope–Gulf Shores, AL

Visible Past (41)
Fairhope Bayfront District
Point Clear Historic District
Montrose Historic District
Lively Arts Calendar (70)
Meyer Civic Center
Touring artists bookings: 25 dates
Outdoor Recreation Assets (21)
Gulf coastal water: 234.52 square miles
Inland water: 98.08 square miles
Federal protected area:
Bon Secour NWR (3,066 acres)
State recreation area:
Gulf SP (6,000 acres)
Good Restaurants (53)
Score: 41.5 Rank: 119

Fayetteville, AR

Visible Past (53)
Shiloh Historic District
Washington-Willow Historic District
Wilson Park Historic District
Lively Arts Calendar (84)
Walton Arts Center
Touring artists bookings: 54 dates
Resident ensemble:
North Arkansas Symphony Orchestra (15 dates)
Outdoor Recreation Assets (14)
Inland water: 5.83 square miles
Federal protected area:
Ozark NF (21,762 acres)
State recreation areas:
Devil's Den SP (1,927 acres)
Prairie Grove SP (130 acres)
Good Restaurants (42)
Score: 56.4 Rank: 88

★ Flagstaff, AZ

Visible Past (86)
Flagstaff Townsite Historic Residential District
North End Historic Residential District
Railroad Addition Historic District
Williams Residential Historic District
Lively Arts Calendar (61)
Ardrey Auditorium
Touring artists bookings: 6 dates
Resident ensemble:
Flagstaff Symphony Orchestra (15 dates)
Outdoor Recreation Assets (82)
Inland water: 43.00 square miles
Federal protected areas:
Coconino NF (1,415,700 acres)
Glen Canyon NRA (44,953 acres)
Grand Canyon NP (662,038 acres)
Kaibab NF (1,528,320 acres)
Lake Mead NRA (83,116 acres)
Navajo NM (40 acres)
Prescott NF (43,695 acres)
Sitgreaves NF (284,707 acres)
Sunset Crater NM (3,040 acres)
Walnut Canyon NM (2,012 acres)
Wupatki NM (35,253 acres)
State recreation areas:
Riordan SHS (5 acres)
Slide Rock SP (43 acres)
Good Restaurants (79)
Score: 93.5 Rank: 14

Florence, OR

Visible Past (79)
Lively Arts Calendar (36)
Touring artists bookings: 4 dates
Outdoor Recreation Assets (91)
Pacific coastal water: 10.36 square miles
Inland water: 64.22 square miles
Federal protected areas:
Oregon Islands NWR (12 acres)
Siuslaw NF (245,576 acres)
Umpqua NF (151,249 acres)
Willamette NF (1,032,247 acres)
State recreation areas:
Alderwood State Wayside (76 acres)
Armitage SP (5,776 acres)
Ben and Kay Dorris SP (92 acres)
Blachly Mountain Forest Wayside (69 acres)
Carl Washburne Memorial SP (1,089 acres)
Darlingtonia State Wayside (18 acres)
Devil's Elbow SP (547 acres)
Elijah Bristow SP (848 acres)
Howard Morton Memorial SP (24 acres)
Jessie Honeyman Memorial SP (522 acres)
Neptune SP (303 acres)
Willamette River Greenway (925 acres)
Good Restaurants (53)
Score: 84.6 Rank: 32

★ = *one of the top 30 places for ambiance.*

★ **Fort Collins–Loveland, CO**

Visible Past (64)

Laurel School Historic District
Old Town Fort Collins

Lively Arts Calendar (93)

Lincoln Center Auditorium
Touring artists bookings: 108 dates
Resident ensembles:
Colorado State University Orchestra (6 dates)
Fort Collins Symphony Orchestra (25 dates)
Opera Fort Collins (3 dates)

Outdoor Recreation Assets (91)

Inland water: 32.56 square miles
Federal protected areas:
Rocky Mountain NP (144,315 acres)
Roosevelt NF (624,049 acres)
State recreation areas:
Boyd Lake SRA (197 acres)
Lory SP (2,479 acres)
Picnic Rock SP (10 acres)

Good Restaurants (72)

Score: 97 Rank: 7

Fort Myers–Cape Coral, FL

Visible Past (36)

Fort Myers Downtown Commercial District

Lively Arts Calendar (92)

Mann Performing Arts Hall
Touring artists bookings: 87 dates
Resident ensemble:
Southwest Florida Symphony Orchestra & Chorus (17 dates)

Outdoor Recreation Assets (65)

Gulf coastal water: 6.05 square miles
Inland water: 236.47 square miles
Federal protected areas:
Caloosahatchee NWR (40 acres)
J.N. "Ding" Darling NWR (4,976 acres)
Matlacha Pass NWR (244 acres)
Pine Island NWR (404 acres)
State recreation areas:
Cayo Costa SP (1,629 acres)
Gasparilla Island SRA (125 acres)
Koreshan SHS (156 acres)
Lovers Key SRA (434 acres)

Good Restaurants (88)

Score: 76.7 Rank: 48

Fredericksburg, TX

Visible Past (60)

Fredericksburg Historic District

Lively Arts Calendar (50)

United Methodist Church
Touring artists bookings: 9 dates

Outdoor Recreation Assets (2)

Inland water: 0.42 square miles
Federal protected area:
Lyndon B. Johnson NHP (504 acres)
State recreation areas:
Admiral Nimitz Museum SHS (5 acres)
Enchanted Rock SNA (1,424 acres)
Lyndon B. Johnson SHS (733 acres)

Good Restaurants (18)

Score: 31.6 Rank: 139

Fredericksburg–Spotsylvania, VA

Visible Past (90)

Fredericksburg Historic District
Spotsylvania Court House Historic District
Woodstock Historic District

Lively Arts Calendar (36)

Dodd Auditorium
Resident ensemble:
Mary Washington College-Community Symphony (4 dates)

Outdoor Recreation Assets (78)

Inland water: 11.41 square miles
Federal protected areas:
Fredericksburg & Spotsylvania NMP (5,235 acres)
Fredericksburg National Cemetery (12 acres)
State recreation area:
Lake Anna SP (2,000 acres)

Good Restaurants (71)

Score: 84.1 Rank: 33

Front Royal, VA

Visible Past (62)

Outdoor Recreation Assets (44)

Inland water: 3.00 square miles
Federal protected areas:
Appalachian National Scenic Trail (1,142 acres)
George Washington NF (6,270 acres)
Shenandoah NP (13,690 acres)

Good Restaurants (9)

Score: 27.2 Rank: 148

Gainesville, FL

Visible Past (80)

City of Alachua Downtown Historic District
High Springs Historic District
Northeast Gainesville Residential District
Pleasant Street Historic District
Southeast Gainesville Residential District
Waldo Historic District

Lively Arts Calendar (87)

University of Florida Performing Arts Center
Touring artists bookings: 72 dates
Resident ensemble:
Gainesville Chamber Orchestra (6 dates)

Outdoor Recreation Assets (6)

Inland water: 94.88 square miles
State recreation areas:
Devil's Millhopper Geological SP (63 acres)
Marjorie Rawlings SHS (12 acres)
O'Leno SP (169 acres)
Paynes Prairie Preserve SP (18,400 acres)
River Rise Preserve SP (1,706 acres)
San Felasco Hammock Preserve SP (6,034 acres)

Good Restaurants (39)

Score: 68.3 Rank: 65

Georgetown, TX

Visible Past (28)

Bartlett Commercial Historic District
Belford Historic District
Round Rock Commercial Historic District
University Avenue–Elm Street Historic District
Williamson County Courthouse Historic District

continued

★ = *one of the top 30 places for ambiance.*

Georgetown, TX (cont.)

Lively Arts Calendar (36)
Southwestern University Fine Arts
Touring artists bookings: 4 dates

Outdoor Recreation Assets (72)
Inland water: 12.48 square miles
Federal protected area:
Balcones Canyonlands NWR (903 acres)

Good Restaurants (9)

Score: 44 **Rank: 114**

Grand Junction, CO

Visible Past (27)
North Seventh Street Historic Residential District

Lively Arts Calendar (58)
Grand Junction HS Auditorium
Touring artists bookings: 5 dates
Resident ensemble:
Grand Junction Symphony Orchestra (9 dates)

Outdoor Recreation Assets (87)
Inland water: 13.36 square miles
Federal protected areas:
Colorado NM (20,454 acres)
Grand Mesa NF (252,647 acres)
Manti-La Sal NF (4,542 acres)
Uncompahgre NF (207,256 acres)
White River NF (83,069 acres)
State recreation areas:
Highline SRA (570 acres)
Island Acres SRA (130 acres)
Vega SRA (898 acres)

Good Restaurants (43)

Score: 67.3 **Rank: 67**

Grants Pass, OR

Visible Past (33)
Grants Pass G Street Historic District

Lively Arts Calendar (45)
Rogue Community College Outdoor Amphitheatre
Touring artists bookings: 6 dates

Outdoor Recreation Assets (75)
Inland water: 2.04 square miles
Federal protected areas:
Oregon Caves NM (484 acres)
Rogue River NF (31,236 acres)
Siskiyou NF (373,949 acres)
State recreation areas:
Gateway State Wayside (272 acres)
Illinois River Forks SP (368 acres)
Rogue River Scenic Waterway (76 acres)

Good Restaurants (31)

Score: 58.4 **Rank: 85**

Grass Valley–Nevada City, CA

Visible Past (43)
Nevada City Downtown Historic District

Outdoor Recreation Assets (97)
Inland water: 16.88 square miles
Federal protected areas:
Tahoe NF (169,686 acres)
Toiyabe NF (2,574 acres)
State recreation areas:
Donner Memorial SP (342 acres)
Empire Mine SHP (801 acres)
Malakoff Diggins SHP (2,963 acres)

Good Restaurants (31)

Score: 46 **Rank: 108**

Hamilton–Bitterroot Valley, MT

Visible Past (38)
Hamilton Southside Historic District

Outdoor Recreation Assets (79)
Inland water: 6.09 square miles
Federal protected areas:
Bitterroot NF (1,109,242 acres)
Lee Metcalf NWR (2,792 acres)
Lolo NF (8,131 acres)
State recreation area:
Painted Rocks SP (263 acres)

Good Restaurants (9)

Score: 34.1 **Rank: 134**

★ **Hanover, NH**

Visible Past (77)
Canaan Street Historic District
Haverhill Corner Historic District
Lyme Common Historic District

Lively Arts Calendar (86)
Hopkins Center
Touring artists bookings: 77 dates

Outdoor Recreation Assets (55)
Inland water: 36.79 square miles
Federal protected areas:
Appalachian National Scenic Trail (6,330 acres)
White Mountain NF (342,449 acres)
State recreation areas:
Bedell Bridge SHS (71 acres)
Crawford Notch SP (25 acres)
Franconia Notch SP (6,692 acres)
George Pond Lot SNA (9 acres)
Plummer Ledge SNA (3 acres)
Sculptured Rocks SNA (272 acres)
Wellington SP (205 acres)

Good Restaurants (83)

Score: 90 **Rank: 20**

Hattiesburg, MS

Visible Past (62)
Hattiesburg Historic Neighborhood District
North Main Street Historic District
Oaks Historic District

Lively Arts Calendar (46)
Mannoni Performing Arts Center
Touring artists bookings: 20 dates
Resident ensembles:
Hattiesburg Civic Light Opera (3 dates)
Southern Mississippi Symphony (12 dates)

Outdoor Recreation Assets (77)
Inland water: 3.12 square miles
Federal protected area:
De Soto NF (50,403 acres)
State recreation area:
Paul B. Johnson SP (744 acres)

Good Restaurants (38)

Score: 46 **Rank: 108**

★ = *one of the top 30 places for ambiance.*

Henderson, NV

Outdoor Recreation Assets (27)

Inland water: 180.20 square miles

Federal protected areas:

Desert NWR (828,794 acres)

Lake Mead NRA (589,024 acres)

Moapa Valley NWR (30 acres)

Toiyabe NF (60,978 acres)

State recreation areas:

Floyd Lamb SP (2,041 acres)

Old Las Vegas Mormon Fort SHS (3 acres)

Spring Mountain Ranch SP (17,608 acres)

Valley of Fire SP (34,880 acres)

Good Restaurants (65)

Score: 1.4 Rank: 200

Hendersonville–East Flat Rock, NC

Visible Past (81)

Druid Hills Historic District

Flat Rock Historic District

Main Street Historic District

Lively Arts Calendar (45)

Hendersonville HS Auditorium

Resident ensemble:

Hendersonville Symphony Orchestra (6 dates)

Outdoor Recreation Assets (25)

Inland water: 1.01 square miles

Federal protected areas:

Blue Ridge Parkway (523 acres)

Carl Sandburg Home NHS (264 acres)

Pisgah NF (17,295 acres)

Good Restaurants (38)

Score: 56.4 Rank: 88

Hilton Head Island, SC

Visible Past (45)

Daufuskie Island Historic District

Lively Arts Calendar (54)

Elizabeth Wallace Theatre

Resident ensemble:

Hilton Head Orchestra (11 dates)

Outdoor Recreation Assets (48)

Atlantic coastal water: 55.81 square miles

Inland water: 109.66 square miles

Federal protected areas:

Ace Basin NWR (833 acres)

Pinckney Island NWR (1,325 acres)

State recreation area:

Hunting Island SP (5,000 acres)

Good Restaurants (78)

Score: 53.4 Rank: 95

Hot Springs, AR

Visible Past (49)

Hot Springs Central Avenue Historic District

Quapaw-Prospect Historic District

Lively Arts Calendar (64)

Ponce de Leon Center

Touring artists bookings: 20 dates

Outdoor Recreation Assets (80)

Inland water: 56.56 square miles

Federal protected areas:

Hot Springs NP (4,564 acres)

Ouachita NF (113,412 acres)

State recreation areas:

Lake Ouachita SP (370 acres)

Mid-America Museum (21 acres)

Good Restaurants (50)

Score: 77.2 Rank: 47

Inverness, FL

Visible Past (13)

Floral City Historic District

Outdoor Recreation Assets (52)

Gulf coastal water: 10.98 square miles

Inland water: 79.80 square miles

Federal protected areas:

Chassahowitzka NWR (23,730 acres)

Crystal River NWR (46 acres)

State recreation areas:

Crystal River SHS (15 acres)

Fort Cooper SP (545 acres)

Homosassa Springs SP (150 acres)

Lake Rousseau SRA (1,684 acres)

Yulee Sugar Mill Ruins SHS (6 acres)

Good Restaurants (25)

Score: 7.4 Rank: 188

Iowa City, IA

Visible Past (59)

Brown Street Historic District

College Green Historic District

South Summit Street District

Lively Arts Calendar (74)

Hancher Auditorium

Touring artists bookings: 35 dates

Outdoor Recreation Assets (8)

Inland water: 8.76 square miles

State recreation area:

Lake Macbride SP (2,180 acres)

Good Restaurants (55)

Score: 48 Rank: 106

Jackson Hole, WY

Visible Past (61)

Outdoor Recreation Assets (100)

Inland water: 214.00 square miles

Federal protected areas:

Bridger NF (6,559 acres)

Grand Teton NP (307,621 acres)

John D. Rockefeller National Parkway (23,777 acres)

National Elk Refuge (24,778 acres)

Shoshone NF (2,682 acres)

Targhee NF (270,988 acres)

Teton NF (1,089,942 acres)

Yellowstone NP (927,616 acres)

Good Restaurants (75)

Score: 61.3 Rank: 78

★ **Kalispell–Flathead Valley, MT**

Visible Past (85)

East Side Historic District

Main Street Commercial Historic District

West Side Historic District

Lively Arts Calendar (67)

Touring artists bookings: 10 dates

Resident ensemble:

Glacier Orchestra & Chorale (11 dates)

continued

★ = *one of the top 30 places for ambiance.*

★ **Kalispell–Flathead Valley, MT (cont.)**

Outdoor Recreation Assets (99)

Inland water: 158.00 square miles

Federal protected areas:

Flathead NF (1,717,996 acres)

Glacier NP (642,749 acres)

Kootenai NF (51,829 acres)

Lolo NF (18,324 acres)

State recreation areas:

Lone Pine SP (182 acres)

Wayfarers SP (68 acres)

Whitefish Lake SP (10 acres)

Good Restaurants (55)

Score: 98 **Rank: 5**

Kauai, HI

Visible Past (34)

Outdoor Recreation Assets (25)

Pacific coastal water: 63.51 square miles

Inland water: 8.86 square miles

Federal protected areas:

Hanalei NWR (917 acres)

Huleia NWR (240 acres)

Kilauea Point NWR (160 acres)

State recreation areas:

Ahukini State Recreation Pier (1 acre)

Ha'ena SP (62 acres)

Hanalei State Recreation Pier (1 acre)

Koke'e SP (4,345 acres)

Na Pali Coast SP (6,175 acres)

Polihale SP (138 acres)

Russian Fort Elizabeth SHP (17 acres)

Wailua River SP (1,126 acres)

Waimea Canyon SP (1,866 acres)

Waimea State Recreation Pier (1 acre)

Good Restaurants (52)

Score: 5.4 **Rank: 192**

Kerrville, TX

Visible Past (5)

Outdoor Recreation Assets (11)

Inland water: 1.49 square miles

State recreation area:

Kerrville-Schreiner SP (517 acres)

Good Restaurants (25)

Score: 0 **Rank: 203**

Ketchum–Sun Valley, ID

Visible Past (22)

Bellevue Historic District

Sun Valley Historic District

Lively Arts Calendar (62)

Sun Valley Center

Touring artists bookings: 18 dates

Outdoor Recreation Assets (74)

Inland water: 16.24 square miles

Federal protected areas:

Challis NF (2,449 acres)

Craters of the Moon NM (13,587 acres)

Minidoka NWR (2,304 acres)

Sawtooth NF (488,667 acres)

Good Restaurants (39)

Score: 60.3 **Rank: 81**

★ **Key West, FL**

Visible Past (98)

Key West Historic District

Pigeon Key Historic District

Lively Arts Calendar (40)

Tennessee Williams Center

Touring artists bookings: 18 dates

Resident ensemble:

Key West Symphony (12 dates)

Outdoor Recreation Assets (98)

Gulf coastal water: 541.00 square miles

Inland water: 407.00 square miles

Federal protected areas:

Big Cypress National Preserve (126,308 acres)

Crocodile Lake NWR (6,560 acres)

Dry Tortugas NP (61,480 acres)

Everglades Expansion (0 acres)

Everglades NP (943,639 acres)

Great White Heron NWR (6,206 acres)

Key West NWR (1,865 acres)

National Key Deer NWR (8,353 acres)

State recreation areas:

Bahia Honda SP (360 acres)

Coral Reef SP (2,437 acres)

Fort Zachary Taylor SHS (51 acres)

Indian Key SHS (17 acres)

Key Largo Hammock SRA (1,701 acres)

Lignumvitae Key Botanical Garden (450 acres)

Long Key SRA (850 acres)

San Pedro Underwater SP

Windley Key Fossil Reef Geological SP (28 acres)

Good Restaurants (87)

Score: 95 **Rank: 11**

Kingman, AZ

Visible Past (37)

Kingman Commercial Historic District

Outdoor Recreation Assets (51)

Inland water: 158.08 square miles

Federal protected areas:

Grand Canyon NP (517,156 acres)

Havasu NWR (12,248 acres)

Kaibab NF (5,468 acres)

Lake Mead NRA (796,812 acres)

Pipe Spring NM (40 acres)

State recreation area:

Lake Havasu SP (13,072 acres)

Good Restaurants (39)

Score: 17.8 **Rank: 166**

Kissimmee–St. Cloud, FL

Visible Past (32)

Kissimmee Historic District

Outdoor Recreation Assets (38)

Inland water: 184.47 square miles

Good Restaurants (43)

Score: 9.9 **Rank: 183**

Laguna Beach–Dana Point, CA

Visible Past (18)

Lively Arts Calendar (95)

Artists Theatre

Touring artists bookings: 70 dates

★ = *one of the top 30 places for ambiance.*

Resident ensembles:
Ballet Pacifica (55 dates)
Capistrano Valley Symphony (10 dates)
Mozart Camerata (7 dates)
Saddleback Chamber Players (8 dates)

Outdoor Recreation Assets (40)
Pacific coastal water: 14.80 square miles
Inland water: 10.23 square miles
Federal protected area:
Cleveland NF (54,343 acres)
State recreation areas:
Bolsa Chica SB (170 acres)
Chino Hills SP (3,115 acres)
Corona Del Mar SB (30 acres)
Crystal Cove SP (3,940 acres)
Doheny SB (274 acres)
Huntington SB (129 acres)
San Clemente SB (117 acres)

Good Restaurants (97)

Score: 58.9 Rank: 84

Lake Conroe, TX

Visible Past (1)

Lively Arts Calendar (45)
Crighton Theatre
Touring artists bookings: 6 dates

Outdoor Recreation Assets (32)
Inland water: 32.58 square miles
Federal protected area:
Sam Houston NF (47,609 acres)
State recreation area:
Lake Houston SP (1,912 acres)

Good Restaurants (27)

Score: 13.3 Rank: 176

Lake Havasu City, AZ

Lively Arts Calendar (26)
Touring artists bookings: 4 dates

Outdoor Recreation Assets (51)
Inland water: 158.08 square miles
Federal protected areas:
Grand Canyon NP (517,156 acres)
Havasu NWR (12,248 acres)
Kaibab NF (5,468 acres)
Lake Mead NRA (796,812 acres)
Pipe Spring NM (40 acres)
State recreation area:
Lake Havasu SP (13,072 acres)

Good Restaurants (42)

Score: 16.8 Rank: 169

Lake of the Cherokees, OK

Visible Past (4)

Outdoor Recreation Assets (19)
Inland water: 51.63 square miles
State recreation areas:
Bernice SP (88 acres)
Honey Creek SP (30 acres)
Lake Eucha SP (51 acres)
Spavinaw SP (51 acres)

Score: 0.9 Rank: 201

Lake of the Ozarks, MO

Visible Past (31)
Camp Pin Oak Historic District

Outdoor Recreation Assets (33)
Inland water: 53.71 square miles
State recreation areas:
Ha Ha Tonka SP (2,696 acres)
Lake Of The Ozarks SP (9,253 acres)

Good Restaurants (43)

Score: 6.4 Rank: 190

Lake Placid, NY

Visible Past (94)
Camp Dudley Road Historic District
Essex Village Historic District
Keeseville Historic District

Lively Arts Calendar (21)
Lake Placid Center of the Arts
Touring artists bookings (12 dates)

Outdoor Recreation Assets (19)
Inland water: 120.00 square miles
State recreation areas:
Crown Point Reservation (351 acres)
Crown Point SHS (380 acres)
John Brown Farm SHS (244 acres)
Lake Harris SRA (28 acres)
Lincoln Pond SRA (605 acres)
Meadowbrook SRA (14 acres)
Paradox Lake SRA (9 acres)
Poke-O-Moonshine SRA (3 acres)
Putnam Pond SRA (62 acres)
Sharp Bridge SRA (19 acres)
Wilmington Notch SRA (9 acres)

Good Restaurants (48)

Score: 32.1 Rank: 138

★ Lake Winnipesaukee, NH

Visible Past (66)
Center Sandwich Historic District
Sanbornton Square Historic District
Wakefield Village Historic District

Outdoor Recreation Assets (87)
Inland water: 125.68 square miles
Federal protected area:
White Mountain NF (145,005 acres)
State recreation areas:
Cathedral Ledge SP (280 acres)
Crawford Notch SP (5,925 acres)
Echo Lake SP (118 acres)
Ellacoya SP (107 acres)
Endicott Rock SHS (1 acre)
Governor Wentworth SHS (96 acres)
Heath Pond Bog SNA (250 acres)
Humphrey Ledge SNA (36 acres)
Madison Boulder SNA (17 acres)
Ossipee Lake SNA (400 acres)
Wentworth Beach SRA (51 acres)
White Lake SP (903 acres)

Good Restaurants (81)

Score: 97.5 Rank: 6

★ = *one of the top 30 places for ambiance.*

Lakeland–Winter Haven, FL

Visible Past (84)

Beacon Hill–Alta Vista Residential District
Dixieland Historic District
East Lake Morton Residential District
Fort Meade Historic District
Lake Wales Historic Residential District
Mountain Lake Estates Historic District
South Bartow Residential District
South Lake Morton Historic District
Winter Haven Heights Historic Residential District

Lively Arts Calendar (84)

The Lakeland Center
Touring artists bookings: 51 dates
Resident ensemble:
Imperial Symphony Orchestra (16 dates)

Outdoor Recreation Assets (22)

Inland water: 135.26 square miles
Federal protected area:
Lake Wales Ridge NWR (154 acres)
State recreation areas:
Lake Arbuckle SP (2,813 acres)
Lake Kissimmee SP (5,030 acres)

Good Restaurants (58)

Score: 75.2 Rank: 51

Largo, FL

Visible Past (8)

Lively Arts Calendar (50)

Touring artists bookings: 9 dates

Outdoor Recreation Assets (50)

Gulf coastal water: 26.30 square miles
Inland water: 64.72 square miles
Federal protected area:
Pinellas NWR (17 acres)
State recreation areas:
Anclote Key Preserve SP (83 acres)
Caladesi Island SP (631 acres)
Honeymoon Island SP (2,400 acres)

Good Restaurants (94)

Score: 29.2 Rank: 144

Las Cruces, NM

Visible Past (64)

Alameda-Depot Historic District
La Mesilla Historic District
Mesquite Street Original Townsite Historic District

Lively Arts Calendar (69)

NMSU Pan American Center
Touring artists bookings: 12 dates
Resident ensemble:
Las Cruces Symphony (12 dates)

Outdoor Recreation Assets (9)

Inland water: 7.44 square miles
Federal protected areas:
San Andres NWR (57,217 acres)
White Sands NM (52,779 acres)
State recreation area:
Leasburg Dam SP (140 acres)

Good Restaurants (50)

Score: 48.5 Rank: 104

Las Vegas, NM

Visible Past (89)

Lincoln Park Historic District
North New Town Historic District
Old Town Residential Historic District

Outdoor Recreation Assets (39)

Inland water: 19.00 square miles
Federal protected areas:
Las Vegas NWR (8,672 acres)
Pecos NM (5,987 acres)
Santa Fe NF (340,428 acres)
State recreation areas:
Conchas Lake SP (9,890 acres)
Morphy Lake SP (35 acres)
Storrie Lake SP (1,180 acres)
Villanueva SP (1,600 acres)

Good Restaurants (16)

Score: 62.3 Rank: 77

Leelanau Peninsula, MI

Visible Past (65)

Leland Historic District

Outdoor Recreation Assets (40)

Great Lakes coastal water: 215.41 square miles
Inland water: 31.22 square miles
Federal protected area:
Sleeping Bear Dunes National Lakeshore (45,835 acres)
State recreation area:
Leelanau SP (1,300 acres)

Good Restaurants (16)

Score: 26.7 Rank: 149

Leesburg–Mount Dora, FL

Visible Past (9)

Lively Arts Calendar (40)

Touring artists bookings: 5 dates

Outdoor Recreation Assets (76)

Inland water: 203.40 square miles
Federal protected areas:
Lake Woodruff NWR (280 acres)
Ocala NF (84,081 acres)
State recreation areas:
Hontoon Island SP (599 acres)
Lake Griffin SRA (255 acres)
Lake Louisa SP (1,790 acres)
Lower Wekiva River Preserve SP (2,580 acres)

Good Restaurants (37)

Score: 37.1 Rank: 128

★ Litchfield Hills, CT

Visible Past (99)

Canaan Village Historic District
Hotchkissville Historic District
Litchfield Historic District
New Milford Center Historic District
Pine Meadow Historic District
Plymouth Center Historic District
Sharon Historic District
Torringford Street Historic District
Watertown Center Historic District
Woodbury Historic District No. 1

★ = *one of the top 30 places for ambiance.*

Lively Arts Calendar (86)
Touring artists bookings: 76 dates
Outdoor Recreation Assets (31)
Inland water: 24.63 square miles
Federal protected area:
Appalachian National Scenic Trail (5,635 acres)
State recreation areas:
American Legion SF (782 acres)
Black Rock SP (443 acres)
Burr Pond SP (436 acres)
Dennis Hill SP (240 acres)
Haystack Mountain SP (224 acres)
Housatonic Meadows SP (451 acres)
John A. Minetto SP (678 acres)
Kent Falls SP (275 acres)
Lake Waramaug SP (95 acres)
Macedonia Brook SP (2,300 acres)
Mohawk Mountain SP (260 acres)
Mohawk SF (3,351 acres)
Mt. Tom SP (223 acres)
Peoples SF (29,544 acres)
Topsmead SF (514 acres)
Good Restaurants (61)
Score: 88.1 Rank: 25

Lower Cape May, NJ
Visible Past (76)
Cape May Historic District
Dennisville Historic District
South Tuckahoe Historic District
Lively Arts Calendar (83)
Touring artists bookings: 26 dates
Resident ensemble:
Ocean City Pops (40 dates)
Outdoor Recreation Assets (42)
Atlantic coastal water: 172.50 square miles
Inland water: 29.99 square miles
Federal protected area:
Cape May NWR (2,587 acres)
State recreation areas:
Cape May Point SP (190 acres)
Cape May Wetlands SNA (3,715 acres)
Corson's Inlet SP (341 acres)
Great Sound SP (217 acres)
Strathmere SNA (95 acres)
Good Restaurants (89)
Score: 83.1 Rank: 35

Madison, WI
Visible Past (92)
Lively Arts Calendar (94)
Oscar Mayer Theatre
Touring artists bookings: 97 dates
Resident ensemble:
Madison Opera (5 dates)
Madison Symphony Orchestra (24 dates)
Wisconsin Chamber Orchestra (11 dates)
Outdoor Recreation Assets (11)
Inland water: 36.18 square miles
State recreation areas:
Blue Mounds SP (178 acres)
Cross Plains Ice Age SR (129 acres)
Governor Nelson SP (433 acres)
Lake Kegonsa SP (343 acres)
Good Restaurants (78)
Score: 81.1 Rank: 39

Marble Falls–Lake LBJ, TX
Visible Past (16)
Outdoor Recreation Assets (12)
Inland water: 56.27 square miles
Federal protected area:
Balcones Canyonlands NWR (2,868 acres)
State recreation areas:
Enchanted Rock SNA (219 acres)
Inks Lake SP (1,202 acres)
Longhorn Cavern SP (639 acres)
Score: 1.9 Rank: 199

Mariposa, CA
Visible Past (87)
Coulterville Main Street Historic District
Mariposa Town Historic District
Outdoor Recreation Assets (90)
Inland water: 11.89 square miles
Federal protected areas:
Sierra NF (91,018 acres)
Stanislaus NF (85,286 acres)
Yosemite NP (264,039 acres)
Good Restaurants (9)
Score: 71.2 Rank: 59

Martha's Vineyard, MA
Visible Past (60)
Edgartown Village Historic District
Martha's Vineyard Campground
William Street Historic District
Lively Arts Calendar (70)
Chilmark Community Center
Touring artists bookings: 5 dates
Outdoor Recreation Assets (35)
Atlantic coastal water: 37.00 square miles
Inland water: 18.00 square miles
Good Restaurants (48)
Score: 63.3 Rank: 75

Maryville, TN
Visible Past (56)
Indiana Avenue Historic District
Lively Arts Calendar (48)
Resident ensemble:
Appalachian Ballet Company (8 dates)
Outdoor Recreation Assets (73)
Inland water: 8.09 square miles
Federal protected areas:
Appalachian National Scenic Trail (115 acres)
Great Smoky Mountains NP (97,741 acres)
Good Restaurants (18)
Score: 71.7 Rank: 58

Maui, HI
Visible Past (52)
Lahaina Historic District
Lively Arts Calendar (77)
Maui Arts and Cultural Center
Touring artists bookings: 32 dates
Resident ensemble:
Maui Symphony Orchestra (15 dates)

continued

★ = *one of the top 30 places for ambiance.*

Maui, HI (cont.)

Outdoor Recreation Assets (16)

Pacific coastal water: 123.60 square miles
Inland water: 3.60 square miles
Federal protected areas:
Haleakala NP (26,911 acres)
Kakahaia NWR (45 acres)
Kalaupapa NHP (23 acres)
State recreation areas:
Haleki'i-Pihana Heiau State Monument (10 acres)
'Iao Valley State Monument (6 acres)
Kaumahina State Wayside (8 acres)
Launiupoko State Wayside (6 acres)
Papalaua State Wayside (7 acres)
Polipoli Spring SRA (10 acres)
Pua'a Ka'a State Wayside (3 acres)
Wahikuli State Wayside (8 acres)
Wai'anapanapa SP (120 acres)
Wailua Valley State Wayside (2 acres)

Good Restaurants (63)

Score: 52.9 Rank: 96

McCall, ID

Visible Past (30)

Outdoor Recreation Assets (100)

Inland water: 55.65 square miles
Federal protected areas:
Boise NF (1,073,921 acres)
Payette NF (884,187 acres
Salmon NF (71,616 acres)

Good Restaurants (25)

Score: 40 Rank: 122

★ Medford–Ashland, OR

Visible Past (91)

Medford Downtown Historic District
Skidmore Academy Historic District
Union Creek Historic District

Lively Arts Calendar (80)

SOU Recital Hall
Touring artists bookings: 8 dates
Resident ensembles:
Britt Festival Orchestra (12 dates)
Rogue Opera (10 dates)
Rogue Valley Symphony (22 dates)

Outdoor Recreation Assets (70)

Inland water: 16.58 square miles
Federal protected areas:
Crater Lake NP (944 acres)
Klamath NF (26,334 acres)
Rogue River NF (411,681 acres)
Umpqua NF (10,628 acres)
State recreation areas:
Casey SRA (80 acres)
Joseph Stewart SRA (911 acres)
Prospect State Wayside (11 acres)
TouVelle SRA (51 acres)
Valley of the Rogue SP (278 acres)

Good Restaurants (61)

Score: 95.5 Rank: 10

★ Melbourne–Palm Bay, FL

Visible Past (59)

Barton Avenue Residential District
Rockledge Drive Residential District
Valencia Subdivision Residential District

Lively Arts Calendar (91)

King Performing Arts Center
Touring artists bookings: 73 dates
Resident ensembles:
Brevard Symphony Orchestra (20 dates)
Space Coast Pops (9 dates)

Outdoor Recreation Assets (67)

Atlantic coastal water: 26.28 square miles
Inland water: 275.96 square miles
Federal protected areas:
Archie Carr NWR (25 acres)
Canaveral NS (29,479 acres)
St. Johns NWR (6,255 acres)
State recreation area:
Sebastian Inlet SP (121 acres)

Good Restaurants (80)

Score: 89.6 Rank: 22

Mendocino–Fort Bragg, CA

Visible Past (56)

Arena Cove Historic District

Outdoor Recreation Assets (27)

Inland water: 7.00 square miles
Federal protected area:
Mendocino NF (179,075 acres)
State recreation areas:
Admiral Standley SRA (45 acres)
Caspar Headlands SR (2 acres)
Greenwood Creek SB (47 acres)
Hendy Woods SP (693 acres)
Jug Handle SR (769 acres)
MacKerricher SP (1,598 acres)
Mailliard Redwoods SR (242 acres)
Manchester SB (1,419 acres)
Mendocino Headlands SP (347 acres)
Montgomery Woods SR (1,142 acres)
Navarro River Redwoods SP (674 acres)
Reynolds SP (66 acres)
Russian Gulch SP (1,300 acres)
Schooner Gulch SB (7 acres)
Sinkyone Wilderness SP (7,000 acres)
Smithe Redwoods SR (822 acres)
Standish-Hickey SRA (1,070 acres)
Van Damme SP (2,163 acres)
Westport-Union Landing SB (41 acres)

Good Restaurants (53)

Score: 43 Rank: 116

Mesa, AZ

Visible Past (38)

Evergreen Historic District
Temple Historic District
West Second Street Historic District
Wilbur Street Historic District

Lively Arts Calendar (82)

Chandler Center for the Arts
Touring artists bookings: 46 dates

★ = *one of the top 30 places for ambiance.*

Resident ensemble:
Mesa Symphony Orchestra (15 dates)
Outdoor Recreation Assets (36)
Inland water: 20.81 square miles
Federal protected area:
Tonto NF (657,695 acres)
Good Restaurants (94)
Score: 59.9 Rank: 82

★ Middle Cape Cod, MA
Visible Past (97)
Brewster Old King's Highway Historic District
Centerville Historic District
Cotuit Historic District
Craigville Historic District
Eastham Center Historic District
Falmouth Village Green Historic District
Harwich Historic District
Hinckley's Corner Historic District
Hyannis Port Historic District
Hyannis Road Historic District
Kennedy Compound
Mill Way Historic District
North Falmouth Village Historic District
Northside Historic District
Old King's Highway Historic District
Old Town Center Historic District
Paine Hollow Road South Historic District
Pleasant–School Street Historic District
Sandy Neck Cultural Resources District
Santuit Historic District
Stony Brook–Factory Village Historic District
Wellfleet Center Historic District
West Barnstable Village–Meetinghouse Way Historic District
West Falmouth Village Historic District
Wianno Historic District
Yarmouth Camp Ground Historic District
Lively Arts Calendar (89)
Barnstable Performing Arts Center
Touring artists bookings: 13 dates
Resident ensembles:
Cape Cod Symphony Orchestra (20 dates)
College Light Opera Company (54 dates)
Outdoor Recreation Assets (46)
Atlantic coastal water: 85.14 square miles
Inland water: 60.05 square miles
Federal protected areas:
Cape Cod NS (27,460 acres)
Monomoy NWR (2,702 acres)
State recreation areas:
Hawksnest SP (218 acres)
Nickerson SP (1,779 acres)
Scusset Beach SR (380 acres)
Shawme-Crowell SF (2,756 acres)
South Cape Beach SP (790 acres)
Washburn Island SNA (355 acres)
Good Restaurants (97)
Score: 94 Rank: 13

Mission–McAllen–Alamo, TX
Visible Past (33)
Lively Arts Calendar (82)
International Civic Center
Touring artists bookings: 4 dates
Resident ensembles:
Rio Grande Valley Ballet (50 dates)
Valley Symphony Orchestra & Chorale (6 dates)
Outdoor Recreation Assets (12)
Inland water: 13.71 square miles
Federal protected areas:
Lower Rio Grande Valley NWR (15,002 acres)
Santa Ana NWR (2,087 acres)
State recreation area:
Bentsen-Rio Grande Valley SP (588 acres)
Good Restaurants (25)
Score: 39.1 Rank: 124

Monadnock Region, NH
Visible Past (93)
Dublin Lake Historic District
Harrisville Historic District
Silver Lake District
Lively Arts Calendar (89)
Colonial Theatre
Touring artists bookings: 22 dates
Outdoor Recreation Assets (18)
Inland water: 22.13 square miles
State recreation areas:
Bear Den SNA (95 acres)
Chesterfield Gorge SNA (13 acres)
Monadnock SP (1,009 acres)
Pisgah Wilderness SP (13,500 acres)
Rhododendron SP (260 acres)
Wantastiquet Mountain SNA (847 acres)
Good Restaurants (43)
Score: 72.2 Rank: 57

Montrose, CO
Visible Past (16)
Outdoor Recreation Assets (69)
Inland water: 1.96 square miles
Federal protected areas:
Black Canyon of the Gunnison NM (20,646 acres)
Curecanti NRA (10,833 acres)
Gunnison NF (11,610 acres)
Manti-La Sal NF (22,563 acres)
Uncompahgre NF (292,997 acres)
State recreation area:
Ute Indian Museum SHS (9 acres)
Good Restaurants (31)
Score: 15.8 Rank: 171

Morro Bay–Cambria, CA
Visible Past (30)
Lively Arts Calendar (68)
San Luis Obispo Performing Arts Center
Touring artists bookings: 5 dates
Resident ensembles:
Pacific Repertory Opera (7 dates)
San Luis Obispo County Symphony (11 dates)

continued

★ *= one of the top 30 places for ambiance.*

Morro Bay–Cambria, CA (cont.)

Outdoor Recreation Assets (32)
Pacific coastal water: 29.31 square miles
Inland water: 18.75 square miles
Federal protected area:
Los Padres NF (188,944 acres)
State recreation areas:
Cayucos SB (16 acres)
Hearst San Simeon State Historical Monument (149 acres)
Los Osos Oaks SR (85 acres)
Montana De Oro SP (8,400 acres)
Morro Bay SP (2,749 acres)
Morro Strand SB (117 acres)
Pismo Dunes SVRA (2,500 acres)
Pismo SB (1,051 acres)
San Simeon SP (541 acres)
William Randolph Hearst SB (8 acres)

Good Restaurants (88)
Score: 40.5 Rank: 121

Murray–Kentucky Lake, KY

Visible Past (34)
Lively Arts Calendar (36)
Lovett Auditorium
Touring artists bookings: 4 dates
Outdoor Recreation Assets (17)
Inland water: 59.94 square miles
State recreation areas:
Kenlake State Resort Park (1,795 acres)
Kentucky Dam Village State Resort Park (1,351 acres)
Good Restaurants (9)
Score: 16.3 Rank: 170

Myrtle Beach, SC

Visible Past (26)
Myrtle Heights–Oak Park Historic District
Lively Arts Calendar (64)
Myrtle Beach Auditorium
Touring artists bookings: 5 dates
Resident ensembles:
Long Bay Symphony Orchestra (5 dates)
Myrtle Beach Philharmonic (5 dates)
Outdoor Recreation Assets (7)
Atlantic coastal water: 10.95 square miles
Inland water: 11.78 square miles
State recreation area:
Myrtle Beach SP (312 acres)
Good Restaurants (96)
Score: 21.7 Rank: 159

Naples, FL

Visible Past (15)
Naples Historic District
Lively Arts Calendar (97)
Philharmonic Center for the Arts
Touring artists bookings: 100 dates
Resident ensemble:
Naples Philharmonic (80 dates)
Outdoor Recreation Assets (89)
Gulf coastal water: 18.88 square miles
Inland water: 90.97 square miles
Federal protected areas:
Big Cypress National Preserve (405,745 acres)
Everglades NP (39,262 acres)
Florida Panther NWR (24,310 acres)
State recreation areas:
Collier-Seminole SP (6,423 acres)
Delnor-Wiggins Pass SP (166 acres)
Fakahatchee Strand Preserve SP (66,367 acres)
Good Restaurants (91)
Score: 82.1 Rank: 36

Natchitoches, LA

Visible Past (58)
Natchitoches Historic District
Lively Arts Calendar (52)
NSU Fine Arts Auditorium
Touring artists bookings: 5 dates
Outdoor Recreation Assets (59)
Inland water: 43.00 square miles
Federal protected areas:
Cane River Creole NHP (60 acres)
Kisatchie NF (130,251 acres)
State recreation areas:
Fort St. Jean Baptiste SHS (7 acres)
Los Adaes SHS (14 acres)
Rebel SHS (46 acres)
Good Restaurants (30)
Score: 65.3 Rank: 70

New Bern, NC

Visible Past (42)
Ghent Historic District
New Bern Historic District
Riverside Historic District
Outdoor Recreation Assets (64)
Inland water: 66.26 square miles
Federal protected area:
Croatan NF (61,296 acres)
Good Restaurants (31)
Score: 28.7 Rank: 145

New Braunfels, TX

Visible Past (10)
Gruene Historic District
Outdoor Recreation Assets (10)
Inland water: 13.15 square miles
State recreation area:
Guadalupe River SP (1,000 acres)
Good Restaurants (37)
Score: 0.4 Rank: 202

New Port Richey, FL

Visible Past (41)
Church Street Historic District
Lively Arts Calendar (48)
Touring artists bookings: 8 dates
Outdoor Recreation Assets (13)
Gulf coastal water: 9.99 square miles
Inland water: 23.13 square miles
State recreation area:
Anclote Key Preserve SP (160 acres)
Good Restaurants (27)
Score: 24.2 Rank: 153

★ = *one of the top 30 places for ambiance.*

Newport–Lincoln City, OR

Visible Past (14)

Lively Arts Calendar (59)

Alice Silverman Theatre

Touring artists bookings: 15 dates

Outdoor Recreation Assets (69)

Pacific coastal water: 20.12 square miles

Inland water: 13.00 square miles

Federal protected areas:

Oregon Islands NWR (38 acres)

Siletz Bay NWR (398 acres)

Siuslaw NF (171,652 acres)

State recreation areas:

Beachside SRA (17 acres)

Beverly Beach SP (130 acres)

Depoe Bay SP (1 acre)

Devil's Lake SRA (109 acres)

Devil's Punch Bowl SNA (8 acres)

Ellmaker State Wayside (76 acres)

Fogarty Creek SRA (142 acres)

Lost Creek SRA (34 acres)

Ona Beach SP (237 acres)

Patterson Memorial SRA (10 acres)

South Beach SP (434 acres)

W.B. Nelson SRA (2 acres)

Yachats SRA (94 acres)

Yaquina Bay SRA (32 acres)

Good Restaurants (60)

Score: 48.5 Rank: 104

Norfork Lake, AR

Visible Past (5)

Outdoor Recreation Assets (66)

Inland water: 32.37 square miles

Federal protected areas:

Buffalo National River (991 acres)

Ozark NF (62,830 acres)

State protected area:

Bull Shoals SP (663 acres)

Good Restaurants (22)

Score: 10.3 Rank: 182

★ **North County San Diego, CA**

Visible Past (67)

Lively Arts Calendar (100)

California Center for the Arts

Touring artists bookings: 246 dates

Resident ensembles:

California Ballet Company (15 dates)

La Jolla Symphony & Chorus (14 dates)

San Diego Chamber Orchestra (22 dates)

San Diego Civic Light Opera Association (20 dates)

San Diego Comic Opera Company (18 dates)

San Diego Opera (23 dates)

Tifereth Israel Community Orchestra (9 dates)

Outdoor Recreation Assets (79)

Pacific coastal water: 26.81 square miles

Inland water: 54.43 square miles

Federal protected areas:

Cabrillo NM (137 acres)

Cleveland NF (290,095 acres)

Sweetwater Marsh NWR (316 acres)

Tijuana Slough NWR (407 acres)

State recreation areas:

Anza-Borrego Desert SP (522,097 acres)

Border Field SP (680 acres)

Cardiff SB (25 acres)

Carlsbad SB (14 acres)

Cuyamaca Rancho SP (24,677 acres)

Leucadia SB (11 acres)

Moonlight SB (14 acres)

Ocotillo Wells SVRA (42,000 acres)

Old Town San Diego SHP (13 acres)

Palomar Mountain SP (1,897 acres)

San Elijo SB (39 acres)

San Onofre SB (3,036 acres)

San Pasqual Battlefield SHP (11 acres)

Silver Strand SB (428 acres)

South Carlsbad SB (135 acres)

Torrey Pines SB (41 acres)

Torrey Pines SR (1,083 acres)

Good Restaurants (100)

Score: 96.5 Rank: 8

Northampton–Amherst, MA

Visible Past (99)

Bradstreet Historic District

Elm Street Historic District

Hadley Center Historic District

Hatfield Center Historic District

Hollis, Thomas, Historic District

Huntington Village Historic District

Northampton Downtown Historic District

Upper Main Street Historic District

Lively Arts Calendar (79)

Calvin Theatre

Touring artists bookings: 31 dates

Resident ensembles:

Amherst Ballet Theatre Company (6 dates)

Commonwealth Opera (6 dates)

Smith College Student Orchestra (4 dates)

University of Massachusetts Symphony Orchestra (4 dates)

Outdoor Recreation Assets (17)

Inland water: 16.44 square miles

State recreation areas:

C.M. Gardner SP (29 acres)

D.A.R. SF (1,517 acres)

Deer Hill SR (259 acres)

East Branch SF (2,000 acres)

Holyoke Range SP (2,252 acres)

Krug Sugarbush SNA (77 acres)

Middlefield SF (1,849 acres)

Skinner SP (390 acres)

Worthington SF (175 acres)

Good Restaurants (34)

Score: 80.6 Rank: 40

Northern Neck, VA

Visible Past (69)

Heathsville Historic District

Irvington

Reedville Historic District

continued

★ = *one of the top 30 places for ambiance.*

Northern Neck, VA (cont.)

Outdoor Recreation Assets (34)
Atlantic coastal water: 150.86 square miles
Inland water: 40.71 square miles
Good Restaurants (15)
Score: 26.2 Rank: 150

Oakhurst–Coarsegold, CA

Visible Past (9)
Outdoor Recreation Assets (84)
Inland water: 14.96 square miles
Federal protected areas:
Devils Postpile NM (799 acres)
Inyo NF (52,241 acres)
Sierra NF (362,049 acres)
Yosemite NP (66,886 acres)
State recreation areas:
Millerton Lake SRA (3,296 acres)
Wassama Round House SHP (27 acres)
Good Restaurants (34)
Score: 20.7 Rank: 161

Ocala, FL

Visible Past (58)
Dunnellon Boomtown Historic District
McIntosh Historic District
Ocala Historic District
Lively Arts Calendar (52)
Lecanto Auditorium
Resident ensemble:
Central Florida Symphony (10 dates)
Outdoor Recreation Assets (77)
Inland water: 84.11 square miles
Federal protected area:
Ocala NF (275,473 acres)
State recreation areas:
Lake Rousseau SRA (696 acres)
Silver River SP (4,432 acres)
Good Restaurants (49)
Score: 74.7 Rank: 52

Ocean City, MD

Visible Past (15)
Outdoor Recreation Assets (60)
Atlantic coastal water: 11.00 square miles
Inland water: 111.46 square miles
Federal protected areas:
Assateague Island NS (7,295 acres)
Chincoteague NWR (418 acres)
State recreation areas:
Assateague SP (756 acres)
Pocomoke River SP (914 acres)
Good Restaurants (77)
Score: 11.8 Rank: 179

Oscoda–Huron Shore, MI

Visible Past (22)
Alabaster Historic District
Outdoor Recreation Assets (53)
Great Lakes coastal water: 132.00 square miles
Inland water: 17.42 square miles
Federal protected area:
Huron NF (111,749 acres)
State recreation area:
Tawas Point SP (175 acres)
Good Restaurants (9)
Score: 11.3 Rank: 180

Oxford, MS

Visible Past (23)
Oxford Courthouse Square Historic District
Lively Arts Calendar (80)
Fulton Chapel
Touring artists bookings: 56 dates
Outdoor Recreation Assets (50)
Inland water: 48.18 square miles
Federal protected area:
Holly Springs NF (38,840 acres)
Score: 59.4 Rank: 83

Pagosa Springs, CO

Visible Past (11)
Outdoor Recreation Assets (92)
Inland water: 5.26 square miles
Federal protected areas:
Rio Grande NF (22,792 acres)
San Juan NF (406,424 acres)
State recreation area:
Navajo SRA (2,672 acres)
Good Restaurants (16)
Score: 25.7 Rank: 151

Pahrump Valley, NV

Visible Past (20)
Outdoor Recreation Assets (50)
Inland water: 12.47 square miles
Federal protected areas:
Ash Meadows NWR (12,849 acres)
Death Valley NM (107,616 acres)
Humboldt NF (248,321 acres)
Toiyabe NF (1,501,601 acres)
State recreation areas:
Belmont Courthouse SHS (1 acre)
Berlin-Ichthyosaur SP (1,248 acres)
Score: 9.4 Rank: 184

★ Palm Springs–Coachella Valley, CA

Visible Past (44)
Lively Arts Calendar (97)
McCallum Theatre for Performing Arts
Touring artists bookings: 174 dates
Resident ensemble:
West Coast Opera Theatre (6 dates)
Outdoor Recreation Assets (68)
Inland water: 95.66 square miles
Federal protected areas:
Cleveland NF (78,133 acres)
Coachella Valley NWR (2,589 acres)
Joshua Tree NM (474,110 acres)
San Bernardino NF (212,871 acres)
State recreation areas:
Anza-Borrego Desert SP (35,177 acres)
California Citrus SHP (247 acres)
Chino Hills SP (296 acres)
Lake Elsinore SRA (2,976 acres)

★ *= one of the top 30 places for ambiance.*

Lake Perris SRA (5,240 acres)
Mount San Jacinto SP (13,718 acres)
Salton Sea SRA (9,000 acres)

Good Restaurants (99)

Score: 85.6 Rank: 30

Palmer–Wasilla, AK

Visible Past (48)

Talkeetna Historic District

Lively Arts Calendar (45)

Machetanz Theatre

Touring artists bookings: 6 dates

Outdoor Recreation Assets (38)

Inland water: 261.27 square miles

Federal protected areas:
Chugach NF (43,386 acres)
Denali National Preserve (634,071 acres)
Denali NP (1,049,451 acres)
Lake Clark NP (6,710 acres)

Score: 41 Rank: 120

Panama City, FL

Visible Past (6)

Lively Arts Calendar (52)

Municipal Auditorium

Touring artists bookings: 10 dates

Outdoor Recreation Assets (42)

Gulf coastal water: 15.07 square miles

Inland water: 118.91 square miles

State recreation area:
St. Andrews SP (1,268 acres)

Good Restaurants (57)

Score: 23.2 Rank: 156

Paradise–Magalia, CA

Visible Past (8)

South of Campus Neighborhood

Lively Arts Calendar (52)

Paradise Auditorium

Touring artists bookings: 5 dates

Resident ensemble:
Paradise Symphony Orchestra (5 dates)

Outdoor Recreation Assets (57)

Inland water: 37.62 square miles

Federal protected areas:
Lassen NF (51,178 acres)
North Central Valley NWR (1,732 acres)
Plumas NF (82,299 acres)
Sacramento River NWR (825 acres)

State recreation areas:
Bidwell-Sacramento River SP (181 acres)
Lake Oroville SRA (28,753 acres)
Mansion SHP (5 acres)

Good Restaurants (22)

Score: 34.6 Rank: 133

Park City, UT

Visible Past (32)

Park City Main Street Historic District

Outdoor Recreation Assets (88)

Inland water: 11.49 square miles

Federal protected areas:
Ashley NF (12,644 acres)
Wasatch NF (501,871 acres)

State recreation areas:
Rail Trail SP (450 acres)
Rockport SP (550 acres)

Good Restaurants (58)

Score: 36.1 Rank: 130

Payson, AZ

Visible Past (46)

Globe Downtown Historic District

Pine Historic District

Outdoor Recreation Assets (94)

Inland water: 28.03 square miles

Federal protected areas:
Coconino NF (3,352 acres)
Tonto NF (1,700,390 acres)
Tonto NM (1,120 acres)

State recreation area:
Tonto Natural Bridge SP (160 acres)

Good Restaurants (22)

Score: 46 Rank: 108

Pendleton District, SC

Visible Past (55)

Newry Historic District

Pendleton Historic District

Seneca Historic District

Outdoor Recreation Assets (71)

Inland water: 102.91 square miles

Federal protected area:
Sumter NF (79,856 acres)

State recreation areas:
Keowee Toxaway SP (1,000 acres)
Lake Hartwell SP (681 acres)
Oconee SP (1,165 acres)
Oconee Station SHS (211 acres)
Sadlers Creek SP (395 acres)
Table Rock SP (3,068 acres)

Score: 38.6 Rank: 125

★ Pensacola, FL

Visible Past (73)

Alger–Sullivan Lumber Company Residential Historic District

North Hill Preservation District

Pensacola Historic District

Lively Arts Calendar (96)

Saenger Theatre

Touring artists bookings: 153 dates

Resident ensemble:
Greater Pensacola Symphony Orchestra (7 dates)

Outdoor Recreation Assets (48)

Gulf coastal water: 14.21 square miles

Inland water: 87.86 square miles

Federal protected area:
Gulf Islands NS (23,212 acres)

State recreation areas:
Big Lagoon SP (698 acres)
Perdido Key SP (285 acres)

Good Restaurants (69)

Score: 88.6 Rank: 24

★ *= one of the top 30 places for ambiance.*

Petoskey–Harbor Springs, MI

Visible Past (73)
Bay View
Four Mile Clearing Rural Historic District

Lively Arts Calendar (71)
Touring artists bookings: 21 dates

Outdoor Recreation Assets (26)
Great Lakes coastal water: 39.80 square miles
Inland water: 16.25 square miles
State recreation areas:
Petoskey SP (298 acres)
Wilderness SP (7,579 acres)

Good Restaurants (72)

Score: 66.3 Rank: 69

Pike County, PA

Visible Past (76)
Milford Historic District

Outdoor Recreation Assets (30)
Inland water: 19.59 square miles
Federal protected areas:
Delaware Water Gap NRA (17,380 acres)
Upper Delaware Scenic River (1 acre)
State recreation area:
Promised Land SP (5,736 acres)

Score: 28.2 Rank: 146

Polson–Mission Valley, MT

Visible Past (19)

Outdoor Recreation Assets (70)
Inland water: 159.94 square miles
Federal protected areas:
Flathead NF (156,602 acres)
National Bison Range NWR (8,694 acres)
Swan River NWR (1,569 acres)
State recreation areas:
Big Arm SP (55 acres)
Finley Point SP (24 acres)
Lake Elmo SP (40 acres)
Lambeth SP (76 acres)
Wild Horse Island SP (2,163 acres)
Yellow Bay SP (10 acres)

Score: 18.8 Rank: 165

Port Angeles–Sequim, WA

Visible Past (21)

Lively Arts Calendar (45)
Port Angeles HS Auditorium
Resident ensemble:
Port Angeles Symphony Orchestra (6 dates)

Outdoor Recreation Assets (84)
Pacific coastal water: 702.17 square miles
Inland water: 35.41 square miles
Federal protected areas:
Dungeness NWR (245 acres)
Flattery Rocks NWR (125 acres)
Olympic NF (199,333 acres)
Olympic NP (865,967 acres)
Protection Island NWR (3 acres)
Quillayute Needles NWR (104 acres)
State recreation areas:
Bogachiel SP (123 acres)
Clallam Bay SP (36 acres)
Dungeness SP (1 acre)
Hoko River SP (33 acres)
Point of Arches SP (21 acres)
Sequim Bay SP (92 acres)

Good Restaurants (70)

Score: 54.9 Rank: 92

Port Charlotte, FL

Visible Past (29)
Punta Gorda Residential District

Lively Arts Calendar (72)
Charlotte County Memorial Auditorium
Touring artists bookings: 21 dates
Resident ensemble:
Charlotte Symphony Orchestra (6 dates)

Outdoor Recreation Assets (45)
Gulf coastal water: 4.32 square miles
Inland water: 122.38 square miles
Federal protected area:
Island Bay NWR (20 acres)
State recreation areas:
Don Pedro Island SP (133 acres)
Port Charlotte Beach SP (213 acres)

Good Restaurants (22)

Score: 50.9 Rank: 98

Port Townsend, WA

Visible Past (67)
Port Townsend Historic District

Outdoor Recreation Assets (94)
Puget Sound coastal water: 168.99 square miles
Inland water: 62.57 square miles
Federal protected areas:
Olympic NF (166,961 acres)
Olympic NP (540,167 acres)
Protection Island NWR (317 acres)
Quillayute Needles NWR (196 acres)
State recreation areas:
Anderson Lake SP (410 acres)
Dosewallips SP (425 acres)
Fort Flagler SP (783 acres)
Fort Worden SP (434 acres)
Kinney Point SP (76 acres)
Mystery Bay SP (10 acres)
Old Fort Townsend SP (377 acres)
Pleasant Harbor (1 acre)
Right Smart Cove (1 acre)
Rothschild House SP (1 acre)
Triton Cove SP (28 acres)

Good Restaurants (55)

Score: 61.3 Rank: 78

Prescott–Prescott Valley, AZ

Visible Past (2)
East Prescott Historic District
Joslin and Whipple Historic District
South Prescott Townsite
West Prescott Historic District

Lively Arts Calendar (64)
Yavapai College Performance Hall
Touring artists bookings: 20 dates

Outdoor Recreation Assets (86)
Inland water: 4.79 square miles

★ = *one of the top 30 places for ambiance.*

Federal protected areas:
Coconino NF (427,107 acres)
Kaibab NF (25,119 acres)
Montezuma Castle NM (841 acres)
Prescott NF (1,194,459 acres)
Tonto NF (316,997 acres)
Tuzigoot NM (58 acres)
State recreation areas:
Dead Horse Ranch SP (320 acres)
Fort Verde SHP (11 acres)
Jerome SHP (3 acres)
Red Rock SP (286 acres)
Good Restaurants (90)
Score: 57.4 Rank: 86

Rabun County, GA
Visible Past (17)
Outdoor Recreation Assets (96)
Inland water: 5.94 square miles
Federal protected areas:
Appalachian National Scenic Trail (190 acres)
Chattahoochee NF (149,652 acres)
State recreation areas:
Black Rock Mountain SP (1,502 acres)
Moccasin Creek SP (32 acres)
Tallulah Gorge SP (3,000 acres)
Good Restaurants (16)
Score: 31.1 Rank: 140

Rehoboth Bay–Indian River Bay, DE
Visible Past (86)
Bridgeville Historic District
Laurel Historic District
Lewes Historic District
Milton Historic District
Outdoor Recreation Assets (24)
Atlantic coastal water: 123.48 square miles
Inland water: 41.34 square miles
Federal protected area:
Prime Hook NWR (8,818 acres)
State recreation areas:
Assawoman Canal SRA (102 acres)
Beach Plum Island Nature Preserve (134 acres)
Cape Henlopen SP (3,270 acres)
Delaware Seashore SP (1,851 acres)
Fenwick Island SP (208 acres)
Fresh Pond SP (475 acres)
Holts Landing SP (301 acres)
Thompson Island Preserve (165 acres)
Trap Pond SP (966 acres)
Good Restaurants (79)
Score: 29.7 Rank: 143

Reno–Sparks, NV
Visible Past (53)
Lively Arts Calendar (85)
Pioneer Center for Performing Arts
Touring artists bookings: 10 dates
Resident ensembles:
Nevada Opera (7 dates)
North Lake Tahoe Symphony (12 dates)
Reno Chamber Orchestra (7 dates)
Reno Philharmonic (18 dates)
Outdoor Recreation Assets (30)
Inland water: 209.01 square miles
Federal protected areas:
Anaho Island NWR (248 acres)
Sheldon NWR (187,240 acres)
Toiyabe NF (66,742 acres)
State recreation areas:
Lake Tahoe SP (10,552 acres)
Washoe Lake SRA (7,778 acres)
Good Restaurants (62)
Score: 64.8 Rank: 72

Rio Rancho, NM
Visible Past (63)
Outdoor Recreation Assets (54)
Inland water: 5.12 square miles
Federal protected areas:
Bandelier NM (25,428 acres)
Cibola NF (45,137 acres)
Santa Fe NF (339,094 acres)
State recreation areas:
Coronado SP (210 acres)
Fenton Lake SP (735 acres)
Good Restaurants (42)
Score: 70.7 Rank: 60

Rockport–Aransas Pass, TX
Visible Past (7)
Outdoor Recreation Assets (95)
Gulf coastal water: 6.87 square miles
Inland water: 207.36 square miles
Federal protected area:
Aransas NWR (52,461 acres)
State recreation areas:
Copano Bay State Fishing Pier (6 acres)
Fulton Mansion SHS (2 acres)
Goose Island SP (314 acres)
Good Restaurants (9)
Score: 25.2 Rank: 152

Roswell, NM
Visible Past (29)
Lively Arts Calendar (40)
Touring artists bookings: 5 dates
Outdoor Recreation Assets (22)
Inland water: 16.12 square miles
Federal protected areas:
Carlsbad Caverns NP (46,427 acres)
Lincoln NF (135,013 acres)
State recreation areas:
Brantley Lake SP (5,800 acres)
Living Desert SP (1,100 acres)
Good Restaurants (27)
Score: 19.8 Rank: 163

Ruidoso, NM
Visible Past (40)
Lincoln Historic District
White Oaks Historic District
Lively Arts Calendar (55)
Touring artists bookings: 12 dates
Outdoor Recreation Assets (41)
Inland water: 0.19 square miles

continued

★ = *one of the top 30 places for ambiance.*

Ruidoso, NM (cont.)
Federal protected areas:
Cibola NF (34,336 acres)
Lincoln NF (364,579 acres)
State recreation area:
Smokey Bear SHP (3 acres)
Good Restaurants (31)
Score: 43.5 Rank: 115

St. Augustine, FL
Visible Past (72)
Abbott Tract Historic District
Lincolnville Historic District
Model Land Company Historic District
St. Augustine Town Plan Historic District
Lively Arts Calendar (59)
Flagler College Auditorium
Touring artists bookings: 15 dates
Outdoor Recreation Assets (33)
Atlantic coastal water: 14.84 square miles
Inland water: 63.99 square miles
Federal protected areas:
Castillo de San Marcos NM (20 acres)
Fort Matanzas NM (228 acres)
State recreation areas:
Anastasia SP (1,522 acres)
Faver-Dykes SP (752 acres)
Guana River SP (2,398 acres)
Good Restaurants (82)
Score: 62.8 Rank: 76

St. George–Zion, UT
Visible Past (49)
Hurricane Historic District
Lively Arts Calendar (61)
Touring artists bookings: 10 dates
Resident ensemble:
Southwest Symphony Orchestra (6 dates)
Outdoor Recreation Assets (81)
Inland water: 2.87 square miles
Federal protected areas:
Dixie NF (394,556 acres)
Zion NP (130,798 acres)
State recreation areas:
Gunlock Lake SP (548 acres)
Quail Creek SP (3,677 acres)
Snow Canyon SP (5,740 acres)
Good Restaurants (46)
Score: 75.7 Rank: 50

St. Jay–Northeast Kingdom, VT
Visible Past (63)
Downtown Hardwick Village Historic District
St. Johnsbury Main Street Historic District
Summer Street Historic District
Lively Arts Calendar (64)
Touring artists bookings: 20 dates
Outdoor Recreation Assets (5)
Inland water: 6.78 square miles
Good Restaurants (38)
Score: 42 Rank: 118

St. Simons–Jekyll Islands, GA
Visible Past (70)
Brunswick Old Town Historic District
Outdoor Recreation Assets (44)
Atlantic coastal water: 6.43 square miles
Inland water: 60.66 square miles
Federal protected area:
Fort Frederica NM (239 acres)
State recreation area:
Hofwyl-Broadfield Plantation SHS (1,268 acres)
Good Restaurants (67)
Score: 32.6 Rank: 137

Salida, CO
Visible Past (50)
St. Elmo Historic District
Salida Downtown Historic District
Outdoor Recreation Assets (96)
Inland water: 2.00 square miles
Federal protected area:
San Isabel NF (456,209 acres)
State recreation area:
Arkansas Headwaters SRA (5,697 acres)
Good Restaurants (46)
Score: 52.4 Rank: 97

San Juan Islands, WA
Visible Past (27)
Lively Arts Calendar (59)
Orcas Theatre & Community Center
Touring artists bookings: 15 dates
Outdoor Recreation Assets (63)
Puget Sound coastal water: 361.99 square miles
Inland water: 81.16 square miles
Federal protected areas:
San Juan Islands NWR (379 acres)
San Juan NHS (1,726 acres)
State recreation areas:
Blind Island SP (3 acres)
Castle Island SP (2 acres)
Clark Island SP (55 acres)
Doe Island SP (6 acres)
Dot Rock SP (1 acre)
Freeman Island SP (1 acre)
Iceberg Island SP (3 acres)
James Island SP (114 acres)
Jones Island SP (188 acres)
Lime Kiln Point SP (36 acres)
Lopez Island Tidelands SP (1 acre)
Matia Island SP (5 acres)
Moran SP (5,176 acres)
Mud Bay Tidelands SP (1 acre)
Northwest McConnel Rock SP (3 acres)
Olga SP (1 acre)
Park Bay Island SP (3 acres)
Patos Island SP (207 acres)
Posey Island SP (1 acre)
Skull Island SP (1 acre)
Spencer Spit SP (130 acres)
Stuart Island SP (148 acres)
Sucia Island SP (564 acres)

Turn Island SP (35 acres)
Twin Rocks SP (1 acre)
Unnamed Islands SP (8 acres)
Victim Island SP (5 acres)

Good Restaurants (63)

Score: 55.4 Rank: 90

Sandpoint–Lake Pend Oreille, ID

Visible Past (35)

Sandpoint Historic District

Lively Arts Calendar (50)

Panida Theatre

Touring artists bookings: 9 dates

Outdoor Recreation Assets (90)

Inland water: 182.00 square miles

Federal protected areas:

Idaho Panhandle NF (439,718)
Kootenai NF (35,909 acres)

State recreation areas:

Priest Lake SP (756 acres)
Round Lake SP (142 acres)

Good Restaurants (27)

Score: 69.3 Rank: 62

★ Santa Barbara, CA

Visible Past (50)

Lively Arts Calendar (94)

Arlington Theatre

Touring artists bookings: 44 dates

Resident ensembles:

Music Academy of the West Summer Festival Orchestra (4 dates)
Santa Barbara Civic Light Opera (30 dates)
Santa Barbara Chamber Orchestra (6 dates)
Santa Barbara Grand Opera (15 dates)
Santa Barbara Symphony Orchestra (28 dates)
The West Coast Symphony (4 dates)

Outdoor Recreation Assets (78)

Pacific coastal water: 103.81 square miles

Inland water: 13.03 square miles

Federal protected areas:

Channel Islands NP (63,552 acres)
Los Padres NF (629,118 acres)

State recreation areas:

Carpinteria SB (57 acres)
Chumash Painted Cave SHP (8 acres)
El Capitan SB (134 acres)
El Presidio de Santa Barbara SHP (4 acres)
Gaviota SP (2,756 acres)
La Purisima Mission SHP (966 acres)
Point Sal SB (84 acres)
Refugio SB (155 acres)

Good Restaurants (89)

Score: 92.5 Rank: 16

★ Santa Fe, NM

Visible Past (70)

Camino del Monte Sol Historic District
Don Gaspar Historic District
Madrid Historic District
Santa Fe Historic District

Lively Arts Calendar (88)

Santa Fe Opera Center

Touring artists bookings: 22 dates

Resident ensembles:

Santa Fe Opera (38 dates)
Santa Fe Pro Musica (13 dates)
Santa Fe Symphony Orchestra & Chorus (8 dates)

Outdoor Recreation Assets (61)

Inland water: 1.60 square miles

Federal protected areas:

Bandelier NM (826 acres)
Pecos NM (87 acres)
Santa Fe NF (245,005 acres)

State recreation areas:

Hyde Memorial SP (350 acres)
Santa Fe River SP (5 acres)

Good Restaurants (91)

Score: 91 Rank: 19

Santa Rosa, CA

Visible Past (66)

Petaluma Historic Commercial District
Railroad Square District
Sonoma Plaza

Lively Arts Calendar (92)

Luther Burbank Center

Touring artists bookings: 23 dates

Resident ensembles:

Redwood Empire Ballet (40 dates)
Rohnert Park Chamber Orchestra (8 dates)
Santa Rosa Symphony Orchestra (43 dates)

Outdoor Recreation Assets (15)

Pacific coastal water: 16.29 square miles

Inland water: 29.21 square miles

Federal protected area:

San Pablo Bay NWR (249 acres)

State recreation areas:

Annadel SP (4,916 acres)
Armstrong Redwoods SR (752 acres)
Austin Creek SRA (4,234 acres)
Bothe-Napa Valley SP (144 acres)
Fort Ross SHP (3,276 acres)
Jack London SHP (983 acres)
Kruse Rhododendron SR (317 acres)
Petaluma Adobe SHP (41 acres)
Robert Louis Stevenson SP (1,538 acres)
Salt Point SP (5,676 acres)
Sonoma Coast SB (5,054 acres)
Sonoma SHP (64 acres)
Sugarloaf Ridge SP (2,514 acres)

Good Restaurants (83)

Score: 67.8 Rank: 66

Sarasota, FL

Visible Past (43)

Caples'-Ringlings' Estates Historic District
Edgewood Historic District
Venezia Park Historic District

Lively Arts Calendar (99)

Van Wezel Auditorium

Touring artists bookings: 116 dates

Resident ensembles:

Florida Symphony Youth Orchestra (12 dates)
Florida West Coast Symphony Orchestra (27 dates)
Sarasota Ballet of Florida (42 dates)

continued

★ = *one of the top 30 places for ambiance.*

Sarasota, FL (cont.)
Sarasota Opera Association (36 dates)
Sarasota Pops (5 dates)
Venice Symphony (20 dates)
Outdoor Recreation Assets (34)
Gulf coastal water: 11.93 square miles
Inland water: 34.21 square miles
State recreation areas:
Myakka River SP (18,725 acres)
Oscar Scherer SP (1,377 acres)
Good Restaurants (98)
Score: 69.3 Rank: 62

★ Savannah, GA
Visible Past (100)
Ardsley Park–Chatham Crescent Historic District
Cuyler–Brownville Historic District
Daffin Park–Parkside Place Historic District
Gordonston Historic District
Isle of Hope Historic District
Savannah Historic District
Thomas Square Streetcar Historic District
Lively Arts Calendar (88)
Savannah Civic Center
Touring artists bookings: 6 dates
Resident ensemble:
Savannah Symphony Orchestra (75 dates)
Outdoor Recreation Assets (57)
Atlantic coastal water: 19.06 square miles
Inland water: 56.43 square miles
Federal protected areas:
Fort Pulaski NM (5,365 acres)
Savannah Coastal NWR (5,527 acres)
Wassaw NWR (10,050 acres)
State recreation areas:
Skidaway Island SP (506 acres)
Wormsloe SHS (8,222 acres)
Good Restaurants (81)
Score: 96 Rank: 9

Scottsdale, AZ
Visible Past (23)
Lively Arts Calendar (93)
Scottsdale Center for the Arts
Touring artists bookings: 112 dates
Resident ensemble:
Scottsdale Symphony Orchestra (5 dates)
Outdoor Recreation Assets (36)
Inland water: 20.81 square miles
Federal protected area:
Tonto NF (657,695 acres)
Good Restaurants (99)
Score: 57.4 Rank: 86

Sebring–Avon Park, FL
Visible Past (19)
Avon Park Historic District
Sebring Downtown Historic District
Lively Arts Calendar (62)
SFCC Auditorium
Touring artists bookings: 18 dates
Outdoor Recreation Assets (21)
Inland water: 77.88 square miles
Federal protected area:
Lake Wales Ridge NWR (504 acres)
State recreation area:
Highlands Hammock SP (370 acres)
Score: 24.2 Rank: 153

Sedona, AZ
Visible Past (7)
Lively Arts Calendar (55)
St. John Vianney Church
Touring artists bookings: 12 dates
Outdoor Recreation Assets (81)
Inland water: 4.79 square miles
Federal protected areas:
Coconino NF (1,415,700 acres)
Glen Canyon NRA (44,953 acres)
Grand Canyon NP (662,038 acres)
Kaibab NF (1,526,993 acres)
Lake Mead NRA (83,116 acres)
Navajo NM (40 acres)
Prescott NF (43,695 acres)
Sitgreaves NF (284,325 acres)
Sunset Crater NM (3,040 acres)
Walnut Canyon NM (2,012 acres)
Wupatki NM (35,253 acres)
State recreation areas:
Riordan SHS (5 acres)
Slide Rock SP (43 acres)
Good Restaurants (74)
Score: 50 Rank: 102

Silver City, NM
Visible Past (51)
Chihuahua Hill Historic District
Pinos Altos Historic District
Silver City Historic District North Addition
Lively Arts Calendar (48)
Touring artists bookings: 8 dates
Outdoor Recreation Assets (83)
Inland water: 1.62 square miles
Federal protected area:
Gila NF (883,394 acres)
Good Restaurants (8)
Score: 73.7 Rank: 54

Smith Mountain Lake, VA
Visible Past (70)
Cahas Mountain Rural Historic District
Cifax Rural Historic District
Rocky Mount Historic District
Outdoor Recreation Assets (23)
Inland water: 34.00 square miles
Federal protected areas:
Appalachian National Scenic Trail (120 acres)
Blue Ridge Parkway (9,328 acres)
Booker T. Washington NM (224 acres)
Jefferson NF (18,810 acres)
State recreation area:
Smith Mountain Lake SP (21,506 acres)
Score: 20.2 Rank: 162

Sonora–Twain Harte, CA
Visible Past (46)
Columbia Historic District
Outdoor Recreation Assets (97)
Inland water: 38.87 square miles

★ = *one of the top 30 places for ambiance.*

Federal protected areas:
Stanislaus NF (612,324 acres)
Yosemite NP (428,605 acres)
State recreation areas:
Calaveras Big Trees SP (497 acres)
Columbia SHP (263 acres)
Railtown 1897 SHP (20 acres)
Good Restaurants (31)
Score: 49.5 Rank: 103

Southern Berkshire County, MA
Visible Past (87)
Mill River Historic District
North Egremont Historic District
Sheffield Center Historic District
Taconic and West Avenues Historic District
Lively Arts Calendar (68)
St. James Church; Norman Rockwell Museum
Touring artists bookings: 23 dates
Outdoor Recreation Assets (53)
Inland water: 14.95 square miles
Federal protected area:
Appalachian National Scenic Trail (4,734 acres)
State recreation areas:
Bash Bish Falls SP (417 acres)
Beartown SF (10,555 acres)
Becket SF (656 acres)
Campbell's Falls SP (5 acres)
Clarksburg SP (3,250 acres)
Cookson SF (2,385 acres)
East Mountain SP (375 acres)
Mt. Everett SR (1,100 acres)
Mt. Greylock SR (10,327 acres)
Natural Bridge SP (17 acres)
October Mountain SF (15,710 acres)
Otis SF (3,861 acres)
Peru SF (3,150 acres)
Pittsfield SF (9,695 acres)
Sandisfield SF (7,785 acres)
Savoy Mountain SF (10,500 acres)
Taconic Trail SP (930 acres)
Tolland SF (8,000 acres)
Wahconah Falls SP (53 acres)
Windsor SF (1,626 acres)
Good Restaurants (86)
Score: 85.1 Rank: 31

Southern Pines–Pinehurst, NC
Visible Past (83)
Aberdeen Historic District
Carthage Historic District
Southern Pines Historic District
Lively Arts Calendar (55)
Touring artists bookings: 12 dates
Outdoor Recreation Assets (6)
Inland water: 7.54 square miles
State recreation area:
Weymouth Woods (628 acres)
Good Restaurants (46)
Score: 50.9 Rank: 98

Southport–Brunswick Islands, NC
Visible Past (39)
Southport Historic District
Outdoor Recreation Assets (16)
Atlantic coastal water: 15.52 square miles
Inland water: 39.97 square miles
Good Restaurants (18)
Score: 4.4 Rank: 194

State College, PA
Visible Past (94)
Aaronsburg Historic District
Bellefonte Historic District
Boalsburg Historic District
College Heights Historic District
Holmes-Foster-Highlands Historic District
Lemont Historic District
Millheim Historic District
Philipsburg Historic District
Rebersburg Historic District
Unionville Historic District
Lively Arts Calendar (81)
PSU Eisenhower Auditorium
Touring artists bookings: 35 dates
Resident ensembles:
Nittany Valley Symphony (6 dates)
Penn State Philharmonic (8 dates)
Pennsylvania Centre Chamber Orchestra (5 dates)
Outdoor Recreation Assets (7)
Inland water: 4.32 square miles
State recreation areas:
Bald Eagle SP (5,900 acres)
Black Moshannon SP (3,481 acres)
McCall Dam SP (8 acres)
Penn Roosevelt SP (100 acres)
Poe Paddy SP (10 acres)
Poe Valley SP (620 acres)
Good Restaurants (50)
Score: 73.2 Rank: 55

Summerville, SC
Visible Past (80)
Summerville Historic District
Outdoor Recreation Assets (3)
Inland water: 2.44 square miles
State recreation areas:
Givhans Ferry SP (888 acres)
Old Dorchester SP (325 acres)
Good Restaurants (58)
Score: 15.3 Rank: 172

Table Rock Lake, MO
Visible Past (4)
Outdoor Recreation Assets (43)
Inland water: 47.68 square miles
Federal protected area:
Mark Twain NF (15,960 acres)
State recreation area:
Table Rock SP (62 acres)
Good Restaurants (22)
Score: 3.9 Rank: 195

★ = *one of the top 30 places for ambiance.*

★ **Taos, NM**

Visible Past (54)
La Loma Plaza Historic District
Taos Downtown Historic District

Lively Arts Calendar (75)
Taos Community Auditorium
Touring artists bookings: 41 dates

Outdoor Recreation Assets (80)
Inland water: 1.46 square miles
Federal protected area:
Carson NF (483,026 acres)

Good Restaurants (69)

Score: 86.6 Rank: 28

Thomasville, GA

Visible Past (91)
Dawson Street Residential Historic District
Stevens Street Historic District
Thomasville Commercial Historic District
Thomasville Historic District

Lively Arts Calendar (45)
Thomasville Cultural Center
Touring artists bookings: 6 dates

Outdoor Recreation Assets (5)
Inland water: 3.69 square miles
State recreation area:
Lapham-Patterson House SHS (1 acre)

Good Restaurants (30)

Score: 47.5 Rank: 107

★ **Toms River–Barnegat Bay, NJ**

Visible Past (83)
Beach Haven Historic District
Cassville Crossroads Historic District
Island Heights Historic District

Lively Arts Calendar (79)
Ocean County College Fine Arts Center
Touring artists bookings: 42 dates
Resident ensemble:
Garden State Symphony Orchestra (7 dates)

Outdoor Recreation Assets (59)
Atlantic coastal water: 15.86 square miles
Inland water: 120.99 square miles
Federal protected area:
Edwin B. Forsythe NWR (13,015 acres)
State recreation areas:
Barnegat Lighthouse SP (32 acres)
Double Trouble SP (5,118 acres)
Island Beach SP (3,002 acres)
Manasquan Canal SRA (5 acres)
Monmouth Battlefield SP (1,520 acres)
Veterans of All Wars Memorial SHS (1 acre)

Good Restaurants (58)

Score: 91.5 Rank: 17

Traverse City, MI

Visible Past (45)
Boardman Neighborhood Historic District
Central Neighborhood Historic District

Lively Arts Calendar (98)
Interlochen Center for the Arts
Touring artists bookings: 180 dates
Resident ensembles:
Interlochen Arts Academy Orchestra (12 dates)
Traverse Symphony Orchestra (12 dates)
World Youth Symphony Orchestra (9 dates)

Outdoor Recreation Assets (18)
Great Lakes coastal water: 11.00 square miles
Inland water: 26.21 square miles
Federal protected area:
Manistee NF (2 acres)
State recreation areas:
Interlochen SP (187 acres)
Old Mission Point SP (513 acres)
Traverse City SP (45 acres)

Good Restaurants (70)

Score: 60.8 Rank: 80

Trinity Peninsula, TX

Visible Past (3)

Outdoor Recreation Assets (55)
Inland water: 21.22 square miles
Federal protected area:
Davy Crockett NF (67,339 acres)

Score: 4.9 Rank: 193

Tryon, NC

Visible Past (26)
Saluda Main Street Historic District

Lively Arts Calendar (36)
Touring artists bookings: 4 dates

Outdoor Recreation Assets (3)
Inland water: 0.75 square miles

Good Restaurants (25)

Score: 6.9 Rank: 189

★ **Tucson, AZ**

Visible Past (96)
Armory Park Historic Residential District
Colonia Solana Residential Historic District
El Encanto Estates Residential Historic District
El Montevideo Neighborhood Residential Historic District
Iron Horse Expansion Historic District
Pie Allen Historic District
Sam Hughes Neighborhood Historic District
Speedway–Drachman Historic District
West University Historic District

Lively Arts Calendar (98)
Convention Center Music Hall
Touring artists bookings: 111 dates
Resident ensembles:
Arizona Opera Company (13 dates)
Catalina Chamber Orchestra (8 dates)
Civic Orchestra of Tucson (4 dates)
Southern Arizona Symphony Orchestra (8 dates)
Tucson Philharmonia Youth Orchestra (3 dates)
Tucson Symphony Orchestra (56 dates)

Outdoor Recreation Assets (67)
Inland water: 2.43 square miles
Federal protected areas:
Buenos Aires NWR (21,977 acres)
Cabeza Prieta NWR (416,211 acres)
Coronado NF (390,474 acres)
Organ Pipe Cactus NM (329,316 acres)
Saguaro NP (82,035 acres)

★ = *one of the top 30 places for ambiance.*

State recreation area:
Catalina SP (5,511 acres)
Good Restaurants (95)
Score: 100 Rank: 1

Vero Beach, FL
Visible Past (14)
Lively Arts Calendar (36)
Riverside Theatre
Touring artists bookings: 4 dates
Outdoor Recreation Assets (23)
Atlantic coastal water: 7.69 square miles
Inland water: 36.79 square miles
Federal protected areas:
Archie Carr NWR (3 acres)
Pelican Island NWR (43 acres)
State recreation area:
Sebastian Inlet SP (457 acres)
Good Restaurants (49)
Score: 10.8 Rank: 181

★ Victorville–Apple Valley, CA
Visible Past (92)
Highland Historic District
Redlands Santa Fe Depot District
Smiley Park Historic District
Lively Arts Calendar (76)
Victor Valley College Center
Touring artists bookings: 40 dates
Resident ensemble:
Victor Valley Symphony Orchestra (4 dates)
Outdoor Recreation Assets (49)
Inland water: 44.61 square miles
Federal protected areas:
Angeles NF (10,289 acres)
Death Valley NM (81,152 acres)
Joshua Tree NM (74,426 acres)
Mohave National Preserve (1,355,637 acres)
San Bernardino NF (457,872 acres)
State recreation areas:
Chino Hills SP (6,775 acres)
Providence Mountains SRA (5,891 acres)
Seccombe Lake SRA (50 acres)
Silverwood Lake SRA (2,201 acres)
Good Restaurants (85)
Score: 89.1 Rank: 23

Virginia Beach, VA
Visible Past (12)
Lively Arts Calendar (73)
Pavilion Center
Touring artists bookings: 24 dates
Resident ensemble:
Virginia Beach Symphony Orchestra (7 dates)
Outdoor Recreation Assets (62)
Atlantic coastal water: 70.83 square miles
Inland water: 58.33 square miles
Federal protected areas:
Back Bay NWR (4,589 acres)
Mackay Island NWR (874 acres)
State recreation areas:
False Cape SP (4,321 acres)
Seashore SP (2,770 acres)
Good Restaurants (92)
Score: 53.9 Rank: 94

Wenatchee, WA
Visible Past (57)
Lively Arts Calendar (36)
Wenatchee HS Auditorium
Resident ensemble:
Wenatchee Valley Symphony (4 dates)
Outdoor Recreation Assets (99)
Inland water: 72.24 square miles
Federal protected areas:
Lake Chelan NRA (59,307 acres)
North Cascades NP (66,751 acres)
Wenatchee NF (1,311,949 acres)
State recreation areas:
Ice Caves SP (160 acres)
Lake Chelan SP (127 acres)
Lake Wenatchee SP (473 acres)
Squilchuck SP (293 acres)
Twenty-Five Mile Creek SP (235 acres)
Good Restaurants (63)
Score: 76.2 Rank: 49

Western St. Tammany Parish, LA
Visible Past (54)
Abita Springs Historic District
Division of St. John Historic District
Lively Arts Calendar (40)
Touring artists bookings: 5 dates
Outdoor Recreation Assets (74)
Inland water: 259.80 square miles
Federal protected areas:
Big Branch Marsh NWR (9,007 acres)
Bogue Chitto NWR (23,112 acres)
State recreation areas:
Fairview-Riverside SP (99 acres)
Fontainebleau SP (2,809 acres)
Slidell SP (71 acres)
Good Restaurants (71)
Score: 64.3 Rank: 73

Whidbey Island, WA
Visible Past (68)
Outdoor Recreation Assets (31)
Pacific coastal water: 295.43 square miles
Inland water: 13.36 square miles
Federal protected areas:
Ebey's Landing National Historic Reserve (1,379 acres)
San Juan Islands NWR (65 acres)
State recreation areas:
Camano Island SP (134 acres)
Deception Pass SP (1,249 acres)
Ebey's Landing SP (46 acres)
Fort Casey SP (417 acres)
Fort Ebey SP (644 acres)
Joseph Whidbey SP (112 acres)
South Whidbey SP (85 acres)
Good Restaurants (53)
Score: 22.7 Rank: 157

★ = *one of the top 30 places for ambiance.*

Wickenburg, AZ

Visible Past (6)

Outdoor Recreation Assets (36)

Inland water: 20.81 square miles

Federal protected area:

Tonto NF (657,695 acres)

Good Restaurants (92)

Score: 3.4 **Rank: 196**

★ Williamsburg, VA

Visible Past (78)

Chandler Court and Pollard Park Historic District

Lively Arts Calendar (69)

Phi Beta Kappa Memorial Hall

Touring artists bookings: 12 dates

Resident ensemble:

Williamsburg Symphonia (12 dates)

Outdoor Recreation Assets (64)

Atlantic coastal water: 14.82 square miles

Inland water: 22.12 square miles

Federal protected area:

Colonial NHP (2,972 acres)

State recreation area:

York River SP (2,505 acres)

Good Restaurants (90)

Score: 87.6 **Rank: 26**

Wimberley, TX

Visible Past (25)

Lively Arts Calendar (40)

Touring artists bookings: 5 dates

Outdoor Recreation Assets (1)

Inland water: 1.92 square miles

Score: 7.9 **Rank: 187**

Woodstock, VT

Visible Past (96)

Chester Village Historic District

Hartford Village Historic District

Norwich Village Historic District

Quechee Historic Mill District

Weston Village Historic District

Wilder Village Historic District

Woodstock Village Historic District

Lively Arts Calendar (81)

Town Hall Theatre

Touring artists bookings: 41 dates

Resident ensemble:

Opera North (12 dates)

Outdoor Recreation Assets (26)

Inland water: 4.77 square miles

Federal protected areas:

Appalachian National Scenic Trail (3,300 acres)

Green Mountain NF (22,008 acres)

Marsh-Billings-Rockefeller NHP (555 acres)

State recreation areas:

Ascutney SP (1,984 acres)

Camp Plymouth SP (300 acres)

Coolidge SP (16,165 acres)

Quechee Gorge SP (612 acres)

Silver Lake SP (34 acres)

Wilgus SP (100 acres)

Good Restaurants (86)

Score: 83.6 **Rank: 34**

York Beaches, ME

Visible Past (84)

Cape Arundel Summer Colony Historic District

Kennebunk Historic District

Kennebunkport Historic District

Saco Historic District

Outdoor Recreation Assets (14)

Atlantic coastal water: 20.11 square miles

Inland water: 31.65 square miles

Federal protected area:

Rachel Carson NWR (3,287 acres)

State recreation areas:

Ferry Beach SP (117 acres)

Fort McClary SHS (27 acres)

John Paul Jones SHS (2 acres)

Vaughan Woods SHS (250 acres)

Good Restaurants (95)

Score: 22.2 **Rank: 158**

Yuma, AZ

Visible Past (47)

Brinley Avenue Historic District

Yuma Century Heights Conservancy Residential Historic District

Yuma Main Street Historic District

Lively Arts Calendar (64)

Touring artists bookings: 20 dates

Outdoor Recreation Assets (73)

Inland water: 4.89 square miles

Federal protected areas:

Cabeza Prieta NWR (443,800 acres)

Kofa NWR (523,040 acres)

State recreation area:

Territorial Prison SHP (9 acres)

Good Restaurants (34)

Score: 74.2 **Rank: 53**

★ = *one of the top 30 places for ambiance.*

ET CETERA: AMBIANCE

RETIREMENT PLACES WITH THE BEST BASS FISHING

Black bass, the premier game fish in North America, are found in lakes and rivers in every state but Alaska. They aren't abundant in all areas, however, and some regions do not have the large bass-holding waters that can withstand extensive public attention. One or more of *Field & Stream*'s 50 best fishing spots in the United States and Canada are within the following retirement places.

Boca Raton, Florida

Lake Okeechobee, at the western edge of this retirement place, is the most renowned of Florida's largemouth bass factories. It has over 200,000 acres of shallow, grass-filled water and is often the least affected Florida bass lake during late winter and early spring, offering phenomenal fishing when the weather is stable.

Champlain Islands, Vermont

With the Green Mountains on the east and the Adirondack Mountains on the west, 120-mile-long Lake Champlain, a natural lake on the Vermont–New York border, is nestled in the midst of some outstanding country. The principal game fish is smallmouth bass, especially in the northern sector. Largemouth bass are abundant, too, particularly in weedy bays. In addition, walleye, trout, salmon, and perch fishing is excellent.

Henderson, Nevada

Near these suburban Las Vegas communities and backed by the Hoover Dam, Lake Mead has lots of good bass cover, resulting in an abundance of 1- to 3-pound largemouth bass. Stripers, too, benefit from the expanded forage base and are popular in this lake, with small fish up to 10 pounds being plentiful.

Hot Springs, Arkansas

Lake Ouachita, a Corps of Engineers lake about 35 miles from Hot Springs, is part of the Ouachita National Forest and is known for a variety of good fishing. Largemouth and spotted (locally called "Kentucky") bass are plentiful here. Stripers, too, are abundant among the rotting timber left standing in this lake when it was flooded.

Kissimmee–St. Cloud, Florida

There are numbers of shallow, grassy lakes in Florida's Kissimmee River chain. Lake Kissimmee (the largest) and East and West Tohopekaliga are among the most prominent. West Tohopekaliga is rated one of the best places for trophy bass, which is high praise in a state that has many trophy largemouth waters.

Lake Havasu City, Arizona

Lake Mohave, an impoundment on the Colorado River downstream from Lake Mead (see Henderson, Nevada, above), is an excellent largemouth bass lake, providing good fishing on points, cliffs, brush, and other habitats that are typical of these weedless desert lakes. Cold water issuing from Hoover Dam makes the upper 15 miles more suitable for trout, but the rest of the 67-mile-long lake offers plenty of bass fishing opportunities.

Lake Winnipesaukee, New Hampshire

Squam Lake, location for the movie *On Golden Pond*, is noted for its smallmouth bass fishing. Its 44,000-acre neighbor, Lake Winnipesaukee, is the largest of New Hampshire's many lakes. Here, trout and land-locked salmon are the locally preferred fish, but many smallmouth and largemouth bass are caught as well.

Lakeland–Winter Haven, Florida

The Florida Phosphate Pits, which are flooded, reclaimed phosphate-mining areas of varying size, possess an abundance of chunky largemouth bass, including plenty of trophy-size fish. There are lots of pits in the south-central mining country, and the newest publicly accessible ones are in the Tenoroc State Reserve outside of Lakeland.

Murray, Kentucky

Kentucky Lake and Barkley Lake, immediately east of this small college town, are magnets for warm water anglers throughout the Midwest. Combined, they are the second-largest man-made water system in America, and their 3,500 miles of shoreline provide countless coves, bays, finders, and hideaways for bass. Largemouth and spotted (Kentucky) bass are plentiful, and smallmouth bass have become especially prominent in recent years.

Norfork Lake, Arkansas

Norfork Lake and nearby Bull Shoals are among the best largemouth bass waters in the Ozarks, have excellent spring and fall fishing, and provide good angling throughout the year for a variety of species, including white bass and crappies. Trout and smallmouth bass are also present.

North County San Diego, California

San Diego's water supply lakes are small and intensively fished. Fifteen of these San Diego County Lakes

are open to the public for fishing, and they have some of the best catch rates in California, including record-size Florida-strain largemouth bass.

Northampton–Amherst, Massachusetts

Located in a wilderness setting just east of Amherst, the 25,000-acre Quabbin Reservoir is the largest body of water in Massachusetts and a principal source of Boston's water supply. In addition to trout and salmon, it sports a good fishery for bass, particularly smallmouth, and is tightly managed for fishing and boating.

Ocala, Florida

Good largemouth fishing can be had in many areas of Florida's lengthy and renowned St. Johns River, particularly Rodman Reservoir at the northern edge of the Ocala National Forest and Lake George, upriver yet south of Rodman Reservoir.

Table Rock Lake, Missouri

Table Rock Lake, an impoundment of the White River in southeastern Missouri, is surrounded by the Mark Twain National Forest. Its 43,100 acres are spread out in a meandering, mazelike configuration of coves and creeks that hide many bass.

Inland Water

Aside from ocean or Great Lakes coastal bays and river estuaries, big lakes in the interior are a recreation draw for miles around. In the 18 locations below, more than 5 percent of the surface area is big-lake water.

PLACE	PERCENTAGE OF SURFACE AREA THAT IS BIG-LAKE WATER
Eagle River–Woodruff, WI	14.2
Burlington, VT	13.0
Polson–Mission Valley, MT	9.7
Sandpoint–Lake Pend Oreille, ID	9.5
Table Rock Lake, MO	9.4
Lake Winnipesaukee, NH	8.6
Cedar Creek Lake, TX	7.9
Hot Springs, AR	7.8
Lake of the Ozarks, MO	7.6
Pendleton District, SC	7.3
Oxford, MS	7.1
Sebring–Avon Park, FL	7.1
Lakeland–Winter Haven, FL	6.7
Lake of the Cherokees, OK	6.6
Murray–Kentucky Lake, KY	6.1
Norfork Lake, AR	5.5
Coeur d'Alene, ID	5.4
Jackson Hole, WY	5.1

Source: Bureau of the Census, unpublished area measurements.

Costs of Living

You get what you pay for, some economists say. High costs are a sign of high quality of life. Expensive places are more desirable; cheaper ones are less so. Tell that to the thousands of older adults who've fled pricey California for Nevada, costly New York for Florida, and even middle-money Florida for the lower-cost Carolinas.

Because of windowed envelopes—interest, dividends, annuities, pensions, and Social Security checks—that can be sent to a forwarding address, you needn't remain rooted in an unaffordable place. The best economic reason you'll need for leaving home is the potential savings you'll find living somewhere else.

RETIREMENT INCOME: GETTING IT

"Money's no problem," an accountant with wit will tell you. "Lack of money . . . now *that's* a problem." Can you afford to stop working? More to the point, can you swing retirement where you're living now—or may there be somewhere else where you can do it more easily?

Lack of enough money causes many people to cling to unsatisfying jobs. For those who do retire, the lack of money crimps plans for travel or for life in a sunny, clean-air place where the bass fishing is good. It indefinitely defers the dream of a small part-time business, the book you've been meaning to write, or the boat you want to build.

The Checks Are in the Mail

In retirement, you'll likely have not one source of income, but many. Apart from Social Security, there is a multitude of annuities, Individual Retirement Accounts (IRAs) and Keogh Plans, thousands of government-employee plans (federal civil service, military, state, and municipal), and nearly a million private pension plans, each of which has different rules for age of eligibility, years of service required, payouts, and how spouses are covered.

For most, the main income sources—in descending dollar amounts—are Social Security benefits, private pensions, and asset income. More and more persons also count on earnings from a job or self-employment.

Replacing Income: Part One

A rule of thumb in retirement planning states: "If your retirement income is 70 to 75 percent of what it was in the last year of work, you'll hardly notice a change in your standard of living." The rule applies mainly to job incomes of between $45,000 and $70,000. To keep up your standard of living after you retire, you'll need the following:

A MINIMUM OF . . .	OR . . .	OF YOUR JOB INCOME OF . . .
$13,400	90%	$15,000
$17,000	85%	$20,000
$20,400	82%	$25,000
$23,700	79%	$30,000
$30,700	77%	$40,000
$36,600	73%	$50,000
$42,800	71%	$60,000
$48,800	70%	$70,000
$54,400	68%	$80,000
$59,000	66%	$90,000

Income figures are pretax amounts. The percentage "replacement rates" do not reflect the impact of future inflation and assume that the household doesn't relocate after retirement to a low-cost area.

Social Security. Money is paid out by the federal government at the end of each month to persons who paid into the system during their working years.

Annual earnings up to the year of eligibility for retirement are averaged and adjusted for inflation to derive an Average Index of Monthly Earnings (AIME). A benefit formula is then applied to the AIME to determine your Primary Insurance Amount (PIA). The percent of the PIA that you actually get depends on when you retire.

In the past, you were eligible for 100 percent of your PIA when you turned 65, the "normal" retirement age defined by the Social Security program back in 1935. This normal age is gradually rising to 67 over the next several decades.

Reduced benefits equal to 80 percent of your PIA are available at age 62. For every month after age 62 you put off claiming your benefits, the 20 percent early retirement penalty is reduced by 0.56 percent (or 6.67 percent a year) so that your full PIA is earned at 65. If you stay on the job after 65, you receive a delayed retirement credit of 3 percent a year. If you work and put off claiming Social Security benefits until you're 68, for instance, you would receive benefits equal to 109 percent of your PIA.

The maximum monthly check comes to $1,721 for a single worker, $2,581 for a couple with one dependent spouse, and $3,442 for a couple when both spouses are eligible. These amounts assume the worker made maximum contributions and retires at full retirement age. The average amount mailed out each month to a couple is much less—$1,487, or $17,844 a year.

Pensions. While pensions are contributed to by everyone working in government, just half of all workers in the private sector are covered by an employer pension plan. And only half of these will ever see the money because of vesting requirements. Not for nothing are persons getting benefits from their former employer called "the pension elite."

Unlike the Social Security system to which workers contribute no matter how many different jobs they hold, private pensions are the equivalent of a corporate loyalty test—at least for the standard 8 or 10 years of service required before an employee is vested and shares in a pension fund.

Unlike Social Security, too, most employer pension plans don't have a cost-of-living escalator clause. The typical amount from a private pension is $12,500 for a married couple age 62 to 65 that is eligible for payments. While the amount isn't paltry, it isn't lavish, either. According to a recent study from the Social Security Administration, just 7 out of 100 couples with private pensions can rely on them for at least half their income.

Assets. Your asset income includes everything from dividends from stock investments you've made over the years; rents from real estate you own; royalties from your invention, song, computer software, book, or oil well; and interest from IRAs, Keogh Plans, CDs, passbook savings accounts, and loans.

Like private pensions and earnings from a job, income from assets supplements Social Security for a more comfortable later life. Nearly eight out of every ten households over 65 count on money from these sources.

Earnings. Earnings from a job or self-employment are the only sure way of boosting your income after you retire. Once you start collecting Social Security and private pension checks, there's almost nothing you can do to dramatically increase their amounts. A job, from part-time or seasonal work all the way to a 50-week-a-year new career, can make the difference between eating out of a dumpster and living comfortably.

Scraping By on $85,323 a Year

One simple way to judge whether you can stop work, take your money, and run to another part of the country is to compare your income with incomes in other places.

The average income in a household in the United States before taxes is $85,323. Among the locations profiled in *Retirement Places Rated,* the average is $70,500. The highest is $134,200 in Park City, Utah, and the lowest is $44,200 in Apache Junction, Arizona.

Households can be a family, a husband and wife, two or more unrelated people, even a single person. Average amounts tend to be high because most households aren't retired and count on wages and salaries—as well as interest and dividends—from more than one member. Still, the figures are useful for making comparisons.

"Replacement Rates"

Get used to the idea of never living comfortably on Social Security. If you are an $87,000-a-year worker retiring at age 65 with maximum earnings in "covered employment" (a job in which Social Security is deducted from wages) each year since you began your career, you can expect $20,652 a year. Even though Social Security increases with inflation, the money comes way short of what you were pulling down at work.

One indicator of how far your Social Security benefits, pension, and asset income will go is the rate at which it would replace different household incomes around the country.

In locations in Rio Grande Country, the Ozarks and Ouachitas, the Rocky Mountains, and the Southern Highlands, for example, your income may go a lot further in replacing local household incomes than it would back home in, say, New York, Denver, or Altoona.

Retired persons who move tend to quit richer areas with high costs for places with more modest average incomes. They are in search of spots where their own money can be stretched. In short, where costs are lower.

Where the Money Comes From

The following table indicates the primary sources of retirement income and the percentage of newly retired couples in the United States who depend on each source:

INCOME SOURCE	PERCENT OF NEWLY RETIRED COUPLES IN U.S.
Social Security	93%
Assets	63%
Private pensions	43%
Earnings	21%
Government pensions	20%

Source: Derived from Social Security Administration, Income of the Population 55 and Over.

RETIREMENT INCOME: SPENDING IT

Do household incomes reflect local prices? For the most part, they do indeed. A Bureau of Labor Statistics study showed that two-thirds of the difference in incomes between, say, Traverse City and Tucson indicates their different costs of living. The rest is due to different employers, worker skills, and prevailing wages.

If you're thinking of moving, consider how far your income would stretch elsewhere. Household incomes in different places provide the first clue. Comparing actual costs completes the picture.

Local Costs of Living

It's a "black hole," the *Wall Street Journal* noted on just what everyone means by cost of living. The government's monthly Consumer Price Index (CPI) offers no help. It reports price inflation, but quotes no prices. While the CPI has gone up eightfold since the start of World War II, it offers no insights on the money you'd need to get by in Santa Barbara versus a small town in the Ozarks.

A few years ago, a group of experts appointed by the Department of Labor to look into better ways to measure cost differences between places threw in the towel. Given the infinite range of consumer tastes and household tactics for saving a dollar, they noted, the few ways to pin down why life in one place is more expensive than in another come down to the following: focus on the weather's effect on clothing costs and household utility bills; then look at taxes.

Replacing Income: Part Two

Just as you want your income after retirement to come close to your on-the-job earnings, you may want to relocate to where your retirement income comes close to your local household average income. This is likelier in parts of the mountain West and interior Texas than it is in wealthy beach communities and ski resorts. The two tables below represent the ten places rated in this book with the lowest average income and the ten retirement places with the highest average income.

Average Income under $50,000

PLACE	INCOME
Apache Junction, AZ	$44,200
Ruidoso, NM	$46,300
Taos, NM	$46,800
Trinity Peninsula, TX	$46,800
Las Vegas, NM	$48,500
Eureka Springs, AR	$49,100
Yuma, AZ	$49,300
Lake of the Cherokees, OK	$49,600
Apalachicola, FL	$49,900

Average Income over $100,000

PLACE	INCOME
Park City, UT	$134,200
Jackson Hole, WY	$130,700
Laguna Beach–Dana Point, CA	$116,700
East End Long Island, NY	$114,600
St. Augustine, FL	$107,500
Naples, FL	$107,400
Ketchum–Sun Valley, ID	$107,200
Boca Raton, FL	$106,000
Carmel–Pebble Beach, CA	$103,800
Santa Barbara, CA	$103,400
Carson City–Carson Valley, NV	$101,900

Source: Woods & Poole Economics, Inc., household income forecasts.

Taxes certainly do make a difference. But clothing and home energy bills? Not that much. According to one retailer, the price difference between cotton and synthetic wardrobes in the Sun Belt and woolen and down-filled Frost Belt clothing amounts to less than 1 percent of a household's annual budget. As for the comparative costs of keeping warm in the North Woods winter and staying cool in the Florida Interior, often the only difference is the season during which local residents pay most of their bill.

One firm that counsels transferred employees uses an 80/20 rule. In its experience, 80 percent of the difference in living costs between where you've come from and where you're going comes down to two items: housing and taxes. The other 20 percent comes from hundreds of things such as spin-balancing the wheels on your car; a six-pack of beer; soap flakes; greens fees for a weekend round of golf; and a shampoo, trim, and blow-dry at a salon.

To measure what it costs to live in each place, *Retirement Places Rated* prices major items in a $55,000-a-year retired couple's budget. In some locations, that couple's income wouldn't be enough to bid on a lower-priced house. In other spots, the income is more than enough to live comfortably.

Housing: The Difference That Makes a Difference

"You can't get too much housing," real estate salespeople say with one hand on the steering wheel and the other on their listings as they drive prospective buyers about for a windshield tour of neighborhoods.

True enough, you never need the space until you don't have it, and there are still tax and investment advantages to owning a home on your own piece of ground. Older adults are no different from everyone else in the kind of roof they prefer overhead: townhouse, apartment, mobile home, or the common detached house. The latter is the overwhelming favorite.

If you open the front door of this typical American home, you'll find yourself in a structure that has a single-level, 1,800-square-foot floor plan enclosing six rooms (three bedrooms, one bath, a living room, and a complete kitchen); an insulated attic and storm windows to conserve the heat from the gas-fired, warm air furnace; and no basement. This house is kept cool during hot spells by a central air-conditioning unit. It is also connected to city water and sewerage lines.

So much for the national composite. Among the millions of single houses in the United States, a buyer can choose from Cape Cods, Cape Annes, and Queen Annes, mountain A-frames, American and Dutch colonials, desert adobes, cabins of peeled pine log, Greek revivals, Puget Sounds, cat-slides, saltboxes, exotic glass solaria, futuristic earth berms, Victorians, plantation cottages, ubiquitous split-levels, and California bungalows.

Having said all that, between a mortgage, property taxes, and utilities, owning a home takes up the lion's share of that $55,000-a-year retired couple's budget. The following outlines these and other expected costs.

Home Mortgage. Claiming an average 18.7 percent of income (or $10,285) among the retirement places profiled here, the mortgage is certainly the most expensive item on the older household's budget. Where the real estate broker touts location, location, location, you may answer rent, rent, rent. While it adds nothing to your net worth, renting permits you to avoid most of the cost differences among places and gives you flexibility. Good rental markets include large college towns and large, seasonal resorts.

Property Taxes. Nevertheless, if you're like most older newcomers, you'll eventually end up owning. Typical property taxes among our 203 retirement places amount to $1,159 on a median-priced home and will account for 2.1 percent of your household budget for as long as you own, unless you settle in a state (1) with low effective tax rates, or (2) generous homestead exemptions for older people with no income tests, or (3) both. Bear in mind, too, that taxes tend to be much lower when the property lies beyond the corporate limits of cities and towns.

Transportation. At 16.46 percent, the cost of getting from one place to another, $9,053, is next. Ask yourself whether you really need more than one car, as the size of this budget item reflects a two-car household. Since there is a national market for cars, meaning you can buy one anywhere for a similar price, the cost of purchasing one doesn't vary much by location. What does vary are taxes, insurance, title and registration fees, and gasoline excise taxes.

Food. This category, which includes groceries *and* dining out, claims another 11.23 percent, or $6,180. While prices for packaged prepared foods generally don't vary enough to hit household budgets around the country with dramatic effect, prices for fresh fruits, vegetables, and dairy products do. In places with an agricultural hinterland, you'll save if you spend money at farmers' markets and roadside produce stands on the back of pickup trucks.

Health Care. Medical expenses take 9.5 percent, or $5,225, and will require more and more of your income each year as you get older. True, basic Medicare covers hospital bills after you turn 65, but it won't cover things such as an outpatient diagnostic visit, a prescription painkiller, or a splint for a broken thumb. Most importantly, Medicare doesn't cover physicians fees.

To measure costs in each place, *Retirement Places Rated* looks at the amounts that Medicare permits five doctors to charge their older patients for specific services. They are:

- Family practitioner—office outpatient visit
- Internist—complete electrocardiogram and report
- Psychiatrist—75–80 minutes of psychotherapy
- Orthopedic surgeon—open reduction of dislocation
- Ophthalmologist—eye exam

Charges for a semi-private room in the area's largest acute-care hospital are also part of this factor.

Utilities. These costs claim 5 percent, or $2,753 of the household's expenses, and cover everything from water and telephone to electricity, piped-in natural gas, and heating oil. Unlike packaged groceries, monthly electric bills vary widely around the country. Climate determines how much money will be needed to keep interiors comfortable. Customer density, distance from oil and coal fuel sources, age of the power plant, and the type and size of equipment used in generating electricity play a part in the charges to consumers.

Recreation. This catch-all covers everything from a health club membership, weekday play at an 18-hole public or semi-private golf course, overnight camping at a state park, and movie tickets. It claims 4.95 percent, or $2,723. Like the dining out part of the food budget, enjoying yourself can be a controllable expense. Costs at large resorts are highest.

State Income Taxes. Though you've chucked the tie and briefcase and bid goodbye to the commuting hassles that go with working full-time, you won't be completely immune from paying taxes, in spite of the many tax breaks coming along when you turn 65. Yes, your tax bracket will be lower after you leave work, but *federal income taxes* may still hit you with the same impact whether you surface in Bellingham, Ocala, or San Antonio. But *state income taxes* vary tremendously. Among the retirement places within states that tax income, they amount to 2.42 percent of the household budget, or $1,331.

Should you move only to one of the handful of no-income-tax states and ignore the alternatives? That may be a mistake. It's better to broaden your search to include other states with two characteristics: (1) a favorable tax treatment of retirement income (see the "State Retirement Income Tax Profiles," later in this chapter) and (2) lower costs of living that offset the state's income tax.

Expensive Neighborhoods

Median home prices mark a point where half the homes are more expensive and half are less. Nationally, the median is $192,000. Among places in *Retirement Places Rated,* the figure is $143,000. Below are places where half the homes cost more than $250,000. Indeed, the top quarter of homes in all of these locations approaches or tops $1 million.

PLACE	MEDIAN HOME PRICE
Carmel–Pebble Beach, CA	$875,000
Laguna Beach–Dana Point, CA	$850,000
St. Simons–Jekyll Islands, GA	$477,000
Jackson Hole, WY	$365,400
Hilton Head Island, SC	$361,000
Sedona, AZ	$320,000
Martha's Vineyard, MA	$304,000
Park City, UT	$296,000
Boca Raton, FL	$295,000
Santa Barbara, CA	$293,000
San Juan Islands, WA	$291,800
Ketchum–Sun Valley, ID	$288,800
Scottsdale, AZ	$286,000
Santa Rosa, CA	$273,200

Source: Places Rated Partnership survey.

Sales Taxes. Finally, for all the annoyance that sales taxes cause, they exact less than 1 percent, or under $550, of our retired couple's expenses on average in the states that levy the tax. In the age of Internet and cross-border shopping, this tax is increasingly seen as easily avoidable.

You'll notice that the major items above add up to 71 percent of the retired household budget. Where does the other 29 percent go? Savings, investments, health insurance, gifts to your grandchildren, tuition for a course at a community college, federal income taxes, a *Wall Street Journal* subscription, a new windbreaker, a bottle of Merlot, and on and on. Aside from federal income taxes, these are discretionary expenses, and their amounts aren't greatly influenced by geography.

A Caution

Let's admit here that pricing costs of living for all people for all the time is impossible. The number of unique items that fill a shopping cart trundled by a household for a year is close to a thousand. Some trade at Wal-Mart and others at convenience stores, some at eBay and other Internet sites; and others at Costco, Price Club, BJ's Wholesale, and Burlington Coat Factory. Having said that, *Retirement Places Rated* nevertheless makes a reasonable attempt at averages.

Scoring: Costs of Living

Will your income stretch further in the Rio Grande Country than in the Desert Southwest? Do prices really vary tremendously among different places, or can sharp-pencil budgeting and bargain-price shopping keep your head above water in Maui or Laguna Beach or anywhere else you choose to live?

To help you compare each place's differences, for each location, *Retirement Places Rated* measures nine expenses on the budget for a hypothetical retired couple with a $55,000 income: (1) **home mortgage,** (2) **transportation,** (3) **food,** (4) **utilities,** (5) **health care,** (6) **recreation,** (7) **property taxes,** (8) **state income taxes,** and (9) **state and local sales taxes.** The expenses are totaled and the result is then compared with all 203 places to get a percentile score. The higher the score, the less expensive the retirement place. A score of 0 is worst, 50 is average, and 100 is the best.

Rankings: Costs of Living

Nine items on a typical retired household's budget are used to rank retirement places for costs of living: (1) **mortgage payments** on a median-priced home; (2) that home's **property taxes;** (3) **utilities,** including water, telephone, electricity, and home heating; (4) **food;** (5) **health care;** (6) **recreation;** (7) **transportation;** (8) **state income taxes;** and (9) **state and local sales taxes.** A place's score is its percentile on a scale of 0 to 100 corresponding to its rank. Lower scores mean more expensive places, and higher scores mean less expensive places. Places that are tied get the same rank and are listed alphabetically.

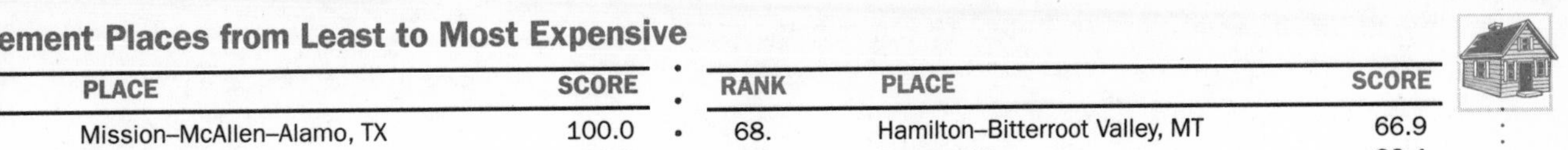

Retirement Places from Least to Most Expensive

RANK	PLACE	SCORE
1.	Mission–McAllen–Alamo, TX	100.0
2.	Natchitoches, LA	99.6
3.	Thomasville, GA	99.1
4.	Roswell, NM	98.6
5.	Alamogordo, NM	98.1
6.	Oscoda–Huron Shore, MI	97.6
7.	Silver City, NM	97.1
8.	Alpine–Big Bend, TX	96.6
9.	Lake of the Cherokees, OK	96.1
10.	Trinity Peninsula, TX	95.6
11.	Murray–Kentucky Lake, KY	95.1
12.	Eufaula, AL	94.6
13.	Eureka Springs, AR	94.1
14.	Aiken, SC	93.6
15.	Pendleton District, SC	93.1
16.	Norfork Lake, AR	92.6
17.	Las Cruces, NM	92.1
18.	Fayetteville, AR	91.6
19.	Hattiesburg, MS	91.1
20.	Crossville, TN	90.6
21.	Sebring–Avon Park, FL	90.1
22.	Las Vegas, NM	89.7
23.	Cedar Creek Lake, TX	89.2
24.	Edenton, NC	88.7
25.	Table Rock Lake, MO	88.2
26.	Maryville, TN	87.7
27.	Ocala, FL	87.2
28.	Oxford, MS	86.7
29.	Inverness, FL	86.2
30.	Summerville, SC	85.7
31.	Berkeley Springs, WV	85.2
32.	Delta County, CO	84.7
33.	Lakeland–Winter Haven, FL	84.2
34.	Smith Mountain Lake, VA	83.7
35.	Bisbee, AZ	83.2
36.	Rehoboth Bay–Indian River Bay, DE	82.7
37.	Kerrville, TX	82.2
38.	Yuma, AZ	81.7
39.	Kingman, AZ	81.2
40.	Branson, MO	80.7
41.	Ruidoso, NM	80.2
42.	Conway, SC	79.8
43.	Lake Havasu City, AZ	79.3
44.	Polson–Mission Valley, MT	78.8
45.	Grants Pass, OR	78.3
46.	Fredericksburg, TX	77.8
47.	Bullhead City, AZ	77.3
48.	Rabun County, GA	76.8
49.	Montrose, CO	76.3
50.	Rockport–Aransas Pass, TX	75.8
51.	Pensacola, FL	75.3
52.	Brevard, NC	74.8
53.	St. Jay–Northeast Kingdom, VT	74.3
54.	Grand Junction, CO	73.8
55.	Lake Placid, NY	73.3
56.	Hot Springs, AR	72.8
57.	New Bern, NC	72.3
58.	New Port Richey, FL	71.8
59.	Rio Rancho, NM	71.3
60.	Daytona Beach, FL	70.8
61.	Lake Winnipesaukee, NH	70.3
62.	Front Royal, VA	69.9
63.	Sandpoint–Lake Pend Oreille, ID	69.4
64.	Marble Falls–Lake LBJ, TX	68.9
65.	Panama City, FL	68.4
66.	Coeur d'Alene, ID	67.9
67.	Asheville, NC	67.4
68.	Hamilton–Bitterroot Valley, MT	66.9
69.	Payson, AZ	66.4
70.	Medford–Ashland, OR	65.9
71.	Monadnock Region, NH	65.4
72.	Athens, GA	64.9
73.	Charles Town–Shepherdstown, WV	64.4
74.	Kalispell–Flathead Valley, MT	63.9
75.	Apalachicola, FL	63.4
76.	Florence, OR	62.9
77.	Tryon, NC	62.4
78.	Petoskey–Harbor Springs, MI	61.9
79.	New Braunfels, TX	61.4
80.	Cedar City, UT	60.9
81.	Brown County, IN	60.4
82.	Bay St. Louis–Pass Christian, MS	60.0
83.	Hanover, NH	59.5
84.	Traverse City, MI	59.0
85.	Fairhope–Gulf Shores, AL	58.5
86.	Myrtle Beach, SC	58.0
87.	Leesburg–Mount Dora, FL	57.5
88.	Melbourne–Palm Bay, FL	57.0
89.	Savannah, GA	56.5
90.	Gainesville, FL	56.0
91.	Columbia, MO	55.5
92.	Camden, ME	55.0
93.	Charleston, SC	54.5
94.	Hendersonville–East Flat Rock, NC	54.0
95.	Apache Junction, AZ	53.5
96.	Oakhurst–Coarsegold, CA	53.0
97.	Cottonwood–Verde Valley, AZ	52.5
98.	McCall, ID	52.0
99.	Flagstaff, AZ	51.5
100.	State College, PA	51.0
101.	Sedona, AZ	50.5
102.	Largo, FL	50.0
103.	Bradenton, FL	49.6
104.	Lake of the Ozarks, MO	49.1
105.	Newport–Lincoln City, OR	48.6
106.	Northern Neck, VA	48.1
107.	Beaufort–Bogue Banks, NC	47.6
108.	Bozeman, MT	47.1
109.	Chewelah, WA	46.6
110.	Prescott–Prescott Valley, AZ	46.1
111.	Bar Harbor, ME	45.6
112.	St. Simons–Jekyll Islands, GA	45.1
113.	Ocean City, MD	44.6
114.	Tucson, AZ	44.1
115.	Taos, NM	43.6
116.	Colorado Springs, CO	43.1
117.	Port Charlotte, FL	42.6
118.	Western St. Tammany Parish, LA	42.1
119.	Vero Beach, FL	41.6
120.	Pahrump Valley, NV	41.1
121.	Salida, CO	40.6
122.	Brookings–Gold Beach, OR	40.1
123.	Eagle River–Woodruff, WI	39.7
124.	Boone–Blowing Rock, NC	39.2
125.	York Beaches, ME	38.7
126.	Virginia Beach, VA	38.2
127.	Charlottesville, VA	37.7
128.	Door Peninsula, WI	37.2
129.	Southern Pines–Pinehurst, NC	36.7
130.	Southern Berkshire County, MA	36.2
131.	Southport–Brunswick Islands, NC	35.7
132.	Kissimmee–St. Cloud, FL	35.2
133.	Palmer–Wasilla, AK	34.7

continued

Retirement Places from Least to Most Expensive (cont.)

RANK	PLACE	SCORE
134.	Paradise–Magalia, CA	34.2
135.	Pagosa Springs, CO	33.7
136.	St. George–Zion, UT	33.2
137.	Wickenburg, AZ	32.7
138.	Pike County, PA	32.2
139.	Fredericksburg–Spotsylvania, VA	31.7
140.	Port Angeles–Sequim, WA	31.2
141.	Iowa City, IA	30.7
142.	Bellingham, WA	30.2
143.	Wimberley, TX	29.8
144.	Dare Outer Banks, NC	29.3
145.	Leelanau Peninsula, MI	28.8
146.	Sarasota, FL	28.3
147.	Scottsdale, AZ	27.8
147.	Mesa, AZ	27.8
149.	Georgetown, TX	26.8
150.	Boerne, TX	26.3
151.	Chestertown, MD	25.8
152.	Wenatchee, WA	25.3
153.	Mariposa, CA	24.8
154.	Sonora–Twain Harte, CA	24.3
155.	Fort Myers–Cape Coral, FL	23.8
156.	Easton–St. Michaels, MD	23.3
157.	Bend, OR	22.8
158.	Woodstock, VT	22.3
159.	Fort Collins–Loveland, CO	21.8
160.	Victorville–Apple Valley, CA	21.3
161.	Northampton–Amherst, MA	20.8
162.	Henderson, NV	20.3
163.	Amador County, CA	19.9
164.	Durango, CO	19.4
165.	Anacortes, WA	18.9
166.	Lake Conroe, TX	18.4
167.	Santa Fe, NM	17.9
168.	Reno–Sparks, NV	17.4
169.	St. Augustine, FL	16.9
170.	Boca Raton, FL	16.4
171.	Carson City–Carson Valley, NV	15.9
172.	Burlington, VT	15.4
173.	Toms River–Barnegat Bay, NJ	14.9
174.	Whidbey Island, WA	14.4
175.	Port Townsend, WA	13.9
176.	Kauai, HI	13.4
177.	Palm Springs–Coachella Valley, CA	12.9
178.	Madison, WI	12.4
179.	Mendocino–Fort Bragg, CA	11.9
180.	Naples, FL	11.4
181.	Annapolis, MD	10.9
182.	Chapel Hill–Carrboro, NC	10.4
183.	Litchfield Hills, CT	10.0
184.	Middle Cape Cod, MA	9.5
185.	Lower Cape May, NJ	9.0
186.	Beaufort, SC	8.5
187.	Grass Valley–Nevada City, CA	8.0
188.	Maui, HI	7.5
189.	Williamsburg, VA	7.0
190.	Hilton Head Island, SC	6.5
191.	Morro Bay–Cambria, CA	6.0
192.	North County San Diego, CA	5.5
193.	Key West, FL	5.0
194.	Ketchum–Sun Valley, ID	4.5
195.	Santa Rosa, CA	4.0
196.	Santa Barbara, CA	3.5
197.	San Juan Islands, WA	3.0
198.	Park City, UT	2.5
199.	Carmel–Pebble Beach, CA	2.0
200.	Laguna Beach–Dana Point, CA	1.5
201.	East End Long Island, NY	1.0
202.	Martha's Vineyard, MA	0.5
203.	Jackson Hole, WY	0.0

PLACE PROFILES: COSTS OF LIVING

The pages that follow detail costs-of-living factors used to rate each place—three costs of home ownership and six other living costs, all measured against the average for a hypothetical couple, age 65, with a gross income of $55,000.

The data come principally from Places Rated Partnership tax and consumer price surveys at the end of 2003. In addition, a number of sources were used. These include American Automobile Association, *Digest of Motor Laws* (state motor vehicle license, registration fees, and gasoline excise taxes), 2003; American Gas Association, *Gas Facts* (residential gas bills), 2003; Commerce Clearing House, *State Tax Guide* (state income and sales tax rates), 2003; Fodor's Travel Publications, *Mobil Travel Guide* (state park fees, dining out costs), 2003; National Golf Foundation (public golf course fees), 2003; U.S. Department of Commerce, Bureau of the Census, Census of Population and Housing (upper, median, and lower home prices; median property taxes; average monthly homeowner costs), 2000; U.S. Department of Energy, *Electric Sales and Revenue* (residential electric bills), 2002; U.S. Department of Health and Human Services, Health Care Financing Administration, unpublished medical procedures costs, geographic adjustment factors, and county managed-care capitation rates, 2003; U.S. Department of Housing and Urban Development, Office of Federal Housing Enterprise Oversight, home price indexes; U.S. Department of Labor, Bureau of Labor Statistics, unpublished data, *Consumer Expenditure Survey* (budget expense weights), 2003, and *Consumer Price Index*, final quarter 2003; U.S. General Services Administration, *Federal Travel Directory* (local per diems for food away from home), monthly, 2003; and Woods & Poole Economics, Inc., unpublished household income figures, 2003.

A star (★) preceding a place's name indicates it is one of the top 30 places for low costs of living.

★ **Aiken, SC**

Household Income: $67,800

Home Prices

Upper: $194,000
Middle: $132,000
Lower: $94,000
Property Taxes: $720
Utilities: $2,428

Retirement Living Costs

Food: $5,880
Health Care: $5,347
Recreation: $1,195
Transportation: $8,658

Retirement Taxes

Income: $0
Sales: $1,290

Score: 93.6 **Rank: 14**

★ **Alamogordo, NM**

Household Income: $50,000

Home Prices

Upper: $160,000
Middle: $116,000
Lower: $85,000
Property Taxes: $710
Utilities: $1,920

Retirement Living Costs

Food: $5,880
Health Care: $4,524
Recreation: $1,498
Transportation: $7,823

Retirement Taxes

Income: $987
Sales: $1,290

Score: 98.1 **Rank: 5**

★ **Alpine–Big Bend, TX**

Household Income: $60,100

Home Prices

Upper: $151,000
Middle: $102,000
Lower: $64,000
Property Taxes: $1,170
Utilities: $2,227

Retirement Living Costs

Food: $5,880
Health Care: $4,524
Recreation: $1,932
Transportation: $9,290

Retirement Taxes

Income: $0
Sales: $1,559

Score: 96.6 **Rank: 8**

Amador County, CA

Household Income: $62,400

Home Prices

Upper: $373,000
Middle: $274,000
Lower: $219,000
Property Taxes: $2,070
Utilities: $2,918

Retirement Living Costs

Food: $5,880
Health Care: $5,768
Recreation: $1,801
Transportation: $9,778

Retirement Taxes

Income: $163
Sales: $1,398

Score: 19.9 **Rank: 163**

Anacortes, WA

Household Income: $76,300

Home Prices

Upper: $326,000
Middle: $238,000
Lower: $186,000
Property Taxes: $2,620
Utilities: $3,235

Retirement Living Costs

Food: $6,180
Health Care: $5,025
Recreation: $2,340
Transportation: $8,831

Retirement Taxes

Income: $0
Sales: $1,828

Score: 18.9 **Rank: 165**

Annapolis, MD

Household Income: $100,000

Home Prices

Upper: $382,000
Middle: $266,000
Lower: $210,000
Property Taxes: $2,860
Utilities: $3,331

Retirement Living Costs

Food: $6,540
Health Care: $6,971
Recreation: $1,656
Transportation: $9,124

Retirement Taxes

Income: $1,362
Sales: $1,075

Score: 10.9 **Rank: 181**

Apache Junction, AZ

Household Income: $44,200

Home Prices

Upper: $226,000
Middle: $146,000
Lower: $100,000
Property Taxes: $1,160
Utilities: $2,390

Retirement Living Costs

Food: $6,540
Health Care: $6,442
Recreation: $1,959
Transportation: $9,743

Retirement Taxes

Income: $527
Sales: $1,344

Score: 53.5 **Rank: 95**

Apalachicola, FL

Household Income: $49,900

Home Prices

Upper: $319,000
Middle: $180,000
Lower: $106,000
Property Taxes: $1,150
Utilities: $2,496

Retirement Living Costs

Food: $6,240
Health Care: $5,460
Recreation: $1,760
Transportation: $9,407

Retirement Taxes

Income: $176
Sales: $1,505

Score: 63.4 **Rank: 75**

Asheville, NC

Household Income: $70,300

Home Prices

Upper: $254,000
Middle: $177,000
Lower: $126,000
Property Taxes: $1,360
Utilities: $2,496

Retirement Living Costs

Food: $6,180
Health Care: $4,651
Recreation: $1,647
Transportation: $8,673

Retirement Taxes

Income: $501
Sales: $1,183

Score: 67.4 **Rank: 67**

Athens, GA

Household Income: $62,000

Home Prices

Upper: $243,000
Middle: $172,000
Lower: $128,000
Property Taxes: $1,440
Utilities: $2,678

Retirement Living Costs

Food: $6,060
Health Care: $5,341
Recreation: $1,607
Transportation: $9,188

Retirement Taxes

Income: $73
Sales: $1,290

Score: 64.9 **Rank: 72**

Bar Harbor, ME

Household Income: $67,500

Home Prices

Upper: $283,000
Middle: $186,000
Lower: $136,000
Property Taxes: $1,920
Utilities: $2,764

continued

★ = *one of the top 30 places for low costs of living.*

Bar Harbor, ME (cont.)
Retirement Living Costs
Food: $6,540
Health Care: $4,524
Recreation: $2,877
Transportation: $9,137
Retirement Taxes
Income: $894
Sales: $1,183
Score: 45.6 **Rank: 111**

Bay St. Louis–Pass Christian, MS
Household Income: $69,500
Home Prices
Upper: $198,000
Middle: $136,000
Lower: $96,000
Property Taxes: $800
Utilities: $2,505
Retirement Living Costs
Food: $6,180
Health Care: $7,157
Recreation: $2,354
Transportation: $8,658
Retirement Taxes
Income: $465
Sales: $1,505
Score: 60 **Rank: 82**

Beaufort, SC
Household Income: $89,200
Home Prices
Upper: $370,000
Middle: $221,000
Lower: $159,000
Property Taxes: $1,050
Utilities: $3,763
Retirement Living Costs
Food: $6,180
Health Care: $4,973
Recreation: $2,433
Transportation: $9,588
Retirement Taxes
Income: $0
Sales: $1,290
Score: 8.5 **Rank: 186**

Beaufort–Bogue Banks, NC
Household Income: $67,100
Home Prices
Upper: $282,000
Middle: $184,000
Lower: $129,000
Property Taxes: $1,050
Utilities: $2,611
Retirement Living Costs
Food: $6,000
Health Care: $4,740
Recreation: $2,240
Transportation: $9,721
Retirement Taxes
Income: $501
Sales: $1,183
Score: 47.6 **Rank: 107**

Bellingham, WA
Household Income: $64,700
Home Prices
Upper: $319,000
Middle: $235,000
Lower: $188,000
Property Taxes: $2,480
Utilities: $3,139
Retirement Living Costs
Food: $6,180
Health Care: $4,524
Recreation: $2,240
Transportation: $7,317
Retirement Taxes
Income: $0
Sales: $1,828
Score: 30.2 **Rank: 142**

Bend, OR
Household Income: $71,700
Home Prices
Upper: $327,000
Middle: $223,000
Lower: $170,000
Property Taxes: $2,430
Utilities: $2,957
Retirement Living Costs
Food: $6,180
Health Care: $4,524
Recreation: $2,569
Transportation: $9,783
Retirement Taxes
Income: $855
Sales: $0
Score: 22.8 **Rank: 157**

Berkeley Springs, WV
Household Income: $51,500
Home Prices
Upper: $181,000
Middle: $134,000
Lower: $100,000
Property Taxes: $740
Utilities: $1,930
Retirement Living Costs
Food: $6,060
Health Care: $5,096
Recreation: $1,500
Transportation: $8,864
Retirement Taxes
Income: $1,827
Sales: $1,290
Score: 85.2 **Rank: 31**

Bisbee, AZ
Household Income: $54,300
Home Prices
Upper: $192,000
Middle: $136,000
Lower: $100,000
Property Taxes: $1,160
Utilities: $2,208
Retirement Living Costs
Food: $6,060
Health Care: $5,616
Recreation: $1,760
Transportation: $9,045
Retirement Taxes
Income: $527
Sales: $1,344
Score: 83.2 **Rank: 35**

Boca Raton, FL
Household Income: $106,000
Home Prices
Upper: $540,000
Middle: $295,000
Lower: $175,000
Property Taxes: $3,100
Utilities: $3,869
Retirement Living Costs
Food: $6,420
Health Care: $7,013
Recreation: $1,937
Transportation: $9,290
Retirement Taxes
Income: $176
Sales: $1,505
Score: 16.4 **Rank: 170**

Boerne, TX
Household Income: $76,900
Home Prices
Upper: $310,000
Middle: $212,000
Lower: $144,000
Property Taxes: $2,750
Utilities: $3,082
Retirement Living Costs
Food: $6,180
Health Care: $4,524
Recreation: $1,643
Transportation: $9,743
Retirement Taxes
Income: $0
Sales: $1,559
Score: 26.3 **Rank: 150**

Boone–Blowing Rock, NC
Household Income: $60,000
Home Prices
Upper: $294,000
Middle: $207,000
Lower: $140,000
Property Taxes: $840
Utilities: $2,131
Retirement Living Costs
Food: $5,880
Health Care: $4,524
Recreation: $2,872
Transportation: $9,783
Retirement Taxes
Income: $501
Sales: $1,183
Score: 39.2 **Rank: 124**

★ = *one of the top 30 places for low costs of living.*

Bozeman, MT

Household Income: $66,600

Home Prices

Upper: $297,000
Middle: $218,000
Lower: $171,000
Property Taxes: $2,240
Utilities: $2,822

Retirement Living Costs

Food: $5,880
Health Care: $4,524
Recreation: $1,836
Transportation: $7,807

Retirement Taxes

Income: $1,934
Sales: $0

Score: 47.1 Rank: 108

Bradenton, FL

Household Income: $81,800

Home Prices

Upper: $294,000
Middle: $204,000
Lower: $145,000
Property Taxes: $2,160
Utilities: $3,206

Retirement Living Costs

Food: $6,060
Health Care: $5,291
Recreation: $2,108
Transportation: $8,355

Retirement Taxes

Income: $176
Sales: $1,505

Score: 49.6 Rank: 103

Branson, MO

Household Income: $56,600

Home Prices

Upper: $216,000
Middle: $144,000
Lower: $108,000
Property Taxes: $840
Utilities: $2,035

Retirement Living Costs

Food: $6,180
Health Care: $5,175
Recreation: $1,585
Transportation: $9,743

Retirement Taxes

Income: $648
Sales: $1,344

Score: 80.7 Rank: 40

Brevard, NC

Household Income: $63,500

Home Prices

Upper: $258,000
Middle: $182,000
Lower: $126,000
Property Taxes: $1,010
Utilities: $2,342

Retirement Living Costs

Food: $5,820
Health Care: $4,524
Recreation: $3,004
Transportation: $7,317

Retirement Taxes

Income: $501
Sales: $1,183

Score: 74.8 Rank: 52

Brookings–Gold Beach, OR

Household Income: $56,900

Home Prices

Upper: $321,000
Middle: $222,000
Lower: $157,000
Property Taxes: $1,640
Utilities: $2,496

Retirement Living Costs

Food: $5,880
Health Care: $4,524
Recreation: $2,082
Transportation: $9,783

Retirement Taxes

Income: $855
Sales: $0

Score: 40.1 Rank: 122

Brown County, IN

Household Income: $85,300

Home Prices

Upper: $232,000
Middle: $168,000
Lower: $133,000
Property Taxes: $1,100
Utilities: $2,477

Retirement Living Costs

Food: $6,180
Health Care: $4,524
Recreation: $2,000
Transportation: $9,316

Retirement Taxes

Income: $1,114
Sales: $1,075

Score: 60.4 Rank: 81

Bullhead City, AZ

Household Income: $50,400

Home Prices

Upper: $190,000
Middle: $157,000
Lower: $120,000
Property Taxes: $1,190
Utilities: $2,227

Retirement Living Costs

Food: $5,820
Health Care: $5,879
Recreation: $1,643
Transportation: $9,124

Retirement Taxes

Income: $527
Sales: $1,344

Score: 77.3 Rank: 47

Burlington, VT

Household Income: $88,700

Home Prices

Upper: $285,000
Middle: $220,000
Lower: $177,000
Property Taxes: $4,230
Utilities: $4,090

Retirement Living Costs

Food: $6,600
Health Care: $5,460
Recreation: $1,780
Transportation: $9,045

Retirement Taxes

Income: $1,163
Sales: $1,075

Score: 15.4 Rank: 172

Camden, ME

Household Income: $67,900

Home Prices

Upper: $288,000
Middle: $192,000
Lower: $141,000
Property Taxes: $2,460
Utilities: $3,149

Retirement Living Costs

Food: $6,180
Health Care: $4,524
Recreation: $1,559
Transportation: $9,188

Retirement Taxes

Income: $894
Sales: $1,183

Score: 55 Rank: 92

Carmel–Pebble Beach, CA

Household Income: $103,800

Home Prices

Upper: $1,340,000
Middle: $875,000
Lower: $519,000
Property Taxes: $2,870
Utilities: $2,957

Retirement Living Costs

Food: $6,600
Health Care: $5,878
Recreation: $4,818
Transportation: $9,778

Retirement Taxes

Income: $163
Sales: $1,398

Score: 2 Rank: 199

Carson City–Carson Valley, NV

Household Income: $101,900

Home Prices

Upper: $410,000
Middle: $284,000
Lower: $220,000
Property Taxes: $1,990
Utilities: $3,072

continued

★ = *one of the top 30 places for low costs of living.*

Carson City–Carson Valley, NV (cont.)

Retirement Living Costs
Food: $6,900
Health Care: $4,591
Recreation: $1,807
Transportation: $9,275
Retirement Taxes
Income: $0
Sales: $1,613
Score: 15.9 **Rank: 171**

Cedar City, UT

Household Income: $57,600
Home Prices
Upper: $213,000
Middle: $160,000
Lower: $128,000
Property Taxes: $1,000
Utilities: $2,179
Retirement Living Costs
Food: $6,180
Health Care: $4,524
Recreation: $2,323
Transportation: $9,397
Retirement Taxes
Income: $865
Sales: $1,344
Score: 60.9 **Rank: 80**

★ Cedar Creek Lake, TX

Household Income: $59,800
Home Prices
Upper: $177,000
Middle: $114,000
Lower: $73,200
Property Taxes: $1,220
Utilities: $2,717
Retirement Living Costs
Food: $5,820
Health Care: $5,831
Recreation: $1,603
Transportation: $9,290
Retirement Taxes
Income: $0
Sales: $1,559
Score: 89.2 **Rank: 23**

Chapel Hill–Carrboro, NC

Household Income: $77,200
Home Prices
Upper: $402,000
Middle: $266,000
Lower: $177,000
Property Taxes: $2,880
Utilities: $3,475
Retirement Living Costs
Food: $6,540
Health Care: $5,611
Recreation: $1,739
Transportation: $9,743
Retirement Taxes
Income: $501
Sales: $1,183
Score: 10.4 **Rank: 182**

Charles Town–Shepherdstown, WV

Household Income: $73,200
Home Prices
Upper: $250,000
Middle: $176,000
Lower: $132,000
Property Taxes: $1,070
Utilities: $2,333
Retirement Living Costs
Food: $5,880
Health Care: $4,571
Recreation: $1,427
Transportation: $8,749
Retirement Taxes
Income: $1,827
Sales: $1,290
Score: 64.4 **Rank: 73**

Charleston, SC

Household Income: $76,900
Home Prices
Upper: $315,000
Middle: $195,000
Lower: $123,000
Property Taxes: $1,080
Utilities: $2,870
Retirement Living Costs
Food: $6,180
Health Care: $5,528
Recreation: $1,484
Transportation: $8,658
Retirement Taxes
Income: $0
Sales: $1,290
Score: 54.5 **Rank: 93**

Charlottesville, VA

Household Income: $89,000
Home Prices
Upper: $398,000
Middle: $267,000
Lower: $188,000
Property Taxes: $1,830
Utilities: $2,726
Retirement Living Costs
Food: $6,540
Health Care: $4,925
Recreation: $1,937
Transportation: $9,179
Retirement Taxes
Income: $29
Sales: $968
Score: 37.7 **Rank: 127**

Chestertown, MD

Household Income: $77,200
Home Prices
Upper: $284,000
Middle: $193,000
Lower: $141,000
Property Taxes: $1,680
Utilities: $2,899
Retirement Living Costs
Food: $6,540
Health Care: $6,971
Recreation: $1,656
Transportation: $9,124
Retirement Taxes
Income: $1,362
Sales: $1,075
Score: 25.8 **Rank: 151**

Chewelah, WA

Household Income: $53,600
Home Prices
Upper: $226,000
Middle: $169,000
Lower: $124,000
Property Taxes: $1,670
Utilities: $2,352
Retirement Living Costs
Food: $6,300
Health Care: $5,356
Recreation: $2,180
Transportation: $9,588
Retirement Taxes
Income: $0
Sales: $1,828
Score: 46.6 **Rank: 109**

Coeur d'Alene, ID

Household Income: $67,600
Home Prices
Upper: $247,000
Middle: $178,000
Lower: $142,000
Property Taxes: $1,790
Utilities: $2,429
Retirement Living Costs
Food: $6,060
Health Care: $4,524
Recreation: $1,682
Transportation: $8,772
Retirement Taxes
Income: $439
Sales: $1,075
Score: 67.9 **Rank: 66**

Colorado Springs, CO

Household Income: $83,400
Home Prices
Upper: $316,000
Middle: $234,000
Lower: $183,000
Property Taxes: $1,250
Utilities: $2,390
Retirement Living Costs
Food: $6,060
Health Care: $5,245
Recreation: $1,506
Transportation: $8,958
Retirement Taxes
Income: $273
Sales: $1,075
Score: 43.1 **Rank: 116**

★ = *one of the top 30 places for low costs of living.*

Columbia, MO

Household Income: $72,100

Home Prices

Upper: $234,000
Middle: $164,000
Lower: $124,000
Property Taxes: $1,610
Utilities: $2,650

Retirement Living Costs

Food: $6,240
Health Care: $5,387
Recreation: $1,910
Transportation: $9,226

Retirement Taxes

Income: $648
Sales: $1,344

Score: 55.5 Rank: 91

Conway, SC

Household Income: $61,700

Home Prices

Upper: $162,000
Middle: $130,000
Lower: $115,000
Property Taxes: $850
Utilities: $2,189

Retirement Living Costs

Food: $5,820
Health Care: $5,023
Recreation: $1,787
Transportation: $8,658

Retirement Taxes

Income: $0
Sales: $1,290

Score: 79.8 Rank: 42

Cottonwood–Verde Valley, AZ

Household Income: $53,500

Home Prices

Upper: $276,000
Middle: $193,000
Lower: $121,000
Property Taxes: $1,240
Utilities: $2,390

Retirement Living Costs

Food: $5,820
Health Care: $4,524
Recreation: $1,708
Transportation: $9,124

Retirement Taxes

Income: $527
Sales: $1,344

Score: 52.5 Rank: 97

★ Crossville, TN

Household Income: $53,900

Home Prices

Upper: $205,000
Middle: $134,000
Lower: $94,000
Property Taxes: $490
Utilities: $1,930

Retirement Living Costs

Food: $5,820
Health Care: $5,207
Recreation: $2,227
Transportation: $8,732

Retirement Taxes

Income: $165
Sales: $1,505

Score: 90.6 Rank: 20

Dare Outer Banks, NC

Household Income: $64,700

Home Prices

Upper: $292,000
Middle: $204,000
Lower: $147,000
Property Taxes: $1,370
Utilities: $2,976

Retirement Living Costs

Food: $6,180
Health Care: $5,065
Recreation: $1,818
Transportation: $9,743

Retirement Taxes

Income: $501
Sales: $1,183

Score: 29.3 Rank: 144

Daytona Beach, FL

Household Income: $58,700

Home Prices

Upper: $207,000
Middle: $150,000
Lower: $116,000
Property Taxes: $1,900
Utilities: $2,650

Retirement Living Costs

Food: $6,060
Health Care: $5,417
Recreation: $1,673
Transportation: $9,783

Retirement Taxes

Income: $176
Sales: $1,505

Score: 70.8 Rank: 60

Delta County, CO

Household Income: $52,200

Home Prices

Upper: $249,000
Middle: $183,000
Lower: $141,000
Property Taxes: $920
Utilities: $2,112

Retirement Living Costs

Food: $5,820
Health Care: $4,720
Recreation: $1,546
Transportation: $8,958

Retirement Taxes

Income: $273
Sales: $1,075

Score: 84.7 Rank: 32

Door Peninsula, WI

Household Income: $72,500

Home Prices

Upper: $288,000
Middle: $181,000
Lower: $124,000
Property Taxes: $2,370
Utilities: $2,842

Retirement Living Costs

Food: $6,060
Health Care: $4,524
Recreation: $1,809
Transportation: $9,401

Retirement Taxes

Income: $1,452
Sales: $1,290

Score: 37.2 Rank: 128

Durango, CO

Household Income: $73,100

Home Prices

Upper: $409,000
Middle: $292,000
Lower: $223,000
Property Taxes: $1,170
Utilities: $2,227

Retirement Living Costs

Food: $6,600
Health Care: $5,042
Recreation: $1,638
Transportation: $8,958

Retirement Taxes

Income: $273
Sales: $1,075

Score: 19.4 Rank: 164

Eagle River–Woodruff, WI

Household Income: $60,800

Home Prices

Upper: $278,000
Middle: $180,000
Lower: $126,000
Property Taxes: $2,150
Utilities: $2,669

Retirement Living Costs

Food: $6,060
Health Care: $4,524
Recreation: $2,060
Transportation: $9,401

Retirement Taxes

Income: $1,452
Sales: $1,290

Score: 39.7 Rank: 123

East End Long Island, NY

Household Income: $114,600

Home Prices

Upper: $450,000
Middle: $320,000
Lower: $250,000
Property Taxes: $8,420
Utilities: $6,336

continued

★ = *one of the top 30 places for low costs of living.*

East End Long Island, NY (cont.)

Retirement Living Costs
Food: $6,840
Health Care: $6,774
Recreation: $3,206
Transportation: $10,527
Retirement Taxes
Income: $0
Sales: $1,290
Score: 1 **Rank: 201**

Easton–St. Michaels, MD

Household Income: $93,500
Home Prices
Upper: $439,000
Middle: $249,000
Lower: $170,000
Property Taxes: $1,550
Utilities: $2,899
Retirement Living Costs
Food: $6,180
Health Care: $4,852
Recreation: $2,288
Transportation: $8,831
Retirement Taxes
Income: $1,362
Sales: $1,075
Score: 23.3 **Rank: 156**

★ Edenton, NC

Household Income: $63,700
Home Prices
Upper: $201,000
Middle: $127,000
Lower: $91,000
Property Taxes: $900
Utilities: $2,630
Retirement Living Costs
Food: $5,880
Health Care: $4,524
Recreation: $1,818
Transportation: $9,743
Retirement Taxes
Income: $501
Sales: $1,183
Score: 88.7 **Rank: 24**

★ Eufaula, AL

Household Income: $58,400
Home Prices
Upper: $159,000
Middle: $103,000
Lower: $67,200
Property Taxes: $310
Utilities: $2,083
Retirement Living Costs
Food: $5,880
Health Care: $5,096
Recreation: $1,980
Transportation: $8,864
Retirement Taxes
Income: $1,043
Sales: $1,290
Score: 94.6 **Rank: 12**

★ Eureka Springs, AR

Household Income: $49,100
Home Prices
Upper: $187,000
Middle: $126,000
Lower: $87,600
Property Taxes: $970
Utilities: $2,179
Retirement Living Costs
Food: $6,000
Health Care: $4,524
Recreation: $1,180
Transportation: $8,774
Retirement Taxes
Income: $735
Sales: $1,344
Score: 94.1 **Rank: 13**

Fairhope–Gulf Shores, AL

Household Income: $70,600
Home Prices
Upper: $270,000
Middle: $183,000
Lower: $128,000
Property Taxes: $540
Utilities: $2,333
Retirement Living Costs
Food: $6,000
Health Care: $5,565
Recreation: $1,888
Transportation: $8,415
Retirement Taxes
Income: $1,043
Sales: $1,290
Score: 58.5 **Rank: 85**

★ Fayetteville, AR

Household Income: $61,200
Home Prices
Upper: $195,000
Middle: $134,000
Lower: $105,000
Property Taxes: $1,080
Utilities: $2,333
Retirement Living Costs
Food: $6,000
Health Care: $4,524
Recreation: $1,168
Transportation: $8,791
Retirement Taxes
Income: $735
Sales: $1,344
Score: 91.6 **Rank: 18**

Flagstaff, AZ

Household Income: $68,700
Home Prices
Upper: $306,000
Middle: $220,000
Lower: $153,000
Property Taxes: $1,300
Utilities: $2,160
Retirement Living Costs
Food: $5,820
Health Care: $4,524
Recreation: $1,708
Transportation: $9,124
Retirement Taxes
Income: $527
Sales: $1,344
Score: 51.5 **Rank: 99**

Florence, OR

Household Income: $69,200
Home Prices
Upper: $279,000
Middle: $211,000
Lower: $166,000
Property Taxes: $2,270
Utilities: $2,688
Retirement Living Costs
Food: $5,880
Health Care: $4,524
Recreation: $2,213
Transportation: $7,317
Retirement Taxes
Income: $855
Sales: $0
Score: 62.9 **Rank: 76**

Fort Collins–Loveland, CO

Household Income: $81,100
Home Prices
Upper: $370,000
Middle: $273,000
Lower: $220,000
Property Taxes: $1,970
Utilities: $2,755
Retirement Living Costs
Food: $6,180
Health Care: $4,914
Recreation: $1,440
Transportation: $8,958
Retirement Taxes
Income: $273
Sales: $1,075
Score: 21.8 **Rank: 159**

Fort Myers–Cape Coral, FL

Household Income: $68,500
Home Prices
Upper: $286,000
Middle: $193,000
Lower: $138,000
Property Taxes: $2,330
Utilities: $3,283
Retirement Living Costs
Food: $6,540
Health Care: $5,910
Recreation: $2,464
Transportation: $9,783
Retirement Taxes
Income: $176
Sales: $1,505
Score: 23.8 **Rank: 155**

★ = *one of the top 30 places for low costs of living.*

Fredericksburg, TX

Household Income: $65,900

Home Prices

Upper: $243,000
Middle: $160,000
Lower: $115,000
Property Taxes: $1,900
Utilities: $2,650

Retirement Living Costs

Food: $6,000
Health Care: $4,524
Recreation: $1,142
Transportation: $9,290

Retirement Taxes

Income: $0
Sales: $1,559

Score: 77.8 **Rank: 46**

Fredericksburg–Spotsylvania, VA

Household Income: $84,000

Home Prices

Upper: $321,000
Middle: $225,000
Lower: $154,000
Property Taxes: $2,380
Utilities: $2,947

Retirement Living Costs

Food: $6,360
Health Care: $5,407
Recreation: $2,437
Transportation: $9,179

Retirement Taxes

Income: $29
Sales: $968

Score: 31.7 **Rank: 139**

Front Royal, VA

Household Income: $71,900

Home Prices

Upper: $234,000
Middle: $181,000
Lower: $142,000
Property Taxes: $1,290
Utilities: $2,333

Retirement Living Costs

Food: $6,240
Health Care: $5,200
Recreation: $2,000
Transportation: $9,226

Retirement Taxes

Income: $29
Sales: $968

Score: 69.9 **Rank: 62**

Gainesville, FL

Household Income: $64,700

Home Prices

Upper: $244,000
Middle: $166,000
Lower: $116,000
Property Taxes: $2,170
Utilities: $2,899

Retirement Living Costs

Food: $6,180
Health Care: $5,561
Recreation: $1,864
Transportation: $9,783

Retirement Taxes

Income: $176
Sales: $1,505

Score: 56 **Rank: 90**

Georgetown, TX

Household Income: $91,500

Home Prices

Upper: $250,000
Middle: $190,000
Lower: $146,000
Property Taxes: $3,740
Utilities: $3,648

Retirement Living Costs

Food: $6,420
Health Care: $4,524
Recreation: $1,656
Transportation: $9,290

Retirement Taxes

Income: $0
Sales: $1,559

Score: 26.8 **Rank: 149**

Grand Junction, CO

Household Income: $68,300

Home Prices

Upper: $258,000
Middle: $189,000
Lower: $145,000
Property Taxes: $1,370
Utilities: $2,246

Retirement Living Costs

Food: $6,180
Health Care: $4,524
Recreation: $1,546
Transportation: $8,958

Retirement Taxes

Income: $273
Sales: $1,075

Score: 73.8 **Rank: 54**

Grants Pass, OR

Household Income: $56,800

Home Prices

Upper: $259,000
Middle: $193,000
Lower: $145,000
Property Taxes: $1,400
Utilities: $2,237

Retirement Living Costs

Food: $6,060
Health Care: $4,524
Recreation: $2,767
Transportation: $7,317

Retirement Taxes

Income: $855
Sales: $0

Score: 78.3 **Rank: 45**

Grass Valley–Nevada City, CA

Household Income: $80,700

Home Prices

Upper: $504,000
Middle: $368,000
Lower: $280,000
Property Taxes: $2,900
Utilities: $3,389

Retirement Living Costs

Food: $6,060
Health Care: $5,295
Recreation: $2,512
Transportation: $9,778

Retirement Taxes

Income: $163
Sales: $1,398

Score: 8 **Rank: 187**

Hamilton–Bitterroot Valley, MT

Household Income: $51,600

Home Prices

Upper: $268,000
Middle: $204,000
Lower: $151,000
Property Taxes: $1,540
Utilities: $2,333

Retirement Living Costs

Food: $5,880
Health Care: $4,524
Recreation: $1,836
Transportation: $7,807

Retirement Taxes

Income: $1,934
Sales: $0

Score: 66.9 **Rank: 68**

Hanover, NH

Household Income: $83,600

Home Prices

Upper: $280,000
Middle: $196,000
Lower: $146,000
Property Taxes: $4,420
Utilities: $3,888

Retirement Living Costs

Food: $6,540
Health Care: $4,596
Recreation: $3,199
Transportation: $7,188

Retirement Taxes

Income: $0
Sales: $0

Score: 59.5 **Rank: 83**

★ **Hattiesburg, MS**

Household Income: $61,200

Home Prices

Upper: $145,000
Middle: $102,000
Lower: $66,000
Property Taxes: $820
Utilities: $2,294

continued

★ = *one of the top 30 places for low costs of living.*

★ **Hattiesburg, MS (cont.)**

Retirement Living Costs
Food: $5,820
Health Care: $5,662
Recreation: $1,900
Transportation: $9,214

Retirement Taxes
Income: $465
Sales: $1,505

Score: 91.1 **Rank: 19**

Henderson, NV

Household Income: $85,100

Home Prices
Upper: $279,000
Middle: $218,000
Lower: $174,000
Property Taxes: $1,850
Utilities: $2,784

Retirement Living Costs
Food: $6,600
Health Care: $6,313
Recreation: $1,965
Transportation: $9,275

Retirement Taxes
Income: $0
Sales: $1,613

Score: 20.3 **Rank: 162**

Hendersonville–East Flat Rock, NC

Household Income: $68,000

Home Prices
Upper: $261,000
Middle: $193,000
Lower: $138,000
Property Taxes: $1,110
Utilities: $2,246

Retirement Living Costs
Food: $6,180
Health Care: $4,524
Recreation: $1,621
Transportation: $9,743

Retirement Taxes
Income: $501
Sales: $1,183

Score: 54 **Rank: 94**

Hilton Head Island, SC

Household Income: $89,200

Home Prices
Upper: $541,000
Middle: $361,000
Lower: $289,000
Property Taxes: $1,950
Utilities: $3,763

Retirement Living Costs
Food: $6,540
Health Care: $4,973
Recreation: $4,409
Transportation: $8,658

Retirement Taxes
Income: $0
Sales: $1,290

Score: 6.5 **Rank: 190**

Hot Springs, AR

Household Income: $61,300

Home Prices
Upper: $207,000
Middle: $128,000
Lower: $86,400
Property Taxes: $790
Utilities: $2,352

Retirement Living Costs
Food: $6,180
Health Care: $5,465
Recreation: $2,921
Transportation: $8,791

Retirement Taxes
Income: $735
Sales: $1,344

Score: 72.8 **Rank: 56**

★ **Inverness, FL**

Household Income: $53,900

Home Prices
Upper: $208,000
Middle: $144,000
Lower: $102,000
Property Taxes: $1,170
Utilities: $2,102

Retirement Living Costs
Food: $5,820
Health Care: $5,522
Recreation: $1,765
Transportation: $9,783

Retirement Taxes
Income: $176
Sales: $1,505

Score: 86.2 **Rank: 29**

Iowa City, IA

Household Income: $77,600

Home Prices
Upper: $268,000
Middle: $195,000
Lower: $148,000
Property Taxes: $2,520
Utilities: $3,283

Retirement Living Costs
Food: $6,060
Health Care: $4,524
Recreation: $2,020
Transportation: $9,316

Retirement Taxes
Income: $507
Sales: $1,290

Score: 30.7 **Rank: 141**

Jackson Hole, WY

Household Income: $130,700

Home Prices
Upper: $1,053,000
Middle: $558,000
Lower: $366,000
Property Taxes: $2,470
Utilities: $4,330

Retirement Living Costs
Food: $6,900
Health Care: $5,408
Recreation: $2,600
Transportation: $8,864

Retirement Taxes
Income: $0
Sales: $1,236

Score: 0 **Rank: 203**

Kalispell–Flathead Valley, MT

Household Income: $63,200

Home Prices
Upper: $264,000
Middle: $192,000
Lower: $141,000
Property Taxes: $2,110
Utilities: $2,563

Retirement Living Costs
Food: $6,060
Health Care: $4,524
Recreation: $1,862
Transportation: $7,807

Retirement Taxes
Income: $1,934
Sales: $0

Score: 63.9 **Rank: 74**

Kauai, HI

Household Income: $76,100

Home Prices
Upper: $478,000
Middle: $346,000
Lower: $261,000
Property Taxes: $990
Utilities: $2,582

Retirement Living Costs
Food: $6,420
Health Care: $4,524
Recreation: $1,502
Transportation: $8,355

Retirement Taxes
Income: $1,401
Sales: $860

Score: 13.4 **Rank: 176**

Kerrville, TX

Household Income: $70,600

Home Prices
Upper: $217,000
Middle: $146,000
Lower: $100,000
Property Taxes: $1,870
Utilities: $2,832

Retirement Living Costs
Food: $6,180
Health Care: $4,524
Recreation: $1,168
Transportation: $9,290

Retirement Taxes
Income: $0
Sales: $1,559

Score: 82.2 **Rank: 37**

★ = *one of the top 30 places for low costs of living.*

Ketchum–Sun Valley, ID

Household Income: $107,200

Home Prices
Upper: $775,000
Middle: $428,000
Lower: $254,000
Property Taxes: $2,060
Utilities: $3,350

Retirement Living Costs
Food: $6,900
Health Care: $5,084
Recreation: $2,117
Transportation: $8,772

Retirement Taxes
Income: $439
Sales: $1,075

Score: 4.5 **Rank: 194**

Key West, FL

Household Income: $89,600

Home Prices
Upper: $613,000
Middle: $411,000
Lower: $282,000
Property Taxes: $3,450
Utilities: $4,704

Retirement Living Costs
Food: $6,360
Health Care: $5,824
Recreation: $1,940
Transportation: $9,769

Retirement Taxes
Income: $176
Sales: $1,505

Score: 5 **Rank: 193**

Kingman, AZ

Household Income: $50,400

Home Prices
Upper: $189,000
Middle: $115,000
Lower: $95,000
Property Taxes: $1,190
Utilities: $2,227

Retirement Living Costs
Food: $5,820
Health Care: $5,879
Recreation: $1,379
Transportation: $9,124

Retirement Taxes
Income: $527
Sales: $1,344

Score: 81.2 **Rank: 39**

Kissimmee–St. Cloud, FL

Household Income: $58,700

Home Prices
Upper: $228,000
Middle: $170,000
Lower: $139,000
Property Taxes: $1,920
Utilities: $2,659

Retirement Living Costs
Food: $6,180
Health Care: $6,959
Recreation: $2,358
Transportation: $9,783

Retirement Taxes
Income: $176
Sales: $1,505

Score: 35.2 **Rank: 132**

Laguna Beach–Dana Point, CA

Household Income: $116,700

Home Prices
Upper: $1,322,000
Middle: $850,000
Lower: $627,000
Property Taxes: $4,127
Utilities: $3,014

Retirement Living Costs
Food: $6,900
Health Care: $7,096
Recreation: $2,841
Transportation: $9,778

Retirement Taxes
Income: $163
Sales: $1,398

Score: 1.5 **Rank: 200**

Lake Conroe, TX

Household Income: $92,700

Home Prices
Upper: $265,000
Middle: $174,000
Lower: $116,000
Property Taxes: $3,050
Utilities: $3,331

Retirement Living Costs
Food: $6,180
Health Care: $8,245
Recreation: $2,249
Transportation: $9,290

Retirement Taxes
Income: $0
Sales: $1,559

Score: 18.4 **Rank: 166**

Lake Havasu City, AZ

Household Income: $50,400

Home Prices
Upper: $210,000
Middle: $147,000
Lower: $117,000
Property Taxes: $1,190
Utilities: $2,227

Retirement Living Costs
Food: $6,000
Health Care: $5,879
Recreation: $1,379
Transportation: $9,124

Retirement Taxes
Income: $527
Sales: $1,344

Score: 79.3 **Rank: 43**

★ Lake of the Cherokees, OK

Household Income: $49,600

Home Prices
Upper: $202,000
Middle: $123,000
Lower: $80,400
Property Taxes: $700
Utilities: $2,064

Retirement Living Costs
Food: $5,880
Health Care: $4,959
Recreation: $1,671
Transportation: $7,899

Retirement Taxes
Income: $899
Sales: $1,290

Score: 96.1 **Rank: 9**

Lake of the Ozarks, MO

Household Income: $59,200

Home Prices
Upper: $274,000
Middle: $190,000
Lower: $126,000
Property Taxes: $950
Utilities: $2,131

Retirement Living Costs
Food: $6,540
Health Care: $5,604
Recreation: $2,350
Transportation: $8,357

Retirement Taxes
Income: $648
Sales: $1,344

Score: 49.1 **Rank: 104**

Lake Placid, NY

Household Income: $59,400

Home Prices
Upper: $182,000
Middle: $134,000
Lower: $100,000
Property Taxes: $2,260
Utilities: $2,918

Retirement Living Costs
Food: $6,120
Health Care: $5,408
Recreation: $1,960
Transportation: $9,950

Retirement Taxes
Income: $0
Sales: $1,290

Score: 73.3 **Rank: 55**

Lake Winnipesaukee, NH

Household Income: $73,400

Home Prices
Upper: $314,000
Middle: $216,000
Lower: $159,000
Property Taxes: $3,300
Utilities: $3,744

continued

★ = *one of the top 30 places for low costs of living.*

Lake Winnipesaukee, NH (cont.)

Retirement Living Costs

Food: $6,180
Health Care: $4,707
Recreation: $2,343
Transportation: $7,188

Retirement Taxes

Income: $0
Sales: $0

Score: 70.3 **Rank: 61**

Lakeland–Winter Haven, FL

Household Income: $65,700

Home Prices

Upper: $201,000
Middle: $142,000
Lower: $102,000
Property Taxes: $1,400
Utilities: $2,534

Retirement Living Costs

Food: $6,060
Health Care: $4,740
Recreation: $1,976
Transportation: $9,783

Retirement Taxes

Income: $176
Sales: $1,505

Score: 84.2 **Rank: 33**

Largo, FL

Household Income: $77,400

Home Prices

Upper: $250,000
Middle: $165,000
Lower: $122,000
Property Taxes: $1,870
Utilities: $2,947

Retirement Living Costs

Food: $6,060
Health Care: $6,197
Recreation: $1,976
Transportation: $9,783

Retirement Taxes

Income: $176
Sales: $1,505

Score: 50 **Rank: 102**

★ Las Cruces, NM

Household Income: $54,900

Home Prices

Upper: $199,000
Middle: $134,000
Lower: $97,000
Property Taxes: $1,030
Utilities: $2,218

Retirement Living Costs

Food: $6,180
Health Care: $4,593
Recreation: $1,656
Transportation: $7,823

Retirement Taxes

Income: $987
Sales: $1,290

Score: 92.1 **Rank: 17**

★ Las Vegas, NM

Household Income: $48,500

Home Prices

Upper: $192,000
Middle: $133,000
Lower: $99,000
Property Taxes: $810
Utilities: $2,323

Retirement Living Costs

Food: $6,360
Health Care: $4,576
Recreation: $2,160
Transportation: $7,960

Retirement Taxes

Income: $987
Sales: $1,290

Score: 89.7 **Rank: 22**

Leelanau Peninsula, MI

Household Income: $66,000

Home Prices

Upper: $415,000
Middle: $249,000
Lower: $168,000
Property Taxes: $1,890
Utilities: $2,803

Retirement Living Costs

Food: $6,180
Health Care: $4,807
Recreation: $1,499
Transportation: $8,412

Retirement Taxes

Income: $0
Sales: $1,290

Score: 28.8 **Rank: 145**

Leesburg–Mount Dora, FL

Household Income: $61,400

Home Prices

Upper: $247,000
Middle: $171,000
Lower: $127,000
Property Taxes: $1,700
Utilities: $2,563

Retirement Living Costs

Food: $5,820
Health Care: $5,511
Recreation: $2,358
Transportation: $9,783

Retirement Taxes

Income: $176
Sales: $1,505

Score: 57.5 **Rank: 87**

Litchfield Hills, CT

Household Income: $93,900

Home Prices

Upper: $569,000
Middle: $262,000
Lower: $199,000
Property Taxes: $4,570
Utilities: $4,301

Retirement Living Costs

Food: $6,900
Health Care: $5,643
Recreation: $2,060
Transportation: $9,372

Retirement Taxes

Income: $257
Sales: $1,290

Score: 10 **Rank: 183**

Lower Cape May, NJ

Household Income: $76,900

Home Prices

Upper: $350,000
Middle: $240,000
Lower: $164,000
Property Taxes: $4,260
Utilities: $4,176

Retirement Living Costs

Food: $6,540
Health Care: $6,714
Recreation: $4,027
Transportation: $9,710

Retirement Taxes

Income: $96
Sales: $1,290

Score: 9 **Rank: 185**

Madison, WI

Household Income: $90,400

Home Prices

Upper: $283,000
Middle: $219,000
Lower: $180,000
Property Taxes: $4,700
Utilities: $4,032

Retirement Living Costs

Food: $6,300
Health Care: $4,598
Recreation: $2,080
Transportation: $9,497

Retirement Taxes

Income: $1,452
Sales: $1,290

Score: 12.4 **Rank: 178**

Marble Falls–Lake LBJ, TX

Household Income: $62,900

Home Prices

Upper: $229,000
Middle: $141,000
Lower: $93,000
Property Taxes: $1,820
Utilities: $2,966

Retirement Living Costs

Food: $6,180
Health Care: $4,934
Recreation: $1,959
Transportation: $9,290

Retirement Taxes

Income: $0
Sales: $1,559

Score: 68.9 **Rank: 64**

★ = *one of the top 30 places for low costs of living.*

Mariposa, CA

Household Income: $58,000

Home Prices

Upper: $318,000
Middle: $254,000
Lower: $200,000
Property Taxes: $1,920
Utilities: $2,573

Retirement Living Costs

Food: $6,420
Health Care: $5,458
Recreation: $1,840
Transportation: $9,783

Retirement Taxes

Income: $163
Sales: $1,398

Score: 24.8 **Rank: 153**

Martha's Vineyard, MA

Household Income: $88,000

Home Prices

Upper: $805,000
Middle: $543,000
Lower: $387,000
Property Taxes: $3,090
Utilities: $3,533

Retirement Living Costs

Food: $6,300
Health Care: $6,032
Recreation: $2,720
Transportation: $9,316

Retirement Taxes

Income: $959
Sales: $1,075

Score: 0.5 **Rank: 202**

★ **Maryville, TN**

Household Income: $65,600

Home Prices

Upper: $212,000
Middle: $153,000
Lower: $114,000
Property Taxes: $890
Utilities: $2,237

Retirement Living Costs

Food: $5,820
Health Care: $4,969
Recreation: $1,594
Transportation: $8,732

Retirement Taxes

Income: $165
Sales: $1,505

Score: 87.7 **Rank: 26**

Maui, HI

Household Income: $75,800

Home Prices

Upper: $556,000
Middle: $400,000
Lower: $297,000
Property Taxes: $1,070
Utilities: $2,496

Retirement Living Costs

Food: $6,420
Health Care: $4,761
Recreation: $1,963
Transportation: $8,367

Retirement Taxes

Income: $1,401
Sales: $860

Score: 7.5 **Rank: 188**

McCall, ID

Household Income: $70,700

Home Prices

Upper: $288,000
Middle: $210,000
Lower: $150,000
Property Taxes: $1,370
Utilities: $2,429

Retirement Living Costs

Food: $6,240
Health Care: $4,524
Recreation: $1,722
Transportation: $8,772

Retirement Taxes

Income: $439
Sales: $1,075

Score: 52 **Rank: 98**

Medford–Ashland, OR

Household Income: $68,200

Home Prices

Upper: $286,000
Middle: $210,000
Lower: $160,000
Property Taxes: $2,140
Utilities: $2,698

Retirement Living Costs

Food: $6,180
Health Care: $4,524
Recreation: $1,910
Transportation: $7,317

Retirement Taxes

Income: $855
Sales: $0

Score: 65.9 **Rank: 70**

Melbourne–Palm Bay, FL

Household Income: $67,700

Home Prices

Upper: $240,000
Middle: $162,000
Lower: $121,000
Property Taxes: $1,790
Utilities: $2,736

Retirement Living Costs

Food: $6,060
Health Care: $6,091
Recreation: $1,845
Transportation: $9,783

Retirement Taxes

Income: $176
Sales: $1,505

Score: 57 **Rank: 88**

Mendocino–Fort Bragg, CA

Household Income: $71,000

Home Prices

Upper: $435,000
Middle: $304,000
Lower: $231,000
Property Taxes: $2,190
Utilities: $2,842

Retirement Living Costs

Food: $6,900
Health Care: $5,824
Recreation: $2,600
Transportation: $9,769

Retirement Taxes

Income: $163
Sales: $1,398

Score: 11.9 **Rank: 179**

Mesa, AZ

Household Income: $84,900

Home Prices

Upper: $285,000
Middle: $200,000
Lower: $147,000
Property Taxes: $1,520
Utilities: $2,755

Retirement Living Costs

Food: $6,540
Health Care: $6,068
Recreation: $1,959
Transportation: $9,124

Retirement Taxes

Income: $527
Sales: $1,344

Score: 27.8 **Rank: 147**

Middle Cape Cod, MA

Household Income: $91,600

Home Prices

Upper: $471,000
Middle: $319,000
Lower: $248,000
Property Taxes: $3,170
Utilities: $3,475

Retirement Living Costs

Food: $6,240
Health Care: $5,999
Recreation: $2,708
Transportation: $9,135

Retirement Taxes

Income: $959
Sales: $1,075

Score: 9.5 **Rank: 184**

★ **Mission–McAllen–Alamo, TX**

Household Income: $53,400

Home Prices

Upper: $121,000
Middle: $79,200
Lower: $50,400
Property Taxes: $1,350
Utilities: $2,198

continued

★ = *one of the top 30 places for low costs of living.*

★ **Mission–McAllen–Alamo, TX (cont.)**

Retirement Living Costs
Food: $5,820
Health Care: $4,816
Recreation: $1,274
Transportation: $9,290
Retirement Taxes
Income: $0
Sales: $1,559
Score: 100 **Rank: 1**

Monadnock Region, NH

Household Income: $75,900
Home Prices
Upper: $248,000
Middle: $189,000
Lower: $152,000
Property Taxes: $4,950
Utilities: $4,166
Retirement Living Costs
Food: $6,420
Health Care: $4,524
Recreation: $2,080
Transportation: $7,688
Retirement Taxes
Income: $0
Sales: $0
Score: 65.4 **Rank: 71**

Montrose, CO

Household Income: $59,400
Home Prices
Upper: $247,000
Middle: $193,000
Lower: $148,000
Property Taxes: $1,140
Utilities: $2,227
Retirement Living Costs
Food: $5,820
Health Care: $4,524
Recreation: $1,809
Transportation: $8,958
Retirement Taxes
Income: $273
Sales: $1,075
Score: 76.3 **Rank: 49**

Morro Bay–Cambria, CA

Household Income: $75,100
Home Prices
Upper: $573,000
Middle: $411,000
Lower: $303,000
Property Taxes: $3,140
Utilities: $2,976
Retirement Living Costs
Food: $6,900
Health Care: $4,791
Recreation: $1,853
Transportation: $9,778
Retirement Taxes
Income: $163
Sales: $1,398
Score: 6.0 **Rank: 191**

★ **Murray–Kentucky Lake, KY**

Household Income: $60,400
Home Prices
Upper: $172,000
Middle: $123,000
Lower: $90,000
Property Taxes: $860
Utilities: $2,131
Retirement Living Costs
Food: $5,880
Health Care: $4,883
Recreation: $1,607
Transportation: $8,821
Retirement Taxes
Income: $0
Sales: $1,290
Score: 95.1 **Rank: 11**

Myrtle Beach, SC

Household Income: $61,700
Home Prices
Upper: $252,000
Middle: $180,000
Lower: $130,000
Property Taxes: $750
Utilities: $2,189
Retirement Living Costs
Food: $6,180
Health Care: $5,023
Recreation: $3,355
Transportation: $8,658
Retirement Taxes
Income: $0
Sales: $1,290
Score: 58 **Rank: 86**

Naples, FL

Household Income: $107,400
Home Prices
Upper: $489,000
Middle: $286,000
Lower: $198,000
Property Taxes: $2,440
Utilities: $3,955
Retirement Living Costs
Food: $6,600
Health Care: $5,634
Recreation: $2,003
Transportation: $9,783
Retirement Taxes
Income: $176
Sales: $1,505
Score: 11.4 **Rank: 180**

★ **Natchitoches, LA**

Household Income: $54,000
Home Prices
Upper: $157,000
Middle: $105,000
Lower: $66,000
Property Taxes: $300
Utilities: $2,150
Retirement Living Costs
Food: $6,000
Health Care: $5,096
Recreation: $1,780
Transportation: $7,688
Retirement Taxes
Income: $248
Sales: $1,290
Score: 99.6 **Rank: 2**

New Bern, NC

Household Income: $69,900
Home Prices
Upper: $217,000
Middle: $144,000
Lower: $105,000
Property Taxes: $1,000
Utilities: $2,669
Retirement Living Costs
Food: $6,000
Health Care: $4,566
Recreation: $2,240
Transportation: $9,743
Retirement Taxes
Income: $501
Sales: $1,183
Score: 72.3 **Rank: 57**

New Braunfels, TX

Household Income: $82,300
Home Prices
Upper: $260,000
Middle: $177,000
Lower: $122,000
Property Taxes: $2,270
Utilities: $2,822
Retirement Living Costs
Food: $6,180
Health Care: $4,524
Recreation: $1,234
Transportation: $9,290
Retirement Taxes
Income: $0
Sales: $1,559
Score: 61.4 **Rank: 79**

New Port Richey, FL

Household Income: $62,700
Home Prices
Upper: $204,000
Middle: $136,000
Lower: $97,000
Property Taxes: $1,360
Utilities: $2,314
Retirement Living Costs
Food: $6,060
Health Care: $6,684
Recreation: $1,581
Transportation: $9,783
Retirement Taxes
Income: $176
Sales: $1,505
Score: 71.8 **Rank: 58**

★ = *one of the top 30 places for low costs of living.*

Newport–Lincoln City, OR

Household Income: $61,600

Home Prices

Upper: $314,000
Middle: $223,000
Lower: $160,000
Property Taxes: $2,420
Utilities: $2,765

Retirement Living Costs

Food: $6,180
Health Care: $4,524
Recreation: $2,451
Transportation: $7,317

Retirement Taxes

Income: $855
Sales: $0

Score: 48.6 **Rank: 105**

★ Norfork Lake, AR

Household Income: $55,200

Home Prices

Upper: $176,000
Middle: $126,000
Lower: $93,000
Property Taxes: $760
Utilities: $2,064

Retirement Living Costs

Food: $5,820
Health Care: $4,587
Recreation: $1,932
Transportation: $8,791

Retirement Taxes

Income: $735
Sales: $1,344

Score: 92.6 **Rank: 16**

North County San Diego, CA

Household Income: $98,800

Home Prices

Upper: $586,000
Middle: $406,000
Lower: $302,000
Property Taxes: $3,000
Utilities: $2,928

Retirement Living Costs

Food: $6,900
Health Care: $6,409
Recreation: $1,722
Transportation: $9,778

Retirement Taxes

Income: $163
Sales: $1,398

Score: 5.5 **Rank: 192**

Northampton–Amherst, MA

Household Income: $74,000

Home Prices

Upper: $326,000
Middle: $254,000
Lower: $204,000
Property Taxes: $3,770
Utilities: $3,514

Retirement Living Costs

Food: $6,060
Health Care: $5,005
Recreation: $1,917
Transportation: $8,821

Retirement Taxes

Income: $959
Sales: $1,075

Score: 20.8 **Rank: 161**

Northern Neck, VA

Household Income: $76,900

Home Prices

Upper: $412,000
Middle: $218,000
Lower: $126,000
Property Taxes: $1,000
Utilities: $2,438

Retirement Living Costs

Food: $6,000
Health Care: $5,248
Recreation: $2,701
Transportation: $9,179

Retirement Taxes

Income: $29
Sales: $968

Score: 48.1 **Rank: 106**

Oakhurst–Coarsegold, CA

Household Income: $66,400

Home Prices

Upper: $280,000
Middle: $212,000
Lower: $156,000
Property Taxes: $1,680
Utilities: $2,563

Retirement Living Costs

Food: $6,060
Health Care: $5,141
Recreation: $1,801
Transportation: $9,778

Retirement Taxes

Income: $163
Sales: $1,398

Score: 53 **Rank: 96**

★ Ocala, FL

Household Income: $58,600

Home Prices

Upper: $195,000
Middle: $139,000
Lower: $103,000
Property Taxes: $1,400
Utilities: $2,256

Retirement Living Costs

Food: $6,060
Health Care: $5,075
Recreation: $1,779
Transportation: $9,783

Retirement Taxes

Income: $176
Sales: $1,505

Score: 87.2 **Rank: 27**

Ocean City, MD

Household Income: $65,400

Home Prices

Upper: $291,000
Middle: $202,000
Lower: $145,000
Property Taxes: $1,530
Utilities: $2,870

Retirement Living Costs

Food: $6,540
Health Care: $4,577
Recreation: $1,959
Transportation: $8,831

Retirement Taxes

Income: $1,362
Sales: $1,075

Score: 44.6 **Rank: 113**

★ Oscoda–Huron Shore, MI

Household Income: $51,100

Home Prices

Upper: $169,000
Middle: $116,000
Lower: $85,200
Property Taxes: $1,050
Utilities: $2,093

Retirement Living Costs

Food: $5,820
Health Care: $5,358
Recreation: $1,433
Transportation: $8,226

Retirement Taxes

Income: $0
Sales: $1,290

Score: 97.6 **Rank: 6**

★ Oxford, MS

Household Income: $54,500

Home Prices

Upper: $229,000
Middle: $148,000
Lower: $92,000
Property Taxes: $740
Utilities: $2,381

Retirement Living Costs

Food: $5,820
Health Care: $4,524
Recreation: $1,722
Transportation: $9,137

Retirement Taxes

Income: $465
Sales: $1,505

Score: 86.7 **Rank: 28**

Pagosa Springs, CO

Household Income: $50,000

Home Prices

Upper: $380,000
Middle: $266,000
Lower: $195,000
Property Taxes: $1,540
Utilities: $2,314

continued

★= *one of the top 30 places for low costs of living.*

Pagosa Springs, CO (cont.)

Retirement Living Costs
Food: $5,880
Health Care: $4,524
Recreation: $1,638
Transportation: $8,958

Retirement Taxes
Income: $273
Sales: $1,075

Score: 33.7 Rank: 135

Pahrump Valley, NV

Household Income: $64,800

Home Prices
Upper: $242,000
Middle: $192,000
Lower: $142,000
Property Taxes: $1,370
Utilities: $2,064

Retirement Living Costs
Food: $6,180
Health Care: $5,703
Recreation: $2,624
Transportation: $9,275

Retirement Taxes
Income: $0
Sales: $1,613

Score: 41.1 Rank: 120

Palm Springs–Coachella Valley, CA

Household Income: $81,100

Home Prices
Upper: $357,000
Middle: $261,000
Lower: $187,000
Property Taxes: $2,410
Utilities: $2,957

Retirement Living Costs
Food: $6,840
Health Care: $6,396
Recreation: $3,171
Transportation: $9,778

Retirement Taxes
Income: $163
Sales: $1,398

Score: 12.9 Rank: 177

Palmer–Wasilla, AK

Household Income: $60,100

Home Prices
Upper: $270,000
Middle: $210,000
Lower: $160,000
Property Taxes: $2,620
Utilities: $3,206

Retirement Living Costs
Food: $6,600
Health Care: $6,167
Recreation: $2,200
Transportation: $9,045

Retirement Taxes
Income: $0
Sales: $0

Score: 34.7 Rank: 133

Panama City, FL

Household Income: $62,900

Home Prices
Upper: $241,000
Middle: $159,000
Lower: $117,000
Property Taxes: $1,160
Utilities: $2,352

Retirement Living Costs
Food: $6,180
Health Care: $5,757
Recreation: $1,680
Transportation: $9,783

Retirement Taxes
Income: $176
Sales: $1,505

Score: 68.4 Rank: 65

Paradise–Magalia, CA

Household Income: $62,300

Home Prices
Upper: $240,000
Middle: $185,000
Lower: $129,000
Property Taxes: $1,850
Utilities: $2,669

Retirement Living Costs
Food: $6,540
Health Care: $5,485
Recreation: $1,471
Transportation: $9,778

Retirement Taxes
Income: $163
Sales: $1,398

Score: 34.2 Rank: 134

Park City, UT

Household Income: $134,200

Home Prices
Upper: $640,000
Middle: $423,000
Lower: $295,000
Property Taxes: $2,330
Utilities: $2,966

Retirement Living Costs
Food: $6,540
Health Care: $4,524
Recreation: $2,240
Transportation: $9,407

Retirement Taxes
Income: $865
Sales: $1,344

Score: 2.5 Rank: 198

Payson, AZ

Household Income: $52,700

Home Prices
Upper: $238,000
Middle: $156,000
Lower: $98,000
Property Taxes: $1,170
Utilities: $2,314

Retirement Living Costs
Food: $5,820
Health Care: $5,779
Recreation: $2,301
Transportation: $9,124

Retirement Taxes
Income: $527
Sales: $1,344

Score: 66.4 Rank: 69

★ Pendleton District, SC

Household Income: $65,700

Home Prices
Upper: $237,000
Middle: $146,000
Lower: $102,000
Property Taxes: $590
Utilities: $2,131

Retirement Living Costs
Food: $5,880
Health Care: $4,524
Recreation: $1,722
Transportation: $8,658

Retirement Taxes
Income: $0
Sales: $1,290

Score: 93.1 Rank: 15

Pensacola, FL

Household Income: $62,300

Home Prices
Upper: $211,000
Middle: $146,000
Lower: $103,000
Property Taxes: $1,100
Utilities: $2,342

Retirement Living Costs
Food: $6,240
Health Care: $5,755
Recreation: $1,740
Transportation: $9,778

Retirement Taxes
Income: $176
Sales: $1,505

Score: 75.3 Rank: 51

Petoskey–Harbor Springs, MI

Household Income: $73,500

Home Prices
Upper: $298,000
Middle: $198,000
Lower: $136,000
Property Taxes: $1,980
Utilities: $2,832

Retirement Living Costs
Food: $6,180
Health Care: $4,524
Recreation: $1,591
Transportation: $8,226

Retirement Taxes
Income: $0
Sales: $1,290

Score: 61.9 Rank: 78

★ = *one of the top 30 places for low costs of living.*

Pike County, PA

Household Income: $60,900

Home Prices

Upper: $246,000
Middle: $186,000
Lower: $141,000
Property Taxes: $3,020
Utilities: $3,187

Retirement Living Costs

Food: $6,180
Health Care: $5,651
Recreation: $2,036
Transportation: $9,248

Retirement Taxes

Income: $0
Sales: $1,290

Score: 32.2 **Rank: 138**

Polson–Mission Valley, MT

Household Income: $51,100

Home Prices

Upper: $265,000
Middle: $178,000
Lower: $124,000
Property Taxes: $1,750
Utilities: $2,294

Retirement Living Costs

Food: $5,880
Health Care: $4,524
Recreation: $1,968
Transportation: $7,807

Retirement Taxes

Income: $1,934
Sales: $0

Score: 78.8 **Rank: 44**

Port Angeles–Sequim, WA

Household Income: $62,100

Home Prices

Upper: $276,000
Middle: $201,000
Lower: $146,000
Property Taxes: $2,040
Utilities: $2,784

Retirement Living Costs

Food: $6,180
Health Care: $4,614
Recreation: $2,069
Transportation: $9,721

Retirement Taxes

Income: $0
Sales: $1,828

Score: 31.2 **Rank: 140**

Port Charlotte, FL

Household Income: $60,000

Home Prices

Upper: $247,000
Middle: $165,000
Lower: $122,000
Property Taxes: $2,020
Utilities: $2,861

Retirement Living Costs

Food: $6,180
Health Care: $6,492
Recreation: $2,042
Transportation: $9,783

Retirement Taxes

Income: $176
Sales: $1,505

Score: 42.6 **Rank: 117**

Port Townsend, WA

Household Income: $66,100

Home Prices

Upper: $397,000
Middle: $260,000
Lower: $187,000
Property Taxes: $2,580
Utilities: $3,379

Retirement Living Costs

Food: $6,060
Health Care: $4,819
Recreation: $2,055
Transportation: $9,721

Retirement Taxes

Income: $0
Sales: $1,828

Score: 13.9 **Rank: 175**

Prescott–Prescott Valley, AZ

Household Income: $53,500

Home Prices

Upper: $304,000
Middle: $213,000
Lower: $151,000
Property Taxes: $1,440
Utilities: $2,390

Retirement Living Costs

Food: $6,180
Health Care: $4,524
Recreation: $1,722
Transportation: $9,124

Retirement Taxes

Income: $527
Sales: $1,344

Score: 46.1 **Rank: 110**

Rabun County, GA

Household Income: $55,400

Home Prices

Upper: $276,000
Middle: $174,000
Lower: $118,000
Property Taxes: $830
Utilities: $2,256

Retirement Living Costs

Food: $5,820
Health Care: $5,893
Recreation: $1,950
Transportation: $8,195

Retirement Taxes

Income: $73
Sales: $1,290

Score: 76.8 **Rank: 48**

Rehoboth Bay–Indian River Bay, DE

Household Income: $59,600

Home Prices

Upper: $283,000
Middle: $198,000
Lower: $141,000
Property Taxes: $880
Utilities: $2,294

Retirement Living Costs

Food: $6,060
Health Care: $5,524
Recreation: $2,016
Transportation: $8,257

Retirement Taxes

Income: $0
Sales: $0

Score: 82.7 **Rank: 36**

Reno–Sparks, NV

Household Income: $98,100

Home Prices

Upper: $351,000
Middle: $253,000
Lower: $204,000
Property Taxes: $2,210
Utilities: $3,446

Retirement Living Costs

Food: $6,180
Health Care: $5,394
Recreation: $2,163
Transportation: $9,275

Retirement Taxes

Income: $0
Sales: $1,613

Score: 17.4 **Rank: 168**

Rio Rancho, NM

Household Income: $68,600

Home Prices

Upper: $230,000
Middle: $170,000
Lower: $132,000
Property Taxes: $1,110
Utilities: $2,237

Retirement Living Costs

Food: $6,540
Health Care: $4,524
Recreation: $1,985
Transportation: $7,823

Retirement Taxes

Income: $987
Sales: $1,290

Score: 71.3 **Rank: 59**

Rockport–Aransas Pass, TX

Household Income: $66,200

Home Prices

Upper: $196,000
Middle: $120,000
Lower: $76,800
Property Taxes: $1,580
Utilities: $2,861

continued

★ = *one of the top 30 places for low costs of living.*

Rockport–Aransas Pass, TX (cont.)

Retirement Living Costs
Food: $6,180
Health Care: $5,813
Recreation: $1,932
Transportation: $9,290

Retirement Taxes
Income: $0
Sales: $1,559

Score: 75.8 **Rank: 50**

★ Roswell, NM

Household Income: $63,100

Home Prices
Upper: $136,000
Middle: $94,000
Lower: $66,000
Property Taxes: $430
Utilities: $1,891

Retirement Living Costs
Food: $6,180
Health Care: $4,524
Recreation: $2,040
Transportation: $8,141

Retirement Taxes
Income: $987
Sales: $1,290

Score: 98.6 **Rank: 4**

Ruidoso, NM

Household Income: $46,300

Home Prices
Upper: $250,000
Middle: $159,000
Lower: $110,000
Property Taxes: $900
Utilities: $2,371

Retirement Living Costs
Food: $6,360
Health Care: $4,524
Recreation: $2,156
Transportation: $7,823

Retirement Taxes
Income: $987
Sales: $1,290

Score: 80.2 **Rank: 41**

St. Augustine, FL

Household Income: $107,500

Home Prices
Upper: $430,000
Middle: $271,000
Lower: $181,000
Property Taxes: $2,700
Utilities: $3,062

Retirement Living Costs
Food: $6,180
Health Care: $5,775
Recreation: $2,042
Transportation: $9,783

Retirement Taxes
Income: $176
Sales: $1,505

Score: 16.9 **Rank: 169**

St. George–Zion, UT

Household Income: $61,200

Home Prices
Upper: $267,000
Middle: $200,000
Lower: $152,000
Property Taxes: $1,110
Utilities: $2,371

Retirement Living Costs
Food: $6,180
Health Care: $4,524
Recreation: $2,323
Transportation: $9,397

Retirement Taxes
Income: $865
Sales: $1,344

Score: 33.2 **Rank: 136**

St. Jay–Northeast Kingdom, VT

Household Income: $61,500

Home Prices
Upper: $166,000
Middle: $132,000
Lower: $105,000
Property Taxes: $2,660
Utilities: $3,130

Retirement Living Costs
Food: $6,060
Health Care: $4,524
Recreation: $2,077
Transportation: $8,711

Retirement Taxes
Income: $1,163
Sales: $1,075

Score: 74.3 **Rank: 53**

St. Simons–Jekyll Islands, GA

Household Income: $79,500

Home Prices
Upper: $609,000
Middle: $477,000
Lower: $258,000
Property Taxes: $1,450
Utilities: $2,746

Retirement Living Costs
Food: $6,060
Health Care: $6,216
Recreation: $2,609
Transportation: $8,673

Retirement Taxes
Income: $73
Sales: $1,290

Score: 45.1 **Rank: 112**

Salida, CO

Household Income: $54,400

Home Prices
Upper: $343,000
Middle: $242,000
Lower: $182,000
Property Taxes: $1,110
Utilities: $2,141

Retirement Living Costs
Food: $6,120
Health Care: $5,252
Recreation: $1,520
Transportation: $8,955

Retirement Taxes
Income: $273
Sales: $1,075

Score: 40.6 **Rank: 121**

San Juan Islands, WA

Household Income: $85,600

Home Prices
Upper: $716,000
Middle: $440,000
Lower: $273,000
Property Taxes: $2,770
Utilities: $3,590

Retirement Living Costs
Food: $5,880
Health Care: $4,524
Recreation: $2,187
Transportation: $9,721

Retirement Taxes
Income: $0
Sales: $1,828

Score: 3 **Rank: 197**

Sandpoint–Lake Pend Oreille, ID

Household Income: $52,000

Home Prices
Upper: $258,000
Middle: $184,000
Lower: $130,000
Property Taxes: $1,290
Utilities: $2,275

Retirement Living Costs
Food: $5,880
Health Care: $4,524
Recreation: $1,722
Transportation: $8,772

Retirement Taxes
Income: $439
Sales: $1,075

Score: 69.4 **Rank: 63**

Santa Barbara, CA

Household Income: $103,400

Home Prices
Upper: $859,000
Middle: $523,000
Lower: $282,000
Property Taxes: $2,950
Utilities: $2,986

Retirement Living Costs
Food: $6,600
Health Care: $4,837
Recreation: $2,051
Transportation: $9,778

Retirement Taxes
Income: $163
Sales: $1,398

Score: 3.5 **Rank: 196**

★ = *one of the top 30 places for low costs of living.*

Santa Fe, NM

Household Income: $81,400

Home Prices

Upper: $428,000
Middle: $278,000
Lower: $205,000
Property Taxes: $1,160
Utilities: $2,554

Retirement Living Costs

Food: $6,540
Health Care: $4,524
Recreation: $2,670
Transportation: $7,823

Retirement Taxes

Income: $987
Sales: $1,290

Score: 17.9 **Rank: 167**

Santa Rosa, CA

Household Income: $98,600

Home Prices

Upper: $667,000
Middle: $488,000
Lower: $374,000
Property Taxes: $3,330
Utilities: $3,168

Retirement Living Costs

Food: $6,600
Health Care: $5,831
Recreation: $1,722
Transportation: $9,778

Retirement Taxes

Income: $163
Sales: $1,398

Score: 4 **Rank: 195**

Sarasota, FL

Household Income: $89,800

Home Prices

Upper: $322,000
Middle: $208,000
Lower: $147,000
Property Taxes: $2,370
Utilities: $3,302

Retirement Living Costs

Food: $6,180
Health Care: $5,653
Recreation: $1,845
Transportation: $9,783

Retirement Taxes

Income: $176
Sales: $1,505

Score: 28.3 **Rank: 146**

Savannah, GA

Household Income: $79,300

Home Prices

Upper: $231,000
Middle: $147,000
Lower: $108,000
Property Taxes: $1,840
Utilities: $3,043

Retirement Living Costs

Food: $6,180
Health Care: $6,227
Recreation: $2,569
Transportation: $8,673

Retirement Taxes

Income: $73
Sales: $1,290

Score: 56.5 **Rank: 89**

Scottsdale, AZ

Household Income: $52,900

Home Prices

Upper: $475,000
Middle: $280,000
Lower: $187,000
Property Taxes: $1,520
Utilities: $2,755

Retirement Living Costs

Food: $6,540
Health Care: $6,068
Recreation: $1,959
Transportation: $9,124

Retirement Taxes

Income: $527
Sales: $1,344

Score: 27.8 **Rank: 147**

★ **Sebring–Avon Park, FL**

Household Income: $55,100

Home Prices

Upper: $170,000
Middle: $124,000
Lower: $92,000
Property Taxes: $1,260
Utilities: $2,227

Retirement Living Costs

Food: $5,820
Health Care: $5,479
Recreation: $1,713
Transportation: $9,783

Retirement Taxes

Income: $176
Sales: $1,505

Score: 90.1 **Rank: 21**

Sedona, AZ

Household Income: $59,400

Home Prices

Upper: $610,000
Middle: $320,000
Lower: $253,000
Property Taxes: $1,300
Utilities: $2,160

Retirement Living Costs

Food: $6,180
Health Care: $4,555
Recreation: $1,379
Transportation: $9,124

Retirement Taxes

Income: $527
Sales: $1,344

Score: 50.5 **Rank: 101**

★ **Silver City, NM**

Household Income: $78,600

Home Prices

Upper: $188,000
Middle: $129,000
Lower: $94,000
Property Taxes: $470
Utilities: $1,814

Retirement Living Costs

Food: $5,820
Health Care: $4,524
Recreation: $1,524
Transportation: $7,823

Retirement Taxes

Income: $987
Sales: $1,290

Score: 97.1 **Rank: 7**

Smith Mountain Lake, VA

Household Income: $58,100

Home Prices

Upper: $292,000
Middle: $211,000
Lower: $150,000
Property Taxes: $1,170
Utilities: $1,920

Retirement Living Costs

Food: $5,820
Health Care: $4,524
Recreation: $2,016
Transportation: $9,179

Retirement Taxes

Income: $29
Sales: $968

Score: 83.7 **Rank: 34**

Sonora–Twain Harte, CA

Household Income: $84,900

Home Prices

Upper: $358,000
Middle: $267,000
Lower: $211,000
Property Taxes: $2,050
Utilities: $2,986

Retirement Living Costs

Food: $5,880
Health Care: $4,980
Recreation: $1,801
Transportation: $9,778

Retirement Taxes

Income: $163
Sales: $1,398

Score: 24.3 **Rank: 154**

Southern Berkshire County, MA

Household Income: $68,700

Home Prices

Upper: $292,000
Middle: $208,000
Lower: $158,000
Property Taxes: $2,820
Utilities: $3,254

continued

★ = *one of the top 30 places for low costs of living.*

Southern Berkshire County, MA (cont.)

Retirement Living Costs
Food: $6,060
Health Care: $5,858
Recreation: $1,719
Transportation: $8,821
Retirement Taxes
Income: $959
Sales: $1,075
Score: 36.2 **Rank: 130**

Southern Pines–Pinehurst, NC

Household Income: $55,900
Home Prices
Upper: $291,000
Middle: $195,000
Lower: $127,000
Property Taxes: $1,210
Utilities: $2,582
Retirement Living Costs
Food: $6,540
Health Care: $4,524
Recreation: $2,306
Transportation: $9,743
Retirement Taxes
Income: $501
Sales: $1,183
Score: 36.7 **Rank: 129**

Southport–Brunswick Islands, NC

Household Income: $77,200
Home Prices
Upper: $278,000
Middle: $189,000
Lower: $130,000
Property Taxes: $1,140
Utilities: $2,746
Retirement Living Costs
Food: $6,180
Health Care: $5,206
Recreation: $2,213
Transportation: $9,743
Retirement Taxes
Income: $501
Sales: $1,183
Score: 35.7 **Rank: 131**

State College, PA

Household Income: $71,400
Home Prices
Upper: $252,000
Middle: $181,000
Lower: $135,000
Property Taxes: $2,300
Utilities: $2,928
Retirement Living Costs
Food: $6,180
Health Care: $5,027
Recreation: $2,062
Transportation: $9,248
Retirement Taxes
Income: $0
Sales: $1,290
Score: 51 **Rank: 100**

★ Summerville, SC

Household Income: $63,400
Home Prices
Upper: $224,000
Middle: $157,000
Lower: $115,000
Property Taxes: $1,090
Utilities: $2,611
Retirement Living Costs
Food: $6,180
Health Care: $4,683
Recreation: $1,580
Transportation: $8,774
Retirement Taxes
Income: $0
Sales: $1,290
Score: 85.7 **Rank: 30**

★ Table Rock Lake, MO

Household Income: $59,700
Home Prices
Upper: $229,000
Middle: $157,000
Lower: $109,000
Property Taxes: $850
Utilities: $2,112
Retirement Living Costs
Food: $6,180
Health Care: $4,741
Recreation: $1,625
Transportation: $8,357
Retirement Taxes
Income: $648
Sales: $1,344
Score: 88.2 **Rank: 25**

Taos, NM

Household Income: $46,800
Home Prices
Upper: $342,000
Middle: $220,000
Lower: $130,000
Property Taxes: $590
Utilities: $2,122
Retirement Living Costs
Food: $6,180
Health Care: $4,524
Recreation: $2,644
Transportation: $7,823
Retirement Taxes
Income: $987
Sales: $1,290
Score: 43.6 **Rank: 115**

★ Thomasville, GA

Household Income: $69,700
Home Prices
Upper: $186,000
Middle: $120,000
Lower: $74,400
Property Taxes: $900
Utilities: $2,333
Retirement Living Costs
Food: $5,820
Health Care: $4,634
Recreation: $1,159
Transportation: $8,195
Retirement Taxes
Income: $73
Sales: $1,290
Score: 99.1 **Rank: 3**

Toms River–Barnegat Bay, NJ

Household Income: $77,700
Home Prices
Upper: $302,000
Middle: $229,000
Lower: $168,000
Property Taxes: $4,860
Utilities: $4,243
Retirement Living Costs
Food: $6,180
Health Care: $6,018
Recreation: $2,183
Transportation: $9,710
Retirement Taxes
Income: $96
Sales: $1,290
Score: 14.9 **Rank: 173**

Traverse City, MI

Household Income: $79,700
Home Prices
Upper: $278,000
Middle: $196,000
Lower: $148,000
Property Taxes: $2,100
Utilities: $2,698
Retirement Living Costs
Food: $6,180
Health Care: $4,956
Recreation: $1,525
Transportation: $8,226
Retirement Taxes
Income: $0
Sales: $1,290
Score: 59 **Rank: 84**

★ Trinity Peninsula, TX

Household Income: $46,800
Home Prices
Upper: $117,000
Middle: $81,600
Lower: $54,000
Property Taxes: $820
Utilities: $2,486
Retirement Living Costs
Food: $5,820
Health Care: $5,761
Recreation: $1,932
Transportation: $9,290
Retirement Taxes
Income: $0
Sales: $1,559
Score: 95.6 **Rank: 10**

★ = *one of the top 30 places for low costs of living.*

Tryon, NC

Household Income: $73,700

Home Prices

Upper: $244,000
Middle: $166,000
Lower: $111,000
Property Taxes: $920
Utilities: $2,227

Retirement Living Costs

Food: $5,820
Health Care: $4,524
Recreation: $2,740
Transportation: $9,743

Retirement Taxes

Income: $501
Sales: $1,183

Score: 62.4 Rank: 77

Tucson, AZ

Household Income: $65,900

Home Prices

Upper: $260,000
Middle: $177,000
Lower: $133,000
Property Taxes: $1,850
Utilities: $2,650

Retirement Living Costs

Food: $6,180
Health Care: $5,753
Recreation: $1,959
Transportation: $9,124

Retirement Taxes

Income: $527
Sales: $1,344

Score: 44.1 Rank: 114

Vero Beach, FL

Household Income: $89,000

Home Prices

Upper: $292,000
Middle: $177,000
Lower: $126,000
Property Taxes: $2,100
Utilities: $3,149

Retirement Living Costs

Food: $6,060
Health Care: $5,793
Recreation: $2,029
Transportation: $9,783

Retirement Taxes

Income: $176
Sales: $1,505

Score: 41.6 Rank: 119

Victorville–Apple Valley, CA

Household Income: $76,300

Home Prices

Upper: $316,000
Middle: $235,000
Lower: $170,000
Property Taxes: $2,160
Utilities: $2,621

Retirement Living Costs

Food: $6,540
Health Care: $6,604
Recreation: $1,853
Transportation: $9,778

Retirement Taxes

Income: $163
Sales: $1,398

Score: 21.3 Rank: 160

Virginia Beach, VA

Household Income: $93,300

Home Prices

Upper: $285,000
Middle: $204,000
Lower: $156,000
Property Taxes: $2,280
Utilities: $3,504

Retirement Living Costs

Food: $6,540
Health Care: $5,270
Recreation: $1,871
Transportation: $9,179

Retirement Taxes

Income: $29
Sales: $968

Score: 38.2 Rank: 126

Wenatchee, WA

Household Income: $70,700

Home Prices

Upper: $302,000
Middle: $224,000
Lower: $169,000
Property Taxes: $2,270
Utilities: $2,794

Retirement Living Costs

Food: $5,880
Health Care: $4,524
Recreation: $1,950
Transportation: $9,721

Retirement Taxes

Income: $0
Sales: $1,828

Score: 25.3 Rank: 152

Western St. Tammany Parish, LA

Household Income: $84,400

Home Prices

Upper: $262,000
Middle: $186,000
Lower: $130,000
Property Taxes: $560
Utilities: $2,496

Retirement Living Costs

Food: $6,180
Health Care: $7,822
Recreation: $1,487
Transportation: $8,257

Retirement Taxes

Income: $248
Sales: $1,290

Score: 42.1 Rank: 118

Whidbey Island, WA

Household Income: $75,500

Home Prices

Upper: $374,000
Middle: $264,000
Lower: $211,000
Property Taxes: $2,340
Utilities: $3,178

Retirement Living Costs

Food: $6,240
Health Care: $4,524
Recreation: $2,108
Transportation: $9,721

Retirement Taxes

Income: $0
Sales: $1,828

Score: 14.4 Rank: 174

Wickenburg, AZ

Household Income: $84,900

Home Prices

Upper: $265,000
Middle: $195,000
Lower: $140,000
Property Taxes: $1,220
Utilities: $2,755

Retirement Living Costs

Food: $5,820
Health Care: $6,068
Recreation: $2,038
Transportation: $9,124

Retirement Taxes

Income: $527
Sales: $1,344

Score: 32.7 Rank: 137

Williamsburg, VA

Household Income: $98,900

Home Prices

Upper: $556,000
Middle: $351,000
Lower: $177,000
Property Taxes: $1,620
Utilities: $3,091

Retirement Living Costs

Food: $6,540
Health Care: $5,490
Recreation: $5,692
Transportation: $9,179

Retirement Taxes

Income: $29
Sales: $968

Score: 7.0 Rank: 189

Wimberley, TX

Household Income: $68,300

Home Prices

Upper: $270,000
Middle: $195,000
Lower: $138,000
Property Taxes: $3,330
Utilities: $3,418

continued

★ = *one of the top 30 places for low costs of living.*

Wimberley, TX (cont.)

Retirement Living Costs

Food: $5,820

Health Care: $4,707

Recreation: $1,959

Transportation: $9,290

Retirement Taxes

Income: $0

Sales: $1,559

Score: 29.8 **Rank: 143**

Woodstock, VT

Household Income: $74,300

Home Prices

Upper: $237,000

Middle: $172,000

Lower: $130,000

Property Taxes: $3,640

Utilities: $3,686

Retirement Living Costs

Food: $6,360

Health Care: $4,524

Recreation: $3,882

Transportation: $8,711

Retirement Taxes

Income: $1,163

Sales: $1,075

Score: 22.3 **Rank: 158**

York Beaches, ME

Household Income: $68,000

Home Prices

Upper: $285,000

Middle: $210,000

Lower: $160,000

Property Taxes: $2,780

Utilities: $3,149

Retirement Living Costs

Food: $6,180

Health Care: $4,536

Recreation: $1,981

Transportation: $9,188

Retirement Taxes

Income: $894

Sales: $1,183

Score: 38.7 **Rank: 125**

Yuma, AZ

Household Income: $49,300

Home Prices

Upper: $183,000

Middle: $132,000

Lower: $104,400

Property Taxes: $1,280

Utilities: $2,554

Retirement Living Costs

Food: $6,000

Health Care: $5,693

Recreation: $1,774

Transportation: $9,124

Retirement Taxes

Income: $527

Sales: $1,344

Score: 81.7 **Rank: 38**

★ = *one of the top 30 places for low costs of living.*

ET CETERA: COSTS OF LIVING

RESALE HOUSES AND NEW HOUSES

If a single, detached home is your preferred form of housing, consider the pluses and minuses of resale houses versus new houses.

In most markets, resale homes are less expensive than equivalent new homes and are available in broader price ranges, with more architectural styles and locations in town. Resale homes usually have had minor defects, often unforeseen when the home was new, corrected by the seller.

But the age of the structure may signal problems. Repairs to the roof, floor coverings, appliances, and mechanical systems, which have depreciated over the years, may be necessary during the first 2 years you own the house. More importantly, as a neighborhood matures, some homes are maintained better than others and price disparities develop, which can affect your own home's value.

New houses in new, homogeneous neighborhoods portend more rapid appreciation in value over equivalent resale houses. You can have a new house covered by an extended homeowner warranty to protect you from major structural defects. If timing permits, you also can "customize" the house with options and extras and have the opportunity to select colors, appliance brands, and technological features such as heating and air-conditioning systems. But the drawback to new homes in many communities is their 10 to 20 percent price premium over equivalent resale homes.

Buying a new home is more complicated, too, since many more decisions have to be made about finish details and landscaping, all of which may mean frequent site visits to confer with the builder.

Duplexes

If you're a first-time investor considering a home for rental income, a duplex (a house divided into apartments for two households) often is a better buy than a single house because of a better relation between price and income. A duplex may be bought for 8 to 10 times its annual rental income, where a single house may cost 13 to 15 times what it could bring in rent.

You may want to consider buying a duplex, renting one of the apartments, and occupying the other yourself. This is particularly attractive in college towns. From Charlottesville, Virginia, to Athens, Georgia, to Madison, Wisconsin, college towns have more rental properties and renters than other places. Aside from the income and depreciation you would have from the rental unit, if you live alone, congenial tenants—perhaps a graduate student and family—can watch the house should you want to do some traveling. You can also trade lower rent for maintenance help.

PROPERTY TAXES

Although the dollar amount of a home's property tax bill seems to inch upward with each reassessment, there is some comfort in knowing that the *rate* at which homes are being taxed is actually going down.

Over the years, while the prices of existing homes were rising, the average effective property tax rate (the tax bill expressed as a percentage of a home's fair market value) dropped from 2 percent to less than 1.15 percent nationwide. Experts expect the downward trend to continue.

Nowhere in the United States can you own a home and escape property taxes without specific income and age qualifications. But homeowners in certain states such as Louisiana, where the statewide average property tax rate is 0.4 percent, shoulder less of a burden than do homeowners in other states such as Wisconsin, which has an average effective tax rate of 3.1 percent, or nearly eight times that of Louisiana.

Homestead Exemptions

When you shop for favorable property taxes around the country, be a little circumspect when you hear of states that give retired people additional property tax relief. Are any of these perks, by themselves, worth the move? Read on.

Homestead exemptions are specific dollar amounts deducted from a home's assessed value. The assessed value minus the exemption equals the amount of taxable value for computing property tax. Homeowners in Florida get a $25,000 exemption, for example, while Hawaiians get a $40,000 exemption if their home is their principal residence. A related break is the *homestead credit,* an amount subtracted from the property tax rather than from the assessed value. Ten states also allow additional exemptions or credits to older homeowners without income qualifications.

Do exemptions translate into much hard cash? Except in Alaska—where you can virtually forget property taxes once you turn 65—not really. Based on statewide average property tax rates, you'll save $204 in Hawaii ($255 if you're over 70), $54 in Illinois, $160 in Kentucky, $144 in South Carolina, and $138 in West Virginia.

Property tax exemptions can be an extra benefit in retirement, but if you're planning a move, you'd do well to put other considerations such as energy cost and house prices first.

STATE/LOCAL SALES TAXES

Sometimes called "retail taxes" or consumption taxes, sales taxes are collected on the purchase of goods at the store level. After property taxes, sales taxes account for the largest source of revenue for state and local governments. Unlike property taxes, however, since 1991 they haven't been deductible from your federal tax return.

Nationally, the median sales tax is 5 percent. If you're living in Mississippi, Rhode Island, or Tennessee, you're paying the nation's highest state rate at 7 percent. But combined state and local sales taxes, in the 34 states that allow it, can top 9 percent.

Alaska, Delaware, Montana, New Hampshire, and Oregon collect no sales taxes at all. To a retired couple, this could mean saving $300 to $600 a year. But you can avoid much of that cost in states where medicine, clothing, and especially groceries are exempt.

STATE RETIREMENT INCOME TAX PROFILES

Question: Where in America can you find rock-bottom property taxes; no personal income tax on any of your retirement income; no sales tax on the basics you'll need, such as food and medicine; no inheritance taxes for your heirs to pay; and a minimum of nickel-and-dime fees for licensing a car or for taking out a fishing license?

Answer: Dream on. The ideal tax haven would have to have the low property taxes of Louisiana, Alaska's forgiveness of taxes on personal income, and the absence of sales taxes as in Oregon. Unfortunately, you just can't find all these tax breaks together in any one state.

The ways states raise revenue differ dramatically. Sales taxes, excise taxes, license taxes, income taxes, intangibles taxes, property taxes, estate taxes, and inheritance taxes are just some of the forms their levies take. Depending on where you live, you may encounter all or only a few.

When federal income taxes were enacted in 1914, two states—Mississippi and Wisconsin—were already collecting income taxes on their own. It was only during

State and Local Sales Tax Rates

	FOOD TAXED	STATE	LOCAL MAXIMUM	STATE/LOCAL MAXIMUM
Alabama *	•	4.00%	6.00%	11.00%
Arizona *		5.60%	3.00%	8.60%
Arkansas *	•	5.125%	4.75%	9.875%
California *		6.00%	2.50%	8.50%
Colorado *		2.90%	5.00%	7.90%
Connecticut		6.00%		6.00%
District of Columbia		5.75%		5.75%
Florida *		6.00%	1.50%	7.50%
Georgia *		4.00%	3.00%	7.00%
Hawaii *	•	4.00%		4.00%
Idaho	•	5.00%	3.00%	8.00%
Illinois *	•	6.25%	3.00%	9.25%
Indiana		6.00%		6.00%
Iowa *		5.00%	2.00%	7.00%
Kansas *	•	5.30%	3.00%	8.30%
Kentucky *		6.00%		6.00%
Louisiana *		4.00%	5.50%	9.50%
Maine		5.00%		5.00%
Maryland		5.00%		5.00%
Massachusetts		5.00%		5.00%
Michigan		6.00%		6.00%
Minnesota *		6.50%	1.00%	7.50%
Mississippi *	•	7.00%	0.25%	7.25%
Missouri *	•	4.225%	4.125%	8.350%
Nebraska *		5.50%	1.50%	7.00%
Nevada *		6.50%	0.75%	7.25%
New Jersey		6.00%		6.00%
New Mexico *		5.00%	2.25%	7.25%
New York *		4.00%	4.50%	8.50%
North Carolina *		4.50%	3.00%	7.50%
North Dakota *		5.00%	2.50%	7.50%
Ohio *		5.00%	2.00%	7.00%
Oklahoma *		4.50%	5.35%	9.85%
Pennsylvania *		6.00%	1.00%	7.00%
Rhode Island		7.00%		7.00%
South Carolina *	•	5.00%	2.00%	7.00%
South Dakota *	•	4.00%	2.00%	6.00%
Tennessee *	•	7.00%	2.75%	9.75%
Texas *		6.25%	2.00%	8.25%
Utah *	•	4.75%	2.25%	7.00%
Vermont *		5.00%	1.00%	6.00%
Virginia *	•	3.50%	1.00%	4.50%
Washington *		6.50%	2.40%	8.90%
West Virginia	•	6.00%		6.00%
Wisconsin *		5.00%	0.60%	5.60%
Wyoming *	•	4.00%	2.00%	6.00%

Source: Federation of Tax Administrators.

• *indicates groceries are taxable. Prescription drugs are tax-exempt everywhere but Illinois and New Mexico.*

* *indicates a flat state sales tax rate. All other states have local additions to their base tax rate.*

the 1920s and 1930s that the majority of states began to raise cash by tapping personal incomes. Today, 41 states impose the tax. Two—New Hampshire and Tennessee—apply it only to income from interest and dividends. Seven—Alaska, Florida, Nevada, South Dakota, Texas, Washington, and Wyoming—don't tax income at all.

Of the 41 states with a broad-based income tax, 35 base the taxes on federal returns, typically taking a portion of what you pay the IRS or using your federal adjusted gross income or taxable income as the starting point for their own computation. Just 4 states—Hawaii, Illinois, Mississippi, and Pennsylvania—fully exempt Social Security and any pensions from taxation. The remaining states take differing views on taxing Social Security, government pensions, and private employer pensions.

The following descriptions of how states tax income include specific features regarding their treatment of retirement income. The best way to learn what your income taxes will be in a new state is to write the state's department of revenue for a ***resident*** income tax form and instructions, fill it out, and compare the bottom line with that of your current state. Of course, you should always consult a tax advisor for help with complex tax issues.

Personal Exemptions and Standard Deductions. Most states specify amounts for taxpayers and each of their dependents that can be used as an offset in determining taxable income. And most of these also specify additional amounts for persons over 65.

Medical and Dental Deductions. Most states treat health care expenses as having already been deducted from federal returns. North Dakota and Oregon grant full deductions for this major retirement expense. Four states in the Great Lakes region—Illinois, Indiana, Michigan, and Ohio—do not permit itemized deductions at all.

Federal Taxes Aren't Deductible Everywhere. Of the 41 states with broad-based income taxes, 12 allow taxpayers to deduct federal income taxes. Is this an advantage? It is if you're deciding between two states with similar tax rates, but only one of them allows you to deduct. In the latter case, your effective tax rate would be less. This makes a big difference to high-income households.

Social Security Exemption. Of the 41 states with a broad-based income tax, 26 of them fully exempt Social Security. The others tax benefits if they are subject to the federal income tax. They are: Colorado, Connecticut, Iowa, Kansas, Minnesota, Missouri, Montana, Nebraska, New Mexico, North Dakota, Rhode Island, Utah, Vermont, West Virginia, and Wisconsin. In the following state tax profiles, Railroad Retirement benefits and Social Security benefits are treated the same.

Public Pension Exemption. Because of legal challenges in the late 1980s and early 1990s, pensions paid by federal, state, and local governments are now treated identically in most states. For example, a state-government pension cannot be taxed more favorably than a federal-government pension. Eleven states now fully exempt public pensions.

Private Pension Exemption. States typically exempt only defined-benefit, or qualified, plans, that is, pensions that provide a specific amount to a retired employee based on years of employment and compensation received. Aside from full exemptions in Hawaii, Illinois, Mississippi, and Pennsylvania, states tend to treat private employer pensions less favorably than public pensions.

Be Aware of Source Taxes. A few years ago, 11 states applied a "source tax" to the pension income of nonresidents. If you worked and earned a pension in one of them, you would be required to pay tax on your pension benefits to that state *even if you no longer lived there.*

Because of a federal law passed in late 1995, all states are now prohibited from taxing nonresident pensions. Four states—Massachusetts, Minnesota, Vermont, and Wisconsin—still tax unqualified retirement plans and various forms of compensation of former state residents still allowed under the new federal law.

ALABAMA

Personal Income Tax Rates

Single or Married Separate Return

Brackets: 3
Lowest: 2% of first $500
Highest: 5% over $3,000

Features

Feature	
Personal Exemptions or Credits	$1,500 single, $3,000 married joint return $300 each dependent
Standard Deduction	$2,000 single, $4,000 married joint return
Medical and Dental Deduction	Limited to excess of 4% of adjusted gross income
Federal Income Tax Deduction	Full
Public Pension Exclusion	Full
Private Pension Exclusion	Full
Social Security Exemption	Full

ALASKA

The personal income tax was repealed in 1979.

ARIZONA

Personal Income Tax Rates

Single or Married Separate Return

Starting point: federal adjusted gross income
Brackets: 5
Lowest: 2.9% of first $10,000
Highest: 5.2% over $150,001

Features

Feature	
Personal Exemptions or Credits	$2,100 single, $4,200 married joint return $2,300 each dependent $2,100, 65 or older
Standard Deduction	$3,500 single, $7,000 married joint return
Medical and Dental Deduction	Limited to excess of 4% of adjusted gross income
Federal Income Tax Deduction	None
Public Pension Exclusion	$2,500
Private Pension Exclusion	None
Social Security Exemption	Full

ARKANSAS

Personal Income Tax Rates

All Taxpayers

Brackets: 6
Lowest: 1% of first $2,999
Highest: 7% over $25,000

Features

Feature	
Personal Exemptions or Credits	$20 credit, single; $40 credit, married $20 credit, each dependent $20 credit, 65 or older
Standard Deduction	10% of gross income to maximum of $1,000
Medical and Dental Deduction	Federal amount
Federal Income Tax Deduction	None
Public Pension Exclusion	$6,000
Private Pension Exclusion	$6,000
Social Security Exemption	Full

CALIFORNIA

Personal Income Tax Rates

Single or Married Separate Return

Starting point: federal adjusted gross income
Brackets: 6
Lowest: 1% of first $5,016
Highest: 9.3% over $32,916

Features

Feature	
Personal Exemptions or Credits	$68 credit, single $136 credit, married joint return $68 credit, each dependent $65 credit, 65 or older
Standard Deduction	$2,431 single, $4,862 married joint return
Medical and Dental Deduction	Federal amount

Federal Income Tax Deduction ....None
Public Pension Exclusion ....$40 credit, military
Private Pension Exclusion ....None
Social Security Exemption ....Full

COLORADO

Personal Income Tax Rates

All Taxpayers

Flat rate of 5% of federal taxable income

Features

Personal Exemptions or Credits ....None
Standard Deduction ....None
Medical and Dental Deduction ....Federal amount
Federal Income Tax Deduction ....None
Public Pension Exclusion ....$20,000 for persons 55–65; $24,000 for persons 65+
Private Pension Exclusion ....$20,000 for persons 55–65; $24,000 for persons 65+
Social Security Exemption ....$20,000 for persons 55–65; $24,000 for persons 65+

CONNECTICUT

Personal Income Tax Rates

All Taxpayers

Flat rate of 4.5% of federal adjusted gross income

Features

Personal Exemptions or Credits ....Up to $12,000 single
Up to $19,000 head of household
Up to $24,000 married joint return
Standard Deduction ....None
Medical and Dental Deduction ....None
Federal Income Tax Deduction ....None
Public Pension Exclusion ....None
Private Pension Exclusion ....None
Social Security Exemption ....None

DELAWARE

Personal Income Tax Rates

All Taxpayers

Starting point: federal adjusted gross income
Brackets: 6
Lowest: 3.1% of first $2,001
Highest: 6.9% over $30,000

Features

Personal Exemptions or Credits ....$100 credit, single
$200 credit, married joint return
$100 credit, 65 or older
Standard Deduction ....$1,300 single, $1,600 married joint return
Additional $1,000, 65 or older
Medical and Dental Deduction ....Federal amount
Federal Income Tax Deduction ....None
Public Pension Exclusion ....$2,000 for persons under 60
$12,500 for persons 60 or older
Private Pension Exclusion ....$2,000 for persons under 60
$12,500 for persons 60 or older
Social Security Exemption ....Full

DISTRICT OF COLUMBIA

Personal Income Tax Rates

All Taxpayers

Starting point: federal adjusted gross income
Brackets: 3
Lowest: 6% of first $10,000
Highest: 9.5% over $20,000

Features

Personal Exemptions or Credits	$1,370, each exemption allowed on federal return $1,370, 65 or older
Standard Deduction	$1,000 married separate return $2,000 single and married joint return
Medical and Dental Deduction	Federal amount
Federal Income Tax Deduction	None
Public Pension Exclusion	$3,000 for persons 62 or older
Private Pension Exclusion	None
Social Security Exemption	Full

FLORIDA

The state does not tax personal income.

GEORGIA

Personal Income Tax Rates

Single or Married Separate Return

Starting point: federal adjusted gross income
Brackets: 6
Lowest: 1% of first $750
Highest: 6% over $7,000

Features

Personal Exemptions or Credits	$1,500 single, $3,000 married joint return $2,500 each dependent
Standard Deduction	$2,300 single, $3,000 married joint return $700 additional, taxpayer over 65 $700 additional, spouse over 65
Medical and Dental Deduction	Federal amount
Federal Income Tax Deduction	None
Public Pension Exclusion	$13,500 for persons 62 or older
Private Pension Exclusion	$13,500 for persons 62 or older
Social Security Exemption	Full

HAWAII

Personal Income Tax Rates

Single or Married Separate Return

Starting point: federal taxable income
Brackets: 8
Lowest: 2% of first $1,500
Highest: 10% over $20,500

Features

Personal Exemptions or Credits	$1,040, each individual $1,040, taxpayer or spouse over 65
Standard Deduction	$1,500 single, $1,900 married joint return
Medical and Dental Deduction	Federal amount

Federal Income Tax Deduction .... None
Public Pension Exclusion .... Full
Private Pension Exclusion .... Full
Social Security Exemption .... Full

IDAHO

Personal Income Tax Rates

Single or Married Separate Return

Starting point: federal taxable income
Brackets: 8
Lowest: 2% of first $1,000
Highest: 8.2% over $20,000

Features

Personal Exemptions or Credits .... Federal amount
Standard Deduction .... Federal amount
Medical and Dental Deduction .... Federal amount
Federal Income Tax Deduction .... None
Public Pension Exclusion .... $17,196 for persons 65+
Private Pension Exclusion .... None
Social Security Exemption .... Full

ILLINOIS

Personal Income Tax Rates

All Taxpayers

Flat rate of 3% of federal adjusted gross income

Features

Personal Exemptions or Credits .... $1,000 personal
$1,000 each additional federal exemption
$1,000 taxpayer or spouse 65 or older
Standard Deduction .... None
Medical and Dental Deduction .... None
Federal Income Tax Deduction .... None
Public Pension Exclusion .... Full
Private Pension Exclusion .... Full
Social Security Exemption .... Full

INDIANA

Personal Income Tax Rates

All Taxpayers

Flat rate of 3.4% of federal adjusted gross income

Features

Personal Exemptions or Credits .... $1,000 individual
$1,000 each dependent
$1,000 taxpayer or spouse 65 or older
Standard Deduction .... None
Medical and Dental Deduction .... None
Federal Income Tax Deduction .... None
Public Pension Exclusion .... $2,000 for federal over 62 and military over 60
Private Pension Exclusion .... None
Social Security Exemption .... Full

IOWA

Personal Income Tax Rates

All Taxpayers

Starting point: federal adjusted gross income
Brackets: 9
Lowest: 0.36% of first $1,136
Highest: 8.98% over $51,120

Features

Personal Exemptions or Credits	$20 credit, single $40 credit, married joint return $15 credit, each dependent $20 credit, 65 or older
Standard Deduction	$1,330 single, $3,270 married joint return
Medical and Dental Deduction	Federal amount
Federal Income Tax Deduction	Full
Public Pension Exclusion	$5,000 for persons 55+
Private Pension Exclusion	$5,000 for persons 55+
Social Security Exemption	Federal amount

KANSAS

Personal Income Tax Rates

Single or Married Separate Return

Starting point: federal adjusted gross income
Brackets: 3
Lowest: 3.5% of first $15,000
Highest: 7.75% over $30,000

Features

Personal Exemptions or Credits	$2,000 each exemption
Standard Deduction	$3,000 single, $5,000 married joint return
Medical and Dental Deduction	Federal amount
Federal Income Tax Deduction	None
Public Pension Exclusion	Full
Private Pension Exclusion	None
Social Security Exemption	Federal amount

KENTUCKY

Personal Income Tax Rates

All Taxpayers

Starting point: federal adjusted gross income
Brackets: 5
Lowest: 2% of first $3,000
Highest: 6% over $8,000

Features

Personal Exemptions or Credits	$20 credit, each exemption $40 credit, 65 or older
Standard Deduction	$650 single, $650 married joint return
Medical and Dental Deduction	Federal amount
Federal Income Tax Deduction	None
Public Pension Exclusion	Full
Private Pension Exclusion	None
Social Security Exemption	Full

LOUISIANA

Personal Income Tax Rates

Single or Married Filing Separately

Starting point: federal adjusted gross income
Brackets: 3
Lowest: 2% of first $10,000
Highest: 6% over $50,000

Features

Personal Exemptions or Credits	$4,500 single, married separate return $9,000 married joint return, head of household $1,000 each dependent $1,000, 65 or older
Standard Deduction	Combined with personal exemptions
Medical and Dental Deduction	Federal amount
Federal Income Tax Deduction	Partial to Full
Public Pension Exclusion	Full
Private Pension Exclusion	$6,000, 65 and older
Social Security Exemption	Full

MAINE

Personal Income Tax Rates

Single or Married Filing Separately

Starting point: federal adjusted gross income
Brackets: 4
Lowest: 2% of first $4,150
Highest: 8.5% over $16,500

Features

Personal Exemptions or Credits	$2,150 each federal exemption
Standard Deduction	$3,800 single, $6,350 married joint return additional $950, single over 65 additional $750, one spouse over 65 additional $1,500, both spouses over 65
Medical and Dental Deduction	Federal amount
Federal Income Tax Deduction	None
Public Pension Exclusion	$6,000 per taxpayer minus SS benefits
Private Pension Exclusion	$6,000 per taxpayer minus SS benefits
Social Security Exemption	Full

MARYLAND

Personal Income Tax Rates

Single or Married Filing Separately

Starting point: federal adjusted gross income
Brackets: 4
Lowest: 2% of first $1,000
Highest: 4.95% over $3,000

Features

Personal Exemptions or Credits	$1,200 each personal and dependent exemption $1,000 personal, 65 or older $1,200 dependent, 65 or older
Standard Deduction	$1,500 or 15% of Maryland adjusted gross income to maximum of $3,000 for single returns; $2,000 to $4,000 married joint return
Medical and Dental Deduction	Federal amount
Federal Income Tax Deduction	None
Public Pension Exclusion	$16,400, 65+, minus SS benefits
Private Pension Exclusion	$16,400, 65+, minus SS benefits
Social Security Exemption	Full

MASSACHUSETTS

Personal Income Tax Rates

All Taxpayers

Taxable Income

Flat rate of 5.95% of federal adjusted gross income

Features

Personal Exemptions or Credits..$2,200 single, $4,400 married joint return
$1,000 each dependent
$700, 65 or older

Standard Deduction ....None

Medical and Dental Deduction ....Federal amount

Federal Income Tax Deduction..None

Public Pension Exclusion ....Full

Private Pension Exclusion ....None

Social Security Exemption...Full

MICHIGAN

Personal Income Tax Rates

All Taxpayers

Flat Rate of 4.4% of federal adjusted gross income

Features

Personal Exemptions or Credits..$2,700 each federal exemption
$2,700 each federal exemption, 65 or older

Standard Deduction ....None

Medical and Dental Deduction ....None

Federal Income Tax Deduction..None

Public Pension Exclusion ....Full

Private Pension Exclusion ....$34,920 single, $69,840 married joint return

Social Security Exemption...Full

MINNESOTA

Personal Income Tax Rates

Single Return

Starting point: federal taxable income

Brackets: 3

Lowest: 6% of first $16,960

Highest: 8.5% over $55,730

Features

Personal Exemptions or Credits..Federal amount

Standard Deduction ....Federal amount

Medical and Dental Deduction ....Federal amount plus full amount of medical insurance premiums for self-employed in excess of that included in federal amount

Federal Income Tax Deduction..None

Public Pension Exclusion ....$14,500 for single persons 65+, $18,000 joint

Private Pension Exclusion ....$14,500 for single persons 65+, $18,000 joint

Social Security Exemption...None

MISSISSIPPI

Personal Income Tax Rates

All Taxpayers

Brackets: 3
Lowest: 3% of first $5,000
Highest: 5% over $10,000

Features

Personal Exemptions or Credits............$6,000 single, $10,000 married joint return
$1,500 each dependent
$1,500 65 or older
Standard Deduction............$2,300 single, $3,400 married joint return
Medical and Dental Deduction............Partial
Federal Income Tax Deduction............None
Public Pension Exclusion............Full
Private Pension Exclusion............Full
Social Security Exemption............Full

MISSOURI

Personal Income Tax Rates

All Taxpayers

Starting point: federal adjusted gross income
Brackets: 10
Lowest: 1.5% of first $1,000
Highest: 6% over $9,000

Features

Personal Exemptions or Credits............$1,200 taxpayer and spouse
$400 each dependent
Standard Deduction............Federal amount
Medical and Dental Deduction............Federal amount
Federal Income Tax Deduction............Full
Public Pension Exclusion............$6,000, single and income less than $25,000 exclusive of Social Security
$6,000, married and income less than $32,000 exclusive of Social Security
Private Pension Exclusion............None
Social Security Exemption............Federal amount
Railroad Retirement Exemption............Full

MONTANA

Personal Income Tax Rates

All Taxpayers

Starting point: federal adjusted gross income
Brackets: 10
Lowest: 2% of first $1,900
Highest: 11% over $67,900

Features

Personal Exemptions or Credits............$1,550 each exemption
$1,550 each 65 or older
Standard Deduction............$2,620 single, $5,240 married joint return
Medical and Dental Deduction............Federal amount
Federal Income Tax Deduction............Full
Public Pension Exclusion............$3,600 maximum, depending on income
Private Pension Exclusion............$3,600 maximum, depending on income
Social Security Exemption............Federal amount

NEBRASKA

Personal Income Tax Rates

Single or Married Filing Separately

Starting point: federal adjusted gross income
Brackets: 4
Lowest: 2.51% of first $2,400
Highest: 6.68% over $26,500

Features

Personal Exemptions or Credits..$88 credit, each federal exemption
Standard Deduction ....Federal amount
Medical and Dental Deduction ....Federal amount
Federal Income Tax Deduction..None
Public Pension Exclusion ....None
Private Pension Exclusion ....None
Social Security Exemption..Federal amount

NEVADA

The state does not tax personal income.

NEW HAMPSHIRE

Personal Income Tax Rates

All Taxpayers

5% tax limited to interest and dividends. Exceptions include interest from bonds issued by the state and its cities and towns, and interest paid by New Hampshire and Vermont banks.

Features

Personal Exemptions or Credits..$1,200 each taxpayer
$1,200 65 or older

NEW JERSEY

Personal Income Tax Rates

Single or Married Filing Separately

Brackets: 6
Lowest: 1.4% of first $20,000
Highest: 6.37% over $75,000

Features

Personal Exemptions or Credits..$1,000 single, $2,000 married joint return
$1,500 each dependent
$1,000 65 or older, taxpayer or spouse
Standard Deduction ....None
Medical and Dental Deduction ....Limited to excess of 2% of gross income
Federal Income Tax Deduction..None
Public Pension Exclusion ....$8,000 single 65+
....$16,000 married joint return 65+
Private Pension Exclusion ....$7,500 single
$5,000 married filing separately
$10,000 married joint return
Social Security Exemption..Full

NEW MEXICO

Personal Income Tax Rates

Single or Married Filing Separately

Starting point: federal adjusted gross income
Brackets: 7
Lowest: 1.7% of first $5,500
Highest: 8.5% over $65,000

Features

Feature	
Personal Exemptions or Credits	Federal amount Maximum $8,000, 65 or older, depending on income
Standard Deduction	Federal amount
Medical and Dental Deduction	3% credit of unreimbursed prescription drug costs
Federal Income Tax Deduction	None
Public Pension Exclusion	$8,000 single 65+, $16,000 married joint
Private Pension Exclusion	None
Social Security Exemption	Federal amount

NEW YORK

Personal Income Tax Rates

Single or Married Filing Separately

Starting point: federal adjusted gross income
Brackets: 5
Lowest: 4% of first $5,500
Highest: 7.125% over $13,000

Features

Feature	
Personal Exemptions or Credits	$1,000 each dependent
Standard Deduction	$6,300 single, $10,200 married joint return
Medical and Dental Deduction	Federal amount
Federal Income Tax Deduction	None
Public Pension Exclusion	Full
Private Pension Exclusion	$20,000 for 59½ or older
Social Security Exemption	Full

NORTH CAROLINA

Personal Income Tax Rates

Single or Married Filing Separately

Starting point: federal taxable income
Brackets: 3
Lowest: 6% of first $12,750
Highest: 7.75% over $60,000

Features

Feature	
Personal Exemptions or Credits	Federal amount
Standard Deduction	$3,000 single, $5,000 married joint return
Medical and Dental Deduction	Federal amount
Federal Income Tax Deduction	None
Public Pension Exclusion	$4,000 per taxpayer if receiving both public and private pensions
Private Pension Exclusion	$2,000 per taxpayer if receiving both public and private pensions
Social Security Exemption	Full

NORTH DAKOTA

Personal Income Tax Rates

All Taxpayers

Starting point: federal taxable income
Brackets: 8
Lowest: 2.67% of first $3,000
Highest: 12% over $50,000

Optional

Taxpayers may forgo state adjustments to federal taxable income and pay 14% of federal tax liability

Features

Feature	
Personal Exemptions or Credits	Federal amount plus $300 married joint return $300 single return, head of household
Standard Deduction	Federal amount
Medical and Dental Deduction	Full
Federal Income Tax Deduction	Full
Public Pension Exclusion	$5,000, less Social Security benefits, for federal pensions and North Dakota public safety pensions
Private Pension Exclusion	None
Social Security Exemption	Federal amount

OHIO

Personal Income Tax Rates

All Taxpayers

Starting point: federal adjusted gross income
Brackets: 9
Lowest: 0.713% of first $5,000
Highest: 7.201% over $200,000

Features

Feature	
Personal Exemptions or Credits.	$950 taxpayer, spouse, each dependent $50 credit, taxpayer over 65
Standard Deduction	None
Medical and Dental Deduction	None
Federal Income Tax Deduction	None
Public Pension Exclusion	$200 maximum credit, based on income
Private Pension Exclusion	$200 maximum credit, based on income
Social Security Exemption	Full

OKLAHOMA

Personal Income Tax Rates

Single or Married Filing Separately

Starting point: federal adjusted gross income
Brackets: 8
Lowest: 0.5% of first $1,000
Highest: 7% over $10,000

Features

Feature	
Personal Exemptions or Credits	$1,000 each taxpayer $1,000 65 or older, depending on federal adjusted gross income
Standard Deduction	$1,000 to $2,000 for single and joint returns $500 to $1,000 for married filing separately
Medical and Dental Deduction	Federal amount

Federal Income Tax Deduction ....Full, but higher rates apply to the remaining taxable income
Public Pension Exclusion $5,500
Private Pension Exclusion $4,400
Social Security Exemption ....Full

OREGON

Personal Income Tax Rates

Single or Married Filing Separately

Starting point: federal taxable income
Brackets: 3
Lowest: 5% of first $2,250
Highest: 9% over $5,700

Features

Personal Exemptions or Credits. ....$124 credit, each federal exemption
Credit equal to 40% of federal credit
Standard Deduction ....$1,800 single, $3,000 married joint return
additional $1,200, single return over 65
additional $2,000, joint return over 65
Medical and Dental Deduction ....Full only for age 59 or older, if itemized
Federal Income Tax Deduction ....$3,000 ($1,500 if married filing separately)
Public Pension Exclusion ....Up to 9% for persons age 59 or older with household income under $45,000 (married joint return) or household income under $22,500 (other filing status)
Private Pension Exclusion ....Identical to public pension exclusion
Social Security Exemption ....Full

PENNSYLVANIA

Personal Income Tax Rates

All Taxpayers

Flat rate of 2.8%

Features

Personal Exemptions or Credits ....None
Standard Deduction ....None
Medical and Dental Deduction ....None
Federal Income Tax Deduction ....None
Public Pension Exclusion ....Full
Private Pension Exclusion ....Full
Social Security Exemption ....Full

RHODE ISLAND

Personal Income Tax Rates

All Taxpayers

27% of federal income tax liability

Features

Personal Exemptions or Credits ....Federal amount
Standard Deduction ....Federal amount
Medical and Dental Deduction ....Federal amount
Federal Income Tax Deduction ....None
Public Pension Exclusion ....None
Private Pension Exclusion ....None
Social Security Exemption ....Federal amount

SOUTH CAROLINA

Personal Income Tax Rates

All Taxpayers

Starting point: federal taxable income
Brackets: 6
Lowest: 2.5% of first $2,280
Highest: 7% over $11,400

Features

Personal Exemptions or Credits....Federal amount
Standard Deduction....Federal amount
Medical and Dental Deduction....Federal amount
Federal Income Tax Deduction....None
Public Pension Exclusion....$3,000 for persons under 65
$10,000 for persons over 65
Private Pension Exclusion....$3,000 for persons under 65
$10,000 for persons over 65
Social Security Exemption....Full

SOUTH DAKOTA

The state does not tax personal income.

TENNESSEE

Personal Income Tax Rates

All Taxpayers

6% tax limited to income from stock dividends and interest from bonds and other obligations. Exceptions include federal obligations and instruments of indebtedness issued to Tennessee banks.

Features

Personal Exemptions or Credits....$1,250 single, $2,500 married joint return

TEXAS

The state does not tax personal income.

UTAH

Personal Income Tax Rates

Single or Married Filing Separately

Starting point: federal taxable income
Brackets: 6
Lowest: 2.3% of first $750
Highest: 7% over $3,750

Features

Personal Exemptions or Credits....75% of federal amount
Standard Deduction....Federal amount
Medical and Dental Deduction....Federal amount
Federal Income Tax Deduction....50% deductible
Public Pension Exclusion....$7,500 maximum, reduced as income rises
Private Pension Exclusion....$7,500 maximum, reduced as income rises
Social Security Exemption....Federal amount

VERMONT

Personal Income Tax Rates

All Taxpayers

25% of federal tax liability

Features

Personal Exemptions or Credits	Federal amount
Standard Deduction	Federal amount
Medical and Dental Deduction	Federal amount
Federal Income Tax Deduction	None
Public Pension Exclusion	None
Private Pension Exclusion	None
Social Security Exemption	Federal amount

VIRGINIA

Personal Income Tax Rates

All Taxpayers

Starting point: federal adjusted gross income
Brackets: 4
Lowest: 2% of first $3,000
Highest: 5.75% over $17,000

Features

Personal Exemptions or Credits	$800 each federal exemption $800 each person 65 or older
Standard Deduction	$3,000 single, $5,000 married joint return
Medical and Dental Deduction	Partial
Federal Income Tax Deduction	None
Public Pension Exclusion	None
Private Pension Exclusion	None
Social Security Exemption	Full
Other	Residents 62 to 64 may exclude up to $6,000 of income from any source; residents 65 or older may exclude up to $12,000 from any source. These exclusions are reduced by the amount of Social Security benefits the taxpayer receives.

WASHINGTON

The state does not tax personal income.

WEST VIRGINIA

Personal Income Tax Rates

Single or Married Filing Separately

Starting point: federal adjusted gross income
Brackets: 5
Lowest: 3% of first $10,000
Highest: 6.5% over $60,000

Features

Personal Exemptions or Credits	$2,000 each federal exemption
Standard Deduction	None
Medical and Dental Deduction	None
Federal Income Tax Deduction	None
Public Pension Exclusion	$2,000; public safety pensions fully exempt
Private Pension Exclusion	None
Social Security Exemption	Federal amount
Other	Each person over 65 may exclude up to $8,000 of income included in federal adjusted income, including pensions deductions.

WISCONSIN

Personal Income Tax Rates

Single or Married Filing Separately

Starting point: federal adjusted gross income
Brackets: 3
Lowest: 4.9% of first $7,500
Highest: 6.93% over $15,001

Features

Personal Exemptions or Credits	$50 credit, each dependent on federal return $25 credit, each taxpayer and spouse over 65
Standard Deduction	Maximum $5,200 single Maximum $8,900 married joint return
Medical and Dental Deduction	5% credit for expenses in excess of standard deduction
Federal Income Tax Deduction	None
Public Pension Exclusion	Federal and benefits from specified Wisconsin retirement systems
Private Pension Exclusion	None
Social Security Exemption	Federal amount

WYOMING

The state does not tax personal income.

Climate

"The fortunate people of the planet," John Kenneth Galbraith once wrote, "are those who live by the seasons. There is far more difference between a Vermont farm in the summer and that farm in the winter than there is between San Diego and São Paulo. This means that people who live where the seasons are good and strong have no need to travel; they can stay at home and let change come to them. This simple truth will one day be recognized and then we will see a great reverse migration from Florida to Maine and on into Quebec."

That extraordinary prediction may cause many a lacquered Sun Belt real estate saleswoman to put down her cellphone and say "Huh?" She can relax. Demographers forecast the march to the sun will continue well into the 21st century.

What else is new? Most of us say we prefer a mild, sunny climate. When asked where in the country these climates are, we point to the lower half of the Pacific Coast, the Desert Southwest, Florida, and anywhere along the South Atlantic and Gulf coasts. Sure enough, this area between 25 and 35 degrees latitude has been drawing older adults for decades.

But other places above the Sun Belt and hundreds of miles from beaches also are drawing older adults. Many of these locations see mild climates, too. The names of some may surprise you.

What always surprises is the variety of global climates found right here at home. Northern maritime, mild Mediterranean, southerly mountain, desert, tropical "paradise," desert highland, rugged northern continental, windward slope, leeward slope, and humid subtropical climates—name it and you'll meet up with it somewhere in the United States.

Climate can't be bought, built, remodeled, or relocated. A place's climate is there for keeps, and the weather events that make up its climate—rain, snow, heat, cold, drought, wind—will have a profound effect on the rest of your life.

FACTORS TO KEEP IN MIND

If you can live anywhere you wish and are open to all the variety this country offers, recognize that a combination of water, latitude and longitude, elevation, prevailing winds, mountains, and urban development lies behind any area's climate.

Water, particularly an ocean, takes the edge off temperature. It warms up slowly, holds much more heat than land, and cools more slowly. Places on the water tend to be cooler in summer and warmer in winter than others inland. The hottest it gets in July on the Santa Monica Pier in Los Angeles is 75°F; meanwhile, 15 miles north in the San Fernando Valley, it's 95°F. Golfers in Boston's western suburbs must store their clubs during the cold weather months from Thanksgiving to the onset of spring. Golfers 45 miles southeast on Cape Cod, with the Gulf Stream flowing by the beaches, can play almost all year-round.

Places located in the heartland see wide swings of temperature. These continental climates tend to be even more rigorous in the higher ***latitudes.*** The closer to the North Pole you get, the more exaggerated are the seasonal shifts because polar and very northerly locations undergo the greatest seasonal variation in the amount and intensity of sunlight.

In Alaska's Palmer–Wasilla area, for example, a December day is only 5 hours long, overcast with occasional snow. In late June, the day lengthens to 18 hours, the sun's heat is intense, and 50-pound cabbages show up in roadside markets.

Far to the southwest from the Alaskan interior, the solar energy pouring over Maui, Hawaii (20.52 N), in June is double what it is in December, but in Palmer–Wasilla (61.36 N) it is 20 times as great. Places in the north and far north, then, experience Siberian winters and short, sunlit summers as well.

Though some medical studies show reduced odds of heart disease and cancer the higher one lives above sea level, a higher ***elevation*** can have the same negative effect on comfort as higher latitude. Each 1,000 feet above sea level lowers a thermometer reading by 3.3 degrees. In New Mexico, there are just 3 degrees difference in annual average temperature between Clayton and Lordsburg, two places with similar elevations. But Clayton is on the edge of the plains while Lordsburg is 440 miles southwest in high desert. However, at two weather stations just 15 miles apart but differing in elevation by 4,700 feet, the average annual temperatures vary by 16 degrees.

To understand how ***prevailing winds*** influence climate, consider a pair of places 3,200 miles apart: Bellingham, Washington, and Bar Harbor, Maine. On their respective coasts, both sit high in northern latitudes and both peek through some of the foggiest mornings in the United States. You'd naturally suppose the two have similar climates. But Bellingham is milder because it is a landfall for air that has moved thousands of miles over the Pacific. Far inland in Washington State, even Wenatchee and Spokane feel the beneficial effects of the Pacific winds. Interior cities in the East, however, experience few consequences of the Atlantic save on rare occasions when the prevailing wind direction turns. Alas, this reversal often means a storm.

The only barriers big enough to deflect and channel winds, rain, and snow are ***mountains.*** Mountain people aren't relating folk tales when they tell visitors that the weather on one side of a mountain range is radically different from that on the other. In winter, the Great Divide shields Colorado Springs from much of the Arctic air that moves down the continent. In summer, the hidden, windward side of the city's mountain vista is a lush, evergreen parkland at lower elevations; the leeward side, where the city sits, a semiarid steppe descending to dry, shortgrass prairie.

Finally, ***urban development*** makes heat islands within the surrounding countryside. Downtown

Climate in Brief

Chambers of commerce and publishers of retirement guidebooks that quote annual average temperatures are misleading. By this measure, San Diego, California, and Oxford, Mississippi, are identical at 60°F.

Beware of promoters highlighting winter temperatures but excluding summer temperatures *adjusted upward by humidity.* One out of three places profiled in this book has a July *humidex* (air temperature heightened by relative humidity) topping 100°F. And the dry Desert Southwest isn't immune: Lake Havasu City, Arizona's humidex is 123°F; Palm Springs, California's is 118°F; and Scottsdale, Arizona's, is 115°F.

Consider the psychological or "seasonal affect" of certain climates. Locations in the Pacific Northwest and Great Lakes area see cloudy skies 3 out of 4 days in the year. Wet days are strongly associated with cloudiness. High latitudes mean much earlier winter darkness. And don't discount periodic hazards such as Rocky Mountain snows, Florida afternoon thunderstorms, Ozark ice storms, and California coastal sea fogs and low stratus. They're nearly everywhere.

If climate is everything to you, consider living in two places. June to October in State College, Pennsylvania, for example, and November to May in Sebring–Avon Park, Florida. Or rotate Yuma, Arizona, winters with Montrose, Colorado, summers. The costs of living in two inexpensive places are still less than the costs in year-round paradise climates of coastal southern California and Hawaii. Living in two places has a less obvious benefit: You have alternating senses of place and sets of friendships.

Scottsdale, Arizona, has night temperatures 8 degrees warmer than they were 50 years ago when the area was a 1-square-mile farming cluster with 2,000 people. Population here has increased 85-fold, concrete and asphalt store the sun's radiant energy better than desert sand ever did, and automobile pollution is trapped overhead in a high-pressure cell. Wind speed, visibility, sunshine, and heating needs are less in the center of cities than in nearby country, but temperature, cloudiness, thunderstorm frequency, and air pollution levels are higher.

CLIMATE REGIONS

Mountains indeed mark the climate regions of the United States. The Pacific Coast is mild and the northern portion of the Great Plains is rigorous. The Great Basin between the Cascade and Sierra Nevada ranges to the west and the Rocky Mountains to the east is dry. Some of the best climates for variety and mildness are found in the southern part of this area. The southern part of the Appalachian Mountains, too, offers mild and variable climates.

Millions of Americans live in the Great Plains and Central Lowlands, ironically the least comfortable region. If you live in the northern part, you're hit by severe winters and hot, humid summers with springs and autumns that are all too short. If you live in the southern part, winters are milder, springs and autumns are longer, but the summer air hits you in the face like a warm, wet towel.

The climate of the East Coast is like the Central Lowlands, but milder and somewhat damper. On the coast, winters are milder and summers are noticeably cooler. Retirement places with excellent climates are here, especially New Jersey's Cape May and Ocean counties, Ocean City in Maryland, and Rehoboth Bay–Indian River Bay in southern Delaware.

The high country that includes the Rockies, the Cascades, the Sierra Nevadas, and the northern half of the Appalachians is home to resort areas owing to the cool, crisp, sunny summers with cold nights and winters that produce snow for outdoor sports. Several places in the valleys are popular with older adults who prefer a stimulating yet not too mild climate.

Hawaii is the only state situated in the tropical zone, officially defined as any area where temperatures don't drop below 64°F. These islands experience small temperature changes, with summer averaging only 4 to 8 degrees higher than winter. Moisture-bearing trade winds from over the Pacific provide a system of natural ventilation for the heat associated with these tropical climates.

SO, WHAT'S COMFORTABLE?

Mop the sweat from pulling a balky lawnmower's starter cord a dozen times on a July afternoon, hack away at the ice on the car's windshield one morning in January, or look out the window on a sodden and gray day and you're forgiven for fantasizing about a place where it's never hot or cold and always bright.

It is a fantasy, indeed. Not only would you likely get bored with an endless sequence of identically dry sunny days with tepid temperatures, you'd also find that none of the places profiled here have climates that match this pattern 365 days a year.

Temperature

Beware of Chamber of Commerce blandishments about a place's annual average temperature. San Francisco's is 57°F. So is St. Louis's. But San Francisco enjoys both a diurnal (24-hour) temperature range of 12 degrees and an annual range (the difference between January's and July's average temperatures) of 12 degrees. St. Louis has a diurnal range of 17 degrees and an annual range of 47 degrees. The temperature swings in these two cities highlight the difference between a marine climate and a continental climate. San Francisco's climate is somewhat cool and remarkably stable year-round. St. Louis's is neither.

Among retirement regions, the greatest annual temperature ranges (up to 77 degrees) are found in the North Woods, the Rocky Mountains, and northern parts of New England. The greatest diurnal temperature swings (up to 40 degrees) are in high desert parts of the Rio Grande and Desert Southwest regions. The smallest diurnal and annual temperature swings are in Hawaii and along the Pacific Coast.

Snowy Places

Most locations profiled in these pages see less than 6 inches of snow, and 34 places experience not even a trace. But some retirement places rated get a bit more than that. Below are 17 that get more than 6 feet in a normal year:

PLACE	ANNUAL SNOWFALL
Palmer–Wasilla, AK	130 inches
Pagosa Springs, CO	116 inches
Flagstaff, AZ	101 inches
Leelanau Peninsula, MI	98 inches
Woodstock, VT	89 inches
Sandpoint–Lake Pend Oreille, ID	89 inches
Petoskey–Harbor Springs, MI	88 inches
Traverse City, MI	88 inches
Jackson Hole, WY	87 inches
Lake Placid, NY	86 inches
McCall, ID	86 inches
St. Jay–Northeast Kingdom, VT	86 inches
Salida, CO	86 inches
Burlington, VT	77 inches
Hanover, NH	77 inches
Bar Harbor, ME	75 inches
Durango, CO	73 inches

Source: NOAA, Climatography of the United States.

Cloudy Places

A day is *clear* if clouds form less than 30 percent of the daytime sky, *partly cloudy* if they form 40 to 70 percent of it, and *cloudy* if they form more than 80 percent. Some spots see cloudiness 2 out of every 3 of their days.

PLACE	ANNUAL CLOUDY DAYS
Palmer–Wasilla, AK	240
Newport–Lincoln City, OR	238
Florence, OR	237
Brookings–Gold Beach, OR	236
Anacortes, WA	231
Bellingham, WA	231
San Juan Islands, WA	231
Port Townsend, WA	230
Port Angeles–Sequim, WA	229
Whidbey Island, WA	228
Kalispell–Flathead Valley, MT	213
Polson–Mission Valley, MT	213
Petoskey–Harbor Springs, MI	210
Traverse City, MI	210
Hamilton–Bitterroot Valley, MT	208

Source: NOAA, Local Climatological Data. Some of the above figures come from the nearest "First Order" station.

Damp Places

Thanks to the humidity, cars can be sponged clean in Florida using nothing more than the heavy morning dew, and mushrooms on the Pacific Northwest coast get enormous quickly.

PLACE	RELATIVE HUMIDITY
Brookings–Gold Beach, OR	75%
Florence, OR	75%
Hattiesburg, MS	75%
Newport–Lincoln City, OR	75%
Port Angeles–Sequim, WA	74%
Port Townsend, WA	74%
Brown County, IN	73%
Iowa City, IA	73%
Leelanau Peninsula, MI	73%
Madison, WI	73%
Natchitoches, LA	73%
Maui, HI	72%
Columbia, MO	72%
Beaufort–Bogue Banks, NC	71%
Summerville, SC	71%
Bellingham, WA	70%
San Juan Islands, WA	70%
Whidbey Island, WA	70%

Source: NOAA, Local Climatological Data. Figures are annual averages nearest to noon. Some of the above figures come from the closest "First Order" station.

Dry Places

In some locations with low humidity, it's cheaper and more efficient to cool interiors with evaporative air conditioners, locally called "swamp coolers," rather than the more expensive refrigerated air conditioners.

PLACE	RELATIVE HUMIDITY
Henderson, NV	24%
Pahrump Valley, NV	24%
St. George–Zion, UT	24%
Tucson, AZ	30%
Wickenburg, AZ	31%
Apache Junction, AZ	32%
Bullhead City, AZ	32%
Kingman, AZ	32%
Lake Havasu City, AZ	32%
Mesa, AZ	32%
Palm Springs–Coachella Valley, CA	32%
Scottsdale, AZ	32%
Victorville–Apple Valley, CA	32%
Yuma, AZ	32%

Source: NOAA, Local Climatological Data. Figures are annual averages nearest to noon. Some of the above figures come from the nearest "First Order" station.

Humidity

After air temperature, humidity is the major factor in climatic comfort. Anyone who has sweated out a hot, humid summer knows humidity heightens heat. In hot, humid climates, heat is retained in the damp air even after the sunset, resulting in nights that are almost as hot as the days.

Wind Chill

Wind chill is the same thing as heat loss. Anyone who has turned their face away from a stiff winter blow swears to this. When the wind rises over 5 miles per hour and the thermometer reads 45°F or less, you'll start to feel temperatures on exposed skin colder than still air.

Approaching a Climatic Ideal

Is searching for the ideal year-round retirement climate an illusion like the quest for perfect health, an honest man, or the Holy Grail?

Perhaps it is. One hundred years ago, the Santa Fe Railroad's *Healthseeker* guidebook advised newcomers to Arizona to winter in Phoenix but head north to Flagstaff's 7,000-foot elevation for the summer. Thousands still take that advice, and many bypass Flagstaff for a place farther north, such as in the Idaho panhandle or the Utah or Colorado Rockies.

In Florida, thousands of retired persons vacate the Sunshine State's summers for a cottage on the Jersey Shore, the New England coast, or a cabin in the southern Appalachians. Still others, absolutely bored by the unvarying paradise-like climate in the Virgin Islands or Hawaii, head back to the mainland for a fix of four-season weather.

This migration isn't exclusively American. Older adults from northern Europe who live in Spain, southern Italy, Greece, or North Africa routinely pack up and return to their native country for a summer climate that's milder than the one on the Mediterranean coast.

Having acknowledged all this, it is still possible to rate places that approach a climatic ideal by pointing to conditions that detract from maximum comfort.

SCORING: CLIMATE

Mild doesn't mean a winterless, perpetually Mediterranean climate. It is simply the absence of great variations or extremes of temperature. As we get older, we tend to be better off in comfortable, stable weather conditions than we are in climates that make large physiological demands and where radical weather changes come on quickly.

WINTER MILDNESS

To measure how mild the winters are, the temperature differences from a high of 65°F each month from November through April, adjusted by wind chill, are totaled. Key West, Florida, has a winter mildness score of 100; Alamogordo, New Mexico's is 50; and Pagosa Springs, Colorado, gets a score of 0. They are respectively the best, average, and worst for winter mildness.

SUMMER MILDNESS

To measure how mild the summers are, the temperature differences from a high of 65°F each month from May through October, adjusted by humidity, are totaled. Bozeman, a college town high in the Montana Rockies, gets a perfect 100; Edenton, on North Carolina's Albemarle coast, gets 50; and Lake Havasu City and Bullhead City, along the Colorado River in westernmost Arizona, each earn a lowly 1. They are respectively the best, average, and worst for summer mildness.

HAZARD FREE

Because they are predictable from decades of weather records, snow, high wind, and thunderstorms are normal but inconvenient weather events in most retirement places. To score for relative freedom from these hazards, *Retirement Places Rated* weights snow three times as heavily as thunderstorms and thunderstorms twice as heavily as wind. Santa Barbara, California's 100 score is best; Tryon, North Carolina, in the Southern Highlands is average at 50; and Salida, Colorado, with 0, is worst.

SEASONAL AFFECT

To measure the local weather's psychological impact, the number of cloudy (more than 80 percent cloud cover) and wet (precipitation greater than 0.1 inch) days are weighted twice as heavily as the number of fog (visibility less than ½ mile) days, and fog days are weighted twice as heavily as latitude. The Palm Springs–Coachella Valley area in California earns a perfect 100; Myrtle Beach, South Carolina, gets 50; and Palmer–Wasilla, Alaska's score is 0. They are respectively the best, average, and worst for seasonal affect.

RANKINGS: CLIMATE

To rank places for mild climate, four factors get equal weight: (1) **summer mildness;** (2) **winter mildness;** (3) **seasonal affect, or the psychological impact of cloudiness, darkness, fog, and rain;** and (4) **hazard free, or the relative absence of snow, thunderstorms, and high wind.** A place's score is its percentile on a scale of 0 to 100 corresponding to its rank. Locations with tie scores get the same rank and are listed alphabetically.

Retirement Places from First to Last

RANK	PLACE	SCORE
1.	North County San Diego, CA	100.0
2.	Carmel–Pebble Beach, CA	99.5
3.	Mendocino–Fort Bragg, CA	99.0
4.	Santa Barbara, CA	98.5
5.	Laguna Beach–Dana Point, CA	98.0
6.	Morro Bay–Cambria, CA	97.5
7.	Kauai, HI	97.0
8.	Maui, HI	96.5
9.	Santa Rosa, CA	96.0
10.	Yuma, AZ	95.5
11.	Paradise–Magalia, CA	95.0
12.	Palm Springs–Coachella Valley, CA	94.0
12.	Scottsdale, AZ	94.0
14.	Bullhead City, AZ	93.5
15.	Lake Havasu City, AZ	93.0
16.	Melbourne–Palm Bay, FL	92.5
17.	Apache Junction, AZ	92.0
18.	Mesa, AZ	91.5
19.	Largo, FL	91.0
20.	Mission–McAllen–Alamo, TX	90.5
21.	Fort Myers–Cape Coral, FL	89.6
23.	New Port Richey, FL	89.1
21.	Sarasota, FL	89.6
24.	Kingman, AZ	88.6
25.	Apalachicola, FL	87.6
25.	Brookings–Gold Beach, OR	87.6

RANK	PLACE	SCORE
27.	Bradenton, FL	87.1
28.	St. Augustine, FL	86.6
29.	St. Simons–Jekyll Islands, GA	86.1
30.	Port Angeles–Sequim, WA	85.6
31.	Port Townsend, WA	85.1
32.	Henderson, NV	84.6
33.	Leesburg–Mount Dora, FL	84.1
34.	Victorville–Apple Valley, CA	83.6
35.	Naples, FL	83.1
36.	Key West, FL	82.6
37.	Lakeland–Winter Haven, FL	82.1
38.	Florence, OR	80.6
38.	Port Charlotte, FL	80.6
38.	Wickenburg, AZ	80.6
41.	Daytona Beach, FL	80.1
42.	Kissimmee–St. Cloud, FL	79.7
43.	Sonora–Twain Harte, CA	79.2
44.	Newport–Lincoln City, OR	78.2
44.	Whidbey Island, WA	78.2
46.	Rockport–Aransas Pass, TX	77.7
47.	Ruidoso, NM	77.2
48.	Inverness, FL	76.7
49.	Bisbee, AZ	76.2
50.	Vero Beach, FL	75.7
51.	Alpine–Big Bend, TX	75.2
52.	Gainesville, FL	74.2
52.	San Juan Islands, WA	74.2
54.	Sebring–Avon Park, FL	73.7
55.	Tucson, AZ	73.2
56.	Hilton Head Island, SC	72.7
57.	Ocala, FL	72.2
58.	Charleston, SC	71.2
58.	Kerrville, TX	71.2
60.	Boca Raton, FL	70.7
61.	Anacortes, WA	70.2
62.	Carson City–Carson Valley, NV	69.8
63.	Boerne, TX	68.8
63.	Marble Falls–Lake LBJ, TX	68.8
65.	Panama City, FL	68.3
66.	Beaufort, SC	67.8
67.	Bellingham, WA	66.8
67.	New Braunfels, TX	66.8
69.	Savannah, GA	66.3
70.	Fredericksburg, TX	65.8
71.	Grass Valley–Nevada City, CA	64.8
71.	Reno–Sparks, NV	64.8
73.	Trinity Peninsula, TX	64.3
74.	Mariposa, CA	63.8
75.	Georgetown, TX	63.3
76.	Oakhurst–Coarsegold, CA	62.8
77.	Thomasville, GA	62.3
78.	Grants Pass, OR	60.8
78.	Prescott–Prescott Valley, AZ	60.8
78.	St. George–Zion, UT	60.8
81.	Bay St. Louis–Pass Christian, MS	60.3
82.	Medford–Ashland, OR	59.4
82.	Pahrump Valley, NV	59.4
84.	Lake Conroe, TX	58.9
85.	Alamogordo, NM	58.4
86.	Amador County, CA	57.9
87.	Aiken, SC	57.4
88.	Athens, GA	56.4
88.	Eufaula, AL	56.4
90.	Pensacola, FL	55.9
91.	Myrtle Beach, SC	55.4
92.	Western St. Tammany Parish, LA	54.9
93.	Cedar Creek Lake, TX	54.4
94.	Payson, AZ	53.9
95.	Beaufort–Bogue Banks, NC	52.9
95.	Sedona, AZ	52.9
97.	Virginia Beach, VA	52.4
98.	Fairhope–Gulf Shores, AL	51.9
99.	Southport–Brunswick Islands, NC	51.4
100.	Bend, OR	50.0
100.	Las Vegas, NM	50.0
100.	Santa Fe, NM	50.0
103.	Dare Outer Banks, NC	48.5
103.	Hot Springs, AR	48.5
103.	Las Cruces, NM	48.5
106.	Silver City, NM	47.5
106.	Summerville, SC	47.5
108.	Wimberley, TX	47.0
109.	Edenton, NC	46.0
109.	Lower Cape May, NJ	46.0
111.	Rio Rancho, NM	45.5
112.	Oxford, MS	45.0
113.	Pendleton District, SC	44.5
114.	Conway, SC	43.5
114.	Smith Mountain Lake, VA	43.5
116.	Montrose, CO	43.0
117.	Hattiesburg, MS	42.5
118.	Natchitoches, LA	42.0
119.	Delta County, CO	41.5
120.	Polson–Mission Valley, MT	41.0
121.	Southern Pines–Pinehurst, NC	40.5
122.	Tryon, NC	40.0
123.	Easton–St. Michaels, MD	39.6
124.	Cottonwood–Verde Valley, AZ	38.6
124.	Northern Neck, VA	38.6
126.	Annapolis, MD	37.6
126.	Chapel Hill–Carrboro, NC	37.6
128.	Asheville, NC	36.1
128.	Hamilton–Bitterroot Valley, MT	36.1
128.	Ocean City, MD	36.1
131.	Kalispell–Flathead Valley, MT	35.6
132.	New Bern, NC	35.1
133.	Chestertown, MD	34.1
133.	Flagstaff, AZ	34.1
135.	Lake of the Cherokees, OK	33.1
135.	Roswell, NM	33.1
137.	Charlottesville, VA	31.6
137.	Wenatchee, WA	31.6
137.	Williamsburg, VA	31.6
140.	Martha's Vineyard, MA	30.6
140.	Rehoboth Bay–Indian River Bay, DE	30.6
142.	Grand Junction, CO	30.1
143.	Fredericksburg–Spotsylvania, VA	29.7
144.	Colorado Springs, CO	28.2
144.	Fort Collins–Loveland, CO	28.2
144.	McCall, ID	28.2
147.	Murray–Kentucky Lake, KY	27.7
148.	Rabun County, GA	27.2
149.	Charles Town–Shepherdstown, WV	26.7
150.	Fayetteville, AR	26.2
151.	Toms River–Barnegat Bay, NJ	25.7
152.	Hendersonville–East Flat Rock, NC	25.2
153.	Eureka Springs, AR	24.7
154.	East End Long Island, NY	23.7
154.	Taos, NM	23.7
156.	Norfork Lake, AR	22.7
156.	Pagosa Springs, CO	22.7
158.	Middle Cape Cod, MA	22.2
159.	Durango, CO	21.7
160.	Maryville, TN	21.2
161.	Brevard, NC	20.7
162.	Table Rock Lake, MO	20.2
163.	Bozeman, MT	19.8
164.	Crossville, TN	18.8
164.	Ketchum–Sun Valley, ID	18.8

continued

Retirement Places from First to Last (cont.)

RANK	PLACE	SCORE
166.	Door Peninsula, WI	17.8
166.	State College, PA	17.8
168.	Lake of the Ozarks, MO	17.3
169.	Coeur d'Alene, ID	16.8
170.	Oscoda–Huron Shore, MI	16.3
171.	Front Royal, VA	15.8
172.	Boone–Blowing Rock, NC	15.3
173.	Branson, MO	14.8
174.	Park City, UT	14.3
175.	Pike County, PA	13.8
176.	Chewelah, WA	13.3
177.	Eagle River–Woodruff, WI	12.8
178.	Cedar City, UT	12.3
179.	Jackson Hole, WY	11.3
179.	York Beaches, ME	11.3
181.	Litchfield Hills, CT	10.8
182.	Southern Berkshire County, MA	10.3
183.	Camden, ME	9.9
184.	Bar Harbor, ME	9.4
185.	Traverse City, MI	8.9
186.	Berkeley Springs, WV	8.4
187.	Lake Winnipesaukee, NH	7.9
188.	Sandpoint–Lake Pend Oreille, ID	7.4
189.	Palmer–Wasilla, AK	6.9
190.	Northampton–Amherst, MA	6.4
191.	Columbia, MO	5.9
192.	Lake Placid, NY	5.4
193.	St. Jay–Northeast Kingdom, VT	4.9
194.	Iowa City, IA	4.4
195.	Hanover, NH	3.9
196.	Madison, WI	3.4
197.	Leelanau Peninsula, MI	2.4
197.	Petoskey–Harbor Springs, MI	2.4
199.	Burlington, VT	1.9
200.	Woodstock, VT	1.4
201.	Brown County, IN	0.9
202.	Salida, CO	0.4
203.	Monadnock Region, NH	0.0

PLACE PROFILES: CLIMATE

The following pages describe climate at weather stations in 203 places. Temperature and precipitation data come from the National Oceanic and Atmospheric Administration (NOAA) *Series 20* publications. Data for humidity, wind speed, days with fog and thunderstorms, as well as the clear, partly cloudy, and cloudy days are derived from the closest station reporting in NOAA's *Local Climatological Data.*

The temperature and precipitation data are NOAA's "30-Year Normals" or averages collected over 3 decades. Every 10 years, the data for the new decade are added into the normal, and the data for the earliest 10 years are dropped to flatten out anomalies and weather extremes. Events such as a freak blizzard in Albuquerque or a heat wave that might occur once every 50 years in Coeur d'Alene have little effect on each place's 30-year normals.

The prose summaries describe each place's location and its distinctive climate and landscape features. Location details the place's elevation and its latitude north of the equator and longitude west of Greenwich, England. With these coordinates, you can roughly determine whether one place is farther north, south, east, or west from another.

When landscape is described, it is usually how the terrain influences a place's climate and what varieties of vegetation grow there naturally. Few people would deny that landscape is an important element on its own; for many, it is as important as climate. Some prefer mountains or seacoasts, others rolling hills or flatwoods forests, while still others favor stark desert vistas. Rather than rating landscapes, they are described briefly here and the decision left up to you.

The descriptions for climate are capsule summaries of each location's type and general features. The tables to the right of each description include monthly high and low temperatures, relative humidity observed nearest to noon, wind speed, precipitation, and snowfall. Each profile also includes a visual legend for the number of days per year that a place experiences such conditions as a partly cloudy sky, temperatures below zero, and thunderstorms (see the sample legend below).

Clear means annual number of clear days [days with less than 30% cloud cover]

Partly Cloudy means annual number of partly cloudy days [days with less than 70% but greater than 30% cloud cover]

Cloudy means annual number of cloudy days [days with greater than 70% cloud cover]

90° — 90° or above means annual number of days temperature tops 90° F

32° — 32° or below means annual number of days temperature hits freezing

0° — 0° or below means annual number of days temperature hits 0°

Foggy days means annual number of days fog limits visibility

Wet days means annual number of days precipitation exceeds .1 inch

Thunderstorms means annual number of days with one or more storm cells

A star (★) preceding a place's name highlights it as one of the top 30 places for climate mildness.

Aiken, SC

Location: 33.33 N and 81.43 W at 490 feet, on the western border of the state directly across the Savannah River from Augusta, Georgia. Atlanta is 150 miles west.

Landscape: Generally flat, with gentle slopes and local relief of less than 100 feet. Aiken is about 500 feet above sea level near the fall line dividing the upcountry Piedmont Plateau and the low country coastal plain. To the west are low-rise sandhills. The trees are a mixed forest of southern yellow pine, oak, and hickory.

Climate: Warm and mild, with occasional hot spells. Precipitation usually falls as rain and is evenly distributed throughout the year. Winters are mild and measurable snow is a rarity and remains on the ground only a short time. While frosts are typical from late fall to early spring, in 100 years of weather records, a temperature of 0°F or colder has never been reached.

Summer mildness: 29 **Seasonal affect:** 49
Winter mildness: 63 **Hazard free:** 69
Score: 57.4 **Rank:** 87

113
108
144
90° 65
32° 46
0° 0
34
72
43

	High °F	Low °F	Hum %	Wind mph	Precip inches	Snow inches
JAN	57	33	56	7.4	4.6	0.2
FEB	61	35	52	8.0	4.5	1.1
MAR	70	43	52	8.1	5.3	0.2
APR	78	49	48	7.9	3.8	0
MAY	84	58	55	6.9	4.2	0
JUN	90	65	59	6.4	5.1	0
JUL	92	69	63	5.9	5.2	0
AUG	91	68	64	5.7	5.3	0
SEP	86	63	62	6.1	3.5	0
OCT	77	51	56	6.5	2.8	0
NOV	69	42	53	6.8	2.9	0
DEC	60	35	55	7.3	3.8	0.3

Alamogordo, NM

Location: 32.54 N and 105.57 W at 4,303 feet, in the south-central part of the state, 200 miles south of Albuquerque and 55 miles north of El Paso, Texas.

Landscape: Near the western base of the Sacramento Mountains that peak around 4,500 feet and form the eastern rim of the Tularosa Basin. The area is typical high desert with native vegetation such as mesquite and creosote bush. White gypsum dunes of the White Sands National Monument stretch across the west toward the San Andreas Mountains. Juniper and pinyon pine forests are in higher elevations and in the Lincoln National Forest.

Climate: Desert character with long, hot, bright, and usually dry summers. Temperature changes from daytime highs to nighttime lows can be dramatic at all seasons. Rains are widespread and usually gentle except for July and August when they typically come in heavy thunderstorms. Winters are moderate but subject to occasional frosts from November through March. Infrequent snowfalls melt within days.

Summer mildness: 16 **Seasonal affect:** 92
Winter mildness: 50 **Hazard free:** 54
Score: 58.4 **Rank:** 85

193
100
72
90° 103
32° 84
0° 0
2
27
36

	High °F	Low °F	Hum %	Wind mph	Precip inches	Snow inches
JAN	57	28	42	8.4	0.7	1.7
FEB	62	32	34	9.2	0.5	1.0
MAR	69	38	27	11.0	0.5	0.5
APR	78	45	21	11.1	0.3	0
MAY	87	54	21	10.3	0.5	0
JUN	95	62	23	9.3	0.9	0
JUL	95	66	35	8.3	2.2	0
AUG	92	64	39	7.8	2.4	0
SEP	86	58	41	7.6	2.0	0
OCT	78	47	36	7.5	1.3	0
NOV	66	36	37	8.0	0.7	0
DEC	58	29	42	7.9	0.8	1.1

Alpine–Big Bend, TX

Location: 30.21 N and 103.39 W at 4,480 feet, in west Texas, 190 miles southeast of El Paso and 75 miles north of the Rio Grande and Mexico.

Landscape: Located in a high desert valley flanked by the Davis Mountains to the north and the Glass Mountains to the east. Dry canyons and extensive, sparse rangeland contrast with the forests of the mountain elevations. In the valleys and on the lower slopes are many varieties of cactus, and after a soaking rain wildflowers are abundant.

Climate: Chihuahuan Desert moderated by altitude. Summers are long and sunny. Winters are brief and mild, though subject to occasional morning frosts, the first of which occurs in early November and the last in early April. Precipitation averages 17 inches annually, with most rains coming July to September afternoons from spectacular thunderheads that build over the mountains and move across the countryside.

Summer mildness: 34 **Seasonal affect:** 92
Winter mildness: 57 **Hazard free:** 57
Score: 75.2 **Rank:** 51

193
100
72
90° 67
32° 60
0° 0
2
28
36

	High °F	Low °F	Hum %	Wind mph	Precip inches	Snow inches
JAN	61	30	42	8.4	0.5	1.1
FEB	65	33	34	9.2	0.5	1.1
MAR	72	39	27	11.0	0.4	0
APR	80	46	21	11.1	0.5	0
MAY	86	54	21	10.3	1.2	0
JUN	90	61	23	9.3	2.2	0
JUL	89	63	35	8.3	2.7	0
AUG	88	61	39	7.8	3.0	0
SEP	83	57	41	7.6	3.3	0
OCT	78	47	36	7.5	1.5	0
NOV	69	38	37	8.0	0.6	0
DEC	62	32	42	7.9	0.5	0.3

★ = *in the top 30 places for climate mildness.*

Amador County, CA

Location: The weather station is the county seat of Jackson, 38.21 N and 120.46 W at 1,975 feet, 45 miles southeast of Sacramento and 100 miles southwest of Reno, Nevada.

Landscape: In the higher grassy foothills of the western slope of the Sierra Nevadas, with steep gradients from mountain to valley. Canyons cut the forested slope giving dramatic relief. Snow-fed rivers, lakes, and reservoirs promote wildflowers and low-growing shrubs. Digger pine and blue oak are found at higher elevations.

Climate: Sierran Forest, in the transition zone between the dry western desert and the wetter Pacific Coast. Mountain temperature changes can vary greatly both daily and seasonally. Prevailing west winds together with elevation influence local conditions. The summers are long, hot, and generally dry. About half of the annual precipitation falls as snow. Frost, as an indicator of the winter season, occurs from early November to late April.

Summer mildness: 16 **Seasonal affect:** 70
Winter mildness: 60 **Hazard free:** 64
Score: 57.9 **Rank:** 86

189
75
100
90° 59
32° 77
0° 0
34
49
14

	High °F	Low °F	Hum %	Wind mph	Precip inches	Snow inches
JAN	57	34	80	7.3	5.2	5.3
FEB	62	37	75	7.4	4.4	3.1
MAR	65	39	65	7.9	5.0	3.0
APR	72	42	55	8.3	2.7	0
MAY	81	47	48	8.3	0.7	0
JUN	90	52	44	8.5	0.3	0
JUL	97	56	44	9.5	0.2	0
AUG	96	55	45	8.9	0.2	0
SEP	90	52	45	7.3	0.6	0
OCT	80	46	53	6.6	1.8	0
NOV	65	40	65	6.9	4.5	0
DEC	57	35	77	7.2	4.5	2.7

Anacortes, WA

Location: 48.30 N and 122.36 W at 75 feet, on Fidalgo Island in upper Puget Sound. Via a bridge eastward to the mainland, Seattle is 80 miles south and Vancouver, British Columbia, is 90 miles north.

Landscape: Fidalgo Island is relatively big with many low-rise hills. The original coniferous forest of Sitka-spruce and western hemlock has largely given way to fruit farms. The shoreline has many small harbors and embayments. Distantly visible on the mainland to the east are Mount Baker and the North Cascade Mountains.

Climate: Marine, characterized by moderate temperatures, a pronounced rainy season, and constant cloud cover during the winter. Anacortes is modified by its position within the rain shadow of the Olympic Mountain range to the south, resulting in more sun and less rain than other Pacific Coast places. Summers are pleasantly cool with low precipitation. Winter days are mild with prevailing temperatures in the 40s; nights are chilly.

Summer mildness: 97 **Seasonal affect:** 0
Winter mildness: 59 **Hazard free:** 75
Score: 70.2 **Rank:** 61

50
84
231
90° 0
32° 68
0° 0
90
95
5

	High °F	Low °F	Hum %	Wind mph	Precip inches	Snow inches
JAN	45	34	77	7.1	3.6	5.2
FEB	49	36	74	7.2	2.5	1.3
MAR	52	38	70	7.4	2.1	2.4
APR	56	41	67	7.4	1.8	0
MAY	62	46	64	6.9	1.6	0
JUN	67	50	62	6.7	1.3	0
JUL	71	52	62	6.2	1.0	0
AUG	72	52	63	6.0	1.0	0
SEP	67	49	68	5.7	1.5	0
OCT	59	44	75	5.9	2.3	0
NOV	50	39	78	6.9	3.6	0
DEC	46	35	80	7.3	3.8	4.4

Annapolis, MD

Location: 38.58 N and 76.29 W at 41 feet, on the Severn River near its mouth on the western shore of the Chesapeake Bay. Baltimore is 27 miles northwest, and Washington, D.C., 35 miles southwest.

Landscape: The wide Severn River drains low, long rolling hills into the upper Bay. The surrounding area is extensively developed suburban and agricultural land. Whatever native vegetation remains flourishes in the mild winters and hot summers of the coastal plains and are typically southern trees, such as the loblolly pine and the magnolia found in the southeastern mixed forest of broadleaf deciduous and needleleaf evergreen trees.

Climate: Subtropical with a definite marine influence. Summer days are hot and humid, though a Bay breeze often lifts in the afternoons. Winters are overcast, chilly and rainy. Frost comes as soon as November 1 and departs in early April. Snowfalls are brief and melt within hours. Spring arrives early for this latitude.

Summer mildness: 57 **Seasonal affect:** 40
Winter mildness: 42 **Hazard free:** 38
Score: 37.6 **Rank:** 126

107
108
150
90° 28
32° 93
0° 0
26
72
28

	High °F	Low °F	Hum %	Wind mph	Precip inches	Snow inches
JAN	42	25	57	9.7	3.3	4.5
FEB	45	27	54	10.3	3.2	5.3
MAR	55	35	50	10.9	3.6	2.6
APR	66	44	49	10.6	3.4	0
MAY	76	54	53	9.2	4.1	0
JUN	84	63	52	8.5	3.4	0
JUL	88	68	53	8.0	3.6	0
AUG	86	67	56	7.8	3.9	0
SEP	80	60	55	8.0	3.3	0
OCT	69	48	54	8.7	3.3	0
NOV	58	39	55	9.3	3.5	0
DEC	47	30	57	9.3	3.4	2.0

★ = *in the top 30 places for climate mildness.*

★ Apache Junction, AZ

Location: 33.25 N and 111.33 W at 1,719 feet in the central Salt River Valley, 25 miles east of Phoenix.

Landscape: Lying within the northern fringe of the Sonoran desert, and surrounded by mountain ranges, including the famous Superstition Mountains to the east. Tonto National Forest lies to the north and east. The surrounding countryside varies from barren rocky waste to fields of cactus and exotic desert vegetation interspersed with mountains and mesas of varied-colored rocks. Creosote bush is common, and paloverde trees, and many varieties of cactus such as cholla, night-blooming cereus, and the giant saguaro flourish.

Climate: Desert. Low humidity levels and clear, sunny, and windless days are the norm. Hot and dry in summer, when daytime temperatures often exceed 100°F. Winters are mild with occasional cold, even below-freezing nights. December 4 brings the first frost, while mid-February is usually the last. The thunderstorm season is July and August when rains are heavy; otherwise, most days are clear and calm.

Summer mildness: 3 **Seasonal affect:** 98
Winter mildness: 77 **Hazard free:** 96
Score: 92.0 **Rank:** 17

	212
	84
	69
90°	163
32°	20
0°	0
	2
	19
	24

	High °F	Low °F	Hum %	Wind mph	Precip inches	Snow inches
JAN	66	40	45	5.3	0.8	0
FEB	71	43	39	5.9	0.8	0
MAR	76	47	34	6.7	0.9	0
APR	84	53	23	7.0	0.3	0
MAY	93	60	18	7.1	0.2	0
JUN	103	68	16	6.8	0.1	0
JUL	106	77	28	7.2	0.9	0
AUG	103	76	33	6.7	1.1	0
SEP	98	69	31	6.3	0.9	0
OCT	88	58	31	5.8	0.7	0
NOV	75	47	37	5.4	0.8	0
DEC	67	40	46	5.1	1.1	0

★ Apalachicola, FL

Location: 29.43 N and 84.59 W at 30 feet at the mouth of the Apalachicola River on Apalachicola Bay and the Gulf of Mexico, 65 miles southwest of Tallahassee, the state capital.

Landscape: Situated in the midst of Florida's flat and irregular outer coastal plain. Much of the area is gently sloping, but nowhere is there relief greater than 100 feet. Marshes, swamps, and lakes are common. The trees include evergreen oaks, short palm, and members of the magnolia and laurel families.

Climate: Subtropical, with warm summers with sporadic heavy thunderstorms and humidity slightly tempered by sea breezes. Winters are extremely mild though somewhat cool, with unpredictable, brief cold spells.

Summer mildness: 38 **Seasonal affect:** 55
Winter mildness: 81 **Hazard free:** 86
Score: 87.6 **Rank:** 25

	106
	123
	136
90°	67
32°	12
0°	0
	178
	66
	68

	High °F	Low °F	Hum %	Wind mph	Precip inches	Snow inches
JAN	61	39	72	9.0	3.9	0
FEB	63	41	70	9.4	3.8	0
MAR	69	48	71	9.7	4.3	0
APR	76	55	71	9.5	2.7	0
MAY	82	62	73	8.6	2.7	0
JUN	87	69	73	7.6	4.6	0
JUL	88	72	76	7.0	7.4	0
AUG	88	71	78	6.7	7.5	0
SEP	86	68	75	7.6	7.5	0
OCT	79	56	70	7.9	3.4	0
NOV	71	48	72	8.4	3.2	0
DEC	64	41	74	8.9	4.1	0

Asheville, NC

Location: 35.36 N and 82.33 W at 2,134 feet, in western North Carolina. Charlotte is 120 miles east, and Knoxville, Tennessee, is 120 miles west.

Landscape: Two miles upstream from the city, the Swannanoa and French Broad rivers join to form the Asheville Plateau valley, flanked on the east and west by mountain ranges. Thirty miles south, the Blue Ridge Mountains form an escarpment with 2,700 feet average elevation. Nearby peaks include Mount Mitchell (6,684 feet) and Big Pisgah (5,721 feet). Tall oak, hickory, walnut, maple, and basswood trees produce a dense canopy in summer. There are lower layers of small trees, dogwood, blueberry, and haw.

Climate: Temperate but invigorating. Considerable variation in temperature occurs from day to day throughout the year. The valley has a pronounced effect on wind direction, which is mostly from the northwest. Destructive weather events are rare. The first frost arrives October 24, and the last frost departs in early April.

Summer mildness: 67 **Seasonal affect:** 25
Winter mildness: 46 **Hazard free:** 38
Score: 36.1 **Rank:** 128

	103
	113
	149
90°	10
32°	86
0°	0
	78
	75
	45

	High °F	Low °F	Hum %	Wind mph	Precip inches	Snow inches
JAN	45	26	59	9.7	2.5	5.0
FEB	49	29	56	9.6	3.3	4.8
MAR	58	37	53	9.4	3.9	2.6
APR	67	45	50	8.9	3.1	0
MAY	74	52	57	7.1	3.6	0
JUN	81	60	59	6.1	3.3	0
JUL	84	64	63	5.8	2.9	0
AUG	83	63	63	5.4	3.8	0
SEP	77	57	64	5.6	3.2	0
OCT	67	45	57	6.8	2.8	0
NOV	58	37	57	8.1	2.9	0
DEC	49	30	59	8.9	2.8	1.9

★ = *in the top 30 places for climate mildness.*

Athens, GA

Location: 33.57 N and 83.22 W at 662 feet, in Georgia's Piedmont Plateau. Atlanta is 60 miles west.

Landscape: Local elevations range between 600 and 800 feet in rolling to hilly terrain. Streams drain eastward to the Savannah River. The countryside is agricultural, with occasional stands of trees dominated by southern yellow pine, with some mixed hardwoods.

Climate: The city's climate is influenced by the Atlantic Ocean 200 miles southeast, the Gulf of Mexico 275 miles south, and the southern Appalachian Mountains to the north and northwest. Summers are warm and humid, but prolonged periods of extreme heat are absent. Precipitation is evenly distributed throughout the year. The mountains to the north partially block extremely cold air. Consequently, the city's winters aren't severe. Cold spells are short-lived, broken up by periods of warm southerly airflow. Frost arrives just after Halloween, and the last frost departs before April Fools Day.

Summer mildness: 42 **Seasonal affect:** 51
Winter mildness: 62 **Hazard free:** 55
Score: 56.4 **Rank:** 88

	114
	106
	146
90°	70
32°	70
0°	0
	39
	70
	51

	High °F	Low °F	Hum %	Wind mph	Precip inches	Snow inches
JAN	52	32	58	8.5	4.6	0.9
FEB	56	35	55	8.9	4.4	0.7
MAR	65	42	53	8.8	5.5	0.4
APR	73	50	50	8.3	4.0	0
MAY	81	58	54	7.1	4.4	0
JUN	87	66	55	6.6	3.9	0
JUL	90	70	59	6.3	4.9	0
AUG	88	69	59	5.8	3.7	0
SEP	83	63	60	6.4	3.4	0
OCT	74	51	54	6.8	3.3	0
NOV	64	42	54	7.4	3.7	0
DEC	55	35	57	8.0	4.1	0.2

Bar Harbor, ME

Location: 44.23 N and 68.12 W at 20 feet, on Maine's Atlantic coast. Augusta, the state capital, is 35 miles west. Boston, Massachusetts, is 165 miles south.

Landscape: Situated on the northeast shore of Mount Desert Island, where glacial features are characteristic in many lakes, islands, and the rocky coastline. Elevations range from sea level to 1,530-foot Mount Cadillac, producing a dramatic combination of mountains, sheer cliff, and ocean. Tortuous trails crisscross Mount Desert. Native vegetation includes a mix of northern hardwoods and spruce.

Climate: Warm continental, with winters that are moderately long and occasionally severe if the predominate weather is coming from the Carolina Coast. The first frost hits October 4. The Atlantic Ocean moderates the cold winds from the Canadian Arctic. Spring arrives late, with the last freeze occurring May 9. Summer weather is mild but changeable, being influenced by the tropical storms that sweep up the Atlantic coast. Autumn is bright and mild.

Summer mildness: 92 **Seasonal affect:** 8
Winter mildness: 10 **Hazard free:** 16
Score: 9.4 **Rank:** 184

	102
	99
	164
90°	4
32°	158
0°	13
	49
	76
	18

	High °F	Low °F	Hum %	Wind mph	Precip inches	Snow inches
JAN	30	11	61	9.2	3.6	20.3
FEB	33	12	58	9.4	3.4	18.2
MAR	41	23	58	10.0	3.7	13.3
APR	52	32	55	10.0	4.1	3.0
MAY	63	42	58	9.2	3.9	0
JUN	73	51	60	8.2	3.2	0
JUL	78	57	59	7.6	3.3	0
AUG	77	56	59	7.5	3.1	0
SEP	69	48	59	7.8	3.7	0
OCT	58	39	50	8.4	3.9	0
NOV	46	31	62	8.8	5.2	4.0
DEC	34	17	62	9.0	4.7	15.9

Bay St. Louis–Pass Christian, MS

Location: 30.18 N and 89.19 W at 28 feet, on the state's thickly settled Gulf Coast. New Orleans, Louisiana, is 60 miles west. Mobile, Alabama, is 70 miles east.

Landscape: Flat, consisting of low-lying delta floodplains sloping to sand beaches and shallow harbors and bays. Native trees are a temperate rain forest of evergreen, oak, laurel, and magnolia, with large stands of loblolly and slash pine in the sandy upland areas.

Climate: Subtropical. The Gulf waters modify local climate. Summers are hot and humid, though temperatures of 90°F or higher occur only half as often here as they do in Hattiesburg, 60 miles north. However, there's no such reverse effect on cold air moving down from the north in winter. November 30 marks the first frost; the last frost occurs in mid-February. Rainfall is plentiful and heaviest in July. Damage from hurricanes and tropical storms can occur six to seven times a year.

Summer mildness: 30 **Seasonal affect:** 51
Winter mildness: 89 **Hazard free:** 47
Score: 60.3 **Rank:** 81

	103
	116
	146
90°	55
32°	15
0°	0
	28
	73
	74

	High °F	Low °F	Hum %	Wind mph	Precip inches	Snow inches
JAN	60	42	66	10.4	5.4	0.3
FEB	63	45	63	10.7	5.9	0.1
MAR	69	52	60	10.9	5.3	0.1
APR	76	60	60	10.2	4.4	0
MAY	83	67	60	8.9	4.8	0
JUN	88	73	63	7.7	5.0	0
JUL	90	75	66	7.0	6.5	0
AUG	90	74	66	6.8	6.6	0
SEP	87	70	65	7.9	5.3	0
OCT	80	60	60	8.2	3.3	0
NOV	71	52	62	9.3	4.1	0
DEC	63	46	66	10.1	5.4	0.2

★ = *in the top 30 places for climate mildness.*

Beaufort, SC

Location: 32.26 N and 80.40 W at 11 feet, on Port Royal, one of the Sea Islands, 45 miles south of Charleston and 35 miles north of Savannah, Georgia.

Landscape: The land is low and flat with elevations averaging less than 25 feet. Port Royal is one of dozens of islands of various shapes and sizes with fresh and saltwater streams, inlets, rivers, and sounds. Most have many swampy areas. Coastal plain forests of beech, sweet gum, magnolia, pine, and oak are common.

Climate: Subtropical. The island group is on the edge of the balmy climate enjoyed by Florida. The surrounding water produces a maritime climate, with mild winters, hot summers with regular thunderstorms, and seasonal temperatures that shift slowly. The inland Appalachian Mountains block cold air from the northern interior, and the Gulf Stream moderates the climate considerably. November 20 heralds the arrival of first frost, and the last frost departs March 9.

Summer mildness: 35 **Seasonal affect:** 45
Winter mildness: 82 **Hazard free:** 65
Score: 67.8 **Rank:** 66

104
109
152
90° 56
32° 28
0° 0
28
71
56

	High °F	Low °F	Hum %	Wind mph	Precip inches	Snow inches
JAN	59	39	57	9.1	3.7	0.1
FEB	62	41	55	9.9	3.3	0.2
MAR	70	48	53	10.0	4.1	0
APR	77	55	50	9.7	2.9	0
MAY	83	63	55	8.7	4.0	0
JUN	88	69	60	8.4	6.1	0
JUL	90	73	66	7.9	6.4	0
AUG	89	72	70	7.4	7.9	0
SEP	85	68	67	7.8	5.0	0
OCT	78	58	70	8.1	2.6	0
NOV	70	49	60	8.1	2.4	0
DEC	62	42	60	8.5	3.2	0

Beaufort–Bogue Banks, NC

Location: 34.4305 N and 76.40 W at 15 feet at the north end of Onslow Bay on the Atlantic coast. Wilmington is 100 miles southwest.

Landscape: The Bogue Banks, a series of offshore island reefs, separate Bogue Sound, part of the Intracoastal Waterway, from the Atlantic. Typical of the Carolina coast, the Banks are composed of dunes, marshes, and maritime forest. Sea oats grow on the dunes. Salt marsh cordgrass, saltmeadow hay, sea oxeye, and black needlebrush predominate in the marsh. The forest includes oak, pine, cedar, yaupon, and wax myrtle.

Climate: Subtropical, moderated by the ocean. Summers are warm and humid, with frequent thunderstorms. Winters are mild with little or no snow. Spring and fall are long lasting and pleasant. Frost first appears November 19 and departs 4 months later in mid-March. Rain falls consistently throughout the year, and tropical storms are a threat from late summer to early fall.

Summer mildness: 48 **Seasonal affect:** 39
Winter mildness: 68 **Hazard free:** 46
Score: 52.9 **Rank:** 95

111
104
150
90° 14
32° 37
0° 0
174
65
47

	High °F	Low °F	Hum %	Wind mph	Precip inches	Snow inches
JAN	55	35	68	9.0	4.6	0.7
FEB	57	36	65	9.7	4.2	1.0
MAR	63	43	67	10.1	4.0	1.1
APR	71	51	64	10.2	2.9	0
MAY	78	60	71	9.1	4.6	0
JUN	84	68	72	8.5	4.4	0
JUL	87	72	75	7.9	6.8	0
AUG	87	72	78	7.4	6.2	0
SEP	83	67	76	7.8	5.3	0
OCT	76	56	72	8.0	3.9	0
NOV	68	47	70	8.1	3.7	0
DEC	59	39	69	8.4	4.2	0.3

Bellingham, WA

Location: 48.45 N and 122.29 W at 60 feet, on Bellingham Bay in the northwest corner of Washington state. Seattle is 90 miles south, and Vancouver, British Columbia, is 50 miles north.

Landscape: Dominated by the broad, glacier-carved Skagit River Valley with fjords and deep undersea troughs. East of Bellingham are the North Cascade Mountains and Mount Baker at 10,775 feet. The San Juan Islands are in nearby Puget Sound. The natural vegetation is a predominately needleleaf forest of Douglas fir, red cedar, and spruce.

Climate: Marine. Winter days are mild, but the nights are chilly. Six months lie between the first frost in November and the last frost in mid-late April. Summers are cool with low precipitation. The cooler air temperatures reduce evaporation and produce a very damp, humid climate with heavy cloud cover.

Summer mildness: 98 **Seasonal affect:** 1
Winter mildness: 53 **Hazard free:** 75
Score: 66.8 **Rank:** 67

50
84
231
90° 0
32° 68
0° 0
90
91
5

	High °F	Low °F	Hum %	Wind mph	Precip inches	Snow inches
JAN	43	32	77	7.1	4.7	5.2
FEB	48	35	74	7.2	3.6	1.3
MAR	51	36	70	7.4	3.0	2.4
APR	56	40	67	7.4	2.7	0
MAY	62	45	64	6.9	2.3	0
JUN	67	51	62	6.7	1.8	0
JUL	71	53	62	6.2	1.3	0
AUG	71	54	63	6.0	1.4	0
SEP	67	48	68	5.7	1.9	0
OCT	58	42	75	5.9	3.4	0
NOV	50	37	78	6.9	5.0	0
DEC	44	33	80	7.3	5.0	4.4

★ = *in the top 30 places for climate mildness.*

Bend, OR

Location: 44.03 N and 121.19 W at 3,629 feet, near the center of the state, along the western border of the Harney Basin and Great Sandy Desert. Portland is 130 miles northwest.

Landscape: The Cascades terrace upward to crests of 10,000 feet about 10 miles west. A rolling plateau extends south and east into California, Nevada, and Idaho. To the north, canyons and streams that feed into the Columbia River cut the plateau. The lower elevation is a shortgrass prairie of grama, needlegrass, and wheatgrass. Mountain forests are Douglas fir, red cedar, and spruce.

Climate: Continental climate of the Great Basin. The Cascades restrain extreme summer temperatures and also block moisture-laden Pacific winds. Rains are generally light, with only a rare rainfall of an inch or more. The average growing season is about 82 days, with frost coming as early as late August and departing as late as July. Moderate days and cool nights characterize temperatures here.

Summer mildness: 80 **Seasonal affect:** 42
Winter mildness: 22 **Hazard free:** 53
Score: 50.0 **Rank:** 100

	117
	79
	169
90°	13
32°	196
0°	4
	50
	31
	8

	High °F	Low °F	Hum %	Wind mph	Precip inches	Snow inches
JAN	42	22	81	4.1	1.8	12.3
FEB	46	25	77	4.5	1.0	4.7
MAR	51	26	66	5.3	0.9	5.6
APR	58	29	57	5.7	0.6	2.0
MAY	65	35	50	5.7	0.8	0
JUN	74	41	44	5.9	0.9	0
JUL	81	45	40	5.8	0.5	0
AUG	81	45	40	5.3	0.6	0
SEP	73	38	42	4.5	0.5	0
OCT	63	32	57	3.7	0.7	0
NOV	48	27	80	3.6	1.6	5.0
DEC	42	22	85	3.6	2.0	9.4

Berkeley Springs, WV

Location: 39.33 N and 78.15 W at 730 feet, at the extreme northern edge of West Virginia's eastern panhandle, some 85 air miles northwest of Washington, D.C.

Landscape: Most of the area is rolling. On the east, the Appalachian Mountains produce high relief. The naturally occurring vegetation is a typical deciduous forest of oak, beech, hickory, and ash. Second growth is rapidly growing pine. In spring, a luxuriant low layer of herbs quickly develops.

Climate: Hot continental, with cold and somewhat snowy winters, but mild summers thanks to elevation. Precipitation is adequate in all months but greater in summer when moisture demands are high. This is one of the cloudier locations for retirement, mainly in winter and spring.

Summer mildness: 74 **Seasonal affect:** 10
Winter mildness: 27 **Hazard free:** 14
Score: 8.4 **Rank:** 186

	58
	103
	204
90°	7
32°	124
0°	5
	178
	71
	35

	High °F	Low °F	Hum %	Wind mph	Precip inches	Snow inches
JAN	34	19	69	10.6	2.4	11.3
FEB	37	20	68	10.5	2.5	9.3
MAR	49	30	65	10.7	3.1	8.7
APR	60	39	65	10.3	3.2	1.7
MAY	71	48	71	8.9	4.1	0.1
JUN	79	57	70	8.0	3.4	0
JUL	83	62	65	7.3	3.5	0
AUG	81	60	65	6.9	3.3	0
SEP	74	54	70	7.4	2.8	0
OCT	63	42	66	8.4	3.4	0.4
NOV	50	34	68	9.8	3.1	3.3
DEC	39	24	68	10.4	2.7	8.3

Bisbee, AZ

Location: 31.23 N and 109.55 W at 5,490 feet in southeast Arizona, just 7 miles north of the Mexico border. Phoenix is 180 miles northwest.

Landscape: The city was built along two steep-sided canyons, Mule Pass Gulch and Brewery Gulch. The surrounding topography is Sonoran Desert and low, dry mountains. The vegetation is very sparse, with bare ground between individual plants. On the rocky slopes of the mountains, paloverde, ocotillo, and saguaro are common.

Climate: Desert, with a long summer that starts in late March and ends in October that produces high temperatures modified by the low humidity. Winters are ideal with warm days and cool nights. Like other locations in the Desert Southwest, nearly every day is clear.

Summer mildness: 4 **Seasonal affect:** 94
Winter mildness: 73 **Hazard free:** 70
Score: 76.2 **Rank:** 49

	194
	90
	81
90°	140
32°	18
0°	0
	3
	12
	42

	High °F	Low °F	Hum %	Wind mph	Precip inches	Snow inches
JAN	64	39	48	8.0	0.9	0.2
FEB	68	41	43	8.1	0.7	0.2
MAR	73	45	39	8.5	0.7	0.1
APR	81	50	29	8.9	0.3	0.1
MAY	90	58	24	8.8	0.2	0
JUN	100	68	23	8.7	0.2	0
JUL	99	74	43	8.4	2.4	0
AUG	97	72	49	7.9	2.2	0
SEP	93	68	41	8.3	1.7	0
OCT	84	57	39	8.2	1.1	0
NOV	73	46	41	8.1	0.7	0.1
DEC	64	40	49	7.8	1.1	0.2

★ = *in the top 30 places for climate mildness.*

Boca Raton, FL

Location: 26.12 N and 80.05 W at 16 feet, along the densely settled Atlantic coast in the southeastern part of the state, between Palm Beach and Miami.

Landscape: The Atlantic Ocean forms the eastern edge of the coastal ridge, and the Gulf Stream flows northward 2 miles offshore, its nearest approach to the Florida coast. Most of the surrounding swampland has been drained for development. Outer coastal plain growth at the eastern edge of the Everglades is primarily saw grass and mangrove.

Climate: Because of its southerly location near the ocean, the area has an equable climate. Winters are pleasantly warm. While the thermometer rarely climbs above 95°F, summers are hot and humid, though tempered by an ocean breeze. Cumulus clouds often shade the land without completely obscuring the sun. The moist unstable air in this area results in frequent short rain showers from May to October.

Summer mildness: 14 **Seasonal affect:** 47
Winter mildness: 99 **Hazard free:** 73
Score: 70.7 **Rank:** 60

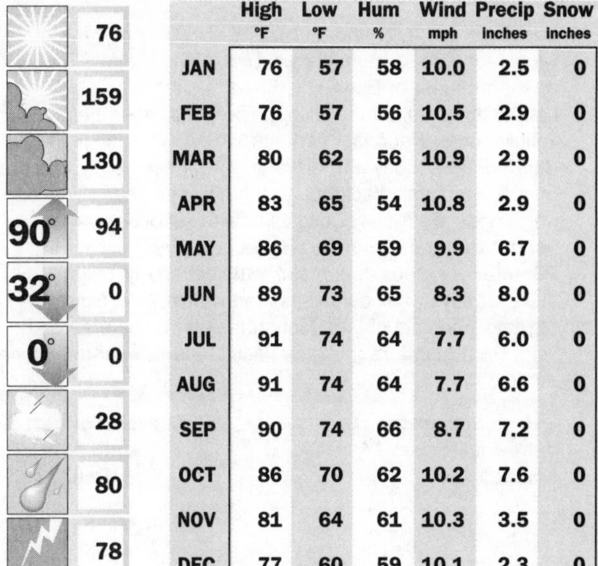

76
159
130
90° 94
32° 0
0° 0
28
80
78

	High °F	Low °F	Hum %	Wind mph	Precip inches	Snow inches
JAN	76	57	58	10.0	2.5	0
FEB	76	57	56	10.5	2.9	0
MAR	80	62	56	10.9	2.9	0
APR	83	65	54	10.8	2.9	0
MAY	86	69	59	9.9	6.7	0
JUN	89	73	65	8.3	8.0	0
JUL	91	74	64	7.7	6.0	0
AUG	91	74	64	7.7	6.6	0
SEP	90	74	66	8.7	7.2	0
OCT	86	70	62	10.2	7.6	0
NOV	81	64	61	10.3	3.5	0
DEC	77	60	59	10.1	2.3	0

Boerne, TX

Location: 29.47 N and 98.44 W at 1,405 feet in the south-central Texas Blacklands, 30 miles northwest of San Antonio.

Landscape: Between the southern rim of the Edwards Plateau and the Gulf Coastal Plain, the area is characterized by rolling hills and open prairie. Limestone caverns, bluffs, and creeks that run to the Guadalupe River are common. Vegetation includes prairie grasses, mesquite, cacti, Texas live oak, cypress, and sycamore.

Climate: Subtropical. Winters are mild, but the rest of the year amounts to one long, hot summer. Moist Gulf air adds humidity to the heat. Rainfall is fairly steady, but is heaviest from May through September. Thunderstorms occur throughout the year. Frost arrives in early November and departs before April.

Summer mildness: 23 **Seasonal affect:** 71
Winter mildness: 67 **Hazard free:** 69
Score: 68.8 **Rank:** 63

108
118
139
90° 90
32° 45
0° 0
22
46
37

	High °F	Low °F	Hum %	Wind mph	Precip inches	Snow inches
JAN	59	33	59	9.0	1.7	0
FEB	63	37	57	9.7	2.1	0.5
MAR	71	44	54	10.4	2.1	0
APR	79	53	56	10.3	3.1	0
MAY	84	61	59	10.0	4.1	0
JUN	89	67	56	9.9	3.8	0
JUL	93	69	51	9.2	2.2	0
AUG	93	68	51	8.5	2.9	0
SEP	88	64	55	8.5	4.2	0
OCT	80	54	54	8.4	3.6	0
NOV	70	44	55	8.8	2.7	0.1
DEC	62	36	57	8.5	1.8	0

Boone–Blowing Rock, NC

Location: 36.13 N and 81.40 W at 3,266 feet, atop the Blue Ridge Mountains in the northwestern corner of the state near the Tennessee line. Asheville is 50 miles southwest.

Landscape: Rough highland with the deep gorges, mountain trails, and rising elevations of the southern Appalachians. Many streams cut through the forests. A typical heavy Appalachian oak forest covers the mountains with a mix of pine, oak, maple, beech, hickory, and birch.

Climate: Hot continental moderated by the altitude. Winters are long and cold with the first frost coming in by October 2 and the last frost not leaving until May 12. The rest of the year is mild and invigorating. Considerable variation in temperature occurs from day to night throughout the year. Precipitation is constant and plentiful, with long, snowy winters and rainy seasons in spring and summer. Destructive weather events are rare.

Summer mildness: 87 **Seasonal affect:** 13
Winter mildness: 26 **Hazard free:** 11
Score: 15.3 **Rank:** 172

103
113
149
90° 0
32° 133
0° 4
78
96
45

	High °F	Low °F	Hum %	Wind mph	Precip inches	Snow inches
JAN	41	20	59	9.7	3.8	11.3
FEB	44	22	56	9.6	3.9	11.4
MAR	53	30	53	9.4	4.8	9.3
APR	60	37	50	8.9	4.2	1.0
MAY	68	45	57	7.1	4.8	0
JUN	74	52	59	6.1	4.5	0
JUL	77	56	63	5.8	4.7	0
AUG	76	55	63	5.4	4.7	0
SEP	71	50	64	5.6	4.1	0
OCT	63	39	57	6.8	4.0	0
NOV	54	31	57	8.1	3.9	4.0
DEC	45	24	59	8.9	3.2	7.9

★ = *in the top 30 places for climate mildness.*

Bozeman, MT

Location: 45.41 N and 111.02 W at 5,950 feet in southwest Montana, 112 miles west of Billings, and 72 miles east southeast of Butte.

Landscape: Gallatin National Forest is near here, and Yellowstone National Park is 45 miles south. The Continental Divide, with elevations well over 10,000 feet, provides a scenic backdrop to the city. The naturally occurring woods are mainly Douglas fir with secondary growth of ponderosa pine, aspen, and lodgepole pine.

Climate: Rigorous mountain, with extremely bright, mild summer days and cool nights, and with severe, cloudy winter days and cold nights. Mountains shield the area somewhat from moisture from the Pacific and from bitterly cold arctic air.

Summer mildness: 100 **Seasonal affect:** 6
Winter mildness: 14 **Hazard free:** 30
Score: 19.8 **Rank:** 163

115
92
153
90° 21
32° 137
0° 15
67
115
23

	High °F	Low °F	Hum %	Wind mph	Precip inches	Snow inches
JAN	32	14	81	8.0	2.8	12.5
FEB	36	20	77	6.0	2.0	7.7
MAR	40	25	69	7.0	2.7	5.9
APR	48	32	61	8.0	3.2	2.1
MAY	58	39	61	8.0	4.6	0.8
JUN	67	46	61	8.0	4.2	0
JUL	76	50	52	8.0	2.1	0
AUG	75	49	51	8.0	2.5	0
SEP	64	40	60	7.0	3.2	0
OCT	54	31	70	7.0	2.7	0.9
NOV	40	24	80	6.0	2.6	5.8
DEC	33	17	83	7.0	2.5	10.6

★ Bradenton, FL

Location: 27.30 N and 82.34 W at 19 feet, on the south bank of the Manatee River near its mouth at Tampa Bay. Tampa is 50 miles north.

Landscape: The southern Gulf Coastal Plains are flat and irregular with less than 300 feet variation in altitude over the gently rolling area. Most of the streams are sluggish. Marshes, swamps, and lakes are numerous. Evergreen oaks, laurel, and magnolia are common, but the trees aren't tall and the leaf canopy isn't dense. There is an understory of various shrubs, with ferns and herbaceous plants as ground cover.

Climate: Subtropical. Summer and winter extremes are checked by the influence of the Gulf. Winter days are bright and warm. Nights are moderately cool. Rainfall averages more than 50 inches annually, with two-thirds coming daily between June and September. Most rain falls as late-afternoon or early-evening thunderstorms, bringing relief from the heat.

Summer mildness: 17 **Seasonal affect:** 69
Winter mildness: 93 **Hazard free:** 77
Score: 87.1 **Rank:** 27

102
142
121
90° 78
32° 0
0° 0
22
69
93

	High °F	Low °F	Hum %	Wind mph	Precip inches	Snow inches
JAN	71	49	56	8.6	2.5	0
FEB	73	51	56	9.2	3.0	0
MAR	77	55	53	9.5	3.2	0
APR	82	59	47	9.3	1.2	0
MAY	87	65	49	8.7	2.8	0
JUN	90	70	56	8.0	7.8	0
JUL	91	72	60	7.2	8.9	0
AUG	91	72	60	7.0	9.5	0
SEP	89	71	60	7.8	8.0	0
OCT	85	65	56	8.5	2.6	0
NOV	79	57	56	8.4	2.1	0
DEC	73	51	56	8.5	2.3	0

Branson, MO

Location: 36.38 N and 93.13 W at 722 feet, 50 miles south of Springfield near the Arkansas state line.

Landscape: There are several important lakes and rivers in this area of the Ozark Plateau. The rounded mountains rise somewhat steeply from river valleys and impounded lakes. Oak-hickory forests are tall, providing a dense high, leafy cover in summer and colorful foliage in fall, but are completely bare in winter. Pines are evidence of second-growth forest. Lower understory layers of shrub and flowering trees are common throughout.

Climate: Hot continental with hot summers and cool winters. Precipitation is adequate throughout the year and usually falls as rain. Winters may be cold enough for snow, but the typical precipitation is icy rain during brief, intense cold snaps that begin with the first frost around October 16. Spring arrives early and is pleasant.

Summer mildness: 41 **Seasonal affect:** 60
Winter mildness: 28 **Hazard free:** 8
Score: 14.8 **Rank:** 173

116
97
153
90° 57
32° 101
0° 1
20
61
56

	High °F	Low °F	Hum %	Wind mph	Precip inches	Snow inches
JAN	45	19	60	11.7	1.9	4.4
FEB	50	23	60	11.9	2.4	4.3
MAR	60	32	56	12.9	3.9	3.4
APR	71	42	55	12.2	3.9	0
MAY	79	50	59	10.4	4.5	0
JUN	86	59	59	9.6	4.3	0
JUL	92	63	56	8.5	3.4	0
AUG	90	61	54	8.6	3.4	0
SEP	83	55	58	9.3	3.9	0
OCT	73	42	54	10.1	3.3	0
NOV	60	33	59	11.3	3.9	1.0
DEC	49	24	63	11.6	3.3	3.0

★ = *in the top 30 places for climate mildness.*

Brevard, NC

Location: 35.14 N and 82.44 W at 2,230 feet, in the mountains near the South Carolina border, near the French Broad River, and 40 miles southwest of Asheville.

Landscape: High rounded slopes of the southern Appalachians, with steep gorges, precipitous cliffs, and numerous waterfalls. Nearby are the Appalachian Trail and Blue Ridge Parkway. Also near are the Pisgah and Nantahala national forests, with oak, beech, walnut, ash, sweet chestnut, and hornbeam. Native laurel blooms in spring along with other common understory trees such as dogwood and redbud.

Climate: Hot continental moderated by the altitude. This is especially notable in summer, with markedly less humidity and cooler nights than cities of similar latitude. Winters are typically cold and cloudy heralded by the first frost around October 8. Early May sees the last frost. Precipitation, mainly mountain rain, is plentiful and well distributed throughout the year.

Summer mildness: 60 **Seasonal affect:** 16
Winter mildness: 36 **Hazard free:** 45
Score: 20.7 **Rank:** 161

	103
	113
	149
90°	9
32°	111
0°	1
	78
	91
	45

	High °F	Low °F	Hum %	Wind mph	Precip inches	Snow inches
JAN	50	25	59	9.7	4.9	3.4
FEB	54	27	56	9.6	5.4	3.5
MAR	62	34	53	9.4	6.4	2.5
APR	70	41	50	8.9	4.7	0
MAY	77	49	57	7.1	5.9	0
JUN	82	57	59	6.1	5.6	0
JUL	85	61	63	5.8	5.9	0
AUG	84	61	63	5.4	6.5	0
SEP	79	55	64	5.6	5.1	0
OCT	71	42	57	6.8	5.3	0
NOV	62	34	57	8.1	5.4	0
DEC	53	28	59	8.9	5.9	1.5

★ Brookings–Gold Beach, OR

Location: 42.03 N and 124.17 W at 113 feet, on southern Oregon's Pacific Coast. The California border is just 10 miles southeast, and Portland is 270 miles north.

Landscape: The shore is backed by the Klamath Mountains to the east, and many streams, including the Rogue River, drain the mountain wilderness. An escarpment rises from the rocky beaches. The Siskiyou National Forest near here includes weeping spruce and Port Orford cedar. Wild azalea, myrtlewood, and redwood are among the native vegetation along the coast.

Climate: Mild marine. Daytime high temperatures can reach 70°F in winter and infrequently top that point in the hottest part of summer. Nights are chilly throughout the year. Overcast skies and precipitation are constant from November to March. First frost arrives as late as December 17, and the last frost leaves by the end of February.

Summer mildness: 97 **Seasonal affect:** 3
Winter mildness: 70 **Hazard free:** 91
Score: 87.6 **Rank:** 25

	52
	77
	236
90°	1
32°	8
0°	0
	41
	101
	8

	High °F	Low °F	Hum %	Wind mph	Precip inches	Snow inches
JAN	55	41	80	9.1	10.9	0.2
FEB	56	42	79	9.1	9.0	0
MAR	57	42	77	9.0	9.3	0.1
APR	60	43	73	8.7	5.2	0
MAY	63	46	71	8.5	3.6	0
JUN	67	50	71	8.6	1.6	0
JUL	68	51	71	8.7	0.5	0
AUG	68	52	72	8.1	1.3	0
SEP	69	51	73	7.6	2.1	0
OCT	64	48	77	7.6	5.7	0
NOV	59	45	78	8.8	11.5	0
DEC	55	41	82	9.1	11.9	0

Brown County, IN

Location: 39.12 N and 86.15 W at 629 feet, 12 miles east of Bloomington, and 60 miles south of Indianapolis.

Landscape: The terrain is rolling with tumbled hills and narrow valleys in contrast to the flat, glacier scoured land of northern Indiana. Ridges, knolls, bluffs, caves, and waterfalls are all found in this area. The surrounding forests have been regrowing for decades, and a wide variety of trees, including oak, maple, beech, sycamore, hickory, walnut, and elm cover the hills.

Climate: Continental. Warm summers and cold winters are the norm. Temperatures may vary widely in winter. The first frost arrives before mid-October, and it will be the end of April before frost departs. Snowfall is moderate with accumulation in the hills. Summers vary from humid to dry. Spring and fall are long and pleasant. Rainfall is moderate, with occasional thunderstorms in summer.

Summer mildness: 63 **Seasonal affect:** 4
Winter mildness: 25 **Hazard free:** 12
Score: 0.9 **Rank:** 201

	88
	99
	179
90°	29
32°	121
0°	6
	163
	78
	43

	High °F	Low °F	Hum %	Wind mph	Precip inches	Snow inches
JAN	37	17	76	10.9	2.6	7.6
FEB	41	20	74	10.8	2.6	4.9
MAR	53	30	71	11.7	4.4	4.8
APR	65	40	68	11.2	4.0	0.2
MAY	74	50	69	9.5	4.8	0
JUN	83	59	69	8.5	4.0	0
JUL	86	63	74	7.5	4.5	0
AUG	85	61	76	7.2	3.9	0
SEP	79	54	74	8.0	2.8	0
OCT	67	41	72	8.8	3.3	0
NOV	54	33	76	10.4	3.7	1.7
DEC	41	22	78	10.5	3.5	3.5

★ = *in the top 30 places for climate mildness.*

★ Bullhead City, AZ

Location: 35.09 N and 114.34 W at 540 feet on the Colorado River in extreme western Arizona. Las Vegas, Nevada, is 78 miles northwest.

Landscape: Deep gorges line the banks of the Colorado, which roars down from impounded Lake Mead past the Black Mountains to the east and the Great Salt Lake Desert west in Nevada. The prevailing vegetation is sagebrush, shadscale, fourwing saltbush, and spiny hopsage that are all tolerant of the poorly drained alkaline soils.

Climate: Desert, with strong daily and seasonal temperature changes. Winters are clear and extremely mild with first frost arriving December 9 and last frost departing by February 7. The flow of air from as far away as the Pacific Ocean moderates the desert climate. There's a long, hot, sunbaked stretch from May to October. Except for a handful of days in spring and summer, there's no measurable precipitation.

Summer mildness: 1 **Seasonal affect:** 99
Winter mildness: 80 **Hazard free:** 98
Score: 93.5 **Rank:** 14

242
75
48
90° 178
32° 14
0° 0
2
11
7

	High °F	Low °F	Hum %	Wind mph	Precip inches	Snow inches
JAN	67	39	40	9.7	0.6	0
FEB	73	44	35	9.6	0.4	0
MAR	79	48	30	9.4	0.5	0
APR	87	54	25	8.9	0.2	0
MAY	96	63	23	7.1	0.1	0
JUN	105	72	22	6.1	0.0	0
JUL	109	79	32	5.8	0.3	0
AUG	107	79	35	5.4	0.5	0
SEP	101	71	35	5.6	0.5	0
OCT	91	59	32	6.8	0.4	0
NOV	77	47	34	8.1	0.5	0
DEC	67	39	41	8.9	0.6	0

Burlington, VT

Location: 44.29 N and 73.13 W on the eastern shore of Lake Champlain, some 75 miles south of Montreal, Quebec.

Landscape: The highest peaks of the Adirondacks are visible 35 miles across the lake, and the Green Mountain foothills begin 10 miles to the east. Northern white pine, eastern hemlock, maple, oak, and beech are common trees in the surrounding forest.

Climate: The last freeze here occurs in late May, followed by a short, extremely pleasant summer. Fall is cool; the first freeze hits in late September. Winters are cold, with brief intense cold snaps formed by high-pressure systems moving down from central Canada and Hudson Bay. Lake Champlain moderates the cold somewhat. This is one of the cloudiest cities in the country.

Summer mildness: 87 **Seasonal affect:** 5
Winter mildness: 7 **Hazard free:** 10
Score: 1.9 **Rank:** 199

58
101
206
90° 6
32° 157
0° 28
120
75
22

	High °F	Low °F	Hum %	Wind mph	Precip inches	Snow inches
JAN	25	8	68	9.7	1.8	18.8
FEB	28	9	68	9.4	1.6	16.8
MAR	39	22	67	9.5	2.2	12.4
APR	54	34	64	9.5	2.8	3.8
MAY	67	45	63	9.0	3.1	0.2
JUN	76	55	66	8.5	3.5	0
JUL	81	60	66	8.0	3.7	0
AUG	78	58	70	7.6	4.1	0
SEP	69	49	74	8.3	3.3	0
OCT	57	39	71	8.8	2.9	0.2
NOV	44	30	72	9.7	3.1	6.6
DEC	30	16	72	9.9	2.4	18.1

Camden, ME

Location: 44.12 N and 69.04 W at 33 feet, on Penobscot Bay in the center of Maine's seacoast. Portland is 70 air miles southwest.

Landscape: Although low-lying, the coastal terrain is very rugged and rocky in most places, allowing for hundreds of bays, islands, peninsulas, and harbors. Immediately to the west are low-rise mountains. Vegetation consists of evergreen coniferous trees, and deciduous maple, birch, and scrub oak. The area inland is dotted with many marshes, ponds, and lakes.

Climate: The Atlantic Ocean has a considerable modifying effect on the local climate, resulting in cool summers and winters that are mild for so northerly a location. Winter snows can be heavy, however. Though fall is generally mild, spring comes late and the weather isn't really warm until late June. Early October will bring in the first frost, and the last frost comes May 9.

Summer mildness: 86 **Seasonal affect:** 8
Winter mildness: 11 **Hazard free:** 22
Score: 9.9 **Rank:** 183

102
99
164
90° 5
32° 155
0° 16
49
76
18

	High °F	Low °F	Hum %	Wind mph	Precip inches	Snow inches
JAN	32	11	61	9.2	3.5	14.4
FEB	35	12	58	9.4	3.3	17.9
MAR	43	23	58	10.0	3.9	10.2
APR	54	32	55	10.0	4.4	2.0
MAY	65	42	58	9.2	4.2	0
JUN	75	51	60	8.2	3.5	0
JUL	80	57	59	7.6	3.1	0
AUG	79	56	59	7.5	3.2	0
SEP	71	48	60	7.8	3.6	0
OCT	60	39	59	8.4	4.3	0
NOV	47	31	62	8.8	5.4	2.0
DEC	36	17	61	9.0	4.9	13.7

★ = *in the top 30 places for climate mildness.*

★ Carmel–Pebble Beach, CA

Location: 36.33 N and 121.55 W at 237 feet, on the Carmel River at the southern point of Monterey Bay, 80 miles south of San Francisco.

Landscape: Monterey Bay is a great sweeping coastal indentation on the Pacific Coast. Sandy and rocky beaches verge on tidepools along the shore. Local relief comes mainly from the Diablo and Santa Lucia mountains that rise to the east in high, grassy bluffs. Cypress and pine groves predominate in the mixed evergreen forest.

Climate: Marine, with year-round mild temperatures moving through gradual transitions. Nighttime cooling produces low-stratus clouds, known as California stratus, and early-morning fog. Most afternoons are clear and sunny. Cool temperatures and sea breezes keep the weather mild year-round. There may be a frost around December 8. Precipitation falls only from October to March. Summers are dry and thunderstorms rare.

Summer mildness: 94 | **Seasonal affect:** 82
Winter mildness: 78 | **Hazard free:** 95
Score: 99.5 | **Rank:** 2

	147
	116
	103
90°	2
32°	1
0°	0
	19
	35
	4

	High °F	Low °F	Hum %	Wind mph	Precip inches	Snow inches
JAN	60	43	57	4.8	3.5	0.1
FEB	62	45	58	6.3	2.7	0
MAR	62	45	60	6.7	3.2	0
APR	63	46	61	7.6	1.7	0
MAY	64	48	63	7.1	0.4	0
JUN	67	50	66	6.8	0.2	0
JUL	68	52	67	6.5	0.1	0
AUG	69	53	68	6.1	0.1	0
SEP	72	53	67	5.8	0.3	0
OCT	70	51	64	5.5	0.9	0
NOV	65	47	57	5.3	2.8	0
DEC	60	44	55	5.0	2.8	0

Carson City–Carson Valley, NV

Location: 39.10 N and 119.46 W at 4,665 feet, 14 miles east of Lake Tahoe. Reno is 30 miles north.

Landscape: Near the eastern foothills and the wind shadow of the Sierra Nevada Range and on the edge of the Great Basin, a major drainage sink for the Rockies. The rivers here flow into landlocked lakes or simply evaporate in the desert. Sagebrush and saltbush are common in this high country desert. The Sierran forest is mountain hemlock, red fir, lodgepole pine, and western white pine.

Climate: Mediterranean highland that is characterized by a long, unbroken, dry summer. Winters are cold but short. The first frost arrives by September 21, and the last frost won't depart until May 29. West winds prevail and influence the temperature and humidity. The mountains block much of the moisture from the Pacific that would otherwise fall as rain. At higher elevations, winter precipitation will fall as snow.

Summer mildness: 58 | **Seasonal affect:** 85
Winter mildness: 22 | **Hazard free:** 67
Score: 69.8 | **Rank:** 62

	159
	93
	112
90°	32
32°	170
0°	4
	7
	23
	0

	High °F	Low °F	Hum %	Wind mph	Precip inches	Snow inches
JAN	47	21	60	5.6	1.9	6.8
FEB	52	24	52	6.2	1.6	4.4
MAR	57	28	44	7.8	1.0	4.7
APR	63	32	36	8.2	0.5	1.0
MAY	72	39	32	8.0	0.6	0
JUN	82	46	29	7.6	0.4	0
JUL	90	50	25	7.0	0.3	0
AUG	88	48	24	6.5	0.3	0
SEP	80	41	30	5.8	0.5	0
OCT	70	32	36	5.4	0.7	0
NOV	55	26	49	5.5	1.4	1.0
DEC	47	21	58	5.2	1.7	6.0

Cedar City, UT

Location: 37.41 N and 113.04 W at 5,834 feet, 45 miles northeast of St. George and 220 miles southwest of Salt Lake City.

Landscape: On a tableland with Zion National Park to the south and Cedar Breaks National Monument to the east. The terrain is moderately to extremely rugged; elevations vary from 3,000 to over 8,000 feet. Lodgepole pine and aspen are dominant trees.

Climate: Rigorous mountain, with cool, pleasant summers and long, cold, snowy winters. Fall and spring are short transitional seasons here. Thanks to elevation, the climate here contrasts sharply with St. George, an hour south.

Summer mildness: 46 | **Seasonal affect:** 35
Winter mildness: 24 | **Hazard free:** 28
Score: 12.3 | **Rank:** 178

	137
	107
	122
90°	62
32°	134
0°	5
	26
	107
	36

	High °F	Low °F	Hum %	Wind mph	Precip inches	Snow inches
JAN	36	15	81	5.7	0.7	7.3
FEB	45	24	77	6.7	0.9	4.2
MAR	56	31	69	8.3	1.4	3.8
APR	66	39	61	9.4	1.1	1.1
MAY	76	48	61	9.6	0.8	0.1
JUN	88	57	61	9.7	0.4	0
JUL	94	64	52	9.3	1.1	0
AUG	91	62	51	9.1	1.5	0
SEP	81	53	60	9.0	1.0	0.1
OCT	68	42	70	7.9	1.0	0.5
NOV	51	29	80	6.8	1.0	2.7
DEC	39	19	83	5.9	0.7	5.3

★ = *in the top 30 places for climate mildness.*

Cedar Creek Lake, TX

Location: 32.10 N and 96.04 W at 460 feet, in East Texas, about 70 air miles southeast of Dallas.
Landscape: The surrounding rolling-to-hilly terrain drains to the Neches River on the east and the Trinity River on the west. The grass is bluestem prairie. The trees are pine, post oak, blackjack oak, and Texas hickory.
Climate: Prairie, with hot summers. Rainfall is about 39 inches annually, evenly distributed, though July and August are somewhat dry. Winters are mild, with temperatures almost always rising above freezing in the daytime, with no zero temperatures on record. Spring and fall are the best seasons. November 20 sees the first frost; the last frost departs March 15. This provides a long growing season, but there are sufficient changes to make the weather interesting. Flowers bloom as late as December and as early as March.

Summer mildness: 20 **Seasonal affect:** 77
Winter mildness: 68 **Hazard free:** 39
Score: 54.4 **Rank:** 93

	138
	98
	130
90°	102
32°	44
0°	0
	11
	50
	45

	High °F	Low °F	Hum %	Wind mph	Precip inches	Snow inches
JAN	55	33	59	11.2	2.2	1.3
FEB	60	37	59	11.9	2.8	1.0
MAR	68	45	57	12.9	3.1	0.2
APR	77	54	56	12.6	3.6	0
MAY	83	62	60	11.2	5.8	0
JUN	90	69	55	10.6	3.1	0
JUL	94	72	48	9.6	2.1	0
AUG	95	72	49	9.0	1.9	0
SEP	88	66	55	9.4	3.4	0
OCT	79	55	54	9.8	4.2	0
NOV	68	44	57	10.8	2.9	0
DEC	58	36	59	11.0	2.9	0.3

Chapel Hill–Carrboro, NC

Location: 35.54 N and 79.03 W at 503 feet, in central North Carolina, 35 miles west of Raleigh, the state capital.
Landscape: The topography of the Piedmont is rolling, with elevations from 200 to 500 feet within a 10-mile radius. Broadleaf deciduous and needleleaf evergreen trees make up the medium tall forests. Loblolly and other southern yellow pine mix with hickory, sweet gum, red maple, and winged elm. Low shrubs of dogwood, viburnum, and blueberry are common.
Climate: Subtropical. Because the Blue Ridge is a partial barrier to cold-air masses moving eastward from the nation's interior, there are very few days in winter when the temperature falls below 20°F. Tropical air is present during much of summer, bringing warm temperatures and high humidity. In midsummer, temperatures reach 90°F or higher every fourth day. Rainfall is well distributed throughout the year. Frost arrives by late October and departs on April 15.

Summer mildness: 49 **Seasonal affect:** 36
Winter mildness: 44 **Hazard free:** 48
Score: 37.6 **Rank:** 126

	112
	106
	147
90°	39
32°	91
0°	0
	34
	74
	44

	High °F	Low °F	Hum %	Wind mph	Precip inches	Snow inches
JAN	49	26	55	8.5	3.7	2.7
FEB	52	28	52	8.9	3.9	2.4
MAR	62	36	49	9.3	4.2	1.9
APR	71	44	45	9.0	3.2	0
MAY	78	53	54	7.7	4.5	0
JUN	85	61	56	7.0	4.4	0
JUL	89	65	58	6.7	4.1	0
AUG	87	64	60	6.4	4.4	0
SEP	82	57	59	6.8	3.2	0
OCT	72	45	53	7.1	3.5	0
NOV	63	37	52	7.6	3.5	0
DEC	53	29	55	8.0	3.5	0.9

Charles Town–Shepherdstown, WV

Location: 39.17 N and 77.51 W at 513 feet, near the meeting point of Virginia, Maryland, and West Virginia. Washington, D.C., is 53 miles southeast.
Landscape: In the midst of rolling farmland and Allegheny Mountain foothills west of the Blue Ridge Parkway, steep hills and mountains rise up in long ridges, curving north to south. The Shenandoah and Potomac rivers offer both white-water rapids and lazy stretches of calm fishing waters. Continuous dense covering is provided in summer by the Appalachian oak forest dominated by tall, broadleaf trees that become bare by November. Common trees are oak, beech, birch, hickory, maple, and shrub undergrowth. Pines are a secondary growth.
Climate: Hot continental with warm, humid summers, cool falls, and somewhat cold and snowy winters. Mid-October brings the first frost, while the last frost is late April. Precipitation is evenly distributed throughout the year, snow or rain in season.

Summer mildness: 62 **Seasonal affect:** 44
Winter mildness: 33 **Hazard free:** 27
Score: 26.7 **Rank:** 149

	102
	113
	150
90°	31
32°	119
0°	1
	23
	71
	36

	High °F	Low °F	Hum %	Wind mph	Precip inches	Snow inches
JAN	39	21	55	9.5	2.4	6.8
FEB	42	23	53	9.7	2.5	7.7
MAR	53	32	51	10.1	3.1	6.1
APR	64	41	50	9.8	3.2	0
MAY	74	50	55	7.9	4.1	0
JUN	83	59	56	6.9	3.4	0
JUL	87	64	58	6.5	3.5	0
AUG	85	62	59	6.1	3.3	0
SEP	78	55	60	6.1	2.8	0
OCT	66	42	56	6.9	3.4	0
NOV	55	34	55	8.3	3.1	1.0
DEC	43	26	55	8.8	2.7	5.6

★ = *in the top 30 places for climate mildness.*

Charleston, SC

Location: 32.46 N and 79.56 W at 118 feet, between the Ashley and Cooper rivers, on the state's central coast.
Landscape: Generally level with sandy to sandy-loam soil. Because of the low elevation, a portion of the city and nearby coastal islands is vulnerable to tidal flooding. The coastal marshes and interior swamps are dominated by moss-draped oak, sweet and black gums, and bald cypress. Grasses and cattails grow in the more open marsh areas.
Climate: Temperate subtropical modified considerably by the ocean. Summer is warm and humid, but temperatures over 100°F are infrequent; nearly half the total rainfall occurs during this time. From late September to early November, the weather is cool and sunny. Pre-winter cold spells begin with the first frost on November 30. Winters are mild; temperatures of 32°F or less are unusual. The last frost departs in late February, leading to a warm, windy, and stormy spring.

Summer mildness: 40 **Seasonal affect:** 52
Winter mildness: 84 **Hazard free:** 58
Score: 71.2 **Rank:** 58

	104
	109
	152
90°	35
32°	19
0°	0
	28
	66
	56

	High °F	Low °F	Hum %	Wind mph	Precip inches	Snow inches
JAN	57	39	57	9.1	3.7	0.1
FEB	60	41	55	9.9	3.5	0.2
MAR	67	48	53	10.0	4.4	0.1
APR	74	56	50	9.7	2.7	0
MAY	81	64	55	8.7	3.5	0
JUN	86	71	60	8.4	5.4	0
JUL	89	74	66	7.9	5.1	0
AUG	88	73	70	7.4	7.1	0
SEP	84	69	67	7.8	4.5	0
OCT	78	59	60	8.1	3.5	0
NOV	70	50	60	8.1	2.9	0
DEC	62	43	59	8.5	3.4	0.3

Charlottesville, VA

Location: 38.01 N and 78.32 W at 480 feet, in the center of Virginia's Piedmont Plateau. Washington, D.C., is 110 miles northeast.
Landscape: The Blue Ridge Mountains rise to the west. These and smaller ranges produce a rolling to steep relief. The land is agricultural, with occasional stands of oak, hickory, sweet gum, red maple, loblolly, and shortleaf pine. There is undergrowth of dogwood, viburnum, blueberry, yaupon, and numerous woody vines.
Climate: Modified continental, with mild winters and warm, humid summers. The first frost arrives November 4, and the last frost leaves April 7. The mountains produce various steering and blocking effects on storms and air masses. Chesapeake Bay further modifies the climate, making it warmer in winter, cooler in summer. Precipitation is well distributed throughout the year, with the maximum in July and August and the minimum in January. Tornadoes and violent storms are rare, but severe thunderstorms occur in July.

Summer mildness: 60 **Seasonal affect:** 40
Winter mildness: 45 **Hazard free:** 28
Score: 31.6 **Rank:** 137

	113
	107
	145
90°	31
32°	87
0°	0
	39
	72
	40

	High °F	Low °F	Hum %	Wind mph	Precip inches	Snow inches
JAN	43	26	55	8.6	3.2	6.7
FEB	47	28	52	8.6	3.3	6.9
MAR	57	36	50	9.1	3.8	5.1
APR	68	45	47	9.0	3.3	0
MAY	76	54	54	7.9	4.9	0
JUN	83	62	56	6.9	3.7	0
JUL	87	66	59	6.5	4.8	0
AUG	85	65	60	6.3	4.7	0
SEP	79	59	60	6.9	4.1	0
OCT	68	48	55	7.3	4.6	0
NOV	59	39	53	7.9	3.7	1.0
DEC	47	29	56	7.9	3.3	3.6

Chestertown, MD

Location: 39.13 N and 76.04 W at 35 feet on the eastern shore of Chesapeake Bay, 30 miles east of Baltimore and 60 miles northeast of Washington, D.C.
Landscape: The topography is generally flat with unvarying relief. Inland from the Bay the land is suburban and developed agricultural. The remaining naturally occurring vegetation is a typical southeastern mixed forest with broadleaf deciduous and needleleaf evergreen.
Climate: Subtropical with a definite marine influence from the Bay. Summer days are hot and humid, and a Bay breeze is welcome. Winters are cloudy, dripping, and chilly. Snowfalls are brief and melt quickly.

Summer mildness: 60 **Seasonal affect:** 26
Winter mildness: 58 **Hazard free:** 29
Score: 34.1 **Rank:** 133

	105
	109
	151
90°	31
32°	97
0°	0
	146
	70
	27

	High °F	Low °F	Hum %	Wind mph	Precip inches	Snow inches
JAN	40	28	65	9.7	3.2	5.9
FEB	43	30	63	10.3	3.1	6.5
MAR	53	38	62	10.8	3.7	3.8
APR	64	48	61	10.5	3.2	0.1
MAY	74	58	65	9.1	4.0	0
JUN	83	67	66	8.5	4.4	0
JUL	87	72	67	8.0	3.7	0
AUG	86	71	70	7.8	4.0	0
SEP	79	63	70	8.0	3.6	0
OCT	68	51	69	8.6	3.1	0
NOV	57	42	67	9.2	3.4	1.0
DEC	45	33	66	9.3	3.8	3.5

★ = *in the top 30 places for climate mildness.*

Chewelah, WA

Location: 48.17 N and 117.44 W at 1,671 feet in northeast Washington state, 50 miles midway between Spokane and the Canadian border.
Landscape: Situated in meadowlands on the floor of the Colville River Valley, the town is surrounded by mountainous benchland. The nearby Selkirk and Huckleberry mountains are forested by a variety of evergreens including cedar, larch, fir, and pine.
Climate: Warm continental. The seasonal temperature shifts are moderated because of mountain protection from wind and severe storms. Summer days are warm with little humidity. The seasons are well defined and include a winter with much snow.

Summer mildness: 82
Winter mildness: 25
Score: 13.3
Seasonal affect: 3
Hazard free: 25
Rank: 176

	86
	87
	192
90°	21
32°	141
0°	5
	101
	78
	11

	High °F	Low °F	Hum %	Wind mph	Precip inches	Snow inches
JAN	33	21	82	8.8	2.4	16.2
FEB	41	26	77	9.2	1.9	7.7
MAR	48	30	68	9.6	1.9	4.1
APR	57	35	61	10.0	1.5	0.6
MAY	66	42	59	9.3	2.0	0.1
JUN	75	49	55	9.2	1.5	0
JUL	83	54	47	8.6	0.9	0
AUG	83	54	46	8.2	1.1	0
SEP	72	46	53	8.3	1.1	0
OCT	59	36	64	8.1	1.3	0.4
NOV	41	29	82	8.6	2.7	6.2
DEC	34	22	86	8.6	3.1	15.1

Coeur d'Alene, ID

Location: 47.40 N and 116.46 W at 2,152 feet, on Coeur d'Alene Lake in the northwest panhandle. Boise is 400 miles south, and Spokane, Washington, is 30 miles west.
Landscape: The Coeur d'Alene Mountains are a division of the Bitterroot Range of the Northern Rockies. They shelter the city with a triangle of forested hills or low mountains for 60 miles along the Montana border from Lake Pend Oreille to the St. Joe River. The Coeur d'Alene National Forest spreads across most of the range. To the north and northwest lies Rathdrum Prairie. Within a 10-mile radius, several mountain peaks rise over 4,000 feet.
Climate: Can be generally described as temperate, with clear, dry summers and rainy, snowy winters. Frost comes in by the first of October, and the last frost is May 11. Though seasonal variation is large, it's less so than most other locations this far north. Precipitation is heaviest from autumn to early spring.

Summer mildness: 71
Winter mildness: 28
Score: 16.8
Seasonal affect: 19
Hazard free: 24
Rank: 169

	86
	87
	192
90°	27
32°	139
0°	3
	47
	66
	11

	High °F	Low °F	Hum %	Wind mph	Precip inches	Snow inches
JAN	36	23	80	8.8	3.5	24.0
FEB	43	26	78	9.3	2.5	9.9
MAR	50	30	65	9.7	2.3	5.1
APR	60	35	55	10.0	1.7	0
MAY	69	42	51	9.2	2.1	0
JUN	77	49	47	9.2	2.0	0
JUL	85	53	37	8.6	0.9	0
AUG	86	53	40	8.2	1.3	0
SEP	76	45	45	8.3	1.2	0
OCT	62	38	59	8.2	1.6	0
NOV	46	32	75	8.7	3.3	5.0
DEC	37	26	83	8.6	3.7	15.9

Colorado Springs, CO

Location: 38.50 N and 104.49 W at 6,008 feet, on the eastern slope of the Colorado Rockies, 75 miles south of Denver.
Landscape: Relatively flat and semiarid. Immediately west, the mountains rise abruptly to heights ranging from 10,000 to 14,000 feet, with forested slopes of mixed spruce. To the east lies the gently undulating prairie of eastern Colorado with typical short grasses and woody shrubs. The land slopes upward to the north, reaching an average height of 8,000 feet at the top of Palmer Lake Divide.
Climate: The wide range of outlying elevations helps to give Colorado Springs the pleasant plains-and-mountain mix that established it as a resort. Precipitation is generally light, with 80 percent of it falling as rain from April to October. Temperatures are on the mild side for a city in this latitude and at this elevation. First frost by October 12; last frost as early as May 3.

Summer mildness: 73
Winter mildness: 16
Score: 28.2
Seasonal affect: 79
Hazard free: 0
Rank: 144

	127
	120
	118
90°	41
32°	121
0°	4
	21
	30
	57

	High °F	Low °F	Hum %	Wind mph	Precip inches	Snow inches
JAN	41	16	41	9.5	0.3	5.1
FEB	45	19	40	10.1	0.4	5.2
MAR	50	25	40	11.3	0.9	9.6
APR	60	33	35	11.7	1.2	6.0
MAY	69	42	37	11.3	2.2	1.0
JUN	79	51	36	10.4	2.3	0
JUL	84	57	36	9.3	2.9	0
AUG	81	55	40	9.0	3.0	0
SEP	74	47	39	9.5	1.3	1.0
OCT	64	36	35	9.6	0.8	3.0
NOV	51	25	39	9.5	0.5	5.0
DEC	42	17	42	9.5	0.5	5.8

★ = *in the top 30 places for climate mildness.*

Columbia, MO

Location: 38.57 N and 92.20 W at 758 feet, in north-central Missouri. Kansas City is 120 miles west, and St. Louis is 100 miles east.
Landscape: Here are the gently rolling plains of the broad Missouri River Valley meeting just at the point where prairie and eastern forest ecologies come together. The natural vegetation is a transitional intermingling of prairie, groves, and woodlands. Efforts are underway to increase the diversity of native species.
Climate: Hot continental. Winters are moderately cold but often interrupted by days that are almost balmy, with temperatures as high as the 50s and 60s. First frost is in by October 30; last frost will be April 10. Summers are warm, with days topping 100°F, and it often is very humid as well. Late spring and early summer are the rainiest.

Summer mildness: 59
Winter mildness: 32
Score: 5.9
Seasonal affect: 21
Hazard free: 5
Rank: 191

	104
	91
	170
90°	40
32°	114
0°	6
	123
	65
	52

	High °F	Low °F	Hum %	Wind mph	Precip inches	Snow inches
JAN	37	19	73	10.8	1.5	5.6
FEB	41	23	72	11.0	1.8	6.5
MAR	53	33	69	12.0	3.2	4.3
APR	66	44	67	11.5	3.8	0.7
MAY	74	53	73	9.1	5.0	0
JUN	83	61	73	8.6	4.3	0
JUL	89	66	72	8.3	3.7	0
AUG	87	64	73	7.9	3.3	0
SEP	79	57	73	8.6	3.9	0
OCT	68	46	71	9.5	3.2	0
NOV	54	35	73	10.6	2.9	1.8
DEC	40	23	75	10.8	2.5	4.2

Conway, SC

Location: 33.50 N and 79.03 W at 25 feet, on South Carolina's coastal plain, inland some 20 miles from Myrtle Beach.
Landscape: Relatively flat, surrounded by low country swamplands drained by the tea-colored Waccamaw River. The hinterland is agricultural, with second-growth tall forests of longleaf, loblolly, and slash pines. Live oaks, azaleas, and other bright flowering shrubs are also native.
Climate: Subtropical. Winter is extremely mild and without snow. First frost hits November 11 and the last frost departs around March 17. The Blue Ridge Mountains block the cold air from the interior. Summer is warm and humid, with frequent heavy thunderstorms. The nearby Atlantic has a pronounced modifying effect on temperatures. Some tropical storms reach here every few years.

Summer mildness: 36
Winter mildness: 65
Score: 43.5
Seasonal affect: 33
Hazard free: 51
Rank: 114

	112
	104
	150
90°	65
32°	51
0°	0
	24
	77
	47

	High °F	Low °F	Hum %	Wind mph	Precip inches	Snow inches
JAN	56	33	56	9.1	4.0	0.3
FEB	60	35	52	9.8	3.7	0.9
MAR	68	43	52	10.2	4.1	0.2
APR	76	50	48	10.3	3.1	0
MAY	83	59	55	9.2	4.5	0
JUN	88	67	59	8.5	5.3	0
JUL	91	70	63	8.0	6.4	0
AUG	89	70	64	7.4	5.9	0
SEP	85	64	62	7.9	5.0	0
OCT	77	52	56	8.1	2.9	0
NOV	69	43	53	8.1	2.7	0
DEC	60	36	55	8.5	3.2	0.1

Cottonwood–Verde Valley, AZ

Location: 34.44 N and 112.00 W at 3,314 feet, 100 miles north of Phoenix and 10 miles east of Prescott.
Landscape: The Verde River runs through this high valley near the western edge of the Mongollon Rim. Near are many high peaks, canyons, and mesas. Cottonwood trees line the river. Ponderosa pine and other conifers are in the high country, and sagebrush and native grasses cover the valley floor. The shrubs must tolerate alkaline conditions, as soils are poorly drained.
Climate: Mountain steppe, with strong daily and seasonal temperature changes. The usual winter flow of air is from the Pacific Ocean, bringing snows. Cold air masses from Canada sometimes force temperatures well below 0°F higher up in the mountains. Frost arrives October 9 and departs as late as May 17. Moisture-bearing winds from the southeast Gulf bring brief summer rains from July to September.

Summer mildness: 9
Winter mildness: 31
Score: 38.6
Seasonal affect: 87
Hazard free: 50
Rank: 124

	212
	84
	69
90°	32
32°	150
0°	0
	11
	39
	24

	High °F	Low °F	Hum %	Wind mph	Precip inches	Snow inches
JAN	59	25	45	5.3	1.6	4.5
FEB	63	28	40	5.9	1.5	3.5
MAR	66	31	36	6.7	1.8	6.8
APR	74	35	25	7.0	0.7	2.0
MAY	84	42	20	7.1	0.4	0
JUN	94	49	18	6.8	0.2	0
JUL	98	61	28	7.2	1.6	0
AUG	95	61	33	6.7	2.4	0
SEP	90	52	34	6.3	1.5	0
OCT	80	40	34	5.8	1.0	0
NOV	68	30	37	5.4	1.6	1.0
DEC	60	26	46	5.1	1.5	5.1

★ = *in the top 30 places for climate mildness.*

Crossville, TN

Location: 35.57 N and 85.50 W at 1,863 feet, on the Cumberland Plateau near the center of the state. Knoxville is 62 miles east, and Nashville is 110 miles west.
Landscape: High, rolling foothills of the Appalachians are on the eastern horizon. This is a timberland plateau of eastern deciduous forest. Common trees are hickory, oak, beech, birch, walnut, and maple. These tall broadleaf trees provide dense foliage during summer and completely shed their leaves in winter. Low shrubs develop in spring.
Climate: Hot continental climate characterized by long, mild summers and cool winters. Daily and seasonal temperature changes aren't dramatic. The first frost will come by October 15, and the last frost is April 26. Precipitation, almost all of it rain, is well distributed throughout the year with slight maxima in the summer.

Summer mildness: 68
Winter mildness: 35
Score: 18.8
Seasonal affect: 12
Hazard free: 32
Rank: 164

	112
	96
	157
90°	10
32°	110
0°	4
	34
	90
	51

	High °F	Low °F	Hum %	Wind mph	Precip inches	Snow inches
JAN	42	21	63	4.8	5.2	5.2
FEB	46	24	62	5.0	4.8	5.2
MAR	56	34	59	5.3	6.2	2.7
APR	65	43	55	5.7	5.0	0
MAY	73	50	60	4.5	5.6	0
JUN	80	58	61	4.2	4.4	0
JUL	83	62	63	3.9	5.5	0
AUG	83	60	63	3.7	3.9	0
SEP	77	55	63	3.8	4.2	0
OCT	67	42	63	3.6	3.7	0
NOV	56	35	64	4.1	5.1	1.0
DEC	46	26	67	4.5	5.7	2.3

Dare Outer Banks, NC

Location: 35.54 N and 75.40 W at 5 feet, on the state's northeast coast, 60 miles south of Virginia Beach, Virginia.
Landscape: Principally barrier islands consisting of white-sand beaches, dunes, wetland habitats, and hardwood forest of Atlantic white cedar, bald cypress, with many types of wildflowers and shrubs. Nags Head Woods is a biologically diverse maritime forest. Its 640 acres of wetland, dune, and hardwood forest habitat make this site one of the best remaining examples of mid-Atlantic maritime forest. Cape Hatteras National Seashore, extending 75 miles along the coast, protects over 30,000 acres.
Climate: Subtropical, with humid, hot summers and mild winters. Frost comes as late as November 4 and the last frost departs April 6. January and February nights can be freezing due to the wind chill. Rain falls throughout the year. Summer brings heavy thunderstorms. Occasional tropical storms from the Atlantic may strike this coastal location.

Summer mildness: 54
Winter mildness: 67
Score: 48.5
Seasonal affect: 31
Hazard free: 44
Rank: 103

	108
	101
	156
90°	32
32°	67
0°	0
	15
	76
	42

	High °F	Low °F	Hum %	Wind mph	Precip inches	Snow inches
JAN	52	34	68	12.1	4.3	0.4
FEB	54	36	65	12.3	3.8	0.6
MAR	61	42	63	12.0	4.2	0.5
APR	70	50	59	11.8	3.4	0
MAY	77	59	65	10.9	4.4	0
JUN	84	67	68	10.7	4.6	0
JUL	87	71	70	10.0	5.5	0
AUG	87	71	69	9.5	5.8	0
SEP	82	66	67	10.5	5.0	0
OCT	72	56	65	11.1	3.9	0
NOV	64	47	64	11.0	3.6	0
DEC	56	39	66	11.5	3.6	0.6

Daytona Beach, FL

Location: 29.12 N and 81.01 W at 10 feet, on the Halifax River and Intracoastal Waterway along Florida's Atlantic coast. Jacksonville is 90 miles north; Miami is 260 miles south.
Landscape: An area of tidewater lagoon. The surrounding land is flat with sandy soil. There is no rise above 35 feet. Coastal plain vegetation in this area is cabbage palm and seagrape. The climax forest is mixed evergreen, oak, and magnolia.
Climate: Nearness to the ocean results in a climate tempered by both onshore and offshore breezes. Summer is hot and humid, but a sea breeze usually starts at midday and common afternoon thundershowers drop temperatures to more comfortable levels. Winters can have cold airflows from the north but usually are mild because of the city's ocean setting and southerly latitude. A late first frost of December 10 and the last frost by February 19 lends to a long growing season.

Summer mildness: 29
Winter mildness: 92
Score: 80.1
Seasonal affect: 48
Hazard free: 79
Rank: 41

	99
	134
	133
90°	98
32°	12
0°	0
	28
	77
	77

	High °F	Low °F	Hum %	Wind mph	Precip inches	Snow inches
JAN	68	47	59	8.9	2.8	0
FEB	70	48	57	9.6	3.1	0
MAR	75	54	55	9.8	2.9	0
APR	80	59	53	9.6	2.2	0
MAY	85	65	57	9.0	3.5	0
JUN	88	71	63	8.1	6.0	0
JUL	90	73	65	7.5	5.4	0
AUG	89	73	67	7.1	6.2	0
SEP	87	72	67	8.3	6.3	0
OCT	82	65	63	9.2	4.1	0
NOV	76	56	60	8.6	2.8	0
DEC	70	50	60	8.5	2.6	0

★ = *in the top 30 places for climate mildness.*

Delta County, CO

Location: Delta, the county seat, is 38.44 N and 108.04 W at 4,953 feet, in the western part of the state. Grand Junction is 45 miles northwest.

Landscape: Within the sage desert and shortgrass prairie of the Colorado Plateau. Ranchland and orchards mark the gently rolling lowland. Lakes and streams are fed from mountain snows. The Gunnison and Uncompahgre rivers flow through steep canyons, where sagebrush and cactus are found. Pine, spruce, and aspen forests cover the subalpine areas.

Climate: Desert steppe brings varied seasonal and daily temperature changes. Summers are dry and comfortable due to the high altitude. Winters are cold with moderate snow cover in the elevations through May. First frost, October 5; last frost, May 17. Humidity is low, and precipitation is scant except for brief mountain thunderstorms.

Summer mildness: 65
Winter mildness: 17
Score: 41.5
Seasonal affect: 80
Hazard free: 20
Rank: 119

	137
	107
	121
90°	23
32°	165
0°	4
	8
	34
	35

	High °F	Low °F	Hum %	Wind mph	Precip inches	Snow inches
JAN	38	15	64	5.6	0.9	10.5
FEB	44	20	52	6.7	0.8	7.9
MAR	52	27	43	8.4	1.2	7.0
APR	62	33	33	9.5	0.9	2.4
MAY	72	41	32	9.6	1.1	0.6
JUN	83	50	34	9.7	0.8	0
JUL	88	56	28	9.3	1.0	0
AUG	85	54	30	9.0	1.2	0
SEP	77	46	33	8.9	1.3	0
OCT	65	36	38	7.9	1.5	0.9
NOV	50	26	51	6.7	1.1	4.9
DEC	40	17	62	5.9	1.1	9.2

Door Peninsula, WI

Location: The weather station is at Sturgeon Bay, 44.51 N and 87.23 W at 660 feet, on Wisconsin's Door Peninsula between Green Bay and Lake Michigan. The site is 180 miles northeast of Madison, the state capital.

Landscape: Characterized by rolling woodlands, limestone bluffs, and 250 miles of rocky shoreline and sandy beaches. Glacier effects predominate. The woods contain northern hardwoods of maple, oak, beech, and birch mixed with pine, eastern hemlock, and eastern red cedar.

Climate: Continental, and largely influenced by lakes Michigan and Superior. This is certainly a four-season climate that is relatively temperate and extends the growing season. Winters are moderately long and can be severe. First frost snaps in by October 8; the last frost departs May 17. Snow falls early and lasts late. Summers are mild, with cool evenings and nights. Springs and autumns are all too short.

Summer mildness: 90
Winter mildness: 9
Score: 17.8
Seasonal affect: 32
Hazard free: 13
Rank: 166

	87
	102
	176
90°	3
32°	159
0°	19
	24
	63
	33

	High °F	Low °F	Hum %	Wind mph	Precip inches	Snow inches
JAN	25	9	72	11.0	1.5	10.4
FEB	28	11	69	10.6	1.1	7.2
MAR	38	22	64	10.9	2.1	8.0
APR	52	33	55	11.3	2.7	2.0
MAY	65	42	50	10.2	3.1	0
JUN	74	51	55	9.2	3.3	0
JUL	80	58	54	8.2	3.4	0
AUG	77	57	60	8.0	3.4	0
SEP	69	50	63	9.0	3.9	0
OCT	57	40	65	9.9	2.7	0
NOV	43	30	73	11.0	2.5	2.0
DEC	30	17	77	10.7	1.9	9.5

Durango, CO

Location: 37.16 N and 107.52 W at 6,523 feet, in Colorado's Four Corners area, 250 air miles southwest of Denver.

Landscape: High in the Animas River Valley surrounded by red bluffs. The sharply uplifted peaks of the San Juan Mountains provide dramatic relief. Much of the area is within the San Juan National Forest, a pine and aspen woods with a subalpine growth of scrub oak and grasses.

Climate: Semiarid continental, which causes definite seasonal temperature variations. Daily temperature changes are notable throughout the year as mountain nights chill considerably. Warm, dry summers blend into short, cool, dry falls. September 18 is when the first frost jacks into the area, and June 4 when the last frost bites. Winters are long and extremely snowy. Due to deep snow accumulations in the mountains, rivers and reservoirs stay relatively full in summer, though city water is frequently rationed.

Summer mildness: 66
Winter mildness: 4
Score: 21.7
Seasonal affect: 77
Hazard free: 11
Rank: 159

	137
	107
	121
90°	18
32°	211
0°	11
	8
	44
	35

	High °F	Low °F	Hum %	Wind mph	Precip inches	Snow inches
JAN	40	10	63	5.6	1.6	20.4
FEB	46	16	55	6.7	1.4	12.6
MAR	53	22	41	8.4	1.7	12.1
APR	62	29	32	9.5	1.2	4.0
MAY	71	36	31	9.6	1.1	0
JUN	82	42	25	9.7	0.7	0
JUL	87	51	27	9.3	1.8	0
AUG	84	49	30	9.0	2.4	0
SEP	76	41	33	8.9	1.9	0
OCT	66	31	37	7.9	2.0	0
NOV	52	22	48	6.7	1.7	6.0
DEC	41	13	60	5.9	1.8	17.4

★ = *in the top 30 places for climate mildness.*

Eagle River–Woodruff, WI

Location: 45.55 N and 89.14 W at 1,647 feet, near where Michigan's Upper Peninsula meets northern Wisconsin. Green Bay is 140 miles southeast.

Landscape: Generally level. The entire area was once part of a great, dense, white pine forest but is now covered with second growth. Within a 20-mile radius of the town are more than 200 lakes, some with identical names.

Climate: Continental, and largely determined by the movement and interaction of large air masses. Weather changes can be expected every few days in winter and spring. Winters are long and cold with an average of 39 days when the temperature drops below 0°F. Summer days are warm and pleasant, with comfortably cool nights. Spring and fall are short, with rapid transition from winter to summer and vice versa. First frost is in by September 23; last frost out May 19.

Summer mildness: 92 **Seasonal affect:** 32
Winter mildness: 1 **Hazard free:** 9
Score: 12.8 **Rank:** 177

87
102
176
90° 3
32° 181
0° 44
24
63
33

	High °F	Low °F	Hum %	Wind mph	Precip inches	Snow inches
JAN	21	-1	72	11.0	1.1	10.6
FEB	26	2	69	10.6	0.8	8.3
MAR	38	15	64	10.9	1.5	9.0
APR	53	29	55	11.3	2.4	2.0
MAY	67	41	50	10.2	3.2	0
JUN	75	50	55	9.2	3.8	0
JUL	80	56	54	8.2	3.4	0
AUG	77	53	60	8.0	4.3	0
SEP	67	45	63	9.0	4.3	0
OCT	55	35	65	9.9	2.6	0
NOV	39	22	73	11.0	1.9	4.0
DEC	25	6	77	10.7	1.4	11.1

East End Long Island, NY

Location: 40.58 N and 72.11 W at 55 feet, at the extreme tip of Long Island. New York City is 120 miles west.

Landscape: The eastern end of Long Island, where the Atlantic Ocean meets Long Island Sound, is divided into two narrow peninsulas by four bays. The surrounding land is suburban and agricultural. Small understory trees and shrubs make up the lower growth of the woodlands. Common specimen trees are oak, beech, birch, hickory, tulip tree, and sweet chestnut.

Climate: Hot continental, with fewer seasonal and daily temperature fluctuations where tempered by the effects of the surrounding salt water. Precipitation is distributed throughout the year. Summers have hot and humid stretches but are generally warm and dry. Winters can be cold with icy rain. Snowfall is light and lasts but a little while. First frost by October 21, and a last frost by April 27 leaves only a modest growing season.

Summer mildness: 72 **Seasonal affect:** 30
Winter mildness: 29 **Hazard free:** 31
Score: 23.7 **Rank:** 154

100
118
148
90° 7
32° 121
0° 2
39
74
28

	High °F	Low °F	Hum %	Wind mph	Precip inches	Snow inches
JAN	39	21	62	9.7	3.9	7.2
FEB	40	22	61	10.1	3.7	4.4
MAR	49	30	56	10.5	4.2	3.4
APR	59	38	56	10.0	4.3	0
MAY	69	47	58	9.0	4.0	0
JUN	78	57	58	8.5	4.0	0
JUL	83	63	62	7.5	3.5	0
AUG	82	62	61	7.4	4.3	0
SEP	76	55	61	7.5	3.4	0
OCT	65	44	59	8.3	3.6	0
NOV	55	36	60	9.9	4.4	1.0
DEC	43	26	58	9.4	4.3	3.9

Easton–St. Michaels, MD

Location: 38.46 N and 76.04 W at 38 feet, in the tidewater region along the eastern shore of Chesapeake Bay near the head of Tred Avon River. Baltimore is 55 miles northwest.

Landscape: There's precious little relief in the long, low hills cut by streams and inlets from the Bay. Inland, the land is developed agricultural fields. The native vegetation is a typical southeastern mixed forest with broadleaf deciduous and needleleaf evergreen trees. In the towns are holly and magnolias.

Climate: Subtropical with a definite marine influence. Summers are hot and humid though often lifted somewhat by a bay breeze. Some winters can be freezing and snowy but normally are chilly and rainy. The first frost comes October 29, but the last frost is out by April 9. Snow is minimal and is quickly gone.

Summer mildness: 55 **Seasonal affect:** 37
Winter mildness: 48 **Hazard free:** 38
Score: 39.6 **Rank:** 123

107
108
150
90° 27
32° 85
0° 0
26
73
28

	High °F	Low °F	Hum %	Wind mph	Precip inches	Snow inches
JAN	43	26	57	9.7	3.6	4.5
FEB	46	28	54	10.3	3.2	5.3
MAR	56	36	50	10.9	3.9	2.6
APR	66	44	49	10.6	3.3	0
MAY	76	54	53	9.2	4.1	0
JUN	84	63	52	8.5	3.5	0
JUL	88	67	52	8.0	4.4	0
AUG	86	66	56	7.8	4.5	0
SEP	81	60	55	8.0	3.4	0
OCT	70	48	55	8.7	3.0	0
NOV	60	40	55	9.3	3.4	0
DEC	49	31	57	9.3	3.6	2.0

★ *= in the top 30 places for climate mildness.*

Edenton, NC

Location: 36.03 N and 76.36 W at 5 feet, on Albemarle Sound in North Carolina's northeast coastal area. Raleigh is 120 miles west, and Virginia Beach, Virginia, is 65 miles north.

Landscape: At the mouth of the Chowan River on Albemarle Sound west of Kitty Hawk and the Barrier Islands. The woods are evergreens, oak, bald cypress, laurel, and magnolia mixed with loblolly and slash pine. The native undergrowth consists of typical coastal plain plants of fern, and other herbaceous plants, small palms, and shrubs.

Climate: Subtropical, with humid, hot, coastal plain summers. Winters are mild but with some freezing nights. First frost delays until November 10; last frost is out by March 24. Snow is negligible, but rain falls throughout the year. Spring and summer can bring heavy thunderstorms, and occasional tropical storms from the Atlantic may reach this location.

Summer mildness: 50
Winter mildness: 63
Score: 46.0
Seasonal affect: 45
Hazard free: 35
Rank: 109

	106
	107
	152
90°	31
32°	52
0°	0
	20
	73
	42

	High °F	Low °F	Hum %	Wind mph	Precip inches	Snow inches
JAN	52	32	60	12.1	4.2	1.7
FEB	55	34	58	12.3	3.8	2.2
MAR	63	41	56	12.0	4.0	1.1
APR	72	49	52	11.8	3.3	0
MAY	79	58	58	10.9	4.5	0
JUN	85	66	58	10.7	4.5	0
JUL	88	70	61	10.0	5.4	0
AUG	87	70	62	9.5	5.4	0
SEP	82	64	62	10.5	4.3	0
OCT	73	53	61	11.1	3.2	0
NOV	65	44	58	11.0	2.8	0
DEC	56	36	60	11.5	3.2	0.5

Eufaula, AL

Location: 31.91 N and 85.15 W at 200 feet in southeastern Alabama, about 90 miles southeast of Montgomery, the state capital. Across the Chattahoochee River is Georgia.

Landscape: The location is at the northern edge of the great outer coastal plain that fronts the Gulf of Mexico. Marshes, swamps, and lakes are numerous. The trees are evergreen oak, magnolia, and laurel.

Climate: Humid subtropical, influenced by the nearby Gulf of Mexico. Winter days are rarely cold. Summers are long, hot, and humid.

Summer mildness: 33
Winter mildness: 87
Score: 56.4
Seasonal affect: 30
Hazard free: 60
Rank: 88

	97
	133
	136
90°	87
32°	22
0°	0
	178
	76
	51

	High °F	Low °F	Hum %	Wind mph	Precip inches	Snow inches
JAN	60	41	66	9.0	4.7	0.3
FEB	63	44	63	9.4	5.4	0.3
MAR	69	51	64	9.7	5.6	0.1
APR	77	59	63	9.5	3.8	0
MAY	83	66	69	8.6	4.2	0
JUN	89	72	70	7.6	6.4	0
JUL	90	74	72	7.0	7.4	0
AUG	89	74	75	6.7	7.4	0
SEP	86	70	74	7.6	5.3	0
OCT	79	59	69	7.9	4.2	0
NOV	70	51	68	8.4	3.5	0
DEC	63	44	67	8.9	4.3	0.2

Eureka Springs, AR

Location: 36.23 N and 93.44 W at 1,420 feet in the Ozark Mountains near the Arkansas and Missouri border, 33 miles northeast of Fayetteville.

Landscape: Encircled by two great lakes and two scenic rivers. The country is rugged and wooded, with farms small and scattered. A dense deciduous forest of oak and hickory surrounds the area. In spring, a luxurious low layer of herbs develops, but this is arrested when the trees leaf out and shade the ground.

Climate: Hot continental, with warm summers due to the elevation and mild winters thanks to the latitude. Each summer can vary from warm and humid maritime to dry continental. Winter occasionally produces dangerous ice storms.

Summer mildness: 44
Winter mildness: 42
Score: 24.7
Seasonal affect: 56
Hazard free: 20
Rank: 153

	127
	103
	136
90°	56
32°	105
0°	1
	92
	62
	50

	High °F	Low °F	Hum %	Wind mph	Precip inches	Snow inches
JAN	46	23	60	10.3	2.0	3.0
FEB	51	27	60	10.8	2.8	3.9
MAR	61	37	56	12.1	4.1	2.4
APR	72	47	55	11.9	4.2	0
MAY	78	55	59	10.6	4.9	0
JUN	85	63	59	10.0	4.4	0
JUL	91	68	56	9.4	3.3	0
AUG	90	66	54	8.9	3.8	0
SEP	82	59	58	9.1	4.1	0
OCT	72	47	54	9.7	3.7	0
NOV	60	37	59	10.3	3.8	1.0
DEC	49	28	63	10.2	3.4	1.0

★ = *in the top 30 places for climate mildness.*

Fairhope–Gulf Shores, AL

Location: 30.31 N and 87.54 W at 122 feet, on the Gulf of Mexico near Mobile Bay, 35 miles south of Mobile.

Landscape: Gulf coastal plain where ecologies appear to be flat plains, but contain coastal lagoons, sandy beaches, swampy lowlands, and salt marshes as well as typical southern forests of loblolly, shortleaf, and pond pines, some sweet gum, and oaks. Local relief ranges from sea level to less than 250 feet inland.

Climate: Subtropical. Destructive hurricanes are extremely infrequent, due more to chance than to location. The area is subject to hurricanes from the West Indies and the Gulf of Mexico. The normal annual rainfall amount is one of the highest in the continental United States. It's evenly distributed year-round, slightly higher at the height of the summer thunderstorm season. First frost arrives by Thanksgiving; last frost departs February 25—a long 274-day growing season, enough for citrus.

Summer mildness: 34
Winter mildness: 83
Score: 51.9
Seasonal affect: 28
Hazard free: 54
Rank: 98

	103
	116
	146
90°	74
32°	21
0°	0
	41
	80
	74

	High °F	Low °F	Hum %	Wind mph	Precip inches	Snow inches
JAN	59	39	61	10.4	5.0	0.1
FEB	63	41	56	10.7	6.1	0.2
MAR	70	49	55	10.9	6.1	0
APR	77	56	52	10.2	4.1	0
MAY	83	63	54	8.9	5.4	0
JUN	89	70	55	7.7	6.6	0
JUL	90	72	60	7.0	7.3	0
AUG	89	72	61	6.8	6.7	0
SEP	87	68	59	7.9	5.7	0
OCT	79	56	52	8.2	3.2	0
NOV	70	49	57	9.3	4.2	0
DEC	62	42	61	10.1	4.9	0

Fayetteville, AR

Location: 36.03 N and 94.09 W at 1,334 feet, in northwest Arkansas, 30 miles from the Oklahoma line and 40 miles south of Missouri. Little Rock is 170 miles southeast.

Landscape: On the White River in the Boston Mountains. Elevations near here reach over 2,000 feet in the highest parts of the Ozark Plateau. This is rugged, wooded mountain country. Broadleaf deciduous oak and hickory predominate, with lower layers of scattered small trees and shrubs, especially redbud and dogwood.

Climate: Modified continental, with hot, humid summers and briefer winters than other locations at this latitude. Winter to winter can vary from warm and humid maritime to cold and dry continental but are relatively free from climatic extremes. Mid-October sees the first frost, and late April marks the last frost. Snowfalls are minimal, but precipitation in January and February can be dangerous icy rain.

Summer mildness: 53
Winter mildness: 43
Score: 26.2
Seasonal affect: 54
Hazard free: 15
Rank: 150

	116
	97
	153
90°	44
32°	103
0°	1
	20
	66
	56

	High °F	Low °F	Hum %	Wind mph	Precip inches	Snow inches
JAN	45	23	60	11.7	1.8	3.0
FEB	50	27	60	11.9	2.5	3.9
MAR	59	37	56	12.9	3.9	2.4
APR	69	47	55	12.2	4.3	0
MAY	76	55	59	10.4	5.0	0
JUN	84	63	59	9.6	5.0	0
JUL	89	68	56	8.5	2.9	0
AUG	88	66	54	8.6	3.6	0
SEP	81	59	58	9.3	4.5	0
OCT	71	47	54	10.1	3.8	0
NOV	59	37	59	11.3	3.7	1.0
DEC	49	28	63	11.6	3.1	1.4

Flagstaff, AZ

Location: 35.08 N and 111.40 W at 7,000 feet, in north-central Arizona, 80 miles south of the Grand Canyon and 120 miles northeast of Phoenix.

Landscape: Part of a geographic region known as the Colorado Plateau, a series of generally level plateaus mostly separated by steep-sided chasms. There is little arable land. Near here is Arizona's highest point, Humphreys Peak in the San Francisco Mountains. The city sits on the northern border of the Prescott National Forest. Lumbering is an important economic base for the area.

Climate: Vigorous, cool to cold winters, with warm summers. Frost arrives by October 21 and departs May 14. Flagstaff gets about 23 inches of precipitation yearly and the surrounding mountains and plateaus receive somewhat more moisture, 20 to 40 inches, with up to 5 feet of snow falling in peak areas.

Summer mildness: 77
Winter mildness: 8
Score: 34.1
Seasonal affect: 83
Hazard free: 6
Rank: 133

	162
	102
	101
90°	1
32°	210
0°	8
	12
	39
	38

	High °F	Low °F	Hum %	Wind mph	Precip inches	Snow inches
JAN	42	15	63	6.8	2.0	20.7
FEB	45	18	60	6.7	2.1	18.3
MAR	49	21	57	7.2	2.6	22.3
APR	58	27	49	7.6	1.5	9.5
MAY	67	33	46	7.3	0.7	1.8
JUN	78	41	38	6.9	0.4	0
JUL	82	51	53	5.5	2.8	0
AUG	79	49	60	5.1	2.8	0
SEP	73	41	55	5.7	2.0	0.1
OCT	63	31	54	5.8	1.6	2.0
NOV	51	22	57	6.8	2.0	10.2
DEC	43	16	62	6.7	2.4	15.9

★ = *in the top 30 places for climate mildness.*

Florence, OR

Location: 43.59 N and 124.06 W at 23 feet, at the mouth of the Siuslaw River near the center of Oregon's Pacific Coast, 60 miles west of Eugene.
Landscape: Minimal elevation from extensive sand dunes and beach. Low growth of sea grass, rhododendrons, and evergreen shrub leads to a taller forest of cedar, hemlock, and Douglas fir in the foothills of the Coast Range. The coastal forest stops at the edge of the dune field except for small islands of conifers. There are also several small lakes found in the dunes.
Climate: Mild marine with heavy rainfall, especially in winter and spring. Humidity is always high, but daily maximum temperatures are comfortable throughout the year. Winters may produce ocean storms and occasional light snow. Falls are clear, lengthy, and pleasant. First frost waits until December 17; the last frost is out by February 28.

Summer mildness: 97
Winter mildness: 70
Score: 80.6
Seasonal affect: 2
Hazard free: 79
Rank: 38

	51
	77
	237
90°	1
32°	8
0°	0
	41
	101
	8

	High °F	Low °F	Hum %	Wind mph	Precip inches	Snow inches
JAN	55	41	80	9.1	10.9	0.9
FEB	56	42	79	9.1	9.0	0.3
MAR	57	42	77	9.0	9.3	0.6
APR	60	43	73	8.7	5.2	0
MAY	63	46	71	8.5	3.6	0
JUN	67	50	71	8.6	1.6	0
JUL	68	51	71	8.7	0.5	0
AUG	68	52	72	8.1	1.3	0
SEP	69	51	73	7.6	2.1	0
OCT	64	48	77	7.6	5.7	0
NOV	59	45	78	8.8	11.5	0
DEC	55	41	82	9.1	11.9	1.2

Fort Collins–Loveland, CO

Location: 40.35 N and 105.05 W at 5,003 feet, on the Cache la Poudre River in the eastern foothills of the Rockies' Front Range, 55 miles north of Denver.
Landscape: Lies near some of the most spectacular mountain terrain in the country. Steep cliffs, high waterfalls, and forested mountain slopes cut by swift rivers are found to the west. Thirty miles east, the landscape settles into grassland prairies of the Great Plains.
Climate: Near the center of the continent, Fort Collins and Loveland are removed from any major source of airborne moisture and are further shielded from rainfall by the high Rockies to the west. In winter, cold air from Canada may bring snow and subfreezing temperatures at night. Frost arrives October 1 and departs by early May. In summer, hot air from the desert southwest brings daytime temperatures of 90°F. However, felt heat is low because of dryness.

Summer mildness: 69
Winter mildness: 14
Score: 28.2
Seasonal affect: 80
Hazard free: 4
Rank: 144

	115
	130
	120
90°	22
32°	167
0°	11
	10
	33
	42

	High °F	Low °F	Hum %	Wind mph	Precip inches	Snow inches
JAN	41	14	46	8.7	0.4	7.3
FEB	46	19	44	8.9	0.4	6.3
MAR	52	25	41	9.7	1.4	12.0
APR	61	34	38	10.1	1.8	6.0
MAY	70	43	38	9.4	2.7	1.0
JUN	80	52	37	8.9	1.9	0
JUL	86	57	35	8.3	1.8	0
AUG	83	55	35	8.0	1.3	0
SEP	75	46	35	8.0	1.3	0
OCT	64	35	37	7.9	1.0	2.0
NOV	51	24	45	8.3	0.7	6.0
DEC	42	16	46	8.5	0.5	6.7

★ Fort Myers–Cape Coral, FL

Location: 26.38 N and 81.52 W at 10 feet, on the broad Caloosahatchee River in southwestern Florida, 120 miles south of Tampa.
Landscape: This area is the western terminus of the Okeechobee Waterway, linking the Atlantic Ocean and the Gulf of Mexico, about 15 miles away. The land is level and low. The climax growth of the coastal plain in this area north of the Everglades is evergreen oak and magnolia. Spanish moss trails from Evangeline oak and bald cypress. Tree ferns, small palms, and shrubs make up the lower layer.
Climate: Subtropical. Summer and winter temperature extremes are checked by the influence of the Gulf. Mild winters have many bright, warm days. Nights are moderately cool. Rainfall averages more than 50 inches annually, two-thirds of this coming daily between June and September. Most rain falls as late-afternoon or early-evening thunderstorms, bringing relief from the heat.

Summer mildness: 12
Winter mildness: 98
Score: 89.6
Seasonal affect: 72
Hazard free: 84
Rank: 21

	100
	168
	98
90°	101
32°	0
0°	0
	21
	72
	93

	High °F	Low °F	Hum %	Wind mph	Precip inches	Snow inches
JAN	74	53	57	8.4	1.8	0
FEB	75	54	55	9.0	2.2	0
MAR	80	59	52	9.4	3.1	0
APR	84	62	47	8.9	1.1	0
MAY	89	68	50	8.1	3.9	0
JUN	90	73	58	7.3	9.5	0
JUL	91	75	59	6.7	8.3	0
AUG	91	75	60	6.8	9.7	0
SEP	90	74	61	7.6	7.8	0
OCT	86	69	56	8.5	2.9	0
NOV	81	61	56	8.2	1.6	0
DEC	76	55	56	8.0	1.5	0

★ = *in the top 30 places for climate mildness.*

Fredericksburg, TX

Location: 30.16 N and 98.52 W at 1,702 feet, on the Pedernales River in central Texas. Austin, the state capital, is 80 miles east, and San Antonio is 80 miles southeast.
Landscape: In a high, green valley as transition from rich Blacklands to Edwards Plateau foothills occurs. Encircled by hills with outcroppings of a large, dissected plateau, formed of thick layers of limestone and other sedimentary rocks lifted about 2,000 feet along the Balcones Escarpment. Erosion carved the uplifted areas into hilly, rocky terrain. Among the peach orchards and many wineries are native vegetation stands of cedar, juniper, oak, and prairie grasses.
Climate: Prairie. Summer days are hot but nights pleasantly cool. Winters are mild with few, brief cold spells. Fall arrives around mid-October though the first frost waits until November 11. The last frost leaves March 24. Snow is negligible. Rainfall is distributed evenly throughout the year. Humidity is generally a comfortable 55 percent.

Summer mildness: 24
Winter mildness: 72
Score: 65.8
Seasonal affect: 74
Hazard free: 56
Rank: 70

	117
	115
	134
90°	97
32°	39
0°	0
	23
	43
	41

	High °F	Low °F	Hum %	Wind mph	Precip inches	Snow inches
JAN	60	35	60	9.7	1.3	0.2
FEB	64	39	59	10.2	1.8	0.7
MAR	72	47	56	10.8	1.4	0.1
APR	79	55	57	10.5	2.5	0
MAY	84	62	60	9.6	4.2	0
JUN	89	67	56	9.1	3.6	0
JUL	93	69	51	8.3	2.2	0
AUG	93	68	50	7.9	2.7	0
SEP	87	64	55	7.9	3.6	0
OCT	79	55	55	8.1	3.6	0
NOV	69	46	58	9.0	1.9	0
DEC	62	38	59	9.2	1.3	0.1

Fredericksburg–Spotsylvania, VA

Location: 38.18 N and 77.27 W at 60 feet, 42 miles south of Washington, D.C., and 40 miles north of Richmond.
Landscape: Rolling hill country at the head of navigation of the Rappahannock River in northeastern Virginia. The woods are a southeastern mixed forest of medium-tall to tall broadleaf deciduous oak, hickory, sweet gum, red maple, and winged elm, together with loblolly and shortleaf pine. The undergrowth is dogwood, viburnum, blueberry, yaupon, and numerous woody vines.
Climate: Modified continental, with cool winters and warm, humid summers. The Blue Ridge Mountains to the west produce various steering and blocking effects on storms and air masses. Chesapeake Bay further modifies the climate, making it warmer in winter and cooler in summer. First frost strikes by October 15; last frost departs April 21. Precipitation is well distributed throughout the year.

Summer mildness: 52
Winter mildness: 34
Score: 29.7
Seasonal affect: 50
Hazard free: 33
Rank: 143

	113
	107
	145
90°	49
32°	112
0°	1
	23
	72
	40

	High °F	Low °F	Hum %	Wind mph	Precip inches	Snow inches
JAN	44	22	60	9.5	3.1	6.2
FEB	47	23	58	9.7	2.9	4.9
MAR	58	33	56	10.1	3.6	3.7
APR	68	41	52	9.8	3.1	0
MAY	77	51	58	7.9	3.9	0
JUN	85	60	58	6.9	3.4	0
JUL	89	65	61	6.5	3.7	0
AUG	87	63	62	6.1	3.6	0
SEP	81	56	62	6.1	3.5	0
OCT	70	43	61	6.9	3.4	0
NOV	59	34	58	8.3	3.4	0
DEC	48	26	60	8.8	3.3	2.1

Front Royal, VA

Location: 38.55 N and 78.10 W at 680 feet in Northern Virginia at the north end of Skyline Drive (Shenandoah National Park extension of Blue Ridge Parkway). Washington, D.C., is 60 miles east.
Landscape: Terrain varies from rolling hills to rugged in the mountains visible to the west. Tall, broadleaf trees that provide a continuous dense canopy in summer dominate the surrounding forest.
Climate: Warm continental, with mild winters and warm, humid summers. The mountains provide steering, blocking, and modifying effects on storms and air masses. All seasons are pleasant, though summer, especially July, can be hot.

Summer mildness: 74
Winter mildness: 37
Score: 15.8
Seasonal affect: 11
Hazard free: 17
Rank: 171

	58
	103
	204
90°	8
32°	134
0°	9
	178
	71
	35

	High °F	Low °F	Hum %	Wind mph	Precip inches	Snow inches
JAN	34	23	55	10.6	2.4	10.1
FEB	37	26	53	10.5	2.4	8.7
MAR	49	35	51	10.7	3.4	5.1
APR	60	43	50	10.3	3.8	0.9
MAY	71	52	55	8.9	4.1	0
JUN	79	60	56	8.0	4.1	0
JUL	83	64	58	7.3	4.3	0
AUG	81	63	59	6.9	3.9	0
SEP	74	57	59	7.4	3.3	0
OCT	63	44	55	8.4	2.8	0.2
NOV	50	36	55	9.8	3.5	2.2
DEC	39	28	57	10.4	3.0	5.1

★ = *in the top 30 places for climate mildness.*

Gainesville, FL

Location: 29.39 N and 82.19 W at 147 feet, in north-central Florida. Jacksonville is 65 miles northeast.

Landscape: Flat-to-rolling ranch and farm country, with some geological relief in limestone sinkholes and caverns. Native trees are longleaf and slash pines. Gallberry, saw palmetto, and fetterbush make up the undergrowth. Plants normally found in ravines of the Appalachian Mountains are at home here. There are lakes and wetlands in the county.

Climate: Subtropical, with a small annual range of temperature change. Humid, hot summer afternoons are cooled by frequent heavy thunderstorms or cool breezes from the Gulf. Winters tend to be dry and mild, with warm days and cool nights. First frost comes as late as November 27, with the last frost as early as March 3 yielding a long growing season. Measurable snowfalls are rare.

Summer mildness: 26 **Seasonal affect:** 53
Winter mildness: 86 **Hazard free:** 74
Score: 74.2 **Rank:** 52

	92
	148
	125
90°	99
32°	18
0°	0
	42
	75
	81

	High °F	Low °F	Hum %	Wind mph	Precip inches	Snow inches
JAN	66	43	61	6.9	3.4	0.1
FEB	68	44	57	7.3	4.2	0
MAR	75	51	55	7.4	3.7	0
APR	81	56	50	7.0	2.6	0
MAY	86	63	50	6.7	3.8	0
JUN	90	68	59	5.9	6.8	0
JUL	91	71	63	5.6	6.8	0
AUG	90	71	65	5.3	8.0	0
SEP	87	69	65	5.9	5.3	0
OCT	81	60	62	6.6	1.8	0
NOV	74	51	63	6.2	2.3	0
DEC	68	45	62	5.9	3.3	0

Georgetown, TX

Location: 30.16 N and 97.44 W at 501 feet, on the Balcones Escarpment separating the Texas Hill Country from the blackland prairies of East Texas. Austin, the state capital, is 20 miles south.

Landscape: Low hills and wide terraces intermingle, supporting a variety of native vegetation, including oak, cedar, walnut, pecan, and mesquite. It varies with some stretches of grasslands, others of cliffs and bluffs. Located on the San Gabriel River, with nearby Lake Georgetown, impounded in 1980, providing a typical highland reservoir.

Climate: Prairie. Summers are hot and humid, though evenings can be cool. Winters are mild, only occasionally reaching below-freezing temperatures. November 25 brings the first frost, while the last frost leaves March 7. Late spring and early fall bring peak precipitation and thunderstorm activity. Winds are predominantly southerly, with occasional strong and cool northerlies. Snowfall is virtually nonexistent.

Summer mildness: 14 **Seasonal affect:** 73
Winter mildness: 72 **Hazard free:** 61
Score: 63.3 **Rank:** 75

	117
	115
	134
90°	106
32°	30
0°	0
	23
	46
	41

	High °F	Low °F	Hum %	Wind mph	Precip inches	Snow inches
JAN	56	35	60	9.7	1.9	0.5
FEB	61	38	59	10.2	2.7	0.3
MAR	70	46	56	10.8	2.5	0
APR	78	55	57	10.5	2.9	0
MAY	84	63	60	9.6	4.6	0
JUN	91	70	56	9.1	3.6	0
JUL	95	73	51	8.3	2.0	0
AUG	96	73	50	7.9	2.3	0
SEP	89	67	55	7.9	3.8	0
OCT	80	57	55	8.1	3.3	0
NOV	69	46	58	9.0	2.9	0
DEC	60	38	59	9.2	2.3	0

Grand Junction, CO

Location: 39.04 N and 108.33 W at 4,597 feet, in the Grand Valley of western Colorado, at the junction of the Colorado and Gunnison rivers. Denver is 250 miles east, and the Utah border is 20 miles west.

Landscape: Near to lake-studded Grand Mesa, the Colorado National Monument, and the Uncompahgre National Forest. Sagebrush and prickly pear cactus are found in the canyons. Pine, spruce, and aspen forests cover the subalpine areas.

Climate: The interior location, coupled with the ring of high mountains, results in low rainfall. Winter snows are frequent and light and don't remain long. First frost arrives in late September, and the last frost is not gone until mid-May. Summer humidity is very low, making the region as dry as parts of Arizona. Sunny days predominate in all seasons. The city's climate is marked by wide seasonal temperature changes. The surrounding mountains protect from sudden and severe weather changes.

Summer mildness: 49 **Seasonal affect:** 82
Winter mildness: 10 **Hazard free:** 30
Score: 30.1 **Rank:** 142

	137
	107
	121
90°	67
32°	174
0°	9
	8
	24
	35

	High °F	Low °F	Hum %	Wind mph	Precip inches	Snow inches
JAN	36	10	64	5.6	0.6	7.4
FEB	46	18	53	6.7	0.5	4.2
MAR	55	26	43	8.4	0.9	4.0
APR	65	33	34	9.5	0.7	1.0
MAY	76	43	31	9.6	0.9	0
JUN	87	50	25	9.7	0.5	0
JUL	92	57	29	9.3	0.8	0
AUG	90	55	31	9.0	0.9	0
SEP	81	45	33	8.9	0.8	0
OCT	69	34	39	7.9	0.9	0
NOV	52	23	50	6.7	0.7	2.0
DEC	40	14	61	5.9	0.7	5.3

★ = *in the top 30 places for climate mildness.*

Grants Pass, OR

Location: 42.26 N and 123.19 W at 948 feet, on the Rogue River in southwestern Oregon. Eugene is 120 miles north, Medford is 20 miles east, and the California border is 60 miles south.

Landscape: This is the rugged terrain of the foothills of the Siskiyous. The Rogue River is swift white water here. Southwest is the Redwood Highway and the Illinois Valley. The common trees in the dense Pacific conifer forest are Douglas fir, western red cedar, western hemlock, silver fir, and Sitka spruce.

Climate: Generally mild highland. The moderate temperatures of the Pacific are altered somewhat by the Coast Range bringing the area a reputation as the "Sun Belt" of southern Oregon. Nights are always cool, as are days but for a brief period between July and August. Winter is the rainy season. Summers are dry. The first frost delays until October 20; last frost bides until April 30.

Summer mildness: 51
Winter mildness: 54
Score: 60.8
Seasonal affect: 25
Hazard free: 89
Rank: 78

	117
	79
	169
90°	53
32°	68
0°	0
	50
	62
	8

	High °F	Low °F	Hum %	Wind mph	Precip inches	Snow inches
JAN	48	33	83	4.1	5.2	2.4
FEB	55	34	77	4.5	3.8	0.7
MAR	61	36	66	5.3	3.5	0.7
APR	67	38	57	5.7	1.8	0
MAY	75	44	50	5.7	1.2	0
JUN	83	50	42	5.9	0.5	0
JUL	90	53	38	5.8	0.2	0
AUG	90	53	39	5.3	0.5	0
SEP	83	47	42	4.5	0.9	0
OCT	70	41	58	3.7	2.4	0
NOV	54	38	80	3.6	5.3	0
DEC	46	34	85	3.6	5.7	1.5

Grass Valley–Nevada City, CA

Location: 39.15 N and 121.01 W at 2,519 feet, on the western slope of the Sierra Nevadas, 60 miles northeast of Sacramento.

Landscape: In a long, steeply sloping mountainous region. The Sacramento Valley to the west softens the terrain somewhat. The transition zone between grassland and Sierran forest is found here. Conifers and shrubs cover the slopes, and at higher elevations, digger pine and blue oak form open stands. At 4,000 to 6,000 feet, the most important trees are western yellow pine, Douglas fir, sugar pine, white fir, and incense cedar.

Climate: Mediterranean, characterized by winter rainfall and dry summers. The higher elevation of the Sierra foothills tempers the summer heat. Winters are milder than at other locations on the eastern slope of the Sierras. There are frequent freezing temperatures at night as well as an occasional blizzard. Mid-October heralds the first frost and the last frost departs May 17.

Summer mildness: 61
Winter mildness: 39
Score: 64.8
Seasonal affect: 66
Hazard free: 55
Rank: 71

	189
	75
	100
90°	39
32°	117
0°	0
	34
	59
	14

	High °F	Low °F	Hum %	Wind mph	Precip inches	Snow inches
JAN	50	30	80	7.2	10.3	6.5
FEB	53	31	75	7.6	8.8	3.5
MAR	56	33	65	8.6	8.4	4.0
APR	62	37	55	8.7	4.2	0
MAY	71	42	48	9.2	1.5	0
JUN	80	49	44	9.7	0.5	0
JUL	88	53	44	9.0	0.2	0
AUG	87	52	45	8.6	0.3	0
SEP	80	47	45	7.5	1.1	0
OCT	70	41	53	6.4	3.3	0
NOV	56	35	65	6.0	8.7	0
DEC	50	30	77	6.6	8.8	2.7

Hamilton–Bitterroot Valley, MT

Location: 46.14 N and 114.09 W at 3,572 feet on the Bitterroot River in extreme western Montana. Missoula is at the head of the valley, 45 miles north.

Landscape: The valley of rolling subalpine woodland is 25 miles wide and 96 miles long. Surrounding is the open parkland of the high valley and the lakes and high, glaciated peaks of the Bitterroot Mountains. Conditions are good for prairie short grasses. Scattered shrubs and low trees give way to forests of ponderosa pine, pinyon-juniper, and Douglas fir.

Climate: Semiarid steppe, with most precipitation falling as snow in winter from October to May. With the variety of elevation and bodies of water, there are many microclimates in the Valley. Snow is especially heavy in the higher altitudes. Winters are cold and long with the first frost arriving September 20 and the last frost not leaving until May 24. Summers are hot, dry, clear, and all too brief.

Summer mildness: 84
Winter mildness: 15
Score: 36.1
Seasonal affect: 39
Hazard free: 37
Rank: 128

	75
	82
	208
90°	17
32°	170
0°	10
	27
	37
	24

	High °F	Low °F	Hum %	Wind mph	Precip inches	Snow inches
JAN	34	16	79	5.2	1.3	12.5
FEB	41	21	76	5.7	0.8	6.2
MAR	48	25	65	6.7	0.8	8.1
APR	57	31	52	7.6	1.0	3.0
MAY	66	38	51	7.3	1.7	0
JUN	74	45	52	7.1	1.6	0
JUL	83	49	42	6.9	0.9	0
AUG	81	47	46	6.6	1.2	0
SEP	70	39	54	6.0	1.2	0
OCT	59	31	65	5.0	0.8	0
NOV	43	23	77	5.1	1.0	4.0
DEC	34	17	81	4.8	1.1	9.5

★ = *in the top 30 places for climate mildness.*

Hanover, NH

Location: 43.42 N and 72.17 W at 531 feet, on the Connecticut River in western New Hampshire. Boston is 135 miles southeast.
Landscape: The Green Mountains of Vermont lie west and the White Mountains lie northeast of this upper Connecticut River Valley location. Low hills flank the river. The surrounding forest is mixed conifer and deciduous, with northern white pine, eastern hemlock, maple, oak, and beech.
Climate: Northerly latitude assures the variety and vigor of a true New England climate. The summer, while not long, is pleasant. Fall is cool and clear and runs through October. First frost comes September 30, and the last frost delays until May 17. Winters are cold, with brief, intense cold snaps formed by high-pressure systems moving down from central Canada and Hudson Bay. Snows are deep and long lasting. Spring is called breakup, or mud season.

Summer mildness: 79 **Seasonal affect:** 9
Winter mildness: 6 **Hazard free:** 18
Score: 3.9 **Rank:** 195

91
110
164
90° 7
32° 167
0° 23
50
75
20

	High °F	Low °F	Hum %	Wind mph	Precip inches	Snow inches
JAN	28	7	58	9.0	2.5	18.7
FEB	33	10	57	9.4	2.4	17.9
MAR	43	21	53	9.9	2.7	13.7
APR	56	32	49	10.0	2.9	3.0
MAY	70	43	49	8.9	3.6	0
JUN	78	52	55	8.1	3.3	0
JUL	83	57	55	7.5	3.3	0
AUG	80	56	57	7.2	3.6	0
SEP	71	48	59	7.3	3.3	0
OCT	59	37	59	7.8	3.3	0
NOV	45	28	60	8.5	3.5	5.0
DEC	32	15	62	8.7	3.1	18.5

Hattiesburg, MS

Location: 31.1937 N and 89.1725 W at 161 feet in southern Mississippi, 70 miles north of Biloxi and the Gulf of Mexico. Jackson, the state capital, is 90 miles northwest.
Landscape: In the Piney Woods section of the Gulf Coastal Plain, a wide belt of longleaf yellow pine that covers southern Mississippi to within a few miles of the coastal-plain grasslands. The DeSoto National Forest lies to the south, southeast, and northeast. Slash and loblolly pine mix with dogwoods along the sloping plains. Marshes, lakes, and swamps are common. The soil is sandstone and clay.
Climate: Subtropical. Hattiesburg averages 60 to 70 inches of rain a year. Thunderstorms are frequent in summer, and hurricanes are a threat from late summer to early autumn. Summers are hot and humid, while winters are mild with negligible amounts of snow and sleet. November 8 will bring the first frost, and March 17 will usher out the last frost.

Summer mildness: 27 **Seasonal affect:** 23
Winter mildness: 69 **Hazard free:** 65
Score: 42.5 **Rank:** 117

111
104
150
90° 95
32° 44
0° 0
195
75
68

	High °F	Low °F	Hum %	Wind mph	Precip inches	Snow inches
JAN	58	34	76	8.4	5.8	0.4
FEB	62	37	74	8.6	5.7	0.3
MAR	70	45	72	9.1	6.3	0
APR	78	54	73	8.5	4.8	0
MAY	84	61	74	7.3	5.2	0
JUN	90	68	74	6.4	4.2	0
JUL	92	71	77	5.9	5.5	0
AUG	92	70	77	5.6	5.2	0
SEP	88	65	76	6.4	3.6	0
OCT	79	52	73	6.5	3.2	0
NOV	70	44	74	7.6	4.8	0
DEC	62	38	76	8.3	6.3	0

Henderson, NV

Location: 36.10 N and 115.08 W at 2,028 feet, just west of the Colorado River Valley. Las Vegas is 15 miles northwest, and Los Angeles is 300 miles southwest.
Landscape: Near the center of a broad desert valley surrounded by mountains from 2,000 to 10,000 feet higher than the valley floor. These mountains act as effective barriers to moisture-laden storms moving in from the Pacific Ocean. The thick-branched Joshua tree grows among creosote bushes and jumbled boulders in the Mohave Desert region.
Climate: Typical desert. Humidity is low with maximum temperatures at the 100°F level. Nearby mountains and Lake Mead contribute to relatively cool nights. Spring and fall are ideal, rarely interrupted by adverse weather conditions. Winters, too, are mild, with daytime averages of 60°F, clear skies, and warm sunshine. First frost is delayed until mid-December; last frost is seen February 17. There are very few overcast or rainy days.

Summer mildness: 6 **Seasonal affect:** 96
Winter mildness: 76 **Hazard free:** 76
Score: 84.6 **Rank:** 32

221
79
65
90° 123
32° 14
0° 0
1
13
14

	High °F	Low °F	Hum %	Wind mph	Precip inches	Snow inches
JAN	55	39	35	7.5	0.6	1.0
FEB	62	43	30	8.6	0.6	0.1
MAR	68	46	25	10.3	0.7	0
APR	77	53	20	11.0	0.3	0
MAY	87	61	17	11.1	0.2	0
JUN	97	70	14	11.1	0.1	0
JUL	102	76	15	10.3	0.5	0
AUG	100	74	19	9.6	0.9	0
SEP	92	68	20	9.0	0.6	0
OCT	80	58	22	8.1	0.3	0
NOV	65	46	30	7.7	0.5	0
DEC	56	39	36	7.3	0.5	0.1

★ = *in the top 30 places for climate mildness.*

Hendersonville–East Flat Rock, NC

Location: 35.19 N and 82.27 W at 2,146 feet, just above the South Carolina border in the western part of the state, 20 miles south of Asheville.

Landscape: The relief is mostly broken, mountainous, and rugged, with some very steep slopes and high waterfalls. The city lies in the midst of a large intermountain valley, with rolling to strongly rolling mountain meadows. The Appalachian oak forest includes the variety of deciduous trees common throughout, including birch, hickory, maple, ash, sweet chestnut, with an understory of small trees and shrubs.

Climate: Warm continental, with considerable temperature differences between winter and summer. It is mild and pleasant from late spring to late fall, and summer nights are always cool even following hot afternoons. Winters are short, with light snowfalls. October 12 will bring in the first frost; April 26 will usher out the last.

Summer mildness: 63 **Seasonal affect:** 18
Winter mildness: 39 **Hazard free:** 43
Score: 25.2 **Rank:** 152

	103
	113
	149
90°	11
32°	109
0°	0
	78
	82
	45

	High °F	Low °F	Hum %	Wind mph	Precip inches	Snow inches
JAN	48	25	59	9.7	3.9	3.2
FEB	51	28	56	9.6	4.5	3.6
MAR	60	35	53	9.4	5.7	2.8
APR	69	42	50	8.9	3.9	0
MAY	76	51	57	7.1	5.0	0
JUN	82	58	59	6.1	4.8	0
JUL	85	62	63	5.8	4.7	0
AUG	83	61	63	5.4	6.0	0
SEP	78	55	64	5.6	4.4	0
OCT	69	43	57	6.8	4.5	0
NOV	59	35	57	8.1	4.3	0
DEC	51	29	59	8.9	4.4	1.4

Hilton Head Island, SC

Location: 32.13 N and 80.45 W at 8 feet, in the Sea Islands, 45 miles south of Charleston.

Landscape: The land is low and flat, with elevations mostly under 25 feet. There are dozens of islands of various shapes and sizes, and on them are fresh- and saltwater streams, inlets, rivers, and sounds. Hilton Head, with excellent beaches, is an exception to the usual swampy conditions of the islands. The interior forests are medium to tall stands of mixed loblolly and shortleaf pines, plus deciduous oak, hickory, red maple, and winged elm.

Climate: Subtropical. The island group is just on the edge of the subtropical climate enjoyed by Florida and the Caribbean. The surrounding water produces a maritime climate, with mild winters, hot and humid summers, and temperatures that shift slowly. The inland mountains block much cold air from the interior. First frost after November 20; last frost leaves March 9.

Summer mildness: 35 **Seasonal affect:** 46
Winter mildness: 82 **Hazard free:** 71
Score: 72.7 **Rank:** 56

	104
	109
	152
90°	56
32°	28
0°	0
	28
	71
	47

	High °F	Low °F	Hum %	Wind mph	Precip inches	Snow inches
JAN	59	39	57	9.1	3.7	0.1
FEB	62	41	55	9.9	3.3	0.2
MAR	70	48	53	10.0	4.1	0
APR	77	55	50	9.7	2.9	0
MAY	83	63	55	8.7	4.0	0
JUN	88	69	60	8.4	6.1	0
JUL	90	73	66	7.9	6.4	0
AUG	89	72	70	7.4	7.9	0
SEP	85	68	67	7.8	5.0	0
OCT	78	58	60	8.1	2.6	0
NOV	70	49	60	8.1	2.4	0
DEC	62	42	59	8.5	3.2	0

Hot Springs, AR

Location: 34.30 N and 93.03 W at 579 feet, 36 miles southwest of Little Rock.

Landscape: On the eastern edge of the Ouachita Mountains and the Ouachita National Forest. There are 47 thermal springs here. In the protected forests, mixed broadleaf deciduous trees such as oak, maple, sweet gum, and hickory thrive. Needleleaf evergreens and lower layers of redbud and dogwood are common.

Climate: The irregular topography, with elevations varying from 400 to 1,000 feet, has a considerable effect on the area's microclimate, particularly on temperature extremes, ground fog, and precipitation. The climate is generally mild not seeing frost until November 9, and bidding farewell to it by late March. However, the area is subject to storms, flash floods, and extreme heat and cold. Winter is short and wet, with temperatures falling below freezing half the nights. Summers are hot, humid, and long. Spring and fall are changeable and usually pleasant.

Summer mildness: 32 **Seasonal affect:** 59
Winter mildness: 60 **Hazard free:** 46
Score: 48.5 **Rank:** 103

	119
	100
	146
90°	78
32°	56
0°	0
	16
	72
	57

	High °F	Low °F	Hum %	Wind mph	Precip inches	Snow inches
JAN	50	29	61	8.6	3.3	2.3
FEB	55	32	59	9.0	3.9	1.4
MAR	65	41	56	9.7	5.4	0.4
APR	74	50	56	9.1	5.5	0
MAY	81	58	58	7.7	6.4	0
JUN	89	66	55	7.2	4.7	0
JUL	93	70	56	6.7	5.0	0
AUG	92	68	56	6.4	3.5	0
SEP	86	62	58	6.7	4.0	0
OCT	76	51	53	6.8	4.3	0
NOV	63	41	59	8.0	5.6	0
DEC	53	32	62	8.2	5.0	0.6

★ = *in the top 30 places for climate mildness.*

Inverness, FL

Location: 28.50 N and 82.20 W at 38 feet in Florida's west-central lakes country, 55 miles north of Tampa.

Landscape: The Green Swamp, the source of five rivers and 70 percent of the state's water, lies east of here. Outside of the towns, the groves and farms are interspersed with lakes, rivers, forests, and sandhills. Withlacoochee State Forest encloses a typical mix of hardwood, longleaf, and slash pine. Aromatic and evergreen bayberry and sweet bay are scattered throughout.

Climate: Subtropical, with a small annual range of temperature. Humid, hot summers are somewhat cooled by regular, heavy afternoon thunderstorms. Winters are extremely mild, but some days in mid-January can touch 32°F. The first frost comes in December 21 while the last frost leaves February 9. Precipitation is distributed throughout the year but rises to high levels during summer.

Summer mildness: 15 | **Seasonal affect:** 57
Winter mildness: 89 | **Hazard free:** 80
Score: 76.7 | **Rank:** 48

92
148
125
90° 109
32° 8
0° 0
27
76
82

	High °F	Low °F	Hum %	Wind mph	Precip inches	Snow inches
JAN	69	44	56	8.9	3.3	0
FEB	71	45	52	9.6	3.5	0
MAR	77	52	50	9.9	3.9	0
APR	82	57	46	9.4	2.1	0
MAY	88	64	49	8.8	3.8	0
JUN	91	70	56	8.0	7.3	0
JUL	92	72	59	7.4	8.1	0
AUG	91	72	60	7.1	8.6	0
SEP	89	70	60	7.7	6.1	0
OCT	83	62	56	8.6	1.9	0
NOV	77	53	55	8.6	2.2	0
DEC	71	46	57	8.6	2.6	0

Iowa City, IA

Location: 41.394 N and 91.3148 W at 654 feet, along both banks of the Iowa River in eastern Iowa. Cedar Rapids is 25 miles northeast, and Des Moines is 110 miles west.

Landscape: In the midst of rolling to steep hills and highly developed farmland. The soil is prairie, high in organic content. The Iowa River provides an extensive drainage basin. Prehistoric coral formations were revealed in the 1993 floods, providing further evidence that the area was part of a huge sea many millions of years ago.

Climate: Continental, with extremes in temperature and precipitation. Summer highs can hit 100°F accompanied by high humidity. Winter temperatures average 15°F to 25°F but can get much colder. First frost by October 11 and the last frost on April 22. Precipitation can be highly variable, with large amounts falling all at once and then long dry periods. The potential for violent storms is high.

Summer mildness: 61 | **Seasonal affect:** 23
Winter mildness: 19 | **Hazard free:** 9
Score: 4.4 | **Rank:** 194

90
100
175
90° 26
32° 139
0° 15
130
59
41

	High °F	Low °F	Hum %	Wind mph	Precip inches	Snow inches
JAN	30	12	74	11.5	1.0	6.7
FEB	35	17	74	11.4	1.0	6.0
MAR	48	28	74	12.4	2.4	5.6
APR	63	40	69	12.7	3.7	1.5
MAY	75	51	68	11.1	4.0	0
JUN	84	60	69	10.0	4.5	0
JUL	88	65	73	8.6	4.9	0
AUG	85	62	75	8.4	4.4	0
SEP	78	54	74	9.2	3.9	0
OCT	66	43	70	10.2	2.8	0.3
NOV	50	31	75	11.2	2.1	1.7
DEC	34	18	77	11.2	1.6	6.8

Jackson Hole, WY

Location: 43.2848 N and 110.4542 W at 6,234 feet, in western Wyoming south of Yellowstone National Park. Billings, Montana, is 110 miles north.

Landscape: In a valley encompassing Bridger–Teton National Forest, Grand Teton National Park, and the National Elk Refuge. Jackson Hole is surrounded by the Rocky Mountains, of which the Teton Range is the youngest. The Snake River cuts through the valley and passes through Jackson Lake. The alpine geography supports a variety of vegetation, including sagebrush, lodgepole pine, fir, spruce, and aspen. Cottonwood, elder, and willow grow in the valley itself.

Climate: The mountains shield the valley from moist air, making for crisp, clear, dry summers. Winters are long with heavy snowfall, but are not too severe. First frost comes early by August 12, and there will be frost potential until July 13. Rainfall amounts are small; most precipitation comes in the form of light, powdery snow from October to April.

Summer mildness: 89 | **Seasonal affect:** 41
Winter mildness: 1 | **Hazard free:** 1
Score: 11.3 | **Rank:** 179

120
90
155
90° 2
32° 252
0° 42
48
45
27

	High °F	Low °F	Hum %	Wind mph	Precip inches	Snow inches
JAN	26	4	60	13.0	1.5	23.3
FEB	32	7	59	12.2	1.0	12.2
MAR	41	16	57	11.4	1.1	12.5
APR	51	24	55	11.5	1.2	6.8
MAY	62	30	56	10.7	2.0	1.3
JUN	72	37	55	10.1	1.7	0.2
JUL	82	41	48	9.5	1.1	0
AUG	80	38	46	9.5	1.3	0
SEP	70	31	51	10.2	1.4	0.3
OCT	58	23	52	11.0	1.2	2.2
NOV	39	16	59	12.1	1.5	9.2
DEC	27	5	60	13.1	1.6	18.6

★ = *in the top 30 places for climate mildness.*

Kalispell–Flathead Valley, MT

Location: 48.11 N and 114.18 W at 2,946 feet, in the Flathead Valley at the western gateway to Glacier National Park, about 70 air miles north of Missoula.

Landscape: The Continental Divide is 50 miles east. In addition to Flathead, the largest natural lake west of the Mississippi, the valley contains four smaller lakes and numerous streams and sloughs. Scattered prairie grasses, shrubs, and low trees give way to evergreen forests. Ponderosa pine, pinyon-juniper, and Douglas fir are frequent associates.

Climate: In winter, the mountains to the east block cold air from Alberta and assure beneficial seasonal rains by cooling the ocean air arriving from the west. There's more precipitation on the eastern side of the valley than the western. It's windy, with intense winds often reaching 30 to 40 mph. Winter is cold and snowy. First frost arrives September 20; last frost departs finally by May 20. Summers are pleasant and dry.

Summer mildness: 93
Winter mildness: 12
Score: 35.6
Seasonal affect: 29
Hazard free: 41
Rank: 131

	71
	81
	213
90°	12
32°	171
0°	12
	33
	44
	22

	High °F	Low °F	Hum %	Wind mph	Precip inches	Snow inches
JAN	28	13	79	6.0	1.5	12.5
FEB	35	18	76	6.2	1.1	6.2
MAR	43	24	65	7.2	1.0	8.1
APR	55	31	52	8.2	1.1	3.0
MAY	64	38	51	7.6	1.9	0
JUN	71	44	52	7.2	2.2	0
JUL	80	47	42	6.7	1.1	0
AUG	79	46	46	6.6	1.4	0
SEP	68	39	54	6.4	1.3	0
OCT	54	29	65	5.3	0.9	0
NOV	38	24	77	5.7	1.3	4.0
DEC	30	16	81	5.6	1.7	9.5

★ Kauai, HI

Location: The weather station is Lihue, 21.59 N and 159.22 W at 207 feet, on the settled east coast of the volcanic island. Honolulu is 95 air miles southeast.

Landscape: The northernmost of the major Hawaiian Islands, it's also the greenest and known as the "Garden Isle." Consisting of Mt. Waialeale and marginal lowlands dissected by fertile valleys and deep fissures, the island is nearly circular. Stands of native plants include varieties of moss lichen, fern, and palm as well as shrubs. There are forests and bogs.

Climate: Mild marine tropical characterized by a two-season year. Temperature conditions are mild and uniform everywhere but high elevations. Waialeale, with an annual rainfall of 40 feet, is the earth's wettest spot, but the leeward coast is much drier. Summers are generally humid, with high cloudiness, except on the driest coasts and high elevations. Easterly trade winds with brisk sea breezes in the afternoon predominate.

Summer mildness: 42
Winter mildness: 99
Score: 97.0
Seasonal affect: 89
Hazard free: 94
Rank: 7

	131
	143
	91
90°	6
32°	0
0°	0
	0
	43
	5

	High °F	Low °F	Hum %	Wind mph	Precip inches	Snow inches
JAN	78	65	73	10.8	5.9	0
FEB	78	65	71	11.1	3.3	0
MAR	79	67	73	12.3	4.2	0
APR	80	69	72	13.3	3.5	0
MAY	81	70	63	13.2	3.2	0
JUN	83	73	61	14.7	1.7	0
JUL	84	74	62	15.6	2.1	0
AUG	85	74	63	14.8	1.8	0
SEP	85	74	62	12.9	2.4	0
OCT	83	72	65	12.0	4.4	0
NOV	81	70	68	11.8	5.5	0
DEC	79	67	70	11.3	5.2	0

Kerrville, TX

Location: 30.03 N and 99.08 W at 1,645 feet, at the edge of the Edwards Plateau. Austin, the state capital, is 80 miles east.

Landscape: Kerr County lies across the hills, valleys, and uplands of the rolling hill country of central Texas. There are breaks into the deep valleys of the Guadalupe River and its tributaries. The area is covered with cedars and live oaks.

Climate: Prairie continental in character, with wide swings of temperature both daily and seasonally, especially in winter. First frost arrives by November 11, and the last frost leaves March 24. Winter precipitation is mostly slow, steady, light rain. Summers are drier and hot. Falls are pleasant but can be stormy due to northers and Gulf storms moving north.

Summer mildness: 24
Winter mildness: 72
Score: 71.2
Seasonal affect: 75
Hazard free: 62
Rank: 58

	117
	115
	134
90°	97
32°	39
0°	0
	23
	43
	41

	High °F	Low °F	Hum %	Wind mph	Precip inches	Snow inches
JAN	60	35	60	9.7	1.3	0.1
FEB	64	39	59	10.2	1.8	0.6
MAR	72	47	56	10.8	1.4	0.1
APR	79	55	57	10.5	2.5	0
MAY	84	62	60	9.6	4.2	0
JUN	89	67	56	9.1	3.6	0
JUL	93	69	51	8.3	2.2	0
AUG	93	68	50	7.9	2.7	0
SEP	87	64	55	7.9	3.6	0
OCT	79	55	55	8.1	3.6	0
NOV	69	46	58	9.0	1.9	0
DEC	62	38	59	9.2	1.3	0

★ = *in the top 30 places for climate mildness.*

Ketchum–Sun Valley, ID

Location: 43.41 N and 114.21 W at 5,821 feet, at the edge of Idaho's Sawtooth National Recreation Area, 100 miles east of Boise.

Landscape: Sits high among even higher, rugged mountains. There are several flat or nearly flat glaciated valleys, some of which are several miles wide. The native vegetation is a mixed coniferous forest comprised of Douglas fir, Engelmann spruce, and cedar-hemlock.

Climate: Semiarid steppe. Summers are crisp, clear, and dry. Winters are long and cold. First frost heralds by September 10, and the frost will last until June 14. Annual precipitation comes almost entirely as light and dry snow and accumulates to some depth. The prevailing winds are westerlies. Seasonal and daily temperature changes are extreme but would be even more so if not moderated by the mountains.

Summer mildness: 74
Seasonal affect: 48
Winter mildness: 2
Hazard free: 23
Score: 18.8
Rank: 164

(clear)	121
(partly cloudy)	90
(cloudy)	154
90°	15
32°	205
0°	20
	47
	36
	15

	High °F	Low °F	Hum %	Wind mph	Precip inches	Snow inches
JAN	29	6	80	8.0	2.4	21.6
FEB	35	9	78	9.0	1.7	9.7
MAR	43	17	65	10.0	1.3	6.7
APR	55	27	55	10.0	1.1	0.7
MAY	67	34	51	9.5	1.2	0.1
JUN	76	41	47	9.0	1.1	0
JUL	86	46	37	8.4	0.7	0
AUG	84	44	40	8.2	0.6	0
SEP	74	35	45	8.2	0.8	0
OCT	63	27	59	8.3	0.8	0.3
NOV	44	19	75	8.4	2.0	6.1
DEC	31	7	83	8.1	2.3	15.0

Key West, FL

Location: 24.33 N, 81.47 W, at 7 feet, at the end of the long island chain swinging in a southwesterly arc from the tip of the Florida peninsula, 160 miles south of Miami.

Landscape: Key West sits on a sand and coral island 3½ miles long and 1 mile wide. The average elevation along the entire island chain is just 8 feet. The waters surrounding these islands are shallow, and there is little wave action because outlying reefs break the surf. Much of the shoreline is filled mangrove swamp.

Climate: Because of the Gulf Stream, the Florida Keys have a notably mild, tropical-maritime climate in which the average winter temperatures are only about 14 degrees lower than in summer. Summers are hot, humid, and stormy, although prevailing easterly tradewinds and sea breezes make the heat tolerable. There is no known record of frost, ice, sleet, or snow.

Summer mildness: 28
Seasonal affect: 47
Winter mildness: 100
Hazard free: 74
Score: 82.6
Rank: 36

(clear)	75
(partly cloudy)	175
(cloudy)	115
90°	139
32°	0
0°	0
	39
	84
	74

	High °F	Low °F	Hum %	Wind mph	Precip inches	Snow inches
JAN	75	59	69	9.5	2.0	0
FEB	75	60	67	10.2	1.8	0
MAR	79	64	66	10.6	1.7	0
APR	82	68	63	10.5	1.8	0
MAY	85	72	65	9.7	3.5	0
JUN	88	75	68	8.4	5.1	0
JUL	89	76	66	8.0	3.6	0
AUG	89	77	67	7.9	5.0	0
SEP	88	76	69	8.2	5.9	0
OCT	84	72	69	9.3	4.4	0
NOV	80	67	69	9.7	2.8	0
DEC	76	62	69	9.2	2.0	0

★ Kingman, AZ

Location: 35.11 N and 114.03 W at 3,334 feet, in the dry Peacock Mountains of northwestern Arizona. Las Vegas, Nevada, is 90 miles northwest.

Landscape: Sits some 2,000 feet above the Colorado River Valley in high plateau country. Lakes Mead, Mohave, and Havasu are principal sources of water and recreation. Ground cover is primarily sagebrush and native grasses. In the upper elevations are sparse conifer stands.

Climate: Arid steppe, with strong daily and seasonal temperature changes. Winters are clear, long, and extremely mild, with some flow of air from as far as the Pacific Ocean. The first frost delays until November 14, and the last frost departs around April 8. There's a short, hot, sunbaked stretch from July to September. Except for brief periods in spring and summer, there's no measurable precipitation.

Summer mildness: 22
Seasonal affect: 95
Winter mildness: 56
Hazard free: 89
Score: 88.6
Rank: 24

(clear)	242
(partly cloudy)	75
(cloudy)	48
90°	101
32°	61
0°	0
	2
	23
	7

	High °F	Low °F	Hum %	Wind mph	Precip inches	Snow inches
JAN	54	31	40	7.3	0.9	0.5
FEB	59	34	35	7.4	0.9	0.3
MAR	63	38	30	7.9	1.1	1.0
APR	71	44	25	8.3	0.6	0
MAY	81	53	23	8.3	0.2	0
JUN	91	62	22	8.5	0.2	0
JUL	96	69	32	9.5	1.1	0
AUG	94	68	35	8.9	1.5	0
SEP	88	60	35	7.3	0.8	0
OCT	78	50	32	6.6	0.7	0
NOV	64	39	34	6.9	0.8	0
DEC	55	32	41	7.2	1.0	0.6

★ = *in the top 30 places for climate mildness.*

Kissimmee–St. Cloud, FL

Location: 28.17 N and 81.24 W at 19 feet at the head of Lake Tohopekaliga in central Florida, 30 miles southwest of Orlando.
Landscape: Situated amid clear lakes in gently rolling hill country. Flood plain grasses and pine flatwoods mix with live oak hammocks. Forests are typical southern coastal mixes of hardwood, longleaf, and slash pine. Aromatic and evergreen bayberry and sweet bay are scattered throughout.
Climate: Subtropical, with a small annual range of temperature change. First frost comes as late as December 27, and the last frost is gone by February 6. Warmed by both the Gulf of Mexico and the Atlantic, winters are sunny, mild, and dry. Summers are hot, humid, and beset by frequent thunderstorms that provide half the area's annual precipitation.

Summer mildness: 12
Winter mildness: 93
Score: 79.7
Seasonal affect: 61
Hazard free: 80
Rank: 42

	92
	148
	125
90°	108
32°	6
0°	0
	27
	74
	82

	High °F	Low °F	Hum %	Wind mph	Precip inches	Snow inches
JAN	73	49	56	8.9	2.2	0
FEB	75	50	52	9.6	3.1	0
MAR	79	55	50	9.9	2.9	0
APR	84	59	46	9.4	1.5	0
MAY	88	65	49	8.8	3.7	0
JUN	91	70	56	8.0	6.1	0
JUL	91	72	59	7.4	7.0	0
AUG	91	72	60	7.1	6.7	0
SEP	90	71	60	7.7	5.7	0
OCT	85	65	56	8.6	2.8	0
NOV	80	57	55	8.6	2.2	0
DEC	75	51	57	8.6	2.2	0

★ Laguna Beach–Dana Point, CA

Location: 33.32 N and 117.47 W at 44 feet, on the Pacific Ocean 40 miles south of Los Angeles. San Diego is another 60 miles south.
Landscape: The shore is somewhat rocky, and steep hills rise from two lagoons at the head of Laguna canyon. Trees and shrubs must withstand severe summer drought and evaporation. Following a wet winter, hard-leaved evergreens such as pinyon and cypress are more abundant.
Climate: Ocean breezes keep the weather mild throughout the year. Days when the temperature tops 90°F or falls to 32°F are rare. It is a long growing season, with the first frost coming in January 5 and the last frost departing by January 25. Morning fog and low clouds are common in cooler seasons. There isn't much precipitation, and what rain there is falls mostly in winter.

Summer mildness: 75
Winter mildness: 75
Score: 98.0
Seasonal affect: 81
Hazard free: 99
Rank: 5

	147
	116
	103
90°	2
32°	3
0°	0
	38
	21
	4

	High °F	Low °F	Hum %	Wind mph	Precip inches	Snow inches
JAN	66	42	55	6.7	2.3	0
FEB	67	43	58	7.4	2.3	0
MAR	66	44	61	8.2	2.2	0
APR	69	46	60	8.5	0.9	0
MAY	70	52	65	8.4	0.3	0
JUN	72	55	68	8.0	0.1	0
JUL	76	59	68	7.8	0.0	0
AUG	77	59	68	7.7	0.1	0
SEP	78	58	65	7.3	0.4	0
OCT	75	53	59	6.9	0.3	0
NOV	70	46	55	6.7	1.7	0
DEC	66	42	53	6.5	1.7	0

Lake Conroe, TX

Location: 30.21 N and 95.33 W at 201 feet, in the Texas Gulf Coastal Plain, 40 miles north of downtown Houston.
Landscape: Rolling hills on a flood plain at the southern edge of the Big Thicket area. The Sam Houston National Forest abuts the northern shore of this 22,000-acre artificial lake. The area is rapidly becoming suburbanized, with some loss to the piney woods and dense deciduous forests.
Climate: Subtropical. Summer days are long, hot, and humid, but the nights are pleasantly cool. Winters are mild with few, brief cold spells. Thanksgiving brings in the first frost, and the last frost is out before St. Patrick's Day. Rainfall is distributed evenly throughout the year but arrives in brief, heavy, and sometimes violent thunderstorms.

Summer mildness: 13
Winter mildness: 81
Score: 58.9
Seasonal affect: 50
Hazard free: 72
Rank: 84

	94
	115
	157
90°	108
32°	28
0°	0
	31
	64
	61

	High °F	Low °F	Hum %	Wind mph	Precip inches	Snow inches
JAN	60	38	63	8.3	3.6	0.1
FEB	64	41	61	8.8	3.2	0.2
MAR	72	48	59	9.4	2.9	0
APR	79	57	57	9.2	3.8	0
MAY	85	63	59	8.2	5.4	0
JUN	91	70	59	7.7	4.5	0
JUL	94	72	58	7.0	3.5	0
AUG	95	72	58	6.3	3.6	0
SEP	89	67	60	6.9	5.0	0
OCT	81	56	56	7.0	3.7	0
NOV	72	48	57	7.9	4.2	0
DEC	63	40	61	8.0	4.0	0

★ = *in the top 30 places for climate mildness.*

★ Lake Havasu City, AZ

Location: 34.29 N and 114.19 W at 602 feet, in extreme western Arizona above Parker Dam on the Colorado River. Las Vegas, Nevada, is 100 miles northwest.

Landscape: On the Colorado River, west of the Mojave Mountains. The center is the 45-mile-long Lake Havasu, with red wall limestone canyons, steep slopes, and gorges. This is the edge of the Sonoran Desert, where growth is low shrub and saguaro. Creosote bush, geraniums, and sedums are common especially after a wet winter.

Climate: Desert, with strong daily and seasonal temperature changes. Winters are clear, long, and extremely mild, with some flow of air from as far away as the Pacific Ocean. First frost comes December 9; last frost is gone by February 7. From May to October is a long, hot, sunbaked stretch. Except for a handful of days in spring and summer, there is no measurable precipitation.

Summer mildness: 1 **Seasonal affect:** 99
Winter mildness: 80 **Hazard free:** 97
Score: 93.0 **Rank:** 15

	242
	75
	48
90°	178
32°	14
0°	0
	2
	11
	7

	High °F	Low °F	Hum %	Wind mph	Precip inches	Snow inches
JAN	67	39	40	7.3	0.6	0
FEB	73	44	35	7.4	0.4	0
MAR	79	48	30	7.9	0.5	0
APR	87	54	25	8.3	0.2	0
MAY	96	63	23	8.3	0.1	0
JUN	105	72	22	8.5	0.0	0
JUL	109	79	32	9.5	0.3	0
AUG	107	79	35	8.9	0.5	0
SEP	101	71	35	7.3	0.5	0
OCT	91	59	32	6.6	0.4	0
NOV	77	47	34	6.9	0.5	0
DEC	67	39	41	7.2	0.6	0

Lake of the Cherokees, OK

Location: 36.33 N and 94.45 W at 739 feet, near the western slope of the Ozark Mountains. Tulsa is 75 miles southwest.

Landscape: The forested hills drop to the 1,300-mile shore of Grand Lake, a major impoundment on the Neosho River. Foothills give way to a low-relief plain and rivers. Forest and prairie grow side by side: deciduous oak-hickory forests with elm, sycamore, bur oak, redbud, and buckeye stand next to vast stretches of bluestem grasses.

Climate: Prairie, with hot summers and winters that are moderate, with occasional hard freezes. October 22 brings in the first frost; last frost departs by April 15. Spring arrives in mid-March and autumn ends in late October. Annual precipitation is moderate and, except for snow in January, usually falls as rain. Humidity is mild.

Summer mildness: 40 **Seasonal affect:** 67
Winter mildness: 40 **Hazard free:** 26
Score: 33.1 **Rank:** 135

	128
	103
	135
90°	72
32°	96
0°	1
	10
	61
	51

	High °F	Low °F	Hum %	Wind mph	Precip inches	Snow inches
JAN	45	23	59	10.5	1.8	3.3
FEB	51	27	57	10.9	2.0	2.4
MAR	61	37	53	12.1	4.0	1.5
APR	72	47	51	12.0	3.8	0
MAY	78	56	58	10.7	5.1	0
JUN	86	64	58	10.0	4.7	0
JUL	92	68	53	9.3	3.0	0
AUG	92	66	53	9.0	3.8	0
SEP	84	60	56	9.2	5.1	0
OCT	73	48	53	9.7	3.8	0
NOV	60	37	57	10.4	3.8	0
DEC	48	27	60	10.3	2.5	1.6

Lake of the Ozarks, MO

Location: 38.00 N and 92.44 W at 1,043 feet, on the Osage River at Bagnell Dam. Kansas City is 170 miles northwest, and St. Louis is 180 miles northeast.

Landscape: There are 1,150 miles of irregular shoreline on the lake, formed when the Osage River was dammed in the rolling, open country of south-central Missouri. The slopes are wooded with oak, maple, sweet gum, and hickory, mixed with second-growth spruce and pine.

Climate: Hot continental with hot, humid summers and cold winters. Apparent temperatures, especially those caused by cold and wind, are pronounced throughout the year. First frost arrives by October 20, and the last frost departs mid-April. Snow is neither deep nor long lasting.

Summer mildness: 47 **Seasonal affect:** 53
Winter mildness: 37 **Hazard free:** 6
Score: 17.3 **Rank:** 168

	116
	97
	153
90°	58
32°	104
0°	3
	20
	66
	56

	High °F	Low °F	Hum %	Wind mph	Precip inches	Snow inches
JAN	43	21	59	11.7	1.6	5.2
FEB	48	26	61	11.9	2.2	4.5
MAR	60	35	57	12.9	3.8	4.3
APR	71	46	57	12.2	4.0	0
MAY	78	55	60	10.4	5.1	0
JUN	85	63	61	9.6	4.2	0
JUL	90	68	60	8.5	3.6	0
AUG	89	66	56	8.6	3.9	0
SEP	82	58	58	9.3	4.5	0
OCT	73	47	57	10.1	4.4	0
NOV	59	37	60	11.3	3.4	1.0
DEC	47	26	64	11.6	2.9	3.4

★ = *in the top 30 places for climate mildness.*

Lake Placid, NY

Location: 44.16 N and 73.59 W at elevation 1,800 feet in northeast New York, in the Adirondack Mountains, surrounding Mirror Lake. Plattsburgh is 40 miles northeast.

Landscape: Lake Placid Trail connects the Adirondack foothills and High Peaks region to the northeast. The land is sharply rolling with relatively deep valleys. Natural lakes abound and a dense mixed conifer and deciduous forest covers the area.

Climate: Rigorous continental, with severe, snowy winters impacted by air and moisture from the Canadian Arctic. Summer days are bright and approach the ideal: a long period of mild, dry days with cool nights. Springs and falls are brief.

Summer mildness: 94 **Seasonal affect:** 11
Winter mildness: 6 **Hazard free:** 3
Score: 5.4 **Rank:** 192

	63
	98
	205
90°	14
32°	189
0°	19
	129
	70
	27

	High °F	Low °F	Hum %	Wind mph	Precip inches	Snow inches
JAN	26	6	72	10.8	2.2	14.0
FEB	29	9	69	10.7	2.0	13.0
MAR	39	22	66	10.8	2.4	10.0
APR	50	33	62	10.5	2.7	9.0
MAY	64	44	66	9.0	3.3	5.0
JUN	72	53	69	8.3	3.8	0
JUL	77	58	70	8.0	3.9	0
AUG	74	56	74	7.7	4.5	0
SEP	67	48	76	8.2	3.8	1.0
OCT	55	37	73	8.8	3.2	9.0
NOV	42	29	73	10.2	3.4	12.0
DEC	30	15	74	10.4	2.8	13.0

Lake Winnipesaukee, NH

Location: 43.36 N and 71.19 W at 504 feet, in central New Hampshire near the southern edge of the White Mountains. Boston is 100 miles south.

Landscape: From the glacier lake to the ski resorts around North Conway, the terrain rises dramatically from elevations of about 2,000 feet to more than 6,000 feet in the Presidential Range. The area is generally rugged, scenic, and heavily forested. Interspersed between ranges and peaks are broad valleys. The mixed conifer and deciduous forest is transitional. Northern white pine, eastern hemlock, maple, oak, and beech are common.

Climate: Rigorous continental, with mild, clear summer days and cool nights. Falls are pleasant and famous throughout the region for bright foliage colors. Winters are long, snowy, and sometimes subfreezing for periods of several days to a week. Springs are changeable. First frost comes early, on September 19; the last frost leaves late, May 24.

Summer mildness: 88 **Seasonal affect:** 6
Winter mildness: 2 **Hazard free:** 29
Score: 7.9 **Rank:** 187

	91
	110
	164
90°	4
32°	181
0°	22
	50
	87
	20

	High °F	Low °F	Hum %	Wind mph	Precip inches	Snow inches
JAN	27	4	58	7.2	3.1	18.0
FEB	31	6	56	7.8	3.0	14.6
MAR	40	18	52	8.1	3.2	10.5
APR	53	29	47	7.8	3.4	2.0
MAY	67	39	48	7.0	4.0	0
JUN	75	49	53	6.4	3.6	0
JUL	80	53	52	5.7	3.9	0
AUG	78	51	53	5.3	3.9	0
SEP	69	43	55	5.5	3.1	0
OCT	58	33	53	6.0	3.7	0
NOV	44	25	59	6.7	4.3	4.0
DEC	31	12	62	7.0	3.8	13.7

Lakeland–Winter Haven, FL

Location: 28.02 N and 81.57 W at 211 feet, in central Florida, 42 miles east of Tampa.

Landscape: In the rolling lake-ridge section, 50 miles from the Gulf of Mexico and 70 miles from the Atlantic Ocean. Here, one can find the highest elevation in the Florida peninsula. Flood-plain prairies and pine flatwoods mix with live oak hammocks. Forests are a typical mix of hardwood, longleaf, and slash pine. Aromatic and evergreen bayberry and sweet bay are scattered throughout.

Climate: Subtropical. The proximity of the Gulf of Mexico and the Atlantic Ocean bring pleasant winters. Days are bright and warm, nights are cool, and rainfall is light to moderate. The high temperature and humidity during the long summers are moderated by afternoon thundershowers. Occasional major cold waves overspread the area, bringing temperatures down below freezing. The first frost comes late on December 27, and the last frost leaves a short time later on February 6.

Summer mildness: 11 **Seasonal affect:** 62
Winter mildness: 96 **Hazard free:** 80
Score: 82.1 **Rank:** 37

	92
	148
	125
90°	108
32°	6
0°	0
	27
	74
	82

	High °F	Low °F	Hum %	Wind mph	Precip inches	Snow inches
JAN	72	50	56	8.9	2.3	0
FEB	74	52	52	9.6	3.0	0
MAR	80	57	50	9.9	3.4	0
APR	84	61	46	9.4	1.4	0
MAY	89	67	49	8.8	4.2	0
JUN	91	71	56	8.0	6.8	0
JUL	92	73	59	7.4	7.0	0
AUG	92	73	60	7.1	7.6	0
SEP	90	72	60	7.7	5.7	0
OCT	85	66	56	8.6	2.0	0
NOV	78	58	55	8.6	2.1	0
DEC	73	53	57	8.6	2.2	0

★ = *in the top 30 places for climate mildness.*

★ Largo, FL

Location: 27.54 N and 82.48 W at 50 feet, on the Gulf Coast, 15 miles west of Tampa and 20 miles north of St. Petersburg.

Landscape: Flat. Largo occupies a high coastal area on the west coast of a peninsula separating the Gulf of Mexico from Tampa Bay. Sand-reef islands line the coast. Coastal vegetation consists of southern yellow pine and laurel, with cultivated citrus groves farther inland.

Climate: Subtropical. The Gulf of Mexico heavily influences the weather. Summers are long, hot, and humid, interrupted by frequent afternoon thunderstorms. Winters are very mild and cool at night, with snow and below-freezing temperatures extremely rare.

Summer mildness: 25 | **Seasonal affect:** 69
Winter mildness: 98 | **Hazard free:** 80
Score: 91.0 | **Rank:** 19

	102
	142
	121
90°	78
32°	0
0°	0
	22
	69
	86

	High °F	Low °F	Hum %	Wind mph	Precip inches	Snow inches
JAN	68	53	59	8.6	2.2	0
FEB	70	54	56	9.2	3.1	0
MAR	75	60	55	9.5	3.6	0
APR	80	65	51	9.3	1.3	0
MAY	86	70	52	8.7	3.1	0
JUN	89	75	60	8.0	6.2	0
JUL	90	76	63	7.2	6.8	0
AUG	90	76	64	7.0	8.6	0
SEP	88	75	62	7.8	7.1	0
OCT	83	69	57	8.5	2.3	0
NOV	76	62	57	8.4	2.1	0
DEC	71	55	59	8.5	2.4	0

Las Cruces, NM

Location: 32.18 N and 106.46 W at 3,883 feet, 40 miles northwest of El Paso, Texas.

Landscape: The wide, level Rio Grande Valley runs northwest to southeast through here. Rolling desert borders the southwest and west. About 12 miles east, the Organ Mountains, with peaks above 8,500 feet, form a rugged backdrop. The northwest portion of the valley narrows to low hills and buttes. The vegetation is dry-desert with negligible ground cover. Only plants adapted to the highly alkaline conditions survive. These include thorn scrub, savanna or steppe grass, prickly pear, and saguaro cactus. In this higher altitude are belts of oak and juniper woodland.

Climate: Desert continental, characterized by low rainfall, hot summers with cool nights, and mild, sunny winters. There are freezes with the first frost coming October 23 and the last frost leaving April 18. The rainfall is light, almost all falling in occasional, brief summer showers. Drizzles are unknown.

Summer mildness: 18 | **Seasonal affect:** 93
Winter mildness: 32 | **Hazard free:** 53
Score: 48.5 | **Rank:** 103

	193
	100
	72
90°	105
32°	120
0°	0
	2
	22
	36

	High °F	Low °F	Hum %	Wind mph	Precip inches	Snow inches
JAN	58	23	42	8.4	0.5	1.3
FEB	63	26	34	9.2	0.4	0.9
MAR	69	33	27	11.0	0.2	0.4
APR	77	40	21	11.1	0.2	0
MAY	86	48	21	10.3	0.3	0
JUN	94	56	23	9.3	0.6	0
JUL	95	63	35	8.3	1.9	0
AUG	92	61	39	7.8	2.2	0
SEP	87	54	41	7.6	1.6	0
OCT	79	41	36	7.5	1.0	0
NOV	67	30	37	8.0	0.6	1.0
DEC	59	23	42	7.9	0.8	1.7

Las Vegas, NM

Location: 35.37 N and 105.13 W at 6,600 feet in northeast New Mexico, some 50 miles east from Santa Fe, the state capital.

Landscape: Mountains of the Mesa Montosa surround this San Miguel County seat. Engleman spruce and subalpine fir cover the higher elevations; ponderosa pine is on the lower, drier more exposed slopes; grasses cover the parks and valleys.

Climate: Highland steppe, with crisp and clear, but cold, winter days. Summers and falls are the best seasons: pleasant, warm, dry, and invigorating. Long periods of cloudiness are unknown.

Summer mildness: 83 | **Seasonal affect:** 83
Winter mildness: 18 | **Hazard free:** 13
Score: 50.0 | **Rank:** 100

	168
	110
	87
90°	23
32°	157
0°	2
	14
	38
	38

	High °F	Low °F	Hum %	Wind mph	Precip inches	Snow inches
JAN	40	18	50	8.0	0.9	5.4
FEB	44	21	42	8.8	0.8	5.4
MAR	50	26	32	10.0	1.2	6.9
APR	59	33	25	10.8	1.0	4.0
MAY	68	42	23	10.5	1.2	0
JUN	78	51	22	9.9	1.4	0
JUL	81	55	30	9.0	3.3	0
AUG	78	53	34	8.2	3.5	0
SEP	71	47	35	8.5	2.1	0
OCT	62	38	35	8.2	1.3	1.0
NOV	49	27	38	7.9	1.0	4.0
DEC	41	19	46	7.7	1.1	7.0

★ = *in the top 30 places for climate mildness.*

Leelanau Peninsula, MI

Location: 45.01 N and 85.45 W at 656 feet in the northwest mainland on the eastern shore of Lake Michigan. Traverse City is 20 miles southeast, Detroit another 250 miles.

Landscape: The peninsula is hilly, ranging from rolling to steep. Dunes predominate in the coastal areas, with lakes and bogs inland. Maples and cherry trees are common, as are pine, hemlock, and birch. Trilliums and other wildflowers grow in the hills. Swamp marigolds can be found in the boglands.

Climate: Winters are severe, with frequent cold snaps and heavy snow. It is a long season, too, with the first frost on October 17 and the last frost on May 10. Summers, however, are mild and pleasant, thanks to the tempering effect of the Great Lakes. Autumns are cool and long. Cloudy to partly cloudy days are the norm throughout the year, but rainfall is light.

Summer mildness: 81
Seasonal affect: 7
Winter mildness: 20
Hazard free: 1
Score: 2.4
Rank: 197

	64
	95
	206
90°	4
32°	155
0°	8
	137
	71
	34

	High °F	Low °F	Hum %	Wind mph	Precip inches	Snow inches
JAN	30	17	77	11.5	2.2	29.1
FEB	33	17	75	10.7	1.5	16.0
MAR	42	24	72	11.1	2.0	11.0
APR	56	35	68	11.0	2.7	3.0
MAY	68	44	66	9.7	2.5	0.3
JUN	76	53	68	8.9	3.3	0
JUL	81	59	70	8.2	2.7	0
AUG	79	58	74	7.9	3.6	0
SEP	72	52	75	8.3	4.0	0
OCT	61	43	74	9.4	3.2	0.6
NOV	47	33	77	10.5	2.9	12.1
DEC	34	22	79	10.7	2.5	26.0

Leesburg–Mount Dora, FL

Location: 28.48 N and 81.52 W at 80 feet, in Florida's central lakes region, 40 miles northwest of Orlando.

Landscape: Composed of lakes, rivers, forests, and sandhills, there is interesting variety. Withlacoochee State Forest is a typical mix of hardwood, longleaf, and slash pine. Aromatic and evergreen bayberry and sweet bay are scattered throughout.

Climate: Subtropical, with a small range of annual temperature change. Humid, hot summers are cooled by frequent afternoon thunderstorms. Winters are extremely mild, with warm days and cool nights. Frost season is quite short, lasting but a few weeks from the first frost on January 2 to the last frost by January 28.

Summer mildness: 18
Seasonal affect: 64
Winter mildness: 91
Hazard free: 80
Score: 84.1
Rank: 33

	92
	148
	125
90°	106
32°	4
0°	0
	27
	73
	82

	High °F	Low °F	Hum %	Wind mph	Precip inches	Snow inches
JAN	70	47	56	8.9	2.7	0
FEB	71	48	52	9.6	3.3	0
MAR	76	53	50	9.9	3.5	0
APR	82	58	46	9.4	2.2	0
MAY	87	64	49	8.8	3.4	0
JUN	90	69	56	8.0	6.5	0
JUL	92	71	59	7.4	6.2	0
AUG	91	72	60	7.1	7.2	0
SEP	89	71	60	7.7	5.9	0
OCT	83	64	56	8.6	3.1	0
NOV	77	56	55	8.6	2.5	0
DEC	72	50	57	8.6	2.4	0

Litchfield Hills, CT

Location: 41.48 N and 73.07 W at 593 feet, in the state's northwest corner, some 35 miles northwest of Hartford.

Landscape: The low Berkshire Mountain foothills surround the area, with many forest-rimmed lakes next to open fields and meadows. The woods are an eastern hardwood forest dominated by tall, broadleaf trees that provide dense cover in summer and brilliant color in fall and are bare in winter. Common varieties are maple, oak, beech, birch, walnut, ash, and sweet chestnut.

Climate: Hot continental, with large temperature variations from season to season. Winters receive Canadian air that sweeps down the Hudson Valley to the west. First frost descends on October 2 and deepens until the last frost on May 14. December to February is cold with long-lasting snow. Spring is short. Summers are clear, warm, and ideal. Falls extend to mid-November. Precipitation is moderate and evenly distributed throughout the year.

Summer mildness: 93
Seasonal affect: 7
Winter mildness: 10
Hazard free: 21
Score: 10.8
Rank: 181

	81
	109
	175
90°	0
32°	165
0°	14
	29
	90
	21

	High °F	Low °F	Hum %	Wind mph	Precip inches	Snow inches
JAN	27	11	58	9.0	4.0	16.3
FEB	30	12	57	9.4	3.9	14.1
MAR	40	22	53	9.9	4.2	10.7
APR	52	32	49	10.0	4.5	2.0
MAY	65	43	49	8.9	4.6	0
JUN	73	52	55	8.1	4.6	0
JUL	78	58	55	7.5	4.2	0
AUG	75	56	57	7.2	4.6	0
SEP	68	48	59	7.3	4.1	0
OCT	56	38	59	7.8	3.9	0
NOV	44	29	60	8.5	4.6	4.0
DEC	32	17	62	8.7	4.4	15.1

Lower Cape May, NJ

Location: 38.56 N and 74.54 W at 10 feet, where the Intracoastal Waterway swings into Delaware Bay. Atlantic City is 50 miles north, and Philadelphia is 85 miles northwest.

Landscape: Surrounding flat terrain is composed of tidal marshes and beach sand. The Wildwood resorts are on a barrier island to the northeast. The interior woods are evergreen and laurel.

Climate: Continental, but the moderating influence of the Atlantic is apparent throughout the year. Summers are cooler, winters warmer than those of other places at the same latitude. During the warm season, sea breezes in the late morning and afternoon prevent excessive heat. On occasion, these may lower the temperature between 15°F and 20°F within half an hour. Fall is long, lasting to mid-November. Warming is somewhat delayed in spring. Precipitation is moderate and well distributed throughout the year.

Summer mildness: 71 **Seasonal affect:** 33
Winter mildness: 48 **Hazard free:** 41
Score: 46.0 **Rank:** 109

95
110
160
90° 8
32° 72
0° 0
44
64
21

	High °F	Low °F	Hum %	Wind mph	Precip inches	Snow inches
JAN	40	26	62	11.0	3.5	4.8
FEB	42	28	59	11.4	3.2	5.4
MAR	50	35	56	11.9	3.9	2.8
APR	59	43	54	11.8	3.4	0
MAY	68	52	55	10.2	3.5	0
JUN	78	61	56	9.2	3.2	0
JUL	83	67	57	8.5	3.3	0
AUG	82	67	58	8.1	3.7	0
SEP	77	60	58	8.4	3.0	0
OCT	66	50	57	9.0	3.1	0
NOV	56	41	57	10.5	3.2	0
DEC	46	31	62	10.6	3.5	2.1

Madison, WI

Location: 43.0423 N and 89.2404 W at 860 feet in southern Wisconsin on an 8-block-wide stretch of land between lakes Mendota and Monona. Milwaukee is 75 miles east.

Landscape: The metro area includes 18,000 acres of lake surface, which is frozen over from December to April. Outside the urban area, dairy farms predominate, with field crops of corn, oats, alfalfa, apples, strawberries, and raspberries.

Climate: Continental. Like much of the interior of North America, summer high and winter low temperatures are extreme, with much variation within seasons. Winters are long and cold due to frequent blasts of arctic air. Even so, the first frost doesn't arrive until October 3, though the last frost will delay leaving until May 6. Snowfall is moderate, however. Summers are warm and often humid.

Summer mildness: 80 **Seasonal affect:** 18
Winter mildness: 5 **Hazard free:** 7
Score: 3.4 **Rank:** 196

90
96
179
90° 7
32° 159
0° 22
140
64
40

	High °F	Low °F	Hum %	Wind mph	Precip inches	Snow inches
JAN	24	6	74	10.5	1.2	8.2
FEB	29	10	73	10.4	1.2	7.3
MAR	41	23	72	11.2	2.6	9.6
APR	57	35	68	11.4	3.2	2.1
MAY	68	46	67	10.0	3.4	0.2
JUN	78	55	69	9.2	3.8	0
JUL	82	60	72	8.1	4.1	0
AUG	79	58	75	8.0	4.4	0
SEP	71	49	76	8.7	3.7	0
OCT	59	39	73	9.6	2.4	0.2
NOV	43	26	76	10.8	2.2	3.3
DEC	29	12	78	10.3	1.8	9.2

Marble Falls–Lake LBJ, TX

Location: 30.45 N and 98.25 W at 1,270 feet, on the Colorado River at the northern end of the Highland Lakes region, 50 miles northwest of Austin, the state capital.

Landscape: Located in the hill country of central Texas. Granite cliffs, limestone bluffs, and caverns are prominent geologic features. Cedar and oak are prevalent; cypress trees grow on the banks of rivers; and Texas bluebonnet and other wildflowers bloom profusely with sufficient spring rainfall.

Climate: Prairie. Summer days are hot but nights pleasantly cool. Winters are mild with few cold spells that also tend to be brief. The first frost arrives November 8; the season's last frost departs March 23. Rainfall is distributed evenly throughout the year. Humidity is generally a comfortable 55 percent.

Summer mildness: 27 **Seasonal affect:** 76
Winter mildness: 66 **Hazard free:** 61
Score: 68.8 **Rank:** 63

117
115
134
90° 118
32° 55
0° 0
23
40
41

	High °F	Low °F	Hum %	Wind mph	Precip inches	Snow inches
JAN	58	32	60	9.7	1.7	0.5
FEB	62	36	59	10.2	2.0	0.3
MAR	69	44	56	10.8	2.1	0
APR	77	54	57	10.5	2.7	0
MAY	83	61	60	9.6	4.8	0
JUN	89	68	56	9.1	3.5	0
JUL	93	70	51	8.3	1.9	0
AUG	93	70	50	7.9	2.0	0
SEP	87	64	55	7.9	3.5	0
OCT	79	53	55	8.1	3.5	0
NOV	68	44	58	9.0	2.1	0
DEC	60	35	59	9.2	1.5	0

★ = *in the top 30 places for climate mildness.*

Mariposa, CA

Location: 37.29 N and 119.57 W at 1,962 feet, 15 miles southwest of Yosemite National Park. Merced and the California central valley lie another 20 miles southwest. San Francisco is 150 miles west.

Landscape: Lying in a canyon valley in the foothills of the Sierra Nevada, the area is surrounded by ranchland, and the hills are covered with a mixed forest of oak and pine. Part of Yosemite National Park and Stanislaus National Forest fall within Mariposa County.

Climate: Continental. The area is protected from the humid air of the Pacific, so warm summers and dry, cool winters are the norm. There is a rain shadow effect cast, so winter snow and summer thunderstorms are rare. It does freeze with the first frost around November 12; the last frost leaves with the tax return, April 15.

Summer mildness: 32 **Seasonal affect:** 74
Winter mildness: 51 **Hazard free:** 64
Score: 63.8 **Rank:** 74

	189
	75
	100
90°	83
32°	64
0°	0
	34
	43
	14

	High °F	Low °F	Hum %	Wind mph	Precip inches	Snow inches
JAN	55	32	80	7.3	5.6	4.3
FEB	59	34	75	7.6	5.0	3.1
MAR	61	36	65	8.7	5.3	3.0
APR	67	40	55	8.7	2.7	0
MAY	77	45	48	9.4	0.8	0
JUN	87	51	44	9.7	0.2	0
JUL	95	57	44	9.1	0.1	0
AUG	94	56	45	8.6	0.2	0
SEP	87	51	45	7.5	0.6	0
OCT	77	43	53	6.4	1.8	0
NOV	62	36	65	6.0	4.8	0
DEC	54	32	77	6.6	4.6	2.7

Martha's Vineyard, MA

Location: The weather station is in Edgartown, 41.23 N and 70.32 W at 20 feet on southeast Martha's Vineyard, and 27 miles southeast of New Bedford in the Atlantic and 70 miles south of Boston.

Landscape: On a 100-square-mile island reachable by ferry off the southeast Massachusetts coast, separated from the Elizabeth Islands and Cape Cod by Vineyard and Nantucket sounds. As a result of glaciation, the island has morainal hills composed of boulders and clay deposits in the north, and low, sandy plains in the south. The island is relatively bare of typical deciduous trees of the northeast forest.

Climate: Mild, cool, and maritime with a distinct four-season climate of warm, damp, foggy summers, cold, wet winters, with brief springs and a long, bright and pleasant fall.

Summer mildness: 89 **Seasonal affect:** 22
Winter mildness: 36 **Hazard free:** 25
Score: 30.6 **Rank:** 140

	98
	104
	163
90°	3
32°	118
0°	1
	24
	75
	19

	High °F	Low °F	Hum %	Wind mph	Precip inches	Snow inches
JAN	38	24	64	13.8	3.8	9.1
FEB	38	25	62	13.8	3.6	9.8
MAR	45	31	62	13.7	3.9	6.1
APR	54	38	60	13.2	4.1	0
MAY	63	46	63	12.2	4.0	0
JUN	72	55	66	11.5	3.4	0
JUL	78	61	67	11.0	2.9	0
AUG	78	61	68	10.8	3.6	0
SEP	71	56	69	11.3	3.5	0
OCT	62	48	67	12.0	3.8	0
NOV	53	39	67	12.9	4.4	0
DEC	43	29	66	13.6	4.3	5.0

Maryville, TN

Location: 35.45 N and 83.58 W at 945 feet, in the foothills of the Great Smoky Mountains of eastern Tennessee. Knoxville is 16 miles north.

Landscape: To the east are the highest peaks in eastern North America. In the nearby Great Smoky Mountains National Park is a large stand of virgin red spruce. Common trees are hickory, oak, beech, birch, walnut, and maple. These tall broadleaf trees provide dense foliage in summer and completely shed their leaves in winter. Low shrubs develop in spring.

Climate: Hot continental, characterized by hot, humid summers and cool, cloudy, and wet winters. Daily and seasonal temperature changes aren't abrupt. The first frost will come by October 27; the last frost leaves by April 13. On summer nights, there's a pleasant moderating effect where a steady wind, a draw caused by the many streams and waterfalls, pulls the cool air down from the mountains to the lowlands.

Summer mildness: 55 **Seasonal affect:** 12
Winter mildness: 47 **Hazard free:** 44
Score: 21.2 **Rank:** 160

	97
	107
	161
90°	39
32°	95
0°	0
	31
	86
	47

	High °F	Low °F	Hum %	Wind mph	Precip inches	Snow inches
JAN	46	26	65	7.9	4.2	4.1
FEB	51	29	61	8.3	4.1	3.7
MAR	61	37	56	8.7	5.1	1.5
APR	70	45	53	8.6	3.7	0
MAY	78	53	60	7.0	4.1	0
JUN	85	62	61	6.5	4.0	0
JUL	87	66	63	6.1	4.7	0
AUG	87	65	63	5.6	3.1	0
SEP	81	59	62	5.8	3.1	0
OCT	71	46	57	5.8	2.8	0
NOV	60	38	60	6.9	3.8	0
DEC	50	30	66	7.3	4.5	1.6

★ = *in the top 30 places for climate mildness.*

★ Maui, HI

Location: The weather station is at Lahaina, 20.52 N and 156.41 W at 20 feet, on the island's west coast, 125 air miles from Honolulu.

Landscape: At 728 square miles, Maui is the second largest of the Hawaiian chain. Created by two volcanoes, which make up east and west peninsulas connected by a valley-like isthmus 7 miles wide, hence the nickname of "Valley Isle." The peaks of west Maui rise to almost 6,000 feet, and those to the southeast to over 10,000 feet. Native plants include varieties of fern and palm, shrub, forest, bog, and moss lichen.

Climate: Mild marine tropical. Daily and seasonal temperature changes are small. Summer days can be hot, owing to high humidity. There's marked variation in rainfall depending on the season and place. Leeward coastal areas are drier than the lower mountains of western Maui. Winds are persistently from the northeast. Severe storms are rare.

Summer mildness: 27 **Seasonal affect:** 90
Winter mildness: 100 **Hazard free:** 93
Score: 96.5 **Rank:** 8

	54
	182
	129
90°	17
32°	0
0°	0
	0
	19
	8

	High °F	Low °F	Hum %	Wind mph	Precip inches	Snow inches
JAN	82	64	74	10.9	3.5	0
FEB	82	63	73	11.4	2.4	0
MAR	83	64	72	12.4	1.8	0
APR	84	65	72	13.2	1.1	0
MAY	85	67	72	12.5	0.6	0
JUN	87	68	70	12.9	0.1	0
JUL	88	69	70	13.5	0.2	0
AUG	88	70	71	12.8	0.2	0
SEP	89	70	71	11.5	0.3	0
OCT	88	69	75	11.3	1.1	0
NOV	86	67	74	12.0	2.2	0
DEC	83	65	74	11.5	3.2	0

McCall, ID

Location: 44.54 N and 116.06 W at 5,031 feet in the Payette River Valley, 100 miles north of Boise, the state capital.

Landscape: Slopes vary from the flat river and lake bottom lands to rolling foothill and steep mountain slopes. Though all aspects are found, most face east and west. Elevations range from about 4,800 to 7,500 feet. Mixed coniferous-deciduous forest predominates. The area's major parent material is granite from the Idaho Batholith. A small area in the northwestern county is underlaid by basalt of the Columbia River formation.

Climate: Highland continental characterized by wide daily and seasonal temperature changes. Winters are severe, with the heaviest snows of any retirement places profiled here. First frost comes early, by August 26; last frost occurs June 23. Summer days are warm to hot and usually dry because westerly air masses draw the dry climate of the Pacific Coast.

Summer mildness: 90 **Seasonal affect:** 34
Winter mildness: 29 **Hazard free:** 15
Score: 28.2 **Rank:** 144

	120
	90
	155
90°	4
32°	224
0°	18
	51
	54
	15

	High °F	Low °F	Hum %	Wind mph	Precip inches	Snow inches
JAN	31	22	76	8.0	3.8	14.0
FEB	37	28	70	8.9	2.8	13.0
MAR	42	32	60	9.9	2.6	10.0
APR	51	37	53	9.9	2.0	9.0
MAY	62	44	52	9.5	2.1	5.0
JUN	71	52	49	9.0	2.1	0
JUL	81	58	38	8.4	0.8	0
AUG	80	57	38	8.2	1.2	0
SEP	70	48	44	8.2	1.7	1.0
OCT	58	39	53	8.3	1.9	9.0
NOV	41	31	69	8.4	3.2	12.0
DEC	32	23	76	8.1	3.5	13.0

Medford–Ashland, OR

Location: 42.19 N and 122.52 W at 1,374 feet, in southwest Oregon, 25 miles north of the California border.

Landscape: Located in a mountain valley formed by the Rogue River and Bear Creek. The valley's outlet to the ocean 80 miles west is the narrow Canyon of the Rogue. Principal trees of the dense coniferous Pacific forest are Douglas fir, western red cedar, western hemlock, silver fir, and Sitka spruce.

Climate: Moderate continental. Late fall, winter, and early spring are cloudy, damp, and cool. The remainder of the year is warm, dry, and sunny. The shadow afforded by the Siskiyous and the Coast Range results in lighter rainfall. Snowfalls are light and usually melt within 24 hours. Winters are mild, with temperatures just dipping below freezing during December and January nights. Summer days can reach 90°F, but nights are cool. Frost arrives by October 20 and leaves by April 30.

Summer mildness: 51 **Seasonal affect:** 27
Winter mildness: 54 **Hazard free:** 85
Score: 59.4 **Rank:** 82

	117
	79
	169
90°	53
32°	68
0°	0
	50
	62
	8

	High °F	Low °F	Hum %	Wind mph	Precip inches	Snow inches
JAN	48	33	83	4.1	5.2	3.7
FEB	55	34	77	4.5	3.8	1.6
MAR	61	36	66	5.3	3.5	1.3
APR	67	38	57	5.7	1.8	0
MAY	75	44	50	5.7	1.2	0
JUN	83	50	42	5.9	0.5	0
JUL	90	53	38	5.8	0.2	0
AUG	90	53	39	5.3	0.5	0
SEP	83	47	42	4.5	0.9	0
OCT	70	41	58	3.7	2.4	0
NOV	54	38	80	3.6	5.3	0
DEC	46	34	85	3.6	5.7	2.3

★ Melbourne–Palm Bay, FL

Location: 28.04 N and 80.36 W at 21 feet, on the Intracoastal Waterway in the center of Florida's Atlantic coast, 58 miles southeast of Orlando.
Landscape: Flat, Florida coastal topography, with miles of hard, sandy beach. Inland, the land rises slightly to 30 feet. Native vegetation includes sea-oat grass, seagrape, and cabbage palm.
Climate: Subtropical. Nearness to the Atlantic results in a climate tempered by land and sea breezes. Temperatures in summer may top 90°F during the late morning or early afternoon, but they're cut short by midday sea breezes and afternoon convective thundershowers lower temperatures to comfortable levels. Winters can have cold airflows from the north, but they're usually mild because of the city's ocean setting and southerly latitude. There is hardly a freezing season, with frost arriving January 16 and departing a few days later, on January 19.

Summer mildness: 28 **Seasonal affect:** 65
Winter mildness: 96 **Hazard free:** 85
Score: 92.5 **Rank:** 16

99
134
133
90° 65
32° 2
0° 0
28
65
77

	High °F	Low °F	Hum %	Wind mph	Precip inches	Snow inches
JAN	71	51	58	8.7	2.2	0
FEB	72	51	56	9.2	2.8	0
MAR	77	56	56	9.9	2.7	0
APR	81	61	54	9.2	1.6	0
MAY	85	67	59	9.1	4.0	0
JUN	88	71	65	7.9	6.1	0
JUL	90	72	64	7.1	5.2	0
AUG	89	73	64	6.5	5.2	0
SEP	88	72	66	7.6	6.6	0
OCT	83	67	62	8.9	4.1	0
NOV	77	59	61	8.9	3.0	0
DEC	73	53	59	8.1	2.1	0

★ Mendocino–Fort Bragg, CA

Location: 39.25 N and 123.21 W at 120 feet in a valley in the Coast Ranges of northwest California, 130 miles north of San Francisco.
Landscape: At the mouth of Big River. Redwood and pine timber are found in Mendocino National Forest off to the east and at Jackson State Forest to the west.
Climate: Mendocino experiences a short growing season, with late frosts in spring, early rains and frosts in fall, and higher average rainfall than Napa and Sonoma counties and the central coast. Summer daytime temperatures are warm, while cold nights often dip into the thirties. This dramatic fluctuation softens the tannins of locally produced cabernet sauvignon and zinfandel.

Summer mildness: 100 **Seasonal affect:** 65
Winter mildness: 88 **Hazard free:** 95
Score: 99.0 **Rank:** 3

160
101
104
90° 0
32° 11
0° 0
100
42
0

	High °F	Low °F	Hum %	Wind mph	Precip inches	Snow inches
JAN	57	46	76	7.2	6.5	0
FEB	57	49	75	8.7	5.5	0
MAR	58	49	73	10.5	6.0	0
APR	61	50	71	12.2	2.8	0
MAY	62	51	71	13.4	1.2	0
JUN	64	53	71	13.9	0.3	0
JUL	65	54	73	13.6	0.1	0
AUG	66	55	74	12.8	0.4	0
SEP	67	56	72	11.1	0.8	0
OCT	64	55	71	9.4	2.9	0
NOV	60	52	73	7.5	6.2	0
DEC	56	47	76	7.1	6.4	0

★ Mesa, AZ

Location: 33.25 N and 111.50 W at 1,234 feet, 15 miles east of Phoenix.
Landscape: The area lies in the center of the Salt River Valley, which is oval and flat. Mountain ranges surround the valley on all sides. The Superstition Mountains are to the east. Though it's a desert, cotton and citrus are cultivated. Native vegetation includes creosote bush, saguaro, cholla, and cereus. An underground water table contributes to the local water supply, along with the Salt and Verde rivers.
Climate: Typical arid desert, with little rainfall and low humidity. Summers are hot, with temperatures frequently above 100°F. Winters are cool, and some nights can fall below freezing. A short freezing period means a long growing season. The first frost comes December 4 and the last frost on February 14. Sunny skies predominate. Cloudy days are rare.

Summer mildness: 3 **Seasonal affect:** 97
Winter mildness: 77 **Hazard free:** 96
Score: 91.5 **Rank:** 18

212
84
69
90° 163
32° 20
0° 0
2
19
24

	High °F	Low °F	Hum %	Wind mph	Precip inches	Snow inches
JAN	66	40	45	5.3	0.8	0
FEB	71	43	39	5.9	0.8	0
MAR	76	47	34	6.7	0.9	0
APR	84	53	23	7.0	0.3	0
MAY	93	60	18	7.1	0.2	0
JUN	103	68	16	6.8	0.1	0
JUL	106	77	28	7.2	0.9	0
AUG	103	76	33	6.7	1.1	0
SEP	98	69	31	6.3	0.9	0
OCT	88	58	31	5.8	0.7	0
NOV	75	47	37	5.4	0.8	0
DEC	67	40	46	5.1	1.1	0

★ = *in the top 30 places for climate mildness.*

Middle Cape Cod, MA

Location: The weather station is Harwich 41.40 N and 70.04 W at 19 feet, 60 miles southeast of Boston on a hooked peninsula jutting out 65 miles into the Atlantic Ocean.

Landscape: The area falls between the hilly western end of the Cape and the flat and treeless eastern or "outer cape." The soil is sandy and arranged in hills and dunes. There are also marshes and lakes. Tree cover is mostly pine wood.

Climate: Cape Cod extends into the Gulf Stream, making for a markedly milder climate than that of the rest of southern New England. Summers are warm, but temperatures rarely exceed 90°F. Winters are mild, with light to moderate snowfall mixed with periods of thaw and rain. First frost arrives on October 22; last frost on April 28.

Summer mildness: 89
Winter mildness: 30
Score: 22.2
Seasonal affect: 17
Hazard free: 23
Rank: 158

	99
	104
	162
90°	1
32°	122
0°	1
	24
	77
	19

	High °F	Low °F	Hum %	Wind mph	Precip inches	Snow inches
JAN	38	21	57	13.9	3.8	9.1
FEB	38	22	56	13.8	3.6	9.8
MAR	45	29	56	13.7	3.9	6.1
APR	54	37	55	13.2	4.1	0.3
MAY	63	46	60	12.2	4.0	0
JUN	72	56	59	11.5	3.4	0
JUL	78	62	57	11.0	2.9	0
AUG	78	62	59	10.8	3.6	0
SEP	71	55	60	11.3	3.5	0
OCT	62	45	58	12.0	3.8	0
NOV	53	37	59	13.0	4.4	0.2
DEC	43	27	59	13.6	4.3	5.2

★ Mission–McAllen–Alamo, TX

Location: 26.12 N and 98.13 W at 124 feet, on the border with Mexico in the lower Rio Grande Valley of southernmost Texas. The river empties into the Gulf of Mexico 75 miles east of here.

Landscape: Flat topography with little relief. Date palms, bougainvillea, and winter poinsettias color the valley towns, but the native upland sage and chaparral has lost out to intensive development, agricultural and urban.

Climate: Subtropical, influenced by the Gulf of Mexico. The valley is usually windy. Winters are clear, with warm days and cool nights. The frost arrives December 29 and departs by the end of January. Summers are long, hot, and humid. The Sierra Madre Oriental Mountains in Mexico block dry air from the Chihuahuan Desert, but both affect the climate of this river plain.

Summer mildness: 6
Winter mildness: 94
Score: 90.5
Seasonal affect: 76
Hazard free: 91
Rank: 20

	98
	132
	135
90°	157
32°	4
0°	0
	27
	34
	26

	High °F	Low °F	Hum %	Wind mph	Precip inches	Snow inches
JAN	68	47	67	11.3	1.4	0
FEB	72	50	63	12.1	1.3	0
MAR	80	57	59	13.4	0.6	0
APR	86	64	59	13.9	1.3	0
MAY	89	70	60	13.1	2.8	0
JUN	93	73	59	12.0	2.7	0
JUL	95	74	55	11.3	1.7	0
AUG	96	74	56	10.3	2.4	0
SEP	92	72	60	9.4	4.4	0
OCT	87	64	59	9.5	2.6	0
NOV	79	56	60	10.7	1.0	0
DEC	71	49	65	10.8	1.1	0

Monadnock Region, NH

Location: 42.561 N and 72.1643 W at 487 feet, in southwestern New Hampshire, 15 miles from the Vermont and Massachusetts borders. Boston is 85 miles southeast.

Landscape: The terrain is hilly to mountainous forestland. Nearby, Mount Monadnock rises to 3,165 feet. The Connecticut River lies to the west and forms the border with Vermont. Vegetation is mixed forest, with pine and maple predominating. Mountain laurel and flowering dogwood are also common in this part of the state.

Climate: The typical New England climate makes for warm summers, long and pleasant autumns, cold winters, and short, wet springs. Heat waves are infrequent in summer, but cold snaps are common in winter. Frost comes in by September 25 and will not leave until May 19. Snowfall amounts can vary greatly from year to year, with limited thaws.

Summer mildness: 72
Winter mildness: 12
Score: 0.0
Seasonal affect: 5
Hazard free: 7
Rank: 203

	98
	104
	163
90°	13
32°	166
0°	18
	185
	81
	19

	High °F	Low °F	Hum %	Wind mph	Precip inches	Snow inches
JAN	32	10	67	13.8	2.9	16.9
FEB	36	13	66	13.8	2.7	16.1
MAR	45	23	65	13.7	2.9	13.2
APR	59	33	62	13.2	3.2	2.8
MAY	71	44	62	12.2	3.8	0.1
JUN	79	53	67	11.5	3.6	0
JUL	84	57	68	11.0	3.6	0
AUG	82	56	71	10.8	3.9	0
SEP	73	48	73	11.3	3.0	0
OCT	62	37	71	12.0	3.2	0.1
NOV	49	30	72	12.9	3.5	3.9
DEC	36	17	71	13.6	3.3	16.1

★ = *in the top 30 places for climate mildness.*

Montrose, CO

Location: 38.28 N and 107.52 W at 5,801 feet, in the Uncompahgre River Valley, 50 miles southeast of Grand Junction.

Landscape: The sage desert and shortgrass prairie of the Colorado Plateau. The western vista is the Uncompahgre Plateau, rising over 9,000 feet. Ranchland and orchards mark the gently rolling lowland. Lakes and streams here are fed from mountain snows. The Uncompahgre River flows through steep canyons. Mixed forests of pine, spruce, and aspen cover the subalpine areas; sagebrush and cactus are found in the canyons.

Climate: Desert steppe brings varied seasonal and daily temperature changes. Summers are dry and comfortable due to the high altitude. Winters are cold with moderate snow cover in the elevations through May. Winters are long, with first the frost arriving October 8 and the last frost not leaving until May 12. Humidity is low, and summer precipitation is scant but for brief mountain thunderstorms.

Summer mildness: 64 **Seasonal affect:** 81
Winter mildness: 13 **Hazard free:** 27
Score: 43.0 **Rank:** 116

	137
	107
	121
90°	34
32°	168
0°	7
	8
	27
	35

	High °F	Low °F	Hum %	Wind mph	Precip inches	Snow inches
JAN	37	12	63	5.6	0.5	7.3
FEB	44	19	54	6.7	0.4	5.7
MAR	53	26	43	8.4	0.7	3.7
APR	62	34	33	9.5	0.8	2.0
MAY	72	42	32	9.6	0.9	0
JUN	83	51	26	9.7	0.6	0
JUL	88	57	28	9.3	1.0	0
AUG	86	54	31	9.0	1.1	0
SEP	77	46	33	8.9	1.2	0
OCT	66	35	38	7.9	1.1	0
NOV	50	25	49	6.7	0.8	4.0
DEC	40	16	60	5.9	0.7	7.5

★ Morro Bay–Cambria, CA

Location: 35.21 N and 120.50 W at 89 feet, on the Pacific Ocean roughly 230 miles midway between San Francisco and Los Angeles.

Landscape: The Santa Lucia Mountains end in cliffs that slice into the ocean to the north, with sandy beaches elsewhere on the coast. Forests are mixed evergreen, with pine and cypress in abundance. Cultivated groves of almond, walnut, and apple trees are common, as are vineyards.

Climate: Weather is stable, ranging from mild and warm in summer to mild and cool in winter. Fog and cloudy mornings usually give way to bright sunshine with cool ocean breezes. The high elevation and coastal location are responsible for the consistently mild climate. There is a long growing season between the last frost of January 25 and the first frost of December 30.

Summer mildness: 70 **Seasonal affect:** 84
Winter mildness: 74 **Hazard free:** 100
Score: 97.5 **Rank:** 6

	147
	116
	103
90°	12
32°	3
0°	0
	19
	28
	4

	High °F	Low °F	Hum %	Wind mph	Precip inches	Snow inches
JAN	63	42	57	4.8	5.0	0
FEB	65	43	58	6.3	4.6	0
MAR	65	43	60	6.7	3.8	0
APR	68	45	61	7.6	1.6	0
MAY	70	47	63	7.1	0.3	0
JUN	74	50	66	6.8	0.0	0
JUL	78	52	67	6.5	0.0	0
AUG	79	53	68	6.1	0.1	0
SEP	79	53	67	5.8	0.4	0
OCT	76	50	64	5.5	1.1	0
NOV	69	46	57	5.3	2.8	0
DEC	64	42	55	5.0	3.8	0

Murray–Kentucky Lake, KY

Location: 36.36 N and 88.19 W at 480 feet, just above the Tennessee line in the extreme western part of the state. Nashville, Tennessee, is 100 miles southeast.

Landscape: Kentucky Lake is one of the world's largest artificial lakes, formed more than 40 years ago by damming the Tennessee River. Relief is minimal. The surrounding country is gently rolling and heavily forested with oak, hickory, walnut, maple, elm, ash, and sweet chestnut, with lower layers of small trees and shrubs.

Climate: Hot continental, with moderately cold winters and warm, humid summers. Precipitation is ample and well distributed throughout the year. October 26 ushers in the first frost; April 5 sees the last frost out. Most days, even those in winter, are suitable for outdoor activity. Spring and fall are the most comfortable seasons. Fall, the sunniest season, is remarkably free from storms or cold.

Summer mildness: 47 **Seasonal affect:** 35
Winter mildness: 52 **Hazard free:** 35
Score: 27.7 **Rank:** 147

	109
	99
	157
90°	51
32°	84
0°	1
	20
	74
	60

	High °F	Low °F	Hum %	Wind mph	Precip inches	Snow inches
JAN	43	25	62	9.3	3.8	4.3
FEB	49	29	65	9.2	4.4	3.1
MAR	60	39	57	9.6	5.1	2.4
APR	71	48	50	8.6	5.1	0
MAY	79	57	56	7.5	4.9	0
JUN	87	65	55	6.5	4.1	0
JUL	90	68	58	6.1	4.7	0
AUG	88	67	59	5.6	3.6	0
SEP	82	60	56	6.2	3.9	0
OCT	71	48	56	6.9	3.6	0
NOV	59	40	61	8.9	5.2	0
DEC	48	30	63	8.9	5.3	1.0

★ = *in the top 30 places for climate mildness.*

Myrtle Beach, SC

Location: 33.41 N and 78.53 W at 30 feet, 100 miles northeast of Charleston.

Landscape: The area known as the "Grand Strand" is flat, has a populated area only a few blocks wide, and extends 60 miles up and down the shore. Elevations are no greater than 50 feet above sea level. There are many more wooded areas than usually found in a beach area. The beaches themselves are white sand. Inland is low and swampy, with stands of southern yellow pine mixed with hickory, sweet gum, and other deciduous trees. The grasses are bluestem, panicums, and longleaf uniola in the coastal marshes.

Climate: Subtropical. Mild winters and warm summers are the rule. The ocean has a pronounced modifying effect on temperatures, and the Blue Ridge Mountains block cold air from the interior. Some tropical storms reach the area every few years. First frost comes by November 20; the last frost leaves by March 11.

Summer mildness: 37 **Seasonal affect:** 50
Winter mildness: 71 **Hazard free:** 50
Score: 55.4 **Rank:** 91

	112
	104
	150
90°	45
32°	35
0°	0
	24
	72
	47

	High °F	Low °F	Hum %	Wind mph	Precip inches	Snow inches
JAN	58	36	56	9.1	3.9	0.5
FEB	62	38	52	9.8	3.7	0.6
MAR	69	45	52	10.2	4.2	0.3
APR	76	52	48	10.3	2.7	0
MAY	83	61	55	9.2	4.4	0
JUN	87	68	59	8.5	5.6	0
JUL	90	71	63	8.0	6.5	0
AUG	89	71	64	7.4	6.5	0
SEP	85	66	62	7.9	5.2	0
OCT	78	55	56	8.1	4.0	0
NOV	70	47	53	8.1	3.1	0
DEC	62	39	55	8.5	3.5	0.3

Naples, FL

Location: 26.08 N and 81.47 W at 9 feet, on Florida's Gulf of Mexico coast, 25 miles south of Ft. Myers.

Landscape: Flat topography. The area lies on a 7-mile mainland beach. Nearby are mangrove islands. To the east is the Big Cypress Swamp and beyond, the Everglades. Native vegetation includes cypress, evergreen oaks, laurel, small palms, and tropical shrubs.

Climate: Subtropical. Summer and winter temperature extremes are checked by the influence of the Gulf. Summer heat is exacerbated by humidity. Winters have many bright, warm days and moderately cool nights. Rainfall averages more than 50 inches annually, with two-thirds coming daily between June and September. Most rain falls as late-afternoon or early-evening thunderstorms, bringing welcome relief from the heat.

Summer mildness: 10 **Seasonal affect:** 66
Winter mildness: 97 **Hazard free:** 77
Score: 83.1 **Rank:** 35

	102
	142
	121
90°	101
32°	0
0°	0
	21
	72
	93

	High °F	Low °F	Hum %	Wind mph	Precip inches	Snow inches
JAN	76	53	56	8.6	1.7	0
FEB	77	54	56	9.2	2.2	0
MAR	81	58	53	9.5	2.3	0
APR	85	61	47	9.3	1.5	0
MAY	88	66	49	8.7	4.1	0
JUN	90	71	56	8.0	8.6	0
JUL	91	72	60	7.2	7.8	0
AUG	92	73	60	7.0	8.2	0
SEP	91	72	60	7.8	8.4	0
OCT	87	67	56	8.5	3.1	0
NOV	82	61	56	8.4	1.8	0
DEC	78	55	56	8.5	1.4	0

Natchitoches, LA

Location: 31.46 N and 93.06 W at 130 feet in northwest Louisiana, 65 miles southeast from Shreveport and 225 miles east of Dallas.

Landscape: The topography is gently sloping, with relief varying from 100 to 250 feet. Most of the numerous streams are sluggish; marshes, swamps, and lakes are numerous. The naturally occurring forest is laurel, magnolia, and evergreen oak.

Climate: Moderately uniform throughout the year: mild winters and hot summers are the rule. Precipitation exceeds evaporation, but summer droughts occur. The growing season is long, but frost occurs every winter. Snow falls rarely but melts almost immediately.

Summer mildness: 19 **Seasonal affect:** 44
Winter mildness: 70 **Hazard free:** 49
Score: 42.0 **Rank:** 118

	114
	100
	151
90°	90
32°	36
0°	0
	107
	64
	57

	High °F	Low °F	Hum %	Wind mph	Precip inches	Snow inches
JAN	57	35	74	9.2	4.9	0.8
FEB	62	38	71	9.6	4.6	0.5
MAR	70	46	70	10.1	4.7	0.2
APR	78	54	72	9.7	4.3	0
MAY	85	62	75	8.3	6.0	0
JUN	91	69	75	7.5	4.3	0
JUL	94	72	74	7.1	3.5	0
AUG	93	71	73	6.7	3.2	0
SEP	88	66	74	7.2	3.4	0
OCT	79	54	72	7.4	3.8	0
NOV	69	45	73	8.5	4.2	0
DEC	60	37	74	8.9	6.1	0.2

★ = *in the top 30 places for climate mildness.*

New Bern, NC

Location: 35.06 N and 77.02 W at 15 feet, on a triangle of land where the Neuse and Trent rivers meet and empty into Pamlico Sound. Raleigh, North Carolina's capital, is 100 miles northwest. The Atlantic Ocean is 35 miles east.
Landscape: In this central tidewater savanna there are bluffs, marshes, lakes, and rivers. Narrow-leafed grasses are found in the salt marshes; cattails, ricegrass, and parrotfeathers are found in the freshwater marshes. The trees are oak-hickory, not as tall, have smaller and more leathery leaves, and a sparse canopy. In town are live oak, laurel, holly, and magnolia, with underbrush of shrubs and herbaceous plants.
Climate: Subtropical, with humid, hot summers and mild winters. Rain falls throughout the year. Spring and summer can bring heavy thunderstorms. Occasional tropical storms from the Atlantic may strike this coastal location. Since first frost comes November 9 and the last frost leaves March 23, the growing season is relatively long.

Summer mildness: 43 **Seasonal affect:** 34
Winter mildness: 64 **Hazard free:** 33
Score: 35.1 **Rank:** 132

	106
	107
	152
90°	39
32°	53
0°	0
	20
	77
	49

	High °F	Low °F	Hum %	Wind mph	Precip inches	Snow inches
JAN	54	33	56	12.1	4.3	1.1
FEB	57	35	52	12.3	4.2	1.0
MAR	65	42	52	12.0	3.9	0.8
APR	73	50	48	11.8	3.2	0
MAY	80	59	55	10.9	4.6	0
JUN	86	66	59	10.7	5.4	0
JUL	88	71	63	10.0	7.0	0
AUG	87	70	64	9.5	6.6	0
SEP	83	64	62	10.5	5.1	0
OCT	75	53	56	11.1	3.0	0
NOV	67	44	53	11.0	3.2	0
DEC	58	36	55	11.5	3.7	0.3

New Braunfels, TX

Location: 29.42 N and 98.07 W at 623 feet, on the Balcones Escarpment in south-central Texas. San Antonio is 30 miles southwest.
Landscape: Arid grassland with shrubs and low trees and low hills. The deep, winding Comal River flows into the Guadalupe. While the spring-fed Comal is predictably smooth and safe, conditions on the white-water Guadalupe frequently change. Nearby Landa Park, Natural Bridge Caverns, and Canyon Lake mark the region. Caladium grows along the riverbanks. As the land rises to the Edwards Plateau, oak, hickory, and juniper mix with mesquite and buffalo grass.
Climate: Prairie, with warm days and cool nights in winter and a long, hot summer. Though miles from the Gulf, the area is influenced by moist, marine air. Most of the annual precipitation falls as rain in May and September. The first frost is around Thanksgiving; the last frost is by March 9.

Summer mildness: 9 **Seasonal affect:** 71
Winter mildness: 76 **Hazard free:** 70
Score: 66.8 **Rank:** 67

	108
	118
	139
90°	122
32°	28
0°	0
	22
	46
	37

	High °F	Low °F	Hum %	Wind mph	Precip inches	Snow inches
JAN	60	37	59	9.0	1.9	0.1
FEB	65	40	57	9.7	2.2	0.4
MAR	73	48	54	10.4	1.8	0
APR	81	56	56	10.3	2.6	0
MAY	86	64	59	10.0	5.0	0
JUN	92	70	56	9.9	4.1	0
JUL	95	72	51	9.2	2.0	0
AUG	96	72	51	8.5	2.5	0
SEP	90	68	55	8.5	4.1	0
OCT	82	57	54	8.4	3.5	0
NOV	72	48	55	8.8	2.8	0
DEC	63	39	57	8.5	2.0	0

★ New Port Richey, FL

Location: 28.14 N and 82.43 W at 30 feet, on Florida's central Gulf coast, 30 miles north of Tampa.
Landscape: Inland is hilly country unusual to Florida. Withlacoochee State Forest is typical mix of oak-gum-cypress hardwood, and needle-leaved evergreens such as longleaf and slash pine. Aromatic and evergreen bayberry and sweet bay are scattered throughout.
Climate: Subtropical, with temperatures modified throughout the year by the waters of the Gulf. Afternoon thunderstorms are frequent during summer, resulting in drastic temperature drops. Snowfall is negligible, and freezing temperatures, even at night, are rare. January 10 brings in the first frost, and January 27 the last frost.

Summer mildness: 21 **Seasonal affect:** 68
Winter mildness: 94 **Hazard free:** 80
Score: 89.1 **Rank:** 23

	102
	142
	121
90°	76
32°	4
0°	0
	22
	70
	86

	High °F	Low °F	Hum %	Wind mph	Precip inches	Snow inches
JAN	70	49	59	8.6	3.0	0
FEB	71	51	56	9.2	3.4	0
MAR	76	56	55	9.5	3.9	0
APR	81	61	51	9.3	1.4	0
MAY	86	67	52	8.7	3.4	0
JUN	89	72	60	8.0	5.6	0
JUL	90	73	63	7.2	7.4	0
AUG	90	73	64	7.0	8.4	0
SEP	89	72	62	7.8	7.2	0
OCT	85	65	57	8.5	2.3	0
NOV	78	57	57	8.4	2.2	0
DEC	73	51	59	8.5	3.0	0

★ = *in the top 30 places for climate mildness.*

Newport–Lincoln City, OR

Location: 44.38 N and 124.03 W at 177 feet, on Oregon's Pacific Coast, 55 miles west of Salem.
Landscape: Parts of the cities sit at the water's edge, and more is built on level benchland about 150 feet above sea level. Just to the east, the foothills of the Coast Range begin a steep ascent to ridges 2,000 to 3,000 feet high. The principal trees of the dense Pacific conifer forests nearby are Douglas fir, western red cedar, western hemlock, silver fir, and Sitka spruce.
Climate: Marine climate typical of Oregon's coastal area. Temperature extremes are almost nonexistent. Warm, moist air from the Pacific makes summers mild and pleasant. In winter, the air releases moisture over the cold landmass, resulting in a constant cloud cover and rain from November to March. Most of the annual precipitation falls during these months. The first frost arrives November 18; the last frost leaves April 16.

Summer mildness: 95
Winter mildness: 61
Score: 78.2
Seasonal affect: 2
Hazard free: 86
Rank: 44

	49
	78
	238
90°	0
32°	30
0°	0
	41
	126
	7

	High °F	Low °F	Hum %	Wind mph	Precip inches	Snow inches
JAN	50	38	80	9.1	11.1	0.8
FEB	53	39	79	9.1	8.1	0.2
MAR	54	39	77	9.0	8.2	0.4
APR	55	40	72	8.7	4.8	0
MAY	59	43	71	8.5	3.5	0
JUN	62	48	71	8.6	2.7	0
JUL	65	50	73	8.7	1.0	0
AUG	65	50	73	8.1	1.3	0
SEP	65	48	72	7.6	2.6	0
OCT	61	45	77	7.6	5.4	0
NOV	55	42	78	8.8	10.9	0
DEC	51	38	80	9.1	12.3	0.6

Norfork Lake, AR

Location: 36.20 N and 92.23 W at 756 feet, near the center of the Arkansas–Missouri border 100 air miles north of Little Rock, the state capital.
Landscape: Though in the center of the Ozark Mountains, gently rolling hills surround Lake Norfork, formed decades ago by damming the White River. The thick woods are broadleaf deciduous forests of oak, hickory, maple, sweet gum, and walnut.
Climate: Hot continental, with warm summers and winters of mild days and freezing nights. In a given year, the climate can vary from warm and humid maritime to cold and dry continental, but it's relatively free from climatic extremes. Winters may be cold enough for snow, but an icy rain is more typical during brief, intense cold snaps. First frost has hit by October 26; last frost strikes April 6, bringing an early spring that is pleasant.

Summer mildness: 43
Winter mildness: 41
Score: 22.7
Seasonal affect: 57
Hazard free: 19
Rank: 156

	116
	97
	153
90°	56
32°	90
0°	1
	20
	63
	56

	High °F	Low °F	Hum %	Wind mph	Precip inches	Snow inches
JAN	45	23	60	11.7	2.5	3.1
FEB	50	27	60	11.9	3.0	3.2
MAR	60	37	56	12.9	4.4	2.0
APR	71	47	55	12.2	4.1	0
MAY	78	55	59	10.4	4.9	0
JUN	85	63	59	9.6	4.1	0
JUL	91	67	56	8.5	2.6	0
AUG	90	66	54	8.6	2.9	0
SEP	82	59	58	9.3	4.1	0
OCT	73	47	54	10.1	3.3	0
NOV	59	37	59	11.3	4.4	1.0
DEC	48	27	63	11.6	3.8	1.6

★ North County San Diego, CA

Location: The weather station is in Oceanside, 33.11 N and 117.22 W at 47 feet on the Pacific Coast, 30 miles north of San Diego.
Landscape: Backed by coastal foothills and mountains to the east. Stream valleys are narrow where they drain the hills. Evergreens with thick, hard leaves like eucalyptus are prevalent. California live oak, tanoak, and California laurel are also common. Chaparral is a low-growing shrub.
Climate: Mediterranean. The ocean and mountains have a tempering effect, meaning no below-freezing days and few over 90°F. In this two-season climate, cool springs give way to dry and mild summers. Fog and dawn/dusk clouds are common, but sunshine is the rule. Storms are virtually nonexistent.

Summer mildness: 84
Winter mildness: 84
Score: 100.0
Seasonal affect: 86
Hazard free: 99
Rank: 1

	147
	116
	101
90°	0
32°	0
0°	0
	24
	19
	3

	High °F	Low °F	Hum %	Wind mph	Precip inches	Snow inches
JAN	65	44	55	5.9	2.0	0
FEB	65	45	58	6.5	1.9	0
MAR	65	47	60	7.4	1.9	0
APR	66	50	59	7.8	0.9	0
MAY	68	54	65	7.9	0.2	0
JUN	70	58	69	7.7	0.1	0
JUL	74	62	69	7.4	0.0	0
AUG	76	63	68	7.3	0.1	0
SEP	75	61	66	7.0	0.3	0
OCT	73	56	61	6.5	0.4	0
NOV	69	49	56	5.9	1.4	0
DEC	65	44	54	5.6	1.6	0

★ = *in the top 30 places for climate mildness.*

Northampton–Amherst, MA

Location: 42.22 N and 72.31 W at 320 feet, in the western part of the state, 70 miles west of Boston and 20 miles north of Springfield.

Landscape: Situated in the center of the long Connecticut Valley, with the Berkshire Hills of the Appalachians visible to the west. This is the Berkshire Taconic forest plateau with curved ridges covered by diverse and transitional forests of red oak, beech, birch, walnut, sugar maple, elm, and sweet chestnut. Cottonwood, basswood, or silver maple are found in poorly drained coves. There are areas of isolated wetlands. Quabbin Reservoir lies to the east.

Climate: Hot continental, with typical New England seasonal temperature extremes. Summers are generally mild and free of thunderstorms, but with occasional hot, muggy days. September 29 heralds the first frost; May 9 bids the last frost adieu. Winters are long with a snow cover that's deep and lasting.

Summer mildness: 68
Winter mildness: 16
Score: 6.4
Seasonal affect: 14
Hazard free: 19
Rank: 190

	81
	109
	175
90°	10
32°	151
0°	11
	29
	75
	33

	High °F	Low °F	Hum %	Wind mph	Precip inches	Snow inches
JAN	35	12	58	9.0	3.2	11.6
FEB	38	15	57	9.4	2.9	11.4
MAR	48	25	53	9.9	3.2	8.8
APR	60	34	49	10.0	3.6	1.0
MAY	72	44	49	8.9	3.9	0
JUN	80	54	55	8.1	3.8	0
JUL	85	59	55	7.5	3.8	0
AUG	83	57	57	7.2	3.7	0
SEP	76	49	59	7.3	3.4	0
OCT	65	39	59	7.8	3.4	0
NOV	52	31	60	8.5	3.8	2.0
DEC	39	19	62	8.7	3.7	10.0

Northern Neck, VA

Location: 37.46 N and 76.28 W at 98 feet, on a peninsula between Virginia's Rappahannock and Potomac rivers extending into Chesapeake Bay. Richmond, the state capital, is 40 miles southeast.

Landscape: Tidewater country of low hills, streams, and marsh of the Chesapeake Bay watershed. The woods inland are a typical southeastern mixed forest, with tall oak, hickory, sweet gum, red maple, and winged elm. At least half of the stands are filled with second-growth loblolly and shortleaf pine. Coastal marshes and interior wetlands are dominated by gums and cypress trees, cattails, and rush. An understory of dogwood, viburnum, blueberry, yaupon, and numerous woody vines is prevalent.

Climate: Subtropical, with mild winters and hot, humid summers. Spring and autumn are especially pleasant. First frost is October 22; last frost is April 15. Precipitation is evenly distributed throughout the year, mostly as rain. Thunderstorms are likely in midsummer.

Summer mildness: 54
Winter mildness: 49
Score: 38.6
Seasonal affect: 54
Hazard free: 22
Rank: 124

	106
	107
	152
90°	39
32°	88
0°	0
	20
	70
	37

	High °F	Low °F	Hum %	Wind mph	Precip inches	Snow inches
JAN	45	26	60	11.5	3.2	5.4
FEB	49	29	58	12.0	2.8	5.4
MAR	59	36	56	12.5	3.5	3.4
APR	69	44	52	11.8	2.9	0
MAY	77	54	58	10.5	4.6	0
JUN	85	62	58	9.8	3.7	0
JUL	88	67	61	9.0	4.2	0
AUG	87	65	62	8.9	4.2	0
SEP	81	59	62	9.6	4.2	0
OCT	70	47	61	10.4	3.4	0
NOV	61	39	58	10.7	3.2	0
DEC	50	31	60	11.2	3.1	2.5

Oakhurst–Coarsegold, CA

Location: 37.19 N and 119.39 W at 2,289 feet, in California's Southern Mines country in the Sierra foothills. San Francisco is 150 miles west.

Landscape: In these high foothills are ravines, buttes, and wooded peaks, watered by streams from the Sierra Nevada Mountains. Yosemite National Park is immediately north with waterfalls, acres of forest, and glacier-carved valleys. Rivers drain into the broad San Joaquin Valley to the west. The lower hills are covered by close-growing cypress and pinyon. In the higher elevations is a combination of digger pine and blue oak.

Climate: Sierran forest climate in the transition zone between the dry west coast desert and the wet west coast farther north. Prevailing west winds influence conditions jointly with elevation. Therefore the summers are long and generally dry, with most of the precipitation falling as rain rather than snow. First frost comes October 22 while the last frost leaves April 15.

Summer mildness: 39
Winter mildness: 46
Score: 62.8
Seasonal affect: 72
Hazard free: 63
Rank: 76

	189
	75
	100
90°	59
32°	77
0°	0
	34
	49
	14

	High °F	Low °F	Hum %	Wind mph	Precip inches	Snow inches
JAN	56	31	80	7.2	6.0	5.3
FEB	58	33	75	7.6	5.6	3.1
MAR	60	35	65	8.6	5.5	3.0
APR	66	38	55	8.7	3.0	0
MAY	75	44	48	9.2	1.0	0
JUN	85	51	44	9.7	0.3	0
JUL	93	57	44	9.0	0.1	0
AUG	93	57	45	8.6	0.1	0
SEP	86	52	45	7.5	0.7	0
OCT	76	44	53	6.4	1.4	0
NOV	64	36	65	6.0	4.3	0
DEC	57	31	77	6.6	4.9	2.7

★ = *in the top 30 places for climate mildness.*

Ocala, FL

Location: 29.11 N and 82.08 W at 99 feet, in north-central Florida, 25 miles south of Gainesville and 90 miles west of Daytona Beach and the Atlantic Ocean.

Landscape: This is low ridge country with deposits of pure limestone, just west of Ocala National Forest. Artesian springs and outlets form the Silver River. Stands of sand pine, longleaf, slash, and other yellow southern pine mix with a variety of hardwoods of the Eastern deciduous forest, evergreen oaks, laurel, and a lower stratum of tree ferns, small palms, and shrubs.

Climate: Subtropical, with a small annual range of temperature changes. Precipitation is light, except from May to September. Summers are hotter and more humid than those of coastal locations but are cooled by afternoon thunderstorms. Winters are mild, with warm days and cool nights. First frost comes early December; the last frost leaves mid-February.

Summer mildness: 10
Seasonal affect: 55
Winter mildness: 90
Hazard free: 80
Score: 72.2
Rank: 57

	92
	148
	125
90°	120
32°	12
0°	0
	27
	77
	82

	High °F	Low °F	Hum %	Wind mph	Precip inches	Snow inches
JAN	70	45	56	8.9	3.2	0
FEB	72	46	52	9.6	3.8	0
MAR	79	53	50	9.9	3.5	0
APR	84	57	46	9.4	2.8	0
MAY	89	63	49	8.8	4.1	0
JUN	92	69	56	8.0	7.2	0
JUL	92	71	59	7.4	7.8	0
AUG	92	71	60	7.1	6.7	0
SEP	90	69	60	7.7	5.5	0
OCT	84	61	56	8.6	2.1	0
NOV	77	53	55	8.6	2.3	0
DEC	72	47	57	8.6	2.7	0

Ocean City, MD

Location: 38.20 N and 75.05 W at 8 feet, on the Atlantic coast of southeastern Maryland, 100 miles southeast of Washington, D.C.

Landscape: A 10-mile barrier beach forming a chain of bays along the Atlantic shore. Assateague Island National Seashore is a narrow barrier island and a southern extension of Ocean City's barrier beach. The coastal marshes and interior swamps of the region are dominated by gums and cypress. There is an understory of grasses and sedges. Undrained shallow depressions in these savannas form upland bogs where evergreen shrubs predominate.

Climate: Subtropical, characterized by milder winters than nearby inland locations, thanks to the Atlantic. Summers are somewhat hot and humid. Precipitation is evenly distributed throughout the year as rain, though there may be summer drought. Snow is infrequent though frost occurs nearly every winter with the first frost on October 19 and the last frost on April 22.

Summer mildness: 62
Seasonal affect: 28
Winter mildness: 43
Hazard free: 43
Score: 36.1
Rank: 128

	97
	104
	164
90°	26
32°	93
0°	0
	34
	70
	28

	High °F	Low °F	Hum %	Wind mph	Precip inches	Snow inches
JAN	43	26	61	9.8	3.6	4.2
FEB	46	28	59	10.4	3.5	3.5
MAR	55	35	53	11.2	4.2	2.4
APR	65	43	52	10.6	3.2	0
MAY	74	53	55	9.1	3.6	0
JUN	82	62	55	8.5	3.6	0
JUL	86	67	55	7.8	4.3	0
AUG	85	66	58	7.5	5.3	0
SEP	79	58	58	7.8	3.7	0
OCT	68	47	58	8.2	3.4	0
NOV	59	38	58	9.2	3.2	0
DEC	48	30	61	9.4	3.7	1.8

Oscoda–Huron Shore, MI

Location: 44.25 N and 83.20 W at 387 feet, in northern Michigan on Lake Huron, 120 miles northeast of Lansing, the state capital.

Landscape: At the mouth of the Au Sable River with the Huron National Forest lying inland. This is a more rugged coast on an upland plateau where relief is minimal. The forest is pine and hemlock.

Climate: The daily and seasonal temperature range is modified by Lake Huron. Rainfall is heaviest in summer. Winters here are cold and snowy, though not as snowy as in locations to the north and west. First frost comes early in late September; the last frost departs in late May. Summer is mild, with cool nights. Cloudiness is greatest in late fall and winter.

Summer mildness: 91
Seasonal affect: 27
Winter mildness: 6
Hazard free: 17
Score: 16.3
Rank: 170

	67
	105
	192
90°	4
32°	166
0°	17
	27
	63
	32

	High °F	Low °F	Hum %	Wind mph	Precip inches	Snow inches
JAN	28	10	70	8.9	1.7	13.8
FEB	30	10	65	8.4	1.2	10.5
MAR	39	20	61	9.0	2.2	9.6
APR	52	32	54	9.2	2.5	2.0
MAY	64	42	51	8.3	2.8	0
JUN	74	51	53	7.6	3.1	0
JUL	80	56	53	7.0	2.8	0
AUG	77	55	58	6.7	3.3	0
SEP	70	48	62	7.1	3.6	0
OCT	58	37	61	7.8	2.4	0
NOV	45	29	69	8.5	2.4	4.0
DEC	33	18	73	8.6	2.2	12.1

★ = *in the top 30 places for climate mildness.*

Oxford, MS

Location: 34.22 N and 89.31 W at 416 feet, in north-central Mississippi, 75 miles southeast of Memphis, Tennessee.
Landscape: Rolling hill country near the Sardis Reservoir and two other lakes. The surrounding Holly Springs National Forest protects a typical southeastern mixed forest. Before the Holly Springs National Forest was formed, much of the land was abandoned farmland with rapidly eroding soils. These rolling hills are now covered with loblolly and shortleaf pines, and upland hardwoods of oak-hickory woodlands.
Climate: Hot continental to subtropical. Though not in the path of storms coming up from the Gulf or down from Canada, the area is influenced by both. Winter is wet with frequent drizzle and infrequent light snowfall. Usually there are mild days and cold nights. October 27 greets the first frost; April 4 bids adieu to the last frost. Summer is hot and humid. Spring and autumn are pleasant and long lasting.

Summer mildness: 36 | **Seasonal affect:** 61
Winter mildness: 55 | **Hazard free:** 40
Score: 45.0 | **Rank:** 112

	120
	96
	149
90°	77
32°	76
0°	0
	10
	72
	53

	High °F	Low °F	Hum %	Wind mph	Precip inches	Snow inches
JAN	49	28	63	10.1	4.6	1.7
FEB	54	31	60	10.2	4.8	1.0
MAR	64	40	56	10.8	6.0	0.2
APR	74	49	53	10.3	5.3	0
MAY	81	57	55	8.8	5.9	0
JUN	88	65	56	8.0	4.1	0
JUL	91	68	57	7.5	4.4	0
AUG	91	66	56	7.0	3.1	0
SEP	85	60	56	7.5	3.7	0
OCT	76	46	51	7.7	3.5	0
NOV	65	39	56	9.1	5.8	0
DEC	54	31	61	9.8	6.1	0.4

Pagosa Springs, CO

Location: 37.16 N and 107.00 W at 7,105 feet, on the San Juan River in southwestern Colorado, 230 air miles from Denver.
Landscape: On a high mountain plateau with peaks of the San Juan Mountains a distant vista to the north and east. The geothermal springs, canyons, mesas, and mountains provide dramatic relief. Mostly forested and dominated by Engelmann spruce and fir forest, scattered aspen groves cover the subalpine areas. The upper reaches grade into alpine tundra.
Climate: Semiarid steppe. High altitude brings just two seasons: an 8-month winter and a 4-month summer. Still, the area averages 300 sunny days a year. Temperature variations are great both daily and annually. Snowfall in this region is legendary. First frost arrives early, by September 3; last frost is late departing, not leaving until June 25.

Summer mildness: 77 | **Seasonal affect:** 78
Winter mildness: 0 | **Hazard free:** 5
Score: 22.7 | **Rank:** 156

	115
	130
	120
90°	2
32°	243
0°	36
	8
	47
	35

	High °F	Low °F	Hum %	Wind mph	Precip inches	Snow inches
JAN	37	1	63	5.6	1.7	31.0
FEB	42	7	55	6.7	1.3	19.9
MAR	48	16	41	8.4	1.6	18.0
APR	57	22	32	9.5	1.2	6.0
MAY	67	30	31	9.6	1.1	1.0
JUN	77	37	25	9.7	0.8	0
JUL	82	46	27	9.3	1.9	0
AUG	80	45	30	9.0	2.5	0
SEP	72	36	33	8.9	2.2	0
OCT	63	26	37	7.9	2.1	3.0
NOV	49	16	48	6.7	1.7	11.0
DEC	39	5	60	5.9	1.8	26.5

Pahrump Valley, NV

Location: 36.10 N and 115.08 W at 2,028 feet, just west of the Colorado River Valley. Los Angeles is 300 miles southwest, and Las Vegas is 40 miles east.
Landscape: A desert valley with mountains from 2,000 to 10,000 feet on the horizon. These mountains act as effective barriers to moisture-laden storms moving in from the Pacific Ocean. In the environs, thick-branched Joshua trees grow among creosote bushes and jumbled boulders.
Climate: Summers are typical of a desert climate. Humidity is low, with maximum temperatures topping 100°F. Falling desert temperatures and nearby mountains contribute to relatively cool nights. Spring and fall are ideal, rarely interrupted by adverse weather conditions. Winters, too, are mild, with daytime averages of 60°F, clear skies, and warm sunshine. First frost comes December 11; last frost leaves February 17. There are very few overcast or rainy days.

Summer mildness: 6 | **Seasonal affect:** 96
Winter mildness: 38 | **Hazard free:** 76
Score: 59.4 | **Rank:** 82

	221
	79
	65
90°	123
32°	14
0°	0
	1
	13
	14

	High °F	Low °F	Hum %	Wind mph	Precip inches	Snow inches
JAN	57	26	35	7.5	0.6	1.0
FEB	62	31	30	8.6	0.6	0.1
MAR	67	36	25	10.3	0.6	0
APR	74	42	20	11.0	0.4	0
MAY	84	51	17	11.1	0.2	0
JUN	95	60	14	11.1	0.1	0
JUL	101	67	15	10.3	0.4	0
AUG	99	65	19	9.6	0.5	0
SEP	91	56	20	9.0	0.3	0
OCT	81	45	22	8.1	0.2	0
NOV	67	33	30	7.7	0.5	0
DEC	57	25	36	7.3	0.4	0.1

★ = *in the top 30 places for climate mildness.*

★ Palm Springs–Coachella Valley, CA

Location: 33.49 N and 116.32 W at 466 feet, in California's desert country, 100 miles east of Los Angeles.
Landscape: In the Coachella Valley at the foot of Mt. San Jacinto, where the San Gorgonio Pass funnels Pacific-warmed air that sometimes includes Los Angeles smog. This is the edge of the Sonoran Desert, known sometimes as the upper Colorado Desert. Joshua Tree National Monument is immediately northeast. Desert cactus, palm, and broadleaf evergreen scrub pine are typical.
Climate: Arid desert surrounding rapid urbanization. Summers are dry and hot with afternoon temperatures topping 100°F. Nights are cooler, as is typical of deserts. Most of the annual precipitation, such as it is, falls in winter as brief rain. The first frost is late arriving in mid-December; the last frost is out by late January.

Summer mildness: 1 **Seasonal affect:** 100
Winter mildness: 85 **Hazard free:** 93
Score: 94.0 **Rank:** 12

	242
	75
	48
90°	180
32°	7
0°	0
	2
	9
	7

	High °F	Low °F	Hum %	Wind mph	Precip inches	Snow inches
JAN	70	43	40	7.3	1.0	0.1
FEB	76	46	35	7.4	0.8	0
MAR	80	49	30	7.9	0.5	0
APR	87	54	25	8.3	0.1	0
MAY	95	61	23	8.3	0.1	0
JUN	104	68	22	8.5	0.1	0
JUL	109	75	32	9.5	0.2	0
AUG	107	75	35	8.9	0.4	0
SEP	101	69	35	7.3	0.4	0
OCT	92	60	32	6.6	0.2	0
NOV	79	49	34	6.9	0.7	0
DEC	70	42	41	7.2	0.8	0

Palmer–Wasilla, AK

Location: 61.36 N and 149.063 W at 239 feet in the Matanuska–Susitna Valley in south-central Alaska, 42 miles northeast of Anchorage. Seattle, Washington, is 1,450 air miles southeast.
Landscape: Level to gently rolling farmland, surrounded by the Chugach and Talkeetna mountain ranges. Pioneer Peak, Knik Glacier, Matanuska Peak, and Lazy Mountain are prominent features in view. The nearby forests are dense conifer stands of Douglas fir, western red cedar, western hemlock, Sitka spruce, and Alaska cedar.
Climate: Four well-marked seasons, though summers are brief. Fifty miles northwest, the Alaska Range blocks much of the cold air from the vast interior. Consequently, winter temperatures are warmer by 30 degrees. The first frost, coming by mid-September signals onset of autumn; the last frost, April 1, shouts spring is coming. By mid-April to the beginning of May, the rivers and lakes have thawed.

Summer mildness: 76 **Seasonal affect:** 0
Winter mildness: 12 **Hazard free:** 32
Score: 6.9 **Rank:** 189

	61
	64
	240
90°	0
32°	178
0°	21
	73
	148
	0

	High °F	Low °F	Hum %	Wind mph	Precip inches	Snow inches
JAN	31	16	73	6.4	6.7	20.4
FEB	35	19	70	6.8	6.8	23.6
MAR	38	22	64	6.9	6.3	27.3
APR	44	29	60	7.2	5.7	16.0
MAY	52	36	56	8.4	6.3	1.5
JUN	58	43	62	8.3	6.0	0
JUL	62	47	68	7.3	5.6	0
AUG	62	46	71	6.9	9.2	0
SEP	56	40	71	6.7	13.8	0
OCT	46	33	72	6.7	13.0	3.7
NOV	37	23	75	6.5	7.7	10.8
DEC	32	18	77	6.2	9.1	26.8

Panama City, FL

Location: 30.09 N and 85.39 W at 33 feet, on the Gulf of Mexico in Florida's northwestern panhandle. Tallahassee, the state capital, is 120 miles east.
Landscape: Sandy coastal region of shallow bays, white beaches, and dunes. Elevations range from a few feet above sea level to more than 100 feet providing relief from usual flat topograghy. The interior swamp includes evergreen oaks and members of the laurel and magnolia families. The longleaf, loblolly, and slash pines represent second-growth forest.
Climate: Subtropical. The Florida panhandle is cooler in summer than the central part of the state and still pleasant in winter. The Yucatan Current runs near here, bringing its moderating influence. This is basically a two-season climate with little temperature swing.

Summer mildness: 25 **Seasonal affect:** 62
Winter mildness: 75 **Hazard free:** 66
Score: 68.3 **Rank:** 65

	108
	122
	135
90°	75
32°	39
0°	0
	35
	66
	69

	High °F	Low °F	Hum %	Wind mph	Precip inches	Snow inches
JAN	60	37	62	9.0	5.0	0.1
FEB	64	39	59	9.4	5.8	0.1
MAR	70	46	59	9.7	5.8	0
APR	78	53	56	9.5	3.7	0
MAY	85	61	58	8.6	4.0	0
JUN	90	68	60	7.6	6.1	0
JUL	91	71	64	7.0	8.5	0
AUG	91	71	65	6.7	7.2	0
SEP	88	66	61	7.6	5.8	0
OCT	80	54	55	7.9	4.3	0
NOV	71	46	60	8.4	4.1	0
DEC	64	40	64	9.0	4.8	0

★ = *in the top 30 places for climate mildness.*

★ Paradise–Magalia, CA

Location: 39.44 N and 121.38 W at 1,708 feet, on Paradise Ridge in the Sierra Nevada foothills, 92 miles north of Sacramento, California's state capital.

Landscape: Known locally as "the Ridge" where steep slopes climb to high mountains. Stream-cut canyons drain to the Sacramento River. Tall digger pine, ponderosa and sugar pine, and blue oak dominate the mixed conifer forest. Lower rounded hills are grass and chaparral scrub covered. Open meadows and woodlands alternate.

Climate: Distinctly four seasons. The altitude moderates temperature. Winter is the rainy season, and summer is long and dry. First frost, mid-October; last frost, mid-May.

Summer mildness: 47 | **Seasonal affect:** 75
Winter mildness: 66 | **Hazard free:** 92
Score: 95.0 | **Rank:** 11

	178
	78
	110
90°	39
32°	117
0°	0
	13
	59
	5

	High °F	Low °F	Hum %	Wind mph	Precip inches	Snow inches
JAN	54	37	80	7.3	10.0	0.2
FEB	57	40	75	7.4	7.6	0
MAR	59	41	65	7.9	7.9	0
APR	66	45	55	8.3	3.8	0
MAY	75	51	48	8.3	1.2	0
JUN	84	58	44	8.5	0.5	0
JUL	91	64	44	9.5	0.1	0
AUG	90	63	45	8.9	0.3	0
SEP	84	59	45	7.3	1.1	0
OCT	74	52	53	6.6	3.2	0
NOV	60	43	65	6.9	8.5	0
DEC	53	37	77	7.2	8.5	0.2

Park City, UT

Location: 40.3846 N and 111.295 W at 6,970 feet, 30 miles east of Salt Lake City.

Landscape: Alpine. The area is located in a high valley of the Wasatch Range with many limestone terraces, lakes, and high mountain streams. Near the junction with the Uinta Mountains where the Wasatch National Forest is mixed conifer, with spruce, fir, and aspen. The many mine tailings are covered and planted with salt grass for erosion control. Open rangeland is nearby. Cottonwood predominates in the valley streams. Alpine wildflowers are abundant in spring and summer.

Climate: This is a four-season area. Summers are warm and dry, winters long and cold. Autumn is short but pleasant, while spring is longer but often stormy. First frost hits early, by September 10; last frost leaves late, June 8. Almost all precipitation falls in the form of snow, some 70 inches in a typical year.

Summer mildness: 67 | **Seasonal affect:** 63
Winter mildness: 4 | **Hazard free:** 3
Score: 14.3 | **Rank:** 174

	125
	101
	139
90°	20
32°	210
0°	21
	42
	43
	38

	High °F	Low °F	Hum %	Wind mph	Precip inches	Snow inches
JAN	34	8	75	7.5	1.8	19.3
FEB	40	13	69	8.1	1.6	13.1
MAR	48	22	59	9.3	1.4	7.9
APR	60	29	53	9.6	1.4	3.2
MAY	70	36	49	9.5	1.2	1.0
JUN	79	42	43	9.4	0.9	0
JUL	87	48	37	9.5	0.9	0
AUG	86	47	39	9.7	1.0	0
SEP	77	39	45	9.1	1.3	0.1
OCT	65	30	55	8.5	1.5	1.9
NOV	48	22	67	7.9	1.7	8.1
DEC	36	12	75	7.5	1.6	13.6

Payson, AZ

Location: 34.14 N and 111.19 W at 4,887 feet, in the Tonto Basin near Arizona's Mogollon Rim. Phoenix is 65 miles southeast.

Landscape: Surrounded by the Tonto National Forest. The Mazatzal Mountains of central Arizona and higher peaks of the White Mountains are nearby, though this is gentle-rolling-hill country. In the higher ridges, the cover is ponderosa, juniper, and pinyon pine. Lower, sagebrush and native grasses grow in the dry alkaline soil.

Climate: Semiarid mountain steppe. There are strong daily and seasonal temperature changes. The usual winter flow of air is from the Pacific Ocean, bringing snow. Cold air masses from Canada sometimes drive temperatures well below freezing in the high plateau and mountainous regions. First frost arrives by October 21; last frost leaves May 14. Moisture-bearing winds from the southeast Gulf region bring rain from July to September.

Summer mildness: 38 | **Seasonal affect:** 91
Winter mildness: 27 | **Hazard free:** 47
Score: 53.9 | **Rank:** 94

	212
	84
	69
90°	64
32°	144
0°	0
	2
	40
	24

	High °F	Low °F	Hum %	Wind mph	Precip inches	Snow inches
JAN	54	24	45	5.3	2.0	5.3
FEB	58	26	40	5.9	1.9	4.1
MAR	62	29	36	6.7	2.4	5.6
APR	70	34	25	7.0	1.1	1.0
MAY	79	41	20	7.1	0.6	0
JUN	90	49	18	6.8	0.4	0
JUL	93	58	28	7.2	2.6	0
AUG	90	57	33	6.7	3.2	0
SEP	84	50	34	6.3	2.1	0
OCT	74	40	34	5.8	1.7	0
NOV	62	30	37	5.4	1.9	2.0
DEC	54	24	46	5.1	2.3	6.4

★ = *in the top 30 places for climate mildness.*

Pendleton District, SC

Location: 34.41 N and 82.57 W at 950 feet in the extreme northwestern part of the state, 25 miles southwest of Greenville.

Landscape: The high parts of the Blue Ridge foothills yield a broken outline. Here's a curving valley with typical upcountry broadleaf forests of beech, sweet gum, magnolia, and oak forests with scattered pine. Rhododendrons, azaleas, and kalmias are the understory bloom in spring.

Climate: Transition between hot continental and subtropical. Winters are brief, with negligible snowfalls. First frost arrives fairly late on November 1; last frost leaves a little early by April 3. Summers are longer than those in more northerly locations and less humid and stormy than those in the low country, 150 miles southeast. Precipitation is distributed throughout the year, with a maximum as early spring rain.

Summer mildness: 48
Winter mildness: 54
Score: 44.5
Seasonal affect: 29
Hazard free: 59
Rank: 113

122
100
143
90° 49
32° 70
0° 0
34
81
43

	High °F	Low °F	Hum %	Wind mph	Precip inches	Snow inches
JAN	51	28	56	7.4	5.2	1.2
FEB	55	31	53	8.0	4.9	1.5
MAR	63	38	52	8.1	6.0	1.1
APR	72	47	49	7.9	4.2	0
MAY	79	55	55	6.9	4.3	0
JUN	86	63	56	6.4	4.2	0
JUL	89	67	58	5.9	4.6	0
AUG	88	67	61	5.7	4.4	0
SEP	82	60	61	6.1	3.7	0
OCT	73	48	53	6.5	4.1	0
NOV	64	39	55	6.8	4.1	0
DEC	54	31	58	7.3	4.8	0.6

Pensacola, FL

Location: 30.25 N and 87.13 W at 39 feet, in the Florida panhandle on Pensacola Bay, 195 miles west of Tallahassee. Mobile, Alabama, is 50 miles west.

Landscape: On a somewhat hilly, sandy slope separated from the Gulf of Mexico by a long, narrow island forming a natural breakwater for the harbor. Salt marshes and white-sand beaches are common. The forested area is southern mixed with various deciduous hardwoods, conifers of loblollies, and shortleaf pine. Elevations don't reach much more than 100 feet above sea level, but most of the city is safely above storm tides.

Climate: Warm, humid summers and cool winters are the expected norm. Rainfall is likely throughout the year, becoming heavy with summer thunderstorms. Sea breezes off the Gulf of Mexico temper the humidity in summer. More than a trace amount of snow per winter is rare.

Summer mildness: 32
Winter mildness: 86
Score: 55.9
Seasonal affect: 24
Hazard free: 66
Rank: 90

106
123
136
90° 84
32° 30
0° 0
178
82
68

	High °F	Low °F	Hum %	Wind mph	Precip inches	Snow inches
JAN	60	41	66	9.0	4.7	0.3
FEB	63	44	63	9.4	5.4	0
MAR	69	51	64	9.7	5.6	0
APR	77	59	63	9.5	3.8	0
MAY	83	66	69	8.6	4.2	0
JUN	89	72	70	7.6	6.4	0
JUL	90	74	72	7.0	7.4	0
AUG	89	74	75	6.7	7.4	0
SEP	86	70	74	7.6	5.3	0
OCT	79	59	69	7.9	4.2	0
NOV	70	51	68	8.4	3.5	0
DEC	63	44	67	8.9	4.3	0

Petoskey–Harbor Springs, MI

Location: 45.22 N and 84.57 W at 786 feet, on the south shore of Little Traverse Bay on Lake Michigan, some 30 miles south of the Mackinac Straits separating Michigan's upper and lower peninsulas. Detroit is 280 miles southeast.

Landscape: Generally level or gently undulating, with sandy and gravelly soils. The region abounds with lakes. Local beaches and gravel pits yield colorful fossilized stones. Elevations in the area provide access to both downhill and cross-country skiing. The forest is pine and hemlock.

Climate: Though rigorous because of its interior and northerly location, the climate is modified by the presence of two Great Lakes. Consequently, summer temperatures average at least 5 degrees cooler than locations in the southern part of the state. However, winters are severe, with cold spells that may last for a week and snowfall that averages almost 75 inches. First frost arrives early, by September 22; the last frost won't leave until May 31.

Summer mildness: 83
Winter mildness: 8
Score: 2.4
Seasonal affect: 17
Hazard free: 2
Rank: 197

67
89
210
90° 5
32° 169
0° 18
23
73
24

	High °F	Low °F	Hum %	Wind mph	Precip inches	Snow inches
JAN	28	12	77	12.6	2.0	23.1
FEB	31	9	72	11.6	1.2	15.4
MAR	41	19	66	11.9	1.5	10.4
APR	55	31	60	11.8	2.4	2.0
MAY	69	40	58	10.1	2.6	0
JUN	77	49	61	9.5	2.8	0
JUL	81	55	63	8.7	2.8	0
AUG	79	53	64	8.5	3.2	0
SEP	71	47	66	9.4	4.3	0
OCT	60	38	68	10.8	3.4	0
NOV	45	30	72	11.9	3.0	12.0
DEC	33	19	78	12.1	2.4	25.5

★ = *in the top 30 places for climate mildness.*

Pike County, PA

Location: 41.19 N and 74.48 W at 1,185 feet, across the Delaware River from New York state. New York City is 80 miles southeast.

Landscape: The Delaware River drains this highland region between the Catskills and the Pocono Mountains. These are long flat-topped or rounded ridges rising to 4,000 feet. Many streams and glacial lakes lie among the wooded hills. White pine, eastern hemlock, and red spruce mix with deciduous trees such as red maple, sassafras, oak, beech, and birch. Mountain laurel, dogwood, dwarf sumac, and fern fill out the lower growth layers.

Climate: Hot continental, with summers moderated by altitude. Winter is cold and cloudy. Precipitation is evenly distributed throughout the year, with snow likely to fall in December and last until spring. The first frost will arrive by October 7; the last frost will leave May 9. Severe weather disturbances are unlikely.

Summer mildness: 70
Winter mildness: 21
Score: 13.8
Seasonal affect: 19
Hazard free: 26
Rank: 175

	69
	113
	183
90°	16
32°	145
0°	6
	19
	76
	32

	High °F	Low °F	Hum %	Wind mph	Precip inches	Snow inches
JAN	34	16	58	8.3	3.1	11.3
FEB	38	18	57	9.0	3.0	10.7
MAR	49	26	53	9.5	3.5	10.4
APR	62	36	49	9.2	3.7	1.0
MAY	73	46	49	7.6	4.5	0
JUN	80	55	55	6.8	3.7	0
JUL	85	60	55	6.2	4.2	0
AUG	82	59	57	5.8	3.6	0
SEP	73	52	59	6.1	3.7	0
OCT	62	40	59	6.6	3.0	0
NOV	51	32	60	7.8	3.9	2.0
DEC	38	22	62	8.0	3.4	9.7

Polson–Mission Valley, MT

Location: 47.41 N and 114.09 W at 2,931 feet, on the southern end of Flathead Lake, 60 miles north of Missoula.

Landscape: The Mission Range of the Rocky Mountains lies east, and the Coeur d'Alene Mountains lie southwest of this valley plateau. Streams and lakes of many sizes are in the area. The Flathead River flows out of Polson. The short prairie grasses, scattered shrubs, and low trees give way to the forests of evergreen. Ponderosa pine, pinyon-juniper, and Douglas fir are frequent associates. Much of the native cover is giving way to farms and orchards.

Climate: Semiarid steppe, with most precipitation falling as winter snow, especially in the higher altitudes. Winters can be cold and long. First frost arrives by September 28; last frost departs May 14. Summers are warm, dry, and seem far too brief.

Summer mildness: 85
Winter mildness: 23
Score: 41.0
Seasonal affect: 31
Hazard free: 41
Rank: 120

	71
	81
	213
90°	12
32°	155
0°	7
	33
	41
	22

	High °F	Low °F	Hum %	Wind mph	Precip inches	Snow inches
JAN	33	20	79	6.0	1.1	12.5
FEB	39	24	76	6.2	0.8	6.2
MAR	47	28	65	7.2	0.9	8.1
APR	58	34	52	8.2	1.1	3.0
MAY	66	41	51	7.6	2.1	0
JUN	74	48	52	7.2	2.2	0
JUL	83	52	42	6.7	1.2	0
AUG	82	52	46	6.6	1.3	0
SEP	70	44	54	6.4	1.3	0
OCT	58	35	65	5.3	0.8	0
NOV	43	28	77	5.7	1.0	4.0
DEC	34	21	81	5.6	1.1	9.5

★ Port Angeles–Sequim, WA

Location: 48.07 N and 123.25 W at 32 feet, on Washington's Olympic Peninsula. Victoria, capital of British Columbia, is 20 miles by ferry across the Strait of Juan de Fuca.

Landscape: A variety of terrain, from the rocky coastline to peaks rising nearly 8,000 feet in the Olympic Mountains immediately to the south. Rivers and lakes drain the forested peninsula. Pacific needleleaf forests grow densely and have some of the world's largest trees. Douglas fir, western red cedar, and Sitka spruce are dominant. There is shrub undergrowth present in the forests.

Climate: Generally mild throughout the year because of the modifying influence of the Pacific Ocean. Annual rainfall is moderate-heavy, with maximum precipitation in winter due to the maritime polar air masses. There are traces of snow. A late first frost arrives November 10; the last frost leaves early, April 7. Summer tends to be foggy.

Summer mildness: 99
Winter mildness: 56
Score: 85.6
Seasonal affect: 13
Hazard free: 87
Rank: 30

	52
	84
	229
90°	0
32°	41
0°	0
	90
	64
	5

	High °F	Low °F	Hum %	Wind mph	Precip inches	Snow inches
JAN	45	34	86	7.1	4.0	2.7
FEB	48	35	83	7.2	2.6	0.8
MAR	51	37	77	7.4	2.0	1.1
APR	55	39	68	7.4	1.3	0
MAY	60	44	64	6.9	1.0	0
JUN	65	48	64	6.7	0.8	0
JUL	69	51	63	6.2	0.5	0
AUG	69	51	64	6.0	0.8	0
SEP	66	48	70	5.7	1.2	0
OCT	58	43	78	5.9	2.3	0
NOV	50	38	82	6.9	4.0	0
DEC	46	34	87	7.3	4.4	1.5

★ = *in the top 30 places for climate mildness.*

Port Charlotte, FL

Location: 26.58 N and 82.05 W at 11 feet, at the northern end of Charlotte Harbor on the Gulf of Mexico, 44 miles south of Sarasota.
Landscape: Flat, level terrain crossed by rivers and streams. The woods are temperate broadleaf evergreen, as well as laurel and magnolia. The lower level of growth includes tree ferns, small palms, and shrubs.
Climate: Subtropical. Summer and winter temperature extremes are checked by the influence of the Gulf. Mild winters have many bright, warm days. Nights are moderately cool. Rainfall averages more than 50 inches annually, with two-thirds of this total coming daily between June and September. Most rain falls as late-afternoon or early-evening thunderstorms, bringing welcome relief from the heat. With a first frost coming late, December 11, and the last frost leaving early, February 16, there is a long growing season.

Summer mildness: 8
Winter mildness: 96
Score: 80.6
Seasonal affect: 67
Hazard free: 77
Rank: 38

	102
	142
	121
90°	120
32°	1
0°	0
	21
	71
	93

	High °F	Low °F	Hum %	Wind mph	Precip inches	Snow inches
JAN	74	51	56	8.6	2.0	0
FEB	76	52	56	9.2	2.5	0
MAR	80	57	53	9.5	2.6	0
APR	85	60	47	9.3	1.3	0
MAY	89	66	49	8.7	3.6	0
JUN	91	71	56	8.0	8.1	0
JUL	92	73	60	7.2	7.3	0
AUG	92	73	60	7.0	7.9	0
SEP	90	72	61	7.8	6.5	0
OCT	86	66	57	8.5	2.8	0
NOV	80	59	57	8.4	1.8	0
DEC	76	53	56	8.5	1.8	0

Port Townsend, WA

Location: 48.07 N and 122.45 W at 16 feet, on Washington's Olympic Peninsula, at the eastern end of the Strait of Juan de Fuca, where Admiralty Inlet leads into Puget Sound. Seattle is 45 air miles south.
Landscape: In the midst of a variety of terrain, from the rocky, glaciated coastline to peaks rising nearly 8,000 feet in the Olympic Mountains to the west. Rivers and lakes drain the forested peninsula. Pacific needleleaf forests grow densely and have some of the world's largest trees. Douglas fir, western red cedar, and Sitka spruce are dominant. There is shrub undergrowth present in the forests.
Climate: Predominantly marine, with cool summers, mild winters, moist air, and small daily temperature variation. Summers are cool and dry. Like most other places in this region, the area is often foggy and cloudy. First frost comes by November 10; the last frost is gone by April 7.

Summer mildness: 99
Winter mildness: 56
Score: 85.1
Seasonal affect: 13
Hazard free: 87
Rank: 31

	53
	83
	230
90°	0
32°	41
0°	0
	90
	64
	5

	High °F	Low °F	Hum %	Wind mph	Precip inches	Snow inches
JAN	45	34	86	7.1	4.0	2.7
FEB	48	35	83	7.2	2.6	0.8
MAR	51	37	77	7.4	2.0	1.1
APR	55	39	68	7.4	1.3	0
MAY	60	44	64	6.9	1.0	0
JUN	65	48	64	6.7	0.8	0
JUL	69	51	63	6.2	0.5	0
AUG	69	51	64	6.0	0.8	0
SEP	66	48	70	5.7	1.2	0
OCT	58	43	78	5.9	2.3	0
NOV	50	38	82	6.9	4.0	0
DEC	46	34	87	7.3	4.4	1.5

Prescott–Prescott Valley, AZ

Location: 34.32 N and 112.28 W at 5,368 feet, in Arizona's mountainous west-central section. Phoenix is 96 miles southeast, Flagstaff is 90 miles northeast.
Landscape: Found in a mile-high basin among pine-dotted mountains rich in minerals. The higher ridges of the Prescott National Forest hold the world's largest stand of ponderosa. Sagebrush and native grasses dominate the dry alkaline soil at lower elevations.
Climate: Semiarid mountain steppe, with strong daily and seasonal temperature changes. Prescott is Arizona's mile-high city, and its high elevation and mountain breezes keep temperatures from reaching the grueling levels of low-lying Phoenix. The usual winter flow of air is from the Pacific Ocean, bringing frequent snow. Cold air masses from Canada sometimes drive temperatures below freezing in the high plateau and mountainous regions. First frost is in by October 9; last frost leaves by May 17. Moisture-bearing winds from the southeast Gulf region bring rain from July to September.

Summer mildness: 56
Winter mildness: 24
Score: 60.8
Seasonal affect: 88
Hazard free: 50
Rank: 78

	212
	84
	69
90°	32
32°	150
0°	0
	11
	39
	24

	High °F	Low °F	Hum %	Wind mph	Precip inches	Snow inches
JAN	50	22	45	5.3	1.5	4.5
FEB	54	24	40	5.9	1.5	3.5
MAR	57	28	36	6.7	1.8	6.8
APR	65	34	25	7.0	0.8	2.0
MAY	74	41	20	7.1	0.6	0
JUN	85	50	18	6.8	0.5	0
JUL	88	58	28	7.2	3.2	0
AUG	85	56	33	6.7	3.4	0
SEP	80	49	34	6.3	2.0	0
OCT	71	38	34	5.8	1.1	0
NOV	60	29	37	5.4	1.5	1.0
DEC	51	22	46	5.1	1.6	5.1

★ = *in the top 30 places for climate mildness.*

Rabun County, GA

Location: The weather station is at Clayton, 34.52 N and 83.24 at 1,925 feet in Georgia's northeast mountains. Atlanta is 90 miles southwest.

Landscape: In the southern Appalachians, terrain is hilly to mountainous, with elevations averaging 1,500 feet. To the north, some mountains rise above 3,000 feet. Chattahoochee National Forest is a mixed deciduous forest, with oak, beech, birch, walnut, maple, ash, and hornbeam. Pines develop where there has been logging or fire.

Climate: Nearby mountains have marked influences on summer heat, producing warm days and cool nights. Winters are cold but not severe. The contrast of valley and hill exposures results in wide variations in winter low temperatures. First frost makes an appearance by October 21; last frost departs by April 24. Generally, places halfway up the mountain slopes remain warmer during winter nights than do places on the valley floor.

Summer mildness: 58 **Seasonal affect:** 15
Winter mildness: 41 **Hazard free:** 52
Score: 27.2 **Rank:** 148

	103
	113
	149
90°	14
32°	93
0°	0
	78
	95
	45

	High °F	Low °F	Hum %	Wind mph	Precip inches	Snow inches
JAN	51	27	65	9.7	6.4	1.6
FEB	55	29	61	9.6	6.1	1.9
MAR	63	35	56	9.4	7.4	1.7
APR	71	42	53	8.9	5.4	0
MAY	77	50	60	7.1	6.8	0
JUN	83	57	61	6.1	5.4	0
JUL	85	62	63	5.8	5.8	0
AUG	84	61	63	5.4	6.1	0
SEP	79	55	62	5.6	5.7	0
OCT	72	43	57	6.8	5.1	0
NOV	63	36	60	8.1	5.9	0
DEC	54	29	66	8.9	6.7	0.8

Rehoboth Bay–Indian River Bay, DE

Location: 38.43 N and 75.04 W at 16 feet, on Delaware Bay and the Atlantic coast, 100 miles east of Washington, D.C.

Landscape: Very nearly a flat topography. A long barrier beach separates the bays from the Atlantic Ocean. Coastal sand dunes and beaches are a sharp contrast with stands of pine. Streams flow from inland lakes to coastal marshlands before emptying into the bays.

Climate: Experiences the northern edge of the subtropical zone. Seasonal and daily temperature variations are moderate. Winters can be cold, with snow that's scant and usually doesn't last long. First frost, October 27; last frost, April 13. Summers can be hot and humid but are tempered by onshore breezes.

Summer mildness: 65 **Seasonal affect:** 24
Winter mildness: 46 **Hazard free:** 36
Score: 30.6 **Rank:** 140

	97
	104
	164
90°	18
32°	91
0°	0
	34
	71
	30

	High °F	Low °F	Hum %	Wind mph	Precip inches	Snow inches
JAN	43	26	62	9.8	3.8	5.1
FEB	45	28	59	10.4	3.3	5.2
MAR	54	35	55	11.2	4.1	2.7
APR	64	43	52	10.6	3.6	0
MAY	73	53	51	9.1	3.8	0
JUN	81	62	51	8.5	3.4	0
JUL	85	67	53	7.8	4.0	0
AUG	84	66	54	7.5	5.2	0
SEP	78	60	54	7.8	3.1	0
OCT	68	49	54	8.2	3.2	0
NOV	59	40	54	9.2	3.3	0
DEC	48	31	57	9.4	3.7	1.9

Reno–Sparks, NV

Location: 39.31 N and 119.48 W at 4,498 feet, near the northern shore of Lake Tahoe. Las Vegas is 445 miles southeast; Sacramento, California, is 135 miles west.

Landscape: The Sierras rise to elevations of 9,000 to 10,000 feet. Hills to the east reach 6,000 to 7,000 feet. The Truckee River, flowing from the Sierra Nevada east through Reno, drains into Pyramid Lake to the northeast. Sagebrush and saltbush are common in the high country desert east of here.

Climate: Desert, with sunshine abundant throughout the year. Temperatures are mild, but the daily range may exceed 45°F. Nights with a minimum temperature over 60°F are rare. The first frost is in September 21; the last frost leaves May 29. Afternoon temperatures are moderate, and only 10 days per year fail to reach a level above freezing. Humidity is very low during summer and moderately low during winter.

Summer mildness: 58 **Seasonal affect:** 84
Winter mildness: 22 **Hazard free:** 59
Score: 64.8 **Rank:** 71

	159
	93
	112
90°	37
32°	169
0°	3
	7
	23
	14

	High °F	Low °F	Hum %	Wind mph	Precip inches	Snow inches
JAN	47	21	60	5.6	1.9	5.7
FEB	52	24	52	6.2	1.6	5.1
MAR	57	28	44	7.8	1.0	4.6
APR	63	32	36	8.2	0.5	1.0
MAY	72	39	32	8.0	0.6	0
JUN	82	46	29	7.6	0.4	0
JUL	90	50	25	7.0	0.3	0
AUG	88	48	24	6.5	0.3	0
SEP	80	41	30	5.8	0.5	0
OCT	70	32	36	5.4	0.7	0
NOV	55	26	49	5.5	1.4	2.0
DEC	47	21	58	5.2	1.7	4.3

★ = *in the top 30 places for climate mildness.*

Rio Rancho, NM

Location: 35.14 N and 106.39 W at 5,290 feet, 10 miles northwest of Albuquerque. Santa Fe, the state capital, is 60 miles northeast.

Landscape: Perched on a mesa overlooking the upper Rio Grande River and bounded by parts of the Cibola National Forest. The Sandia and Manzano mountains are to the east. The land is a typical steppe or shortgrass prairie, with scattered shrubs and low trees. Common vegetation includes sagebrush or shadscale and a mixture of short grasses. There may be willows and sedges along streams.

Climate: Arid continental. The dry air lessens the effect of the heat, which frequently tops 100°F in summer. Summer nights are cool. Winters are cool also, with light snow in higher elevations. First frost is in by October 11; last frost is out by May 5. In mid- to late summer there are frequent and intense thunderstorms, accounting for half the area's annual precipitation.

Summer mildness: 41
Winter mildness: 31
Score: 45.5
Seasonal affect: 89
Hazard free: 31
Rank: 111

	169
	111
	85
90°	75
32°	151
0°	1
	6
	24
	41

	High °F	Low °F	Hum %	Wind mph	Precip inches	Snow inches
JAN	47	22	50	8.1	0.4	2.5
FEB	54	26	42	8.9	0.5	2.2
MAR	61	32	32	10.1	0.5	1.8
APR	71	40	25	11.0	0.5	0.6
MAY	80	49	23	10.6	0.5	0
JUN	90	58	22	10.0	0.6	0
JUL	93	64	30	9.1	1.4	0
AUG	89	63	34	8.3	1.6	0
SEP	82	55	35	8.6	1.0	0
OCT	71	43	35	8.3	0.9	0.1
NOV	57	31	38	7.9	0.4	1.3
DEC	48	23	46	7.7	0.5	2.6

Rockport–Aransas Pass, TX

Location: 28.01 N and 97.03 W at 6 feet, on the Gulf of Mexico, 30 miles northeast of Corpus Christi.

Landscape: Aransas County is a flat coastal plain, with many bays and inlets. Elevations range from sea level to a mere 50 feet. The sandy loam and coastal clay soils are dotted with mesquite and live oak.

Climate: Humid subtropical. The heat is moderated by the prevailing southeasterly winds off the Gulf, producing a climate that's predominantly marine. Summers are warm and humid. Winters are pleasantly mild, with freezing temperatures occurring only at night, and only about 10 times per year. First frost is late arriving on December 9; last frost departs early, by February 16. Spring and fall are the most pleasant, with moderate temperatures and changeable weather.

Summer mildness: 7
Winter mildness: 91
Score: 77.7
Seasonal affect: 68
Hazard free: 77
Rank: 46

	103
	121
	140
90°	135
32°	9
0°	0
	29
	38
	29

	High °F	Low °F	Hum %	Wind mph	Precip inches	Snow inches
JAN	68	45	68	12.1	1.5	0.1
FEB	72	48	65	13.0	1.8	0
MAR	79	55	61	14.1	0.9	0
APR	85	63	62	14.3	1.6	0
MAY	89	68	66	12.8	3.4	0
JUN	92	72	63	11.8	4.0	0
JUL	95	74	57	11.5	2.2	0
AUG	96	73	58	11.0	2.9	0
SEP	92	70	62	10.4	4.3	0
OCT	86	62	59	10.3	2.7	0
NOV	78	55	62	11.6	1.4	0
DEC	71	47	64	11.5	1.0	0

Roswell, NM

Location: 33.2342 N and 104.3136 W at 3,557 feet, roughly 175 miles midway between El Paso, Texas, and Lubbock, Texas. Albuquerque is 180 miles northwest.

Landscape: The area is situated in the high desert plains of the Pecos Valley, with mountains to the west and south. The dry land forms into cliffs, terraces, buttes, mesas, and canyons. Carlsbad Caverns National Park lies to the south and Lincoln National Forest to the west. Mesquite, creosote, yucca, and cacti mix with desert willows, Rio Grande cottonwood, and native grasses.

Climate: Typical desert, with long, hot, and dry summers. Winters range from daytime warm to cold nights. The first frost arrives in late October; the last frost leaves by April 13. Most precipitation falls in the form of summer thunderstorms, with trace snowfall in winter.

Summer mildness: 21
Winter mildness: 40
Score: 33.1
Seasonal affect: 78
Hazard free: 34
Rank: 135

	157
	104
	104
90°	105
32°	107
0°	1
	57
	21
	47

	High °F	Low °F	Hum %	Wind mph	Precip inches	Snow inches
JAN	54	25	57	7.7	0.4	2.4
FEB	60	29	50	8.5	0.5	2.9
MAR	68	36	40	10.1	0.3	1.5
APR	77	45	37	10.1	0.5	0.2
MAY	85	55	42	9.8	1.0	0
JUN	94	62	45	9.5	1.6	0
JUL	95	67	51	8.7	1.7	0
AUG	92	65	55	7.8	2.6	0
SEP	86	59	57	8.0	2.0	0
OCT	77	47	53	7.8	1.1	0.2
NOV	66	35	53	7.8	0.5	1.2
DEC	56	26	55	7.5	0.5	1.9

★ = *in the top 30 places for climate mildness.*

Ruidoso, NM

Location: 33.20 N and 105.41 W at 6,641 feet, in south-central New Mexico. El Paso, Texas, is 155 miles south.
Landscape: On the eastern slope of the Sacramento Mountains with the Tularosa Valley to the west. Thorny desert shrubs of mesquite and creosote bush thrive in lower elevations; juniper and pinyon are found in higher elevations to the east.
Climate: Highland, with cold winters, and short hot summers. Daily and seasonal temperature changes are pronounced. Because of the mountain location, the first frost arrives early, by September 19; and the last frost does not leave until June 11. There are traces of snow, but most precipitation falls as light rain and is evenly distributed throughout the year. The higher elevations of the Lincoln National Forest, which includes the ski area, usually remain snow-covered all winter.

Summer mildness: 95 **Seasonal affect:** 85
Winter mildness: 17 **Hazard free:** 45
Score: 77.2 **Rank:** 47

	193
	100
	72
90°	5
32°	200
0°	4
	6
	49
	36

	High °F	Low °F	Hum %	Wind mph	Precip inches	Snow inches
JAN	42	20	42	8.4	1.6	2.7
FEB	43	21	34	9.2	1.4	1.7
MAR	49	25	27	11.0	1.5	1.1
APR	57	32	21	11.1	0.5	0
MAY	65	38	21	10.3	1.0	0
JUN	73	46	23	9.3	2.0	0
JUL	72	49	35	8.3	4.4	0
AUG	70	47	39	7.8	5.0	0
SEP	66	43	41	7.6	3.3	0
OCT	59	35	36	7.5	1.8	0
NOV	49	26	37	8.0	1.3	1.0
DEC	43	22	42	7.9	2.0	2.6

★ St. Augustine, FL

Location: 29.51 N and 81.16 W at 5 feet, on the Atlantic coast in northeastern Florida, 40 miles south of Jacksonville.
Landscape: Located on a peninsula with the Matanzas and North rivers on the east and south and the San Sebastian on the west. These rivers and saltwater lagoons lie between the city and Anastasia Island and the Atlantic Ocean beyond, serving as a port of entry on the Atlantic Intracoastal Waterway. There are coquina quarries. The surrounding terrain is level. The pines begin to yield to palms. Broadleaf deciduous trees are a rarity in the coastal pine forest.
Climate: Subtropical. The atmosphere is heavily humid. Average daily sunshine ranges from 5½ hours in December to 9 hours in May. The greatest amount of rain, mostly in the form of daily afternoon thundershowers, falls during late summer. There is a short frost season with first frost delayed until mid-December; last frost exits mid-February.

Summer mildness: 30 **Seasonal affect:** 49
Winter mildness: 90 **Hazard free:** 88
Score: 86.6 **Rank:** 28

	97
	127
	141
90°	104
32°	8
0°	0
	38
	73
	66

	High °F	Low °F	Hum %	Wind mph	Precip inches	Snow inches
JAN	66	46	57	8.2	3.1	0
FEB	68	47	53	9.0	3.8	0
MAR	74	53	50	9.0	3.6	0
APR	79	58	48	8.6	2.4	0
MAY	84	64	50	8.0	3.6	0
JUN	88	70	57	7.8	5.5	0
JUL	90	72	58	7.1	5.5	0
AUG	89	72	60	6.8	6.3	0
SEP	86	71	62	7.6	6.1	0
OCT	81	64	58	8.1	3.7	0
NOV	74	55	56	7.7	2.3	0
DEC	69	48	58	7.8	3.0	0

St. George–Zion, UT

Location: 37.06 N and 113.34 W at 2,880 feet, in southwestern Utah. Las Vegas, Nevada, is 130 miles southwest.
Landscape: Fifteen miles north, the Pine Valley Mountains rise to over 10,000 feet. The same distance west are the Beaver Dam Mountains, rising to 7,000 feet. Canyon walls of red, gray, yellow, and brown sandstone and volcanic cinder-cone rock formations provide relief. As it's on the northern edge of the Mohave Desert, vegetation is sparse. Cacti, thorny shrubs, creosote bush, and chamiso are most prevalent.
Climate: Semiarid desert steppe. The most striking features are bright sunshine, small annual precipitation, dryness, and purity of air, and large daily variations in temperature. Summers are characterized by hot, dry weather and low humidity. Winters are short and mild, with the Rocky Mountains blocking cold air masses from the north and east. First frost comes in November 4; last frost leaves on March 31.

Summer mildness: 5 **Seasonal affect:** 94
Winter mildness: 48 **Hazard free:** 72
Score: 60.8 **Rank:** 78

	221
	79
	65
90°	125
32°	89
0°	0
	1
	20
	14

	High °F	Low °F	Hum %	Wind mph	Precip inches	Snow inches
JAN	54	27	35	7.5	1.1	1.6
FEB	61	32	30	8.6	0.9	0.7
MAR	68	38	25	10.3	1.1	0
APR	77	44	20	11.0	0.5	0
MAY	86	53	17	11.1	0.4	0
JUN	97	62	14	11.1	0.2	0
JUL	102	69	15	10.3	0.6	0
AUG	100	67	19	9.6	0.8	0
SEP	93	58	20	9.0	0.5	0
OCT	81	46	22	8.1	0.5	0
NOV	65	35	30	7.7	0.9	0
DEC	54	28	36	7.3	0.7	0.7

★ *= in the top 30 places for climate mildness.*

St. Jay–Northeast Kingdom, VT

Location: 44.25 N and 72.01 W at 588 feet, in Vermont's upper Connecticut River Valley, 33 miles east of Montpelier, the state capital, and 75 miles east of Burlington.

Landscape: The Green Mountains form the western boundary, the Connecticut River the eastern. This area is comprised of low rugged hills, lowlands dotted with glacial lakes, ponds, bogs, and swamps. The Passumpsic, Moose, and Sleeper river valleys create interesting relief. The woods are a transitional forest of mixed conifer and deciduous trees. Northern white pine, eastern hemlock, maple, oak, and beech are common.

Climate: Northerly latitude assures the variety and vigor of a true New England climate. Summers, while not long, are pleasant. Falls are cool, extending through October. Winters are cold and snowy, with brief, intense cold snaps formed by high-pressure systems moving down from central Canada and Hudson Bay. The first frost arrives September 25; the last frost departs May 22.

Summer mildness: 78 **Seasonal affect:** 16
Winter mildness: 3 **Hazard free:** 16
Score: 4.9 **Rank:** 193

	91
	110
	164
90°	9
32°	173
0°	28
	15
	81
	20

	High °F	Low °F	Hum %	Wind mph	Precip inches	Snow inches
JAN	27	6	58	9.0	2.3	21.3
FEB	31	7	57	9.4	2.1	19.5
MAR	42	19	53	9.9	2.5	14.3
APR	55	31	49	10	2.7	3.0
MAY	70	42	49	8.9	3.3	0
JUN	78	52	55	8.1	3.8	0
JUL	82	56	55	7.5	3.7	0
AUG	80	55	57	7.2	4.0	0
SEP	71	47	59	7.3	3.1	0
OCT	59	36	59	7.8	3.1	0
NOV	44	28	60	8.5	3.5	6.0
DEC	31	13	62	8.7	3.2	21.9

★ St. Simons–Jekyll Islands, GA

Location: 31.13 N and 81.21 W at 10 feet, on the Intracoastal Waterway, 65 miles south of Savannah, and 54 miles north of Jacksonville, Florida.

Landscape: Flat, with no elevation higher than 20 feet. Shell beaches blend into the surrounding marshlands. The low terrain and low latitude location is vulnerable to occasional tropical storms, though their full force is felt infrequently. The outer coastal plain, reached by a causeway, is a temperate rain forest with Evangeline oak, longleaf pine, laurel, Bayonet palmettos, holly, and magnolia. Flowers bloom through the winter, and climbing vines are prevalent.

Climate: The area enjoys mild and relatively short winters due to the moderating effect of coastal waters. Summers are warm and humid, but very high temperatures are rare. Heat waves are usually interrupted by thundershowers. Even in summer the nights are usually pleasant. With first frost on December 3 and last frost on February 24, there is a long growing season.

Summer mildness: 39 **Seasonal affect:** 58
Winter mildness: 87 **Hazard free:** 73
Score: 86.1 **Rank:** 29

	97
	127
	141
90°	42
32°	16
0°	0
	38
	68
	66

	High °F	Low °F	Hum %	Wind mph	Precip inches	Snow inches
JAN	60	42	54	8.2	3.3	0
FEB	62	44	50	9.0	3.9	0.1
MAR	69	51	48	9.0	3.9	0
APR	76	58	45	8.6	2.5	0
MAY	82	66	50	8.0	3.3	0
JUN	87	72	54	7.8	5.0	0
JUL	90	74	57	7.1	5.6	0
AUG	88	74	61	6.8	7.0	0
SEP	85	71	60	7.6	6.5	0
OCT	77	61	53	8.1	2.9	0
NOV	70	52	52	7.7	2.6	0
DEC	63	45	55	7.8	3.1	0

Salida, CO

Location: 38.31 N and 106.00 W at 7,036 feet in central Colorado, on the Arkansas River, between the Sangre de Cristo and Sawatch mountains, 80 miles west northwest of Pueblo and 130 miles southwest of Denver.

Landscape: Up against the eastern slope of the Continental Divide, with visible, snowcapped peaks rising to 14,000 feet. The lower forest is aspen and ponderosa pine, and the upper forest is Douglas fir.

Climate: Semiarid steppe in which considerable precipitation falls in winter, principally as snow. Summers are bright, cool, and short. Winters can be severe. Falls and springs are transition seasons.

Summer mildness: 46 **Seasonal affect:** 43
Winter mildness: 15 **Hazard free:** 0
Score: 0.4 **Rank:** 202

	127
	120
	118
90°	61
32°	154
0°	18
	26
	89
	50

	High °F	Low °F	Hum %	Wind mph	Precip inches	Snow inches
JAN	36	16	52	9.5	0.4	14.0
FEB	45	19	50	10.0	0.5	13.0
MAR	56	25	50	11.2	0.7	10.0
APR	66	33	48	11.7	0.7	9.0
MAY	76	42	52	11.2	1.0	5.0
JUN	88	51	51	10.4	0.8	0
JUL	94	57	54	9.3	1.6	0
AUG	91	55	56	9.0	1.7	0
SEP	81	47	52	9.4	1.1	1.0
OCT	68	36	47	9.6	1.0	9.0
NOV	51	25	53	9.5	0.6	12.0
DEC	39	17	53	9.4	0.7	13.0

★ = *in the top 30 places for climate mildness.*

San Juan Islands, WA

Location: The weather station is at Friday Harbor, 48.32 N and 123.00 W at 91 feet, in the midst of an archipelago of 172 islands that make up San Juan County in northwestern Washington. Bellingham is 20 miles east by ferry.

Landscape: The islands are a submerged mountain chain in upper Puget Sound, where the straits of Juan de Fuca and Georgia meet at the Canadian border. Mt. Constitution, at 2,409 feet, is the highest point on the islands. Many are low flat or flat-topped hills, with wooded forests of Sitka spruce and western hemlock. Madroña, with a red-skinned trunk, is scattered throughout the coniferous forests at these low levels.

Climate: Marine, with mild summers and cool winters, moist air, and small daily temperature variation. First frost comes October 20; last frost leaves April 21. Summers are dry. Like most other places in this region, the area is often foggy and cloudy.

Summer mildness: 98 **Seasonal affect:** 1
Winter mildness: 53 **Hazard free:** 87
Score: 74.2 **Rank:** 52

	50
	84
	231
90°	0
32°	68
0°	0
	90
	91
	5

	High °F	Low °F	Hum %	Wind mph	Precip inches	Snow inches
JAN	43	32	77	7.1	4.7	2.7
FEB	48	35	74	7.2	3.6	0.6
MAR	51	36	71	7.4	3.0	1.1
APR	56	40	68	7.4	2.7	0
MAY	62	45	65	6.9	2.3	0
JUN	67	51	64	6.7	1.8	0
JUL	71	53	63	6.2	1.3	0
AUG	71	54	63	6.0	1.4	0
SEP	67	48	67	5.7	1.9	0
OCT	58	42	74	5.9	3.4	0
NOV	50	37	77	6.9	5.0	0
DEC	44	33	79	7.3	5.0	1.8

Sandpoint–Lake Pend Oreille, ID

Location: 48.16 N and 116.33 W at 2,086 feet, in the Idaho panhandle, 50 miles south of the Canadian border. Spokane, Washington, is 75 miles south.

Landscape: Lake Pend Oreille, near the outflow of the Pend Oreille River, is 43 miles long and 6 miles at its widest. The surface of the lake reflects the surrounding Selkirk, Cabinet, and Coeur d'Alene mountain ranges, with peaks rising over 6,000 feet. The Kaniksu National Forest is mixed coniferous and deciduous. Douglas fir, hemlock, and cedar predominate in this high valley surrounded by mountain ranges.

Climate: Continental and generally described as rigorous. Summers are dry and bright. Falls are pleasant but all too short. Winters are long, cold, and snowy. First frost by September 11; last frost by June 3. Though seasonal temperature variation is large, it's less so than in most other locations this far north.

Summer mildness: 86 **Seasonal affect:** 4
Winter mildness: 19 **Hazard free:** 14
Score: 7.4 **Rank:** 188

	86
	87
	192
90°	15
32°	187
0°	7
	47
	80
	11

	High °F	Low °F	Hum %	Wind mph	Precip inches	Snow inches
JAN	30	19	80	8.8	4.0	31.0
FEB	37	22	78	9.3	3.1	14.1
MAR	45	26	65	9.7	2.8	8.3
APR	56	31	55	10.0	2.1	0
MAY	66	38	51	9.2	2.4	0
JUN	74	45	47	9.2	2.1	0
JUL	82	47	37	8.6	1.2	0
AUG	82	47	40	8.2	1.5	0
SEP	71	40	45	8.3	1.5	0
OCT	56	33	59	8.2	2.0	0
NOV	38	28	75	8.7	4.3	10.0
DEC	30	22	83	8.6	4.5	25.9

★ Santa Barbara, CA

Location: 34.25 N and 119.42 W at 100 feet, in the Santa Maria Valley, 150 miles northwest of Los Angeles.

Landscape: The valley is flat and fertile, opening onto the Pacific Ocean at the base of the Santa Ynez Mountains. The foothills of the San Rafael Mountains, the Solomon Hills, and the Casmalia Hills bound it. Cypress and pine groves predominate in the mixed evergreen forest.

Climate: Mediterranean, including a rainy season typical of the California Coast in winter. Particularly from June to October, there's little or no precipitation. Clear, sunny afternoons prevail on most days. At night and in the morning, however, the California stratus and fog appear.

Summer mildness: 79 **Seasonal affect:** 88
Winter mildness: 74 **Hazard free:** 100
Score: 98.5 **Rank:** 4

	147
	116
	103
90°	3
32°	0
0°	0
	19
	17
	3

	High °F	Low °F	Hum %	Wind mph	Precip inches	Snow inches
JAN	64	40	56	4.8	3.2	0
FEB	65	43	57	6.3	3.6	0
MAR	65	45	59	6.7	2.8	0
APR	67	47	60	7.6	1.1	0
MAY	69	50	62	7.1	0.2	0
JUN	71	54	66	6.8	0.0	0
JUL	74	57	66	6.5	0.0	0
AUG	75	58	67	6.1	0.1	0
SEP	75	57	65	5.8	0.5	0
OCT	73	52	62	5.5	0.5	0
NOV	69	45	56	5.3	2.0	0
DEC	64	40	54	5.0	2.2	0

★ = *in the top 30 places for climate mildness.*

Santa Fe, NM

Location: 35.40 N and 105.56 W at 6,947 feet, in the north-central part of the state, 60 miles from Albuquerque.
Landscape: In the northern Rio Grande Valley on the Santa Fe River in the rolling foothills of the rugged Sangre de Cristo Mountains. Westward, the terrain slopes to the Rio Grande River some 20 miles away. The high mountains protect the city from much of the winter cold. Engelmann spruce and subalpine fir cover the higher slopes; ponderosa pine is on the lower, drier, and more exposed slopes.
Climate: Highland steppe. Winters are crisp, clear, and sunny, with considerable daytime warming. First frost makes an appearance by October 6; last frost lingers until May 15. Summers are warm, pleasant, dry, and invigorating. Long cloudy periods are unknown.

Summer mildness: 82
Winter mildness: 18
Score: 50.0
Seasonal affect: 87
Hazard free: 10
Rank: 100

	169
	111
	85
90°	8
32°	169
0°	4
	6
	33
	41

	High °F	Low °F	Hum %	Wind mph	Precip inches	Snow inches
JAN	40	18	50	8.1	0.9	5.4
FEB	44	21	42	8.9	0.8	5.4
MAR	50	26	32	10.1	1.2	6.9
APR	59	33	25	11.0	1.0	4.0
MAY	68	42	23	10.6	1.2	0
JUN	78	51	22	10.0	1.4	0
JUL	81	55	30	9.1	3.3	0
AUG	78	53	34	8.3	3.5	0
SEP	71	47	35	8.6	2.1	0
OCT	62	38	35	8.3	1.3	1.0
NOV	49	27	38	7.9	1.0	4.0
DEC	41	19	46	7.7	1.1	7.0

★ Santa Rosa, CA

Location: 38.26 N and 122.42 W at 177 feet, in the Russian River Valley, 50 miles north of San Francisco.
Landscape: This valley runs parallel to the Pacific Coast with only low hills, 300 feet to 500 feet, between it and the ocean 25 miles southwest. Higher hills rise 10 miles to the east, leading into the foothills of the Coast Ranges. The principal trees of the conifer forest are Douglas fir, western red cedar, western hemlock, and Sitka spruce.
Climate: The nearness of the ocean and the surrounding topography join with the prevailing westerly circulation to produce a predominantly southerly airflow year-round. However, the area is sufficiently far inland to assure it a varied climate. First frost arrives November 19; last frost is gone March 26. Summers are warm and winters cool, and there is a daily temperature shift also. There's less fog and drizzle here than in other points south.

Summer mildness: 56
Winter mildness: 65
Score: 96.0
Seasonal affect: 79
Hazard free: 94
Rank: 9

	161
	101
	103
90°	34
32°	37
0°	0
	15
	46
	2

	High °F	Low °F	Hum %	Wind mph	Precip inches	Snow inches
JAN	58	37	70	7.2	6.5	0
FEB	63	40	70	8.6	4.7	0
MAR	65	41	68	10.5	4.2	0
APR	70	43	62	12.1	1.9	0
MAY	75	46	61	13.4	0.5	0
JUN	81	50	61	13.9	0.2	0
JUL	84	51	62	13.6	0.1	0
AUG	84	52	64	12.8	0.2	0
SEP	83	51	64	11.1	0.5	0
OCT	77	47	64	9.4	2.0	0
NOV	66	42	68	7.4	4.6	0
DEC	58	38	71	7.0	5.1	0

★ Sarasota, FL

Location: 27.20 N and 82.32 W at 27 feet, sheltered from the Gulf of Mexico behind Longboat Key on Sarasota Bay. Tampa is 50 miles north; Fort Myers is 75 miles south.
Landscape: The southern Gulf Coastal Plains are flat and irregular. There's less than 200 feet variation in altitude over the gently rolling areas. Most of the numerous streams are sluggish; and marshes, swamps, and lakes are numerous. Evergreen oaks, laurel, and magnolia are common. Trees aren't tall, and the leaf canopy is less dense. There is a well-developed underbrush of ferns, shrubs, and herbaceous plants.
Climate: Subtropical. The waters of the Gulf of Mexico and surrounding bays modify temperature throughout the year. Thunderstorms are frequent during late-summer afternoons, rapidly cooling the hot, humid days. Winters are mild. Snow and freezing temperatures are rare.

Summer mildness: 20
Winter mildness: 97
Score: 89.6
Seasonal affect: 70
Hazard free: 80
Rank: 21

	102
	142
	121
90°	78
32°	0
0°	0
	22
	69
	86

	High °F	Low °F	Hum %	Wind mph	Precip inches	Snow inches
JAN	72	52	56	8.6	2.2	0
FEB	72	53	56	9.2	2.7	0
MAR	77	58	53	9.5	3.2	0
APR	81	61	47	9.3	1.6	0
MAY	86	67	49	8.7	2.6	0
JUN	89	72	56	8.0	6.5	0
JUL	90	73	60	7.2	6.5	0
AUG	91	73	60	7.0	7.9	0
SEP	89	73	60	7.8	7.2	0
OCT	85	66	56	8.5	2.6	0
NOV	79	59	56	8.4	2.1	0
DEC	74	54	56	8.5	2.1	0

★ = *in the top 30 places for climate mildness.*

Savannah, GA

Location: 32.05 N and 81.06 W at 42 feet, at the mouth of the Savannah River and Atlantic Ocean. Jacksonville, Florida, is 140 miles down the coast, and Charleston, South Carolina, is 100 miles up the coast.

Landscape: Surrounded by flat land, low and marshy to the north and east, rising to several feet above sea level to the west and south. About half the land to the west and south is clear of trees and the other half is woods, much of which lie in swamp. The outer coastal plain is a temperate rain forest that includes live oak, loblolly pine, laurel, and magnolia.

Climate: Subtropical. Summer temperatures are moderated by thundershowers almost every afternoon. Sunshine is adequate in all seasons; seldom are there more than 2 or 3 days in succession without it. First frost makes an appearance by November 14; last frost is gone by March 11. There's abundant rain during the long growing season.

Summer mildness: 33 **Seasonal affect:** 46
Winter mildness: 79 **Hazard free:** 68
Score: 66.3 **Rank:** 69

	104
	111
	150
90°	76
32°	33
0°	0
	39
	70
	61

	High °F	Low °F	Hum %	Wind mph	Precip inches	Snow inches
JAN	60	38	54	8.5	3.6	0.1
FEB	62	41	50	9.2	3.2	0.2
MAR	70	48	48	9.2	3.8	0
APR	78	55	45	8.7	3.0	0
MAY	84	63	50	7.7	4.1	0
JUN	89	69	54	7.5	5.7	0
JUL	91	72	57	7.1	6.4	0
AUG	90	72	61	6.6	7.5	0
SEP	85	68	60	7.2	4.5	0
OCT	78	57	53	7.4	2.4	0
NOV	70	48	52	7.5	2.2	0
DEC	62	41	54	7.9	3.0	0.1

★ Scottsdale, AZ

Location: 33.30 N and 111.53 W at 1,259 feet, 10 miles immediately east of Phoenix.

Landscape: The area lies in the center of the oval-shaped flat Salt River Valley. Mountain ranges surround the valley on all sides, with the famous Superstition Mountain to the east. Although this is a desert, cotton and citrus are cultivated. Native vegetation includes creosote bush, saguaro, cholla, and cereus. An underground water table contributes to the local water supply, along with the Salt and Verde rivers.

Climate: Arid desert climate, with little rainfall and low humidity. Summers are hot with temperatures frequently above 100°F. Winters are cool and can drop below freezing at night. The growing season is long, with the first frost coming late, on December 4 and the last frost coming early, February 14. Cloudy days are rare, as sunshine predominates.

Summer mildness: 2 **Seasonal affect:** 97
Winter mildness: 85 **Hazard free:** 96
Score: 94.0 **Rank:** 12

	212
	84
	69
90°	163
32°	20
0°	0
	2
	19
	24

	High °F	Low °F	Hum %	Wind mph	Precip inches	Snow inches
JAN	66	41	45	5.3	0.7	0
FEB	71	45	39	5.9	0.7	0
MAR	76	49	34	6.7	0.9	0
APR	85	55	23	7.0	0.2	0
MAY	94	64	18	7.1	0.1	0
JUN	104	73	16	6.8	0.1	0
JUL	106	81	28	7.2	0.8	0
AUG	104	79	33	6.7	1.0	0
SEP	98	73	31	6.3	0.9	0
OCT	88	61	31	5.8	0.7	0
NOV	75	49	37	5.4	0.7	0
DEC	66	42	46	5.1	1.0	0

Sebring–Avon Park, FL

Location: 27.29 N and 81.26 W at 131 feet, circling Lake Jackson in south-central Florida. Orlando is 90 miles north. Sarasota, on the Gulf coast, is 60 miles west. Ft. Pierce, on the Atlantic coast, is 60 miles east.

Landscape: Highland lakes region, with sandy ridges giving relief to low-level muckland and flatland. Most of the surrounding acreage is citrus groves and ranches. Hardwood hammock and cabbage palms are dense in the rain forest of Highlands Hammock State Park.

Climate: Subtropical, with a surplus of moisture. As in other Florida locations, the humid, hot summer is cooled by afternoon thunderstorms. Winters are mild and the first frost comes late, December 31; the last frost leaves early, January 23. Annual range of temperature changes is small.

Summer mildness: 8 **Seasonal affect:** 58
Winter mildness: 92 **Hazard free:** 80
Score: 73.7 **Rank:** 54

	92
	148
	125
90°	137
32°	4
0°	0
	27
	76
	82

	High °F	Low °F	Hum %	Wind mph	Precip inches	Snow inches
JAN	73	48	56	8.9	2.2	0
FEB	75	49	52	9.6	2.8	0
MAR	79	54	50	9.9	3.0	0
APR	85	59	46	9.4	1.7	0
MAY	89	65	49	8.8	4.0	0
JUN	91	70	56	8.0	8.4	0
JUL	92	71	59	7.4	7.7	0
AUG	92	72	60	7.1	7.2	0
SEP	90	71	60	7.7	6.1	0
OCT	85	64	56	8.6	2.8	0
NOV	80	57	55	8.6	1.9	0
DEC	74	51	57	8.6	1.9	0

★ *= in the top 30 places for climate mildness.*

Sedona, AZ

Location: 34.52 N and 111.45 W at 4,280 feet, in Oak Creek Canyon. Phoenix is 90 miles south, and Flagstaff is 20 miles north.

Landscape: Overlooks red-hued rocks and buttes of the canyon whose steep walls rise 1,200 feet. The forest is ponderosa pine, Douglas fir, and (at higher elevations) subalpine fir and Engelmann spruce.

Climate: Semiarid mountain steppe. There are strong daily and seasonal temperature changes. The usual winter flow of air is from the Pacific Ocean, bringing frequent snows. Cold air from Canada sometimes drives temperatures below freezing. First frost, October 13; last frost, May 17. Moisture-bearing winds from the southeast Gulf region bring brief rains from July to September.

Summer mildness: 19 **Seasonal affect:** 90
Winter mildness: 44 **Hazard free:** 48
Score: 52.9 **Rank:** 95

	212
	84
	69
90°	66
32°	155
0°	0
	11
	29
	24

	High °F	Low °F	Hum %	Wind mph	Precip inches	Snow inches
JAN	56	29	45	7.0	1.7	4.5
FEB	60	32	40	6.9	1.8	3.5
MAR	64	35	36	7.5	2.2	6.8
APR	73	41	25	7.9	1.2	2.0
MAY	82	48	20	7.5	0.6	0
JUN	93	56	18	7.1	0.4	0
JUL	97	64	28	5.7	1.8	0
AUG	94	62	33	5.3	2.1	0
SEP	88	56	34	6.0	2.0	0
OCT	78	47	34	6.1	1.5	0
NOV	65	36	37	7.1	1.6	1.0
DEC	56	30	46	7.0	1.8	5.1

Silver City, NM

Location: 32.46 N and 108.16 W at 5,851 feet, in southwestern New Mexico. Tucson, Arizona, is 170 miles west, and El Paso, Texas, is 140 miles east.

Landscape: East of the Continental Divide in the foothills of the Pinos Altos Range at the edge of the Gila National Forest. There are wild ranges, high cliffs, and remote canyons. The Chihuahuan Desert vegetation includes creosote, ceniza, and ocotillo shrubs. Juniper and pinyons are common on rocky outcrops. Ponderosa pine, Douglas fir, white fir, and spruce occur in the high forests.

Climate: Desert continental. The rainfall, at 8 inches per year, is light and falls in brief showers through late summer and fall. Drizzles are unknown. Summers are hot, but the nights are cool. Winters tend to be mild and sunny, with freezing nights. The arrival of the first frost on October 30 and the departure of the last frost on April 22 makes for a short growing season.

Summer mildness: 11 **Seasonal affect:** 93
Winter mildness: 34 **Hazard free:** 56
Score: 47.5 **Rank:** 106

	193
	100
	72
90°	112
32°	110
0°	0
	2
	23
	24

	High °F	Low °F	Hum %	Wind mph	Precip inches	Snow inches
JAN	58	25	42	8.4	0.9	2.1
FEB	63	27	34	9.2	0.6	1.8
MAR	70	33	27	11.0	0.7	1.9
APR	78	39	21	11.1	0.2	0
MAY	87	47	21	10.3	0.3	0
JUN	96	57	23	9.3	0.5	0
JUL	96	65	35	8.3	2.0	0
AUG	93	62	39	7.8	2.1	0
SEP	88	56	41	7.6	1.5	0
OCT	79	43	36	7.5	1.2	0
NOV	67	31	37	8.0	0.7	0
DEC	58	25	42	7.9	1.2	0.8

Smith Mountain Lake, VA

Location: 37.02 N and 79.32 W at 795 feet, in foothills on the eastern slope of the Blue Ridge Mountains in southwest Virginia. Roanoke is 30 miles northwest, and Greensboro, North Carolina, is 100 miles south.

Landscape: This 22,000-acre artificial lake is located in a natural notch in a 7-mile-long ridge, Smith Mountain, just below the confluence of the Blackwater and Roanoke rivers. The woods on the slopes are a typical southeastern mixed forest of medium-tall to tall oak, hickory, sweet gum, and red maple, together with loblolly and shortleaf pine. The undergrowth is dogwood, viburnum, blueberry, yaupon, and numerous woody vines.

Climate: Hot continental, with four distinct seasons. First frost arrives by October 14; last frost departs on April 26. Winters are short, summers somewhat hot and humid. Spring and autumn are ideal. Precipitation is evenly distributed throughout the year, mostly as rain. In midsummer, mountain thunderstorms are likely.

Summer mildness: 66 **Seasonal affect:** 52
Winter mildness: 26 **Hazard free:** 42
Score: 43.5 **Rank:** 114

	102
	113
	150
90°	17
32°	123
0°	2
	23
	69
	36

	High °F	Low °F	Hum %	Wind mph	Precip inches	Snow inches
JAN	42	20	55	9.5	2.3	5.8
FEB	45	22	52	9.7	2.3	4.7
MAR	55	30	50	10.1	2.9	3.5
APR	65	38	47	9.8	2.8	0
MAY	73	48	54	7.9	3.6	0
JUN	81	56	56	6.9	2.8	0
JUL	85	61	59	6.5	3.5	0
AUG	84	59	60	6.1	3.7	0
SEP	77	52	60	6.1	3.5	0
OCT	67	39	55	6.9	3.6	0
NOV	57	32	53	8.3	3.0	0
DEC	46	24	56	8.8	2.4	2.0

★ = *in the top 30 places for climate mildness.*

Sonora–Twain Harte, CA

Location: The weather station is at Sonora, 37.59 N and 120.23 W at 1,854 feet. Sacramento is 90 miles northwest. Modesto, in the central valley, is 40 miles southwest.
Landscape: Found in the foothills of the Sierra Nevada Mountains at the edge of the Stanislaus National Forest. There are five rivers that drain the region. Chaparral in the low elevations gives way to digger pine and several oak species in the higher mountains.
Climate: Sierran forest climate in the transition zone between the dry west coast desert and the wet west coast farther north. Prevailing west winds influence conditions jointly with elevation. Therefore the summers are long and generally dry. Most of the annual precipitation falls as rain rather than snow. The first frost arrives on November 12, and the last frost leaves April 14.

Summer mildness: 32 **Seasonal affect:** 73
Winter mildness: 51 **Hazard free:** 90
Score: 79.2 **Rank:** 43

	189
	75
	100
90°	83
32°	64
0°	0
	34
	43
	14

	High °F	Low °F	Hum %	Wind mph	Precip inches	Snow inches
JAN	55	32	80	7.2	5.6	0.4
FEB	59	34	75	7.6	5.0	0
MAR	61	36	65	8.6	5.3	0.4
APR	67	40	55	8.7	2.7	0
MAY	77	45	48	9.2	0.8	0
JUN	87	51	44	9.7	0.2	0
JUL	95	57	44	9.0	0.1	0
AUG	94	56	45	8.6	0.2	0
SEP	87	51	45	7.5	0.6	0
OCT	77	43	53	6.4	1.8	0
NOV	62	36	65	6.0	4.8	0
DEC	54	32	77	6.6	4.6	0.1

Southern Berkshire County, MA

Location: The weather station is at Great Barrington, 42.11 N and 73.21 W at 721 feet, in the rural corner where Massachusetts, New York, and Connecticut meet.
Landscape: The Berkshire Plateau in the east and the Taconic Mountains in the west enclose the Berkshire Valley. Rolling, open meadows are watered by the headwaters of the Housatonic River. A typical northern deciduous forest covers the uplands with maple, birch, beech, oak, and a scattering of pine. The low growth is shrub, herb, and fern.
Climate: Hot continental, with large temperature variations from season to season. Winters receive Canadian air sweeping down the Hudson Valley to the west and bring the first frost by October 15; the last frost departs a little late, April 27. December to February is cold, with long-lasting snow. Springs are short. Summers are clear, warm, and ideal. Falls are bright and extend through mid-November.

Summer mildness: 85 **Seasonal affect:** 15
Winter mildness: 9 **Hazard free:** 21
Score: 10.3 **Rank:** 182

	81
	109
	175
90°	19
32°	135
0°	6
	29
	75
	21

	High °F	Low °F	Hum %	Wind mph	Precip inches	Snow inches
JAN	31	9	58	9.0	3.0	16.3
FEB	33	12	57	9.4	2.9	14.1
MAR	43	22	53	9.9	3.2	10.7
APR	56	32	49	10.0	3.8	2.0
MAY	68	42	49	8.9	4.5	0
JUN	76	51	55	8.1	4.1	0
JUL	80	56	55	7.5	4.0	0
AUG	78	54	57	7.2	4.6	0
SEP	71	46	59	7.3	3.7	0
OCT	60	35	59	7.8	3.5	0
NOV	48	28	60	8.5	3.9	4.0
DEC	35	17	62	8.7	3.6	15.1

Southern Pines–Pinehurst, NC

Location: 35.10 N and 79.23 W at 512 feet, 75 miles south of Chapel Hill in the southern heartland of the state.
Landscape: This area is in gently rolling sandhill country between the foothills of the Uwharrie Mountains and the coastal plains. The woods are a hardwood swamp forest, with broadleaf deciduous and needleleaf evergreens.
Climate: Subtropical, with mild winters and hot, humid summers. Precipitation is evenly distributed throughout the year, but peaks slightly in midsummer or early spring thunderstorms. Occasionally there will be summer droughts. Unprotected by the mountains, the first frost will come by September 29, and the last frost departs on May 9. Snow is rare.

Summer mildness: 52 **Seasonal affect:** 38
Winter mildness: 38 **Hazard free:** 52
Score: 40.5 **Rank:** 121

	112
	106
	147
90°	43
32°	111
0°	0
	34
	74
	44

	High °F	Low °F	Hum %	Wind mph	Precip inches	Snow inches
JAN	49	24	55	8.5	4.0	2.1
FEB	53	27	52	8.9	4.0	1.8
MAR	62	35	49	9.3	4.4	1.3
APR	71	43	45	9.0	3.2	0
MAY	78	52	54	7.7	4.5	0
JUN	85	60	56	7.0	4.0	0
JUL	88	64	58	6.7	4.9	0
AUG	87	63	60	6.4	4.8	0
SEP	82	56	60	6.8	3.5	0
OCT	72	43	54	7.1	3.7	0
NOV	63	35	55	7.6	3.2	0
DEC	53	28	55	8.0	3.5	0.5

★ = *in the top 30 places for climate mildness.*

Southport–Brunswick Islands, NC

Location: 33.55 N and 78.01 W at 34 feet, on the Atlantic Ocean in North Carolina's extreme southeastern corner. Wilmington is 30 miles north.

Landscape: The surrounding low-lying terrain is typical of the state's coastal plain. The average elevation is less than 40 feet and level. Many rivers, creeks, and lakes are nearby, with considerable swampy growth surrounding them. Large tracts of southern mixed forest alternate with cultivated fields.

Climate: A strong marine influence. Summers are warm and humid, but excessive heat is rare. During the colder part of the year, polar air reaches the coastal areas, causing sharp temperature drops. Rainfall is ample and well distributed, with most occurring in summer thundershowers. In winter, rain may fall steadily for several days. Snowfall is slight. Some tropical storms reach the Cape Fear area every few years. November 11 sees the first frost, and March 21 sees the last frost.

Summer mildness: 44 **Seasonal affect:** 43
Winter mildness: 62 **Hazard free:** 49
Score: 51.4 **Rank:** 99

112
104
150
90° 20
32° 42
0° 0
24
74
48

	High °F	Low °F	Hum %	Wind mph	Precip inches	Snow inches
JAN	55	32	56	9.1	4.7	0.5
FEB	57	34	52	9.8	4.4	0.6
MAR	64	42	52	10.2	4.4	0.3
APR	72	50	48	10.3	3.0	0
MAY	79	59	55	9.2	4.0	0
JUN	85	67	59	8.5	4.9	0
JUL	88	71	63	8.0	6.9	0
AUG	88	70	64	7.4	7.1	0
SEP	83	64	62	7.9	6.8	0
OCT	75	52	56	8.1	3.3	0
NOV	68	43	53	8.1	3.3	0
DEC	59	35	55	8.5	4.1	0.3

State College, PA

Location: 40.47 N and 77.51 W at 1,157 feet. Philadelphia is 190 miles east, and Pittsburgh is 140 miles west.

Landscape: The ridges and valleys of the Appalachians run northeast to southwest, with elevations varying from 977 to 2,400 feet. In the Nittany Valley are rolling meadows, and the foothills of the Allegheny Plateau rise to the west. Forests of pine, hemlock, and hardwoods of beech, maple, oak, ash, and cherry were once more common before the clear-cut harvests. The surrounding higher elevations are now covered with second-growth forests.

Climate: Hot continental, with temperatures moderated by the surrounding mountain elevations. The city is protected by its eastern slope location, producing drier, somewhat less humid seasons. Winters are cold and relatively dry, with thick cloud cover. The first frost comes on October 15; the last frost leaves April 27. Summer and fall are the most pleasant seasons.

Summer mildness: 76 **Seasonal affect:** 21
Winter mildness: 23 **Hazard free:** 24
Score: 17.8 **Rank:** 166

87
109
169
90° 8
32° 131
0° 5
19
76
32

	High °F	Low °F	Hum %	Wind mph	Precip inches	Snow inches
JAN	33	17	58	8.3	2.4	11.7
FEB	36	18	55	9.0	2.6	11.7
MAR	46	27	52	9.5	3.2	11.1
APR	58	37	49	9.2	2.9	1.0
MAY	70	48	52	7.6	3.6	0
JUN	78	56	53	6.8	4.0	0
JUL	82	61	52	6.2	3.6	0
AUG	80	59	55	5.8	3.2	0
SEP	73	52	56	6.1	3.2	0
OCT	62	41	54	6.6	2.8	0
NOV	49	33	57	7.8	3.2	3.0
DEC	37	23	58	8.0	2.7	9.5

Summerville, SC

Location: 33.0106 N and 80.1033 W at 75 feet, 25 miles northwest of Charleston.

Landscape: The local terrain is mostly swampland and forest. Southeast is the Atlantic Ocean, and east is the Francis Marion National Forest. Tree cover includes oak, sweet and black gums, and bald cypress.

Climate: Subtropical, with moderation from the ocean. Summer is a period of heat and humidity, with frequent thunderstorms. Fall and winter are cool but rarely cold. With the first frost arriving fairly late, on November 6, and the last frost leaving rather early, on March 27, the growing season is extended. Spring is warm, windy, and sunny.

Summer mildness: 37 **Seasonal affect:** 36
Winter mildness: 64 **Hazard free:** 58
Score: 47.5 **Rank:** 106

104
109
152
90° 59
32° 50
0° 0
28
74
56

	High °F	Low °F	Hum %	Wind mph	Precip inches	Snow inches
JAN	57	33	70	9.1	4.0	0
FEB	61	35	67	9.9	3.6	0.6
MAR	69	43	67	10.0	4.5	0
APR	76	49	67	9.7	3.1	0
MAY	83	58	69	8.7	4.3	0
JUN	88	66	72	8.4	6.1	0
JUL	90	70	75	7.9	6.1	0
AUG	89	69	77	7.4	6.9	0
SEP	85	64	76	7.8	4.8	0
OCT	77	52	72	8.1	3.1	0
NOV	70	43	70	8.1	2.5	0
DEC	61	36	69	8.5	3.3	0.1

★ = *in the top 30 places for climate mildness.*

Table Rock Lake, MO

Location: 36.40 N and 93.52 W at 1,324 feet, just above the Arkansas state line. Springfield is 50 miles north.

Landscape: One of several lakes on the Ozark Plateau formed by river impoundment. The rounded mountains rise somewhat steeply from river valleys and the lakeshore. Oak-hickory forests are tall, providing a dense cover in summer and colorful foliage in fall, but are bare of leaves in winter. Pines are evidence of second-growth forest. Lower layers of shrub, dogwood, and redbud are common.

Climate: Hot continental, with hot summers and cold winters. Precipitation is adequate throughout the year, usually falling as rain. Winters may be cold enough for snow, but an icy rain is more typical during brief, intense cold snaps. First frost arrives October 16; last frost departs April 21. Spring comes in early and is pleasant.

Summer mildness: 54 **Seasonal affect:** 59
Winter mildness: 31 **Hazard free:** 8
Score: 20.2 **Rank:** 162

	116
	97
	153
90°	57
32°	101
0°	1
	20
	61
	56

	High °F	Low °F	Hum %	Wind mph	Precip inches	Snow inches
JAN	43	19	60	11.7	2.0	4.4
FEB	48	23	60	11.9	2.4	4.3
MAR	58	33	56	12.9	4.2	3.4
APR	69	43	55	12.2	4.5	0
MAY	76	52	59	10.4	4.9	0
JUN	84	60	59	9.6	4.5	0
JUL	89	65	56	8.5	3.1	0
AUG	89	62	54	8.6	3.8	0
SEP	81	56	58	9.3	4.4	0
OCT	70	43	54	10.1	3.6	0
NOV	58	33	59	11.3	3.8	1.0
DEC	46	23	63	11.6	3.4	3.0

Taos, NM

Location: 36.24 N and 105.34 W at 6,983 feet, 40 miles south of the Colorado border. Santa Fe, the state capital, is 70 miles south, and Albuquerque is 130 miles southwest.

Landscape: In an area where the western flank of the Sangre de Cristo range meets the semiarid high desert of the upper Rio Grande Valley. Wheeler Peak (13,161 feet), the highest point in New Mexico, is nearby. The relief includes deep gorges, mountainous skylines, and wide valleys. Typical steppe vegetation consists of numerous short grasses, scattered shrubs, and low trees. Engelmann spruce and subalpine fir cover the intermediate slopes, and ponderosa pine is on the lower, drier, more exposed areas.

Climate: Steppe and semiarid continental. Precipitation is evenly distributed throughout the year, falling as rain in summer storms and snow in the cold winters. Summers are clear, mild, and ideal. First frost comes by October 4; last frost departs May 12.

Summer mildness: 69 **Seasonal affect:** 86
Winter mildness: 3 **Hazard free:** 4
Score: 23.7 **Rank:** 154

	169
	111
	85
90°	9
32°	163
0°	5
	6
	34
	41

	High °F	Low °F	Hum %	Wind mph	Precip inches	Snow inches
JAN	39	7	50	8.1	0.6	8.2
FEB	44	14	42	8.9	0.5	7.5
MAR	52	21	32	10.1	0.8	6.8
APR	61	28	25	11.0	0.8	5.0
MAY	71	37	23	10.6	0.9	1.0
JUN	81	45	22	10.0	1.1	0
JUL	85	51	30	9.1	1.6	0
AUG	82	49	34	8.3	2.0	0
SEP	75	42	35	8.6	1.5	0
OCT	65	31	35	8.3	1.1	2.0
NOV	51	20	38	7.9	0.8	7.0
DEC	41	10	46	7.7	0.8	8.2

Thomasville, GA

Location: 30.50 N and 83.58 W at 250 feet, in the extreme southern part of the state. Tallahassee, Florida, is 35 miles southwest.

Landscape: At the western edge of the coastal plain in low, gently sloping pinelands near the Ochlockonee River. Stands of temperate rain forest of evergreen and laurel occur. The city is noted for a profusion of moss-covered live oaks and roses, azaleas, camellias, and other ornamental shrubs.

Climate: Subtropical, with no freezing winters. Summers are hot and humid. The annual temperature range is small to moderate. Rainfall is abundant and well distributed throughout the year. The first frost comes in November 11, and the last frost goes March 12.

Summer mildness: 17 **Seasonal affect:** 56
Winter mildness: 78 **Hazard free:** 68
Score: 62.3 **Rank:** 77

	102
	130
	133
90°	94
32°	34
0°	0
	50
	71
	83

	High °F	Low °F	Hum %	Wind mph	Precip inches	Snow inches
JAN	63	39	58	6.8	4.5	0.1
FEB	67	41	54	7.4	5.0	0.3
MAR	74	48	52	7.5	5.1	0
APR	81	54	47	6.9	3.6	0
MAY	87	61	50	6.3	4.2	0
JUN	91	68	55	5.8	5.4	0
JUL	92	71	61	5.2	6.2	0
AUG	92	70	62	5.0	5.1	0
SEP	89	66	59	5.9	3.6	0
OCT	82	55	52	6.3	2.2	0
NOV	74	47	55	6.1	3.1	0
DEC	66	41	52	6.4	4.3	0

★ = *in the top 30 places for climate mildness.*

Toms River–Barnegat Bay, NJ

Location: 39.57 N and 74.12 W at 40 feet, in the center of New Jersey's Atlantic coast. New York City is 95 miles north, and Atlantic City is 50 miles south.

Landscape: Surrounding flat terrain is composed of tidal marshes and beach sand. The dunes provide vantages for observing bird migrations along the Atlantic flyway. Inland is a forest of mixed evergreens.

Climate: Hot continental, with the moderating influence of the Atlantic apparent throughout the year. Summers are relatively cooler and winters warmer than those of other places at the same latitude. During the warm season, sea breezes in the late morning and afternoon prevent excessive heat and may lower the temperature 15 degrees within half an hour. Fall is long, lasting until mid-November. On the other hand, warming is delayed in spring. Precipitation is moderate and well distributed throughout the year. First frost as early as October 30; last frost as soon as April 11.

Summer mildness: 75 **Seasonal affect:** 20
Winter mildness: 35 **Hazard free:** 34
Score: 25.7 **Rank:** 151

	95
	110
	160
90°	12
32°	98
0°	0
	44
	73
	27

	High °F	Low °F	Hum %	Wind mph	Precip inches	Snow inches
JAN	39	22	58	11.0	3.6	5.3
FEB	41	24	56	11.4	3.4	5.5
MAR	49	32	54	11.9	4.1	2.6
APR	58	40	52	11.8	4.1	0
MAY	68	50	56	10.2	4.3	0
JUN	77	59	56	9.2	3.5	0
JUL	82	65	57	8.5	4.4	0
AUG	81	64	58	8.1	4.4	0
SEP	75	58	60	8.4	3.6	0
OCT	65	47	60	9.0	3.5	0
NOV	55	38	64	10.5	4.2	0
DEC	44	28	67	10.6	4.0	2.3

Traverse City, MI

Location: 44.45 N and 85.37 W at 599 feet, on Grand Traverse Bay. Detroit is 250 miles southeast.

Landscape: The tip of the 20-mile Old Mission Peninsula, jutting into the bay from the city, is exactly midway between the Equator and the North Pole. The terrain is generally level or gently undulating, with sandy and gravelly soils. The region abounds with lakes. The forest is second-growth pine and hemlock. Maple, oak, and birch are occasional deciduous trees.

Climate: Though rigorous because of its interior and northerly location, the climate is modified by the Great Lakes on either side of the Michigan peninsula. Consequently, summer temperatures average at least 5 degrees cooler than in locations in the southern part of the state. However, winters are severe, with cold spells that may last for a week and snowfall that averages almost 75 inches. First frost comes by October 17; last frost after May 10.

Summer mildness: 81 **Seasonal affect:** 22
Winter mildness: 20 **Hazard free:** 2
Score: 8.9 **Rank:** 185

	67
	89
	210
90°	5
32°	143
0°	5
	23
	71
	23

	High °F	Low °F	Hum %	Wind mph	Precip inches	Snow inches
JAN	30	17	77	12.6	2.2	23.1
FEB	33	17	72	11.6	1.5	15.4
MAR	42	24	66	11.9	2.0	10.4
APR	56	35	60	11.8	2.7	2.0
MAY	68	44	58	10.1	2.5	0
JUN	76	53	61	9.5	3.3	0
JUL	81	59	63	8.7	2.7	0
AUG	79	58	64	8.5	3.6	0
SEP	72	52	66	9.4	4.0	0
OCT	61	43	68	10.8	3.2	0
NOV	47	33	72	11.9	2.9	12.0
DEC	34	22	78	12.1	2.5	25.5

Trinity Peninsula, TX

Location: The weather station is in Trinity, 30.37 N and 95.01 W at 131 feet, between Lake Livingston and the Trinity River, the longest river entirely in Texas. Huntsville is 20 miles southeast; Houston is 75 miles south.

Landscape: This is the southern edge of Big Thicket area, with rolling hills and many large lakes. Native vegetation includes post and blackjack oak, and Texas hickory stands mixed with dense forests of piney woods.

Climate: Lies within the south temperate humid section of the Gulf Coast region. Spring arrives early. Summers are long and hot. Winters though are short and mild, with a few brief overnight cold spells. Light snow is a possibility. A first frost arrives in late November; the last frost exits in early March. Rainfall is distributed fairly evenly throughout the year.

Summer mildness: 15 **Seasonal affect:** 63
Winter mildness: 83 **Hazard free:** 61
Score: 64.3 **Rank:** 73

	94
	115
	157
90°	106
32°	27
0°	0
	11
	62
	61

	High °F	Low °F	Hum %	Wind mph	Precip inches	Snow inches
JAN	58	38	63	8.3	3.6	0.2
FEB	62	41	61	8.8	3.1	0.6
MAR	71	49	59	9.4	3.1	0
APR	79	57	57	9.2	3.5	0
MAY	85	64	59	8.2	5.2	0
JUN	91	70	59	7.7	4.2	0
JUL	94	72	58	7.0	2.4	0
AUG	95	72	58	6.3	3.3	0
SEP	89	67	60	6.9	5.0	0
OCT	80	57	56	7.0	3.6	0
NOV	70	49	57	7.9	4.2	0
DEC	61	41	61	8.0	3.8	0

★ = *in the top 30 places for climate mildness.*

Tryon, NC

Location: 35.12 N and 82.14 W at 1,085 feet, just above the South Carolina border. Asheville is 30 miles north.
Landscape: Central mountain region, with the Blue Ridge Mountains to the north. Nearby are waterfalls and valleys of rolling farmland, together with lakes and ski areas. The surrounding Appalachian oak forest includes tulip trees, sweet chestnut, birch, hickory, walnut, and maple. In spring, a low layer of herbaceous plants quickly develops but is reduced after the trees reach full foliage.
Climate: Hot continental, with a strong annual cycle of cool winters and warm summers. The surrounding mountains and valleys produce a variety of microclimates, and the presence of thermal winds provides a pleasingly mild climate in lower elevations. Precipitation, usually rain, is adequate in all months. Spring comes earlier in this "thermal belt" than just a few miles north or south. First frost won't arrive until late October; last frost leaves in early April.

Summer mildness: 45 **Seasonal affect:** 26
Winter mildness: 59 **Hazard free:** 50
Score: 40.0 **Rank:** 122

	122
	100
	143
90°	41
32°	70
0°	0
	34
	83
	43

	High °F	Low °F	Hum %	Wind mph	Precip inches	Snow inches
JAN	52	30	55	7.4	5.2	2.7
FEB	56	32	53	8.0	5.4	2.8
MAR	66	39	52	8.1	6.5	1.7
APR	74	46	48	7.9	4.7	0
MAY	81	55	54	6.9	5.9	0
JUN	86	62	54	6.4	5.7	0
JUL	88	66	60	5.9	5.3	0
AUG	87	65	62	5.7	5.9	0
SEP	82	59	62	6.1	5.4	0
OCT	73	48	55	6.5	5.4	0
NOV	64	40	54	6.8	4.8	0
DEC	55	33	55	7.3	5.1	1.0

Tucson, AZ

Location: 32.13 N and 110.55 W at 2,437 feet, on the Santa Cruz River, 120 miles southeast of Phoenix and 60 miles north of the Mexican border.
Landscape: At the foot of the Catalina Mountains in a broad, flat to gently rolling valley floor rimmed by mountains. Northeast, the Coronado National Forest is typical of pine, spruce, and fir forests of the higher elevations.
Climate: Desert, with a sunny, dry climate and a unique desert-mountain location. There's a long, hot season beginning in April and ending in October. High temperatures are modified by low humidity. Tucson lies in the zone receiving more sunshine than any other in the United States. Clear skies or very thin, high clouds permit intense surface heating during the day and active radiation cooling at night. Summer is the rainy season with robust, active thunderstorms.

Summer mildness: 5 **Seasonal affect:** 91
Winter mildness: 73 **Hazard free:** 67
Score: 73.2 **Rank:** 55

	195
	90
	80
90°	93
32°	112
0°	0
	2
	33
	42

	High °F	Low °F	Hum %	Wind mph	Precip inches	Snow inches
JAN	64	39	40	7.9	0.9	0.3
FEB	68	41	35	8.1	0.7	0.2
MAR	73	45	29	8.5	0.7	0.3
APR	81	50	21	8.9	0.3	0
MAY	90	58	17	8.7	0.2	0
JUN	100	68	17	8.6	0.2	0
JUL	99	74	33	8.4	2.4	0
AUG	97	72	38	7.8	2.2	0
SEP	93	68	32	8.3	1.7	0
OCT	84	57	30	8.1	1.1	0
NOV	73	46	32	8.1	0.7	0
DEC	64	40	39	7.8	1.1	0.3

Vero Beach, FL

Location: 27.38 N and 80.24 W at 17 feet, near the center of Florida's Atlantic coast. Palm Beach is 50 miles south.
Landscape: There are miles of dunes and barrier beach on the coastal plain northeast of Lake Okeechobee. Native vegetation includes sea-oat grass, seagrape, and cabbage palm. Live oaks shade many of the residential streets while oleander, hibiscus, and bougainvillea lend a tropical atmosphere.
Climate: Subtropical, on the northern border of Florida's warmest thermal belt. Nearness to the Atlantic results in a climate tempered by land and sea breezes. Apparent temperatures in summer may top 90°F during the late morning or early afternoon but are cut short by midday sea breezes and afternoon convective thundershowers. Winters can have cold airflows from the north but usually are mild because of the area's ocean setting and southerly latitude.

Summer mildness: 22 **Seasonal affect:** 60
Winter mildness: 95 **Hazard free:** 63
Score: 75.7 **Rank:** 50

	99
	134
	133
90°	58
32°	1
0°	0
	15
	77
	70

	High °F	Low °F	Hum %	Wind mph	Precip inches	Snow inches
JAN	73	50	59	8.7	2.2	0
FEB	74	51	56	9.2	2.9	0
MAR	78	56	56	9.9	3.1	0
APR	82	60	52	9.2	2.0	0
MAY	86	65	57	9.1	4.6	0
JUN	88	70	64	7.9	6.7	0
JUL	90	72	65	7.1	6.4	0
AUG	90	72	64	6.5	6.5	0
SEP	89	72	64	7.6	7.4	0
OCT	84	66	61	8.9	5.8	0
NOV	79	59	62	8.9	3.3	0
DEC	74	53	59	8.1	2.1	0.2

★ = *in the top 30 places for climate mildness.*

Victorville–Apple Valley, CA

Location: 34.32 N and 117.17 W at 2,715 feet, in the high desert of the Victor Valley, 78 miles northeast of Los Angeles.

Landscape: On the southwestern edge of the Mohave Desert and north of the San Bernardino Mountains and National Forest. This is dramatic country where mountain peaks thousands of feet high look down on valleys lying below sea level.

Climate: Desert. Nights are invariably much cooler than the days. Springs and summers in the Victor Valley are warm to hot, often topping 100°F. Humidity remains low during those months. In contrast, fall and winter temperatures occasionally drop to freezing or below. The first frost is late on November 5; last frost a little early on April 13. Most of the annual precipitation falls in the winter as rain on the lower slopes and in great amounts of snow in the higher mountains and just a trace on the valley floor.

Summer mildness: 13 **Seasonal affect:** 98
Winter mildness: 50 **Hazard free:** 90
Score: 83.6 **Rank:** 34

	242
	75
	48
90°	104
32°	79
0°	0
	2
	12
	7

	High °F	Low °F	Hum %	Wind mph	Precip inches	Snow inches
JAN	58	30	40	7.3	0.8	0.8
FEB	63	34	35	7.4	0.9	0.1
MAR	66	37	30	7.9	0.9	0.1
APR	73	41	25	8.3	0.4	0
MAY	81	48	23	8.3	0.2	0
JUN	91	55	22	8.5	0.1	0
JUL	97	61	32	9.5	0.2	0
AUG	96	61	35	8.9	0.3	0
SEP	90	55	35	7.3	0.4	0
OCT	80	45	32	6.6	0.3	0
NOV	67	36	34	6.9	0.6	0
DEC	59	30	41	7.2	0.7	0.2

Virginia Beach, VA

Location: 36.51 N and 75.58 W at 16 feet, at the entrance to Chesapeake Bay. Norfolk borders the city. Richmond is 90 miles northwest.

Landscape: Low-level land extending south to the North Carolina border. Back Bay is a brackish lagoon and a national wildlife refuge south of the city that parallels the ocean. Stands of medium-tall to tall oak, hickory, sweet gum, red maple, and winged elm are present. At least half of the stands also contain loblolly and shortleaf pine. Gums and bald cypress dominate the extensive coastal marshes and interior swamps.

Climate: Subtropical, in a position north of hurricane tracks and tropical storms and south of high-latitude storm systems. Winters are mild. First frost appears in early November; last frost disappears April 5. Springs and falls are especially pleasant. Summers are warm, humid, and long. Though there's occasional snow, a temperature of 0°F has never been recorded here.

Summer mildness: 59 **Seasonal affect:** 41
Winter mildness: 60 **Hazard free:** 40
Score: 52.4 **Rank:** 97

	106
	107
	152
90°	37
32°	76
0°	0
	20
	74
	37

	High °F	Low °F	Hum %	Wind mph	Precip inches	Snow inches
JAN	47	31	60	11.5	3.8	2.8
FEB	50	32	58	12.0	3.5	3.0
MAR	58	39	56	12.5	3.7	1.0
APR	67	47	52	11.8	3.1	0
MAY	75	57	58	10.5	3.8	0
JUN	83	65	58	9.8	3.8	0
JUL	86	70	61	9.0	5.1	0
AUG	85	69	62	8.9	4.8	0
SEP	80	64	62	9.6	3.9	0
OCT	70	53	61	10.4	3.2	0
NOV	61	44	58	10.7	2.9	0
DEC	52	35	60	11.2	3.2	0.9

Wenatchee, WA

Location: 47.25 N and 120.18 W at 645 feet, in central Washington, roughly 150 miles midway between Seattle to the west and Spokane to the east.

Landscape: Here is the juncture of the Wenatchee and Columbia rivers. The rounded, shrubbed Wenatchee Mountains are off to the southwest, and the Columbia plain stretches east in juniper grasslands. The uplands are moderately dissected, hilly, and steep. The tablelands are fertile and covered with loess.

Climate: Steppe grassland, generally shielded from the wet Pacific-driven weather by the Cascade Range. Summers are warm and nearly rainless. Winters are cool, foggy, and rainy. Snow is plentiful in the higher mountains. The first frost arrives October 20; last frost leaves April 17.

Summer mildness: 65 **Seasonal affect:** 38
Winter mildness: 33 **Hazard free:** 37
Score: 31.6 **Rank:** 137

	86
	87
	192
90°	33
32°	118
0°	1
	48
	26
	11

	High °F	Low °F	Hum %	Wind mph	Precip inches	Snow inches
JAN	35	22	80	8.8	1.3	11.7
FEB	43	27	77	9.3	0.9	4.1
MAR	55	33	67	9.7	0.6	1.8
APR	64	40	53	10.0	0.6	0
MAY	73	48	49	9.2	0.5	0
JUN	81	55	45	9.2	0.6	0
JUL	88	60	37	8.6	0.2	0
AUG	87	59	38	8.2	0.5	0
SEP	78	50	40	8.3	0.4	0
OCT	64	40	56	8.2	0.5	0
NOV	47	32	79	8.7	1.3	3.0
DEC	36	25	84	8.6	1.5	10.1

Western St. Tammany Parish, LA

Location: 30.28 N and 90.06 W at 30 feet, on the north shore of Lake Pontchartrain. A 24-mile causeway across the lake connects the parish with New Orleans.

Landscape: On a low-level area of alluvial plain in the Lower Mississippi Valley. Swamp and marshlands support cypress, small palms, tree ferns, shrubs, and herbaceous plants. Evergreen-oak and magnolia forests are the natural climax vegetation.

Climate: Subtropical and best described as humid. Lake Pontchartrain and the nearby Gulf of Mexico modify the temperature and decrease its range. Heavy and frequent rains are typical, with daily afternoon thunderstorms from mid-June to September. From December to March, precipitation is likely to be steady rain of 2 or 3 day's duration. During winter and spring, cold rain forms fogs. The first frost comes in November 11, and the last frost goes March 14. Hurricanes are an occasional threat from July to October.

Summer mildness: 23 **Seasonal affect:** 42
Winter mildness: 80 **Hazard free:** 60
Score: 54.9 **Rank:** 92

	103
	119
	144
90°	91
32°	32
0°	0
	28
	76
	69

	High °F	Low °F	Hum %	Wind mph	Precip inches	Snow inches
JAN	61	39	66	9.4	5.0	0.2
FEB	65	41	63	9.9	6.1	0.2
MAR	72	48	60	9.9	5.9	0
APR	79	55	59	9.4	4.7	0
MAY	85	62	60	8.1	5.0	0
JUN	90	68	63	6.9	4.9	0
JUL	92	70	66	6.1	6.5	0
AUG	91	70	66	6.0	5.8	0
SEP	88	66	65	7.3	5.1	0
OCT	80	55	59	7.5	3.2	0
NOV	71	48	62	8.7	4.5	0
DEC	64	42	66	9.1	6.0	0.1

Whidbey Island, WA

Location: The weather station is at Coupeville, 48.08 N and 122.35 W at 50 feet, on the Saratoga Passage in Puget Sound, 40 miles above Seattle.

Landscape: At 40 miles long, Whidbey is one of the largest offshore islands in the continental United States. The coast has rocky banks indented by coves and inlets. Inland there are gently rolling hills with patches of Garry oak, fir, red cedar, and spruce. Penn Cove and Crockett's Lake are important feeding grounds for shorebirds and waterfowl.

Climate: Marine, characterized by moderate temperatures, a pronounced though not sharply defined rainy season, and considerable cloudiness, particularly during winter. Occasionally, severe winter storms come in from the north. Summers are warm and pleasant and winters mild and rainy. The first frost glazes foliage by October 28, deepens until the last frost departs April 15.

Summer mildness: 96 **Seasonal affect:** 20
Winter mildness: 57 **Hazard free:** 71
Score: 78.2 **Rank:** 44

	57
	81
	228
90°	0
32°	52
0°	0
	43
	62
	7

	High °F	Low °F	Hum %	Wind mph	Precip inches	Snow inches
JAN	45	34	77	9.8	2.5	2.9
FEB	49	35	74	9.6	1.8	1.1
MAR	53	37	70	9.8	1.8	1.1
APR	57	40	67	9.6	1.8	0
MAY	63	44	64	8.9	1.7	0
JUN	68	48	62	8.7	1.3	0
JUL	72	50	62	8.3	0.8	0
AUG	73	50	63	7.9	1.0	0
SEP	68	46	68	8.1	1.4	0
OCT	59	42	75	8.5	1.7	0
NOV	50	38	78	9.3	2.6	0
DEC	45	35	80	9.6	2.9	1.5

Wickenburg, AZ

Location: 33.58 N and 112.43 W at 2,903 feet, in west-central Arizona. Phoenix is 30 miles southeast.

Landscape: In the Harcuvar Mountains on the Hassayampa River at the northern edge of the Sonoran Desert. A typical desert river, the Hassayampa moves underground for much of the 100-mile length. Where it appears, there is an oasis with cottonwood and willows and supporting a diverse riparian culture. Native vegetation includes mixed grasses, chaparral brush, and oak-juniper woodlands. These uplands of high desert also include the Joshua tree, saguaro, cholla, and ironwood.

Climate: Semiarid mountain steppe, with strong daily and seasonal temperature changes. The usual winter flow of air is from the Pacific, though cold air from Canada sometimes drives temperatures below freezing in the high plateau and mountainous regions. Mid-November ushers in the first frost; late March sees the last frost exit. Summer is dry with daytime temperatures topping 100°F.

Summer mildness: 4 **Seasonal affect:** 95
Winter mildness: 58 **Hazard free:** 92
Score: 80.6 **Rank:** 38

	212
	84
	69
90°	152
32°	63
0°	0
	2
	20
	24

	High °F	Low °F	Hum %	Wind mph	Precip inches	Snow inches
JAN	65	32	44	5.3	1.2	0
FEB	69	35	37	5.9	1.1	0
MAR	74	39	32	6.7	1.6	0
APR	82	43	22	7.0	0.5	0
MAY	91	51	27	7.1	0.2	0
JUN	101	59	15	6.8	0.1	0
JUL	105	69	27	7.2	1.4	0
AUG	102	68	32	6.7	1.9	0
SEP	96	60	30	6.3	1.4	0
OCT	87	48	30	5.8	0.7	0
NOV	74	38	35	5.4	1.0	0
DEC	66	32	44	5.1	1.3	0.2

★ = *in the top 30 places for climate mildness.*

Williamsburg, VA

Location: 37.16 N and 76.42 W at 86 feet, on a tidewater peninsula between the James and York rivers, 40 miles midway between Richmond and Norfolk.

Landscape: Elevated slightly on a ridge, the country is low and level to gently rolling field. Salt flats along brackish rivers are predominantly marsh grass. The southeastern mixed forest has medium-tall to tall oak, hickory, sweet gum, red maple, and winged elm. At least half the stands are filled with loblolly and shortleaf pine. Gums and cypress dominate the coastal marshes and interior swamps. Live oak and wax myrtle grow only in tidewater.

Climate: Hot continental. Winter is mild, while spring and fall are ideal. First frost arrives by October 28; last frost leaves by April 14. Summers are warm, humid, and long. Precipitation is evenly distributed as rain, though there's occasional snow. The area lies north of the hurricane and tropical storm track and south of high-latitude storm systems.

Summer mildness: 51 **Seasonal affect:** 37
Winter mildness: 49 **Hazard free:** 36
Score: 31.6 **Rank:** 137

106
107
152
90° 37
32° 85
0° 0
20
75
37

	High °F	Low °F	Hum %	Wind mph	Precip inches	Snow inches
JAN	48	27	60	11.5	3.8	4.2
FEB	51	29	58	12.0	3.5	2.5
MAR	61	36	56	12.5	4.2	1.8
APR	70	44	52	11.8	3.0	0
MAY	78	54	58	10.5	4.5	0
JUN	85	62	58	9.8	4.0	0
JUL	88	67	61	9.0	5.0	0
AUG	87	66	62	8.9	4.7	0
SEP	81	60	62	9.6	4.3	0
OCT	71	48	61	10.4	3.2	0
NOV	63	39	58	10.7	3.5	0
DEC	52	31	60	11.2	3.4	1.2

Wimberley, TX

Location: 29.59 N and 98.03 W at 840 feet, in the central Texas Hill Country, 35 miles midway between Austin and San Antonio.

Landscape: The San Marcos River rises from springs here. Caves and lakes dot the nearby green meadows and low-rise hill country. Along the watercourses are cypress and juniper-oak stands.

Climate: Prairie. Though summers are hot, night temperatures usually drop into the 70s. Winters are mild. November 17 sees the first frost arrive; March 17 bids the last frost farewell. Prevailing winds are southerly, though strong northers may bring cold spells that rarely last more than a few days. Precipitation is well distributed but heaviest in late spring, with a secondary rainfall peak in September. Summer brings some heavy thunderstorms. Winter rains are slow and steady.

Summer mildness: 10 **Seasonal affect:** 64
Winter mildness: 61 **Hazard free:** 57
Score: 47.0 **Rank:** 108

116
114
135
90° 107
32° 21
0° 0
115
47
41

	High °F	Low °F	Hum %	Wind mph	Precip inches	Snow inches
JAN	59	32	69	9.6	1.7	0.5
FEB	63	35	67	10.1	2.2	0.3
MAR	72	42	64	10.8	1.9	0
APR	79	49	67	10.4	2.6	0
MAY	85	58	72	9.5	4.8	0
JUN	91	66	70	9.1	3.7	0
JUL	95	70	65	8.3	2.0	0
AUG	96	69	64	7.9	2.1	0
SEP	91	63	68	7.9	3.3	0
OCT	82	50	67	8.1	3.4	0
NOV	72	42	68	9.0	2.4	0.1
DEC	62	35	68	9.1	1.9	0

Woodstock, VT

Location: 43.37 N and 72.31 W at 705 feet, just west of the Connecticut River and New Hampshire line and 60 miles south of Montpelier, the state capital.

Landscape: In the upper Connecticut River Valley with the Green Mountains rising to the west. Rivers cut through steep gorges giving high relief to the winding valleys. The forests are transitional stands of mixed conifer and deciduous trees. Northern white pine, eastern hemlock, maple, oak, and beech are common.

Climate: Northerly latitude assures the variety and vigor of a true New England climate. The summer, while not long, is clear and warm. Fall is cool, extending through October. Winters are cold, with brief, intense cold snaps formed by high-pressure systems moving down from central Canada and Hudson Bay. Snows are deep and long lasting. First frost comes in late September; last frost delays leaving until mid-May. Spring is called breakup or mud season.

Summer mildness: 79 **Seasonal affect:** 10
Winter mildness: 6 **Hazard free:** 12
Score: 1.4 **Rank:** 200

91
110
164
90° 7
32° 167
0° 23
50
75
20

	High °F	Low °F	Hum %	Wind mph	Precip inches	Snow inches
JAN	28	7	58	9.0	2.5	20.9
FEB	33	10	57	9.4	2.4	20.6
MAR	43	21	53	9.9	2.7	16.9
APR	56	32	49	10.0	2.9	5.0
MAY	70	43	49	8.9	3.6	0
JUN	78	52	55	8.1	3.3	0
JUL	83	57	55	7.5	3.3	0
AUG	80	56	57	7.2	3.6	0
SEP	71	48	59	7.3	3.3	0
OCT	59	37	59	7.8	3.3	0
NOV	45	28	60	8.5	3.5	5.0
DEC	32	15	62	8.7	3.1	20.9

★ = *in the top 30 places for climate mildness.*

York Beaches, ME

Location: 43.23 N and 70.32 W at 51 feet, on Maine's southern Atlantic coast. Portland is 35 miles north, and Boston, Massachusetts, is 60 miles south.

Landscape: Low hills drained by marsh and stream rise at the mouth of the York River on the Atlantic Ocean. Coastal watersheds include upstream areas, wetlands, estuaries, beaches, near-shore waters, and offshore habitats. Natural harbors, inlets, and sandy beaches mark the shore. Native vegetation is mixed evergreen of pine and spruce, with some maple and oak. The low-lying areas support typical marsh grasses and cattails.

Climate: Hot continental. Moderated somewhat by the ocean, winters can be cold, damp, and snowy. Spring arrives late. Summer days are clear and warm; the nights pleasantly cool. Fall is bright, mild, and long lasting.

Summer mildness: 91 **Seasonal affect:** 9
Winter mildness: 13 **Hazard free:** 18
Score: 11.3 **Rank:** 179

	Days
	102
	99
	164
90°	6
32°	157
0°	14
	49
	76
	19

	High °F	Low °F	Hum %	Wind mph	Precip inches	Snow inches
JAN	30	11	62	9.2	3.5	19.3
FEB	33	14	59	9.4	3.3	17.2
MAR	41	25	59	10.0	3.7	12.3
APR	52	34	57	10.0	4.1	2.0
MAY	63	43	57	9.2	3.6	0
JUN	73	52	60	8.2	3.4	0
JUL	79	58	60	7.6	3.1	0
AUG	77	57	60	7.5	2.9	0
SEP	69	49	60	7.8	3.1	0
OCT	59	38	60	8.4	3.9	0
NOV	47	30	62	8.8	5.2	3.0
DEC	35	18	62	9.0	4.6	14.9

★ Yuma, AZ

Location: 32.43 N and 114.37 W at 137 feet, in the extreme southwestern corner of Arizona, 21 miles north of the Mexican border. The city is 150 miles midway between Phoenix to the east and San Diego to the west.

Landscape: The land is typical desert steppe, with dry, sandy, and dusty soil. There's scant vegetation. Craggy buttes and mountains take their characteristic texture from wind erosion. The surrounding Trigo, Chocolate, Castle Dome, Mohawk, and Gila ranges are the dominant geologic feature.

Climate: Desert, with many places in the world receiving more rain in a year than has fallen here in the past century. There is a first frost by December 9 and a last frost by February 7. Home heating is necessary during the nights from late October to mid-April. Of all of America's First Order weather stations, the one here records the highest number of sunny days.

Summer mildness: 2 **Seasonal affect:** 100
Winter mildness: 88 **Hazard free:** 97
Score: 95.5 **Rank:** 10

	Days
	242
	75
	48
90°	178
32°	14
0°	0
	2
	11
	7

	High °F	Low °F	Hum %	Wind mph	Precip inches	Snow inches
JAN	69	44	40	7.3	0.4	0
FEB	74	47	35	7.4	0.2	0
MAR	79	51	30	7.9	0.2	0
APR	86	57	25	8.3	0.1	0
MAY	94	64	23	8.3	0.0	0
JUN	103	72	22	8.5	0.0	0
JUL	107	81	32	9.5	0.3	0
AUG	105	80	35	8.9	0.6	0
SEP	101	73	35	7.3	0.3	0
OCT	90	62	32	6.6	0.3	0
NOV	77	51	34	6.9	0.2	0
DEC	69	44	41	7.2	0.5	0

★ = *in the top 30 places for climate mildness.*

ET CETERA: CLIMATE

CLIMATE AND HEALTH

A bogus fact sometimes getting into print has it that men get an extra 12 months of life and women an extra 18 simply by moving to Florida.

There is no proven link between longevity and climate. True, the three places with the highest portion of centenarians—the Caucasus Mountains, the mountains of Bolivia, and northwestern India—are in southern latitudes at high elevations. But in America, the longest average life spans are recorded in three states with northern latitudes, flat terrain, and severe winters—Minnesota, North Dakota, and Iowa.

People with specific chronic diseases are much more comfortable in some climates than in others. Asthmatics do best in warm, dry places that have a minimum of airborne allergens and no molds. People with rheumatism or arthritis find comfort in warm, moist southerly climates where the weather is constant and the atmospheric pressure swings least. Those suffering from tuberculosis or emphysema seem to do best in the lower elevations of mountains with lots of clear air and sunshine.

A small classic in bioclimatology is H.E. Landsberg's *Weather and Health,* which details the relationships between climate and the aggravation of physical afflictions. Drawing on this and other sources, *Retirement Places Rated* describes some basic weather phenomena and suggests how they can affect the way you feel.

Weather Stages: Beware of 3 and 4

The weather changes that cause the body to react have been studied by meteorologists and classified into six basic stages that make up the clear–stormy–clear cycle repeated all over the planet. The stages in the cycle are linked to some of the joys and tragedies of existence.

- **Stage 1:** Cool, high-pressure air, with few clouds and moderate winds, followed by . . .
- **Stage 2:** Perfectly clear, dry air, high pressure, and little wind, leading to . . .
- **Stage 3:** Considerable warming, steady or slightly falling pressure, and some high clouds, until . . .
- **Stage 4:** The warm, moist air gets into the lower layers; pressure falls, clouds thicken, precipitation is common, and the wind picks up speed; then . . .
- **Stage 5:** An abrupt change takes place; showery precipitation is accompanied by cold, gusty winds, rapidly rising pressure, and falling humidity as the moisture in the air is released.
- **Stage 6:** Gradually, the pressure rises still further and the clouds diminish; temperatures reach low levels and the humidity continues to drop, leading back to . . .
- **Stage 1:** Cool, high-pressure air . . .

Of course, these phases aren't equally long, either in any given sequence or in the course of a year. During winter, all 6 stages may follow one another within 3 days while in the summer 2 weeks may pass before the cycle is completed.

The beautiful-weather stages 1 and 2 stimulate the body very little. They make no demands that can't be met by adequate clothing and shelter. In contrast, weather stages 4 and 5 are often violent. They stir us up mentally and physically.

There is no question but weather stages affect the body. Hospital birth and death records prove it. In pregnancy, in far more cases than statistical accident permits, labor begins on days that are in weather stage 3. Heart attacks peak in weather stages 3 and 4 and drop in stages 1 and 6. Bleeding ulcers and migraines peak in stage 4.

Weather influences mood and conduct. There is a strong link between weather stage 3 and suicide, behavior problems in schoolchildren, and street riots. A study in Poland showed that accident rates in factory workers doubled during cyclonic weather conditions (stages 3 and 4: periods of falling pressure, rising temperatures, and humidity signaling the onset of stormy weather) and returned to normal low levels in fair weather. Animals are affected, too. Dogcatchers are busiest during stages 3, 4, and 5 because dogs become restless, stray from their homes, and wander through the streets.

More on Comfort

As the six weather stages suggest, everyday comfort is influenced by three basic climatic factors: humidity, temperature, and barometric pressure.

Humidity. The amount of moisture in the air is closely related to air temperature in determining the comfort level of the atmosphere. Much of the discomfort and nervous tension experienced at the approach of stormy weather (weather stage 4) is the product of rising temperatures and humidity.

High levels of atmospheric moisture, such as those felt most of the time in the Pacific Northwest and along the Gulf Coast and South Atlantic Coast, aren't usually the cause of direct discomfort except in persons suffering from certain types of arthritis or rheumatism. But even in these cases, the mild temperatures found in these locations do much to offset discomfort. In fact, the stability of the barometric pressure in these areas makes them ideal for people with muscle and joint pain.

But damp air combined with low temperatures can be uncomfortable. Most people who live through damp winters, especially in places with high winds, complain that the cold, wet wind goes right through them. Moreover, the harmful effect of cold, damp air on pulmonary diseases has long been known. With this in mind, it's smart to think carefully about moving

to New England coastal locations—Cape Cod and the Maine coast, for example—where these conditions are winter trademarks.

Perhaps the most noticeable drawback to very moist air is the variety of organisms it supports. Bacteria and the spores of fungi and molds thrive in moist air but are almost absent in dry air. If the air is moist and also warm, the problem is multiplied. People susceptible to bacterial skin infections, fungal infections such as athlete's foot, or mold allergies should consider places with high humidity carefully.

On the other end of the spectrum, very dry air produces perceptible effects immediately and can cause discomfort within a day. When the relative humidity falls below 50 percent, most persons experience dry nasal passages and perhaps a dry, tickling throat. In the Desert Southwest, where the humidity can drop to 20 percent or less in some locations, many people experience nosebleeds, flaking skin, and constant sore throats.

Temperature. Some bioclimatologists maintain that the body is most comfortable and productive at "65-65," meaning an air temperature of 65° with 65 percent humidity. High relative humidity intensifies the felt effect of high temperatures because it impairs the evaporative cooling effect of sweating.

At apparent temperatures as low as 80°F to 90°F, a person may begin to suffer symptoms of heat stress. The degree of heat stress experienced will vary depending on age, health, and body characteristics. Infants, young children, and older adults are most likely to be affected by high temperature/humidity combinations.

The map "Apparent Temperatures (July)" shows how felt temperatures vary across the country. The places with the highest temperatures are in the southern half of the plateau between the Sierra Nevada to the west and the Rocky Mountains to the east, the Great Interior Valley of California, and parts of the high plains regions of New Mexico, Oklahoma, and Texas. These areas are generally dry, so the effects of the high temperatures on the body are not particularly noticeable or damaging. This is especially true of locations west of eastern New Mexico.

States along the Gulf Coast and the South Atlantic Coast have temperatures that are less spectacularly high but humidity that can be oppressive. Most people would find a 90°F day in Savannah, Georgia, Daytona Beach, Florida, or Rockport–Aransas Pass, Texas, far more uncomfortable than they would a day of the same temperature in Silver City, New Mexico, or Yuma, Arizona.

What about cold temperatures? Throughout the 1960s and 1970s, older adults shunned cold weather in favor of the hot and sunny beach climates of the Sun Belt. Now, many are discovering the benefits of seasonal change and some cold weather, particularly around the holiday season.

But cold weather can have an adverse effect on persons with heart or circulatory ailments. These diseases follow a seasonal pattern, with a peak of deaths occurring in January and February. The cooling of the extremities places greater stress on the heart as it tries to maintain a safe body temperature. Breathing very cold air can tax the heart-lung system, and some persons who have hardening of the coronary arteries may get chest pains when outdoors in a cold wind.

Cold weather can also increase blood pressure with adverse consequences for those with circulatory problems. Although polar weather inhibits the survival of respiratory germs, these microbes thrive in a damp, cloudy, cool climate and contribute to a high incidence of influenza, bronchitis, and colds.

As the body gets older, its circulatory system gets less effective. Add to this another natural consequence of aging—the decreased rate of metabolism that keeps the body warm—and you have explained older adults' needs for higher household temperatures. The expense of heating costs in a cool climate, therefore, may offset the appeal of seasonal changes and winter weather.

But despite the dangers of heat or cold extremes, sudden wide shifts of temperature in either direction constitute a threat to health. When the weather—and especially the temperature—changes suddenly and dramatically, the rates of cardiac arrest, respiratory distress, stroke, and other medical emergencies skyrocket.

Sudden atmospheric cooling can bring on attacks of asthma, bronchitis, and stroke. Heart attacks and associated symptoms are more frequent following these periods. Often, autumn changing-air masses produce these symptoms, particularly by the passage of a cold frontal system following a dropping barometer.

A sudden rise in the temperature may precipitate its own assortment of medical emergencies, among them heat stroke, heart attack, and stroke. Because the body recuperates during the night, the nighttime maximum air temperature is far more significant than the daytime maximum during a heat wave. A hot night prevents the body from reestablishing its thermal

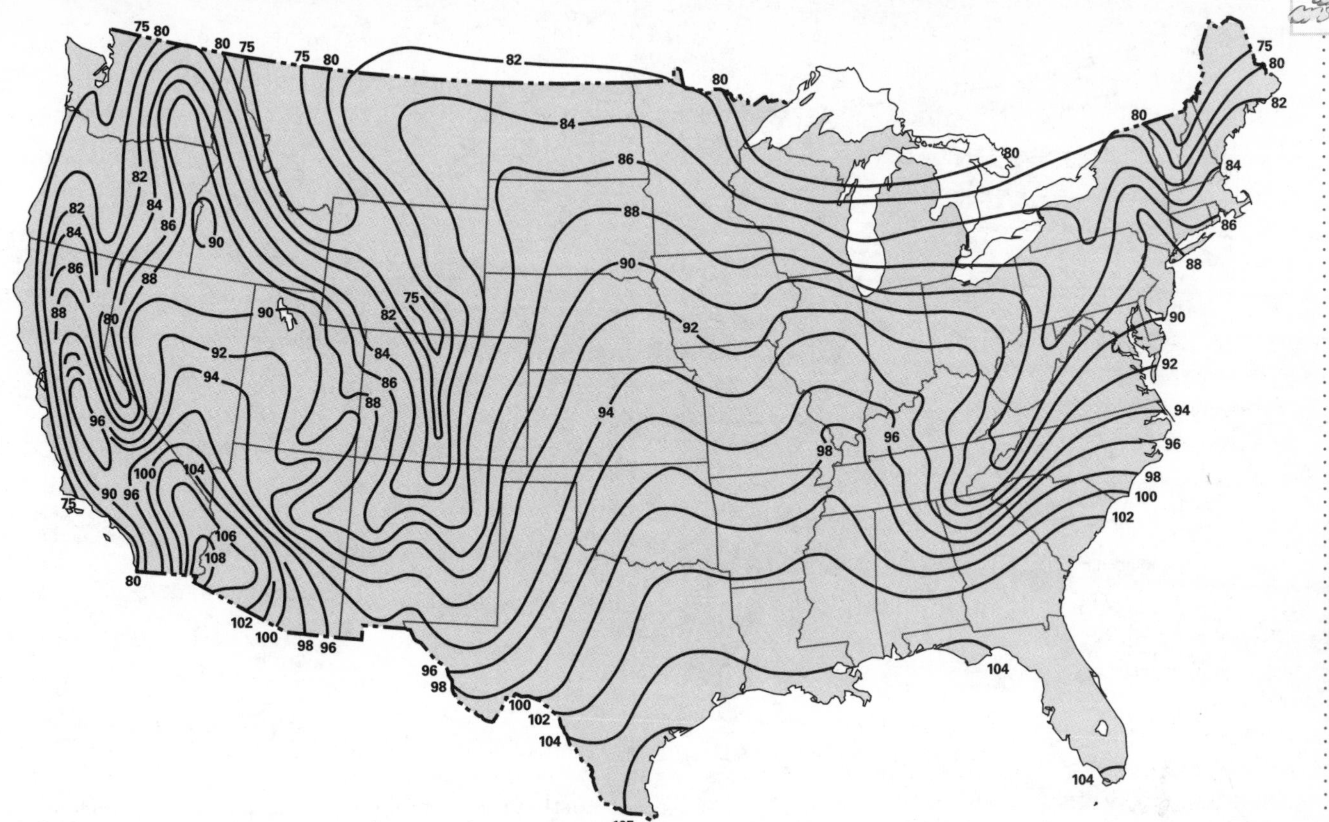

equilibrium and tends to lessen the amount of sleep a person gets, increasing fatigue. Hospital employees call these sudden temperature shifts, which cause so much discomfort and harm, "ambulance weather."

Barometric Pressure. Though most people may be unaware of the source of their discomfort, barometric pressure and its wide and rapid fluctuations are powerful influences on performance, comfort, and health. Pressure changes are felt more keenly by older adults, whose bodies are generally more sensitive to change.

Recalling weather stage 4, the rapid fall of pressure that signals the arrival of storms and advancing cold fronts can trigger episodes of asthma, heart disease, stroke, and pain in the joints. People with rheumatism or arthritis may suffer unduly if they live in places where pressure changes are continual and rapid. The map "Pressure Changes from Day to Day (February)" shows the regions with greatest and least pressure changes during an average day in February, when joint pain and other discomforts reach their peak.

As the map shows, the northern and eastern sections of the country experience the biggest swings, averaging a barometric change of .20 inch to .25 inch from one day to the next. In summer, when pressure changes are relatively small, the average change in these regions is approximately .10 inch. States in the southern latitudes, particularly Florida and southern California, show the least change, only about .10 inch in February and less than .05 inch in summer. Of course, these figures are averages; and along the Gulf and Atlantic coasts, large and rapid pressure changes are occasionally caused by hurricanes.

The map offers another reason why so many older adults choose Florida and the Gulf Coast. Additionally, due to the stabilizing and modifying effects that large bodies of water have on temperature and pressure, weather conditions by seacoasts are steadier than those of most inland, desert, or mountain locations.

Although the year-round climates found in Florida and the other Gulf states aren't as pleasant as they are hyped to be, subtropical climates—hot, humid, monotonous, and even wearying as they are to some—are just about perfect for people with severe rheumatoid joint pain or those who cannot tolerate sudden changes in the weather.

Pressure Changes from Day to Day (February)

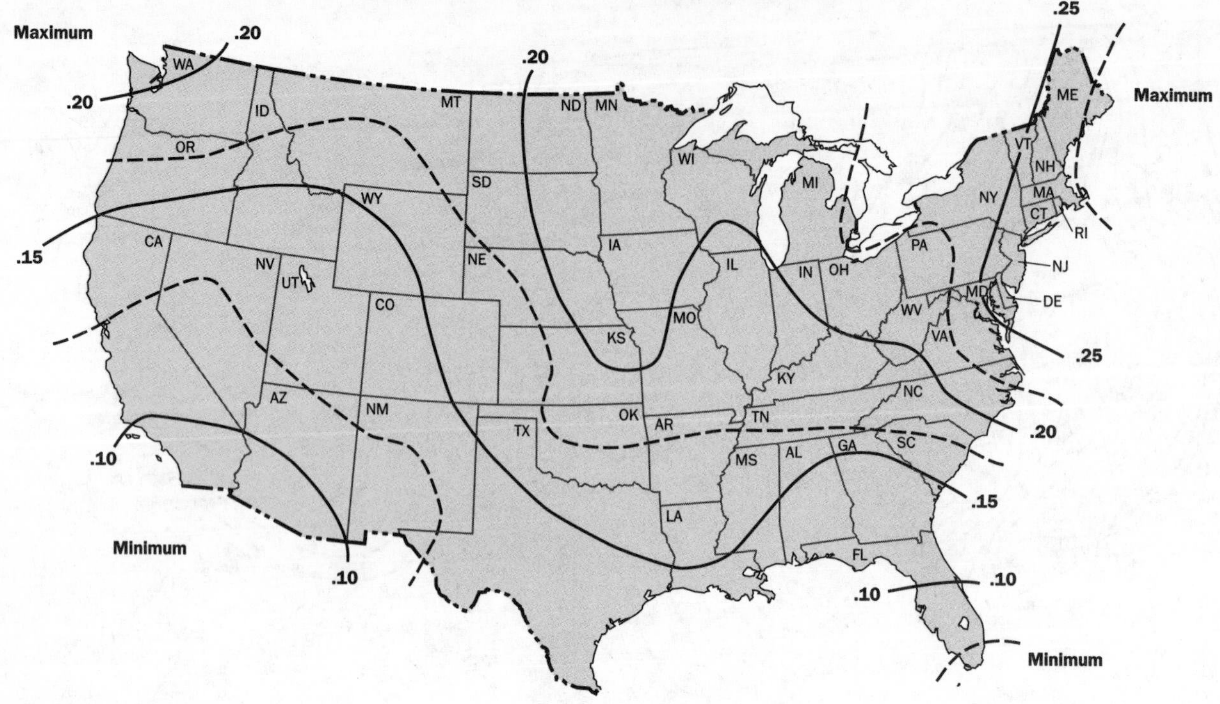

Questing for Relief

People with heart conditions should definitely avoid extreme heat and cold, rapid temperature variations, and wide and sudden pressure swings. This can rule out most interior regions as well as northerly ones, even those on coastal locations.

Recommended are places that have warm, mild, and steady weather. Mountains and high altitudes should be avoided on two counts: less oxygen and strain caused by steep grades. Best bets are southerly coastal locations where sea level, oxygen-rich air, and stable pressures and temperatures predominate most of the year.

Look along the coast of the Mid-Atlantic Metro Belt southward all the way around the Florida peninsula and westward along the Gulf. Also look along the southern third of the Pacific coastline.

Emphysema brings a completely different set of problems and solutions. In general, excessive dampness combined with cool or cold weather is harmful. This eliminates the Pacific Northwest, New England, and the North Woods. Southerly coastal locations are better, but the air is perhaps still too damp. Seek out warm, sunny, and dry climates such as those found in Arizona, New Mexico, Utah, Nevada, and the interior valleys of California. Remember to avoid high elevations.

Asthma is a complex disorder not completely understood. While it is believed to be an autoimmune disorder similar to allergies, it may be precipitated or worsened by different things in different individuals. Your wisest course is to consult medical specialists first to determine the specific cause of your attacks. Asthmatics seem to do best in the pollen free, dry, warm air found in the Desert Southwest. Because the air on the desert floor can be dusty, seeking a moderate altitude there may be beneficial.

Tuberculosis, recently considered a waning disease, is on the rise. It generally strikes people who have weakened resistance to infection, making older adults more susceptible than the rest of the population. Treatment is multifaceted, but an area that is mild, dry, sunny, and has clear air helps a great deal.

Mountain locations have always been popular and can provide relief if the altitude isn't excessive. Because dampness isn't recommended, the dry, sunny places in the southern Rockies are preferable to locations in the Southern Highlands. Ocean breezes are thought to be beneficial, too, and may be better for people who cannot tolerate the more rugged climate of the interior mountains. Hawaii or the southern California Coast is ideal.

For people with rheumatic pains and discomfort in amputated limbs or in old scar tissue, the warm and steady climates of the subtropics are perfect. Here the surrounding water keeps temperatures and pressures from shifting quickly, and the prevailing warmth is soothing. It would be hard to miss with any seafront location from Myrtle Beach, South Carolina, south to the Florida Keys, around and up the west coast of the Florida peninsula, westward along the Gulf and down all the way to the mouth of the Rio Grande.

Life at the Top

Mountain resorts usually got their start as 19th-century health retreats when "night air" and "bad air" were seen as causes for chronic respiratory diseases. The antidote prescribed was "pine air" and a high altitude.

While mountain air tends to be clear and relatively free from pollutants, it also contains less oxygen. A rapid change to a high altitude is risky for people with heart diseases and arteriosclerosis. If you suffer from asthma, emphysema, or anemia, you should consult local physicians before moving to any place more than 2,000 feet above sea level. Even if all indications point to a positive reaction, it would be wise to take up residence for at least several months before making a permanent move.

Since altitude puts a certain amount of stress on the body's circulatory system and lungs, becoming acclimated to high places leads to good health. A higher altitude accelerates respiration and increases the lung capacity, strengthens the heart, increases the metabolic rate, and boosts the number and proportion of red blood cells.

In the United States, the highest town with a post office is Climax, Colorado. At 11,350 feet, Climax is beyond the comfort range of many older adults. Up here, a 3-minute egg takes 7 minutes to boil, corn on the cob needs to be on the fire 45 minutes, and home-brewed beer matures in half the expected time. Yet many of the 4,000 residents love it. The incidence of infection is amazingly low, and insects are practically unknown. In the East, the highest town of any size is Highlands, North Carolina, in the Great Smoky Mountains. Though less than half as high as Climax, Highlands and the neighboring towns offer the cool, clear air and invigorating climate that has long drawn people to the mountains.

MILE HIGH PLACES

The 17 places below are all over 1 mile in elevation in the Rockies. In the East, the highest spot profiled in these pages is Boone–Blowing Rock, NC. It sits up in the Blue Ridge Mountains at 3,266 feet.

PLACE	ELEVATION
Pagosa Springs, CO	7,105 feet
Salida, CO	7,036 feet
Flagstaff, AZ	7,000 feet
Taos, NM	6,983 feet
Park City, UT	6,970 feet
Santa Fe, NM	6,947 feet
Ruidoso, NM	6,641 feet
Las Vegas, NM	6,600 feet
Durango, CO	6,523 feet
Jackson Hole, WY	6,234 feet
Colorado Springs, CO	6,008 feet
Bozeman, MT	5,950 feet
Silver City, NM	5,851 feet
Cedar City, UT	5,834 feet
Ketchum–Sun Valley, ID	5,821 feet
Montrose, CO	5,801 feet
Prescott–Prescott Valley, AZ	5,368 feet

Source: U.S. Geological Survey.

NATURAL HAZARDS

Risk management firms whose clients include the insurance industry now rate areas as small as a zip code for the damage from future hurricanes, tornadoes, and earthquakes. These natural hazards follow definite geographic patterns, and some places are at greater risk than others.

The Sun Belt Is Also a Storm Belt

Most severe storms occur in the southern half of the nation. For this reason, you might say the Sun Belt is also a storm belt.

Thunderstorms and Lightning. Thunderstorms are common and don't usually cause death. But lightning kills 200 Americans a year. The most common natural danger, at any given moment there are about 2,000 thunderstorms in progress around the globe. In the time it takes you to read this paragraph, lightning will have struck 700 times.

Florida, the "Sunshine State," is actually the country's stormiest state, with three times as much thunder and lightning as any other. California, Oregon, and Washington are the three most storm-free

Florida's Stormy Coast

The minimum requirement for the recording of a thunderstorm is the presence of a single storm cell. On a bad day in summer, locations on Florida's west coast can record three or four in a single afternoon.

PLACE	STORMS PER YEAR
Bradenton, FL	93
Fort Myers–Cape Coral, FL	93
Naples, FL	93
Port Charlotte, FL	93
Largo, FL	86
New Port Richey, FL	86
Sarasota, FL	86
Thomasville, GA	83
Inverness, FL	82
Kissimmee–St. Cloud, FL	82
Lakeland–Winter Haven, FL	82
Leesburg–Mount Dora, FL	82
Ocala, FL	82
Sebring–Avon Park, FL	82
Gainesville, FL	81

Source: NOAA, Local Climatological Data. Some of the above figures come from the nearest "First Order" station.

states. In a typical year, coastal California locations average between two and five thunderstorm episodes. Most American locations average between 35 and 50. Florida's Gulf Coast averages 90.

The Place Profiles earlier in this chapter tell how many thunderstorm days each place can expect in an average year. The southeastern quadrant of our country generally receives more rain and thunderstorms than the rest, although the thunderstorms of the Great Plains are awesome spectacles.

Tornadoes. While they aren't nearly as large or long-lived as hurricanes and release much less force, tornadoes have more killing power concentrated in a small area than any other storm. For absolute ferocity and wind speed, a tornado hasn't a rival.

The hallmark of this vicious inland storm is the huge funnel cloud that sweeps and bounces along the ground, destroying buildings, sweeping up cars, trains, livestock, and trees, and sucking them up hundreds of feet into the whirling vortex. Wind speeds close to 300 miles per hour have been recorded.

Although no one can tell for certain just where particular tornadoes might touch down, their season, origin, and direction of travel are predictable using decades of records. Tornado season reaches its peak in late spring and early summer. After forming in the intense heat and rising air of the plains, these storms proceed toward the northeast at speeds averaging 25 to 40 miles per hour. Most tornadoes do not last long or travel far. Half of all tornadoes reported travel less than 5 miles on the ground; a rare few have been tracked for more than 200 miles.

Nearly one-third of all twisters ever reported in the United States touched down somewhere in Kansas, Oklahoma, and Texas. Indeed, Tornado Alley is an area 150 miles on either side of a line drawn from Abilene, Texas, to Omaha, Nebraska. Among retirement spots, the lake locations in Oklahoma and Missouri, any location in Texas or Arkansas, and even spots in Kentucky and Tennessee have a high potential for tornado damage and danger. The map, "Tornado and Hurricane Risk Areas," shows the nation's danger areas for these natural hazards.

Hurricanes. On the North Carolina coast from the Brunswick Islands up to the Outer Banks in September of 1996, blue hurricane evacuation markers along the back routes directed travelers to inland safety from Fran, a category 3 hurricane.

Giant tropical cyclonic storms that start at sea, hurricanes are unmatched for sheer power over a very large area. They last for days, measure hundreds of miles across, and release tremendous energy in the form of high winds, torrential rains, lightning, and tidal surges. They usually occur in late summer and fall, and strike the Gulf states and southern segments of the Atlantic coast. Like thunderstorms, hurricanes are much less frequent and less severe on the Pacific Coast.

Hurricanes usually originate in the tropical waters of the Atlantic Ocean. They occur toward summer's end because it takes that long for the water temperature and evaporation rate to rise sufficiently to begin the cyclonic, counterclockwise rotation of a wind system around a low-pressure system. When the winds are less than 39 miles per hour, the cyclone becomes a tropical depression. When winds speed up to between 39 and 74 miles per hour, the depression becomes a tropical storm. When the winds top 74 miles per hour, the storm becomes a hurricane.

Often the greatest danger and destruction from hurricanes aren't winds but tidal surges that sweep ashore with seas 15 feet or more higher than normal high tides. Although Florida and the southern coasts are most vulnerable to hurricanes, low-lying locations as far north as Cape Cod and the Maine coast aren't invulnerable. The map, "Tornado and Hurricane Risk

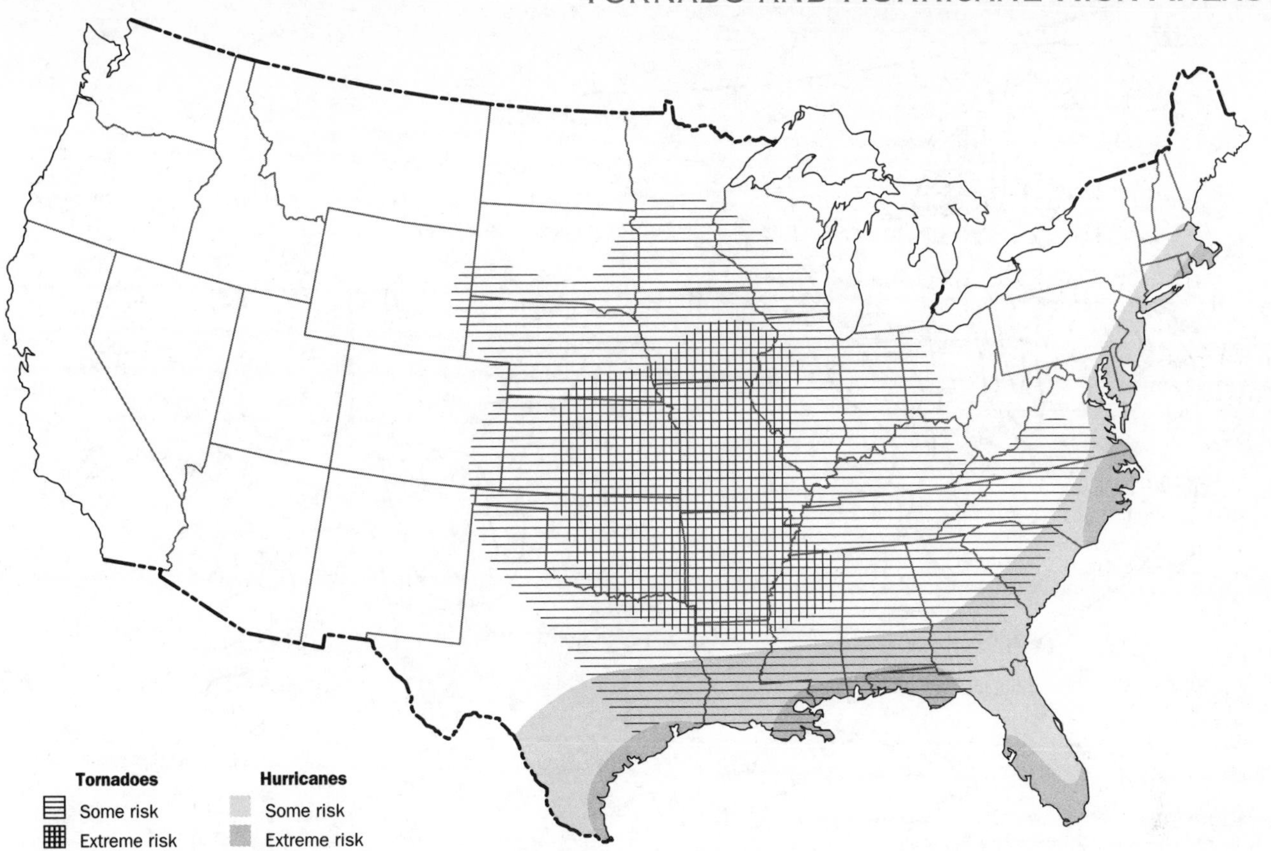

Areas," shows the nation's danger areas for these natural hazards.

Earthquake Risks

California and the Pacific Northwest may be relatively free of the thunderstorms, tornadoes, and hurricanes that buffet other parts of the country. But these states are in the area most prone to earthquake damage. A glance at the map, "Earthquake Hazard Zones," which predicts not only the probability of earthquakes but also their severity, confirms this.

All retirement places in California, Nevada, and Utah have the potential for substantial earthquake damage. Locations in Oregon are relatively safe, but the Puget Sound area of Washington has experienced three major shocks in the past 35 years. Portions of Montana and Idaho also are vulnerable.

Other pockets of earthquake risk may surprise you. In New Mexico, Albuquerque is situated in a danger area, and so is Silver City. The resorts on the South Carolina and Georgia coasts sit in the middle of a quake-sensitive zone that was the site of the 1886 Charleston quake, the strongest ever measured east of the Mississippi. The entire New England region shares a danger roughly comparable to this area. Boston has suffered a severe quake and remains prone today. A series of quakes occurred in southeastern Missouri in 1811–12, changing the course of the Mississippi River and creating a major lake. There is still some risk in this area, which includes retirement places in western Kentucky and Tennessee and part of the Ozarks.

Can Anyone Win?

After studying the maps, you may come to the dismal conclusion that you cannot win: where one natural disaster area stops, another begins. Some areas, like the coasts of South Carolina and Georgia, appear to possess a triple-whammy combination of earthquake, tornado, and hurricane hazards.

Studying the map more closely, you might begin to detect retirement areas that seem safer than others. One such area is the Pacific Northwest, with the exception of the significant earthquake risk around Puget Sound. Parts of Arizona, Utah, and New Mexico, too, are relatively free from disaster risk. The southern Appalachians, despite a moderate earthquake risk, do not experience many storms due to the protection of the mountains. But some parts of that

EARTHQUAKE HAZARD ZONES

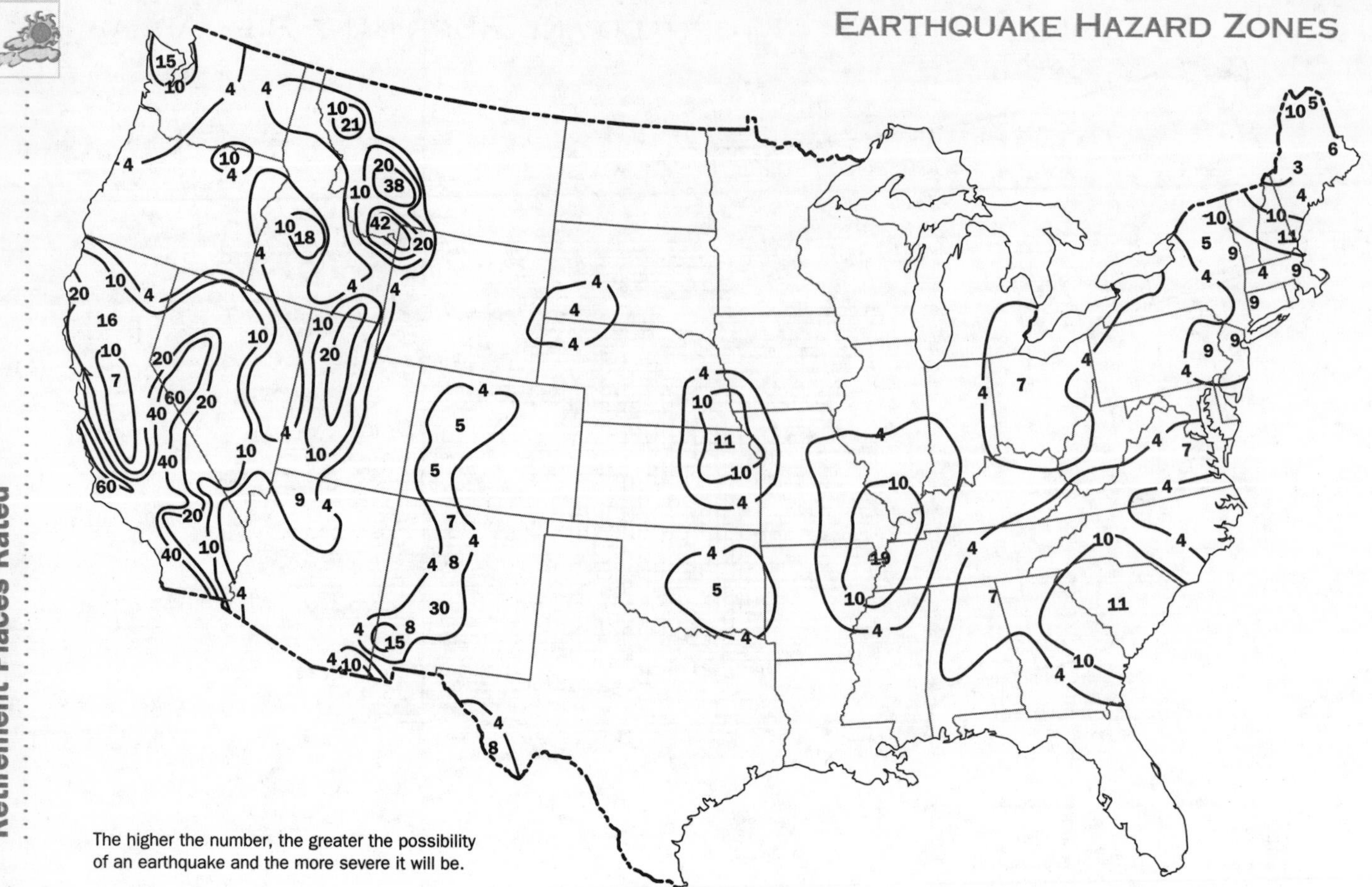

The higher the number, the greater the possibility of an earthquake and the more severe it will be.

region are flood-prone. And moderate earthquake risk seems almost unavoidable anywhere but the frigid north central plains or the steamy, tornado-ridden flatlands of Texas and the Gulf states.

So, as with most things in life, when it comes to avoiding natural disasters, you can only pay your money and take your chances.

HAY FEVER SUFFERERS, TAKE NOTE

It does not come from hay nor does it cause a fever, but that's little consolation to the 18 million Americans afflicted. Hay fever is an allergic reaction of the eyes, nose, or throat to certain airborne particles. These particles may be any pollen from seed-bearing trees, grasses, and weeds, or spores from certain molds. The term originated in Britain when people assumed its fever-like symptoms had something to do with the fall haying.

Most persons might think that once they're into adulthood, they already know whether they have hay fever. But if you move, would you suddenly develop a baffling runny nose and minor sore throat? Allergy problems aren't always alleviated by relocation, and sometimes a new allergen, absent where you used to live, can turn up to cause you problems.

In the Arctic, because of low temperature, poor soil, and small and primitive vegetation, nobody suffers from it. In the tropics and subtropics, because the plants are generally flowered and produce pollen so heavy it cannot become airborne, few complain of it.

Live in a temperate region and you'll find irritating pollen. The best market for over-the-counter antihistamines in America is the Heartland where grasses and trees without flowers predominate. Farming disrupts the soil here, encouraging the growth of weeds (especially the most devilish of them all, ragweed). It extends from the Rockies to the Appalachian chain, and from the Canadian border down to the mid-South.

Alas, nowhere in this country except Alaska and the southern half of Florida will you entirely escape. It's simply a question of degree. Some places that were once havens for asthmatics and hay fever sufferers aren't any longer. Examples include many of the fast-growing areas of the Desert Southwest. In the 1950s, Tucson was virtually free of ragweed pollen. Its desert location prevented the growth of weeds, grasses, and trees that cause hay fever. As more and more people moved into the area, more trees were planted and lawns seeded. The result? A pollen index that's still good but not nearly as good as it used to be.

Personal Safety

In Chapel Hill, North Carolina, the cops are worried about gun thefts in town and in nearby Carrboro. Several sporting goods shops have been hit, and in many home burglaries, the take includes a rifle or handgun. Everyone notes the irony: houses are broken into for the guns that homeowners bought to protect themselves from a rash of break-ins. The rising spiral means more guns on the street.

In Barnstable District Court on Cape Cod one spring day, two dozen persons are arraigned for offenses that wouldn't open the eyes of a reporter on the *Miami Herald* police beat: possession of marijuana and conspiracy to violate controlled substance laws, operating under the influence and speeding, breaking and entering with intent to commit a felony, giving a false name to a police officer, and assault and battery.

In a coffee shop up in Wisconsin's Door County peninsula, the talk one winter morning concerns a condo break-in. Missing are a shopping bag of Pampers and a baby's crib. Left behind are a state-of-the-art stereo system, Waterford crystal, the silver, and a closet full of high-fashion skiwear. Maybe we should all start locking our doors, the locals in the coffee shop agree.

Chapel Hill does have a modest crime problem, Door County has none, and Cape Cod hasn't much of one until the summer tourists come. Indeed, the odds of your being a crime victim in 3 out of 4 of the 203 places profiled in *Retirement Places Rated* are below the national average.

Check the police log printed in the newspapers of some places or the website of the local police department (see the upcoming sidebar, "E-Blotters") and you'll wonder whether anything interesting goes on there at all. A drunk-and-disorderly, a car break-in, a bar fight that spills out into the parking lot, a graffiti artist loose downtown, a husband-wife donnybrook—all are just occasional items hidden among the traffic accidents, animal complaints, and fishing violations.

Some places seem so safe you couldn't pay someone to punch you. Others, by comparison, are just plain dangerous. If you decide on settling in rural Brown County, Indiana, the rough odds of your being involved in a violent crime are 1 in 1,149. Should you settle in Myrtle Beach, South Carolina, the chances rise to 1 in 95, or slightly better than being injured in your own home. One could say that life along South Carolina's Grand Strand is more than 12 times more dangerous than it is in the rolling limestone belt in the south-central part of Indiana.

EVERYONE'S A VICTIM

But quoting raw odds distorts the crime picture. In spite of the popular idea that older persons are the preferred targets of crooks, you are more likely to have your pocket picked or your purse snatched than you are of being victimized by all other crimes. So why the need for a chapter on personal safety if your retirement years are statistically safer than all the years preceding?

The simple answer is that you are a different kind of crime victim whenever you have to trim back shrubbery along your home's foundation to limit a thief's potential hiding places, or have to get rid of the mailbox and install a mail slot in your front door, or have to check your car's door locks when driving down a darkened avenue, or have to keep feeling for your wallet at street festivals, or have to use only empty elevators, or have to stay indoors evenings more than you really care to. In some places, such tactics are advised; in others, they are merely prudent; and in still others, they may not be necessary at all.

CRIME IN BRIEF

Crime isn't declining everywhere. In 27 retirement places—many having community policing, professional cops, and tough judges—lawbreaking still rose at least 15 percent over the last 5 years.

Consider local crime rates carefully. Usually they are quoted in promotion brochures or on websites as a single number and then only if that number is under the national average. But most offenses are either against property or against people. The latter, designated *violent crimes,* are much more serious.

Consider, too, that police in some kinds of places are busier than in others. Sun Belt resorts such as Daytona Beach, Florida, and Myrtle Beach, South Carolina, and even Branson in the Missouri Ozarks, see tens of thousands of visitors year-round and have serious *property crime* problems. Places along the notorious "drug highways" of I-5, I-10, I-75, and I-95 are sometimes caught in the drug-trafficking (and occasional gun) crossfire. Places with large military bases see a higher rate of aggravated assaults.

There are defensive tactics older adults can use to avoid being a crime victim, the best of which are detailed in the *Et Cetera* section at the end of this chapter. Ultimately, a prudent selection of neighborhoods makes all the difference. The local police department's Community Relations officer can help by identifying dangerous areas for you. He or she can also do a quick security check of your new home.

E-BLOTTERS

The local newspaper isn't the only source of information on criminal activity, nor even the best. The facts now come directly from 24-hour crime reports on the police department's website.

Consider three sample items that recently appeared on police blotters from around the country in the investigating officer's own words:

Shoplifting in Myrtle Beach, South Carolina: "A 48-year-old woman was arrested after she put a pair of Tommy Hilfiger overalls under her dress at Belk at Myrtle Square Mall. As she ran out of the store, the overalls fell onto the floor. Police arrested her."

Burglary in Santa Fe, New Mexico: "Someone broke into a gray 1989 Saab between 3 p.m. Monday and midnight Tuesday on the 2600 block of Cerrillos Road. A Social Security card and a Kenwood stereo were reported stolen."

Assault in Annapolis, Maryland: "Officers responded to an assault report at a restaurant and found an adult male victim suffering from a cut on his left ear. The victim told the officers that his companion threw a baked potato that struck a nearby adult male, staining his shirt. They got into a physical fight with blows being exchanged."

To find these and similar accounts, simply do an Internet search for your city's name with the term "police department" before or after the city's name. Electronic crime blotters are the most popular part of the police department's website. Some departments even e-mail the 24-hour reports free of charge to subscribers throughout the world.

CRIME RISK: SEVERAL CONNECTIONS

Why some places are safer than others is a subject certain to get politicians, police, and citizens into arguments. For all the debate, experts recognize several factors.

Climate has a striking connection with lawbreaking. Police respond to more disturbance calls on the day after summer temperatures are highest than on any other days of the year. The numbers of burglaries, vandalisms, and rapes increase when ambient temperatures are 85°F.

Indeed, in the Sun Belt and in the Frost Belt, cops and criminals are busiest throughout July and August when all crimes except robbery are the likeliest to happen. Since people spend more time outdoors during these months, they are more exposed. Homes, too, are more unprotected during this time of year because they are left with open windows and unlocked doors. Robbery is the cold-weather exception. It is highest in

December when shoppers and retail stores doing brisk holiday business make tempting targets.

Time of day and the ***photoperiod***, or length of the day, are two other factors. After sundown is the time most cars are stolen, most persons and businesses are robbed, most persons are assaulted, and most thefts are committed. Burglaries, purse-snatchings, and pocket-pickings, on the other hand, happen more often during daylight hours. Some police dispatchers contend that the number of daylight minutes is a predictor of the kind of 911 calls they handle.

Population size is closely tied to crime rates. Safer places—Fredericksburg in the Texas Hill Country and the Leelanau Peninsula in northern Michigan, for instance—are rural. More dangerous places are urban. There are exceptions, certainly. Mariposa, California, has a crime rate resembling that of Tucson, Arizona.

Even local ***traffic*** plays a role. The ease with which a criminal can drive off down the street, escape onto an arterial road, and disappear among commuters on the interstate is an encouragement. One reason places on islands and peninsulas have lower crime rates is that few crooks are dumb enough to commit robberies if their only escape is over a long bridge or causeway.

Age and ***sex*** figure into the equation. Some 40 million persons in this country have arrest records for misdeeds other than traffic violations. The proportion of suspects who are male is much higher than their proportion in the general population. Half the persons picked up by police for violent and property crimes are under 20 years of age and four-fifths are male. None of this should be taken to mean that persons hold up convenience stores, boost Chevrolet Camaros, or duke it out in disco parking lots because they are young and male, but these characteristics are associated with other factors in crime.

The ***economy*** also plays a role. In most places, each time the unemployment rate goes up, the police make more arrests. But joblessness and loss of income won't automatically make a place unsafe. Many of the safer places in this book are poorer than average and suffer job losses during business slumps. More affluent areas, given similar sets of circumstances, aren't nearly as safe as they seem: rich offenders are arrested less often than poor ones, especially on suspicion. Once arrested, they are convicted with less frequency. This is especially true in juvenile cases involving thefts and break-ins.

Crime Compared with Other Events in Life

The rates of some violent crimes are higher than those of other harmful life events. For example, the risk of being a victim of violent crime is higher than the risk of divorce, death from cancer, or injury or death from a fire. Anyone over 15 years old runs a greater risk of being a violent crime victim, with or without injury, than being hurt in a traffic accident. Still, a person is much more likely to die from natural causes than from being a victim of crime. In the following table, so-called violent crimes are in bold.

EVENT	RATE PER 1,000 ADULTS
Accidental injury, all circumstances	290
Accidental injury at home	105
Personal Theft	**82**
Accidental injury at work	68
Accidental injury in an automobile	23
Divorce	23
Death, all causes	11
Aggravated Assault	**9**
Death of a spouse	9
Robbery	**7**
Heart disease death	4
Cancer death	2
Accidental death, all circumstances	0.5
Pneumonia/influenza death	0.3
Automobile accidental death	0.2
Suicide	0.2
Injury from fire	0.1
Murder	**0.1**
Death from fire	0.003

Source: Bureau of Justice Statistics, Report to the Nation on Crime and Justice.

Transience affects crime rates. A warning sign for crooks is a stable neighborhood where people know one another and look out for one another's safety and property no matter how many police cruise the area. High neighborhood turnover leading to more strangers living next to each other leads to higher crime rates. Resort areas that draw transients—Branson, Missouri, Myrtle Beach, South Carolina, or Pensacola, Florida, for instance—have serious crime problems. When visitors are added to the year-round residents, the higher population betters the odds that victim and crook will meet.

Police strength, too, is linked to the local crime rate. In Manhattan, there are 1,300 police officers per square mile; in most rural counties, there are between 1 and 3 sworn uniformed officers for every 1,000 residents. In the sparsely settled Montana Rockies and parts of the California desert well east of Los Angeles, however, state police need an average of 30 minutes or more to respond to calls.

It's natural to think that personal safety in a place rises or falls in proportion to the size of the local police force, but it just isn't so. Police enforce traffic codes, investigate accidents, find lost children, and calm down fighting spouses. They battle crime, too, but most of what they do is after the fact. They respond to complaints; they interview victims and fill out reports; they follow up on tips; and they collar suspects and bring them to book. A large number of police per capita, however, is usually an indication of a high-crime area rather than an area where crime is being foiled.

Other factors related to criminal activity include the practices of local prosecutors, judges, juries, and parole boards; the attitudes of the community toward crime; and the willingness of ordinary citizens to report crime.

CRIME INDEXES

Every year, some 11,000 police departments send figures of the number of crimes reported in their cities and towns to the FBI in Washington. Because of their seriousness, frequency, and probability of being reported, eight crimes make up the FBI's Crime Index. Four are classified as "violent" crimes; the other four are "property" crimes.

Violent Crime

It seemed too good to be true: throughout the 1990s, violent crime rates dropped to their lowest level in a generation. Police chiefs and mayors celebrated in front of television cameras and declared that strategies such as community policing, zero tolerance, reclaiming public spaces, rapid deployment, accurate intelligence, and relentless follow-up were working. In most regions of the country, for the rest of the decade and into the new millennium, each year was safer than the one before.

FLORIDA'S "NOT SO GUILTY" PLEA

In 1931, while researching his famous piece "The Worst American State," H.L. Mencken found that the best source of data on causes of death was the life insurance industry, and that when it came to homicide, Florida had the highest rate.

After 7 decades, not much has changed. Most large cities in Florida rank near the bottom in personal safety. Of all the states, Florida has the highest rates for violent crime and for property crime. The state is the setting for the best-selling crime fiction of Edna Buchanan, Carl Hiaasen, Elmore Leonard, and John D. MacDonald.

Miami, the state's best-known city, was the tropical backdrop for a bloody Friday-night television series in the early 1980s in which hip undercover narcs and drug lords brandished locally made TEC-9 machine pistols at each other. Today, tour buses leave the Dade Cultural Center for sightseeing excursions to the sites of Gianni Versace's murder, the FDR assassination attempt, the Candy Mossler murder, and the Barbara Mackle kidnapping.

All of the above may not be fair to the Sunshine State. Crime rates are figured per 100,000 year-round residents. But Florida draws millions of visitors who stay for a good part of the year. A truer way to measure crime rates, notes Florida's Department of Law Enforcement, would be to add a place's average daily number of tourists to its number of year-round residents, then determine the rate. The results would produce dramatically lower crime rates and improve the state's national image.

But 2001 ended the optimism. That year, the rates for major crimes shot up. Some criminologists predicted that parolees returning to the streets from their convictions during the crack-cocaine epidemic, plus surging numbers of teenagers (historically, the age group likeliest to commit crime) and joblessness would mark the end of good news for some time to come.

Of all criminal offenses, ***murder*** is the likeliest to be reported and has the highest rate of charges being brought. Half of all murdered persons knew their killers, perhaps even sat across from them at the breakfast table the morning of the crime or loaned them money the week before. Among the retirement places profiled in this book, Savannah, Georgia, has the highest murder rate. Typical of southern cities, killings here are often the result of drug deals gone bad or new slights and old scores settled with a gun or knife.

Victims and killers around the country are becoming less connected, however. One murder in eight involves a victim and a stranger, one in twenty a juvenile gang killing. Based on the number of unsolved killings each year and an increase in slayings involving strangers, the FBI estimates at least 25 serial killers are on the loose.

Rape, too, frequently involves acquainted victims and aggressors. It is the most under-reported of crimes and also has the highest proportion of "unfounded" complaints. Rape victims are always female by current crime-reporting standards.

Thanks to branch bank and convenience store holdups as well as attempted stickups in nightclub parking lots, the ***robbery*** rate in Myrtle Beach, South Carolina, is four times that of the typical retirement place profiled in *Retirement Places Rated.* It is the one violent crime that most often involves more than one criminal, and the one committed less out of impulsive anger than as a way of making a living. It differs from common theft because it involves force or threat, thereby placing the victim in fear.

Assault is simply an attempt, successful or not, to injure another person. Its rate is highest in August and lowest in February, higher in the West than in other parts of the country, and higher in areas with resort or military economies. A high rate of assault, like that in Palmer–Wasilla, Alaska, more often indicates strictly enforced domestic-abuse laws than it does a bar fight.

Property Crime

Branson, Missouri, isn't just home to semi-retired singers and comedians and their dinner theaters. The town has the highest burglary rate among the 203 retirement places profiled here.

Burglary can be either forcible entry, unlawful entry where no force is used, or attempted forcible entry—all to commit a felony or theft. Most burglaries, say professional crooks in prison, are planned for hours and pulled off in minutes. The typical target is the home or apartment; in Branson, it's the parked car. Nearly half of the incidents involve simply walking in rather than breaking in. The typical time is between 9:00 and 11:00 a.m. or between 1:00 and 3:00 p.m. when you're least likely to be inside.

Safer Versus More Dangerous Places

A look at the crime rates in the "Place Profiles" later in this chapter makes one thing stand out. Whether speaking of violent crimes (which account for just 12 percent of lawbreaking) or property crimes, small, rural places outside the Sun Belt can surpass not only larger resorts but also the country itself by a wide margin.

Property Crime

WORST	RATE
Branson, MO	16,817
Kingman, AZ	9,118
Panama City, FL	8,779
Conway, SC	8,541
Myrtle Beach, SC	8,541

BEST	RATE
Norfork Lake, AR	1,197
Northern Neck, VA	1,333
Smith Mountain Lake, VA	1,340
Leelanau Peninsula, MI	1,416
Brown County, IN	1,417

Note: The property crime rate is the sum of rates for burglary, theft, and auto theft. The U.S. average is 4,790.

Violent Crime

WORST	RATE
Las Vegas, NM	1,843
Annapolis, MD	1,330
Gainesville, FL	1,226
Branson, MO	1,200
Mariposa, CA	1,123

BEST	RATE
Door Peninsula, WI	34
San Juan Islands, WA	63
Camden, ME	83
Woodstock, VT	83
Brown County, IN	86

Note: The violent crime rate is the sum of rates for murder, rape, robbery, and aggravated assault. The U.S. average is 712.

Larceny-theft, after drunk driving and drug offenses, is the most common crime in North America. Skipping out of a self-serve gas station is one example.

Shoplifting a Russian sable coat is another. Except for purse snatches and picked pockets, in almost all of the larceny-theft cases, the victim never sees the offender.

Auto theft, it's been said, is a victimless crime because you get over your loss with a check from the insurance company. The typical incident, peaking in the summer during school recess, involves an unlocked car in a parking lot at a shopping mall, hospital, discount store, or movie theater. In the Phoenix suburbs of Mesa and Scottsdale and in larger cities along Interstate 10 in the California desert, stealing cars is an underground art. Along the Rio Grande in southernmost Texas, eight of ten cars stolen in McAllen and Brownsville are driven over international bridges to Mexico, often before the victims realize their cars are gone.

Arson was added to the Crime Index in 1979 following a congressional mandate. It includes any willful or malicious burning or attempt to burn, with or without the intent to defraud, a building or a vehicle or personal property of someone else. It doesn't include fires of suspicious or unknown origin.

Caveats

Crime rates are derived from the number of offenses actually reported to local police. But more than 60 percent of all crime goes *unreported,* according to victim surveys, and that percentage varies from one place to another.

Because victims often believe it futile to file complaints, many crimes never become known. This affects the accuracy of the Crime Index. Even if a complaint is filed, the investigating officer's definition of the crime may affect the numbers. A snatched purse, for instance, is either a robbery or a larceny depending on the jurisdiction. Likewise, a slap in the face is either an aggravated or simple assault depending on motive.

Moreover, some police departments have either padded the figures to oust a judge considered soft on crime or to persuade the city council to increase the department's budget, or they fudged the number of crimes to create an image of effective law enforcement.

In some rural areas, too, car thefts and parking-lot fights growing out of teenage high jinks aren't added to the statistics. Wise sheriffs punish the offenders informally with a night in jail, restitution, and some community service.

It's important to distinguish between the *incidence* of crime and the crime *rate.* Incidence is simply how many crimes are reported in a given place. The more people living in a place, the greater the crime incidence.

Police in greater Tucson, Arizona, log 5,500 violent crimes a year. Far to the east, their counterparts in Gainesville, Florida, investigate 2,000. Is Tucson more dangerous than Gainesville? Hardly. Tucson's violent crime rate per 100,000 residents is 660; Gainesville's is 961. While Tucson is safer than Gainesville, neither one has a violent crime rate below the national average—560.

SCORING: PERSONAL SAFETY

The one crime that cops file the most reports on is theft: a stolen bike, a necklace missing from a jewelry retailer's display case, hubcaps disappearing from a used-car lot, a customer skipping out of a fast-food restaurant. Yet these heists are counted as heavily as homicides to determine crime rates. When it comes to comparing places, this method doesn't show relative danger.

A more realistic way to grade for personal safety is simple: For each place, *Retirement Places Rated* averages the rates for violent and property crimes for the latest 5-year period, but since property crimes are much less serious than crimes against people, they get one-tenth the weight of violent crimes. Note: although arson is a property crime, arson figures aren't included in the scoring because they aren't available for many retirement places. Each place's score begins with the addition of two factors:

1. **Violent crime rate.** The rates for murder, robbery, and aggravated assault are added together.
2. **Property crime rate.** The rates for burglary, theft, and auto theft are totaled, and the result is divided by 10.

This sum is then scaled against a standard where the average for all 203 places is set at 50. Wimberley, in the Texas Hill Country, with a score of 50, is the typical retirement place for relative freedom from crime.

Places with *lower* crime rates than the average earn scores *greater* than 50. Norfork Lake, in the Arkansas Ozarks, gets a perfect 100 score.

Places with *higher* crime rates than average get scores *lower* than 50. While not as crime-ridden as other locations in the United States, Branson, Missouri, does have a shockingly high property crime rate—the main reason why the resort in the Missouri Ozarks earns the worst score, 0.

SCORING EXAMPLES

A New England college town, a Texas college town, and a spa in the Arkansas Ouachitas demonstrate the scoring method for crime.

Northampton–Amherst, Massachusetts (Score: 78.8)

If higher crime rates go with younger populations, Northampton–Amherst is certainly an exception to that rule. One of every four people here is a student at the Five Colleges—Amherst, Hampshire, Mount Holyoke, Smith, and the University of Massachusetts. Yet the area sees crime rates far below the national average. Moreover, crime rates that fell throughout the 1980s continued to fall throughout the 1990s.

Among the 3,500 crimes reported to the police in a typical year, one-third involves theft. Comparing Northampton–Amherst's violent crime rate (287) and one-tenth its property crime rate (235) against the average for all retirement places produces a score of 78.8.

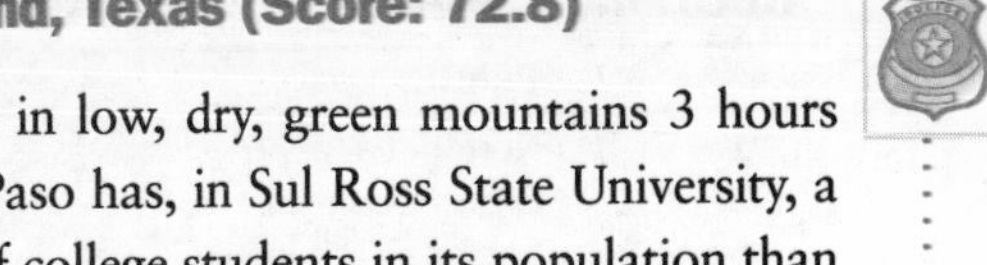

Alpine–Big Bend, Texas (Score: 72.8)

This small place in low, dry, green mountains 3 hours southeast of El Paso has, in Sul Ross State University, a higher portion of college students in its population than Northampton–Amherst. The area experiences few stick-ups and break-ins, and the rate for car theft is a tiny fraction of the national average. Escape only leads out into empty Chihuahua Desert ranching country, where you may outrun a Ford Crown Victoria police cruiser but you won't outrun Motorola and a helicopter.

Alpine has had several sensational murders, however. Recently, prisoners in the county lockup were moved to more secure facilities in a neighboring county seat to cut down on drug smuggling. For all that, the area's violent crime rate (340) and one-tenth the property crime rate (225) give the area a better-than-average score of 72.8.

Hot Springs, Arkansas (Score: 34.7)

If Sun Belt resorts are saddled with high crime rates, this one is an exception. Adding its violent crime rate (430) to one-tenth its property crime rate (475) results in a total of 905, a less-than-middling record good for a score of 34.7.

It wasn't always this way. Up until 1967, when Governor Winthrop Rockefeller ordered state troopers to break up the craps tables, bulldoze the slot machines into a gravel pit, and close down the brothels, Hot Springs had a 100-year, wide-open tradition for lawlessness.

Today, the locals will tell you that one-third of the annual crime occurs during the spring racing season at Oaklawn Park, and that the only other thing that distinguishes this retirement place in the eyes of the law is the phenomenal number of speeding tickets handed out on 1-30 and on US 270 by the Arkansas Highway Patrol's Troop K.

RANKINGS: PERSONAL SAFETY

To rank each place for freedom from crime, *Retirement Places Rated* adds two numbers: (1) the **violent crime rate** and (2) the **property crime rate** divided by 10. The result is then scaled against the average for all 203 places to get a percentile score. The higher the score, the safer the retirement place. Places with tie scores get the same rank and are listed in alphabetical order.

Retirement Places from Best to Worst

RANK	PLACE	SCORE
1.	Norfork Lake, AR	100.0
2.	Brown County, IN	99.6
3.	Leelanau Peninsula, MI	99.1
4.	Smith Mountain Lake, VA	98.6
5.	Door Peninsula, WI	98.1
6.	Northern Neck, VA	97.6
7.	Berkeley Springs, WV	97.1
8.	Whidbey Island, WA	96.6
9.	Woodstock, VT	96.1
10.	Fredericksburg, TX	95.6
11.	Bar Harbor, ME	95.1
12.	Camden, ME	94.6
13.	Polson–Mission Valley, MT	94.1
14.	San Juan Islands, WA	93.6
15.	Monadnock Region, NH	93.1
16.	Charles Town–Shepherdstown, WV	92.6
17.	Delta County, CO	92.1
18.	Brookings–Gold Beach, OR	91.6
19.	Front Royal, VA	91.1
20.	State College, PA	90.6
21.	Lake of the Cherokees, OK	90.1
22.	York Beaches, ME	89.7
23.	Hanover, NH	89.2
24.	Boerne, TX	88.7
25.	Litchfield Hills, CT	88.2
26.	Eagle River–Woodruff, WI	87.7
27.	Tryon, NC	87.2
28.	Chewelah, WA	86.7
29.	Lake Placid, NY	86.2
30.	Lake Havasu City, AZ	85.7
31.	Lake Winnipesaukee, NH	85.2
32.	St. Jay–Northeast Kingdom, VT	84.7
33.	Bozeman, MT	84.2
34.	Boone–Blowing Rock, NC	83.7
35.	Pagosa Springs, CO	83.2
36.	Amador County, CA	82.7
37.	Murray–Kentucky Lake, KY	82.2
38.	Hendersonville–East Flat Rock, NC	81.7
39.	Brevard, NC	81.2
40.	Pike County, PA	80.7
41.	Salida, CO	80.2
42.	Traverse City, MI	79.8
43.	Sedona, AZ	79.3
44.	Northampton–Amherst, MA	78.8
45.	Toms River–Barnegat Bay, NJ	78.3
46.	Hamilton–Bitterroot Valley, MT	77.8
47.	Georgetown, TX	77.3
48.	Port Angeles–Sequim, WA	76.8
49.	Fredericksburg–Spotsylvania, VA	76.3
50.	Port Charlotte, FL	75.8
51.	Montrose, CO	75.3
52.	Chestertown, MD	74.8
53.	Eureka Springs, AR	74.3
54.	Oscoda–Huron Shore, MI	73.8
55.	Marble Falls–Lake LBJ, TX	73.3
56.	Alpine–Big Bend, TX	72.8
57.	Henderson, NV	72.3
58.	Wickenburg, AZ	71.8
59.	Apalachicola, FL	71.3
60.	Kauai, HI	70.8
61.	Inverness, FL	70.3
62.	St. George–Zion, UT	69.9
63.	Williamsburg, VA	69.4
64.	Rio Rancho, NM	68.9
65.	Southport–Brunswick Islands, NC	68.4
66.	Kerrville, TX	67.9
67.	Port Townsend, WA	67.4
68.	Fort Collins–Loveland, CO	66.9
69.	Burlington, VT	66.4
70.	Ketchum–Sun Valley, ID	65.9
71.	Santa Fe, NM	65.4
72.	Grass Valley–Nevada City, CA	64.9
73.	Sandpoint–Lake Pend Oreille, ID	64.4
74.	East End Long Island, NY	63.9
75.	Grants Pass, OR	63.4
76.	Southern Berkshire County, MA	62.9
77.	Cedar City, UT	62.4
78.	Fayetteville, AR	61.9
79.	Bisbee, AZ	61.4
80.	Fairhope–Gulf Shores, AL	60.9
81.	Iowa City, IA	60.4
82.	Pahrump Valley, NV	60.0
83.	Eufaula, AL	59.5
84.	Beaufort–Bogue Banks, NC	59.0
85.	Pendleton District, SC	58.5
86.	Virginia Beach, VA	58.0
87.	Edenton, NC	57.5
88.	Table Rock Lake, MO	57.0
89.	Kalispell–Flathead Valley, MT	56.5
90.	Madison, WI	56.0
91.	Southern Pines–Pinehurst, NC	55.5
92.	Durango, CO	55.0
93.	Grand Junction, CO	54.5
94.	Scottsdale, AZ	54.0
95.	Park City, UT	53.5
96.	Bend, OR	53.0
97.	Trinity Peninsula, TX	52.5
98.	Anacortes, WA	52.0
99.	Maryville, TN	51.5
100.	Morro Bay–Cambria, CA	51.0
101.	Jackson Hole, WY	50.5
102.	Wimberley, TX	50.0
103.	Cedar Creek Lake, TX	49.6
104.	Payson, AZ	49.1
105.	Easton–St. Michaels, MD	48.6
106.	Charlottesville, VA	48.1
107.	Santa Barbara, CA	47.6
108.	Largo, FL	47.1
109.	Bellingham, WA	46.6
110.	Crossville, TN	46.1
111.	Alamogordo, NM	45.6
112.	Lake Conroe, TX	45.1
113.	Rabun County, GA	44.6
114.	Santa Rosa, CA	44.1
115.	Western St. Tammany Parish, LA	43.6
116.	Asheville, NC	43.1
117.	Paradise–Magalia, CA	42.6
118.	Newport–Lincoln City, OR	42.1
119.	McCall, ID	41.6
120.	Laguna Beach–Dana Point, CA	41.1
121.	Petoskey–Harbor Springs, MI	40.6
122.	Carson City–Carson Valley, NV	40.1
123.	Sonora–Twain Harte, CA	39.7
124.	Medford–Ashland, OR	39.2
125.	Lake of the Ozarks, MO	38.7
126.	Prescott–Prescott Valley, AZ	38.2
127.	Coeur d'Alene, ID	37.7
128.	New Port Richey, FL	37.2

RANK	PLACE	SCORE	RANK	PLACE	SCORE
129.	Maui, HI	36.7	167.	Taos, NM	17.9
130.	Columbia, MO	36.2	168.	St. Augustine, FL	17.4
131.	Yuma, AZ	35.7	169.	Naples, FL	16.9
132.	Wenatchee, WA	35.2	170.	Las Cruces, NM	16.4
133.	Hot Springs, AR	34.7	171.	Mesa, AZ	15.9
134.	Colorado Springs, CO	34.2	172.	Kingman, AZ	15.4
135.	Cottonwood–Verde Valley, AZ	33.7	173.	Melbourne–Palm Bay, FL	14.9
136.	Roswell, NM	33.2	174.	Victorville–Apple Valley, CA	14.4
137.	Florence, OR	32.7	175.	Sebring–Avon Park, FL	13.9
138.	Mendocino–Fort Bragg, CA	32.2	176.	Ocean City, MD	13.4
139.	Oxford, MS	31.7	177.	Palm Springs–Coachella Valley, CA	12.9
140.	Dare Outer Banks, NC	31.2	178.	Fort Myers–Cape Coral, FL	12.4
141.	Chapel Hill–Carrboro, NC	30.7	179.	Mariposa, CA	11.9
142.	Martha's Vineyard, MA	30.2	180.	Ocala, FL	11.4
143.	Silver City, NM	29.8	181.	Daytona Beach, FL	10.9
144.	Bullhead City, AZ	29.3	182.	Ruidoso, NM	10.4
145.	Summerville, SC	28.8	183.	Savannah, GA	10.0
146.	New Braunfels, TX	28.3	184.	Beaufort, SC	9.5
147.	Lower Cape May, NJ	27.8	184.	Hilton Head Island, SC	9.5
148.	New Bern, NC	27.3	186.	Tucson, AZ	8.5
149.	Reno–Sparks, NV	26.8	187.	Athens, GA	8.0
150.	Flagstaff, AZ	26.3	188.	Lakeland–Winter Haven, FL	7.5
151.	Rehoboth Bay–Indian River Bay, DE	25.8	189.	Key West, FL	7.0
152.	Carmel–Pebble Beach, CA	25.3	190.	Pensacola, FL	6.5
153.	Vero Beach, FL	24.8	191.	Kissimmee–St. Cloud, FL	6.0
154.	Leesburg–Mount Dora, FL	24.3	192.	Bradenton, FL	5.5
155.	Thomasville, GA	23.8	193.	Boca Raton, FL	5.0
156.	Middle Cape Cod, MA	23.3	194.	Panama City, FL	4.5
157.	Bay St. Louis–Pass Christian, MS	22.8	195.	Charleston, SC	4.0
158.	Aiken, SC	22.3	196.	Annapolis, MD	3.5
159.	Rockport–Aransas Pass, TX	21.8	197.	St. Simons–Jekyll Islands, GA	3.0
160.	Hattiesburg, MS	21.3	198.	Palmer–Wasilla, AK	2.5
161.	Natchitoches, LA	20.8	199.	Conway, SC	2.0
162.	Mission–McAllen–Alamo, TX	20.3	199.	Myrtle Beach, SC	2.0
163.	North County San Diego, CA	19.9	201.	Gainesville, FL	1.0
164.	Oakhurst–Coarsegold, CA	19.4	202.	Las Vegas, NM	0.5
165.	Apache Junction, AZ	18.9	203.	Branson, MO	0.0
166.	Sarasota, FL	18.4			

PLACE PROFILES: PERSONAL SAFETY

The following Place Profiles show each retirement place's average annual rates for seven crimes: murder, rape, robbery, aggravated assault, burglary, theft, and motor-vehicle theft for the latest 5 years that data are available.

The rates for these crimes are grouped into **Violent** and **Property** categories. The next-to-last column indicates the crime trend over 5 years: 27 places have arrows pointing up (↑), meaning their *Retirement Places Rated* crime rates rose more than 15 percent during that time period; 39 places have an arrow pointing down (↓), meaning their crime rates have dropped more than 15 percent. A dash for the remaining 137 places means their crime rates have neither risen nor fallen more than 15 percent.

All figures are derived from the FBI's unpublished "Crime by County" annual reports for the latest 5 years for which data is available. A star (★) preceding a place's name highlights it as one of the top 30 places for personal safety.

	Violent Crime Rates				Property Crime Rates					
	MURDER	RAPE	ROBBERY	ASSAULT	BURGLARY	THEFT	AUTO THEFT	TREND	SCORE	RANK
Average 203 Retirement Places	**4.5**	**34.9**	**70.3**	**330.1**	**997**	**2,938**	**266**	**–**	**–**	**–**
Aiken, SC	9.6	49.0	120.6	496.0	1,177	2,600	378	–	22.3	158
Alamogordo, NM	5.9	53.4	36.1	306.0	758	3,131	138	–	45.6	111
Alpine-Big Bend, TX	3.3	30.9	16.7	288.6	736	1,412	98	↓	72.8	56
Amador County, CA	1.9	23.0	11.5	229.9	751	1,391	130	–	82.7	36
Anacortes, WA	2.6	47.6	39.7	84.5	932	4,570	229	–	52.0	98
Annapolis, MD	11.0	30.2	423.4	866.1	916	4,003	360	↑	3.5	196
Apache Junction, AZ	7.2	44.8	76.3	518.2	1,343	3,674	421	–	18.9	165
Apalachicola, FL	8.3	34.8	12.6	200.5	653	2,392	155	↑	71.3	59
Asheville, NC	6.2	26.4	110.2	282.2	1,065	2,560	293	–	43.1	116
Athens, GA	9.3	57.3	237.8	424.9	1,589	5,941	555	–	8.0	187
★ Bar Harbor, ME	2.4	15.2	3.8	74.2	574	1,757	91	–	95.1	11
Bay St. Louis-Pass Christian, MS	8.1	74.4	169.2	207.3	1,480	4,268	424	–	22.8	157
Beaufort, SC	5.7	57.1	141.5	683.4	1,462	4,423	308	–	9.5	184
Beaufort-Bogue Banks, NC	4.2	21.3	55.3	193.6	1,184	2,753	147	–	59.0	84
Bellingham, WA	2.7	63.4	48.5	173.0	1,019	3,879	242	–	46.6	109
Bend, OR	1.8	30.9	45.1	129.7	976	4,050	303	–	53.0	96
★ Berkeley Springs, WV	5.6	9.2	16.7	78.0	732	1,000	118	↑	97.1	7
Bisbee, AZ	4.4	9.0	34.2	230.3	894	2,665	366	–	61.4	79
Boca Raton, FL	7.0	42.5	281.6	623.4	1,782	4,599	806	–	5.0	193
★ Boerne, TX	1.5	13.2	6.4	166.8	636	1,616	100	↓	88.7	24
Boone-Blowing Rock, NC	3.3	15.6	13.6	125.3	760	2,339	114	–	83.7	34
Bozeman, MT	1.2	18.9	12.9	122.6	426	2,544	222	↑	84.2	33
Bradenton, FL	5.6	46.3	214.0	819.5	1,668	3,734	452	–	5.5	192
Branson, MO	5.0	46.3	130.9	1,017.8	2,930	13,425	463	↑	0.0	203
Brevard, NC	2.5	28.8	14.1	250.6	704	1,233	87	↑	81.2	39
★ Brookings-Gold Beach, OR	2.5	20.2	9.0	92.8	673	1,936	132	–	91.6	18
★ Brown County, IN	0.0	0.0	13.4	73.5	348	1,010	60	↑	99.6	2
Bullhead City, AZ	5.7	31.5	77.3	438.0	1,222	2,882	315	–	29.3	144
Burlington, VT	1.6	34.2	22.9	82.0	934	3,867	199	–	66.4	69
★ Camden, ME	1.9	20.0	10.2	51.2	484	1,962	102	↓	94.6	12
Carmel-Pebble Beach, CA	7.9	33.5	184.3	445.5	863	2,643	346	–	25.3	152
Carson City-Carson Valley, NV	1.6	31.0	41.7	449.3	704	2,358	178	–	40.1	122
Cedar City, UT	1.9	24.2	14.0	188.6	699	3,403	229	–	62.4	77
Cedar Creek Lake, TX	7.7	26.9	30.1	361.1	1,183	1,971	159	↓	49.6	103
Chapel Hill-Carrboro, NC	4.3	27.0	125.9	275.9	1,272	3,996	246	–	30.7	141
★ Charles Town-Shepherdstown, WV	4.6	8.6	31.0	106.4	585	1,565	129	–	92.6	16
Charleston, SC	10.0	62.7	281.4	794.7	1,363	4,929	756	–	4.0	195
Charlottesville, VA	4.5	37.6	84.3	255.5	603	3,320	188	↓	48.1	106
Chestertown, MD	2.6	21.3	32.4	276.5	698	1,345	101	–	74.8	52
★ Chewelah, WA	5.2	17.6	16.3	89.4	767	2,326	145	–	86.7	28
Coeur d'Alene, ID	4.1	47.0	28.8	338.0	959	3,410	212	–	37.7	127
Colorado Springs, CO	4.9	56.5	102.9	268.4	929	3,559	302	–	34.2	134
Columbia, MO	4.7	35.5	92.2	290.5	697	3,847	185	–	36.2	130
Conway, SC	9.7	64.0	216.0	765.7	2,011	5,887	642	–	2.0	199
Cottonwood-Verde Valley, AZ	0.0	21.6	34.6	354.2	1,041	3,714	410	↑	33.7	135
Crossville, TN	1.8	10.3	36.2	356.8	1,052	2,495	422	↑	46.1	110
Dare Outer Banks, NC	7.3	38.5	25.7	176.8	2,357	4,777	175	–	31.2	140
Daytona Beach, FL	6.2	60.2	204.4	624.7	1,570	3,412	481	–	10.9	181
★ Delta County, CO	2.5	17.3	7.2	137.7	602	1,521	102	↓	92.1	17
★ Door Peninsula, WI	0.4	8.3	4.6	20.3	448	1,754	78	–	98.1	5
Durango, CO	3.9	75.7	18.2	201.7	772	3,371	172	–	55.0	92
★ Eagle River-Woodruff, WI	2.7	19.5	6.4	153.3	717	1,591	203	–	87.7	26
East End Long Island, NY	3.1	7.2	92.5	178.6	744	2,610	386	–	63.9	74
Easton-St. Michaels, MD	6.5	29.5	72.5	343.1	751	2,343	139	–	48.6	105
Edenton, NC	6.3	21.1	60.9	255.3	1,072	2,339	96	–	57.5	87
Eufaula, AL	8.1	19.9	58.9	319.2	515	2,178	72	↑	59.5	83
Eureka Springs, AR	6.2	24.4	14.1	236.1	687	1,861	158	–	74.3	53
Fairhope-Gulf Shores, AL	4.8	24.7	50.9	240.6	827	2,542	142	–	60.9	80
Fayetteville, AR	4.1	36.4	27.9	211.4	734	2,883	240	–	61.9	78
Flagstaff, AZ	4.9	42.7	56.1	325.4	965	5,006	214	–	26.3	150
Florence, OR	2.6	40.9	108.7	200.6	1,191	4,290	427	–	32.7	137
Fort Collins-Loveland, CO	1.8	59.5	22.7	188.8	603	2,912	149	–	66.9	68
Fort Myers-Cape Coral, FL	7.2	56.2	252.8	533.0	1,417	3,342	832	↑	12.4	178
★ Fredericksburg, TX	2.1	10.0	6.7	110.3	448	1,454	66	–	95.6	10
Fredericksburg-Spotsylvania, VA	4.2	18.8	53.0	154.5	352	2,556	183	↑	76.3	49

★ = *in the top 30 places for personal safety.*

	Violent Crime Rates				Property Crime Rates					
	MURDER	RAPE	ROBBERY	ASSAULT	BURGLARY	THEFT	AUTO THEFT	TREND	SCORE	RANK
Average 203 Retirement Places	**4.5**	**34.9**	**70.3**	**330.1**	**997**	**2,938**	**266**	–	–	–
★ Front Royal, VA	2.4	23.2	26.7	58.2	502	2,230	205	–	91.1	19
Gainesville, FL	5.6	78.7	248.8	893.0	1,973	5,351	576	–	1.0	201
Georgetown, TX	2.3	34.3	30.5	195.4	635	1,936	143	↓	77.3	47
Grand Junction, CO	6.1	25.8	34.9	208.4	886	3,477	204	–	54.5	93
Grants Pass, OR	5.2	34.3	57.6	102.7	1,010	3,231	354	–	63.4	75
Grass Valley-Nevada City, CA	2.9	25.2	22.8	326.4	715	1,823	204	–	64.9	72
Hamilton-Bitterroot Valley, MT	9.2	6.7	2.7	176.5	276	2,903	133	↑	77.8	46
★ Hanover, NH	2.0	26.4	9.1	59.1	459	2,690	94	–	89.2	23
Hattiesburg, MS	10.3	48.7	129.1	310.1	1,713	4,112	265	↓	21.3	160
Henderson, NV	4.9	53.6	105.5	119.0	776	1,549	491	↓	72.3	57
Hendersonville-East Flat Rock, NC	4.5	28.4	42.6	149.4	862	1,709	153	–	81.7	38
Hilton Head Island, SC	5.7	57.1	141.5	683.4	1,462	4,423	308	–	9.5	184
Hot Springs, AR	10.8	44.3	154.4	220.7	1,322	3,136	288	–	34.7	133
Inverness, FL	1.7	15.3	29.9	280.5	851	1,537	123	–	70.3	61
Iowa City, IA	1.4	36.1	27.6	328.6	595	2,132	125	↑	60.4	81
Jackson Hole, WY	2.5	48.7	28.2	206.6	733	3,673	236	↓	50.5	101
Kalispell-Flathead Valley, MT	5.0	53.1	17.2	151.7	725	3,772	251	–	56.5	89
Kauai, HI	3.9	35.8	24.3	78.5	993	3,184	174	–	70.8	60
Kerrville, TX	6.7	46.3	32.5	232.2	721	2,268	125	↓	67.9	66
Ketchum-Sun Valley, ID	0.0	31.2	5.4	233.5	746	2,792	172	↓	65.9	70
Key West, FL	4.2	44.1	152.7	649.6	1,530	5,148	550	↓	7.0	189
Kingman, AZ	4.8	24.1	62.6	274.6	1,806	6,802	511	–	15.4	172
Kissimmee-St. Cloud, FL	6.0	57.7	198.9	684.8	2,248	4,453	457	–	6.0	191
Laguna Beach-Dana Point, CA	5.1	21.2	174.0	257.7	824	2,357	621	↓	41.1	120
Lake Conroe, TX	5.3	33.5	67.8	347.3	929	2,303	305	–	45.1	112
★ Lake Havasu City, AZ	2.3	0.0	11.5	131.4	526	2,395	240	↓	85.7	30
★ Lake of the Cherokees, OK	4.3	19.5	7.2	183.8	657	1,110	201	–	90.1	21
Lake of the Ozarks, MO	1.9	29.1	14.4	345.3	997	3,568	214	↑	38.7	125
★ Lake Placid, NY	3.3	17.3	6.7	241.8	619	1,228	51	–	86.2	29
Lake Winnipesaukee, NH	2.1	53.6	12.1	78.6	643	2,469	119	–	85.2	31
Lakeland-Winter Haven, FL	6.7	49.0	204.9	593.7	2,024	4,156	787	↓	7.5	188
Largo, FL	1.4	32.3	91.3	299.3	732	2,819	204	↓	47.1	108
Las Cruces, NM	8.4	61.7	98.9	443.2	1,470	4,229	363	↑	16.4	170
Las Vegas, NM	13.0	64.3	123.1	1,642.9	2,101	4,335	386	–	0.5	202
★ Leelanau Peninsula, MI	0.6	34.8	3.6	64.1	298	1,066	52	–	99.1	3
Leesburg-Mount Dora, FL	3.7	42.1	73.9	590.9	1,097	2,178	240	–	24.3	154
★ Litchfield Hills, CT	1.2	15.0	19.6	126.5	581	1,838	215	–	88.2	25
Lower Cape May, NJ	2.9	50.3	116.1	259.1	1,360	4,481	175	–	27.8	147
Madison, WI	1.5	32.4	102.0	178.2	642	3,050	261	–	56.0	90
Marble Falls-Lake LBJ, TX	3.9	55.3	13.9	208.2	788	1,883	146	–	73.3	55
Mariposa, CA	5.1	35.0	14.5	1,068.6	1,178	1,707	158	–	11.9	179
Martha's Vineyard, MA	1.4	23.2	5.3	442.0	1,102	3,854	187	↓	30.2	142
Maryville, TN	2.5	67.7	43.2	314.9	704	2,229	266	↓	51.5	99
Maui, HI	3.7	36.0	75.2	115.6	1,443	4,830	325	–	36.7	129
McCall, ID	2.8	56.2	11.7	327.8	1,450	2,668	259	↓	41.6	119
Medford-Ashland, OR	3.4	40.4	44.3	267.2	846	3,913	260	–	39.2	124
Melbourne-Palm Bay, FL	4.7	42.8	127.1	599.5	1,225	3,619	334	–	14.9	173
Mendocino-Fort Bragg, CA	6.8	48.2	57.9	486.3	1,158	2,193	257	–	32.2	138
Mesa, AZ	4.1	25.9	110.2	473.4	1,052	3,932	1,112	↓	15.9	171
Middle Cape Cod, MA	1.4	27.9	32.1	656.7	1,081	2,293	205	–	23.3	156
Mission-McAllen-Alamo, TX	6.9	24.5	99.2	428.0	1,673	3,832	612	–	20.3	162
★ Monadnock Region, NH	0.5	42.7	15.0	109.9	353	1,476	77	–	93.1	15
Montrose, CO	1.9	25.9	19.1	133.5	614	2,852	146	–	75.3	51
Morro Bay-Cambria, CA	2.5	37.9	37.0	368.1	733	2,152	158	–	51.0	100
Murray-Kentucky Lake, KY	1.6	29.9	22.0	194.1	628	1,724	121	–	82.2	37
Myrtle Beach, SC	9.7	64.0	216.0	765.7	2,011	5,887	642	–	2.0	199
Naples, FL	5.8	61.6	138.3	522.7	1,373	3,124	361	–	16.9	169
Natchitoches, LA	9.4	31.8	114.0	541.1	1,245	2,907	143	↑	20.8	161
New Bern, NC	6.0	32.1	122.9	425.2	1,245	3,072	211	–	27.3	148
New Braunfels, TX	3.4	39.7	47.0	477.7	956	3,283	209	↓	28.3	146
New Port Richey, FL	3.3	35.7	69.9	356.4	1,102	2,790	268	–	37.2	128
Newport-Lincoln City, OR	4.3	36.4	42.3	218.3	1,190	3,793	258	–	42.1	118
★ Norfolk Lake, AR	1.7	5.7	3.1	96.0	132	997	69	–	100.0	1
North County San Diego, CA	6.6	31.4	220.5	487.9	937	2,409	928	↓	19.9	163

continued

★ = *in the top 30 places for personal safety.*

	Violent Crime Rates				Property Crime Rates					
	MURDER	RAPE	ROBBERY	ASSAULT	BURGLARY	THEFT	AUTO THEFT	TREND	SCORE	RANK
Average 203 Retirement Places	**4.5**	**34.9**	**70.3**	**330.1**	**997**	**2,938**	**266**	–	–	–
Northampton-Amherst, MA	0.8	27.6	21.4	237.4	536	1,607	210	–	78.8	44
★ Northern Neck, VA	1.8	18.3	11.5	127.5	452	819	62	–	97.6	6
Oakhurst-Coarsegold, CA	9.5	50.1	164.2	544.9	1,415	2,164	637	–	19.4	164
Ocala, FL	6.0	61.2	149.2	742.3	1,391	3,039	262	↓	11.4	180
Ocean City, MD	5.2	48.4	101.6	597.5	1,192	4,929	268	–	13.4	176
Oscoda-Huron Shore, MI	1.3	64.7	8.3	179.7	944	1,938	134	–	73.8	54
Oxford, MS	2.9	26.5	110.5	209.1	1,309	4,696	212	↓	31.7	139
Pagosa Springs, CO	0.0	10.2	4.6	173.2	474	2,449	128	↓	83.2	35
Pahrump Valley, NV	5.2	0.0	17.3	383.1	1,252	1,434	83	↑	60.0	82
Palm Springs-Coachella Valley, CA	9.3	35.5	212.8	633.0	1,579	2,690	814	↓	12.9	177
Palmer-Wasilla, AK	4.4	54.8	59.2	943.2	781	7,225	419	↓	2.5	198
Panama City, FL	5.4	72.8	109.0	650.5	1,772	6,586	420	↑	4.5	194
Paradise-Magalia, CA	4.0	42.9	69.2	282.1	1,195	2,694	363	–	42.6	117
Park City, UT	2.4	39.5	18.9	146.5	806	4,338	183	–	53.5	95
Payson, AZ	3.9	35.4	17.3	357.5	789	2,641	175	–	49.1	104
Pendleton District, SC	5.1	18.0	33.7	374.1	742	1,754	119	–	58.5	85
Pensacola, FL	6.8	57.7	217.2	803.4	1,442	3,457	291	–	6.5	190
Petoskey-Harbor Springs, MI	1.2	109.9	18.4	189.3	1,537	3,601	151	↑	40.6	121
Pike County, PA	2.0	27.6	13.3	188.3	1,257	1,291	150	–	80.7	40
★ Polson-Mission Valley, MT	3.4	12.8	5.8	134.5	364	1,351	170	–	94.1	13
Port Angeles-Sequim, WA	2.6	43.8	26.0	119.0	704	2,621	152	–	76.8	48
Port Charlotte, FL	3.1	13.5	54.6	182.9	716	1,964	189	–	75.8	50
Port Townsend, WA	1.2	37.3	15.1	203.4	909	2,683	178	–	67.4	67
Prescott-Prescott Valley, AZ	5.0	22.0	26.2	404.1	965	2,961	225	–	38.2	126
Rabun County, GA	9.4	10.3	10.5	549.2	953	1,190	204	↑	44.6	113
Rehoboth Bay-Indian River Bay, DE	4.2	62.6	90.5	536.1	946	2,556	118	–	25.8	151
Reno-Sparks, NV	6.7	60.6	180.1	282.8	1,029	3,710	364	–	26.8	149
Rio Rancho, NM	4.6	28.5	28.2	337.0	575	1,425	138	–	68.9	64
Rockport-Aransas Pass, TX	3.7	49.0	27.0	498.3	1,589	3,425	238	↓	21.8	159
Roswell, NM	6.1	41.5	37.2	360.7	1,202	3,479	181	↑	33.2	136
Ruidoso, NM	7.5	55.5	47.0	806.4	2,132	3,158	242	↑	10.4	182
St. Augustine, FL	6.7	26.8	117.2	582.8	1,067	3,496	225	–	17.4	168
St. George-Zion, UT	2.2	45.7	14.9	143.8	642	2,980	227	–	69.9	62
St. Jay-Northeast Kingdom, VT	1.2	36.0	5.8	74.4	1,047	2,318	173	↓	84.7	32
St. Simons-Jekyll Islands, GA	8.0	45.5	203.1	915.7	1,369	5,282	392	–	3.0	197
Salida, CO	3.5	15.0	5.6	152.9	611	2,533	104	–	80.2	41
★ San Juan Islands, WA	0.8	6.5	3.4	52.0	732	1,974	117	↓	93.6	14
Sandpoint-Lake Pend Oreille, ID	2.6	31.7	13.7	257.0	896	2,390	192	↓	64.4	73
Santa Barbara, CA	3.0	33.2	84.8	334.0	886	2,355	178	–	47.6	107
Santa Fe, NM	3.0	40.4	62.3	257.5	1,084	1,592	196	↑	65.4	71
Santa Rosa, CA	3.4	41.4	76.6	304.3	929	2,689	267	–	44.1	114
Sarasota, FL	3.6	32.7	179.3	445.5	1,313	3,781	288	–	18.4	166
Savannah, GA	16.3	45.0	384.9	352.6	1,433	4,605	730	–	10.0	183
Scottsdale, AZ	4.8	27.7	93.5	169.3	1,269	2,504	656	↓	54.0	94
Sebring-Avon Park, FL	7.3	32.0	131.7	630.9	1,946	3,193	368	–	13.9	175
Sedona, AZ	0.0	37.9	56.9	94.8	579	2,428	171	↓	79.3	43
Silver City, NM	7.0	28.8	41.2	471.1	1,155	3,077	170	↓	29.8	143
★ Smith Mountain Lake, VA	3.4	14.1	10.2	83.3	329	935	76	–	98.6	4
Sonora-Twain Harte, CA	3.7	21.4	28.6	458.9	1,222	1,865	295	↑	39.7	123
Southern Berkshire County, MA	0.8	24.7	29.9	361.2	720	1,566	150	–	62.9	76
Southern Pines-Pinehurst, NC	6.1	20.5	69.4	285.0	1,120	2,040	202	–	55.5	91
Southport-Brunswick Islands, NC	11.4	19.2	43.8	194.3	1,494	1,888	219	↑	68.4	65
★ State College, PA	1.9	29.4	16.8	95.0	392	2,160	78	–	90.6	20
Summerville, SC	4.9	50.2	84.2	461.8	919	2,757	307	–	28.8	145
Table Rock Lake, MO	4.0	18.1	11.1	456.5	866	1,042	196	–	57.0	88
Taos, NM	6.9	21.4	41.5	741.3	965	2,740	187	↑	17.9	167
Thomasville, GA	8.0	25.5	153.1	382.7	1,326	3,380	274	–	23.8	155
Toms River-Barnegat Bay, NJ	1.9	17.1	52.9	142.3	649	2,297	145	–	78.3	45
Traverse City, MI	0.8	70.5	12.9	118.9	496	2,411	116	–	79.8	42
Trinity Peninsula, TX	8.2	11.8	30.2	412.3	1,204	1,394	191	–	52.5	97
★ Tryon, NC	2.6	15.9	27.4	185.7	863	1,098	141	–	87.2	27
Tucson, AZ	8.9	55.4	185.3	506.1	1,242	5,391	928	–	8.5	186
Vero Beach, FL	4.1	60.8	93.5	378.6	1,311	3,629	300	–	24.8	153
Victorville-Apple Valley, CA	12.0	36.6	263.5	503.4	1,427	2,535	928	↓	14.4	174

★ = *in the top 30 places for personal safety.*

	Violent Crime Rates				Property Crime Rates					
	MURDER	RAPE	ROBBERY	ASSAULT	BURGLARY	THEFT	AUTO THEFT	TREND	SCORE	RANK
Average 203 Retirement Places	**4.5**	**34.9**	**70.3**	**330.1**	**997**	**2,938**	**266**	–	–	–
Virginia Beach, VA	4.7	28.8	123.6	95.0	723	3,458	240	–	58.0	86
Wenatchee, WA	4.1	56.5	43.6	198.7	1,095	4,644	274	–	35.2	132
Western St. Tammany Parish, LA	5.4	30.4	57.7	332.6	868	2,764	263	–	43.6	115
★ Whidbey Island, WA	1.8	27.6	11.8	58.6	504	1,492	81	–	96.6	8
Wickenburg, AZ	0.0	0.0	0.0	190.2	1,008	2,397	418	↓	71.8	58
Williamsburg, VA	4.9	31.2	66.1	168.4	358	2,849	140	–	69.4	63
Wimberley, TX	3.9	56.0	48.5	266.5	887	2,671	196	–	50.0	102
★ Woodstock, VT	1.1	13.8	6.0	62.0	499	1,767	78	↓	96.1	9
★ York Beaches, ME	1.8	20.8	19.1	57.9	760	2,256	139	–	89.7	22
Yuma, AZ	4.4	21.7	44.3	339.3	1,058	3,418	385	↓	35.7	131

★ = *in the top 30 places for personal safety.*

ET CETERA: PERSONAL SAFETY

ARE NEWCOMERS MORE VULNERABLE THAN LOCALS?

As we age, our dread of crime can grow out of proportion to the odds of actually ending up a victim. But the outcomes of a burglary, robbery, or a fraud are certainly deeper and longer lasting for older adults than they are for younger persons.

Aside from staying away from unfamiliar dark streets; locking your doors and windows; not talking to strangers; and being alert, aware, and accompanied when going out, here are other common-sense tactics for avoiding crime that are drawn from police departments in several retirement places. The time for unlocking your doors or leaving the keys in your car in a new destination comes—if ever—only after you've become the equal of the natives in your knowledge of what's safe and what isn't.

Burglary Defenses

For most homes, minimum security—defined by police as foiling entry into a home through any door or window except by destructive force—is enough to stop all but the dumbest or most dogged burglars. It's usually *after* they've been burglarized, experts note, that people learn additional ways to make their homes secure.

If your home is going to be hit, the chances are greater that it will happen during the day while you are out—even if you're gardening in the backyard—than at night when you're asleep. The probability is high, too, that the burglar will be an unemployed young person who knows the neighborhood, and that the job will be done on the spur of the moment because the home looks empty and easy to enter.

From the viewpoint of the crook, the job's quick rewards also entail the risk of doing time in jail. He may turn back at any of three points:

Casing the House. If doors and windows are in plain sight and the sounds are unmistakable that someone is inside, most intruders will turn down the risk and search for an easier target. Here are some defensive tactics:

- If you leave the house during the day, walk out to the sidewalk and turn and wave at the front door whether or not the house is occupied.
- Close the garage door if you are away—an empty garage is a sign of absent people. If you'll be away for more than a day or two, unplug the garage door opener, lock the garage door, and leave the house through the front door. Using high-tech apparatus, expert crooks can crack electronic codes for garage door openers.
- Turn down the ringer on the telephone—an unanswered telephone is a giveaway. And don't announce your absence on your telephone answering-machine or voicemail greeting.
- Plant thorny bushes under windows and near doors or trim back existing shrubbery to limit an intruder's potential hiding places.
- Leave your air conditioner's fan on when you are out. Most burglaries occur in August and a silent air conditioner is the crook's tip to an empty house.
- Tune in a radio or a television to a talk program, and turn on a porch light and yard light and one or two interior lights—the bathroom is one of the best rooms in which to leave a light on—if you are going out for the evening.

Entering the House. Even if the front door is unlocked, an intruder commits a crime once he is inside the house—whether or not anything is stolen. If doors and windows are locked and it looks as if it will take time and energy to break in, he will often go elsewhere.

Prowling the House. A burglar inside a target house is a very dangerous person to confront. He may be discouraged if he cannot quickly find loot or if he thinks the police are on their way. Here are several defensive tactics:

- Maintain a secure closet (not a safe) with an outward-opening door for storing furs, cameras, guns, silverware, and jewelry; on the door, install a 1-inch deadbolt lock. Place an annunciator alarm on the inside. If the door is paneled or of hollow-core construction, strengthen it with ¾-inch plywood or galvanized sheet steel backing.
- Install a telephone extension in your bedroom and add a rim lock with a 1-inch deadbolt to the interior side of the bedroom door (ideally, a "thumb turn" with no exterior key); then if you hear an intruder, you can retreat to the bedroom, lock the door, and call the police.

In addition, avoid:

- Displaying guns on interior walls that can be seen from the street. Guns are big drawing cards for burglars.
- Hiding door keys in the mailbox, under the doormat, atop the door casing, in a flowerpot, or any secret place seasoned burglars search first.
- Keeping a safe in your house. If an intruder finds a safe, he will assume you have something of great value and may come back later and force you to open it.
- Leaving window fans and air conditioners in unlocked windows when you are away from home.
- Entering your home or calling out if you find a window or door forced when you return home. Go to a neighbor and call the police. Wait there until the police come.
- Attaching tags on your key ring that identify you, your car, or your address.

Personal Larceny Defenses

Personal larceny with contact, a police blotter term for purse-snatching and pocket-picking, is the only crime that strikes older adults more frequently than the rest of the population. It is a common way a street crook gets cash in a hurry. The target is the person who looks the easiest to attack, has the most money or valuables to lose, and appears the least likely to give chase.

- **Purses.** If you can do without a purse, do without it. Instead, tuck money and credit cards in an inside pocket. If you must carry a purse, carry it under your arm with its opening facing down; if you're attacked, let the purse's contents fall to the ground, then sit down on the sidewalk before you are knocked down.
- **Wallets.** Never carry a wallet in your back pocket; even an amateur can lift it and escape before you realize what's happening. Carry it in the front pocket of your trousers. Wrap a large rubber band around the wallet so that it can't be withdrawn smoothly and can't fall through if your pocket is cut by a razor blade.

In addition, you should avoid:

- Walking without energy, purpose, or assurance. Predators sense vulnerability if you lack confidence.
- Letting strangers stop you for conversation.
- Approaching cars parked on the street with motors running.
- Flashing your jewelry or cash. This is a signal to street thugs, especially if you seem neither strong nor quick. They may follow you to a more convenient spot for a holdup.
- Walking close to building entrances or shrubbery.
- Getting separated from your purse or wallet in a crowded rest room or other public place, or leaving your purse or wallet unattended in a shopping cart, or on a counter.
- Mingling with adolescents leaving school or groups of adolescents anywhere.
- Using shortcuts, alleys, or dark ways, and walking through sparsely traveled areas or near thick trees and shrubs.

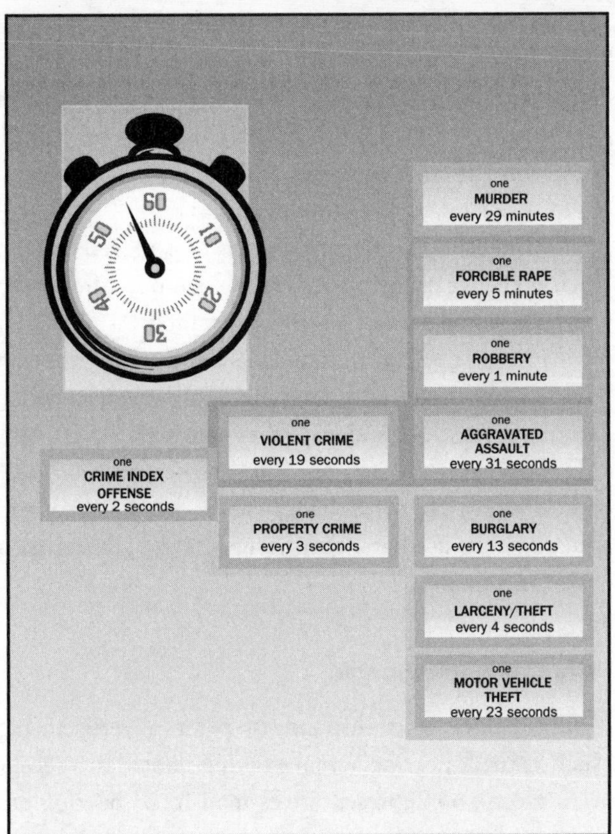

Source: Federal Bureau of Investigation, Crime in the United States, *1998.*

SECURE HOUSING DEVELOPMENTS

If you are considering life in a development—whether a high-rise apartment or condominium, mobile home park, townhouse complex, housing tract, or enclosed dwelling with adjoining courtyards and interior patios—check for these basic security factors.

Opportunity for Surveillance

The ease with which residents and police patrols can watch what is going on is determined by the design of the building complex. The ability to see and question strangers depends on how each residence is designed and its relationship to neighboring dwellings. The nearness of elevator doors to apartment entrances, the number of apartments opening onto each landing, the location and nearness of parking lots and open spaces, the layout of streets and walkways, the evenness and intensity of exterior and interior lighting—all of these factors affect ease of surveillance.

All entryways and walkways should be clearly visible to residents and police at any time of day or night. This means the landscaping surrounding them

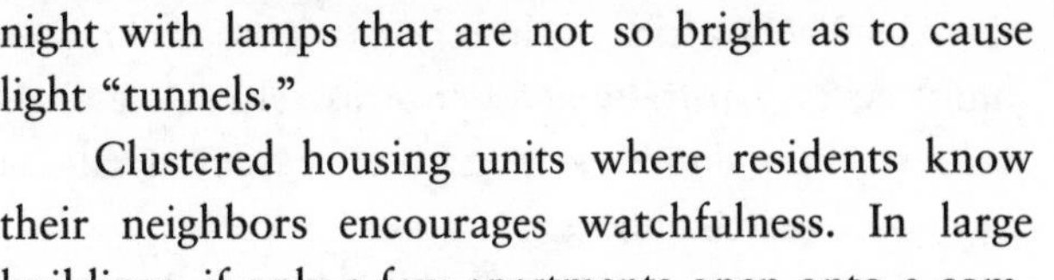

should be low and free from obstacles and heavy foliage. Walkways should be evenly illuminated at night with lamps that are not so bright as to cause light "tunnels."

Clustered housing units where residents know their neighbors encourages watchfulness. In large buildings, if only a few apartments open onto a common landing or hallway, the same sort of neighborly concern is promoted.

Differentiation of Space and Territory

The most dangerous places within large buildings are interior public areas with no definite territorial boundaries. Areas seemingly belonging to no one are, in effect, open to everyone. When places are definitely marked off, an intruder will be more obvious, and owners and neighbors will be alerted to potential danger more quickly.

Access Control

Obviously, the quality of locks, doors, door frames, and windows affects the ease with which your residence can be entered. Yet many builders give little attention to these details. Still less attention may be given to entrances, a surprising fact when you consider that the design and layout of entrances are crucial elements in security, since they define territory and boundaries to residents, visitors, and intruders.

Entrances and exits to a complex should be limited in number, and entrance routes should pass near activity areas so that many people can observe those who come and go. An increasingly popular type of retirement community designed for metropolitan areas high in crime—like many found in Florida or Texas—consists of an enclosed complex of either condominium townhouses or cluster homes surrounded by a wall or secure fence and connected by courtyards and terraces. Entrance in these developments is usually through a single gate guarded by a watchman who has closed-circuit television and an elaborate communications system.

Siting and Clustering

The placement of buildings on the grounds and their relationship to one another affect the ease of access. The opportunity for crime increases in complexes where the design allows anyone to wander at will between dwellings or through courtyards. When residences are clustered so that entrances face each

other and access is limited, strangers are less likely to wander through and are more apt to be questioned if they do. The practice of clustering units together, then, limits access naturally and unobtrusively, while at the same time providing a setting for the casual social contacts between neighbors that assures security.

Despite the feeling of safety that walls, fences, guard posts, and television scanners provide for persons in a community setting, too heavy a concentration of these may be a warning flag. Security measures piled on top of one another, such as excessive numbers of police with attack dogs, indicate high crime in the area. If you sense an excessive preoccupation with security, it's wise to ask about crime or simply eliminate the community from your list altogether.

TYPICAL FRAUDS

P.T. Barnum is credited with the wise but cynical comment that there is "a sucker born every minute and two [con men] to take advantage of him." He spoke from bitter experience; twice in his lifetime he was the victim of swindlers.

Why do older adults fall for con games? The answer is that the proposals sound too good to pass up and are presented with urgency by persons who appear to be honest and sincere. The favorite target of these crooks are older adults who are likely to have liquid assets in their savings accounts.

It's hard to believe that people can still be taken in by the "pigeon drop," a thousand-year-old scam in which the "mark" is expected to ante up some of his or her own money in order to be cut in on an imaginary find of a small fortune. A similar game involves persuading a victim to help bank examiners and the FBI catch an embezzler by withdrawing some of his or her funds and turning them over to the supposed law enforcement officer.

Both of these scams have been exposed time after time, yet victims continue to be bilked out of millions of dollars every year. Consumer and business frauds, too, net billions for their perpetrators. Here are some common examples.

Building Inspector and Contractor Scams

Crooks working in tandem pull off code violation frauds with newcomers as their frequent victims. One poses as a building inspector who "discovers" serious violations and the need for immediate repairs to a homeowner's furnace. Shortly afterward the accomplice arrives, pretending to be a repairman who can perform the needed work at low cost. Typically, little or nothing is done to the furnace, but the victim gets a bill for several hundred dollars.

Home improvement swindles are played by con men who usually show up late in the day offering to perform some service such as installing insulation at half price. They claim they have just finished a job in the neighborhood and have material left over, which accounts for the good deal they can pass on to you. You have to make up your mind on the spot and pay immediately. The job probably never gets finished, and the materials used are worth even less than the bargain price you paid.

Work-at-Home Scams

Older adults who respond to print advertisements such as the following actual examples noted in a recent U.S. House of Representatives mail-fraud hearing are prime targets for work-at-home scams:

> IDEAS, INVENTIONS, new products needed by innovative manufacturers. Marketing assistance available to individuals, tinkerers, universities, companies. Call free: 1-800-528-6050. Arizona residents: 1-800-352-0458, extension 831.
>
> EARN $200 weekly, part-time taking short phone messages at home. Call 1-615-779-3235 extension 267.
>
> Assemble electronic devices in your home during spare time. $300.00 to $600.00/week possible. Experience, knowledge, not necessary. No investment. Write for free information. Electronic Development Lab, Drawer 1560-L, Pinellas Park, FL 33565.

The ads promise extra income each month, all yours for addressing envelopes, making wreaths or plaques in your living room, knitting baby bootees, assembling fishing tackle in your basement, growing earthworms, watching television, or raising house plants at home. U.S. Postal Service investigators, who have been looking into these scams for years, say that they haven't encountered one legitimate work-at-home offer that requires payment from the person who responds to the ad.

Neighborhood Crime Watches

It is possible to see a crime in progress without recognizing it as such. Here are some situations that might be observed in any neighborhood. These are situations a trained police officer would investigate if he or she were making the observation.

Situations Involving Vehicles

SITUATIONS	POSSIBLE SIGNIFICANCE
Moving vehicles, especially if moving slowly without lights, following an aimless or repetitive course.	Casing for a place to rob or burglarize; drug pusher, sex offender, or vandal.
Parked, occupied vehicle, especially at an unusual hour.	Lookout for burglary in progress (sometimes two people masquerading as lovers).
Vehicle parked in neighbor's drive being loaded with valuables, even if the vehicle looks legitimate, i.e., moving van or commercial van.	Burglary or larceny in progress.
Abandoned vehicle with or without license plate.	Stolen or abandoned after being used in a crime.
Persons loitering around parked cars.	Burglary of vehicle contents, theft of accessories, vandalism.
Persons detaching accessories and mechanical parts.	Theft or vandalism.
Apparent business transactions from a vehicle near school, park, or quiet residential neighborhood.	Drug sales.
Persons being forced into vehicle.	Kidnapping, rape, robbery.
Objects thrown from a moving vehicle.	Disposal of contraband.

Situations Involving Property

SITUATION	POSSIBLE SIGNIFICANCE
Property in homes, garages, or storage areas, especially if several items of the same kind such as TVs and bicycles.	Storage of stolen property.
Property in vehicles, especially meaningful at night or if property is household goods, appliances, unmounted tape decks, stereo equipment.	Stolen property, burglary in progress.
Property being removed from a house or building; meaningful if residents are at work, on vacation, or are known to be absent.	Burglary or larceny in progress.
Open doors, broken doors or windows, or other signs of a forced entry.	Burglary in progress or the scene of a recent burglary.

Situations Involving Persons

SITUATION	POSSIBLE SIGNIFICANCE
Door-to-door solicitors—especially significant if one goes to the back of the house and one stays in front. Can be men or women, clean-cut and well dressed.	Casing for burglary, burglary in progress, soliciting violation.
Waiting in front of a house.	Lookout for burglary in progress.
Forced entry or entry through window.	Burglary, vandalism, theft.
Persons shortcutting through yards.	Fleeing the scene of a crime.
Persons running, especially if carrying items of value.	Fleeing the scene of a crime.
Person carrying property, especially if property isn't boxed or wrapped.	Offender leaving the scene of a burglary, robbery, or larceny.
High volume of human traffic in and out of residence.	Drug sales, vice activities, "fence" operation.

That's the key to work-at-home scams. A fee is required in order for the person to get in on the opportunity. The promoter claims that the money is for a start-up kit or for other expenses. The promise is that the promoter will buy back the finished product or that he will arrange for it to be purchased by others in the marketplace. Unfortunately, the promoter seldom if ever buys back the products, and the consumer is not only robbed of his or her initial cash outlay but is also stuck with a large quantity of products for which there is no market.

Commodities Sales

Commodities swindles have become one of the biggest consumer frauds in years. Government investigators estimate these schemes are defrauding the public of as much as $1 billion a year.

The term commodities refers to a wide range of investments, from metals and gems to wholesale food products and foreign currencies. Although most investment firms are reputable, there are a growing number of firms that illegally sell or exchange investments to the unwary. Because commodity issues are complex, even highly educated persons are taken in. Indeed, convicted swindlers have testified in recent congressional hearings that the preferred customer is a retired physician, engineer, college professor, or military officer. Moreover, according to these crooks, the best telephone area codes in the country to call are the Midwest and Far West because, they allege, people there are less cynical.

Commodity investments are perfect vehicles for swindlers, since the payment of profits to investors can often be deferred for 6 months to a year, leaving plenty of time for the operators to skip town before the investors suspect a scam. Moreover, since commodities are by nature very complicated and risky investments, many investors are never sure whether they've been had or not.

There are two basic ways to invest in commodities. The first is to pay the full price and take immediate possession of the items. The second is to buy on margin, which involves putting up a percentage of the total purchase price with the balance being due on a future date.

A commodities scheme typically involves a boiler room full of telephones in which 10 to 100 salespeople make calls to persons who responded to newspaper advertising. The salespeople work on commission and high-pressure pitches are the name of the game. In many cases, a sale is consummated on the telephone. If the person called doesn't agree to purchase anything in the initial call, he or she will be inundated with literature and harassed until a sale is made. The salesperson usually requires the deposit to be wired from the investor's bank, leaving no time for second thoughts.

Services

"Here comes the Gray Peril," local planners in many an attractive rural spot whispered to one another a generation ago. "They'll bid up real estate, string out the visiting nurses, slow down traffic, tap into Meals on Wheels, and vote down school bond issues, all without contributing a nickel to the economy."

How times change. Today, places are courting retired persons as ardently as they're chasing fickle tourists and light industry. A few years ago, Alamagordo, New Mexico, offered to pay half your moving costs. Hot Springs, Arkansas, calls out the volunteer Blue Coats to show you around and even buy you lunch. Mississippi cancels taxes on Social Security and all public and private pensions and ponders free license plates.

Not for nothing. A retired household moving in from outside can have the same impact as three new light industrial jobs, some planners figure. Local economies get better when they float on a cushion of Social Security, pensions, and asset income. Talk to a trust officer in a bank in downtown Grand Junction, Colorado, or Eagle River, Wisconsin, and he or she will bend your ear about how they wouldn't be in business if not for the millions they oversee for older depositors.

Some rural spots owe their growth to older adults who moved there *because* the area was short on services—and short on taxes too. To the confusion of municipal officials, after bouncing over dirt roads, smelling landfill effluvia, and looking in vain for the *Wall Street Journal* at the public library, the newcomers soon show up at public meetings demanding better services and offer higher property taxes in return.

But in many rural areas, the myth lingers that footloose older adults want big-city benefits without paying for them. This chapter examines four services: **general hospital services, office-based physicians, public libraries,** and **continuing education.**

GENERAL HOSPITAL SERVICES

For many of us, health care tips the balance in deciding whether to stay in familiar territory or move to a distant place. In later life, sitting in a doctor's waiting room becomes a more frequent activity. Checking into the hospital for a short stay is a likelihood. With each passing year, the bills for physician fees and prescriptions get bigger and bigger.

Retirement Places Rated doesn't judge the quality of health care; it simply looks at the place's supply. While larger places have an edge, this doesn't mean quality health care in a small Ozark clinic is a contradiction in terms. Nor does it necessarily mean you're better off in a university medical center in Chapel Hill. The quality of medical care people get depends on their ability to pay for it, the luck of the draw, professional competence, and human error.

The word *health* can also mean its opposite: illness. A hospital isn't really a health care institution; its business is to take care of sick people. The truly healthy need little medical care except for an occasional shot or checkup; the unhealthy need a lot more.

Just as not all M.D.s see patients, not all hospitals handle typical illnesses and emergencies. Many of the 5,801 facilities certified by Medicare for inpatient treatment are hospitals that exclusively treat chronic diseases or alcohol and drug addiction, or they may be burn centers, psychiatric hospitals, or rehabilitation hospitals. *Retirement Places Rated* counts only general hospitals where most patients stay less than 30 days. In addition to Medicare certification, most are accredited for acute care by the Joint Commission on Accreditation of Health Care Organizations (JCAHO).

Though most operate as nonprofits, general hospitals are actually businesses that can't afford to go deeply into the red. They offer common services such as an emergency department, respiratory therapy, intensive care, ultrasound, a blood bank, a histopathology laboratory, and outpatient surgery. Some stake out market niches with an additional menu—a sports medicine clinic, a women's health center, an open-heart surgery unit, a certified trauma center, or an x-ray radiation therapy unit.

Two of every three hospitals are *nonteaching*. That is, they're staffed almost entirely by "attending physicians" who have an outside practice, are paid by the patient, and have admitting privileges at the hospital.

Teaching hospitals grant admitting privileges to attending physicians, but they also employ full-time "house staff," taking in first-year and advanced residents and a teaching faculty. The attending physician heads a team of house staff members to make important decisions about a patient's care. The patient pays the attending physician; the hospital pays the house staff.

If an area appeals to you but it doesn't have a hospital, don't be discouraged. There are usually good facilities a short drive away. Residents of Ocean City on Maryland's eastern shore may have to drive to Baltimore for specialized care, but Dorchester General Hospital up the shore in Cambridge or Peninsula General Hospital in Salisbury are more than adequate for routine care.

OFFICE-BASED PHYSICIANS

Not every M.D. is listed in the Yellow Pages. Some are hospital administrators, medical school professors, journalists, lawyers, or researchers for pharmaceutical companies. Others work for the federal government's Public Health Service, Veteran's Administration, or Department of Defense. Still others are in residency training or are full-time members of hospital staffs. When it comes to doctors, what really counts is the numbers who have offices and see patients.

SERVICES IN BRIEF: CONSIDER COLLEGE TOWNS

Of course your health is excellent. For a time in life that's supposed to be upbeat, *acute care, Medicare,* and *continuing care* are discouraging words indeed. Sure you detest niggling taxes that fund an elaborate menu of municipal services. Fleeing these taxes is one reason you're moving. Education after retirement? You haven't thought about it and probably won't. Your race is run; there's no further need for courses and credentials.

If you agree with all of the above, heed some advice from others who had the same convictions about learning, death, and taxes when they made their own move.

You won't miss the congestion and tension of city life if you settle in the bucolic sticks, but you will miss the services you've taken for granted before you moved.

Though you'll rarely see sobering pictures of physicians and hospitals in slick literature promoting retirement places, in time the whole household will become a big consumer of medical care. Make sure specialists and hospitals are available *before* you settle in.

Position and possessions ultimately won't matter in later life. What matters are friends, a sense of humor, and a well-furnished mind. It's said that college towns have high percentages of young people *and* retired people because both groups are there for a good time. But college towns also offer an unrecognized advantage: a higher level of human services than places of similar or even larger size. In retirement, these human services truly count.

Paging Dr. Finder

Learning whether cardiologists, urologists, psychiatrists, or other specialists practice in a distant area needn't be a telephonic drudgery. Call the local hospital's public relations office for a free copy of their Physician Locator or M.D. Directory. Hospitals in competitive markets know they'll more likely have you as a customer when you're ill if they can introduce you early on to an M.D. who uses their facilities.

These "Dr. Finders" aren't mere telephone contact sheets. Often they're photo galleries of physicians with capsule résumés on their education from college through medical school to residency, their specialties, and their board certifications. You can also learn if they take walk-in patients or accept Medicare assignments and whether another doctor will cover for them on their day off. Some of these guides even detail their civic clubs and what they like to do on weekends.

AMA Physician Categories

The American Medical Association (AMA) classifies a physician as a family practitioner, general practitioner, medical specialist, surgeon, or other specialist by 34 specialties in which the physician reports spending the largest number of his or her professional hours.

General/Family Practitioners

- General Practice
- Family Practice

Medical Specialists

- Allergy
- Cardiovascular Diseases
- Dermatology
- Gastroenterology
- Internal Medicine
- Pediatric Allergy
- Pediatric Cardiology
- Pediatrics
- Pulmonary Diseases

Surgical Specialists

- Colon and Rectal Surgery
- General Surgery
- Neurological Surgery
- Obstetrics and Gynecology
- Ophthalmology
- Orthopedic Surgery
- Otolaryngology
- Plastic Surgery
- Thoracic Surgery
- Urology

Other Specialists

- Aerospace Medicine
- Anesthesiology
- Child Psychiatry
- Diagnostic Radiology
- Forensic Pathology
- General Preventive Medicine
- Neurology
- Occupational Medicine
- Pathology
- Physical Medicine and Rehabilitation
- Psychiatry
- Public Health

Radiology

- Therapeutic Radiology

Sentiment, their perceptions of local quality of life, or both help to determine where doctors end up practicing. But mainly it's economics. The beginning physician has invested 3 to 7 years in graduate medical education and frequently has to start out with an enormous loan to repay. Some begin work on a hospital staff, develop a practice, get loose from the hospital, and open an office. Others are recruited into partnerships or group practices through ads like these from the *Journal of the American Medical Association:*

> North Carolina: Expanding group recruiting two experienced Emergency Physicians. Double coverage and flexible schedule. Excellent total compensation package includes paid vacation. CME time and occurrence malpractice. 22,000 census. Waterfront community. Community hospital closest to Outer Banks and ocean. Send C.V. to Box 1945, c/o JAMA.

> Cardiologist—BC/BE wanted to join a well-established solo, Board Certified, noninvasive Cardiologist in a nice Oregon coastal community. Facility available for Echo-Doppler, Holter, Stress test, Cardiac Nuclear Studies, Temporary and Permanent Pacemaker, Swan Ganz, HIS bundle. Excellent salary and benefits. Early partnership. Send C.V. to Box 6199, c/o JAMA.

Hospital Services

The American Hospital Association (AHA) classifies hospital services into these 84 categories:

Adult day-care program
Alcohol/drug abuse or dependency inpatient unit
Alcohol/drug abuse or dependency outpatient services
Alzheimer's diagnostic/assessment services
Angioplasty
Arthritis treatment center
Birthing room/LDRP room
Blood bank
Burn-care unit
Cardiac catheterization laboratory
Cardiac intensive-care unit
Cardiac rehabilitation program
Chaplaincy/pastoral care services
Chronic obstructive pulmonary disease services
Community health promotion
Comprehensive geriatric assessment
CT scanner
Diagnostic radioisotope facility
Emergency department
Emergency department social work services
Emergency response (geriatric)
Ethics committee
Extracorporeal shock wave lithotripter
Fitness center
General inpatient care for AIDS/ARC
Genetic counseling/screening services
Geriatric acute-care unit
Geriatric clinics
Health sciences library
Hemodialysis
Histopathology laboratory
HIV/AIDS unit
Home health services
Hospice
Magnetic resonance imaging
Mammography diagnostic
Mammography screening
Medical surgical or other intensive-care unit
Megavoltage radiation therapy
Neonatal intensive-care unit
Noninvasive cardiac assessment services
Obstetrics unit
Occupational health services
Occupational therapy services
Oncology services
Open-heart surgery
Organ/tissue transplant
Organized outpatient services
Organized social work services
Orthopedic surgery
Outpatient social work services
Outpatient surgery services
Patient education
Patient representative services
Pediatric acute inpatient unit
Physical therapy services
Psychiatric child/adolescent services
Psychiatric consultation/liaison services
Psychiatric education services
Psychiatric emergency services
Psychiatric geriatric services
Psychiatric inpatient services
Psychiatric outpatient services
Psychiatric partial hospitalization program
Radioactive implants
Recreational therapy services
Rehabilitation inpatient unit
Rehabilitation outpatient services
Reproductive health services
Respiratory therapy services
Respite care
Senior membership program
Single photon emission computerized tomography (SPECT)
Skilled nursing or other long-term-care facility
Specialized outpatient program for AIDS/ARC
Speech therapy services
Sports medicine clinic/services
Therapeutic radioisotope facility
Trauma center (certified)
Ultrasound
Volunteer services department
Women's health center/services
Worksite health promotion
X-ray radiation therapy

By whatever means they launch themselves professionally, the major concern of new M.D.s who wish to specialize is a place's covered (insured) census (population size).

The American Medical Association (AMA) classifies office-based physicians into four groups, depending on how they spend their professional hours. Unless they specialize in pediatrics, obstetrics, or child psychiatry, physicians are waking up to the reality that their typical patients are now older than 55—in contrast to a generation just past when they were younger than 50.

General/family practitioners use all accepted methods of medical care. They treat diseases and injuries, provide preventive care, give routine checkups, prescribe drugs, and do some surgery. They also refer patients to medical specialists.

Medical specialists focus on specific medical disciplines such as cardiology, allergy, gastroenterology, and dermatology. They're the largest of the AMA groups because, frankly, specializing is where the money is. They're likely to give attention to surgical and nonsurgical approaches to treatment. If it's decided that surgery is the method of treatment, they refer patients to surgeons.

Surgical specialists, the best paid of the AMA's groups, operate on a regular basis several times a week. The letters F.A.C.S. (Fellow of the American College of Surgeons) after a surgeon's name indicate he or she has passed an evaluation of surgical training and skills as well as ethical fitness.

Other specialists concentrate on disciplines as familiar as psychiatry and neurology or as exotic as diagnostic radiology, aerospace medicine, and forensic pathology.

Show Me Your Recently Used Library Card: Reading Quotients

How many books sit on a library's shelves tells half the story of local reading. How often people check them out—the library's circulation—is the other half.

When circulation is added to the number of books and the sum is divided by the population served, the result is the reading quotient, a rough indicator of reading habits. The average reading quotient for the 203 retirement places in this book is 10.8. In several places, it's more than twice that number.

PLACE	READING QUOTIENT
Martha's Vineyard, MA	70.3
Bar Harbor, ME	38.4
Taos, NM	38.0
Brookings–Gold Beach, OR	32.3
Toms River–Barnegat Bay, NJ	28.1
San Juan Islands, WA	27.4
Pahrump Valley, NV	26.2
McCall, ID	26.1
Eagle River–Woodruff, WI	24.9
Williamsburg, VA	23.3
Fredericksburg–Spotsylvania, VA	23.2
East End Long Island, NY	22.8
Port Townsend, WA	21.9
Chewelah, WA	21.4
Camden, ME	21.1
Lake Placid, NY	21.0
Santa Fe, NM	20.7

Source: Derived from National Center for Education Statistics, unpublished Federal-State Cooperative System library data.

PUBLIC LIBRARIES

Enter the handsome Craven County library on a summer afternoon in the heart of New Bern, North Carolina, plop down in an armchair among the local histories, best-sellers, out-of-town newspapers, and data terminals, and you'll get so comfortable in the air-conditioned quiet you'll want to hang out there all day long.

Until its door is padlocked after a municipal budget cut or a treasured librarian is laid off, one service taken for granted is the local public library. There are more than 9,000 systems in this country. From all that, you may expect libraries to be the most plentiful of public services. They are. Though you'll find current fiction and nonfiction on the shelves everywhere, you won't always locate issues of the *Wall Street Journal, Morningstar, Vanity Fair,* or *Wired.* Nor will you always find a community fax machine or an Internet connection to look up that book mentioned on one of the talk shows.

Libraries and library resources are concentrated in larger places. Tucson's 1.2 million books are shelved in the main building on North Stone Avenue and in 18 neighborhood branches throughout surrounding Pima

County. Laguna Beach is part of the huge Orange County Public Library system, with over 2.5 million books dispersed among 28 branches. But the size of the collection tells only half the story. Measured by the number of books per person, the supply is greater in smaller places, especially college towns and towns in New England, where some endowed public libraries are beginning their third century of operation.

CONTINUING EDUCATION

When we look back over our lives, the autobiographies we wanted to write are different from the ones that finally get written. There's one thread imbedded in the stories: the quick passage through school in youth to a long period of raising a family and working throughout the middle years, ending up in a retirement that's all too short. "Is that all there is?" sang Peggy Lee.

School, then a job, then retirement—the *linear life pattern* some call it—no longer fits people's lengthening life spans. For those who miss the world of work, retirement may turn into a period of boredom and anxiety. For others, it would be an empty time indeed if there weren't opportunities for learning new things.

Read the smarmy feature articles in newspapers 20 or so years ago about the grandmother who started her masters in social work or the retired U.S. Marine Corps Major-General who got an A in Art History and you'll realize older students were looked on as interlopers in the classroom.

They aren't any longer. Gray-haired students cruise the stadium parking lot at the University of Arkansas looking for an open slot. They push a tray down the cafeteria line at the Viking Union at Western Washington University, and they scold you for smoking on the steps at the University of Vermont's library. Like any student, they buttonhole instructors after class, bang out assigned papers, and cram for final exams.

The average age of students is rising, particularly at public colleges. To fill classrooms, colleges and universities cut tuition fees or waive them for retired people who want to earn a degree, finish one, or just study for no reason other than fulfillment.

Of the 203 places featured in this book, 141 have at least one college. ***Two-year colleges*** include junior colleges, community colleges, and technical institutes that offer at least 1 year of college-level courses leading to an associate degree or are creditable toward a bachelor's degree. Most 2-year colleges are nonprofit and public. ***Four-year colleges*** offer undergraduate courses leading to a Bachelor of Arts or Bachelor of Science degree and may also offer graduate courses. Though most students in 4-year colleges are attending publicly controlled ones, most 4-year colleges are nonprofit and private.

SCORING: SERVICES

That services are in greater supply in bigger places than in smaller ones is simple common sense. This doesn't mean your need for a cardiologist or an allergist, a public library that gets *Value Line* and *Architectural Digest,* and a schedule of college courses can be met only in places the scale of Tucson or San Diego.

Rating places by their services can't be done to everyone's satisfaction, let's first admit. Services constitute a laundry list of everything from trash pickup and street repair to emergency medical teams and firefighters to gypsy moth spraying and sewage treatment.

If you agree that a broad range of hospital services, a choice of general practice and specialist physicians who treat patients, public libraries that are well looked after, and the chance to take a college course or finish a degree is as good a set of services as any other, then you won't always be disappointed by smaller places, particularly college towns with a medical school.

In spotlighting these services, *Retirement Places Rated* doesn't judge the quality of local hospitals, the credentials of local physicians, the breadth of local college course offerings, or the staff attentiveness at the local public library. This guide simply indicates the presence of selected services that most persons agree enhance retirement living.

A place's final score is derived from the scores it receives in the following four areas.

GENERAL HOSPITAL SERVICES

Grading here is based on the availability in local hospitals of services defined by the American Hospital Association (AHA). This figure is then scaled against a standard where the availability of all 85 AHA services gets a 100, the average number of services a 50, and no services a 0.

For example, the menu of services available at Durango, Colorado's hospital—the Mercy Medical Center—is good for a middling score of 49. Consider retirement places with medical schools: Columbia, Missouri; Iowa City, Iowa; and Hanover, New Hampshire. The choice of hospital services in those smaller areas is nearly as good as it is in Maricopa County in Arizona and California's Orange and San Diego counties, where retirement places found in each of those populous areas earn a score of 100 in this category.

OFFICE-BASED PHYSICIANS

Among every 100,000 people within the 203 retirement places featured in this book, 47 are M.D.s in general/family practice, another 61 are medical specialists, and 44 are surgeons.

Each place's figures for their own three physician groups are totaled and then scaled against a standard where the highest number gets 100, the average a 50, and the lowest a 0. Not surprisingly, the three locations with top scores in this factor—Chapel Hill–Carrboro, North Carolina; Charlottesville, Virginia; and Iowa City, Iowa—are college towns with medical schools.

PUBLIC LIBRARIES

The 767 million books in America's public libraries works out to 2.69 per person. The $902 million these libraries spend on books each year works out to $3.16 per person.

Each place's books per person and dollars per person figures are scaled against a standard where the highest number gets 100, the average a 50, and the lowest a 0. Places that are part of larger library systems are graded by the figures for the library system's entire legal service area. Martha's Vineyard off the coast of Massachusetts, Norfork Lake in northwestern Arkansas, and Cedar Creek Lake in Texas are, respectively, the best, average, and worst for public libraries.

CONTINUING EDUCATION

Grading here is based on the percentage of a place's population enrolled in colleges and universities. Because 2-year institutions cost less and are more likely to grant fee waivers to older adults, they're weighted one and a half times that of private 4-year colleges. Because public 4-year colleges have the same cost advantages plus a greater variety of courses listed in their catalogs as 2-year institutions, they're weighted two and a half times that of private 4-year colleges.

The resulting weighted percentage figure is then scaled against a standard where the highest number gets 100, the average a 50, and the lowest a 0. Enrollment figures are the sum of full-time and part-time students. Institutions offering only graduate-level courses aren't counted.

RANKINGS: SERVICES

Four criteria make up the score for a retirement place's supply of selected services: (1) ***short-term general hospital services,*** (2) ***physicians who treat patients,*** (3) ***public libraries,*** and (4) ***continuing education.*** Scores are rounded one decimal place. Locations with tie scores, usually within the same county, get the same rank and are listed alphabetically.

Retirement Places from First to Last

RANK	PLACE	SCORE
1.	Iowa City, IA	100.0
2.	Gainesville, FL	99.5
3.	Charlottesville, VA	99.0
4.	Columbia, MO	98.5
5.	Madison, WI	98.0
6.	Hanover, NH	97.5
7.	Chapel Hill–Carrboro, NC	97.0
8.	East End Long Island, NY	96.5
9.	Northampton–Amherst, MA	96.0
10.	Charleston, SC	95.5
11.	Southern Berkshire County, MA	95.0
12.	Williamsburg, VA	94.5
13.	Burlington, VT	94.0
14.	Fort Collins–Loveland, CO	93.5
15.	Traverse City, MI	93.0
16.	Boca Raton, FL	92.5
17.	York Beaches, ME	92.0
18.	North County San Diego, CA	91.5
19.	Tucson, AZ	91.0
20.	Grand Junction, CO	90.5
21.	Thomasville, GA	90.0
22.	Bellingham, WA	89.6
23.	Laguna Beach–Dana Point, CA	89.1
24.	Carmel–Pebble Beach, CA	88.6
25.	Savannah, GA	88.1
26.	Southern Pines–Pinehurst, NC	87.6
27.	Fayetteville, AR	87.1
28.	Hattiesburg, MS	86.6
29.	Scottsdale, AZ	85.6
29.	Wickenburg, AZ	85.6
31.	Flagstaff, AZ	84.6
31.	Sedona, AZ	84.6
33.	Reno–Sparks, NV	84.1
34.	Monadnock Region, NH	83.6
35.	Asheville, NC	83.1
36.	Bar Harbor, ME	82.6
37.	Florence, OR	82.1
38.	Athens, GA	81.6
39.	Daytona Beach, FL	81.1
40.	Wenatchee, WA	80.6
41.	Largo, FL	80.1
42.	Anacortes, WA	79.2
42.	Santa Barbara, CA	79.2
44.	Port Angeles–Sequim, WA	78.7
45.	Middle Cape Cod, MA	77.7
45.	Toms River–Barnegat Bay, NJ	77.7
47.	Fredericksburg–Spotsylvania, VA	76.7
47.	Santa Rosa, CA	76.7
49.	Pensacola, FL	76.2
50.	Durango, CO	75.2
50.	Sarasota, FL	75.2
52.	Western St. Tammany Parish, LA	74.7
53.	Annapolis, MD	73.7
53.	Petoskey–Harbor Springs, MI	73.7
55.	Hendersonville–East Flat Rock, NC	73.2
56.	Melbourne–Palm Bay, FL	72.7
57.	Litchfield Hills, CT	72.2
58.	Mesa, AZ	71.7
59.	Medford–Ashland, OR	71.2
60.	Rehoboth Bay–Indian River Bay, DE	70.7
61.	Colorado Springs, CO	70.2
62.	Lake Winnipesaukee, NH	69.8
63.	Henderson, NV	69.3
64.	Boone–Blowing Rock, NC	68.3
64.	Carson City–Carson Valley, NV	68.3
66.	Paradise–Magalia, CA	67.8
67.	Chestertown, MD	67.3
68.	Silver City, NM	66.3
68.	State College, PA	66.3
70.	Conway, SC	65.3
70.	Myrtle Beach, SC	65.3
72.	Brevard, NC	64.8
73.	Jackson Hole, WY	64.3
74.	Leesburg–Mount Dora, FL	63.8
75.	Fort Myers–Cape Coral, FL	63.3
76.	Las Cruces, NM	62.8
77.	Santa Fe, NM	62.3
78.	Palm Springs–Coachella Valley, CA	61.8
79.	Murray–Kentucky Lake, KY	61.3
80.	Morro Bay–Cambria, CA	60.8
81.	St. Jay–Northeast Kingdom, VT	60.3
82.	Oxford, MS	59.9
83.	Victorville–Apple Valley, CA	59.4
84.	Bend, OR	58.9
85.	New Port Richey, FL	58.4
86.	Hot Springs, AR	57.9
87.	Lakeland–Winter Haven, FL	57.4
88.	Virginia Beach, VA	56.9
89.	Smith Mountain Lake, VA	56.4
90.	Kerrville, TX	55.9
91.	Kalispell–Flathead Valley, MT	55.4
92.	Martha's Vineyard, MA	54.9
93.	Coeur d'Alene, ID	54.4
94.	Kauai, HI	53.9
95.	Taos, NM	53.4
96.	Bradenton, FL	52.9
97.	Easton–St. Michaels, MD	52.4
98.	Lake Placid, NY	51.9
99.	Naples, FL	51.4
100.	Camden, ME	50.9
101.	Mendocino–Fort Bragg, CA	50.4
102.	Maui, HI	50.0
103.	Beaufort, SC	48.5
103.	Hilton Head Island, SC	48.5
103.	McCall, ID	48.5
106.	Branson, MO	48.0
107.	Cottonwood–Verde Valley, AZ	47.0
107.	Prescott–Prescott Valley, AZ	47.0
109.	Fairhope–Gulf Shores, AL	46.5
110.	Bozeman, MT	46.0
111.	San Juan Islands, WA	45.5
112.	Northern Neck, VA	44.5
112.	St. Augustine, FL	44.5
114.	Panama City, FL	44.0
115.	Cedar City, UT	43.5
116.	Norfork Lake, AR	43.0
117.	Mission–McAllen–Alamo, TX	42.5
118.	Las Vegas, NM	42.0
119.	Wimberley, TX	41.5
120.	St. Simons–Jekyll Islands, GA	41.0
121.	Grants Pass, OR	40.5
122.	Sonora–Twain Harte, CA	40.0
123.	New Bern, NC	39.6
124.	Bay St. Louis–Pass Christian, MS	39.1
125.	Newport–Lincoln City, OR	38.6
126.	Park City, UT	38.1
127.	Natchitoches, LA	37.6
128.	Aiken, SC	37.1
129.	Vero Beach, FL	36.6
130.	Door Peninsula, WI	35.1
130.	Maryville, TN	35.1
130.	Pendleton District, SC	35.1

RANK	PLACE	SCORE
133.	Key West, FL	34.6
134.	Ketchum–Sun Valley, ID	34.1
135.	Montrose, CO	33.6
136.	Salida, CO	33.1
137.	Port Townsend, WA	32.6
138.	Georgetown, TX	32.1
139.	Ocean City, MD	31.6
140.	Ocala, FL	31.1
141.	Palmer–Wasilla, AK	30.6
142.	Alpine–Big Bend, TX	30.1
143.	Polson–Mission Valley, MT	29.7
144.	Lower Cape May, NJ	28.7
144.	Woodstock, VT	28.7
146.	Charles Town–Shepherdstown, WV	28.2
147.	Brookings–Gold Beach, OR	27.7
148.	Ruidoso, NM	27.2
149.	Pagosa Springs, CO	26.7
150.	Eagle River–Woodruff, WI	26.2
151.	Whidbey Island, WA	25.7
152.	Sebring–Avon Park, FL	24.7
152.	Yuma, AZ	24.7
154.	Chewelah, WA	24.2
155.	Grass Valley–Nevada City, CA	23.7
156.	Delta County, CO	23.2
157.	Fredericksburg, TX	22.7
158.	Bisbee, AZ	22.2
159.	Leelanau Peninsula, MI	21.7
160.	Edenton, NC	21.2
161.	St. George–Zion, UT	20.7
162.	Beaufort–Bogue Banks, NC	20.2
163.	Bullhead City, AZ	18.8
163.	Kingman, AZ	18.8
163.	Lake Havasu City, AZ	18.8
166.	Alamogordo, NM	18.3
167.	Summerville, SC	17.8
168.	New Braunfels, TX	17.3
169.	Apache Junction, AZ	16.8
170.	Payson, AZ	16.3
171.	Tryon, NC	15.8
172.	Eufaula, AL	15.3
173.	Sandpoint–Lake Pend Oreille, ID	14.8
174.	Port Charlotte, FL	14.3
175.	Roswell, NM	13.8
176.	Rio Rancho, NM	13.3
177.	Pahrump Valley, NV	12.8
178.	Eureka Springs, AR	11.8
178.	Oakhurst–Coarsegold, CA	11.8
180.	Cedar Creek Lake, TX	11.3
181.	Boerne, TX	10.8
182.	Lake of the Ozarks, MO	10.3
183.	Lake Conroe, TX	9.9
184.	Inverness, FL	9.4
185.	Front Royal, VA	8.9
186.	Marble Falls–Lake LBJ, TX	8.4
187.	Oscoda–Huron Shore, MI	7.9
188.	Brown County, IN	7.4
189.	Amador County, CA	6.9
190.	Southport–Brunswick Islands, NC	6.4
191.	Rabun County, GA	5.9
192.	Hamilton–Bitterroot Valley, MT	5.4
193.	Crossville, TN	4.9
194.	Kissimmee–St. Cloud, FL	4.4
195.	Berkeley Springs, WV	3.9
196.	Mariposa, CA	3.4
197.	Trinity Peninsula, TX	2.9
198.	Lake of the Cherokees, OK	2.4
199.	Apalachicola, FL	1.9
200.	Dare Outer Banks, NC	1.4
201.	Rockport–Aransas Pass, TX	0.9
202.	Table Rock Lake, MO	0.4
203.	Pike County, PA	0.0

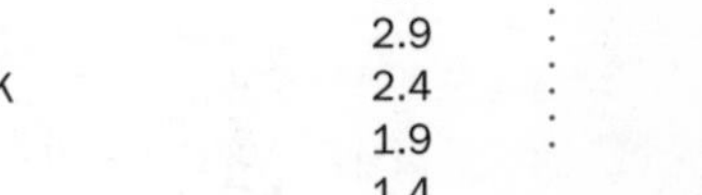

PLACE PROFILES: SERVICES

The following pages detail short-term general hospital services, the number of physicians treating patients, figures for local public libraries, and college-level continuing-education opportunities in each of the 203 places.

Under the heading **General Hospital Services** are the names of short-stay, acute-care general hospitals accredited by the Joint Commission on Accreditation of Health Care Organizations (JCAHO) and certified for Medicare participation by the U.S. Department of Health and Human Services. Hospitals that are listed in all capital letters are AMA-approved teaching hospitals. Veterans (VA) hospitals and military hospitals are also named. Because VA hospitals aren't part of the Medicare system and only military veterans may be patients, they aren't counted when determining a place's score.

Office-Based Physicians, the second heading, details how many patient-treating M.D.s practice in the county according to the AMA's basic classifications of general/family practice, medical specialties, and surgery.

Under **Public Libraries** is a listing of the libraries in the library system serving the retirement place, including all central city, suburban, and rural branches.

Under the heading **Continuing Education** are the names of community or 2-year colleges and their enrollment figures (in parentheses) and the names and enrollment figures (in parentheses) of local 4-year institutions—defined here as granting at least a bachelor's degree. Public 4-year institutions are italicized.

The sources for the information include the American Hospital Association, *Guide to the Health Care Field* (hospital accreditation and services), 2003;

American Library Association, *American Library Directory* (public library locations), 2001, and Output Measures for Public Libraries (public library quality standards), 1987; American Medical Association, *Physician Characteristics and Distribution* (office-based physician classifications and number by county), 2003; Places Rated Partnership survey of state library association annual reports, 2002; U.S. Department of Defense, Veterans Administration, Annual Report (VA hospital locations), 2003; U.S. Department of Education, National Center for Education Statistics, *Directory of Postsecondary Institutions* (college and university types and enrollments), 2003; *Public Libraries in the United States* (public library collections and budgets), 2003; and U.S. Department of Health and Human Services, Bureau of Health-Care Professions, Area Resource File (hospital services by county), 2003.

A star (★) preceding a place's name highlights it as one of the top 30 for services.

Aiken, SC

General Hospital Services
Aiken Regional Medical Center
Office-Based Physicians
General/Family Practice: 24
Specialists: 47
Surgeons: 42
Public Libraries
Part of Aiken–Bamberg–Barnwell Regional Library
Continuing Education
Two-Year
Aiken Technical College (2,260)
Four-Year
University of South Carolina (3,256)
Score: 37.1 **Rank: 128**

Alamogordo, NM

General Hospital Services
Gerald Champion Memorial Hospital
Holloman (Air Force) Hospital
Office-Based Physicians
General/Family Practice: 15
Specialists: 13
Surgeons: 14
Public Libraries
Alamogordo Public Library
Continuing Education
Two-Year
New Mexico State University (2,061)
Score: 18.3 **Rank: 166**

Alpine–Big Bend, TX

General Hospital Services
Big Bend Regional Medical Center
Office-Based Physicians
General/Family Practice: 3
Surgeons: 2
Public Libraries
Alpine Public Library
Continuing Education
Four-Year
Sul Ross State University (3,212)
Score: 30.1 **Rank: 142**

Amador County, CA

General Hospital Services
Sutter Amador Hospital
Office-Based Physicians
General/Family Practice: 14
Specialists: 11
Surgeons: 5
Public Libraries
Amador County Library
Score: 6.9 **Rank: 189**

Anacortes, WA

General Hospital Services
Island Hospital
Skagit Valley United General Hospital
Office-Based Physicians
General/Family Practice: 45
Specialists: 44
Surgeons: 49
Public Libraries
Anacortes Public Library
Continuing Education
Two-Year
Skagit Valley College (5,813)
Score: 79.2 **Rank: 42**

Annapolis, MD

General Hospital Services
Anne Arundel Medical Center
Crownsville Hospital Center
Kimborough (Army) Community Hospital
North Arundel Hospital
Office-Based Physicians
General/Family Practice: 77
Specialists: 342
Surgeons: 226
Public Libraries
Annapolis and Anne Arundel Public Library
Continuing Education
Two-Year
Anne Arundel Community College (11,890)
Four-Year
St. John's College (513)
Score: 73.7 **Rank: 53**

Apache Junction, AZ

General Hospital Services
Casa Grande Regional Medical Center
Central Arizona Medical Center
Office-Based Physicians
General/Family Practice: 12
Specialists: 24
Surgeons: 19
Public Libraries
Part of Pinal County Library District
Continuing Education
Two-Year
Central Arizona College (5,576)
Score: 16.8 **Rank: 169**

Apalachicola, FL

General Hospital Services
George E. Weems Memorial Hospital
Office-Based Physicians
General/Family Practice: 2
Specialists: 2
Surgeons: 2
Public Libraries
Apalachicola Municipal Library
Score: 1.9 **Rank: 199**

Asheville, NC

General Hospital Services
ASHEVILLE (VA) MEDICAL CENTER
MEMORIAL MISSION MEDICAL CENTER
St. Joseph's Hospital
Office-Based Physicians
General/Family Practice: 113
Specialists: 204
Surgeons: 164
Public Libraries
Asheville–Buncombe Library System
Continuing Education
Two-Year
Asheville Buncombe Community College (6,361)
Four-Year
University of North Carolina (3,222)
Warren Wilson College (675)
Score: 83.1 **Rank: 35**

★ = *one of the top 30 places for services.*

Athens, GA

General Hospital Services

Athens Regional Medical Center
St. Mary's Hospital

Office-Based Physicians

General/Family Practice: 15
Specialists: 77
Surgeons: 85

Public Libraries

Athens Regional Library System

Continuing Education

Two-Year

Athens Area Technical Institute (1,622)

Four-Year

University of Georgia (30,149)

Score: 81.6 **Rank: 38**

Bar Harbor, ME

General Hospital Services

Blue Hill Memorial Hospital
Maine Coast Memorial Hospital
Mt. Desert Island Hospital

Office-Based Physicians

General/Family Practice: 25
Specialists: 24
Surgeons: 22

Public Libraries

25 independent libraries

Continuing Education

Four-Year

College of the Atlantic (653)

Score: 82.6 **Rank: 36**

Bay St. Louis–Pass Christian, MS

General Hospital Services

Biloxi Regional Medical Center
BILOXI (VA) MEDICAL CENTER
Columbia Garden Park Hospital
Gulf Coast Medical Center
Gulfport Memorial Hospital
Hancock General Hospital
KEESLER (AIR FORCE) HOSPITAL
Sand Hill Hospital

Office-Based Physicians

General/Family Practice: 28
Specialists: 145
Surgeons: 138

Public Libraries

Part of Hancock County and Harrison County Library Systems

Score: 39.1 **Rank: 124**

Beaufort, SC

General Hospital Services

Beaufort Memorial Hospital
Beaufort (Naval) Hospital
Hilton Head Hospital
Low Country General Hospital

Office-Based Physicians

General/Family Practice: 19
Specialists: 67
Surgeons: 85

Public Libraries

Part of Beaufort County Library

Continuing Education

Two-Year

Technical College of the Lowcountry (1,382)
University of South Carolina at Beaufort (1,147)

Score: 48.5 **Rank: 103**

Beaufort–Bogue Banks, NC

General Hospital Services

Carteret General Hospital

Office-Based Physicians

General/Family Practice: 13
Specialists: 15
Surgeons: 22

Public Libraries

Part of Craven–Pamlico–Carteret Regional Library

Continuing Education

Two-Year

Carteret Community College (1,428)

Score: 20.2 **Rank: 162**

★ Bellingham, WA

General Hospital Services

ST. JOSEPH'S HOSPITAL

Office-Based Physicians

General/Family Practice: 64
Specialists: 78
Surgeons: 66

Public Libraries

Bellingham Public Library
Whatcom County Rural Library District

Continuing Education

Two-Year

Bellingham Technical College (3,714)
Northwest Indian College (1,572)
Whatcom Community College (3,517)

Four-Year

Western Washington University (10,708)

Score: 89.6 **Rank: 22**

Bend, OR

General Hospital Services

Central Oregon District Hospital
St. Charles Medical Center

Office-Based Physicians

General/Family Practice: 32
Specialists: 46
Surgeons: 70

Public Libraries

Deschutes County Library

Continuing Education

Two-Year

Central Oregon Community College (5,412)

Score: 58.9 **Rank: 84**

Berkeley Springs, WV

General Hospital Services

Morgan County War Memorial Hospital

Office-Based Physicians

General/Family Practice: 4
Specialists: 4
Surgeons: 1

Public Libraries

Morgan County Public Library

Score: 3.9 **Rank: 195**

Bisbee, AZ

General Hospital Services

Benson Hospital
Copper Queen Community Hospital
Northern Cochise Community Hospital
Sierra Vista Community Hospital
Southeast Arizona Medical Center

Office-Based Physicians

General/Family Practice: 11
Specialists: 30
Surgeons: 20

Public Libraries

Cochise County Library District

Continuing Education

Two-Year

Cochise College (4,319)

Score: 22.2 **Rank: 158**

★ Boca Raton, FL

General Hospital Services

Boca Raton Community Hospital
Palm Beach Gardens (VA) Medical Center
West Boca Medical Center

Office-Based Physicians

General/Family Practice: 153
Specialists: 1,021
Surgeons: 695

Public Libraries

23 independent libraries

Continuing Education

Two-Year

Palm Beach Community College (18,310)

Four-Year

Florida Atlantic University (17,704)
Lynn University (1,566)
Northwood University, Florida (566)
Palm Beach Atlantic College (1,953)

Score: 92.5 **Rank: 16**

Boerne, TX

Office-Based Physicians

General/Family Practice: 9
Specialists: 16
Surgeons: 8

Public Libraries

3 independent libraries

Score: 10.8 **Rank: 181**

★ = *one of the top 30 places for services.*

Retirement Places Rated

Boone–Blowing Rock, NC

General Hospital Services

Blowing Rock Hospital
Watauga Medical Center

Office-Based Physicians

General/Family Practice: 13
Specialists: 21
Surgeons: 28

Public Libraries

Part of Appalachian Regional Library

Continuing Education

Four-Year

Appalachian State University (12,457)

Score: 68.3 **Rank: 64**

Bozeman, MT

General Hospital Services

Deaconess Hospital

Office-Based Physicians

General/Family Practice: 28
Specialists: 24
Surgeons: 33

Public Libraries

5 independent libraries

Continuing Education

Four-Year

Montana State University (11,232)

Score: 46 **Rank: 110**

Bradenton, FL

General Hospital Services

Columbia Blake Medical Center
Manatee Memorial Hospital

Office-Based Physicians

General/Family Practice: 41
Specialists: 152
Surgeons: 113

Public Libraries

Manatee County Public Library System

Continuing Education

Two-Year

Manatee Community College (7,808)

Score: 52.9 **Rank: 96**

Branson, MO

General Hospital Services

Skaggs Community Health Center

Office-Based Physicians

General/Family Practice: 8
Specialists: 16
Surgeons: 8

Public Libraries

Part of Forsyth Public Library and Taneyhills Community Library Systems

Continuing Education

Four-Year

College of the Ozarks (1,509)

Score: 48 **Rank: 106**

Brevard, NC

General Hospital Services

Transylvania Community Hospital

Office-Based Physicians

General/Family Practice: 10
Specialists: 11
Surgeons: 14

Public Libraries

Transylvania County Library

Continuing Education

Four-Year

Brevard College (658)

Score: 64.8 **Rank: 72**

Brookings–Gold Beach, OR

General Hospital Services

Curry General Hospital

Office-Based Physicians

General/Family Practice: 7
Specialists: 3
Surgeons: 1

Public Libraries

5 independent libraries

Score: 27.7 **Rank: 147**

Brown County, IN

Office-Based Physicians

General/Family Practice: 2
Specialists: 1
Surgeons: 1

Public Libraries

Brown County Public Library

Score: 7.4 **Rank: 188**

Bullhead City, AZ

General Hospital Services

Mohave Valley Hospital
Western Arizona Regional Medical Center

Office-Based Physicians

General/Family Practice: 17
Specialists: 38
Surgeons: 38

Public Libraries

Part of Mohave County Library District

Continuing Education

Two-Year

Mohave Community College (5,223)

Score: 18.8 **Rank: 163**

★ Burlington, VT

General Hospital Services

FLETCHER ALLEN HOSPITAL

Office-Based Physicians

General/Family Practice: 72
Specialists: 279
Surgeons: 172

Public Libraries

15 independent libraries

Continuing Education

Four-Year

Champlain College (2,060)
Saint Michaels College (2,628)
Trinity College (1,062)
University of Vermont (10,351)

Score: 94 **Rank: 13**

Camden, ME

General Hospital Services

Penobscot Bay Medical Center

Office-Based Physicians

General/Family Practice: 11
Specialists: 27
Surgeons: 20

Public Libraries

16 independent libraries

Score: 50.9 **Rank: 100**

★ Carmel–Pebble Beach, CA

General Hospital Services

Community Hospital of Monterey Peninsula
George Mee Memorial Hospital
NATIVIDAD MEDICAL CENTER
Salinas Valley Memorial Hospital

Office-Based Physicians

General/Family Practice: 95
Specialists: 182
Surgeons: 144

Public Libraries

22 independent libraries

Continuing Education

Two-Year

Hartnell College (6,784)
Healf Business College (436)
Monterey Peninsula College (8,933)

Four-Year

California State University, Monterey Bay (654)
Monterey Institute of International Studies (701)

Score: 88.6 **Rank: 24**

Carson City–Carson Valley, NV

General Hospital Services

Carson Tahoe Hospital

Office-Based Physicians

General/Family Practice: 23
Specialists: 43
Surgeons: 30

Public Libraries

Carson City Library
Douglas County Library

Continuing Education

Two-Year

Western Nevada Community College (4,409)

Score: 68.3 **Rank: 64**

Cedar City, UT

General Hospital Services

East Texas Medical Center Athens

Office-Based Physicians

General/Family Practice: 6
Specialists: 7
Surgeons: 9

★ = *one of the top 30 places for services.*

Public Libraries
Cedar City Public Library
Continuing Education
Four-Year
Southern Utah University (5,159)
Score: 43.5 **Rank: 115**

Cedar Creek Lake, TX
General Hospital Services
East Texas Medical Center
Office-Based Physicians
General/Family Practice: 14
Specialists: 8
Surgeons: 12
Public Libraries
Clint W. Murchison Memorial Library
Continuing Education
Two-Year
Trinity Valley Community College (4,808)
Score: 11.3 **Rank: 180**

★ Chapel Hill–Carrboro, NC
General Hospital Services
UNIVERSITY OF NORTH CAROLINA HOSPITAL
Office-Based Physicians
General/Family Practice: 79
Specialists: 408
Surgeons: 244
Public Libraries
Chapel Hill Public Library
Continuing Education
Four-Year
University of North Carolina (24,439)
Score: 97 **Rank: 7**

Charles Town–Shepherdstown, WV
General Hospital Services
Jefferson Memorial Hospital
Office-Based Physicians
General/Family Practice: 12
Specialists: 12
Surgeons: 8
Public Libraries
4 independent libraries
Continuing Education
Four-Year
Shepherd College (3,602)
Score: 28.2 **Rank: 146**

★ Charleston, SC
General Hospital Services
Bon Secours–St. Francis Xavier Hospital
CHARLESTON MEMORIAL HOSPITAL
CHARLESTON (NAVAL) HOSPITAL
CHARLESTON (VA) MEDICAL CENTER
Columbia Trident Medical Center
East Cooper Regional Medical Center
MEDICAL UNIVERSITY HOSPITAL
ROPER HOSPITAL
Office-Based Physicians
General/Family Practice: 123
Specialists: 582
Surgeons: 441
Public Libraries
Charleston County Library
Continuing Education
Two-Year
Trident Technical College (9,292)
Four-Year
Johnson & Wales University (1,197)
Charleston Southern University (2,562)
Citadel Military College (4,316)
College of Charleston (10,537)
Medical University of South Carolina (2,256)
Score: 95.5 **Rank: 10**

★ Charlottesville, VA
General Hospital Services
Martha Jefferson Hospital
UNIVERSITY OF VIRGINIA HOSPITAL
Office-Based Physicians
General/Family Practice: 79
Specialists: 407
Surgeons: 247
Public Libraries
Part of Jefferson–Madison Regional Library
Continuing Education
Two-Year
Piedmont Virginia Community College (4,011)
Four-Year
University of Virginia (21,728)
Score: 99 **Rank: 3**

Chestertown, MD
General Hospital Services
Kent & Queen Annes Hospital
Office-Based Physicians
General/Family Practice: 8
Specialists: 12
Surgeons: 9
Public Libraries
Kent County Public Library
Continuing Education
Four-Year
Washington College (981)
Score: 67.3 **Rank: 67**

Chewelah, WA
General Hospital Services
MOUNT CARMEL HOSPITAL
Office-Based Physicians
General/Family Practice: 15
Specialists: 5
Surgeons: 5
Public Libraries
2 independent libraries
Score: 24.2 **Rank: 154**

Coeur d'Alene, ID
General Hospital Services
Kootenai Medical Center
Office-Based Physicians
General/Family Practice: 38
Specialists: 31
Surgeons: 47
Public Libraries
Coeur d'Alene Public Library
Kootenai County District Library
Continuing Education
Two-Year
North Idaho College (3,312)
Score: 54.4 **Rank: 93**

Colorado Springs, CO
General Hospital Services
(Air Force) Academy Hospital
Evan (Army) Community Hospital
Memorial Hospital
PENROSE ST. FRANCIS HEALTH SYSTEM
Office-Based Physicians
General/Family Practice: 87
Specialists: 219
Surgeons: 212
Public Libraries
Pikes Peak Library District
Continuing Education
Two-Year
Pikes Peak Community College (6,726)
Four-Year
Beth El College of Nursing (460)
Colorado College (2,014)
Fuller Theological Seminary (2,276)
Nazarene Bible College (418)
University of Colorado (5,906)
Score: 70.2 **Rank: 61**

★ Columbia, MO
General Hospital Services
BOONE HOSPITAL CENTER
CHARTER HOSPITAL OF COLUMBIA
Columbia Regional Hospital
Truman Memorial (VA) Hospital
UNIVERSITY OF MISSOURI HOSPITALS
Office-Based Physicians
General/Family Practice: 76
Specialists: 287
Surgeons: 208
Public Libraries
Daniel Boone Regional Library
Continuing Education
Four-Year
Columbia College (6,229)
Stephens College (889)
University of Missouri (22,356)
Score: 98.5 **Rank: 4**

★ = *one of the top 30 places for services.*

Conway, SC

General Hospital Services

Coastal Carolina Hospital
Columbia Grand Strand Regional Medical Center
Conway Hospital
Loris Community Hospital

Office-Based Physicians

General/Family Practice: 36
Specialists: 83
Surgeons: 76

Public Libraries

Part of Horry County Memorial Library System

Continuing Education

Two-Year

Horry-Georgetown Technical College (3,166)

Four-Year

Coastal Carolina University (4,468)

Score: 65.3 **Rank: 70**

Cottonwood–Verde Valley, AZ

General Hospital Services

Marcus Lawrence Memorial Hospital
Yavapai Regional Medical Center

Office-Based Physicians

General/Family Practice: 28
Specialists: 48
Surgeons: 47

Public Libraries

Part of Yavapai County Library District

Continuing Education

Two-Year

Yavapai College (6,082)

Four-Year

Prescott College (736)

Score: 47 **Rank: 107**

Crossville, TN

General Hospital Services

Cumberland Medical Center

Office-Based Physicians

General/Family Practice: 5
Specialists: 21
Surgeons: 17

Public Libraries

Art Circle Public Library

Score: 4.9 **Rank: 193**

Dare Outer Banks, NC

Office-Based Physicians

General/Family Practice: 4
Specialists: 3
Surgeons: 4

Public Libraries

Part of East Albemarle Regional Library

Score: 1.4 **Rank: 200**

Daytona Beach, FL

General Hospital Services

Atlantic Medical Centers
Bert Fish Medical Center
Florida Hospital Fish Memorial
HALIFAX MEDICAL CENTER
Ormond Beach Memorial Hospital
West Volusia Memorial Hospital

Office-Based Physicians

General/Family Practice: 119
Specialists: 202
Surgeons: 170

Public Libraries

Volusia County Public Library

Continuing Education

Two-Year

Daytona Beach Community College (12,004)

Four-Year

Bethune Cookman College (2,402)
Embry-Riddle Aeronautical University (11,714)
Stetson University (2,897)

Score: 81.1 **Rank: 39**

Delta County, CO

General Hospital Services

Delta County Memorial Hospital

Office-Based Physicians

General/Family Practice: 11
Specialists: 4
Surgeons: 7

Public Libraries

5 independent libraries

Score: 23.2 **Rank: 156**

Door Peninsula, WI

General Hospital Services

Door County Memorial Hospital

Office-Based Physicians

General/Family Practice: 7
Specialists: 9
Surgeons: 10

Public Libraries

Door County Library

Score: 35.1 **Rank: 130**

Durango, CO

General Hospital Services

Mercy Medical Center

Office-Based Physicians

General/Family Practice: 22
Specialists: 24
Surgeons: 37

Public Libraries

Durango Public Library

Continuing Education

Four-Year

Fort Lewis College (4,267)

Score: 75.2 **Rank: 50**

Eagle River–Woodruff, WI

General Hospital Services

Eagle River Memorial Hospital

Office-Based Physicians

General/Family Practice: 9
Surgeons: 3

Public Libraries

9 independent libraries

Score: 26.2 **Rank: 150**

★ East End Long Island, NY

General Hospital Services

Brookhaven Memorial Hospital
Brunswick Hospital
Eastern Long Island Hospital
NORTHPORT (VA) MEDICAL CENTER
Southampton Hospital
SOUTHSIDE HOSPITAL
UNIVERSITY HOSPITAL, STONY BROOK

Office-Based Physicians

General/Family Practice: 270
Specialists: 1,334
Surgeons: 761

Public Libraries

61 independent libraries

Continuing Education

Two-Year

Suffolk County Community College (10,800)

Four-Year

Dowling College (5,855)
Long Island University, Brentwood (588)
Long Island University, Southampton College (1,410)
New York Institute of Technology, Central Islip (1,142)
Saint Josephs College, Suffolk Campus (2,464)
SUNY at Stony Brook (17,665)
SUNY College of Technology at Farmingdale (6,209)

Score: 96.5 **Rank: 8**

Easton–St. Michaels, MD

General Hospital Services

Easton Memorial Hospital

Office-Based Physicians

General/Family Practice: 11
Specialists: 40
Surgeons: 35

Public Libraries

Talbot County Free Library

Score: 52.4 **Rank: 97**

Edenton, NC

General Hospital Services

Chowan Hospital

Office-Based Physicians

General/Family Practice: 5
Specialists: 3
Surgeons: 10

★ = *one of the top 30 places for services.*

Public Libraries
Part of Pettigrew Regional Library
Score: 21.2 **Rank: 160**

Eufaula, AL
General Hospital Services
Lakeview Community Hospital
Office-Based Physicians
General/Family Practice: 5
Specialists: 4
Surgeons: 6
Public Libraries
Eufaula Carnegie Library
Score: 15.3 **Rank: 172**

Eureka Springs, AR
General Hospital Services
Carroll Medical Center
Eureka Springs Hospital
Office-Based Physicians
General/Family Practice: 13
Specialists: 2
Surgeons: 5
Public Libraries
Eureka Spring Carnegie Library
Continuing Education
Two-Year
Chauncey Sparks State Technical College (635)
Score: 11.8 **Rank: 178**

Fairhope–Gulf Shores, AL
General Hospital Services
North Baldwin Hospital
South Baldwin Medical Center
Thomas Hospital
Office-Based Physicians
General/Family Practice: 45
Specialists: 55
Surgeons: 49
Public Libraries
10 independent libraries
Continuing Education
Two-Year
James H. Faulkner State Community College (3,042)
Score: 46.5 **Rank: 109**

★ Fayetteville, AR
General Hospital Services
Fayetteville City Hospital
Fayetteville (VA) Medical Center
Northwest Medical Center
WASHINGTON REGIONAL MEDICAL CENTER
Office-Based Physicians
General/Family Practice: 71
Specialists: 74
Surgeons: 75
Public Libraries
Part of Ozarks Regional Library
Continuing Education
Four-Year
University of Arkansas (14,692)
Score: 87.1 **Rank: 27**

Flagstaff, AZ
General Hospital Services
Flagstaff Medical Center
Page Hospital
Office-Based Physicians
General/Family Practice: 40
Specialists: 62
Surgeons: 55
Public Libraries
Flagstaff City/Coconino County Library
Continuing Education
Two-Year
Coconino County Community College (2,738)
Four-Year
Northern Arizona University (20,131)
Score: 84.6 **Rank: 31**

Florence, OR
General Hospital Services
Cottage Grove Hospital
Peace Harbor Hospital
Office-Based Physicians
General/Family Practice: 108
Specialists: 185
Surgeons: 140
Public Libraries
Siuslaw Public Library District
Continuing Education
Two-Year
Lane Community College (8,799)
Four-Year
Northwest Christian College (404)
University of Oregon (17,470)
Score: 82.1 **Rank: 37**

★ Fort Collins–Loveland, CO
General Hospital Services
Estes Park Medical Center
McKee Medical Center
POUDRE VALLEY HOSPITAL
Office-Based Physicians
General/Family Practice: 122
Specialists: 104
Surgeons: 106
Public Libraries
6 independent libraries
Continuing Education
Four-Year
Colorado State University (25,333)
National Technological University (1,571)
Score: 93.5 **Rank: 14**

Fort Myers–Cape Coral, FL
General Hospital Services
Cape Coral Hospital
East Pointe Hospital
Gulf Coast Hospital
Lee Memorial Hospital
Southwest Florida Regional Medical Center
Office-Based Physicians
General/Family Practice: 51
Specialists: 257
Surgeons: 217
Public Libraries
Lee County Library System
Continuing Education
Two-Year
Edison Community College (9,810)
Score: 63.3 **Rank: 75**

Fredericksburg, TX
General Hospital Services
Hill Country Memorial Hospital
Office-Based Physicians
General/Family Practice: 12
Specialists: 11
Surgeons: 11
Public Libraries
Pioneer Memorial Library
Score: 22.7 **Rank: 157**

Fredericksburg–Spotsylvania, VA
General Hospital Services
Mary Washington Hospital
Office-Based Physicians
General/Family Practice: 16
Specialists: 69
Surgeons: 64
Public Libraries
Part of Central Rappahannock Regional Library
Continuing Education
Four-Year
Mary Washington College (3,755)
Score: 76.7 **Rank: 47**

Front Royal, VA
General Hospital Services
Warren Memorial Hospital
Office-Based Physicians
General/Family Practice: 5
Specialists: 6
Surgeons: 8
Public Libraries
Samuels Public Library
Score: 8.9 **Rank: 185**

★ Gainesville, FL
General Hospital Services
ALACHUA GENERAL HOSPITAL
GAINESVILLE (VA) MEDICAL CENTER
North Florida Regional Medical Center
SHANDS HOSPITAL, UNIVERSITY OF FLORIDA
Office-Based Physicians
General/Family Practice: 109
Specialists: 453
Surgeons: 298
Public Libraries
Alachua County Library District

continued

★ = *one of the top 30 places for services.*

★ **Gainesville, FL (cont.)**

Continuing Education

Two-Year

Santa Fe Community College (12,283)

Four-Year

University of Florida (39,412)

Score: 99.5 Rank: 2

Georgetown, TX

General Hospital Services

Georgetown Hospital
John's Community Hospital
Round Rock Hospital

Office-Based Physicians

General/Family Practice: 57
Specialists: 58
Surgeons: 47

Public Libraries

6 independent libraries

Continuing Education

Four-Year

Southwestern University (1,261)

Score: 32.1 Rank: 138

★ **Grand Junction, CO**

General Hospital Services

Community Hospital
Family Health West
Grand Junction (VA) Medical Center
ST. MARY'S HOSPITAL & MEDICAL CENTER

Office-Based Physicians

General/Family Practice: 69
Specialists: 58
Surgeons: 58

Public Libraries

Mesa Public Library District

Continuing Education

Four-Year

Mesa State College (4,721)

Score: 90.5 Rank: 20

Grants Pass, OR

General Hospital Services

Three Rivers Community Hospital

Office-Based Physicians

General/Family Practice: 23
Specialists: 24
Surgeons: 24

Public Libraries

Josephine County Library System

Continuing Education

Two-Year

Rogue Community College (2,858)

Score: 40.5 Rank: 121

Grass Valley–Nevada City, CA

General Hospital Services

Sierra Nevada Memorial Hospital
Tahoe Forest Hospital District

Office-Based Physicians

General/Family Practice: 31
Specialists: 37
Surgeons: 40

Public Libraries

Nevada County Library

Score: 23.7 Rank: 155

Hamilton–Bitterroot Valley, MT

General Hospital Services

Marcus Daly Memorial Hospital

Office-Based Physicians

General/Family Practice: 10
Specialists: 9
Surgeons: 9

Public Libraries

3 independent libraries

Score: 5.4 Rank: 192

★ **Hanover, NH**

General Hospital Services

Alice Peck Day Memorial Hospital
Cottage Hospital
Littleton Hospital
MARY HITCHCOCK MEMORIAL HOSPITAL
Speare Memorial Hospital

Office-Based Physicians

General/Family Practice: 46
Specialists: 217
Surgeons: 142

Public Libraries

40 independent libraries

Continuing Education

Two-Year

Lebanon College (588)

Four-Year

Dartmouth College (5,123)
Plymouth State College (4,357)

Score: 97.5 Rank: 6

★ **Hattiesburg, MS**

General Hospital Services

Forrest General Hospital
Wesley Medical Center

Office-Based Physicians

General/Family Practice: 32
Specialists: 83
Surgeons: 88

Public Libraries

The Library of Hattiesburg, Petal & Forrest County

Continuing Education

Four-Year

William Carey College (2,172)
University of Southern Mississippi (13,657)

Score: 86.6 Rank: 28

Henderson, NV

General Hospital Services

St. Rose Dominican Hospital

Office-Based Physicians

General/Family Practice: 170
Specialists: 693
Surgeons: 467

Public Libraries

Henderson Public District Library

Continuing Education

Two-Year

Community College of Southern Nevada (20,417)

Four-Year

University of Nevada, Las Vegas (19,715)

Score: 69.3 Rank: 63

Hendersonville–East Flat Rock, NC

General Hospital Services

MARGARET PARDEE MEMORIAL HOSPITAL
Park Ridge Hospital

Office-Based Physicians

General/Family Practice: 35
Specialists: 47
Surgeons: 44

Public Libraries

Henderson County Public Library

Continuing Education

Two-Year

Blue Ridge Community College (1,573)

Score: 73.2 Rank: 55

Hilton Head Island, SC

General Hospital Services

Hilton Head Hospital

Office-Based Physicians

General/Family Practice: 19
Specialists: 67
Surgeons: 85

Public Libraries

Part of Beaufort County Library

Continuing Education

Two-Year

Technical College of the Lowcountry (1,382)
University of South Carolina at Beaufort (1,147)

Score: 48.5 Rank: 103

Hot Springs, AR

General Hospital Services

National Park Medical Center
St. Joseph's Regional Health Center

Office-Based Physicians

General/Family Practice: 29
Specialists: 58
Surgeons: 54

Public Libraries

Part of Tri-Lakes Regional Library

Continuing Education

Two-Year

Garland County Community College (1,902)

Score: 57.9 Rank: 86

★ = *one of the top 30 places for services.*

Inverness, FL

General Hospital Services

Citrus Memorial Hospital

Seven Rivers Community Hospital

Office-Based Physicians

General/Family Practice: 18

Specialists: 62

Surgeons: 41

Public Libraries

Citrus County Library System

Score: 9.4 **Rank: 184**

★ Iowa City, IA

General Hospital Services

IOWA CITY (VA) MEDICAL CENTER

MERCY HOSPITAL

UNIVERSITY OF IOWA HOSPITAL

Office-Based Physicians

General/Family Practice: 80

Specialists: 315

Surgeons: 301

Public Libraries

Iowa City Public Library

Continuing Education

Four-Year

University of Iowa (28,052)

Score: 100 **Rank: 1**

Jackson Hole, WY

General Hospital Services

St. John's Hospital

Office-Based Physicians

General/Family Practice: 8

Specialists: 12

Surgeons: 15

Public Libraries

Teton County Library

Score: 64.3 **Rank: 73**

Kalispell–Flathead Valley, MT

General Hospital Services

Kalispell Regional Hospital

North Valley Hospital

Office-Based Physicians

General/Family Practice: 27

Specialists: 34

Surgeons: 43

Public Libraries

Flathead County Library

Continuing Education

Two-Year

Flathead Valley Community College (1,645)

Score: 55.4 **Rank: 91**

Kauai, HI

General Hospital Services

Kauai Veterans Memorial Hospital

Mahelona Memorial Hospital

Wilcox Memorial Hospital

Office-Based Physicians

General/Family Practice: 18

Specialists: 29

Surgeons: 18

Public Libraries

Part of Hawaii State Library System

Continuing Education

Two-Year

Kauai Community College (1,461)

Score: 53.9 **Rank: 94**

Kerrville, TX

General Hospital Services

Kerrville (VA) Medical Center

Peterson Memorial Hospital

Office-Based Physicians

General/Family Practice: 9

Specialists: 32

Surgeons: 30

Public Libraries

Butt–Holdsworth Memorial Library

Continuing Education

Four-Year

Schreiner College (676)

Score: 55.9 **Rank: 90**

Ketchum–Sun Valley, ID

General Hospital Services

Wood River Medical Center

Office-Based Physicians

General/Family Practice: 13

Specialists: 10

Surgeons: 22

Public Libraries

3 independent libraries

Score: 34.1 **Rank: 134**

Key West, FL

General Hospital Services

Fishermens Hospital

Mariners Hospital

Office-Based Physicians

General/Family Practice: 15

Specialists: 30

Surgeons: 45

Public Libraries

Monroe County Public Library System

Continuing Education

Two-Year

Florida Keys Community College (2,120)

Score: 34.6 **Rank: 133**

Kingman, AZ

General Hospital Services

Kingman Regional Medical Center

Office-Based Physicians

General/Family Practice: 17

Specialists: 38

Surgeons: 38

Public Libraries

Part of Mohave County Library District

Continuing Education

Two-Year

Mohave Community College (5,223)

Score: 18.8 **Rank: 163**

Kissimmee–St. Cloud, FL

General Hospital Services

Columbia Osceola Regional Medical Center

FLORIDA HOSPITAL KISSIMMEE

Office-Based Physicians

General/Family Practice: 19

Specialists: 62

Surgeons: 44

Public Libraries

Osceola County Library System

Score: 4.4 **Rank: 194**

★ Laguna Beach–Dana Point, CA

General Hospital Services

Mission Hospital Regional Medical Center

Saddleback Memorial Medical Center

South Coast Medical Center

Office-Based Physicians

General/Family Practice: 698

Specialists: 2,280

Surgeons: 1,519

Public Libraries

Part of Orange County Public Library

Continuing Education

Two-Year

Coastline Community College (7,747)

Cypress College (13,426)

Fullerton College (17,874)

Golden West College (11,732)

Irvine Valley College (8,027)

Orange Coast College (21,135)

Rancho Santiago College (24,460)

Saddleback College (14,093)

Four-Year

California Graduate School of Theology (835)

California State University, Fullerton (22,604)

Chapman University (3,476)

Chapman University-Academic Centers (6,239)

Christ College Irvine (931)

Pacific Christian College (892)

Southern California College (1,200)

University of California, Irvine (17,256)

Score: 89.1 **Rank: 23**

Lake Conroe, TX

General Hospital Services

CONROE REGIONAL MEDICAL CENTER

The Woodlands Memorial Hospital

Office-Based Physicians

General/Family Practice: 42

Specialists: 36

Surgeons: 37

Public Libraries

Montgomery County Library

Score: 9.9 **Rank: 183**

★ = *one of the top 30 places for services.*

Lake Havasu City, AZ

General Hospital Services

Havasu Samaritan Regional Hospital

Office-Based Physicians

General/Family Practice: 17

Specialists: 38

Surgeons: 38

Public Libraries

Mohave County Library District

Continuing Education

Two-Year

Mohave Community College (5,223)

Score: 18.8 Rank: 163

Lake of the Cherokees, OK

General Hospital Services

Grove General Hospital

Office-Based Physicians

General/Family Practice: 7

Specialists: 4

Surgeons: 3

Public Libraries

Part of Eastern Oklahoma Library District

Score: 2.4 Rank: 198

Lake of the Ozarks, MO

General Hospital Services

Lake of the Ozarks General Hospital

Office-Based Physicians

General/Family Practice: 4

Specialists: 2

Surgeons: 8

Public Libraries

Camden County Library District

Score: 10.3 Rank: 182

Lake Placid, NY

General Hospital Services

Moses Ludington Hospital

Office-Based Physicians

General/Family Practice: 12

Specialists: 8

Surgeons: 4

Public Libraries

Lake Placid Public Library

Continuing Education

Two-Year

North Country Community College (1,148)

Score: 51.9 Rank: 98

Lake Winnipesaukee, NH

General Hospital Services

Huggins Hospital

Lakes Region General Hospital

Office-Based Physicians

General/Family Practice: 23

Specialists: 37

Surgeons: 53

Public Libraries

29 independent libraries

Continuing Education

Two-Year

New Hampshire Technical College, Laconia (927)

Score: 69.8 Rank: 62

Lakeland–Winter Haven, FL

General Hospital Services

Bartow Memorial Hospital

Heart of Florida Medical Center

Lakeland Medical Center

Winter Haven Hospital

Office-Based Physicians

General/Family Practice: 49

Specialists: 226

Surgeons: 181

Public Libraries

12 independent libraries

Continuing Education

Two-Year

Polk Community College (5,461)

Four-Year

Florida Southern College (2,571)

Southeastern College (1,065)

Warner Southern College (581)

Webber College (453)

Whitefield Theological Seminary (835)

Score: 57.4 Rank: 87

Largo, FL

General Hospital Services

Bay Pines (VA) Medical Center

Largo Medical Center

Sun Coast Hospital

Office-Based Physicians

General/Family Practice: 196

Specialists: 716

Surgeons: 464

Public Libraries

Part of Pinellas Public Library Cooperative

Continuing Education

Two-Year

Saint Petersburg Junior College (21,176)

Four-Year

Clearwater Christian College (528)

Eckerd College (1,335)

Score: 80.1 Rank: 41

Las Cruces, NM

General Hospital Services

MEMORIAL GENERAL HOSPITAL

Office-Based Physicians

General/Family Practice: 39

Specialists: 61

Surgeons: 44

Public Libraries

3 independent libraries

Continuing Education

Two-Year

New Mexico State University-Dona Ana (3,788)

Four-Year

New Mexico State University-Main Campus (15,127)

Score: 62.8 Rank: 76

Las Vegas, NM

General Hospital Services

Northeastern Regional Hospital

Office-Based Physicians

General/Family Practice: 10

Specialists: 11

Surgeons: 5

Public Libraries

Carnegie Public Library

Continuing Education

Two-Year

Luna Vocational Technical Institute (1,568)

Four-Year

New Mexico Highlands University (2,813)

Score: 42 Rank: 118

Leelanau Peninsula, MI

General Hospital Services

Leelanau Memorial Health Center

Office-Based Physicians

General/Family Practice: 4

Specialists: 3

Surgeons: 1

Public Libraries

4 independent libraries

Score: 21.7 Rank: 159

Leesburg–Mount Dora, FL

General Hospital Services

Florida Hospital Waterman

Leesburg Regional Medical Center

South Lake Memorial Hospital

Office-Based Physicians

General/Family Practice: 42

Specialists: 88

Surgeons: 77

Public Libraries

Lake County Library System

Leesburg Public Library

Continuing Education

Two-Year

Lake–Sumter Community College (2,584)

Score: 63.8 Rank: 74

Litchfield Hills, CT

General Hospital Services

Charlotte Hungerford Hospital

New Milford Hospital

Sharon Hospital

Office-Based Physicians

General/Family Practice: 24

Specialists: 125

Surgeons: 66

Public Libraries

30 independent libraries

★ = *one of the top 30 places for services.*

Continuing Education
Two-Year
Northwestern Connecticut Community College (2,089)
Score: 72.2 **Rank: 57**

Lower Cape May, NJ
General Hospital Services
Burdete Tomlin Memorial Hospital
Office-Based Physicians
General/Family Practice: 10
Specialists: 33
Surgeons: 22
Public Libraries
9 independent libraries
Score: 28.7 **Rank: 144**

★ Madison, WI
General Hospital Services
MERITER HOSPITAL
MIDDLETON MEMORIAL (VA) HOSPITAL
ST. MARY'S HOSPITAL
Stoughton Hospital
UNIVERSITY OF WISCONSIN HOSPITAL
Office-Based Physicians
General/Family Practice: 213
Specialists: 566
Surgeons: 357
Public Libraries
24 independent libraries
Continuing Education
Two-Year
University of Wisconsin Centers (9,084)
Wisconsin Area Vocational Tech (18,900)
Four-Year
Edgewood College (2,056)
University of Wisconsin (39,125)
Score: 98 **Rank: 5**

Marble Falls–Lake LBJ, TX
General Hospital Services
Highland Lakes Medical Center
Office-Based Physicians
General/Family Practice: 11
Specialists: 6
Surgeons: 3
Public Libraries
Burnet County Library System
Score: 8.4 **Rank: 186**

Mariposa, CA
General Hospital Services
John Fremont Healthcare District
Office-Based Physicians
General/Family Practice: 4
Specialists: 2
Surgeons: 1
Public Libraries
Mariposa County Library
Score: 3.4 **Rank: 196**

Martha's Vineyard, MA
General Hospital Services
Martha's Vineyard Hospital
Office-Based Physicians
General/Family Practice: 4
Specialists: 13
Surgeons: 5
Public Libraries
Edgartown Free Public Library
Oak Bluffs Public Library
Vineyard Haven Public Library
Score: 54.9 **Rank: 92**

Maryville, TN
General Hospital Services
Blount Memorial Hospital
Office-Based Physicians
General/Family Practice: 20
Specialists: 56
Surgeons: 30
Public Libraries
Blount County Public Library
Continuing Education
Four-Year
Maryville College (885)
Score: 35.1 **Rank: 130**

Maui, HI
General Hospital Services
Maui Memorial Hospital
Molokai General Hospital
Office-Based Physicians
General/Family Practice: 27
Specialists: 66
Surgeons: 55
Public Libraries
Part of Hawaii State Library System
Continuing Education
Two-Year
Maui Community College (2,765)
Score: 50 **Rank: 102**

McCall, ID
General Hospital Services
Cascade Medical Center
McCall Memorial Hospital
Office-Based Physicians
General/Family Practice: 5
Specialists: 2
Surgeons: 3
Public Libraries
2 independent libraries
Score: 48.5 **Rank: 103**

Medford–Ashland, OR
General Hospital Services
Ashland Community Hospital
Providence Medford Medical Center
Rogue Valley Medical Center
Office-Based Physicians
General/Family Practice: 43
Specialists: 114
Surgeons: 92
Public Libraries
Jackson County Library
Continuing Education
Four-Year
Southern Oregon University (4,962)
Score: 71.2 **Rank: 59**

Melbourne–Palm Bay, FL
General Hospital Services
Cape Canaveral Hospital
Holmes Regional Medical Center
Patrick (Air Force) Hospital
Sea Pines Hospital
Wuesthoff Memorial Hospital
Office-Based Physicians
General/Family Practice: 93
Specialists: 274
Surgeons: 192
Public Libraries
Brevard County Library System
Continuing Education
Two-Year
Brevard Community College (14,188)
Four-Year
Florida Institute of Technology (4,232)
Score: 72.7 **Rank: 56**

Mendocino–Fort Bragg, CA
General Hospital Services
Howard Memorial Hospital
Mendocino Coast Hospital
Ukiah Valley Medical Center
Office-Based Physicians
General/Family Practice: 39
Specialists: 41
Surgeons: 43
Public Libraries
Mendocino County Library
Continuing Education
Two-Year
Mendocino College (3,489)
Score: 50.4 **Rank: 101**

Mesa, AZ
General Hospital Services
Desert Samaritan Medical Center
Desert Vista Hospital
Mesa General Hospital Medical Center
Mesa Lutheran Hospital
Valley Lutheran Hospital
Office-Based Physicians
General/Family Practice: 646
Specialists: 1,768
Surgeons: 1,316
Public Libraries
Mesa Public Library

continued

★ = *one of the top 30 places for services.*

Mesa, AZ (cont.)

Continuing Education

Two-Year

Chandler/Gilbert Community College (3,527)

Estrella Mountain Community College (2,165)

Gateway Community College (6,806)

Glendale Community College (17,699)

Mesa Community College (21,244)

Paradise Valley Community College (5,576)

Phoenix College (11,689)

Rio Salado Community College (8,754)

Scottsdale Community College (9,775)

South Mountain Community College (2,418)

Four-Year

Arizona State University (42,040)

Arizona State University-West (4,770)

Grand Canyon University (2,119)

Ottawa University (1,635)

Western International University (1,195)

Score: 71.7 **Rank: 58**

Middle Cape Cod, MA

General Hospital Services

Cape Cod Hospital

Falmouth Hospital

Office-Based Physicians

General/Family Practice: 33

Specialists: 177

Surgeons: 105

Public Libraries

34 independent libraries

Continuing Education

Two-Year

Cape Cod Community College (3,640)

Score: 77.7 **Rank: 45**

Mission–McAllen–Alamo, TX

General Hospital Services

Edinburg Regional Medical Center

Knapp Medical Center

McAllen Heart Hospital

MCALLEN MEDICAL CENTER

Mission Hospital

Rio Grande Regional Hospital

Office-Based Physicians

General/Family Practice: 119

Specialists: 186

Surgeons: 123

Public Libraries

9 independent libraries

Continuing Education

Two-Year

South Texas Community College (3,298)

Four-Year

University of Texas-Pan American (13,360)

Score: 42.5 **Rank: 117**

Monadnock Region, NH

General Hospital Services

Cheshire Medical Center

Office-Based Physicians

General/Family Practice: 26

Specialists: 31

Surgeons: 18

Public Libraries

25 independent libraries

Continuing Education

Four-Year

Antioch New England Graduate School (1,147)

Franklin Pierce College (3,017)

Keene State College (4,736)

Score: 83.6 **Rank: 34**

Montrose, CO

General Hospital Services

Montrose Memorial Hospital

Office-Based Physicians

General/Family Practice: 4

Specialists: 11

Surgeons: 13

Public Libraries

Montrose Library District

Score: 33.6 **Rank: 135**

Morro Bay–Cambria, CA

General Hospital Services

French Hospital

San Luis Obispo General Hospital

Sierra Vista Regional Medical Center

Office-Based Physicians

General/Family Practice: 67

Specialists: 135

Surgeons: 108

Public Libraries

Part of San Luis Obispo City-County Library

Continuing Education

Two-Year

Cuesta College (7,880)

Four-Year

California Polytechnic State University (16,023)

Score: 60.8 **Rank: 80**

Murray–Kentucky Lake, KY

General Hospital Services

Murray-Calloway County Hospital

Office-Based Physicians

General/Family Practice: 5

Specialists: 13

Surgeons: 13

Public Libraries

Calloway County Public Library

Continuing Education

Four-Year

Murray State University (8,148)

Score: 61.3 **Rank: 79**

Myrtle Beach, SC

General Hospital Services

Grand Strand Regional Medical Center

Office-Based Physicians

General/Family Practice: 36

Specialists: 83

Surgeons: 76

Public Libraries

Part of Horry County Memorial Library System

Continuing Education

Two-Year

Horry-Georgetown Technical College (3,166)

Four-Year

Coastal Carolina University (4,468)

Score: 65.3 **Rank: 70**

Naples, FL

General Hospital Services

Naples Community Hospital

Office-Based Physicians

General/Family Practice: 35

Specialists: 160

Surgeons: 138

Public Libraries

Collier County Public Library

Score: 51.4 **Rank: 99**

Natchitoches, LA

General Hospital Services

Natchitoches Parish Hospital

Office-Based Physicians

General/Family Practice: 4

Specialists: 12

Surgeons: 9

Public Libraries

Natchitoches Parish Library

Continuing Education

Four-Year

Northwestern State University (9,040)

Score: 37.6 **Rank: 127**

New Bern, NC

General Hospital Services

Cherry Point (Naval) Hospital

Craven Regional Medical Center

Office-Based Physicians

General/Family Practice: 16

Specialists: 63

Surgeons: 53

Public Libraries

Part of Craven–Pamlico–Carteret Regional Library

Continuing Education

Two-Year

Craven Community College (2,238)

Score: 39.6 **Rank: 123**

★ = *one of the top 30 places for services.*

New Braunfels, TX

General Hospital Services
McKenna Memorial Hospital

Office-Based Physicians
General/Family Practice: 26
Specialists: 20
Surgeons: 23

Public Libraries
3 independent libraries

Score: 17.3 **Rank: 168**

New Port Richey, FL

General Hospital Services
Bayonet Regional Medical Center
East Pasco Medical Center
New Port Richey Hospital
North Bay Medical Center

Office-Based Physicians
General/Family Practice: 39
Specialists: 196
Surgeons: 91

Public Libraries
Pasco County Library System

Continuing Education

Two-Year
Pasco-Hernando Community College (5,685)

Four-Year
Saint Leo College (7,176)

Score: 58.4 **Rank: 85**

Newport–Lincoln City, OR

General Hospital Services
North Lincoln Hospital
Pacific Communities Hospital

Office-Based Physicians
General/Family Practice: 6
Specialists: 14
Surgeons: 10

Public Libraries
7 independent libraries

Continuing Education

Two-Year
Oregon Coast Community College (923)

Score: 38.6 **Rank: 125**

Norfork Lake, AR

General Hospital Services
Baxter County Regional Hospital

Office-Based Physicians
General/Family Practice: 10
Specialists: 16
Surgeons: 23

Public Libraries
Baxter County Library

Continuing Education

Two-Year
Arkansas State University (614)

Score: 43 **Rank: 116**

★ **North County San Diego, CA**

General Hospital Services
CAMP PENDLETON (NAVAL) HOSPITAL
Fallbrook Hospital
Palomar Medical Center
SAN DIEGO (NAVAL) MEDICAL CENTER
San Diego (VA) Medical Center
Scripps Encinitas Memorial Hospital
Tri-City Medical Center

Office-Based Physicians
General/Family Practice: 624
Specialists: 2,112
Surgeons: 1,452

Public Libraries
76 independent libraries

Continuing Education

Two-Year
Cuyamaca College (4,409)
Grossmont College (14,560)
Kelsey-Jenney Business College (422)
Mira Costa College (9,020)
Palomar College (20,569)
San Diego City College (13,130)
San Diego Mesa College (19,904)
San Diego Miramar College (6,145)
Southwestern College (15,133)

Four-Year
California Pacific University (835)
California School of Professional Psychology (629)
California State University, San Marcos (3,642)
Christian Heritage College (454)
Coleman College (827)
National University (10,068)
Point Loma Nazarene College (2,459)
San Diego State University (29,350)
U.S. International University (1,307)
University of California (18,315)
University of San Diego (6,416)
Vision Christian University (835)

Score: 91.5 **Rank: 18**

★ **Northampton–Amherst, MA**

General Hospital Services
Cooley Dickinson Hospital
Mary Lane Hospital

Office-Based Physicians
General/Family Practice: 52
Specialists: 189
Surgeons: 52

Public Libraries
25 independent libraries

Continuing Education

Four-Year
Amherst College (1,623)
Hampshire College (1,094)
Mount Holyoke College (1,896)
Smith College (3,189)
University of Massachusetts (25,267)

Score: 96 **Rank: 9**

Northern Neck, VA

General Hospital Services
Rappahannock General Hospital

Office-Based Physicians
General/Family Practice: 11
Specialists: 21
Surgeons: 13

Public Libraries
Lancaster County Public Library
Northumberland County Public Library

Score: 44.5 **Rank: 112**

Oakhurst–Coarsegold, CA

General Hospital Services
Chowchilla District Memorial Hospital
Madera Community Hospital

Office-Based Physicians
General/Family Practice: 11
Specialists: 43
Surgeons: 19

Public Libraries
Madera County Library

Score: 11.8 **Rank: 178**

Ocala, FL

General Hospital Services
Ocala Regional Medical Center
Munroe Regional Medical Center

Office-Based Physicians
General/Family Practice: 35
Specialists: 122
Surgeons: 97

Public Libraries
Part of Central Florida Regional Library System

Continuing Education

Two-Year
Central Florida Community College (6,330)

Score: 31.1 **Rank: 140**

Ocean City, MD

General Hospital Services
Atlantic General Hospital

Office-Based Physicians
General/Family Practice: 11
Specialists: 8
Surgeons: 4

Public Libraries
Worcester County Library

Score: 31.6 **Rank: 139**

★ = *one of the top 30 places for services.*

Oscoda–Huron Shore, MI

General Hospital Services
Tawas St. Joseph Hospital

Office-Based Physicians
General/Family Practice: 4
Specialists: 5
Surgeons: 5

Public Libraries
Part of Iosco–Arenac District Library

Score: 7.9 **Rank: 187**

Oxford, MS

General Hospital Services
Baptist Memorial Hospital North Mississippi

Office-Based Physicians
General/Family Practice: 8
Specialists: 19
Surgeons: 24

Public Libraries
Part of First Regional Library

Continuing Education
Four-Year
University of Mississippi (10,635)

Score: 59.9 **Rank: 82**

Pagosa Springs, CO

Office-Based Physicians
General/Family Practice: 7
Specialists: 2
Surgeons: 3

Public Libraries
Part of Upper San Juan Library District

Score: 26.7 **Rank: 149**

Pahrump Valley, NV

General Hospital Services
Nye Regional Medical Center

Office-Based Physicians
General/Family Practice: 6
Specialists: 2
Surgeons: 1

Public Libraries
Pahrump Community Library

Score: 12.8 **Rank: 177**

Palm Springs–Coachella Valley, CA

General Hospital Services
Desert Regional Medical Center
Eisenhower Medical Center
Heart Hospital
John Kennedy Memorial Hospital
Menifee Valley Medical Center

Office-Based Physicians
General/Family Practice: 235
Specialists: 539
Surgeons: 417

Public Libraries
Palm Springs Public Library
Parts of Riverside City & County Public Library

Continuing Education
Two-Year
College of the Desert (8,078)
Mount San Jacinto College (5,579)
Palo Verde College (929)
Riverside Community College (19,123)
Four-Year
California Baptist College (1,239)
La Sierra University (1,536)
University of California (8,906)

Score: 61.8 **Rank: 78**

Palmer–Wasilla, AK

General Hospital Services (18)
Valley Hospital

Office-Based Physicians
General/Family Practice: 15
Specialists: 5
Surgeons: 11

Public Libraries
2 independent libraries

Score: 30.6 **Rank: 141**

Panama City, FL

General Hospital Services
Bay Medical Center
Gulf Coast Medical Center
Tyndall (Air Force) Hospital

Office-Based Physicians
General/Family Practice: 24
Specialists: 71
Surgeons: 82

Public Libraries
Part of Northwest Regional Library System

Continuing Education
Two-Year
Gulf Coast Community College (5,988)

Score: 44 **Rank: 114**

Paradise–Magalia, CA

General Hospital Services
Biggs-Gridley Memorial Hospital
Enloe Memorial Hospital
Feather River Hospital
Oroville Hospital

Office-Based Physicians
General/Family Practice: 51
Specialists: 93
Surgeons: 90

Public Libraries
Butte County Library

Continuing Education
Two-Year
Butte College (8,921)
Four-Year
California State University (13,798)

Score: 67.8 **Rank: 66**

Park City, UT

Office-Based Physicians
General/Family Practice: 17
Specialists: 20
Surgeons: 12

Public Libraries
Park City Library

Score: 38.1 **Rank: 126**

Payson, AZ

General Hospital Services
Cobre Valley Community Hospital
Payson Regional Medical Center

Office-Based Physicians
General/Family Practice: 15
Specialists: 12
Surgeons: 12

Public Libraries
Part of Gila County Library District

Score: 16.3 **Rank: 170**

Pendleton District, SC

General Hospital Services
Oconee Memorial Hospital

Office-Based Physicians
General/Family Practice: 25
Specialists: 17
Surgeons: 22

Public Libraries
Oconee County Library

Continuing Education
Four-Year
Clemson University (16,318)

Score: 35.1 **Rank: 130**

Pensacola, FL

General Hospital Services
Baptist Hospital
Columbia West Florida Regional Medical Center
PENSACOLA (NAVAL) HOSPITAL
SACRED HEART HOSPITAL

Office-Based Physicians
General/Family Practice: 98
Specialists: 219
Surgeons: 175

Public Libraries
Part of West Florida Regional Library

Continuing Education
Two-Year
Pensacola Junior College (11,250)
Four-Year
Pensacola Christian College (3,255)
University of West Florida (8,052)

Score: 76.2 **Rank: 49**

Petoskey–Harbor Springs, MI

General Hospital Services
Northern Michigan Hospitals

Office-Based Physicians
General/Family Practice: 9
Specialists: 39
Surgeons: 33

★ = *one of the top 30 places for services.*

Public Libraries
6 independent libraries
Continuing Education
Two-Year
North Central Michigan College (2,032)
Score: 73.7 **Rank: 53**

Pike County, PA
Office-Based Physicians
General/Family Practice: 3
Specialists: 8
Surgeons: 4
Public Libraries
Pike County Public Library
Score: 0 **Rank: 203**

Polson–Mission Valley, MT
General Hospital Services
St. Joseph Hospital
St. Luke Community Hospital
Office-Based Physicians
General/Family Practice: 14
Specialists: 2
Surgeons: 3
Public Libraries
5 independent libraries
Continuing Education
Four-Year
Salish Kootenai Community College (844)
Score: 29.7 **Rank: 143**

Port Angeles–Sequim, WA
General Hospital Services
Olympic Memorial Hospital
Office-Based Physicians
General/Family Practice: 31
Specialists: 25
Surgeons: 25
Public Libraries
Part of North Olympic Library System
Continuing Education
Two-Year
Peninsula College (3,147)
Score: 78.7 **Rank: 44**

Port Charlotte, FL
General Hospital Services
Charlotte Regional Medical Center
Fawcett Memorial Hospital
St. Joseph Hospital
Office-Based Physicians
General/Family Practice: 14
Specialists: 97
Surgeons: 60
Public Libraries
Charlotte–Glades Library System
Score: 14.3 **Rank: 174**

Port Townsend, WA
General Hospital Services
Jefferson General Hospital
Office-Based Physicians
General/Family Practice: 13
Specialists: 8
Surgeons: 6
Public Libraries
Jefferson County Rural Library District
Port Townsend Public Library
Score: 32.6 **Rank: 137**

Prescott–Prescott Valley, AZ
General Hospital Services
Prescott (VA) Medical Center
Yavapai Regional Medical Center
Office-Based Physicians
General/Family Practice: 28
Specialists: 48
Surgeons: 47
Public Libraries
Part of Yavapai County Library District
Continuing Education
Two-Year
Yavapai College (6,082)
Four-Year
Prescott College (736)
Score: 47 **Rank: 107**

Rabun County, GA
General Hospital Services
Rabun County Memorial Hospital
Office-Based Physicians
General/Family Practice: 4
Specialists: 4
Surgeons: 6
Public Libraries
Part of Northeast Georgia Regional Library
Score: 5.9 **Rank: 191**

Rehoboth Bay–Indian River Bay, DE
General Hospital Services
Beebe Medical Center
Nanticoke Memorial Hospital
Office-Based Physicians
General/Family Practice: 31
Specialists: 84
Surgeons: 62
Public Libraries
14 independent libraries
Continuing Education
Two-Year
Delaware Technical College (4,377)
Score: 70.7 **Rank: 60**

Reno–Sparks, NV
General Hospital Services
LOUGARIS (VA) MEDICAL CENTER
Northern Nevada Medical Center
St. Mary's Regional Medical Center
WASHOE MEDICAL CENTER
Office-Based Physicians
General/Family Practice: 100
Specialists: 234
Surgeons: 194
Public Libraries
Washoe County Library
Continuing Education
Two-Year
Truckee Meadows Community College (9,203)
Four-Year
Sierra Nevada College (466)
University of Nevada (11,989)
Score: 84.1 **Rank: 33**

Rio Rancho, NM
Office-Based Physicians
General/Family Practice: 26
Specialists: 30
Surgeons: 9
Public Libraries
Rio Rancho Public Library
Score: 13.3 **Rank: 176**

Rockport–Aransas Pass, TX
Office-Based Physicians
General/Family Practice: 6
Specialists: 2
Surgeons: 3
Public Libraries
Aransas County Public Library
Score: 0.9 **Rank: 201**

Roswell, NM
General Hospital Services
Artesia General Hospital
Columbia Medical Center of Carlsbad
Office-Based Physicians
General/Family Practice: 4
Specialists: 10
Surgeons: 15
Public Libraries
Roswell Public Library
Continuing Education
Two-Year
New Mexico State University (1,151)
Score: 13.8 **Rank: 175**

Ruidoso, NM
General Hospital Services
Lincoln County Medical Center
Office-Based Physicians
General/Family Practice: 4
Specialists: 2
Surgeons: 11
Public Libraries
Ruidoso Public Library
Continuing Education
Two-Year
Eastern New Mexico University (516)
Score: 27.2 **Rank: 148**

★ = *one of the top 30 places for services.*

St. Augustine, FL

General Hospital Services

Flagler Hospital West

Office-Based Physicians

General/Family Practice: 27
Specialists: 101
Surgeons: 58

Public Libraries

St. Johns County Public Library

Continuing Education

Four-Year

Flagler College (1,426)

Score: 44.5 Rank: 112

St. George–Zion, UT

General Hospital Services

Dixie Medical Center

Office-Based Physicians

General/Family Practice: 21
Specialists: 25
Surgeons: 28

Public Libraries

Washington County Public Library

Continuing Education

Two-Year

Dixie College (4,921)

Score: 20.7 Rank: 161

St. Jay–Northeast Kingdom, VT

General Hospital Services

Northeastern Vermont Hospital

Office-Based Physicians

General/Family Practice: 9
Specialists: 14
Surgeons: 11

Public Libraries

17 independent libraries

Continuing Education

Four-Year

Lyndon State College (1,145)

Score: 60.3 Rank: 81

St. Simons–Jekyll Islands, GA

General Hospital Services

Southeast Georgia Medical Center

Office-Based Physicians

General/Family Practice: 12
Specialists: 48
Surgeons: 43

Public Libraries

Part of Brunswick–Glynn County Regional Library

Continuing Education

Two-Year

Brunswick College (1,920)

Score: 41 Rank: 120

Salida, CO

General Hospital Services

Heart of the Rockies Medical Center

Office-Based Physicians

General/Family Practice: 7
Specialists: 3
Surgeons: 6

Public Libraries

Salida/South Chaffee County Library

Score: 33.1 Rank: 136

San Juan Islands, WA

Office-Based Physicians

General/Family Practice: 8
Specialists: 5
Surgeons: 7

Public Libraries

Lopez Island Library
Orcas Island Library District
San Juan Island Library District

Score: 45.5 Rank: 111

Sandpoint–Lake Pend Oreille, ID

General Hospital Services

Bonner General Hospital

Office-Based Physicians

General/Family Practice: 7
Specialists: 6
Surgeons: 10

Public Libraries

3 independent libraries

Score: 14.8 Rank: 173

Santa Barbara, CA

General Hospital Services

Goleta Valley Cottage Hospital
Marian Medical Center
St. Francis Medical Center
SANTA BARBARA COTTAGE HOSPITAL
Santa Inez Valley Hospital
Valley Community Hospital
Vandenberg (Air Force) Hospital

Office-Based Physicians

General/Family Practice: 97
Specialists: 311
Surgeons: 222

Public Libraries

Santa Barbara Public Library

Continuing Education

Two-Year

Allan Hancock College (12,979)
Santa Barbara City College (11,409)

Four-Year

The Fielding Institute (843)
University of California (18,224)
Westmont College (1,255)

Score: 79.2 Rank: 42

Santa Fe, NM

General Hospital Services

Pinon Hills Hospital
ST. VINCENT HOSPITAL

Office-Based Physicians

General/Family Practice: 41
Specialists: 85
Surgeons: 61

Public Libraries

Santa Fe Public Library

Continuing Education

Two-Year

Santa Fe Community College (3,128)

Four-Year

College of Santa Fe (1,433)
St. John's College (466)

Score: 62.3 Rank: 77

Santa Rosa, CA

General Hospital Services

Kaiser Foundation Hospital
SANTA ROSA COMMUNITY HOSPITAL
Santa Rosa Memorial Hospital
Sutter Medical Center
Warrack Medical Center Hospital

Office-Based Physicians

General/Family Practice: 224
Specialists: 247
Surgeons: 209

Public Libraries

Sonoma County Library

Continuing Education

Two-Year

Santa Rosa Junior College (23,164)

Four-Year

Sonoma State University (6,778)

Score: 76.7 Rank: 47

Sarasota, FL

General Hospital Services

Bon Secours Venice Hospital
Doctors' Hospital
Englewood Community Hospital
Sarasota Memorial Hospital

Office-Based Physicians

General/Family Practice: 81
Specialists: 317
Surgeons: 241

Public Libraries

Sarasota County Public Library System

Continuing Education

Four-Year

Ringling School of Art and Design (823)

Score: 75.2 Rank: 50

★ Savannah, GA

General Hospital Services

Candler Hospital
MEMORIAL MEDICAL CENTER
St. Joseph's Hospital

Office-Based Physicians

General/Family Practice: 60
Specialists: 218
Surgeons: 193

Public Libraries

Part of Chatham–Effingham–Liberty Regional Library

★ = *one of the top 30 places for services.*

Continuing Education

Two-Year

Savannah Technical Institute (1,811)

Four-Year

Armstrong State College (5,348)

Savannah College of Art and Design (2,782)

Savannah State College (3,211)

Score: 88.1 **Rank: 25**

★ Scottsdale, AZ

General Hospital Services

MAYO CLINIC SCOTTSDALE

SCOTTSDALE HEALTHCARE–OSBORN

SCOTTSDALE HEALTHCARE–SHEA

Office-Based Physicians

General/Family Practice: 646

Specialists: 1,768

Surgeons: 1,316

Public Libraries

Scottsdale Public Library

Continuing Education

Two-Year

Chandler/Gilbert Community College (3,527)

Estrella Mountain Community College (2,165)

Gateway Community College (6,806)

Glendale Community College (17,699)

Mesa Community College (21,244)

Paradise Valley Community College (5,576)

Phoenix College (11,689)

Rio Salado Community College (8,754)

Scottsdale Community College (9,775)

South Mountain Community College (2,418)

Four-Year

Arizona State University (42,040)

Arizona State University-West (4,770)

Grand Canyon University (2,119)

Ottawa University (1,635)

Western International University (1,195)

Score: 85.6 **Rank: 29**

Sebring–Avon Park, FL

General Hospital Services

Florida Hospital Heartland Medical Center

Highlands Regional Medical Center

Office-Based Physicians

General/Family Practice: 11

Specialists: 38

Surgeons: 26

Public Libraries

Highlands County Library System

Continuing Education

Two-Year

South Florida Community College (2,717)

Score: 24.7 **Rank: 152**

Sedona, AZ

General Hospital Services

Flagstaff Medical Center

Office-Based Physicians

General/Family Practice: 40

Specialists: 62

Surgeons: 55

Public Libraries

Part of Flagstaff City/Coconino County Library District

Continuing Education

Two-Year

Coconino County Community College (2,738)

Four-Year

Northern Arizona University (20,131)

Score: 84.6 **Rank: 31**

Silver City, NM

General Hospital Services

Gila Regional Medical Center

Office-Based Physicians

General/Family Practice: 10

Specialists: 13

Surgeons: 11

Public Libraries

The Public Library

Continuing Education

Four-Year

Western New Mexico University (2,530)

Score: 66.3 **Rank: 68**

Smith Mountain Lake, VA

General Hospital Services

Carilion Franklin Memorial Hospital

Office-Based Physicians

General/Family Practice: 32

Specialists: 14

Surgeons: 12

Public Libraries

Franklin County Public Library

Continuing Education

Two-Year

Paul D. Camp Community College (1,509)

Four-Year

Ferrum College (1,091)

Score: 56.4 **Rank: 89**

Sonora–Twain Harte, CA

General Hospital Services

Sonora Community Hospital

Tuolumne General Hospital

Office-Based Physicians

General/Family Practice: 11

Specialists: 26

Surgeons: 19

Public Libraries

Tuolumne County Free Library

Continuing Education

Two-Year

Columbia College (2,159)

Score: 40 **Rank: 122**

★ Southern Berkshire County, MA

General Hospital Services

BERKSHIRE MEDICAL CENTER

Fairview Hospital

Hillcrest Hospital

Office-Based Physicians

General/Family Practice: 18

Specialists: 154

Surgeons: 73

Public Libraries

31 independent libraries

Continuing Education

Two-Year

Berkshire Community College (2,388)

Four-Year

North Adams State College (1,725)

Williams College (2,055)

Score: 95 **Rank: 11**

★ Southern Pines–Pinehurst, NC

General Hospital Services

Firsthealth Moore Regional Hospital

Office-Based Physicians

General/Family Practice: 13

Specialists: 46

Surgeons: 63

Public Libraries

Sandhill Regional Library System

Southern Pines Public Library

Continuing Education

Two-Year

Sandhills Community College (2,287)

Score: 87.6 **Rank: 26**

Southport–Brunswick Islands, NC

General Hospital Services

Brunswick Community Hospital

Dosher Memorial Hospital

Office-Based Physicians

General/Family Practice: 10

Specialists: 12

Surgeons: 14

Public Libraries

Brunswick County Library

Continuing Education

Two-Year

Brunswick Community College (829)

Score: 6.4 **Rank: 190**

★ = *one of the top 30 places for services.*

State College, PA

General Hospital Services
Centre Community Hospital
Office-Based Physicians
General/Family Practice: 23
Specialists: 71
Surgeons: 48
Public Libraries
4 independent libraries
Continuing Education
Four-Year
Pennsylvania State University (39,646)
Score: 66.3 Rank: 68

Summerville, SC

Office-Based Physicians
General/Family Practice: 23
Specialists: 10
Surgeons: 12
Public Libraries
Dorchester County Library
Continuing Education
Four-Year
Cummins Memorial Theological Seminary (835)
Score: 17.8 Rank: 167

Table Rock Lake, MO

Office-Based Physicians
General/Family Practice: 3
Specialists: 3
Surgeons: 2
Public Libraries
Stone County Library
Score: 0.4 Rank: 202

Taos, NM

General Hospital Services
Holy Cross Hospital
Office-Based Physicians
General/Family Practice: 9
Specialists: 9
Surgeons: 9
Public Libraries
Taos Public Library
Continuing Education
Two-Year
University of New Mexico, Taos (770)
Score: 53.4 Rank: 95

★ Thomasville, GA

General Hospital Services
John Archbold Memorial Hospital
Office-Based Physicians
General/Family Practice: 8
Specialists: 39
Surgeons: 33
Public Libraries
Thomas County Public Library
Continuing Education
Two-Year
Thomas Technical Institute (995)
Four-Year
Thomas College (757)
Score: 90 Rank: 21

Toms River–Barnegat Bay, NJ

General Hospital Services
Kimball Medical Center
Medical Center of Ocean County
Southern Ocean County Hospital
Office-Based Physicians
General/Family Practice: 25
Specialists: 316
Surgeons: 165
Public Libraries
Ocean County Library
Continuing Education
Two-Year
Ocean County College (8,122)
Four-Year
Beth Medrash Govoha (1,848)
Georgian Court College (2,509)
Score: 77.7 Rank: 45

★ Traverse City, MI

General Hospital Services
MUNSON MEDICAL CENTER
Office-Based Physicians
General/Family Practice: 30
Specialists: 79
Surgeons: 58
Public Libraries
Traverse Area District Library
Continuing Education
Two-Year
Northwestern Michigan College (3,937)
Score: 93 Rank: 15

Trinity Peninsula, TX

General Hospital Services
East Texas Medical Center Trinity
Office-Based Physicians
General/Family Practice: 2
Specialists: 1
Public Libraries
2 independent libraries
Score: 2.9 Rank: 197

Tryon, NC

General Hospital Services
St. Luke's Hospital
Office-Based Physicians
General/Family Practice: 4
Specialists: 5
Surgeons: 8
Public Libraries
Polk County Public Library
Score: 15.8 Rank: 171

★ Tucson, AZ

General Hospital Services
Carondelet St. Joseph's Hospital
Carondelet St. Mary's Hospital
Columbia El Dorado Hospital
Columbia Northwest Hospital
KINO COMMUNITY HOSPITAL
Tucson General Hospital
Tucson Heart
TUCSON MEDICAL CENTER
TUCSON (VA) MEDICAL CENTER
UNIVERSITY MEDICAL CENTER
Office-Based Physicians
General/Family Practice: 190
Specialists: 708
Surgeons: 480
Public Libraries
Tucson-Pima Public Library
Continuing Education
Two-Year
Pima Community College (27,866)
Four-Year
University of Arizona (34,777)
Score: 91 Rank: 19

Vero Beach, FL

General Hospital Services
Indian River Memorial Hospital
Sebastian River Medical Center
Office-Based Physicians
General/Family Practice: 22
Specialists: 85
Surgeons: 74
Public Libraries
Indian River County Library
Score: 36.6 Rank: 129

Victorville–Apple Valley, CA

General Hospital Services
Desert Valley Hospital
JERRY PETTIS MEMORIAL (VA) HOSPITAL
St. Mary Regional Medical Center
Victor Valley Community Hospital
Office-Based Physicians
General/Family Practice: 329
Specialists: 825
Surgeons: 585
Public Libraries
San Bernardino County Library
Continuing Education
Two-Year
Barstow College (2,321)
Chaffey Community College (13,334)
Crafton Hills College (4,654)
San Bernardino Valley College (9,873)
Victor Valley College (7,283)
Four-Year
California State University (11,957)
Calvary Chapel Bible College (533)
Loma Linda University (3,167)
San Bernardino Bible College (835)
University of Redlands (3,723)
Score: 59.4 Rank: 83

★ = *one of the top 30 places for services.*

Virginia Beach, VA

General Hospital Services

Sentara Bayside Hospital
VIRGINIA BEACH GENERAL HOSPITAL

Office-Based Physicians

General/Family Practice: 116
Specialists: 239
Surgeons: 207

Public Libraries

Virginia Beach Public Library

Continuing Education

Four-Year

Regent University (1,452)

Score: 56.9 Rank: 88

Wenatchee, WA

General Hospital Services

Central Washington Hospital
Lake Chelan Community Hospital

Office-Based Physicians

General/Family Practice: 44
Specialists: 49
Surgeons: 44

Public Libraries

Part of North Central Regional Library

Continuing Education

Two-Year

Wenatchee Valley College (2,634)

Score: 80.6 Rank: 40

Western St. Tammany Parish, LA

General Hospital Services

Lakeview Regional Medical Center
Northshore Regional Medical Center
St. Tammany Parish Hospital
Slidell Memorial Hospital

Office-Based Physicians

General/Family Practice: 30
Specialists: 173
Surgeons: 114

Public Libraries

Part of St. Tammany Parish Library System

Continuing Education

Four-Year

LaSalle University (6,226)

Score: 74.7 Rank: 52

Whidbey Island, WA

General Hospital Services

Oak Harbor (Naval) Hospital
Whidbey General Hospital

Office-Based Physicians

General/Family Practice: 21
Specialists: 12
Surgeons: 19

Public Libraries

Part of Sno-Isle Regional Library

Score: 25.7 Rank: 151

★ **Wickenburg, AZ**

General Hospital Services

Wickenburg Regional Hospital

Office-Based Physicians

General/Family Practice: 646
Specialists: 1,768
Surgeons: 1,316

Public Libraries

Wickenburg Public Library

Score: 85.6 Rank: 29

★ **Williamsburg, VA**

General Hospital Services

Williamsburg Community Hospital

Office-Based Physicians

General/Family Practice: 26
Specialists: 51
Surgeons: 51

Public Libraries

Williamsburg Regional Library

Continuing Education

Four-Year

College of William and Mary (7,709)

Score: 94.5 Rank: 12

Wimberley, TX

General Hospital Services

Central Texas Medical Center

Office-Based Physicians

General/Family Practice: 14
Specialists: 29
Surgeons: 21

Public Libraries

5 independent libraries

Continuing Education

Four-Year

Southwest Texas State University (20,917)

Score: 41.5 Rank: 119

Woodstock, VT

General Hospital Services

Mt. Ascutney Hospital Health Center
Springfield Hospital
WHITE RIVER JUNCTION (VA) MEDICAL CENTER

Office-Based Physicians

General/Family Practice: 12
Specialists: 59
Surgeons: 30

Public Libraries

26 independent libraries

Score: 28.7 Rank: 144

★ **York Beaches, ME**

General Hospital Services

Henrietta Goodall Hospital
Southern Maine Medical Center
York Hospital

Office-Based Physicians

General/Family Practice: 30
Specialists: 60
Surgeons: 48

Public Libraries

33 independent libraries

Continuing Education

Four-Year

University of New England (1,783)

Score: 92 Rank: 17

Yuma, AZ

General Hospital Services

Yuma Regional Medical Center

Office-Based Physicians

General/Family Practice: 15
Specialists: 50
Surgeons: 41

Public Libraries

Yuma County Library District

Continuing Education

Two-Year

Arizona Western College (5,754)

Score: 24.7 Rank: 152

★ = *one of the top 30 places for services.*

ET CETERA: SERVICES

FINDING THE RIGHT DOCTOR

Chances are good you'll have to choose a new physician at some point; even if you don't move after retirement, your doctor might. Finding a replacement for the person in whom you've put so much trust isn't always easy.

Think about the kind of doctor with whom you're most comfortable. Do you want to place complete faith in your physician? Do you have questions about your treatment? Do you like a cooperative arrangement, in which you and your doctor work as a

team? It's very important to most people that they have a doctor who'll listen to their complaints, worries, and concerns, rather than one who may make patients feel they're questioning the doctor's authority.

If you're planning to move, you might ask your present doctor if he or she knows anything about the doctors in the area where you're going. Or you can get names from the nearest hospital at the new location, from friends you make, from medical societies, and from new neighbors.

When you've decided whom you want to contact, call that doctor's office, say you're a prospective patient, and ask to speak to the doctor briefly. You may have to agree to call back, but making a connection with a professional voice is an important step. If you can't arrange this, if the doctor is too busy, you probably ought to go to the next name on your list. You need a physician who's readily accessible.

When you do make contact, tell the doctor enough about yourself so that he or she has a good idea of who you are and what your problems may be. If the doctor sounds right to you, you could ask about fees, house calls (yes, they're again being made when necessary), and emergencies. Or you may wish to save some of these questions for a personal visit. It's important to establish through the initial phone call or visit that you and the doctor will be at ease with each other.

Evaluate the doctor's attitude. If he or she doesn't want to bother with you now, you'll probably get that don't-bother-me treatment sooner or later when dealing with specific problems. Make sure:

- You can openly discuss your feelings and personal concerns about sexual and emotional problems.
- The doctor isn't vague, impatient, or unwilling to answer all your questions about the causes and treatment of your physical problems.
- The doctor takes a thorough history on you and asks about past physical and emotional problems, family medical history, medication you're taking, and other matters affecting your health.
- The doctor doesn't always attribute your problems to getting older and he or she doesn't automatically prescribe drugs rather than deal with real causes of your medical problems.
- The doctor has an associate to whom you can turn should your doctor retire or die.

Talk with the doctor about the transfer of your medical records. Some doctors like to have them, especially if there's any specific medical problem or chronic condition. Other doctors prefer not to see them and to develop new records.

Even if you feel fine, arrange to have a physical or at least a quick checkup. This is more for the doctor's benefit than for yours, but it will help you too. Should an emergency occur, the doctor will have basic information about you and some knowledge of your needs, and you'll avoid the stress of trying to work with a doctor who has to learn about you in an emergency.

FINDING THE RIGHT LAWYER

When you move from one state to another, you enter a new legal environment. Even if your will is legal in your new state (and it may not be), it may not do the best possible job. When you resettle, see a lawyer in your new area to make certain your will is one your state will recognize. Some states, for example, require that the executor of a will be a resident of the state where the deceased lived. For a legal checkup, you may have to contact a family lawyer.

Lawyering is a competitive field. In the past, lawyers and clients usually found each other in the Rotary Club, at a church supper, or on the golf course. Since 1977, when the Supreme Court struck down laws barring the legal profession from advertising, many lawyers have gotten quite adept at promoting themselves. Just look up "Lawyers" in a telephone book's Yellow Pages and you'll be surprised by the techniques many firms borrow from consumer goods advertising. Specialists for 24-hour divorces, personal bankruptcy, workers' compensation, and personal injury claims abound. Somewhere hidden among the listings is a professional who can advise you. How do you find him or her?

- **Satisfied clients:** If a friend or neighbor has used a lawyer's services, ask what sort of matter the lawyer handled. Some lawyers, especially in large cities, specialize in a certain branch of law and aren't interested in taking on cases outside their specialty. They aren't family lawyers.
- **Lawyers referral service:** Most state bar associations have a referral service with a toll-free phone number. Typically, the name you're given is an attorney who practices where you live, specializes in your legal problem, and is next up in the association's

database to be referred. You can have a first interview with him or her for a stated—and very modest—fee. In that interview, you can find out whether you'll need further legal services, and, if so, you can decide whether you want to continue with the lawyer to whom you were referred.

- **Local bar association:** If the state bar association referral service lists no lawyer in your area, try the local bar association. If you don't find it in the telephone book, inquire for the president's name at the county courthouse. You can then ask him or her for the name of a good lawyer. Be sure to make it clear you're asking them, in their capacity as president of the local association, for the name of a reliable attorney who can perform the kind of service you're seeking.

Don't Put Off Your Will

It's human nature to avoid thinking about the need for a will. Seven out of every ten people die without one, and eight of ten who do have a will fail to keep it up to date. If you don't have a will when you die, the state where you live in your retirement years will write one for you according to its own statutes, and the assets you may have worked hard to accumulate will be distributed according to its laws.

Don't put off making a will because of imagined costs. A lawyer can tell you the basic fee in advance; it's usually $500 to $1,000 for a simple document. And it may save your heirs thousands. Once you have a will, make a note to yourself in your calendar to review it every year. Births, marriages, deaths, hard feelings, the patching up of hard feelings, plus changes in your finances, your health, or federal or state laws—any of these may affect your will. Periodic review helps ensure you won't forget to make needed adjustments.

If death and taxes are inevitable—as the old saying goes—so are taxes after death. But it isn't all bad. As of 2004, no estate smaller than $850,000 is subject to federal tax. State tax exemptions vary greatly and often change, another reason for keeping the document up to date.

Where should you keep your will? Put it in a safe place, but don't hide it behind a painting or under a rug. If you conceal it too well, a court may rule you don't have one! Your lawyer should have a signed copy, and the original should be in a logical place, such as a safety-deposit box or your desk. Be sure your spouse, a close relative, or a friend knows where both the copies and the original are.

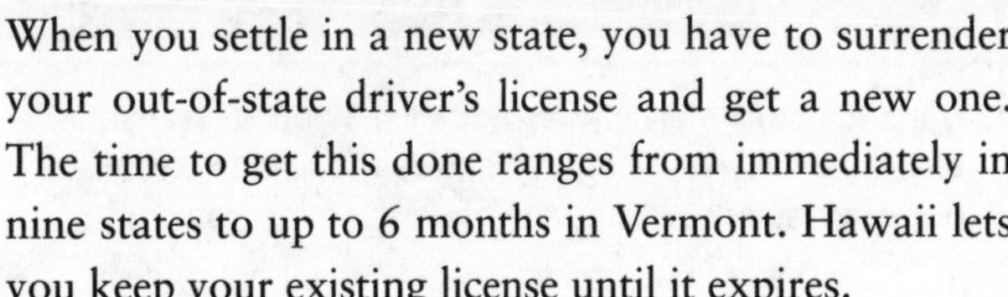

DRIVER LICENSING

When you settle in a new state, you have to surrender your out-of-state driver's license and get a new one. The time to get this done ranges from immediately in nine states to up to 6 months in Vermont. Hawaii lets you keep your existing license until it expires.

Required Tests

For a new resident with a valid driver's license from a former state, the requirements for getting a license from the new state vary. All states now require vision testing. In Connecticut and New Hampshire, all other tests aside from vision may be waived. Washington requires you to get behind the wheel with a license examiner for a road test; in 29 other states, a road test may be waived or required at the discretion of the examiner.

Problem Drivers

Forty-six states belong to the National Driver License Compact, an agreement among states to share information on drivers who accumulate tickets in one jurisdiction and try to escape control in another. If your license has been revoked, you won't get a new one simply by moving to another state. Every license application is checked with the National Driver Register, a federal data file of persons whose license to drive has been revoked.

Driving Danger Signals

Researching the records of insurance companies and state police agencies, Dr. Leon Pastalan of the University of Michigan found that older drivers receive a high number of tickets for the following five traffic violations:

- Rear-end collisions
- Dangerously slow driving
- Failure to yield the right-of-way
- Driving the wrong way on one-way streets
- Illegal turns

Even though people age at different rates, normal changes that affect eyesight, muscle reflexes, and hearing are the reasons older adults are ticketed for these moving violations more often than the rest of the population. Simply recognizing your limitations will help you become a better driver.

Driver Age Discrimination?

Once you start feeling your age, will insurance companies and state highway safety committees consider you dangerous when you get behind the wheel of your automobile?

On the face of it, older drivers have a better accident record than younger drivers. People over 60 represent one in eight persons in this country yet are involved in only one in fifteen of the automobile accidents. But the National Safety Council notes that people over 60 drive much less than younger people and actually have a poorer accident record when comparing the number of miles driven.

The American Medical Association and the American Association of Motor Vehicle Administrators have recommended that, while no one's license should be placed in jeopardy just because the driver is older, states should reexamine older drivers more frequently than younger drivers. Twenty-four states and Washington, D.C., now require special examinations or accelerated license renewal based solely on age; these requirements are detailed below. In addition, California, Delaware, Georgia, Nevada, New Jersey, Oregon, and Pennsylvania require doctors to report conditions that impair driving ability. Tennessee takes the opposing view: licenses issued to drivers over 65 "do not expire."

Alaska	No mail-in renewals after age 69. Vision test required at age 69.
Arizona	License renewal every 5 years after age 65. No mail-in renewals after age 70.
California	Reexamination waived for "clean record" drivers under age 70. No mail-in renewals after age 70. Vision and rules of the road written test required at age 70.
Colorado	License renewal every 5 years after age 61.
Connecticut	License renewal every 2 years after age 65.
Florida	Vision test required after age 79.
Hawaii	License renewal every 2 years for drivers over age 65.
Idaho	Drivers over 63 must renew every 4 years. No mail-in renewals after age 69.
Illinois	Complete reexamination every 4 years for drivers age 69 to 80, every 2 years for drivers age 81 to 86, every year age 87 and older. Renewal applicants over 75 must take a road test.
Indiana	Complete reexamination every 3 years for drivers over age 75.
Iowa	License renewal every 2 years for drivers over age 70.
Kansas	License renewal every 4 years for drivers over age 65.
Louisiana	Physical reexamination every 4 years for drivers over age 60.
Maine	Vision reexamination at age 40, 52, and 65 and over. License renewal every 4 years for drivers over age 65.
Missouri	License renewal every 3 years after age 70.
Montana	License renewal every 6 years for drivers over age 68 and every 4 years for drivers over age 75.
New Hampshire	Complete reexamination for drivers over age 75.
New Mexico	License renewal every year for drivers over age 75.
Oregon	Vision reexamination at 50 and over.
Pennsylvania	Physical examination on a random basis for drivers over age 45.
Rhode Island	License renewal every 2 years for drivers over age 70.
South Carolina	License renewal with vision test every 5 years for drivers over 65.
Utah	Vision examination required at age 65.
Washington, D.C.	Vision and reaction examination for drivers over age 70; complete reexamination at age 75 and over.
Wisconsin	No mail-in renewals after age 70.

Source: Insurance Institute for Highway Safety.

Eyesight. Ninety percent of all sensory input needed to drive a car comes through the eyes. As vision loses its sharpness, the typical rectangular black-and-white road signs become hard to read. Night driving is especially risky because the older we get, the more illumination we need to see. For example, an 80-year-old needs three times the light that a 20-year-old needs to read. Other problems include loss of depth perception (a major cause of rear-end collisions) and limited peripheral vision (dangerous when making turns at intersections).

You can adjust to these dangers by not driving at night, having regular eye checkups, wearing gray- or green-tinted sunglasses on days with high sun glare, and replacing your car's standard rearview mirror with a wide-angle one to aid peripheral vision.

Muscle Reflexes. Many people slow down as they get older. Strength may dwindle, neck and shoulder joints may stiffen, and you may tire sooner. Most important to driving, your reflex reactions may slow. All these symptoms can affect how safely you enter

Establishing Residency for Tuition Benefits

Legal residency not only is important for tax purposes but also is a necessary step to qualify for in-state tuition fees or tuition waivers at local public colleges.

Of the states that offer some form of tuition reduction or waiver, most require proof of at least 1 year of residency. Here are several steps to take to satisfy that requirement:

- Ask the local county clerk for a certificate of domicile.
- Get a driver's license and register your car in the new state.
- If you don't drive, ask the driver's license authority for a nondriver ID card. All states now issue them; some are similar to the driver's license format. Delaware, Illinois, and Minnesota will issue an ID card to all persons, not just nondrivers.
- File your final state income tax in your former state; file state and federal income taxes in the new state.
- At your first opportunity, register and vote in an election in your new state.

a busy freeway, change lanes to pass a plodding 18-wheel truck, or avoid a rear-end fender bender.

Ask your physician if any of the medications you're taking might decrease your alertness and ability to drive defensively. On long road trips, take along a companion to share the driving and break the day's distance into short stretches to reduce fatigue. Don't get caught on freeways and major arterial streets during morning and evening rush hours.

Hearing. One in every five persons over 55 and one of every three persons over 65 has impaired hearing. It's a gradual condition and can go unnoticed for a long time. When you can't hear an ambulance siren, a ticket for failing to yield the right-of-way to an emergency vehicle is the likely consequence.

You can compensate for hearing loss by having periodic checkups. When you drive, open a window, turn off the radio, keep the air-conditioner fan on low speed, and cut unnecessary conversation.

COLLEGE TUITION BREAKS

Forty-two states waive or reduce tuition in their public colleges for persons who've reached a specific age. For attendance at both 2- and 4-year institutions, it's the law in 15 states; in another 7 states, it's a formal policy adopted by the state's Board of Regents or Board of Higher Education. California, Florida, and New York statutes cover tuition waivers only at 4-year institutions. It's common practice for individual colleges and universities in all 50 states to establish their own tuition reduction policies.

The limitations on this benefit vary. States that permit tuition waivers grant it on a space-available basis, which simply means older students who want to take advantage of the tuition break are admitted to courses only after tuition-paying students have enrolled. Eight states grant the benefit only for auditing courses (enrolling for no credit). Four states—Illinois, Indiana, Maryland, and Virginia—look at the student's income to determine eligibility.

College Tuition Waivers for Older Adults

STATE	MINIMUM AGE	2-YEAR COLLEGES	4-YEAR COLLEGES
Alabama	60	○	
Alaska	60	●	●
Arkansas	60	■	■
California	60		■
Colorado	65	○	○
Connecticut	62	■	■
Delaware	60	■	○
District of Columbia	65		●
Florida	60	○	■
Georgia	62	●	●
Hawaii	60		■
Idaho	60	○	●
Illinois	65	■	■
Indiana	60	○	○
Kansas	60	○	●
Kentucky	65	■	■
Louisiana	60	■	■
Maine	65		●
Maryland	60	■	■
Massachusetts	60	●	●
Michigan	60	●	●
Minnesota	62	○	○
Missouri	65	○	○
Montana	62	●	●
Nebraska	65	○	○
Nevada	62	●	●
New Jersey	65	■	■
New Mexico	65	■	■
New York	60		■
North Carolina	65	■	■
Ohio	60	■	■
Oklahoma	65	●	●
Oregon	65		●
Rhode Island	60	■	■
South Carolina	60	■	■
South Dakota	65		●
Tennessee	65	■	■
Texas	65	○	○
Utah	62	○	○
Vermont	62	○	○
Virginia	60	■	■
Washington	60	■	■
Wyoming	62	○	○

■ = *state statute*, ● = *formal policy*, ○ = *discretion of each institution*

Source: State Higher Education Executive Officers, State Tuition and Fee Policies, 1997; Places Rated Partnership survey.

DRIVER'S LICENSE AND CAR REGISTRATION AFTER MOVING

A Guide for Persons with Current Paperwork from a Former Jurisdiction

	Driver's Licensing				Vehicle Registration		
	TIME LIMIT	WRITTEN TEST	VISION TEST	ROAD TEST	NDL COMPACT	TIME LIMIT	INSPECTION REQUIRED
Alabama	30 days	●	Yes		Yes	30 days	
Alaska	90 days	●	Yes		Yes	10 days	
Arizona	immediately	○	Yes	○	Yes	immediately	
Arkansas	30 days		Yes		Yes	10 days	s
California	10 days	●	Yes	○	Yes	20 days	e
Colorado	30 days	●	Yes	○	Yes	immediately	e
Connecticut	30 days	○	Yes	○	Yes	60 days	e
Delaware	60 days	●	Yes	○	Yes	60 days	s/e
District of Columbia	30 days	●	Yes	○	Yes	*	s/e
Florida	30 days	○	Yes	○	Yes	10 days	e
Georgia	30 days	●	Yes		No	30 days	e
Hawaii	*	●	Yes	○	Yes	10 days	s
Idaho	90 days	●	Yes		Yes	90 days	
Illinois	90 days	●	Yes		Yes	30 days	e
Indiana	60 days	●	Yes		Yes	60 days	e
Iowa	immediately	●	Yes		Yes	90 days	
Kansas	90 days	●	Yes		Yes	*	
Kentucky	immediately	●	Yes		No	15 days	
Louisiana	90 days		Yes		Yes	immediately	s/e
Maine	30 days	●	Yes	○	Yes	30 days	s
Maryland	30 days	○	Yes	○	Yes	30 days	e
Massachusetts	immediately		Yes		No	immediately	s/e
Michigan	immediately	●	Yes		No	immediately	e
Minnesota	60 days	●	Yes	○	Yes	60 days	
Mississippi	60 days	●	Yes	○	Yes	30 days	s
Missouri	immediately	●	Yes	○	Yes	30 days	s/e
Montana	90 days	○	Yes	○	Yes	immediately	
Nebraska	30 days	●	Yes	○	Yes	*	
Nevada	30 days	○	Yes	○	Yes	45 days	e
New Hampshire	60 days	○	Yes	○	Yes	60 days	s
New Jersey	60 days	●	Yes	○	Yes	60 days	s/e
New Mexico	30 days	●	Yes		Yes	30 days	
New York	30 days	●	Yes		Yes	30 days	s/e
North Carolina	30 days	●	Yes	○	Yes	immediately	s/e
North Dakota	60 days	●	Yes	○	Yes	immediately	
Ohio	30 days	●	Yes	○	Yes	immediately	e
Oklahoma	immediately	●	Yes	○	Yes	60 days	s/e
Oregon	immediately	●	Yes	○	Yes	immediately	e
Pennsylvania	60 days	●	Yes	○	Yes	60 days	s/e
Rhode Island	30 days	●	Yes		Yes	30 days	s/e
South Carolina	90 days		Yes	○	Yes	45 days	s
South Dakota	90 days	○	Yes	○	Yes	90 days	
Tennessee	30 days	○	Yes	○	Yes	immediately	
Texas	30 days	○	Yes	○	Yes	30 days	s/e
Utah	60 days	●	Yes		Yes	60 days	s/e
Vermont	6 months	○	Yes	○	Yes	6 months	s
Virginia	30 days	○	Yes		Yes	30 days	s
Washington	30 days	●	Yes	●	Yes	30 days	
West Virginia	30 days	●	Yes		Yes	30 days	s/e
Wisconsin	immediately	●	Yes	○	No	immediately	e
Wyoming	120 days	●	Yes	○	Yes	immediately	

● = *required*, ○ = *may be waived*, * = *existing license or registration valid until expiration, s = safety inspection, e = emissions test, s/e = both*

Source: American Automobile Association, Digest of Motor Laws, 2003; Federal Highway Administration, Driver License Administration Requirements and Fees, 2002; Places Rated Partnership survey.

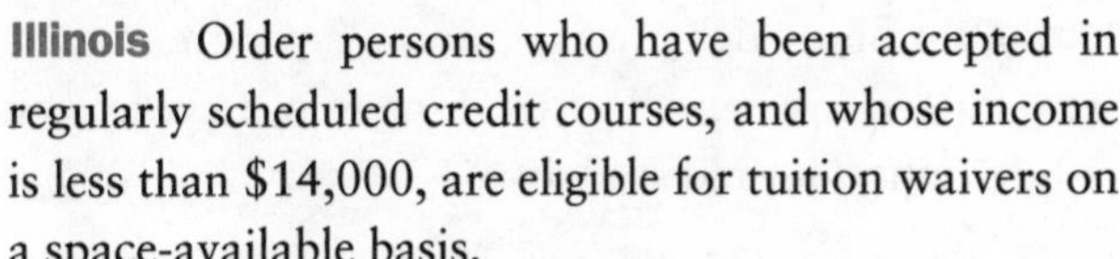

Alabama There's no legislation or state policy to waive or reduce tuition for older adults in state-funded colleges and universities. Tuition and general student fees are waived for courses in all state-funded 2-year colleges.

Alaska State policy waives tuition for residents 60 years or older at state-funded institutions on a space-available basis.

Arizona There's no legislation or state policy within the university or community college system to waive or reduce tuition for older adults.

Arkansas Tuition and general student fees are waived for credit courses on a space-available basis for older adults at any state institutions of higher learning.

California Tuition and general student fees may be waived only at participating campuses of the California State University system for credit courses on a space-available basis.

Colorado State higher education policy permits each state-funded institution, at its discretion, to waive or reduce tuition for older adults.

Connecticut State law waives tuition at all state-funded 2-year colleges; unless student is admitted to degree-granting programs at state universities, tuition is waived only on a space-available basis.

Delaware State law waives application, course, registration, and other fees for credit courses on a space-available basis. Students must be formal degree candidates.

District of Columbia Tuition is waived in courses taken for credit or audited at all University of the District of Columbia campuses.

Florida Tuition fees are waived for courses taken by residents over 60 who attend classes at state universities on a space-available basis. No academic credit is given under the waiver.

Georgia State higher education policy allows tuition fees to be waived only for credit courses on a space-available basis. Dental, medical, veterinary, and law school courses are excluded.

Hawaii Tuition and general student fees are waived at the University of Hawaii campuses for regularly scheduled credit courses on a space-available basis.

Idaho State policy reduces the registration fee to $20, plus a $5 fee per credit hour is charged for courses on a space-available basis.

Illinois Older persons who have been accepted in regularly scheduled credit courses, and whose income is less than $14,000, are eligible for tuition waivers on a space-available basis.

Indiana With certain limitations, 50 percent of the tuition fee is waived for older adults who aren't working full-time and have a high school degree.

Iowa There's no legislation or state policy within the university or community college system to waive or reduce tuition for older adults.

Kansas Tuition and general student fees at state-funded universities are waived only for auditing courses on a space-available basis.

Kentucky Tuition and general student fees are waived at any state-funded institution of higher learning, for residents only, for regularly scheduled credit courses on a space-available basis.

Louisiana Tuition and other registration fees are waived for courses on a space-available basis, provided sufficient funds are appropriated by the legislature to reimburse colleges and universities affected.

Maine Tuition and fees are waived for undergraduate courses on a space-available basis at state-supported colleges and universities.

Maryland Tuition fees are waived for 2-year college courses on a space-available basis, and up to three university or 4-year college courses per term on a space-available basis for students whose income is derived from retirement benefits and who aren't employed full-time.

Massachusetts Tuition fees are waived for courses if the college or university isn't over-enrolled.

Michigan Community colleges and state colleges and universities may waive tuition for older students meeting admission requirements.

Minnesota Except for an administration fee of $6 per credit hour, collected only when a course is taken for credit, tuition and activity fees are waived to attend courses for credit, to audit any course offered for credit, or to enroll in any noncredit adult vocational education courses on a space-available basis.

Mississippi There's no legislation or state policy within the university or community college system to waive or reduce tuition for older adults.

Missouri State higher education policy permits each state-funded institution, at its discretion, to waive or reduce tuition for older adults.

Montana State higher education policy permits tuition to be waived at the discretion of the regents of the Montana university system.

Nebraska State higher education policy permits each state-funded institution, at its discretion, to waive or reduce tuition for older adults.

Nevada Registration fees are waived only for regularly scheduled courses that may be audited or taken for credit. Consent of the instructor may be required.

New Hampshire There's no state legislation or policy waiving tuition fees for older adults.

New Jersey Tuition fees may be waived for courses on a space-available basis at each public institution of higher education.

New Mexico Tuition may be reduced to $5 per credit hour up to a maximum of six credit hours per semester for older residents on a space-available basis.

New York Tuition fees may be waived only for auditing courses on a space-available basis at institutions of the state university system.

North Carolina Tuition fees are waived for auditing courses or for taking courses for credit on a space-available basis.

North Dakota There's no state legislation or policy waiving tuition fees for older adults.

Ohio Tuition and matriculation fees are waived only for auditing courses on a space-available basis.

Oklahoma State higher education policy allows tuition fees to be waived only for auditing courses on a space-available basis.

Oregon Tuition fees are waived for auditing courses on a space-available basis.

Pennsylvania There's no legislation or state policy within the university or community college system to waive or reduce tuition for older adults.

Rhode Island Tuition and general student fees are waived for credit courses on a space-available basis at the discretion of the institution.

South Carolina Tuition fees are waived for courses, for credit or audit, at any state-supported institution on a space-available basis.

South Dakota Tuition fees are reduced to 50 percent of resident tuition at state universities.

Tennessee Tuition and registration fees are waived for auditing or taking for credit courses on a space-available basis. The board of regents may charge a service fee not to exceed $50 per quarter or $75 per semester. The waiver doesn't apply at medical, dental, or pharmacy schools.

Texas State higher education policy allows tuition fees to be waived for auditing courses on a space-available basis by the governing board of any state-supported institution.

Utah Tuition fees (but not quarterly registration fees) may be waived for courses on a space-available basis at each state-funded college and university.

Vermont Tuition fees may be waived for courses on a space-available basis at each state-funded college and university.

Virginia Tuition and registration fees are waived on a space-available basis, if the student has a federal taxable income not exceeding $10,000. Registration is limited to no more than three courses in any one term, quarter, or semester if the person isn't enrolled for academic credit.

Washington Depending on the institution and for no more than two courses per term, tuition and general student fees may be waived for courses taken for credit and waived entirely for courses taken for audit. There may be a nominal fee of $5 charged per term for auditing.

West Virginia There's no legislation or state policy within the university or community college system to waive or reduce tuition for older adults.

Wisconsin There's no legislation or state policy within the university or community college system to waive or reduce tuition for older adults.

Wyoming The university or community college system may waive or reduce tuition for older adults at each institution's discretion.

The Economy

For years, economic boosters in attractive locations throughout the country kicked around an interesting possibility: Enticing affluent persons to move in is a much cleaner and easier strategy than chasing after smokestack employers. The impact of just one couple moving in and spending their retirement income locally, so the argument goes, could be the same as three new jobs in light industry.

For all that, diesel logging trucks—their exhaust stacks roaring—are still a common sight on coastal U.S. 17 from Virginia Beach, Virginia, to Savannah, Georgia; on route 12 in Vermont; and on U.S. 93 in western Montana. On Colorado's western slope, Montrose still has a huge candy factory, an experimental airplane plant, and several boutique fishing-gear manufacturers. In the Arkansas Ozarks, FM stations still broadcast help-wanted ads for workers at local chicken processors. On the Chesapeake Bay, fishing boats still lightly bob and bump at wooden docks.

If places had to rely on free-spending older newcomers for their economic futures, they'd starve. Paychecks everywhere are still earned the old-fashioned way—in agriculture, mining, manufacturing, construction, and a lot of retail trade and services. Still, if you're thinking of starting a second career or finding an interesting part-time job, which places aren't prone to recession and which can expect to gain new jobs over the next 5 years is an important consideration.

OLDER PERSONS DO WORK

Near Fayetteville, Arkansas, a husband and wife, both retired from the U.S. Army Corps of Engineers, breed AKC Schipperke dogs and take in stray animals for later adoption. They advertise their Skips in *Dog World,* and buyers come from all over the Mississippi and Ohio valleys. For them, it's a matter of being your own boss and doing something you love rather than working a temporary job at Tyson's Foods, in nearby Springdale, when that employer is especially busy.

In a Chapel Hill, North Carolina, haberdashery, a woman stands near the Kenneth Cole and Pendleton shelves in the shirt alcove. The boys from Duke, UNC, and State are her customers, especially during the job-interviewing season. They haven't a clue about what goes into a good shirt or even how best to wash it. She likes this retail job much better than the one she had selling linens and bedding at a department store in a mall near Raleigh.

In Eagle River, Wisconsin, a World War II veteran tells how his teenage friend is mystified that the man doesn't quit his penny-ante commander's job at American Legion Post #431 and get behind the counter at McDonald's out on Highway 17. The teenager promises to pull strings with the day manager to start the older friend at $6.00. For some odd reason, says the man, he can't drum into the kid's head that the commander's job requires organizational and human relations skills, and is far more fun and interesting than fast food, even if it were done for free.

A thousand miles south, a charming woman runs the visitor's drop-in center on Central Avenue in downtown Hot Springs, Arkansas. Amid racks full of brochures, booklets, maps, pamphlets, and broadsides, she talks with American and foreign tourists all day long. "Ask me a question and I'll be happy to answer it. And if I don't know the answer," she adds, "I'll be happy to make one up." Her work is voluntary; so are other options at St. Joseph's Health Center's hospital auxiliary, or helping high school kids with reading problems.

All are retired and work in their own way—as a volunteer, through self-employment, or at a part-time job. Though having a job after retirement is by no means a concern of every older adult, it is to many. In the years immediately after retirement, nearly one in four people takes a short-schedule, seasonal, or temporary job. Another one in four would do the same thing according to surveys, but several things stand in the way.

FARMS, FORESTS, AND MINES

Just outside the residential fringe of many retirement places is a kind of muscular outback. Equipment-sales yards along the commercial strips leading into town offer the clue: John Deere tractors, Ingersoll-Rand pumps, Dresser rock drills, and Homelite chain saws. At least one in ten workers in the following areas has a job in the slow-growing or no-growing farming, forestry, and mining industries.

- Berkeley Springs, WV
- Cedar Creek Lake, TX
- Chewelah, WA
- Delta County, CO
- Eureka Springs, AR
- Fredericksburg, TX
- Hamilton–Bitterroot Valley, MT
- Lake of the Cherokees, OK
- Leelanau Peninsula, MI
- Marble Falls-Lake LBJ, TX
- Oakhurst–Coarsegold, CA
- Pahrump Valley, NV
- Polson–Mission Valley, MT
- Roswell, NM
- Silver City, NM
- Trinity Peninsula, TX
- Wenatchee, WA

Source: Woods & Poole Economics, Inc., employment forecasts.

Social Security Rules

If you're going back to work, "Social Security giveth, and Social Security taketh away," notes retirement expert Bob Menchin. The amount of money you can earn on the job and still collect the benefits coming to you is limited. If you're under FRA, or *full retirement age* (in 2004, FRA is 66), and your income exceeds $11,520, your benefits will be reduced by $1 for every $2 you're earning over that amount. In the year you reach FRA, $1 in benefits will be deducted from every $3 you earn above a new limit of $30,720. *Starting with the month you hit FRA,* however, you get your benefits with no limit on your earnings.

Keeping your earnings under the exempt amount is understandable. Not only would half or more of your excess earnings be lost through Social Security reductions, but they also would be subject to income taxes as well as Social Security withholding. Unfortunately, explaining this to an employer makes it seem as if you're limited in motivation.

The Market for Part-Time Jobs

In spite of the rapid growth in the number of part-time jobs, most of these positions are dead-end, low-skill, mind-numbing, low-paid ones with few benefits.

The big reason that there aren't more better-paying and challenging part-time jobs is the high cost to employers. Training and administrative costs, for instance, are the same for full- and part-time workers. A short workweek boosts the hourly costs to employers for these expenses. In contrast, jobs that require little training—such as hamburger flipping, counter help, aisle sweeping, or cashiering—won't significantly raise the costs to employers, particularly if the job has no benefit package.

Age Discrimination

In spite of the law protecting anyone between the ages of 40 and 70 from being passed over in hiring or being involuntarily retired solely on the basis of age, this kind of discrimination still happens everywhere in the job market.

It is also one of the most difficult job-market issues to identify. Few, if any, employers support discriminatory business practices; they are open to lawsuits if they do. Yet a large number of older workers have experienced discrimination. About the only advice career counselors can offer is that fair treatment usually comes from working for a supervisor older than yourself.

MILITARY ECONOMIES

At least one in every twenty workers in the locations below gets a paycheck from the Department of Defense. Not for nothing are their representatives sitting on Congressional Armed Services Committees. To the relief of local officials, planned cutbacks and base closings have been put on hold here since the terrorist attacks of September 11, 2001.

- Alamogordo, NM
- Annapolis, MD
- Bay St. Louis–Pass Christian, MS
- Beaufort, SC
- Bisbee, AZ
- Colorado Springs, CO
- Hilton Head Island, SC
- New Bern, NC
- North County San Diego, CA
- Panama City, FL
- Pensacola, FL
- Virginia Beach, VA
- Whidbey Island, WA
- Yuma, AZ

Source: Woods & Poole Economics, Inc., employment forecasts.

JOB FORECASTS IN RETIREMENT PLACES

Economists who follow job trends have an old joke: If you take each local planner's numbers for job growth in his or her area and add them all together, the total jobs forecasted would require that every man, woman, and child hold down one day-job and moonlight two others.

Fortunately, economists with a national view have a better perspective. Although no one sees the future with certainty, forecasting where jobs will be plentiful over the next few years isn't a matter of gazing into a crystal ball.

Start by asking the question: Do people move to where the jobs are, or do jobs come to where the people are? While this is a good topic to argue about over beers at an academic convention, most economists think jobs come to where the people are. In other words, any growing place that has a concentration of people with a variety of worker skills will be a jobs mecca.

But there's more to it than that. Some spots are saddled with sunset industries—shipbuilding, textiles, sawmills, and mining, for example—while others have sunrise industries—health care, higher education, software, and, yes, government. Most locations have varying mixes of the dying and the growing.

Forecasting which spots will gain jobs is as much a matter of determining the prospects for certain industries as it is predicting population shifts. The great American job machine has churned out record numbers of jobs for decades and, depending on which expert is talking, the machine is either showing wear and tear or has shifted into a new and different gear. Still, millions of new jobs will be added to the U.S. economy by 2010. Although employment increases will occur at half the pace of the 1990s, the prospects for certain occupations look quite rosy.

The hot industries—retail trade; services; and finance, insurance, and real estate (known as FIRE in employment shorthand)—will stay hot. With variation between places, this is where the real action is expected to occur. And with variation among employers, these hot industries are precisely the ones where *good* part-time jobs are found.

UNEMPLOYMENT RISK

If you see a good number of light-manufacturing plants with full parking lots and notice lots of hard-hat construction workers aboard growling earth-moving machines at new residential and commercial developments, you'll know that in flush times jobs are easy to find here and the pay is just great. You can also assume that, should a recession roll in, this place may be hard hit by unemployment.

One of the few things you'll find economists agreeing on is that places with large numbers of workers in manufacturing and construction are harshly affected during business slumps.

In contrast to boom-and-bust places, there are others where the pace isn't quite as fast, and where

Ski Towns, College Towns, and Competition

For all the lively goings-on in places dominated by the higher-education calendar or winter skiing, they aren't ideal places for older adults to track down an interesting part-time or seasonal job. The competition is especially stiff in the following places, where the number of younger persons who look for a part-time job is more than three-and-a-half times the number of persons in their early 60s searching for the same thing.

- Athens, GA
- Boone–Blowing Rock, NC
- Bozeman, MT
- Cedar City, UT
- Chapel Hill–Carrboro, NC
- Columbia, MO
- Flagstaff, AZ
- Gainesville, FL
- Hattiesburg, MS
- Iowa City, IA
- Natchitoches, LA
- Northampton–Amherst, MA
- Oxford, MS
- State College, PA
- Wimberley, TX

Source: Woods & Poole Economics, Inc., employment forecasts.

large numbers of white-collar workers commute to downtown or suburban jobs with financial, real estate, and insurance firms. Others find their work at colleges and universities, at big medical centers in the area, or at local resorts. The employment mix in these areas is more balanced, with most of the weight going to the white-collar sector.

Finally, there are places at the opposite extreme from industrial places, not because they are thriving, but because manufacturing plays no part in their existence. These have nearly pure white-collar economies characterized by people working almost exclusively in retail trade, services, finance, insurance, and real estate.

Even though in retirement you may have little to worry about regarding being without a full-time job, local unemployment may still affect you in unforeseen ways. By boosting the competition for available work, high unemployment limits your chances of finding a part-time job should you ever want one.

Just as places can be rated for mild climates and their supply of public golf links, so also can they be rated for how vulnerable they are to joblessness during a bad business cycle. The two yardsticks are the local portion of workers in manufacturing, construction, and the military, plus the place's most recent 60-month unemployment record versus national averages. Among *Retirement Places Rated*'s 203 locations, the unemployment threat is very high (↑ ↑) in 27, high (↑) in 32, average (↔) in 39, low (↓) in 53, and very low (↓ ↓) in 52.

THE PART-TIME JOB MARKET

If relocation is a definite option in your retirement and if finding work in your destination isn't a hallucination, are there any immutable laws for finding a comfortable, well-paying, flexible, interesting, challenging part-time job with a sympathetic employer?

Gee no, there aren't. But there are common-sense rules for judging whether one place is more promising than another. Consider the variety of jobs, their quality, and the competition to land one of them.

Job Quality: Show Me the Money

Sure, somewhere over the rainbow there's a job waiting where colleagues are like family, fringes are fabulous, the cafeteria is gourmet, the parking close in, and where there's no pecking order, no performance reviews, and no prohibition on catnaps.

A quality job? For some, perhaps. But in the view of economists, there is just one benchmark that counts: the worker's paycheck. The big difference between earnings in North County San Diego and the Trinity Peninsula in Texas is somewhat due to cost-of-living differences. But it's mainly due to differences in skills and the employer productivity.

To broadly describe job quality, we adopt this simple view: a quality job pays more. Based on earnings figures for people in FIRE (finance, insurance, and real estate industries), services, and retail trade in each retirement place, it's possible to break the places into five groups: Where the quality of jobs is very high (↑ ↑), where it's high (↑), where it's just average (↔), where the quality is low (↓), and where it's very low (↓ ↓).

Tinker, Tailor . . . Parachute Packer

The U.S. Department of Labor's *Dictionary of Occupational Titles* should be recommended bedtime reading for job seekers. You'll either quickly nod off or you'll sit right up when you read how many jobs are there somewhere that you've never heard of—some 20,000 job titles between "abalone diver" and "zoo veterinarian."

All of which leads into something important: If you spent your career as an actuary, geographer, real-estate appraiser, or webmaster, are there any part-time or seasonal opportunities in retirement places besides the Wal-Mart, the county hospital, or the fish bait concession at the local State Park?

Answer: of course, but almost always in bigger places. When it comes to the *variety* of interesting jobs, size does matter. By looking at how many new jobs in hot industries are projected by 2009, it's possible to break our retirement places into five groups: Where the variety of jobs is very high (↑ ↑), where it's high (↑), where it's just average (↔), where the variety is low (↓), and where it's very low (↓ ↓).

What Are the Odds?

Think of how much competition you'll meet in tracking down a good seasonal or short-schedule job. Are there crowds of voluntary part-time workers pounding the pavement everywhere, or are the odds more favorable in Colorado Springs, Colorado, and Chapel Hill, North Carolina, than in Las Cruces, New Mexico, or Port Angeles, Washington?

"Voluntary" part-timers are persons who want only part-time jobs rather than persons who resignedly take a temporary, seasonal, or short-schedule job because there's nothing else available. There are 20 million voluntary part-timers in this country. Most are older adults, 19- to 24-year-old college students, and women aged 38 to 54 easing back into the workplace.

To measure competition, *Retirement Places Rated* compares the population of these two latter groups to persons in their early 60s. In each place, the part-time job competition is:

- Very High (↑ ↑) if the number of college-age persons and women reentering the job market is more than six-and-a-half times the number of persons in their early 60s.
- High (↑) if the number of college-age persons and women reentering the job market is between five-and-a-half and six-and-a-half times the number of persons in their early 60s.
- Average (↔) if the number of college-age persons and women reentering the job market is between four-and-a-half and five-and-a-half times the number of persons in their early 60s.
- Low (↓) if the number of college-age persons and women reentering the job market is between three-and-a-half and four-and-a-half times the number of persons in their early 60s.
- Very Low (↓ ↓) if the number of college-age persons and women reentering the job market is less than three-and-a-half times the number of persons in their early 60s.

SCORING: THE ECONOMY

If you've taken early retirement from your lifelong career and want to launch a new one or simply land an interesting part-time job, are the prospects rosier in Rehoboth Bay, Reno, or Ruidoso (Delaware, Nevada, and New Mexico, respectively)?

To help you answer the question, *Retirement Places Rated* compares three factors in each place: (1) the rate of job growth to the year 2009, (2) the total number of new full-time equivalent jobs forecasted in retail trade, services, and the FIRE industries (finance, insurance, and real estate), and (3) job quality, determined by how much local workers in these industries see on their paychecks in each place. Note: One worker typically holds a full-time equivalent job; occasionally, two workers share it. Two full-time equivalent jobs roughly translate into three part-time jobs of 25 hours per week.

Which of these factors is more important? A rosy growth forecast, such as the 18 percent for Southport–Brunswick Islands, always looks good at first view, and it does translate into some 4,700 new jobs in services, retail trade, and FIRE each year. In

contrast, the more modest 8.8 percent forecast for Annapolis and surrounding Anne Arundel County results in 20,000 new jobs in these industries during the same period.

And what about job quality in these two locations? Not only do full- and part-time workers in Maryland's capital make more money than similar workers to the south in Southport–Brunswick Islands; they also make more money than the national average. True, the difference points to different costs of living but it also points to the quality of the work.

To produce a score, the three factors—number of new jobs, job quality, and rate of growth—get equal weight. The result is then scaled against a standard from 0 to 100 where 50 is average. Three places in Arizona's Maricopa County—Mesa, Scottsdale, and Wickenburg—have a score of 99. Anacortes, high up on Washington's Puget Sound coast, scores a 50.0. The Trinity Peninsula in the Texas interior has a score of 0.0. These three areas are respectively the best, average, and worst retirement places for job growth between now and 2009.

RANKINGS: THE ECONOMY

To rank 203 places for part-time job potential, *Retirement Places Rated* weights four criteria equally: (1) the **number of new jobs projected by the year 2009 in services, retail trade, and the FIRE industries** (finance, insurance, and real estate), (2) the **rate of growth,** (3) the **quality of new jobs,** and (4) **how resistant the location is to unemployment.**

Forecasts are for the entire county in which the place is located. Scores are rounded to one decimal place. Locations with tie scores, usually within the same county, get the same rank and are listed alphabetically.

Retirement Places from First to Last

RANK	PLACE	SCORE
1.	Mesa, AZ	99.0
1.	Scottsdale, AZ	99.0
1.	Wickenburg, AZ	99.0
4.	Henderson, NV	98.5
5.	North County San Diego, CA	98.0
6.	Laguna Beach–Dana Point, CA	97.5
7.	Boca Raton, FL	97.0
8.	Palm Springs–Coachella Valley, CA	96.5
9.	Victorville–Apple Valley, CA	96.0
10.	Bradenton, FL	95.5
11.	Colorado Springs, CO	95.0
12.	Georgetown, TX	94.5
13.	Tucson, AZ	94.0
14.	Fort Myers–Cape Coral, FL	93.5
15.	Lake Conroe, TX	93.0
16.	Naples, FL	92.5
17.	Annapolis, MD	92.0
18.	Charleston, SC	91.5
19.	Bay St. Louis–Pass Christian, MS	91.0
20.	Sarasota, FL	90.5
21.	Conway, SC	89.6
21.	Myrtle Beach, SC	89.6
23.	Mission–McAllen–Alamo, TX	89.1
24.	Reno–Sparks, NV	88.6
25.	Santa Rosa, CA	88.1
26.	Largo, FL	87.6
27.	Madison, WI	87.1
28.	Cottonwood–Verde Valley, AZ	86.1
28.	Prescott–Prescott Valley, AZ	86.1
30.	Melbourne–Palm Bay, FL	85.6
31.	Park City, UT	85.1
32.	New Port Richey, FL	84.6
33.	Western St. Tammany Parish, LA	84.1
34.	Beaufort, SC	83.1
34.	Hilton Head Island, SC	83.1
36.	Branson, MO	82.6
37.	Virginia Beach, VA	82.1
38.	Lakeland–Winter Haven, FL	81.6
39.	East End Long Island, NY	81.1
40.	Fairhope–Gulf Shores, AL	80.6
41.	Kissimmee–St. Cloud, FL	80.1
42.	Port Charlotte, FL	79.7
43.	Medford–Ashland, OR	79.2
44.	Lake Winnipesaukee, NH	78.7
45.	Fort Collins–Loveland, CO	78.2
46.	Florence, OR	77.7
47.	Morro Bay–Cambria, CA	77.2
48.	St. Augustine, FL	76.7
49.	Wimberley, TX	76.2
50.	St. George–Zion, UT	75.7
51.	Santa Fe, NM	75.2
52.	Carson City–Carson Valley, NV	74.7
53.	Bend, OR	74.2
54.	Flagstaff, AZ	73.2
54.	Sedona, AZ	73.2
56.	Carmel–Pebble Beach, CA	72.7
57.	Santa Barbara, CA	72.2
58.	Fayetteville, AR	71.7
59.	Paradise–Magalia, CA	71.2
60.	Coeur d'Alene, ID	70.7
61.	Southport–Brunswick Islands, NC	70.2
62.	Toms River–Barnegat Bay, NJ	69.8
63.	Chapel Hill–Carrboro, NC	69.3
64.	Asheville, NC	68.8
65.	Bullhead City, AZ	67.3
65.	Kingman, AZ	67.3

RANK	PLACE	SCORE
65.	Lake Havasu City, AZ	67.3
68.	Middle Cape Cod, MA	66.8
69.	Traverse City, MI	66.3
70.	Ocala, FL	65.8
71.	Daytona Beach, FL	65.3
72.	Gainesville, FL	64.8
73.	Grass Valley–Nevada City, CA	64.3
74.	Vero Beach, FL	63.8
75.	Fredericksburg–Spotsylvania, VA	63.3
76.	Apache Junction, AZ	62.8
77.	Pensacola, FL	62.3
78.	Bellingham, WA	61.8
79.	Panama City, FL	61.3
80.	Charlottesville, VA	60.8
81.	Leesburg–Mount Dora, FL	60.3
82.	Williamsburg, VA	59.9
83.	Savannah, GA	59.4
84.	Maui, HI	58.9
85.	Dare Outer Banks, NC	58.4
86.	Iowa City, IA	57.9
87.	Ketchum–Sun Valley, ID	57.4
88.	Inverness, FL	56.9
89.	Lake of the Ozarks, MO	56.4
90.	Key West, FL	55.9
91.	Durango, CO	55.4
92.	Burlington, VT	54.9
93.	Oakhurst–Coarsegold, CA	54.4
94.	Las Cruces, NM	53.9
95.	Bozeman, MT	53.4
96.	Rehoboth Bay–Indian River Bay, DE	52.9
97.	New Braunfels, TX	52.4
98.	Kalispell–Flathead Valley, MT	51.9
99.	Columbia, MO	51.4
100.	Maryville, TN	50.9
101.	Yuma, AZ	50.4
102.	Anacortes, WA	50.0
103.	Grand Junction, CO	49.5
104.	Rio Rancho, NM	49.0
105.	Bisbee, AZ	48.5
106.	State College, PA	48.0
107.	Hanover, NH	47.5
108.	Cedar Creek Lake, TX	47.0
109.	York Beaches, ME	46.5
110.	Marble Falls–Lake LBJ, TX	46.0
111.	Southern Pines–Pinehurst, NC	45.5
112.	Payson, AZ	45.0
113.	Cedar City, UT	44.5
114.	St. Simons–Jekyll Islands, GA	44.0
115.	Summerville, SC	43.5
116.	Jackson Hole, WY	43.0
117.	Amador County, CA	42.5
118.	Taos, NM	42.0
119.	Athens, GA	41.5
120.	Grants Pass, OR	41.0
121.	Litchfield Hills, CT	40.5
122.	Northampton–Amherst, MA	40.0
123.	Pahrump Valley, NV	39.6
124.	Hendersonville–East Flat Rock, NC	39.1
125.	Aiken, SC	38.6
126.	Boone–Blowing Rock, NC	38.1
127.	Sebring–Avon Park, FL	37.6
128.	Mendocino–Fort Bragg, CA	37.1
129.	Port Townsend, WA	36.6
130.	Sandpoint–Lake Pend Oreille, ID	36.1
131.	Hot Springs, AR	35.6
132.	Crossville, TN	35.1
133.	Wenatchee, WA	34.6
134.	Lower Cape May, NJ	34.1
135.	Beaufort–Bogue Banks, NC	33.6
136.	Monadnock Region, NH	33.1
137.	Kerrville, TX	32.6
138.	Boerne, TX	32.1
139.	Whidbey Island, WA	31.6
140.	Door Peninsula, WI	31.1
141.	New Bern, NC	30.6
142.	Woodstock, VT	30.1
143.	Palmer–Wasilla, AK	29.7
144.	Norfork Lake, AR	29.2
145.	Petoskey–Harbor Springs, MI	28.7
146.	Hamilton–Bitterroot Valley, MT	28.2
147.	Port Angeles–Sequim, WA	27.7
148.	Newport–Lincoln City, OR	27.2
149.	Pagosa Springs, CO	26.7
150.	Table Rock Lake, MO	26.2
151.	Lake of the Cherokees, OK	25.7
152.	Easton–St. Michaels, MD	25.2
153.	Montrose, CO	24.7
154.	Oxford, MS	24.2
155.	Camden, ME	23.7
156.	Martha's Vineyard, MA	23.2
157.	Sonora–Twain Harte, CA	22.7
158.	Ocean City, MD	22.2
159.	Pike County, PA	21.7
160.	Ruidoso, NM	21.2
161.	Bar Harbor, ME	20.7
162.	Polson–Mission Valley, MT	20.2
163.	Hattiesburg, MS	19.8
164.	Southern Berkshire County, MA	19.3
165.	Las Vegas, NM	18.8
166.	Murray–Kentucky Lake, KY	18.3
167.	Brookings–Gold Beach, OR	17.8
168.	Kauai, HI	17.3
169.	Fredericksburg, TX	16.8
170.	Charles Town–Shepherdstown, WV	16.3
171.	San Juan Islands, WA	15.8
172.	Eureka Springs, AR	15.3
173.	Eagle River–Woodruff, WI	14.8
174.	Leelanau Peninsula, MI	14.3
175.	Silver City, NM	13.8
176.	St. Jay–Northeast Kingdom, VT	13.3
177.	Alamogordo, NM	12.8
178.	Pendleton District, SC	12.3
179.	Front Royal, VA	11.8
180.	Delta County, CO	11.3
181.	Brevard, NC	10.8
182.	Tryon, NC	10.3
183.	Chewelah, WA	9.9
184.	Roswell, NM	9.4
185.	Northern Neck, VA	8.9
186.	Salida, CO	8.4
187.	Eufaula, AL	7.9
188.	McCall, ID	7.4
189.	Thomasville, GA	6.9
190.	Rabun County, GA	6.4
191.	Brown County, IN	5.9
192.	Lake Placid, NY	5.4
193.	Smith Mountain Lake, VA	4.9
194.	Oscoda–Huron Shore, MI	4.4
195.	Chestertown, MD	3.9
196.	Rockport–Aransas Pass, TX	3.4
197.	Mariposa, CA	2.9
198.	Alpine–Big Bend, TX	2.4
199.	Natchitoches, LA	1.9
200.	Edenton, NC	1.4
201.	Apalachicola, FL	0.9
202.	Berkeley Springs, WV	0.4
203.	Trinity Peninsula, TX	0.0

PLACE PROFILES: THE ECONOMY

The following capsule descriptions show job features for each place. The percent figure after ***Job Growth Forecast*** is the rate of growth forecasted for 2004 to 2009 in all industries. Detailed under ***New Jobs in . . .*** are the number of new positions forecasted in FIRE (finance, insurance, and real estate industries), retail trade, and services—industries where older adults find opportunity and also where most part-time, seasonal, and short-schedule jobs are found.

The symbols seen throughout stand for five intervals: very high (↑ ↑), high (↑), average (↔), low (↓), and very low (↓ ↓). ***Unemployment Risk*** is based on each area's portion of blue-collar and military jobs and its most recent 60-month unemployment rate compared with the national average. Under ***Part-Time Job Market,*** *Quality* describes typical earnings for workers in FIRE, retail trade, and services compared with the average figure for all of the retirement places; *Variety* describes the absolute number of new jobs in those industries; and *Competition* compares the number of persons in their early 20s and women in their late 40s reentering the job market with the number of persons in their early 60s.

All forecasts are county totals and are derived from current Complete Economic and Demographic Data Source (CEDDS) data from July 1, 2004, to July 1, 2009, by Woods & Poole Economics, Inc., and are used here with permission. Forecasts are uncertain and future data may differ substantially from Woods & Poole projections. The use of these data and the conclusions drawn from them are solely the responsibility of the author.

A star (★) in front of a place's name highlights it as one of the top 30 places for part-time job opportunities between 2004 and 2009.

Aiken, SC
Job Growth Forecast: +6.82%
Unemployment Risk: ↔
New Jobs in . . .
FIRE: 297
Retail: 1,061
Services: 980
Part-Time Job Market
Quality: ↔
Variety: ↔
Competition: ↔
Score: 38.6 **Rank: 125**

Alamogordo, NM
Job Growth Forecast: +5.30%
Unemployment Risk: ↑
New Jobs in . . .
FIRE: 279
Retail: 106
Services: 671
Part-Time Job Market
Quality: ↑ ↑
Variety: ↓
Competition: ↑
Score: 12.8 **Rank: 177**

Alpine–Big Bend, TX
Job Growth Forecast: +5.37%
Unemployment Risk: ↓ ↓
New Jobs in . . .
FIRE: 7
Retail: 69
Services: 181
Part-Time Job Market
Quality: ↓
Variety: ↓ ↓
Competition: ↔
Score: 2.4 **Rank: 198**

Amador County, CA
Job Growth Forecast: +11.65%
Unemployment Risk: ↔
New Jobs in . . .
FIRE: 153
Retail: 227
Services: 1,262
Part-Time Job Market
Quality: ↔
Variety: ↓
Competition: ↓
Score: 42.5 **Rank: 117**

Anacortes, WA
Job Growth Forecast: +8.55%
Unemployment Risk: ↑ ↑
New Jobs in . . .
FIRE: 315
Retail: 1,399
Services: 1,678
Part-Time Job Market
Quality: ↑
Variety: ↔
Competition: ↔
Score: 50 **Rank: 102**

★ Annapolis, MD
Job Growth Forecast: +8.78%
Unemployment Risk: ↓ ↓
New Jobs in . . .
FIRE: 2,818
Retail: 2,428
Services: 15,248
Part-Time Job Market
Quality: ↑ ↑
Variety: ↑ ↑
Competition: ↑
Score: 92 **Rank: 17**

Apache Junction, AZ
Job Growth Forecast: +12.31%
Unemployment Risk: ↑
New Jobs in . . .
FIRE: 438
Retail: 943
Services: 2,883
Part-Time Job Market
Quality: ↔
Variety: ↑
Competition: ↓
Score: 62.8 **Rank: 76**

Apalachicola, FL
Job Growth Forecast: +4.87%
Unemployment Risk: ↓
New Jobs in . . .
FIRE: 50
Retail: 20
Services: 185
Part-Time Job Market
Quality: ↓ ↓
Variety: ↓ ↓
Competition: ↓
Score: 0.9 **Rank: 201**

Asheville, NC
Job Growth Forecast: +7.41%
Unemployment Risk: ↓ ↓
New Jobs in . . .
FIRE: 734
Retail: 2,466
Services: 5,020
Part-Time Job Market
Quality: ↑
Variety: ↑
Competition: ↔
Score: 68.8 **Rank: 64**

★ = *one of the top 30 places for part-time job opportunities between 2004 and 2009.*

Athens, GA
Job Growth Forecast: +5.83%
Unemployment Risk: ↓ ↓
New Jobs in . . .
FIRE: 414
Retail: 611
Services: 1,546
Part-Time Job Market
Quality: ↑
Variety: ↔
Competition: ↑ ↑
Score: 41.5 Rank: 119

Bar Harbor, ME
Job Growth Forecast: +5.31%
Unemployment Risk: ↔
New Jobs in . . .
FIRE: 96
Retail: 340
Services: 926
Part-Time Job Market
Quality: ↔
Variety: ↓
Competition: ↔
Score: 20.7 Rank: 161

★ Bay St. Louis–Pass Christian, MS
Job Growth Forecast: +17.05%
Unemployment Risk: ↓
New Jobs in . . .
FIRE: 621
Retail: 2,265
Services: 8,138
Part-Time Job Market
Quality: ↔
Variety: ↑ ↑
Competition: ↑
Score: 91 Rank: 19

Beaufort, SC
Job Growth Forecast: +12.67%
Unemployment Risk: ↓ ↓
New Jobs in . . .
FIRE: 1,001
Retail: 3,820
Services: 3,348
Part-Time Job Market
Quality: ↑ ↑
Variety: ↑
Competition: ↔
Score: 83.1 Rank: 34

Beaufort–Bogue Banks, NC
Job Growth Forecast: +7.91%
Unemployment Risk: ↔
New Jobs in . . .
FIRE: 378
Retail: 783
Services: 539
Part-Time Job Market
Quality: ↓
Variety: ↓
Competition: ↓
Score: 33.6 Rank: 135

Bellingham, WA
Job Growth Forecast: +8.18%
Unemployment Risk: ↑
New Jobs in . . .
FIRE: 490
Retail: 2,109
Services: 3,329
Part-Time Job Market
Quality: ↔
Variety: ↑
Competition: ↑
Score: 61.8 Rank: 78

Bend, OR
Job Growth Forecast: +12.33%
Unemployment Risk: ↑
New Jobs in . . .
FIRE: 743
Retail: 1,745
Services: 4,031
Part-Time Job Market
Quality: ↑
Variety: ↑
Competition: ↔
Score: 74.2 Rank: 53

Berkeley Springs, WV
Job Growth Forecast: +5.34%
Unemployment Risk: ↓ ↓
New Jobs in . . .
FIRE: 19
Retail: 33
Services: 122
Part-Time Job Market
Quality: ↓ ↓
Variety: ↓ ↓
Competition: ↓
Score: 0.4 Rank: 202

Bisbee, AZ
Job Growth Forecast: +8.60%
Unemployment Risk: ↔
New Jobs in . . .
FIRE: 380
Retail: 910
Services: 2,441
Part-Time Job Market
Quality: ↓
Variety: ↔
Competition: ↔
Score: 48.5 Rank: 105

★ Boca Raton, FL
Job Growth Forecast: +11.22%
Unemployment Risk: ↔
New Jobs in . . .
FIRE: 8,487
Retail: 8,446
Services: 42,334
Part-Time Job Market
Quality: ↑ ↑
Variety: ↑ ↑
Competition: ↓
Score: 97 Rank: 7

Boerne, TX
Job Growth Forecast: +11.90%
Unemployment Risk: ↓ ↓
New Jobs in . . .
FIRE: 563
Retail: 222
Services: 564
Part-Time Job Market
Quality: ↓ ↓
Variety: ↓
Competition: ↔
Score: 32.1 Rank: 138

Boone–Blowing Rock, NC
Job Growth Forecast: +8.15%
Unemployment Risk: ↓ ↓
New Jobs in . . .
FIRE: 141
Retail: 841
Services: 741
Part-Time Job Market
Quality: ↑
Variety: ↓
Competition: ↓ ↓
Score: 38.1 Rank: 126

Bozeman, MT
Job Growth Forecast: +11.17%
Unemployment Risk: ↓ ↓
New Jobs in . . .
FIRE: 467
Retail: 1,115
Services: 1,819
Part-Time Job Market
Quality: ↔
Variety: ↔
Competition: ↔
Score: 53.4 Rank: 95

★ Bradenton, FL
Job Growth Forecast: +17.41%
Unemployment Risk: ↓ ↓
New Jobs in . . .
FIRE: 678
Retail: 1,916
Services: 24,757
Part-Time Job Market
Quality: ↓
Variety: ↑ ↑
Competition: ↓
Score: 95.5 Rank: 10

Branson, MO
Job Growth Forecast: +20.38%
Unemployment Risk: ↑ ↑
New Jobs in . . .
FIRE: 558
Retail: 1,713
Services: 3,521
Part-Time Job Market
Quality: ↑
Variety: ↑
Competition: ↓
Score: 82.6 Rank: 36

★ = *one of the top 30 places for part-time job opportunities between 2004 and 2009.*

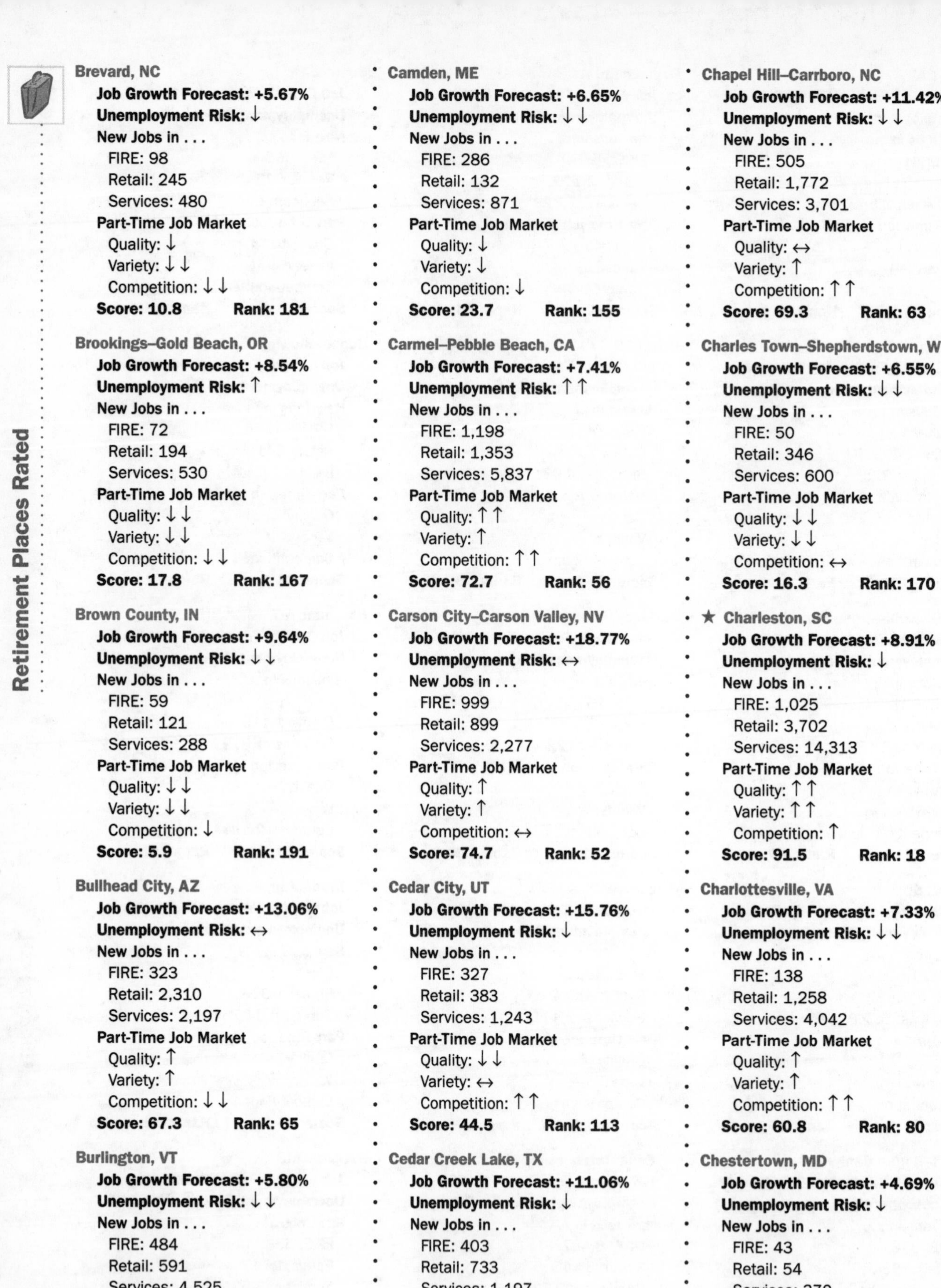

Brevard, NC
Job Growth Forecast: +5.67%
Unemployment Risk: ↓
New Jobs in . . .
FIRE: 98
Retail: 245
Services: 480
Part-Time Job Market
Quality: ↓
Variety: ↓ ↓
Competition: ↓ ↓
Score: 10.8 Rank: 181

Brookings–Gold Beach, OR
Job Growth Forecast: +8.54%
Unemployment Risk: ↑
New Jobs in . . .
FIRE: 72
Retail: 194
Services: 530
Part-Time Job Market
Quality: ↓ ↓
Variety: ↓ ↓
Competition: ↓ ↓
Score: 17.8 Rank: 167

Brown County, IN
Job Growth Forecast: +9.64%
Unemployment Risk: ↓ ↓
New Jobs in . . .
FIRE: 59
Retail: 121
Services: 288
Part-Time Job Market
Quality: ↓ ↓
Variety: ↓ ↓
Competition: ↓
Score: 5.9 Rank: 191

Bullhead City, AZ
Job Growth Forecast: +13.06%
Unemployment Risk: ↔
New Jobs in . . .
FIRE: 323
Retail: 2,310
Services: 2,197
Part-Time Job Market
Quality: ↑
Variety: ↑
Competition: ↓ ↓
Score: 67.3 Rank: 65

Burlington, VT
Job Growth Forecast: +5.80%
Unemployment Risk: ↓ ↓
New Jobs in . . .
FIRE: 484
Retail: 591
Services: 4,525
Part-Time Job Market
Quality: ↑
Variety: ↑
Competition: ↑ ↑
Score: 54.9 Rank: 92

Camden, ME
Job Growth Forecast: +6.65%
Unemployment Risk: ↓ ↓
New Jobs in . . .
FIRE: 286
Retail: 132
Services: 871
Part-Time Job Market
Quality: ↓
Variety: ↓
Competition: ↓
Score: 23.7 Rank: 155

Carmel–Pebble Beach, CA
Job Growth Forecast: +7.41%
Unemployment Risk: ↑ ↑
New Jobs in . . .
FIRE: 1,198
Retail: 1,353
Services: 5,837
Part-Time Job Market
Quality: ↑ ↑
Variety: ↑
Competition: ↑ ↑
Score: 72.7 Rank: 56

Carson City–Carson Valley, NV
Job Growth Forecast: +18.77%
Unemployment Risk: ↔
New Jobs in . . .
FIRE: 999
Retail: 899
Services: 2,277
Part-Time Job Market
Quality: ↑
Variety: ↑
Competition: ↔
Score: 74.7 Rank: 52

Cedar City, UT
Job Growth Forecast: +15.76%
Unemployment Risk: ↓
New Jobs in . . .
FIRE: 327
Retail: 383
Services: 1,243
Part-Time Job Market
Quality: ↓ ↓
Variety: ↔
Competition: ↑ ↑
Score: 44.5 Rank: 113

Cedar Creek Lake, TX
Job Growth Forecast: +11.06%
Unemployment Risk: ↓
New Jobs in . . .
FIRE: 403
Retail: 733
Services: 1,197
Part-Time Job Market
Quality: ↓
Variety: ↔
Competition: ↓
Score: 47 Rank: 108

Chapel Hill–Carrboro, NC
Job Growth Forecast: +11.42%
Unemployment Risk: ↓ ↓
New Jobs in . . .
FIRE: 505
Retail: 1,772
Services: 3,701
Part-Time Job Market
Quality: ↔
Variety: ↑
Competition: ↑ ↑
Score: 69.3 Rank: 63

Charles Town–Shepherdstown, WV
Job Growth Forecast: +6.55%
Unemployment Risk: ↓ ↓
New Jobs in . . .
FIRE: 50
Retail: 346
Services: 600
Part-Time Job Market
Quality: ↓ ↓
Variety: ↓ ↓
Competition: ↔
Score: 16.3 Rank: 170

★ Charleston, SC
Job Growth Forecast: +8.91%
Unemployment Risk: ↓
New Jobs in . . .
FIRE: 1,025
Retail: 3,702
Services: 14,313
Part-Time Job Market
Quality: ↑ ↑
Variety: ↑ ↑
Competition: ↑
Score: 91.5 Rank: 18

Charlottesville, VA
Job Growth Forecast: +7.33%
Unemployment Risk: ↓ ↓
New Jobs in . . .
FIRE: 138
Retail: 1,258
Services: 4,042
Part-Time Job Market
Quality: ↑
Variety: ↑
Competition: ↑ ↑
Score: 60.8 Rank: 80

Chestertown, MD
Job Growth Forecast: +4.69%
Unemployment Risk: ↓
New Jobs in . . .
FIRE: 43
Retail: 54
Services: 370
Part-Time Job Market
Quality: ↓ ↓
Variety: ↓ ↓
Competition: ↓
Score: 3.9 Rank: 195

★ = *one of the top 30 places for part-time job opportunities between 2004 and 2009.*

Chewelah, WA
Job Growth Forecast: +6.47%
Unemployment Risk: ↑ ↑
New Jobs in . . .
FIRE: 62
Retail: 198
Services: 415
Part-Time Job Market
Quality: ↓
Variety: ↓ ↓
Competition: ↓
Score: 9.9 **Rank: 183**

Coeur d'Alene, ID
Job Growth Forecast: +13.72%
Unemployment Risk: ↑ ↑
New Jobs in . . .
FIRE: 708
Retail: 2,150
Services: 2,872
Part-Time Job Market
Quality: ↔
Variety: ↑
Competition: ↔
Score: 70.7 **Rank: 60**

★ **Colorado Springs, CO**
Job Growth Forecast: +11.28%
Unemployment Risk: ↔
New Jobs in . . .
FIRE: 4,492
Retail: 9,469
Services: 13,027
Part-Time Job Market
Quality: ↑ ↑
Variety: ↑ ↑
Competition: ↑
Score: 95 **Rank: 11**

Columbia, MO
Job Growth Forecast: +8.09%
Unemployment Risk: ↓ ↓
New Jobs in . . .
FIRE: 117
Retail: 1,232
Services: 2,726
Part-Time Job Market
Quality: ↑
Variety: ↑
Competition: ↑ ↑
Score: 51.4 **Rank: 99**

★ **Conway, SC**
Job Growth Forecast: +11.93%
Unemployment Risk: ↓
New Jobs in . . .
FIRE: 1,948
Retail: 5,053
Services: 5,796
Part-Time Job Market
Quality: ↑ ↑
Variety: ↑ ↑
Competition: ↓
Score: 89.6 **Rank: 21**

★ **Cottonwood–Verde Valley, AZ**
Job Growth Forecast: +17%
Unemployment Risk: ↓ ↓
New Jobs in . . .
FIRE: 1,113
Retail: 2,459
Services: 6,504
Part-Time Job Market
Quality: ↓
Variety: ↑ ↑
Competition: ↓ ↓
Score: 86.1 **Rank: 28**

Crossville, TN
Job Growth Forecast: +8.42%
Unemployment Risk: ↑
New Jobs in . . .
FIRE: 84
Retail: 492
Services: 868
Part-Time Job Market
Quality: ↑
Variety: ↓
Competition: ↓ ↓
Score: 35.1 **Rank: 132**

Dare Outer Banks, NC
Job Growth Forecast: +14.30%
Unemployment Risk: ↑
New Jobs in . . .
FIRE: 529
Retail: 1,437
Services: 1,118
Part-Time Job Market
Quality: ↔
Variety: ↔
Competition: ↓
Score: 58.4 **Rank: 85**

Daytona Beach, FL
Job Growth Forecast: +6.20%
Unemployment Risk: ↓
New Jobs in . . .
FIRE: 406
Retail: 1,779
Services: 6,382
Part-Time Job Market
Quality: ↑
Variety: ↑
Competition: ↓
Score: 65.3 **Rank: 71**

Delta County, CO
Job Growth Forecast: +8.76%
Unemployment Risk: ↔
New Jobs in . . .
FIRE: 158
Retail: 274
Services: 237
Part-Time Job Market
Quality: ↓ ↓
Variety: ↓ ↓
Competition: ↓
Score: 11.3 **Rank: 180**

Door Peninsula, WI
Job Growth Forecast: +8.58%
Unemployment Risk: ↔
New Jobs in . . .
FIRE: 192
Retail: 334
Services: 874
Part-Time Job Market
Quality: ↓
Variety: ↓
Competition: ↓
Score: 31.1 **Rank: 140**

Durango, CO
Job Growth Forecast: +13.07%
Unemployment Risk: ↓
New Jobs in . . .
FIRE: 419
Retail: 591
Services: 1,994
Part-Time Job Market
Quality: ↔
Variety: ↔
Competition: ↑
Score: 55.4 **Rank: 91**

Eagle River–Woodruff, WI
Job Growth Forecast: +7.47%
Unemployment Risk: ↔
New Jobs in . . .
FIRE: 5
Retail: 199
Services: 542
Part-Time Job Market
Quality: ↓ ↓
Variety: ↓ ↓
Competition: ↓ ↓
Score: 14.8 **Rank: 173**

East End Long Island, NY
Job Growth Forecast: +4.34%
Unemployment Risk: ↓
New Jobs in . . .
FIRE: 1,887
Retail: 4,288
Services: 13,912
Part-Time Job Market
Quality: ↑ ↑
Variety: ↑ ↑
Competition: ↑
Score: 81.1 **Rank: 39**

Easton–St. Michaels, MD
Job Growth Forecast: +5.79%
Unemployment Risk: ↓ ↓
New Jobs in . . .
FIRE: 192
Retail: 250
Services: 993
Part-Time Job Market
Quality: ↔
Variety: ↓
Competition: ↓ ↓
Score: 25.2 **Rank: 152**

★ = *one of the top 30 places for part-time job opportunities between 2004 and 2009.*

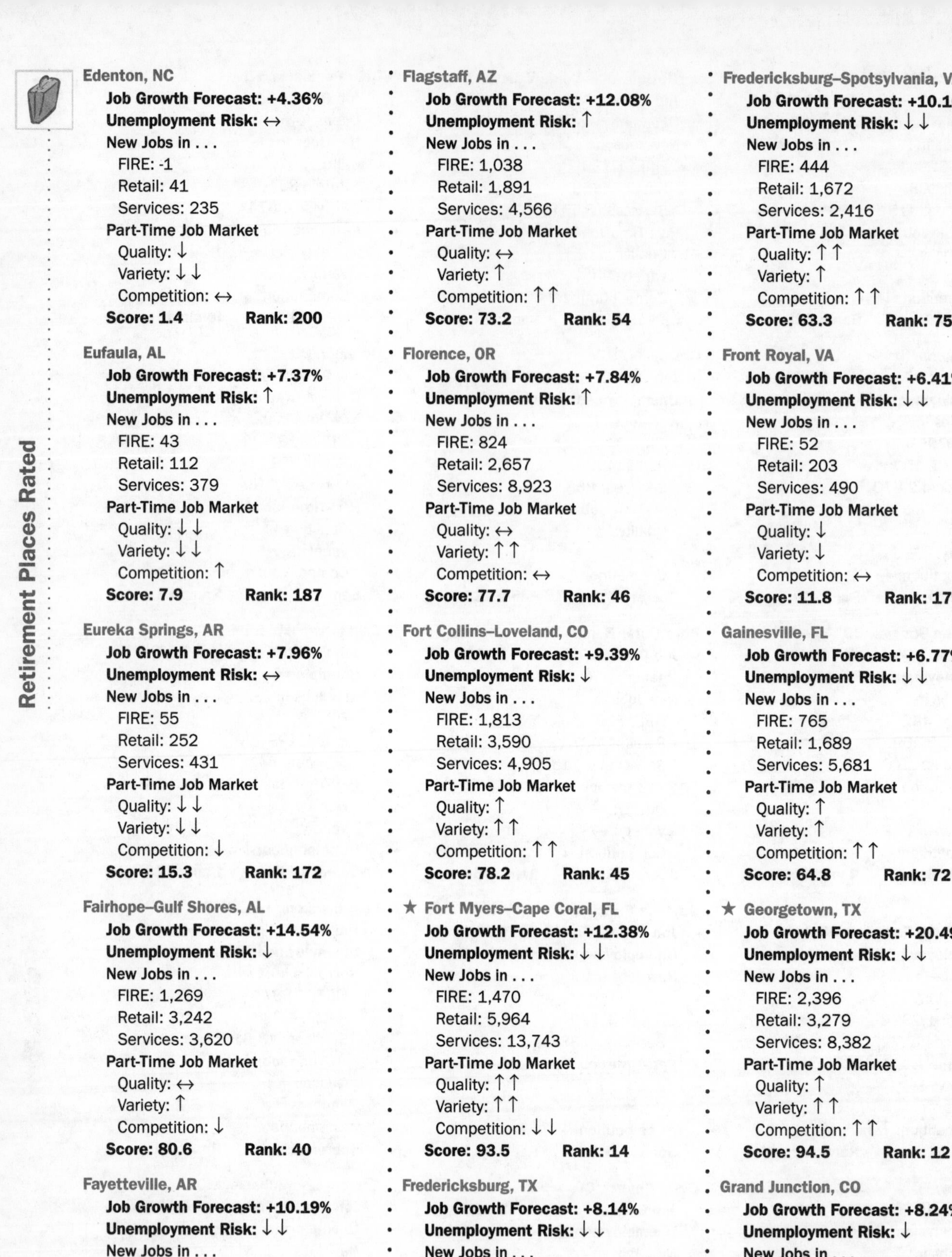

Edenton, NC

Job Growth Forecast: +4.36%
Unemployment Risk: ↔
New Jobs in . . .
FIRE: -1
Retail: 41
Services: 235
Part-Time Job Market
Quality: ↓
Variety: ↓ ↓
Competition: ↔
Score: 1.4 Rank: 200

Eufaula, AL

Job Growth Forecast: +7.37%
Unemployment Risk: ↑
New Jobs in . . .
FIRE: 43
Retail: 112
Services: 379
Part-Time Job Market
Quality: ↓ ↓
Variety: ↓ ↓
Competition: ↑
Score: 7.9 Rank: 187

Eureka Springs, AR

Job Growth Forecast: +7.96%
Unemployment Risk: ↔
New Jobs in . . .
FIRE: 55
Retail: 252
Services: 431
Part-Time Job Market
Quality: ↓ ↓
Variety: ↓ ↓
Competition: ↓
Score: 15.3 Rank: 172

Fairhope–Gulf Shores, AL

Job Growth Forecast: +14.54%
Unemployment Risk: ↓
New Jobs in . . .
FIRE: 1,269
Retail: 3,242
Services: 3,620
Part-Time Job Market
Quality: ↔
Variety: ↑
Competition: ↓
Score: 80.6 Rank: 40

Fayetteville, AR

Job Growth Forecast: +10.19%
Unemployment Risk: ↓ ↓
New Jobs in . . .
FIRE: 477
Retail: 2,449
Services: 3,902
Part-Time Job Market
Quality: ↑
Variety: ↑
Competition: ↑ ↑
Score: 71.7 Rank: 58

Flagstaff, AZ

Job Growth Forecast: +12.08%
Unemployment Risk: ↑
New Jobs in . . .
FIRE: 1,038
Retail: 1,891
Services: 4,566
Part-Time Job Market
Quality: ↔
Variety: ↑
Competition: ↑ ↑
Score: 73.2 Rank: 54

Florence, OR

Job Growth Forecast: +7.84%
Unemployment Risk: ↑
New Jobs in . . .
FIRE: 824
Retail: 2,657
Services: 8,923
Part-Time Job Market
Quality: ↔
Variety: ↑ ↑
Competition: ↔
Score: 77.7 Rank: 46

Fort Collins–Loveland, CO

Job Growth Forecast: +9.39%
Unemployment Risk: ↓
New Jobs in . . .
FIRE: 1,813
Retail: 3,590
Services: 4,905
Part-Time Job Market
Quality: ↑
Variety: ↑ ↑
Competition: ↑ ↑
Score: 78.2 Rank: 45

★ Fort Myers–Cape Coral, FL

Job Growth Forecast: +12.38%
Unemployment Risk: ↓ ↓
New Jobs in . . .
FIRE: 1,470
Retail: 5,964
Services: 13,743
Part-Time Job Market
Quality: ↑ ↑
Variety: ↑ ↑
Competition: ↓ ↓
Score: 93.5 Rank: 14

Fredericksburg, TX

Job Growth Forecast: +8.14%
Unemployment Risk: ↓ ↓
New Jobs in . . .
FIRE: 148
Retail: 190
Services: 425
Part-Time Job Market
Quality: ↓ ↓
Variety: ↓ ↓
Competition: ↓ ↓
Score: 16.8 Rank: 169

Fredericksburg–Spotsylvania, VA

Job Growth Forecast: +10.10%
Unemployment Risk: ↓ ↓
New Jobs in . . .
FIRE: 444
Retail: 1,672
Services: 2,416
Part-Time Job Market
Quality: ↑ ↑
Variety: ↑
Competition: ↑ ↑
Score: 63.3 Rank: 75

Front Royal, VA

Job Growth Forecast: +6.41%
Unemployment Risk: ↓ ↓
New Jobs in . . .
FIRE: 52
Retail: 203
Services: 490
Part-Time Job Market
Quality: ↓
Variety: ↓
Competition: ↔
Score: 11.8 Rank: 179

Gainesville, FL

Job Growth Forecast: +6.77%
Unemployment Risk: ↓ ↓
New Jobs in . . .
FIRE: 765
Retail: 1,689
Services: 5,681
Part-Time Job Market
Quality: ↑
Variety: ↑
Competition: ↑ ↑
Score: 64.8 Rank: 72

★ Georgetown, TX

Job Growth Forecast: +20.49%
Unemployment Risk: ↓ ↓
New Jobs in . . .
FIRE: 2,396
Retail: 3,279
Services: 8,382
Part-Time Job Market
Quality: ↑
Variety: ↑ ↑
Competition: ↑ ↑
Score: 94.5 Rank: 12

Grand Junction, CO

Job Growth Forecast: +8.24%
Unemployment Risk: ↓
New Jobs in . . .
FIRE: 758
Retail: 1,337
Services: 1,879
Part-Time Job Market
Quality: ↔
Variety: ↔
Competition:↔
Score: 49.5 Rank: 103

★ = *one of the top 30 places for part-time job opportunities between 2004 and 2009.*

Grants Pass, OR

Job Growth Forecast: +8.07%
Unemployment Risk: ↑↑
New Jobs in . . .
FIRE: 181
Retail: 583
Services: 1,471
Part-Time Job Market
Quality: ↔
Variety: ↔
Competition: ↓↓
Score: 41 **Rank: 120**

Grass Valley–Nevada City, CA

Job Growth Forecast: +12.18%
Unemployment Risk: ↓
New Jobs in . . .
FIRE: 414
Retail: 995
Services: 3,399
Part-Time Job Market
Quality: ↔
Variety: ↑
Competition: ↓
Score: 64.3 **Rank: 73**

Hamilton–Bitterroot Valley, MT

Job Growth Forecast: +11.48%
Unemployment Risk: ↔
New Jobs in . . .
FIRE: 114
Retail: 275
Services: 781
Part-Time Job Market
Quality: ↓
Variety: ↓
Competition: ↓
Score: 28.2 **Rank: 146**

Hanover, NH

Job Growth Forecast: +6.26%
Unemployment Risk: ↓↓
New Jobs in . . .
FIRE: 62
Retail: 799
Services: 2,298
Part-Time Job Market
Quality: ↑↑
Variety: ↔
Competition: ↑
Score: 47.5 **Rank: 107**

Hattiesburg, MS

Job Growth Forecast: +4.48%
Unemployment Risk: ↓
New Jobs in . . .
FIRE: 67
Retail: –92
Services: 1,402
Part-Time Job Market
Quality: ↔
Variety: ↔
Competition: ↑↑
Score: 19.8 **Rank: 163**

★ Henderson, NV

Job Growth Forecast: +14.83%
Unemployment Risk: ↔
New Jobs in . . .
FIRE: 16,378
Retail: 24,762
Services: 55,280
Part-Time Job Market
Quality: ↑↑
Variety: ↑↑
Competition: ↔
Score: 98.5 **Rank: 4**

Hendersonville–East Flat Rock, NC

Job Growth Forecast: +7.51%
Unemployment Risk: ↓↓
New Jobs in . . .
FIRE: 178
Retail: 841
Services: 915
Part-Time Job Market
Quality: ↑
Variety: ↔
Competition: ↓↓
Score: 39.1 **Rank: 124**

Hilton Head Island, SC

Job Growth Forecast: +12.67%
Unemployment Risk: ↓↓
New Jobs in . . .
FIRE: 1,001
Retail: 3,820
Services: 3,348
Part-Time Job Market
Quality: ↑↑
Variety: ↑
Competition: ↔
Score: 83.1 **Rank: 34**

Hot Springs, AR

Job Growth Forecast: +6.48%
Unemployment Risk: ↔
New Jobs in . . .
FIRE: 245
Retail: 767
Services: 1,298
Part-Time Job Market
Quality: ↔
Variety: ↔
Competition: ↓
Score: 35.6 **Rank: 131**

Inverness, FL

Job Growth Forecast: +11.99%
Unemployment Risk: ↔
New Jobs in . . .
FIRE: 213
Retail: 1,101
Services: 2,769
Part-Time Job Market
Quality: ↓
Variety: ↑
Competition: ↑↑
Score: 56.9 **Rank: 88**

Iowa City, IA

Job Growth Forecast: +8.65%
Unemployment Risk: ↓↓
New Jobs in . . .
FIRE: 359
Retail: 1,760
Services: 2,816
Part-Time Job Market
Quality: ↔
Variety: ↑
Competition: ↑↑
Score: 57.9 **Rank: 86**

Jackson Hole, WY

Job Growth Forecast: +10.41%
Unemployment Risk: ↓↓
New Jobs in . . .
FIRE: 611
Retail: 382
Services: 746
Part-Time Job Market
Quality: ↑
Variety: ↓
Competition: ↑
Score: 43 **Rank: 116**

Kalispell–Flathead Valley, MT

Job Growth Forecast: +9.98%
Unemployment Risk: ↑
New Jobs in . . .
FIRE: 269
Retail: 775
Services: 3,001
Part-Time Job Market
Quality: ↓
Variety: ↑
Competition: ↔
Score: 51.9 **Rank: 98**

Kauai, HI

Job Growth Forecast: +3.97%
Unemployment Risk: ↑
New Jobs in . . .
FIRE: 193
Retail: 197
Services: 748
Part-Time Job Market
Quality: ↑
Variety: ↓
Competition: ↔
Score: 17.3 **Rank: 168**

Kerrville, TX

Job Growth Forecast: +8.71%
Unemployment Risk: ↓↓
New Jobs in . . .
FIRE: 357
Retail: 379
Services: 821
Part-Time Job Market
Quality: ↓
Variety: ↓
Competition: ↓
Score: 32.6 **Rank: 137**

★ = *one of the top 30 places for part-time job opportunities between 2004 and 2009.*

Ketchum–Sun Valley, ID
Job Growth Forecast: +16.04%
Unemployment Risk: ↓
New Jobs in . . .
FIRE: 374
Retail: 582
Services: 1,162
Part-Time Job Market
Quality: ↑↑
Variety: ↔
Competition: ↔
Score: 57.4 Rank: 87

Key West, FL
Job Growth Forecast: +8.85%
Unemployment Risk: ↓↓
New Jobs in . . .
FIRE: 346
Retail: 1,144
Services: 2,479
Part-Time Job Market
Quality: ↑
Variety: ↔
Competition: ↓
Score: 55.9 Rank: 90

Kingman, AZ
Job Growth Forecast: +13.06%
Unemployment Risk: ↔
New Jobs in . . .
FIRE: 323
Retail: 2,310
Services: 2,197
Part-Time Job Market
Quality: ↑
Variety: ↑
Competition: ↓↓
Score: 67.3 Rank: 65

Kissimmee–St. Cloud, FL
Job Growth Forecast: +14.38%
Unemployment Risk: ↓
New Jobs in . . .
FIRE: 1,003
Retail: 2,832
Services: 3,051
Part-Time Job Market
Quality: ↑
Variety: ↑
Competition: ↑
Score: 80.1 Rank: 41

★ Laguna Beach–Dana Point, CA
Job Growth Forecast: +7.93%
Unemployment Risk: ↓↓
New Jobs in . . .
FIRE: 26,654
Retail: 15,863
Services: 61,754
Part-Time Job Market
Quality: ↑↑
Variety: ↑↑
Competition: ↑↑
Score: 97.5 Rank: 6

★ Lake Conroe, TX
Job Growth Forecast: +16.90%
Unemployment Risk: ↓
New Jobs in . . .
FIRE: 1,736
Retail: 4,603
Services: 8,136
Part-Time Job Market
Quality: ↑↑
Variety: ↑↑
Competition: ↑
Score: 93 Rank: 15

Lake Havasu City, AZ
Job Growth Forecast: +13.06%
Unemployment Risk: ↔
New Jobs in . . .
FIRE: 323
Retail: 2,310
Services: 2,197
Part-Time Job Market
Quality: ↑
Variety: ↑
Competition: ↓↓
Score: 67.3 Rank: 65

Lake of the Cherokees, OK
Job Growth Forecast: +11.19%
Unemployment Risk: ↓
New Jobs in . . .
FIRE: 183
Retail: 439
Services: 418
Part-Time Job Market
Quality: ↓↓
Variety: ↓
Competition: ↓↓
Score: 25.7 Rank: 151

Lake of the Ozarks, MO
Job Growth Forecast: +13.96%
Unemployment Risk: ↑
New Jobs in . . .
FIRE: 465
Retail: 1,075
Services: 1,331
Part-Time Job Market
Quality: ↔
Variety: ↔
Competition: ↓↓
Score: 56.4 Rank: 89

Lake Placid, NY
Job Growth Forecast: +4.61%
Unemployment Risk: ↑
New Jobs in . . .
FIRE: 104
Retail: 158
Services: 390
Part-Time Job Market
Quality: ↓
Variety: ↓↓
Competition: ↔
Score: 5.4 Rank: 192

Lake Winnipesaukee, NH
Job Growth Forecast: +17.44%
Unemployment Risk: ↓↓
New Jobs in . . .
FIRE: 205
Retail: 1,458
Services: 3,336
Part-Time Job Market
Quality: ↑↑
Variety: ↑
Competition: ↔
Score: 78.7 Rank: 44

Lakeland–Winter Haven, FL
Job Growth Forecast: +7.12%
Unemployment Risk: ↑
New Jobs in . . .
FIRE: 802
Retail: 3,767
Services: 9,031
Part-Time Job Market
Quality: ↑↑
Variety: ↑↑
Competition: ↓
Score: 81.6 Rank: 38

★ Largo, FL
Job Growth Forecast: +5.71%
Unemployment Risk: ↓
New Jobs in . . .
FIRE: 783
Retail: 2,425
Services: 21,456
Part-Time Job Market
Quality: ↑
Variety: ↑↑
Competition: ↓
Score: 87.6 Rank: 26

Las Cruces, NM
Job Growth Forecast: +8.61%
Unemployment Risk: ↑↑
New Jobs in . . .
FIRE: 295
Retail: 1,148
Services: 3,349
Part-Time Job Market
Quality: ↓
Variety: ↑
Competition: ↑↑
Score: 53.9 Rank: 94

Las Vegas, NM
Job Growth Forecast: +9.48%
Unemployment Risk: ↑
New Jobs in . . .
FIRE: 65
Retail: 140
Services: 588
Part-Time Job Market
Quality: ↓↓
Variety: ↓↓
Competition: ↑
Score: 18.8 Rank: 165

★ = *one of the top 30 places for part-time job opportunities between 2004 and 2009.*

Leelanau Peninsula, MI
Job Growth Forecast: +8.05%
Unemployment Risk: ↓
New Jobs in . . .
FIRE: 37
Retail: 89
Services: 605
Part-Time Job Market
Quality: ↓↓
Variety: ↓↓
Competition: ↓
Score: 14.3 **Rank: 174**

Leesburg–Mount Dora, FL
Job Growth Forecast: +8.56%
Unemployment Risk: ↓
New Jobs in . . .
FIRE: 430
Retail: 1,628
Services: 3,241
Part-Time Job Market
Quality: ↔
Variety: ↑
Competition: ↓↓
Score: 60.3 **Rank: 81**

Litchfield Hills, CT
Job Growth Forecast: +3.77%
Unemployment Risk: ↓↓
New Jobs in . . .
FIRE: 402
Retail: 818
Services: 2,632
Part-Time Job Market
Quality: ↑
Variety: ↔
Competition: ↔
Score: 40.5 **Rank: 121**

Lower Cape May, NJ
Job Growth Forecast: +4.89%
Unemployment Risk: ↑↑
New Jobs in . . .
FIRE: 335
Retail: 529
Services: 1,274
Part-Time Job Market
Quality: ↑
Variety: ↔
Competition: ↓
Score: 34.1 **Rank: 134**

★ **Madison, WI**
Job Growth Forecast: +7.34%
Unemployment Risk: ↓↓
New Jobs in . . .
FIRE: 2,153
Retail: 2,669
Services: 12,913
Part-Time Job Market
Quality: ↑↑
Variety: ↑↑
Competition: ↑↑
Score: 87.1 **Rank: 27**

Marble Falls–Lake LBJ, TX
Job Growth Forecast: +14.56%
Unemployment Risk: ↓
New Jobs in . . .
FIRE: 659
Retail: 351
Services: 1,292
Part-Time Job Market
Quality: ↓↓
Variety: ↔
Competition: ↓
Score: 46 **Rank: 110**

Mariposa, CA
Job Growth Forecast: +5.57%
Unemployment Risk: ↑
New Jobs in . . .
FIRE: 31
Retail: 66
Services: 193
Part-Time Job Market
Quality: ↓
Variety: ↓↓
Competition: ↓
Score: 2.9 **Rank: 197**

Martha's Vineyard, MA
Job Growth Forecast: +8.74%
Unemployment Risk: ↓
New Jobs in . . .
FIRE: 148
Retail: 222
Services: 416
Part-Time Job Market
Quality: ↑
Variety: ↓↓
Competition: ↔
Score: 23.2 **Rank: 156**

Maryville, TN
Job Growth Forecast: +9.95%
Unemployment Risk: ↓
New Jobs in . . .
FIRE: 302
Retail: 769
Services: 1,825
Part-Time Job Market
Quality: ↑↑
Variety: ↔
Competition: ↑
Score: 50.9 **Rank: 100**

Maui, HI
Job Growth Forecast: +7.53%
Unemployment Risk: ↔
New Jobs in . . .
FIRE: 321
Retail: 1,349
Services: 3,609
Part-Time Job Market
Quality: ↑
Variety: ↑
Competition: ↑
Score: 58.9 **Rank: 84**

McCall, ID
Job Growth Forecast: +10.43%
Unemployment Risk: ↑↑
New Jobs in . . .
FIRE: 77
Retail: 127
Services: 169
Part-Time Job Market
Quality: ↓↓
Variety: ↓↓
Competition: ↓
Score: 7.4 **Rank: 188**

Medford–Ashland, OR
Job Growth Forecast: +10.39%
Unemployment Risk: ↑
New Jobs in . . .
FIRE: 711
Retail: 2,909
Services: 5,914
Part-Time Job Market
Quality: ↑
Variety: ↑↑
Competition: ↔
Score: 79.2 **Rank: 43**

★ **Melbourne–Palm Bay, FL**
Job Growth Forecast: +7.60%
Unemployment Risk: ↓
New Jobs in . . .
FIRE: 1,012
Retail: 4,101
Services: 10,698
Part-Time Job Market
Quality: ↑
Variety: ↑↑
Competition: ↔
Score: 85.6 **Rank: 30**

Mendocino–Fort Bragg, CA
Job Growth Forecast: +6.45%
Unemployment Risk: ↑
New Jobs in . . .
FIRE: 144
Retail: 602
Services: 1,430
Part-Time Job Market
Quality: ↔
Variety: ↔
Competition: ↔
Score: 37.1 **Rank: 128**

★ **Mesa, AZ**
Job Growth Forecast: +12.94%
Unemployment Risk: ↓
New Jobs in . . .
FIRE: 35,288
Retail: 39,202
Services: 112,257
Part-Time Job Market
Quality: ↑↑
Variety: ↑↑
Competition: ↑
Score: 99 **Rank: 1**

★ = *one of the top 30 places for part-time job opportunities between 2004 and 2009.*

Middle Cape Cod, MA
Job Growth Forecast: +6.88%
Unemployment Risk: ↓
New Jobs in . . .
FIRE: 1,147
Retail: 1,880
Services: 4,617
Part-Time Job Market
Quality: ↑↑
Variety: ↑
Competition: ↓
Score: 66.8 Rank: 68

★ **Mission–McAllen–Alamo, TX**
Job Growth Forecast: +11.74%
Unemployment Risk: ↑↑
New Jobs in . . .
FIRE: 1,302
Retail: 4,607
Services: 9,074
Part-Time Job Market
Quality: ↔
Variety: ↑↑
Competition: ↑↑
Score: 89.1 Rank: 23

Monadnock Region, NH
Job Growth Forecast: +4.93%
Unemployment Risk: ↓↓
New Jobs in . . .
FIRE: 144
Retail: 764
Services: 1,291
Part-Time Job Market
Quality: ↑
Variety: ↔
Competition: ↑
Score: 33.1 Rank: 136

Montrose, CO
Job Growth Forecast: +9.09%
Unemployment Risk: ↔
New Jobs in . . .
FIRE: 205
Retail: 444
Services: 410
Part-Time Job Market
Quality: ↓
Variety: ↓
Competition: ↔
Score: 24.7 Rank: 153

Morro Bay–Cambria, CA
Job Growth Forecast: +9.51%
Unemployment Risk: ↓↓
New Jobs in . . .
FIRE: 1,119
Retail: 1,813
Services: 6,121
Part-Time Job Market
Quality: ↑
Variety: ↑↑
Competition: ↑
Score: 77.2 Rank: 47

Murray–Kentucky Lake, KY
Job Growth Forecast: +8.21%
Unemployment Risk: ↔
New Jobs in . . .
FIRE: -29
Retail: 394
Services: 226
Part-Time Job Market
Quality: ↑↑
Variety: ↓↓
Competition: ↔
Score: 18.3 Rank: 166

★ **Myrtle Beach, SC**
Job Growth Forecast: +11.93%
Unemployment Risk: ↓
New Jobs in . . .
FIRE: 1,948
Retail: 5,053
Services: 5,796
Part-Time Job Market
Quality: ↑↑
Variety: ↑↑
Competition: ↓
Score: 89.6 Rank: 21

★ **Naples, FL**
Job Growth Forecast: +13.70%
Unemployment Risk: ↓
New Jobs in . . .
FIRE: 1,461
Retail: 4,243
Services: 10,359
Part-Time Job Market
Quality: ↑↑
Variety: ↑↑
Competition: ↓↓
Score: 92.5 Rank: 16

Natchitoches, LA
Job Growth Forecast: +3.96%
Unemployment Risk: ↑
New Jobs in . . .
FIRE: 16
Retail: 10
Services: 236
Part-Time Job Market
Quality: ↔
Variety: ↓↓
Competition: ↑↑
Score: 1.9 Rank: 199

New Bern, NC
Job Growth Forecast: +5.79%
Unemployment Risk: ↔
New Jobs in . . .
FIRE: 77
Retail: 498
Services: 1,360
Part-Time Job Market
Quality: ↔
Variety: ↔
Competition: ↑
Score: 30.6 Rank: 141

New Braunfels, TX
Job Growth Forecast: +11.73%
Unemployment Risk: ↓
New Jobs in . . .
FIRE: 605
Retail: 1,019
Services: 1,517
Part-Time Job Market
Quality: ↔
Variety: ↔
Competition: ↔
Score: 52.4 Rank: 97

New Port Richey, FL
Job Growth Forecast: +12.54%
Unemployment Risk: ↓
New Jobs in . . .
FIRE: 492
Retail: 3,423
Services: 5,639
Part-Time Job Market
Quality: ↑
Variety: ↑↑
Competition: ↓
Score: 84.6 Rank: 32

Newport–Lincoln City, OR
Job Growth Forecast: +7.22%
Unemployment Risk: ↑↑
New Jobs in . . .
FIRE: 65
Retail: 379
Services: 1,087
Part-Time Job Market
Quality: ↓
Variety: ↓
Competition: ↓↓
Score: 27.2 Rank: 148

Norfork Lake, AR
Job Growth Forecast: +8.07%
Unemployment Risk: ↔
New Jobs in . . .
FIRE: 95
Retail: 348
Services: 982
Part-Time Job Market
Quality: ↓
Variety: ↓
Competition: ↓↓
Score: 29.2 Rank: 144

★ **North County San Diego, CA**
Job Growth Forecast: +8.26%
Unemployment Risk: ↓
New Jobs in . . .
FIRE: 10,051
Retail: 15,858
Services: 89,576
Part-Time Job Market
Quality: ↑↑
Variety: ↑↑
Competition: ↑↑
Score: 98 Rank: 5

★ = *one of the top 30 places for part-time job opportunities between 2004 and 2009.*

Northampton–Amherst, MA
Job Growth Forecast: +4.72%
Unemployment Risk: ↓↓
New Jobs in . . .
FIRE: 33
Retail: 48
Services: 3,426
Part-Time Job Market
Quality: ↔
Variety: ↔
Competition: ↑↑
Score: 40 Rank: 122

Northern Neck, VA
Job Growth Forecast: +9.77%
Unemployment Risk: ↑↑
New Jobs in . . .
FIRE: 21
Retail: 88
Services: 262
Part-Time Job Market
Quality: ↔
Variety: ↓↓
Competition: ↓↓
Score: 8.9 Rank: 185

Oakhurst–Coarsegold, CA
Job Growth Forecast: +10.42%
Unemployment Risk: ↑↑
New Jobs in . . .
FIRE: 238
Retail: 572
Services: 2,569
Part-Time Job Market
Quality: ↑
Variety: ↔
Competition: ↑↑
Score: 54.4 Rank: 93

Ocala, FL
Job Growth Forecast: +8.96%
Unemployment Risk: ↔
New Jobs in . . .
FIRE: 464
Retail: 2,294
Services: 3,716
Part-Time Job Market
Quality: ↑
Variety: ↑
Competition: ↓
Score: 65.8 Rank: 70

Ocean City, MD
Job Growth Forecast: +5.22%
Unemployment Risk: ↑↑
New Jobs in . . .
FIRE: 228
Retail: 502
Services: 645
Part-Time Job Market
Quality: ↔
Variety: ↓
Competition: ↓↓
Score: 22.2 Rank: 158

Oscoda–Huron Shore, MI
Job Growth Forecast: +5.46%
Unemployment Risk: ↑↑
New Jobs in . . .
FIRE: 35
Retail: 164
Services: 271
Part-Time Job Market
Quality: ↓
Variety: ↓↓
Competition: ↓↓
Score: 4.4 Rank: 194

Oxford, MS
Job Growth Forecast: +7.26%
Unemployment Risk: ↓↓
New Jobs in . . .
FIRE: 124
Retail: 178
Services: 790
Part-Time Job Market
Quality: ↔
Variety: ↓
Competition: ↑↑
Score: 24.2 Rank: 154

Pagosa Springs, CO
Job Growth Forecast: +16.62%
Unemployment Risk: ↔
New Jobs in . . .
FIRE: 200
Retail: 216
Services: 430
Part-Time Job Market
Quality: ↓↓
Variety: ↓↓
Competition: ↓
Score: 26.7 Rank: 149

Pahrump Valley, NV
Job Growth Forecast: +11.73%
Unemployment Risk: ↑
New Jobs in . . .
FIRE: 245
Retail: 316
Services: 612
Part-Time Job Market
Quality: ↑
Variety: ↓
Competition: ↓↓
Score: 39.6 Rank: 123

★ **Palm Springs–Coachella Valley, CA**
Job Growth Forecast: +11.05%
Unemployment Risk: ↑
New Jobs in . . .
FIRE: 4,414
Retail: 16,745
Services: 24,092
Part-Time Job Market
Quality: ↑
Variety: ↑↑
Competition: ↑↑
Score: 96.5 Rank: 8

Palmer–Wasilla, AK
Job Growth Forecast: +8.80%
Unemployment Risk: ↑↑
New Jobs in . . .
FIRE: 90
Retail: 371
Services: 822
Part-Time Job Market
Quality: ↔
Variety: ↓
Competition: ↑↑
Score: 29.7 Rank: 143

Panama City, FL
Job Growth Forecast: +8.05%
Unemployment Risk: ↑
New Jobs in . . .
FIRE: 621
Retail: 1,489
Services: 3,688
Part-Time Job Market
Quality: ↔
Variety: ↑
Competition: ↔
Score: 61.3 Rank: 79

Paradise–Magalia, CA
Job Growth Forecast: +9.24%
Unemployment Risk: ↑↑
New Jobs in . . .
FIRE: 328
Retail: 1,216
Services: 6,380
Part-Time Job Market
Quality: ↔
Variety: ↑
Competition: ↑
Score: 71.2 Rank: 59

Park City, UT
Job Growth Forecast: +22.98%
Unemployment Risk: ↑
New Jobs in . . .
FIRE: 945
Retail: 1,162
Services: 3,102
Part-Time Job Market
Quality: ↑
Variety: ↑
Competition: ↑↑
Score: 85.1 Rank: 31

Payson, AZ
Job Growth Forecast: +12.63%
Unemployment Risk: ↑
New Jobs in . . .
FIRE: 391
Retail: 571
Services: 1,081
Part-Time Job Market
Quality: ↓↓
Variety: ↔
Competition: ↓↓
Score: 45 Rank: 112

★ = *one of the top 30 places for part-time job opportunities between 2004 and 2009.*

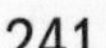

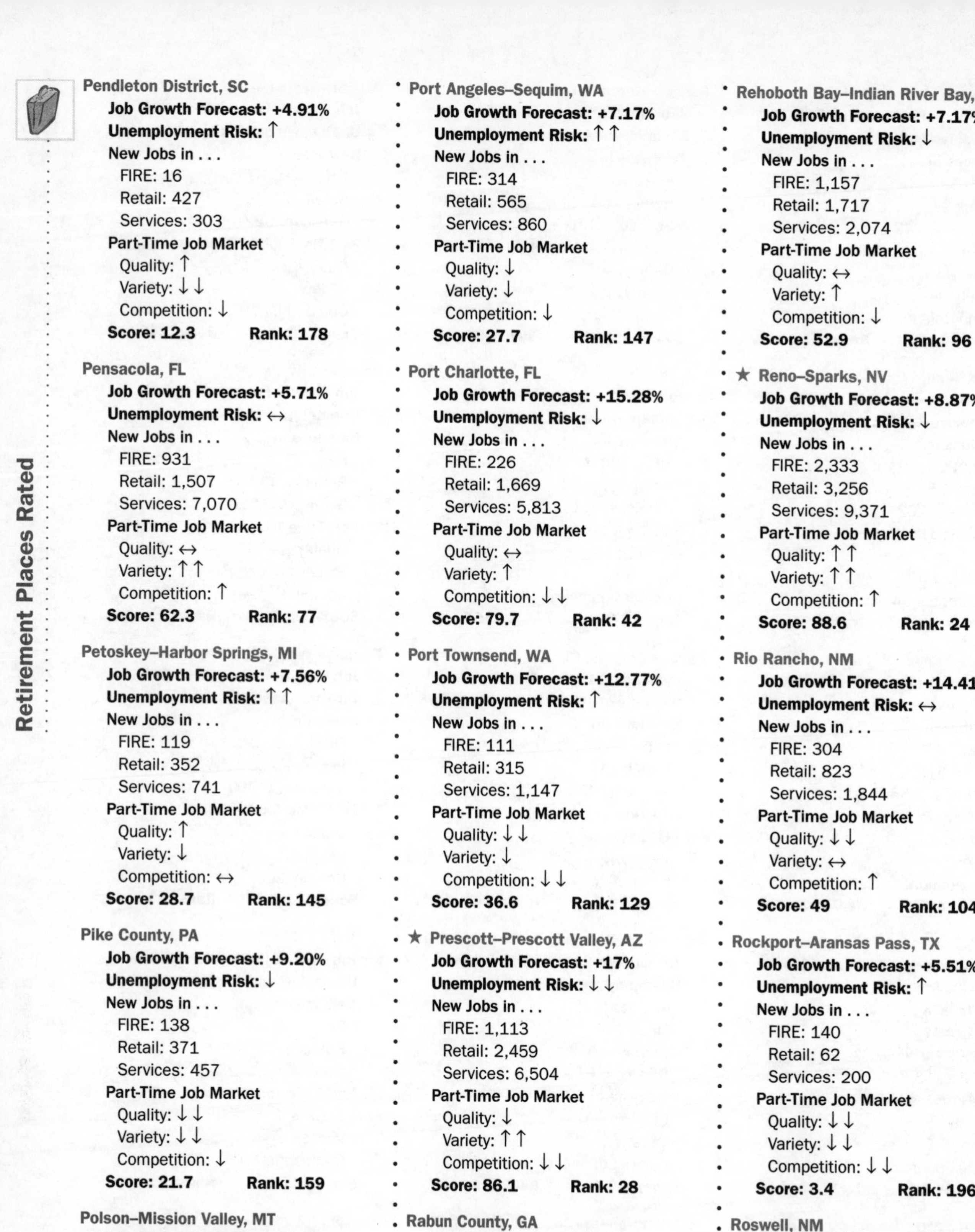

Pendleton District, SC
Job Growth Forecast: +4.91%
Unemployment Risk: ↑
New Jobs in . . .
FIRE: 16
Retail: 427
Services: 303
Part-Time Job Market
Quality: ↑
Variety: ↓↓
Competition: ↓
Score: 12.3 **Rank: 178**

Pensacola, FL
Job Growth Forecast: +5.71%
Unemployment Risk: ↔
New Jobs in . . .
FIRE: 931
Retail: 1,507
Services: 7,070
Part-Time Job Market
Quality: ↔
Variety: ↑↑
Competition: ↑
Score: 62.3 **Rank: 77**

Petoskey–Harbor Springs, MI
Job Growth Forecast: +7.56%
Unemployment Risk: ↑↑
New Jobs in . . .
FIRE: 119
Retail: 352
Services: 741
Part-Time Job Market
Quality: ↑
Variety: ↓
Competition: ↔
Score: 28.7 **Rank: 145**

Pike County, PA
Job Growth Forecast: +9.20%
Unemployment Risk: ↓
New Jobs in . . .
FIRE: 138
Retail: 371
Services: 457
Part-Time Job Market
Quality: ↓↓
Variety: ↓↓
Competition: ↓
Score: 21.7 **Rank: 159**

Polson–Mission Valley, MT
Job Growth Forecast: +9.08%
Unemployment Risk: ↑↑
New Jobs in . . .
FIRE: 41
Retail: 133
Services: 815
Part-Time Job Market
Quality: ↓↓
Variety: ↓↓
Competition: ↔
Score: 20.2 **Rank: 162**

Port Angeles–Sequim, WA
Job Growth Forecast: +7.17%
Unemployment Risk: ↑↑
New Jobs in . . .
FIRE: 314
Retail: 565
Services: 860
Part-Time Job Market
Quality: ↓
Variety: ↓
Competition: ↓
Score: 27.7 **Rank: 147**

Port Charlotte, FL
Job Growth Forecast: +15.28%
Unemployment Risk: ↓
New Jobs in . . .
FIRE: 226
Retail: 1,669
Services: 5,813
Part-Time Job Market
Quality: ↔
Variety: ↑
Competition: ↓↓
Score: 79.7 **Rank: 42**

Port Townsend, WA
Job Growth Forecast: +12.77%
Unemployment Risk: ↑
New Jobs in . . .
FIRE: 111
Retail: 315
Services: 1,147
Part-Time Job Market
Quality: ↓↓
Variety: ↓
Competition: ↓↓
Score: 36.6 **Rank: 129**

★ Prescott–Prescott Valley, AZ
Job Growth Forecast: +17%
Unemployment Risk: ↓↓
New Jobs in . . .
FIRE: 1,113
Retail: 2,459
Services: 6,504
Part-Time Job Market
Quality: ↓
Variety: ↑↑
Competition: ↓↓
Score: 86.1 **Rank: 28**

Rabun County, GA
Job Growth Forecast: +7.54%
Unemployment Risk: ↓↓
New Jobs in . . .
FIRE: 13
Retail: 80
Services: 378
Part-Time Job Market
Quality: ↓
Variety: ↓↓
Competition: ↓↓
Score: 6.4 **Rank: 190**

Rehoboth Bay–Indian River Bay, DE
Job Growth Forecast: +7.17%
Unemployment Risk: ↓
New Jobs in . . .
FIRE: 1,157
Retail: 1,717
Services: 2,074
Part-Time Job Market
Quality: ↔
Variety: ↑
Competition: ↓
Score: 52.9 **Rank: 96**

★ Reno–Sparks, NV
Job Growth Forecast: +8.87%
Unemployment Risk: ↓
New Jobs in . . .
FIRE: 2,333
Retail: 3,256
Services: 9,371
Part-Time Job Market
Quality: ↑↑
Variety: ↑↑
Competition: ↑
Score: 88.6 **Rank: 24**

Rio Rancho, NM
Job Growth Forecast: +14.41%
Unemployment Risk: ↔
New Jobs in . . .
FIRE: 304
Retail: 823
Services: 1,844
Part-Time Job Market
Quality: ↓↓
Variety: ↔
Competition: ↑
Score: 49 **Rank: 104**

Rockport–Aransas Pass, TX
Job Growth Forecast: +5.51%
Unemployment Risk: ↑
New Jobs in . . .
FIRE: 140
Retail: 62
Services: 200
Part-Time Job Market
Quality: ↓↓
Variety: ↓↓
Competition: ↓↓
Score: 3.4 **Rank: 196**

Roswell, NM
Job Growth Forecast: +5.57%
Unemployment Risk: ↑
New Jobs in . . .
FIRE: 5
Retail: 282
Services: 471
Part-Time Job Market
Quality: ↓
Variety: ↓↓
Competition: ↑
Score: 9.4 **Rank: 184**

★ = *one of the top 30 places for part-time job opportunities between 2004 and 2009.*

Ruidoso, NM

Job Growth Forecast: +10.29%
Unemployment Risk: ↓
New Jobs in . . .
FIRE: 121
Retail: 307
Services: 537
Part-Time Job Market
Quality: ↓↓
Variety: ↓↓
Competition: ↓↓
Score: 21.2 Rank: 160

St. Augustine, FL

Job Growth Forecast: +13.35%
Unemployment Risk: ↓↓
New Jobs in . . .
FIRE: 710
Retail: 2,154
Services: 3,325
Part-Time Job Market
Quality: ↑
Variety: ↑
Competition: ↓
Score: 76.7 Rank: 48

St. George–Zion, UT

Job Growth Forecast: +16.48%
Unemployment Risk: ↓
New Jobs in . . .
FIRE: 1,106
Retail: 1,925
Services: 2,851
Part-Time Job Market
Quality: ↔
Variety: ↑
Competition: ↑
Score: 75.7 Rank: 50

St. Jay–Northeast Kingdom, VT

Job Growth Forecast: +6.53%
Unemployment Risk: ↔
New Jobs in . . .
FIRE: 42
Retail: 124
Services: 591
Part-Time Job Market
Quality: ↓
Variety: ↓
Competition: ↔
Score: 13.3 Rank: 176

St. Simons–Jekyll Islands, GA

Job Growth Forecast: +6.97%
Unemployment Risk: ↓
New Jobs in . . .
FIRE: 190
Retail: 916
Services: 1,753
Part-Time Job Market
Quality: ↔
Variety: ↔
Competition: ↔
Score: 44 Rank: 114

Salida, CO

Job Growth Forecast: +8.09%
Unemployment Risk: ↓↓
New Jobs in . . .
FIRE: 170
Retail: 283
Services: 55
Part-Time Job Market
Quality: ↓↓
Variety: ↓↓
Competition: ↓
Score: 8.4 Rank: 186

San Juan Islands, WA

Job Growth Forecast: +10.05%
Unemployment Risk: ↓
New Jobs in . . .
FIRE: 101
Retail: 93
Services: 468
Part-Time Job Market
Quality: ↓↓
Variety: ↓↓
Competition: ↓↓
Score: 15.8 Rank: 171

Sandpoint–Lake Pend Oreille, ID

Job Growth Forecast: +9.71%
Unemployment Risk: ↑↑
New Jobs in . . .
FIRE: 239
Retail: 660
Services: 692
Part-Time Job Market
Quality: ↓
Variety: ↓
Competition: ↓
Score: 36.1 Rank: 130

Santa Barbara, CA

Job Growth Forecast: +6.05%
Unemployment Risk: ↓
New Jobs in . . .
FIRE: 941
Retail: 2,421
Services: 6,353
Part-Time Job Market
Quality: ↑↑
Variety: ↑↑
Competition: ↑↑
Score: 72.2 Rank: 57

Santa Fe, NM

Job Growth Forecast: +10.89%
Unemployment Risk: ↓↓
New Jobs in . . .
FIRE: 1,053
Retail: 2,108
Services: 4,035
Part-Time Job Market
Quality: ↑
Variety: ↑
Competition: ↔
Score: 75.2 Rank: 51

★ Santa Rosa, CA

Job Growth Forecast: +8.27%
Unemployment Risk: ↓↓
New Jobs in . . .
FIRE: 2,061
Retail: 2,950
Services: 10,405
Part-Time Job Market
Quality: ↑↑
Variety: ↑↑
Competition: ↑
Score: 88.1 Rank: 25

★ Sarasota, FL

Job Growth Forecast: +9.86%
Unemployment Risk: ↓↓
New Jobs in . . .
FIRE: 1,883
Retail: 2,502
Services: 13,124
Part-Time Job Market
Quality: ↑
Variety: ↑↑
Competition: ↓↓
Score: 90.5 Rank: 20

Savannah, GA

Job Growth Forecast: +5.10%
Unemployment Risk: ↓
New Jobs in . . .
FIRE: 58
Retail: 2,707
Services: 4,668
Part-Time Job Market
Quality: ↑↑
Variety: ↑
Competition: ↑
Score: 59.4 Rank: 83

★ Scottsdale, AZ

Job Growth Forecast: +12.94%
Unemployment Risk: ↓
New Jobs in . . .
FIRE: 35,288
Retail: 39,202
Services: 112,257
Part-Time Job Market
Quality: ↑↑
Variety: ↑↑
Competition: ↑
Score: 99 Rank: 1

Sebring–Avon Park, FL

Job Growth Forecast: +9.39%
Unemployment Risk: ↑
New Jobs in . . .
FIRE: 1
Retail: 214
Services: 1,631
Part-Time Job Market
Quality: ↓
Variety: ↔
Competition: ↔
Score: 37.6 Rank: 127

★ = *one of the top 30 places for part-time job opportunities between 2004 and 2009.*

Sedona, AZ
Job Growth Forecast: +12.08%
Unemployment Risk: ↑
New Jobs in . . .
FIRE: 1,038
Retail: 1,891
Services: 4,566
Part-Time Job Market
Quality: ↔
Variety: ↑
Competition: ↑ ↑
Score: 73.2 **Rank: 54**

Silver City, NM
Job Growth Forecast: +7.97%
Unemployment Risk: ↑ ↑
New Jobs in . . .
FIRE: 138
Retail: 259
Services: 331
Part-Time Job Market
Quality: ↓ ↓
Variety: ↓ ↓
Competition: ↓
Score: 13.8 **Rank: 175**

Smith Mountain Lake, VA
Job Growth Forecast: +5.18%
Unemployment Risk: ↔
New Jobs in . . .
FIRE: 41
Retail: 133
Services: 371
Part-Time Job Market
Quality: ↓
Variety: ↓ ↓
Competition: ↓
Score: 4.9 **Rank: 193**

Sonora–Twain Harte, CA
Job Growth Forecast: +6.98%
Unemployment Risk: ↑
New Jobs in . . .
FIRE: 154
Retail: 256
Services: 725
Part-Time Job Market
Quality: ↔
Variety: ↓
Competition: ↓
Score: 22.7 **Rank: 157**

Southern Berkshire County, MA
Job Growth Forecast: +2.46%
Unemployment Risk: ↓
New Jobs in . . .
FIRE: –3
Retail: 5
Services: 2,075
Part-Time Job Market
Quality: ↑ ↑
Variety: ↔
Competition: ↔
Score: 19.3 **Rank: 164**

Southern Pines–Pinehurst, NC
Job Growth Forecast: +7.74%
Unemployment Risk: ↔
New Jobs in . . .
FIRE: 197
Retail: 508
Services: 1,873
Part-Time Job Market
Quality: ↑
Variety: ↔
Competition: ↓
Score: 45.5 **Rank: 111**

Southport–Brunswick Islands, NC
Job Growth Forecast: +17.93%
Unemployment Risk: ↔
New Jobs in . . .
FIRE: 1,217
Retail: 1,214
Services: 2,334
Part-Time Job Market
Quality: ↓
Variety: ↑
Competition: ↓ ↓
Score: 70.2 **Rank: 61**

State College, PA
Job Growth Forecast: +7.55%
Unemployment Risk: ↓ ↓
New Jobs in . . .
FIRE: 402
Retail: 876
Services: 1,936
Part-Time Job Market
Quality: ↑
Variety:↔
Competition: ↑ ↑
Score: 48 **Rank: 106**

Summerville, SC
Job Growth Forecast: +9.76%
Unemployment Risk: ↓
New Jobs in . . .
FIRE: 68
Retail: 501
Services: 1,628
Part-Time Job Market
Quality: ↔
Variety: ↔
Competition: ↑
Score: 43.5 **Rank: 115**

Table Rock Lake, MO
Job Growth Forecast: +11.62%
Unemployment Risk: ↑ ↑
New Jobs in . . .
FIRE: 81
Retail: 172
Services: 785
Part-Time Job Market
Quality: ↓ ↓
Variety: ↓
Competition: ↓ ↓
Score: 26.2 **Rank: 150**

Taos, NM
Job Growth Forecast: +13.10%
Unemployment Risk: ↑ ↑
New Jobs in . . .
FIRE: 316
Retail: 388
Services: 1,004
Part-Time Job Market
Quality: ↓ ↓
Variety: ↓
Competition: ↓
Score: 42 **Rank: 118**

Thomasville, GA
Job Growth Forecast: +3.87%
Unemployment Risk: ↔
New Jobs in . . .
FIRE: 41
Retail: 174
Services: 479
Part-Time Job Market
Quality: ↑
Variety: ↓ ↓
Competition: ↔
Score: 6.9 **Rank: 189**

Toms River–Barnegat Bay, NJ
Job Growth Forecast: +6.45%
Unemployment Risk: ↔
New Jobs in . . .
FIRE: 1,001
Retail: 2,657
Services: 5,713
Part-Time Job Market
Quality: ↑ ↑
Variety: ↑ ↑
Competition: ↓
Score: 69.8 **Rank: 62**

Traverse City, MI
Job Growth Forecast: +10.34%
Unemployment Risk: ↔
New Jobs in . . .
FIRE: 342
Retail: 1,152
Services: 3,763
Part-Time Job Market
Quality: ↑ ↑
Variety: ↑
Competition: ↑
Score: 66.3 **Rank: 69**

Trinity Peninsula, TX
Job Growth Forecast: +5.89%
Unemployment Risk: ↔
New Jobs in . . .
FIRE: 12
Retail: 40
Services: 99
Part-Time Job Market
Quality: ↓ ↓
Variety: ↓ ↓
Competition: ↓ ↓
Score: 0 **Rank: 203**

★ = *one of the top 30 places for part-time job opportunities between 2004 and 2009.*

Tryon, NC
Job Growth Forecast: +9.07%
Unemployment Risk: ↓
New Jobs in . . .
FIRE: 49
Retail: 124
Services: 377
Part-Time Job Market
Quality: ↓ ↓
Variety: ↓ ↓
Competition: ↓ ↓
Score: 10.3 **Rank: 182**

★ **Tucson, AZ**
Job Growth Forecast: +9.75%
Unemployment Risk: ↓
New Jobs in . . .
FIRE: 2,831
Retail: 4,118
Services: 27,664
Part-Time Job Market
Quality: ↔
Variety: ↑ ↑
Competition: ↑
Score: 94 **Rank: 13**

Vero Beach, FL
Job Growth Forecast: +10.36%
Unemployment Risk: ↑ ↑
New Jobs in . . .
FIRE: 404
Retail: 868
Services: 3,447
Part-Time Job Market
Quality: ↑
Variety: ↑
Competition: ↓
Score: 63.8 **Rank: 74**

★ **Victorville–Apple Valley, CA**
Job Growth Forecast: +9.36%
Unemployment Risk: ↔
New Jobs in . . .
FIRE: 4,499
Retail: 13,767
Services: 22,008
Part-Time Job Market
Quality: ↑ ↑
Variety: ↑ ↑
Competition: ↑ ↑
Score: 96 **Rank: 9**

Virginia Beach, VA
Job Growth Forecast: +8.37%
Unemployment Risk: ↓ ↓
New Jobs in . . .
FIRE: 2,265
Retail: 2,439
Services: 9,225
Part-Time Job Market
Quality: ↑
Variety: ↑ ↑
Competition: ↑ ↑
Score: 82.1 **Rank: 37**

Wenatchee, WA
Job Growth Forecast: +5.98%
Unemployment Risk: ↑ ↑
New Jobs in . . .
FIRE: 78
Retail: 380
Services: 1,412
Part-Time Job Market
Quality: ↑
Variety: ↔
Competition: ↔
Score: 34.6 **Rank: 133**

Western St. Tammany Parish, LA
Job Growth Forecast: +13.67%
Unemployment Risk: ↓
New Jobs in . . .
FIRE: 1,198
Retail: 2,871
Services: 5,646
Part-Time Job Market
Quality: ↔
Variety: ↑ ↑
Competition: ↑
Score: 84.1 **Rank: 33**

Whidbey Island, WA
Job Growth Forecast: +7.70%
Unemployment Risk: ↔
New Jobs in . . .
FIRE: 352
Retail: 580
Services: 1,001
Part-Time Job Market
Quality: ↓
Variety: ↔
Competition: ↔
Score: 31.6 **Rank: 139**

★ **Wickenburg, AZ**
Job Growth Forecast: +12.94%
Unemployment Risk: ↓
New Jobs in . . .
FIRE: 35,288
Retail: 39,202
Services: 112,257
Part-Time Job Market
Quality: ↑ ↑
Variety: ↑ ↑
Competition: ↑
Score: 99 **Rank: 1**

Williamsburg, VA
Job Growth Forecast: +9.89%
Unemployment Risk: ↓ ↓
New Jobs in . . .
FIRE: 783
Retail: 1,154
Services: 2,444
Part-Time Job Market
Quality: ↔
Variety: ↑
Competition: ↑
Score: 59.9 **Rank: 82**

Wimberley, TX
Job Growth Forecast: +16.20%
Unemployment Risk: ↓
New Jobs in . . .
FIRE: 1,080
Retail: 1,682
Services: 3,726
Part-Time Job Market
Quality: ↓
Variety: ↑
Competition: ↑ ↑
Score: 76.2 **Rank: 49**

Woodstock, VT
Job Growth Forecast: +6.31%
Unemployment Risk: ↓ ↓
New Jobs in . . .
FIRE: 86
Retail: 282
Services: 1,525
Part-Time Job Market
Quality: ↓
Variety: ↔
Competition: ↓
Score: 30.1 **Rank: 142**

York Beaches, ME
Job Growth Forecast: +5.56%
Unemployment Risk: ↓
New Jobs in . . .
FIRE: 312
Retail: 808
Services: 2,919
Part-Time Job Market
Quality: ↔
Variety: ↑
Competition: ↔
Score: 46.5 **Rank: 109**

Yuma, AZ
Job Growth Forecast: +7.74%
Unemployment Risk: ↑ ↑
New Jobs in . . .
FIRE: 146
Retail: 1,409
Services: 2,508
Part-Time Job Market
Quality: ↑
Variety: ↑
Competition: ↔
Score: 50.4 **Rank: 101**

★ = *one of the top 30 places for part-time job opportunities between 2004 and 2009.*

It's dryly said that finding any job means having to listen to No, No, No, No, No . . . and No one more time, before finally hearing Yes. Landing a good part-time job isn't any different, except when it means *creating* one with an employer who isn't looking, or interviewing with an employer who is looking but hasn't the slightest idea what to do with an older applicant. In these situations, you may be in for a long series of No's.

SOME UNVOICED EMPLOYER OBJECTIONS

While job discrimination on the basis of age is against the law, you may still be a victim of what labor economists call "statistical" discrimination when an employer makes assumptions—including the following—about all older persons applying for a job:

- You want a job that isn't available.
- You have old-fashioned, conservative values.
- You haven't the same economic incentive to work that younger workers have.
- You don't have the stamina or the flexibility.
- You want more money because you have more experience.
- You'll call in sick more often than younger workers.
- Your fringe coverage—life insurance, health insurance, and pension benefits—will cost more than fringes for younger applicants.
- Your prospects for staying with a job and justifying the employer's investment in on-the-job training are less than those of a younger worker.
- You're preoccupied with the past; a slate upon which nothing more can be written.

All of these objections somehow work themselves into the "overqualified" catchall; it's the word most frequently used by an employer when turning down older people who've applied for a job.

Anyone who has worked 20, 30, or 40 years is overqualified by standard definition. Why not ask the employer what he or she means by being overqualified? If you'll go to work at the going rate, plus bring experience and maturity to the job, won't that mean that the cost of your productivity will be less than or equal to a younger worker's? If you're already covered by Medicare and Social Security, won't the employer avoid the cost of health insurance and a pension plan if you're hired? If the average tenure of younger workers in certain jobs is less than the shelf life of yogurt, mightn't that make you a better bet for longevity?

JOB SEARCHING

The number of part-time jobs has rocketed since the 1990s, often as a consequence of corporate downsizing. Most of these jobs are found in retail trade; services; and in finance, insurance, and real estate. Here are some useful strategies for searching out good opportunities.

Focus on Small Businesses and Nonprofit Organizations

Large employers often have policies against part-time employment. Smaller companies are more flexible. Moreover, small businesses compete with larger employers for good workers, not by offering more money, but by offering informal, adaptable working conditions. Finally, older workers cast off from large corporations start small businesses (fewer than 250 employees), and economists expect more job creation in these organizations than in larger firms.

Many of the most interesting jobs are found in the nonprofit sector—libraries, museums, colleges and universities, hospitals, and human service organizations. Like small businesses, they offer flexibility instead of big money.

RESPOND TO FULL-TIME JOB OPENINGS

If you've identified an employer that can use your skills, buttonhole the boss for a full-time job. If he or she hasn't any, suggest a part-time alternative. If the company has no experience with part-timers, suggest a trial period.

Too often part-timers pass by advertised positions that are full-time. Many 8-hour-a-day jobs can be shared.

DON'T FORGET THE GOVERNMENT

Part-time opportunities are expanding within the federal government, partly because of a regulation that requires federal agencies to introduce short-schedule positions and prorate compensation and benefits according to the number of hours worked. The good jobs, however, are reserved for persons who've previously worked for Uncle Sam for at least 3 years.

All state governments have agencies with part-time positions. The key is identifying the agencies and where in the state the positions are (don't assume there are no state government jobs outside of the capital city). A good place to start is the state's aging or adult services office.

Try Temporary Work

One major reason why agencies that supply temporary workers are hiring older persons is that the work is usually full-time for a limited period. For job seekers with child-care needs, this isn't the most attractive situation. Agencies specializing in clerical work dominate the Yellow Pages, but firms that engage part-time engineers, accountants, and health care professionals are growing.

Volunteer

The "Me Decade" has given way to the "Decency Decade," if you follow pop sociologists on the talk shows. Today, one of every four Americans over the age of 14 is involved in some kind of volunteer work. The value of all their volunteered time adds up to more than $100 billion a year.

Volunteer positions frequently turn into paid positions. If anything, they provide the setting for polishing up existing job skills and acquiring new skills and experience for seeking paid employment.

PART-TIME EMPLOYERS: A SHORT DIRECTORY

Depending on the product or service they sell, America's millions of private businesses are pigeonholed into more than 20,000 slots by the federal government. Here's a selected list, grouped under the three broadest classes—retail trade; finance, insurance, and real estate; and services—that (1) are found nearly everywhere, (2) offer part-time and seasonal flexibility, and (3) are businesses where older adults are finding jobs.

RETAIL TRADE

Building Materials and Garden Supplies

- Lumber and Other Building Materials
- Paint, Glass, and Wallpaper Stores
- Hardware Stores
- Retail Nurseries and Garden Stores
- Mobile Home Dealers

General Merchandise Stores

- Department Stores
- Variety Stores

Food Stores

- Grocery Stores
- Meat and Fish Markets
- Fruit and Vegetable Markets
- Candy, Nut, and Confectionery Stores
- Dairy Products Stores
- Retail Bakeries

Automotive Dealers and Service Stations

- New and Used Car Dealers
- Auto and Home Supply Stores
- Gasoline Service Stations
- Boat Dealers
- Recreational Vehicle Dealers
- Motorcycle Dealers

Apparel and Accessory Stores

- Men's and Boys' Clothing Stores
- Women's Clothing Stores
- Women's Accessory and Specialty Stores
- Children's and Infants' Wear Stores
- Family Clothing Stores
- Shoe Stores

Furniture and Home Furnishings Stores

- Furniture Stores
- Household Appliance Stores
- Radio, TV, and Electronic Stores

Miscellaneous Retail

- Drug Stores and Proprietary Stores
- Liquor Stores
- Used Merchandise Stores
- Nonstore Retailers (Mail Order Firms)

FINANCE, INSURANCE, AND REAL ESTATE

Depository Institutions

- Commercial Banks
- Savings Institutions
- Credit Unions

Nondepository Institutions

- Federally Sponsored Credit Institutions
- Personal Credit Institutions
- Business Credit Institutions
- Mortgage Bankers and Brokers

continued

Part-Time Employers: A Short Directory (cont.)

Insurance Carriers

- Life Insurance
- Medical Service and Health Insurance
- Fire, Marine, and Casualty Insurance
- Surety Insurance
- Title Insurance
- Pension, Health, and Welfare Funds

Real Estate

- Real Estate Operators and Lessors
- Real Estate Agents and Managers
- Title Abstract Offices
- Subdividers and Developers

SERVICES

Hotels and Other Lodging Places

- Hotels and Motels
- Rooming and Boarding Houses
- Camps and Recreational Vehicle Parks
- Membership-Basis Organization Hotels

Personal Services

- Laundry, Cleaning, and Garment Services
- Photographic Studios, Portrait
- Beauty Shops
- Barber Shops
- Shoe Repair and Shoeshine Parlors
- Funeral Service and Crematories

Business Services

- Advertising
- Credit Reporting and Collection
- Mailing, Reproduction, Stenographic
- Services to Buildings
- Miscellaneous Equipment Rental and Leasing
- Personnel Supply Services
- Computer and Data Processing Services

Auto Repair, Services, and Parking

- Automotive Rentals
- Automobile Parking
- Automotive Repair Shops

Miscellaneous Repair Services

- Electrical Repair Shops
- Watch, Clock, and Jewelry Repair
- Reupholstery and Furniture Repair

Motion Pictures

- Motion Picture Production and Services
- Motion Picture Distribution and Services
- Motion Picture Theaters
- Videotape Rental

Amusement and Recreation Services

- Dance Studios, Schools, and Halls
- Producers, Orchestras, Entertainers
- Bowling Centers
- Commercial Sports
- Miscellaneous Amusement, Recreation Services

HEALTH SERVICES

- Offices and Clinics of Medical Doctors
- Offices and Clinics of Dentists
- Offices of Osteopathic Physicians
- Offices of Other Health Practitioners
- Nursing and Personal Care Facilities
- Hospitals
- Medical and Dental Laboratories
- Home Health Care Services

LEGAL SERVICES

- Legal Services

EDUCATIONAL SERVICES

- Elementary and Secondary Schools
- Colleges and Universities
- Libraries
- Vocational Schools

SOCIAL SERVICES

- Individual and Family Services
- Job Training and Related Services
- Child Day Care Services
- Residential Care

MUSEUMS, BOTANICAL, ZOOLOGICAL GARDENS

- Museums and Art Galleries
- Botanical and Zoological Gardens

MEMBERSHIP ORGANIZATIONS

- Business Associations
- Professional Organizations
- Labor Organizations
- Civic and Social Associations
- Political Organizations
- Religious Organizations

ENGINEERING AND MANAGEMENT SERVICES

- Engineering and Architectural Services
- Accounting, Auditing, and Bookkeeping
- Research and Testing Services
- Management and Public Relations

Putting It All Together

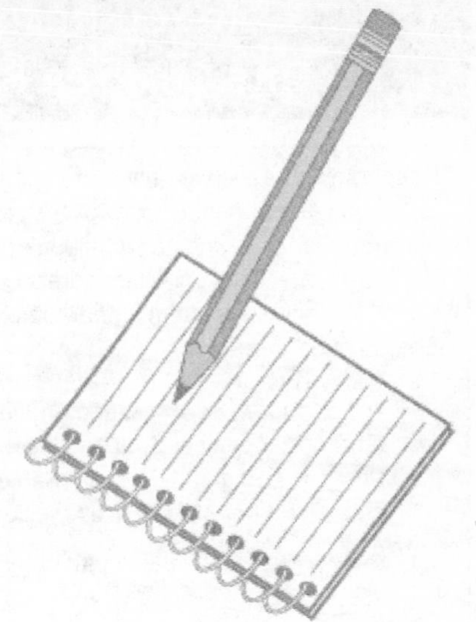

Is there really an ideal place for retirement in America? Various chambers of commerce, real estate promoters, and state tourism and economic development agencies may claim the title for their own locales. After all, with 20 million persons between 50 and 60 years of age pondering where they'll live after they retire, attracting the footloose among them is a highly promising growth industry.

By this book's criteria, however, the ideal place would have the climate of Maui, Hawaii, where a southerly latitude and the Pacific Ocean keeps the air temperature from ever dropping below 65°F or from topping 90°F much of the time.

It would have to be a rural place if it were to match the low crime rate of Rabun County in the northeast Georgia mountains, or the inexpensive housing around Roswell in southeastern New Mexico cattle country.

Yet the ideal spot would also have to be a large college town to match the full range of health care facilities and continuing education opportunities available in Gainesville, Florida, or Chapel Hill, North Carolina.

For ambiance, you may choose a place like Middle Cape Cod, Massachusetts, which not only has good restaurants and a calendar of symphony orchestra performances and guest artist dates, but opportunities for outdoor activities as well—all in a setting filled with reminders of a historic past.

For finding part-time work, the place should have the prospects of North County San Diego, California, or Henderson, Nevada, for job growth in the retail trade; services; and finance, insurance, and real estate (FIRE) industries.

Finally, the ideal place should offer the low living costs of Mission–McAllen–Alamo on the north bank of the Rio Grande in southernmost Texas.

Obviously, this ideal haven is a fiction. You can explore the geography at length and with care, but you will never find the single place that combines all the firsts according to this book's criteria. Moreover, because one person's haven can often be another's purgatory and your rural retreat someone else's boondocks, one can argue that there really is no such thing as the ideal place.

Having said all this, one can still try to discover which of the 203 places come close to the ideal.

If You Read This Chapter First

Readers who've skipped ahead to see how it all comes out may be surprised by many of the results shown in the chart on the upcoming pages. If you're curious about how a place is rated in a particular category, see the explanation of the scoring system in the appropriate chapter. Bear in mind that:

- The Economy, Services, and Ambiance chapters favor larger places. Smaller places have the edge in Costs of Living and Personal Safety. Climate favors neither big nor small places.
- Scores are expressed in percentages where 50 is average, 100 best, and 0 worst.
- When you review the rankings in each of the chapters, be sure to note the close groupings of scores. With such close results, ranking places from 1 to 203 may give the impression of greater differences among them than actually exist.
- Throughout this guide, the places compared aren't towns or cities. Almost all of them are counties where older newcomers settle in town, suburb, and rural hinterland.
- Though this guide does not profile every desirable retirement destination in America, each of the 203 places it does include are among the country's best.

FINDING THE BEST ALL-AROUND PLACES

The method for determining America's best all-around places is simple: The scores of each place for all six factors—Ambiance, Costs of Living, Climate, Personal Safety, Services, and the Economy—are averaged for a final score. Pensacola, Florida, for instance, has a score of 88.6 in Ambiance, 75.3 in Costs of Living, 55.9 in Climate, 6.5 in Personal Safety, 76.2 in Services, and 62.3 in the Economy. The mean of all these score is 60.8, much better than the average for all of the retirement places. Because the system is based on scores, the higher the mean score, the better the place is judged to be all-around. (Pensacola places 29th overall.)

In some respects, the list of the Top 30 in this edition of *Retirement Places Rated* resembles that of the previous edition, published in 1999. Although their rankings have changed, 15 of the places in this edition's Top 30 were in the previous edition's Top 30.

By no means are the Top 30 flawless. Sixteen rank near the bottom in one or more of the six categories. Just one—Sedona, Arizona—ranks in the upper half in all of them.

America's Top Retirement Places

RANK	RETIREMENT PLACE	MEAN SCORE
1.	Florence, OR	70.1
2.	Scottsdale, AZ	69.6
3.	Charleston, SC	69.3
4.	Melbourne–Palm Bay, FL	68.7
5.	North County San Diego, CA	68.6
6.	Tucson, AZ	68.5
7.	Medford–Ashland, OR	68.4
8.	Lake Winnipesaukee, NH	68.2
9.	Daytona Beach, FL	66.9
10.	Fayetteville, AR	65.8
11.	Bellingham, WA	65.8
12.	Santa Barbara, CA	65.6
13.	Sedona, AZ	65.1
14.	Lakeland–Winter Haven, FL	64.7
15.	Hanover, NH	64.6
16.	Laguna Beach–Dana Point, CA	64.4
17.	Fort Collins–Loveland, CO	64.3
18.	Largo, FL	64.2
19.	Mission–McAllen–Alamo, TX	63.6
20.	Asheville, NC	63.4
21.	Santa Rosa, CA	62.8
22.	Savannah, GA	62.7
23.	Wickenburg, AZ	62.2
24.	Sarasota, FL	61.9
25.	Traverse City, MI	61.3
26.	Mesa, AZ	61.0
27.	Grand Junction, CO	61.0
28.	New Port Richey, FL	60.9
29.	Pensacola, FL	60.8
30.	East End Long Island, NY	60.8

Though several ties are indicated above, there are none because of rounding.

RANKINGS: PUTTING IT ALL TOGETHER

The following chart gives each place's score in each of *Retirement Places Rated*'s six chapters. On the right side, the average of these six scores is shown, as is the place's overall rank—the higher the average, the higher the rank. For example, Asheville's average score of 63.4 places it 20th overall among 203 locations. The best possible average score is 100.0, meaning perfection in all six categories. Scores that are truly tied get the same rank. Because of rounding, there are fewer ties than indicated. A star (★) in front of a place's name identifies it as one of the overall Top 30.

Within each column, the entries in green represent the top 30 places within that particular category. For example, Aiken, South Carolina; Alamogordo, New Mexico; and Alpine–Big Bend, Texas, all rank among the top 30 for the Costs of Living category.

RETIREMENT PLACE	AMBIANCE	COSTS OF LIVING	CLIMATE	PERSONAL SAFETY	SERVICES	THE ECONOMY	MEAN SCORE	RANK
Aiken, SC	44.5	**93.6**	57.4	22.3	37.1	38.6	48.9	109
Alamogordo, NM	14.3	**98.1**	58.4	45.6	18.3	12.8	41.3	161
Alpine–Big Bend, TX	30.6	**96.6**	75.2	72.8	30.1	2.4	51.3	92
Amador County, CA	23.7	19.9	57.9	82.7	6.9	42.5	38.9	169
Anacortes, WA	27.7	18.9	70.2	52.0	79.2	50.0	49.7	104
Annapolis, MD	78.2	10.9	37.6	3.5	73.7	**92.0**	49.3	107
Apache Junction, AZ	12.3	53.5	**92.0**	18.9	16.8	62.8	42.7	151
Apalachicola, FL	55.4	63.4	**87.6**	71.3	1.9	0.9	46.8	125
★ Asheville, NC	82.1	67.4	36.1	43.1	83.1	68.8	**63.4**	20
Athens, GA	39.6	64.9	56.4	8.0	81.6	41.5	48.7	112
Bar Harbor, ME	81.6	45.6	9.4	**95.1**	82.6	20.7	55.8	66
Bay St. Louis–Pass Christian, MS	50.4	60.0	60.3	22.8	39.1	**91.0**	53.9	76
Beaufort, SC	54.4	8.5	67.8	9.5	48.5	83.1	45.3	133
Beaufort–Bogue Banks, NC	50.9	47.6	52.9	59.0	20.2	33.6	44.0	142
★ Bellingham, WA	**99.5**	30.2	66.8	46.6	**89.6**	61.8	**65.8**	11
Bend, OR	45.5	22.8	50.0	53.0	58.9	74.2	50.7	98
Berkeley Springs, WV	35.6	85.2	8.4	**97.1**	3.9	0.4	38.4	172
Bisbee, AZ	35.1	83.2	76.2	61.4	22.2	48.5	54.4	75
Boca Raton, FL	45.0	16.4	70.7	5.0	**92.5**	**97.0**	54.4	74
Boerne, TX	2.4	26.3	68.8	**88.7**	10.8	32.1	38.2	175
Boone–Blowing Rock, NC	33.6	39.2	15.3	83.7	68.3	38.1	46.4	128
Bozeman, MT	**91.5**	47.1	19.8	84.2	46.0	53.4	57.0	58
Bradenton, FL	19.3	49.6	**87.1**	5.5	52.9	**95.5**	51.7	88
Branson, MO	8.9	80.7	14.8	0.0	48.0	82.6	39.2	168
Brevard, NC	79.7	74.8	20.7	81.2	64.8	10.8	55.3	68
Brookings–Gold Beach, OR	30.1	40.1	**87.6**	**91.6**	27.7	17.8	49.2	108
Brown County, IN	12.8	60.4	0.9	**99.6**	7.4	5.9	31.2	198
Bullhead City, AZ	17.8	77.3	**93.5**	29.3	18.8	67.3	50.7	99
Burlington, VT	**87.1**	15.4	1.9	66.4	**94.0**	54.9	53.3	81
Camden, ME	79.7	55.0	9.9	**94.6**	50.9	23.7	52.3	85
Carmel–Pebble Beach, CA	65.3	2.0	**99.5**	25.3	**88.6**	72.7	58.9	45
Carson City–Carson Valley, NV	77.7	15.9	69.8	40.1	68.3	74.7	57.8	51
Cedar City, UT	21.2	60.9	12.3	62.4	43.5	44.5	40.8	163
Cedar Creek Lake, TX	2.9	**89.2**	54.4	49.6	11.3	47.0	42.4	153
Chapel Hill–Carrboro, NC	68.8	10.4	37.6	30.7	**97.0**	69.3	52.3	85
Charles Town–Shepherdstown, WV	63.8	64.4	26.7	**92.6**	28.2	16.3	48.7	112
★ Charleston, SC	**99.0**	54.5	71.2	4.0	**95.5**	**91.5**	**69.3**	3
Charlottesville, VA	**86.1**	37.7	31.6	48.1	**99.0**	60.8	60.6	35
Chestertown, MD	78.7	25.8	34.1	74.8	67.3	3.9	47.4	120
Chewelah, WA	17.3	46.6	13.3	**86.7**	24.2	9.9	33.0	194
Coeur d'Alene, ID	72.7	67.9	16.8	37.7	54.4	70.7	53.4	80
Colorado Springs, CO	79.2	43.1	28.2	34.2	70.2	**95.0**	58.3	47
Columbia, MO	42.5	55.5	5.9	36.2	**98.5**	51.4	48.3	115
Conway, SC	5.9	79.8	43.5	2.0	65.3	**89.6**	47.7	118
Cottonwood–Verde Valley, AZ	**90.0**	52.5	38.6	33.7	47.0	**86.1**	58.0	48
Crossville, TN	36.6	**90.6**	18.8	46.1	4.9	35.1	38.7	171
Dare Outer Banks, NC	37.6	29.3	48.5	31.2	1.4	58.4	34.4	191
★ Daytona Beach, FL	**93.0**	70.8	80.1	10.9	81.1	65.3	**66.9**	9
Delta County, CO	14.8	84.7	41.5	**92.1**	23.2	11.3	44.6	138
Door Peninsula, WI	66.8	37.2	17.8	**98.1**	35.1	31.1	47.7	118
Durango, CO	**94.5**	19.4	21.7	55.0	75.2	55.4	53.5	79
Eagle River–Woodruff, WI	38.1	39.7	12.8	**87.7**	26.2	14.8	36.6	184
★ East End Long Island, NY	**98.5**	1.0	23.7	63.9	**96.5**	81.1	**60.8**	30
Easton–St. Michaels, MD	70.2	23.3	39.6	48.6	52.4	25.2	43.2	149
Edenton, NC	33.1	**88.7**	46.0	57.5	21.2	1.4	41.3	160
Eufaula, AL	13.8	**94.6**	56.4	59.5	15.3	7.9	41.3	161
Eureka Springs, AR	8.4	**94.1**	24.7	74.3	11.8	15.3	38.1	177

continued

RETIREMENT PLACE	AMBIANCE	COSTS OF LIVING	CLIMATE	PERSONAL SAFETY	SERVICES	THE ECONOMY	MEAN SCORE	RANK
Fairhope–Gulf Shores, AL	41.5	58.5	51.9	60.9	46.5	80.6	56.7	60
★ Fayetteville, AR	56.4	**91.6**	26.2	61.9	**87.1**	71.7	**65.8**	10
Flagstaff, AZ	**93.5**	51.5	34.1	26.3	84.6	73.2	60.5	36
★ Florence, OR	84.6	62.9	80.6	32.7	82.1	77.7	**70.1**	1
★ Fort Collins–Loveland, CO	**97.0**	21.8	28.2	66.9	**93.5**	78.2	**64.3**	17
Fort Myers–Cape Coral, FL	76.7	23.8	**89.6**	12.4	63.3	**93.5**	59.9	42
Fredericksburg, TX	31.6	77.8	65.8	**95.6**	22.7	16.8	51.7	87
Fredericksburg–Spotsylvania, VA	84.1	31.7	29.7	76.3	76.7	63.3	60.3	38
Front Royal, VA	27.2	69.9	15.8	**91.1**	8.9	11.8	37.5	179
Gainesville, FL	68.3	56.0	74.2	1.0	**99.5**	64.8	60.6	31
Georgetown, TX	44.0	26.8	63.3	77.3	32.1	**94.5**	56.3	61
★ Grand Junction, CO	67.3	73.8	30.1	54.5	**90.5**	49.5	**61.0**	27
Grants Pass, OR	58.4	78.3	60.8	63.4	40.5	41.0	57.1	57
Grass Valley–Nevada City, CA	46.0	8.0	64.8	64.9	23.7	64.3	45.3	134
Hamilton–Bitterroot Valley, MT	34.1	66.9	36.1	77.8	5.4	28.2	41.4	158
★ Hanover, NH	**90.0**	59.5	3.9	**89.2**	**97.5**	47.5	**64.6**	15
Hattiesburg, MS	46.0	**91.1**	42.5	21.3	**86.6**	19.8	51.2	93
Henderson, NV	1.4	20.3	84.6	72.3	69.3	**98.5**	57.7	53
Hendersonville–East Flat Rock, NC	56.4	54.0	25.2	81.7	73.2	39.1	54.9	70
Hilton Head Island, SC	53.4	6.5	72.7	9.5	48.5	83.1	45.6	130
Hot Springs, AR	77.2	72.8	48.5	34.7	57.9	35.6	54.5	73
Inverness, FL	7.4	**86.2**	76.7	70.3	9.4	56.9	51.2	95
Iowa City, IA	48.0	30.7	4.4	60.4	**100.0**	57.9	50.2	101
Jackson Hole, WY	61.3	0.0	11.3	50.5	64.3	43.0	38.4	173
Kalispell–Flathead Valley, MT	**98.0**	63.9	35.6	56.5	55.4	51.9	60.2	40
Kauai, HI	5.4	13.4	**97.0**	70.8	53.9	17.3	43.0	150
Kerrville, TX	0.0	82.2	71.2	67.9	55.9	32.6	51.6	89
Ketchum–Sun Valley, ID	60.3	4.5	18.8	65.9	34.1	57.4	40.2	164
Key West, FL	**95.0**	5.0	82.6	7.0	34.6	55.9	46.7	126
Kingman, AZ	17.8	81.2	**88.6**	15.4	18.8	67.3	48.2	116
Kissimmee–St. Cloud, FL	9.9	35.2	79.7	6.0	4.4	80.1	35.9	187
★ Laguna Beach–Dana Point, CA	58.9	1.5	**98.0**	41.1	**89.1**	**97.5**	**64.4**	16
Lake Conroe, TX	13.3	18.4	58.9	45.1	9.9	**93.0**	39.8	165
Lake Havasu City, AZ	16.8	79.3	**93.0**	**85.7**	18.8	67.3	60.2	41
Lake of the Cherokees, OK	0.9	**96.1**	33.1	**90.1**	2.4	25.7	41.4	159
Lake of the Ozarks, MO	6.4	49.1	17.3	38.7	10.3	56.4	29.7	199
Lake Placid, NY	32.1	73.3	5.4	**86.2**	51.9	5.4	42.4	154
★ Lake Winnipesaukee, NH	**97.5**	70.3	7.9	85.2	69.8	78.7	**68.2**	8
★ Lakeland–Winter Haven, FL	75.2	84.2	82.1	7.5	57.4	81.6	**64.7**	14
★ Largo, FL	29.2	50.0	**91.0**	47.1	80.1	**87.6**	**64.2**	18
Las Cruces, NM	48.5	**92.1**	48.5	16.4	62.8	53.9	53.7	78
Las Vegas, NM	62.3	**89.7**	50.0	0.5	42.0	18.8	43.9	145
Leelanau Peninsula, MI	26.7	28.8	2.4	**99.1**	21.7	14.3	32.2	196
Leesburg–Mount Dora, FL	37.1	57.5	84.1	24.3	63.8	60.3	54.5	72
Litchfield Hills, CT	**88.1**	10.0	10.8	**88.2**	72.2	40.5	51.6	89
Lower Cape May, NJ	83.1	9.0	46.0	27.8	28.7	34.1	38.1	176
Madison, WI	81.1	12.4	3.4	56.0	**98.0**	**87.1**	56.3	61
Marble Falls–Lake LBJ, TX	1.9	68.9	68.8	73.3	8.4	46.0	44.6	139
Mariposa, CA	71.2	24.8	63.8	11.9	3.4	2.9	29.7	200
Martha's Vineyard, MA	63.3	0.5	30.6	30.2	54.9	23.2	33.8	193
Maryville, TN	71.7	**87.7**	21.2	51.5	35.1	50.9	53.0	83
Maui, HI	52.9	7.5	**96.5**	36.7	50.0	58.9	50.4	100
McCall, ID	40.0	52.0	28.2	41.6	48.5	7.4	36.3	186
★ Medford–Ashland, OR	**95.5**	65.9	59.4	39.2	71.2	79.2	**68.4**	7
★ Melbourne–Palm Bay, FL	**89.6**	57.0	**92.5**	14.9	72.7	**85.6**	**68.7**	4
Mendocino–Fort Bragg, CA	43.0	11.9	**99.0**	32.2	50.4	37.1	45.6	131
★ Mesa, AZ	59.9	27.8	**91.5**	15.9	71.7	**99.0**	**61.0**	26
Middle Cape Cod, MA	**94.0**	9.5	22.2	23.3	77.7	66.8	48.9	109
★ Mission–McAllen–Alamo, TX	39.1	**100.0**	**90.5**	20.3	42.5	**89.1**	**63.6**	19
Monadnock Region, NH	72.2	65.4	0.0	**93.1**	83.6	33.1	57.9	49
Montrose, CO	15.8	76.3	43.0	75.3	33.6	24.7	44.8	137
Morro Bay–Cambria, CA	40.5	6.0	**97.5**	51.0	60.8	77.2	55.5	67
Murray–Kentucky Lake, KY	16.3	**95.1**	27.7	82.2	61.3	18.3	50.2	102
Myrtle Beach, SC	21.7	58.0	55.4	2.0	65.3	**89.6**	48.7	112
Naples, FL	82.1	11.4	83.1	16.9	51.4	**92.5**	56.2	63
Natchitoches, LA	65.3	**99.6**	42.0	20.8	37.6	1.9	44.5	140
New Bern, NC	28.7	72.3	35.1	27.3	39.6	30.6	38.9	170
New Braunfels, TX	0.4	61.4	66.8	28.3	17.3	52.4	37.8	178

RETIREMENT PLACE	AMBIANCE	COSTS OF LIVING	CLIMATE	PERSONAL SAFETY	SERVICES	THE ECONOMY	MEAN SCORE	RANK
★ New Port Richey, FL	24.2	71.8	**89.1**	37.2	58.4	84.6	**60.9**	28
Newport–Lincoln City, OR	48.5	48.6	78.2	42.1	38.6	27.2	47.2	122
Norfork Lake, AR	10.3	**92.6**	22.7	**100.0**	43.0	29.2	49.6	105
★ North County San Diego, CA	**96.5**	5.5	**100.0**	19.9	**91.5**	**98.0**	**68.6**	5
Northampton–Amherst, MA	80.6	20.8	6.4	78.8	**96.0**	40.0	53.8	77
Northern Neck, VA	26.2	48.1	38.6	**97.6**	44.5	8.9	44.0	144
Oakhurst–Coarsegold, CA	20.7	53.0	62.8	19.4	11.8	54.4	37.0	182
Ocala, FL	74.7	**87.2**	72.2	11.4	31.1	65.8	57.1	56
Ocean City, MD	11.8	44.6	36.1	13.4	31.6	22.2	26.6	202
Oscoda–Huron Shore, MI	11.3	**97.6**	16.3	73.8	7.9	4.4	35.2	189
Oxford, MS	59.4	**86.7**	45.0	31.7	59.9	24.2	51.2	95
Pagosa Springs, CO	25.7	33.7	22.7	83.2	26.7	26.7	36.5	185
Pahrump Valley, NV	9.4	41.1	59.4	60.0	12.8	39.6	37.1	181
Palm Springs–Coachella Valley, CA	**85.6**	12.9	**94.0**	12.9	61.8	**96.5**	60.6	33
Palmer–Wasilla, AK	41.0	34.7	6.9	2.5	30.6	29.7	24.2	203
Panama City, FL	23.2	68.4	68.3	4.5	44.0	61.3	45.0	135
Paradise–Magalia, CA	34.6	34.2	**95.0**	42.6	67.8	71.2	57.6	54
Park City, UT	36.1	2.5	14.3	53.5	38.1	85.1	38.3	174
Payson, AZ	46.0	66.4	53.9	49.1	16.3	45.0	46.1	129
Pendleton District, SC	38.6	**93.1**	44.5	58.5	35.1	12.3	47.0	124
★ Pensacola, FL	**88.6**	75.3	55.9	6.5	76.2	62.3	**60.8**	29
Petoskey–Harbor Springs, MI	66.3	61.9	2.4	40.6	73.7	28.7	45.6	131
Pike County, PA	28.2	32.2	13.8	80.7	0.0	21.7	29.4	201
Polson–Mission Valley, MT	18.8	78.8	41.0	**94.1**	29.7	20.2	47.1	123
Port Angeles–Sequim, WA	54.9	31.2	**85.6**	76.8	78.7	27.7	59.2	44
Port Charlotte, FL	50.9	42.6	80.6	75.8	14.3	79.7	57.3	55
Port Townsend, WA	61.3	13.9	85.1	67.4	32.6	36.6	49.5	106
Prescott–Prescott Valley, AZ	57.4	46.1	60.8	38.2	47.0	**86.1**	55.9	65
Rabun County, GA	31.1	76.8	27.2	44.6	5.9	6.4	32.0	197
Rehoboth Bay–Indian River Bay, DE	29.7	82.7	30.6	25.8	70.7	52.9	48.7	111
Reno–Sparks, NV	64.8	17.4	64.8	26.8	84.1	**88.6**	57.8	51
Rio Rancho, NM	70.7	71.3	45.5	68.9	13.3	49.0	53.1	82
Rockport–Aransas Pass, TX	25.2	75.8	77.7	21.8	0.9	3.4	34.1	192
Roswell, NM	19.8	**98.6**	33.1	33.2	13.8	9.4	34.7	190
Ruidoso, NM	43.5	80.2	77.2	10.4	27.2	21.2	43.3	148
St. Augustine, FL	62.8	16.9	**86.6**	17.4	44.5	76.7	50.8	97
St. George–Zion, UT	75.7	33.2	60.8	69.9	20.7	75.7	56.0	64
St. Jay–Northeast Kingdom, VT	42.0	74.3	4.9	84.7	60.3	13.3	46.6	127
St. Simons–Jekyll Islands, GA	32.6	45.1	**86.1**	3.0	41.0	44.0	42.0	157
Salida, CO	52.4	40.6	0.4	80.2	33.1	8.4	35.9	188
San Juan Islands, WA	55.4	3.0	74.2	**93.6**	45.5	15.8	47.9	117
Sandpoint–Lake Pend Oreille, ID	69.3	69.4	7.4	64.4	14.8	36.1	43.6	147
★ Santa Barbara, CA	**92.5**	3.5	**98.5**	47.6	79.2	72.2	**65.6**	12
Santa Fe, NM	**91.0**	17.9	50.0	65.4	62.3	75.2	60.3	38
★ Santa Rosa, CA	67.8	4.0	**96.0**	44.1	76.7	**88.1**	**62.8**	21
★ Sarasota, FL	69.3	28.3	**89.6**	18.4	75.2	**90.5**	**61.9**	24
★ Savannah, GA	**96.0**	56.5	66.3	10.0	**88.1**	59.4	**62.7**	22
★ Scottsdale, AZ	57.4	27.8	**94.0**	54.0	**85.6**	**99.0**	**69.6**	2
Sebring–Avon Park, FL	24.2	**90.1**	73.7	13.9	24.7	37.6	44.0	142
★ Sedona, AZ	50.0	50.5	52.9	79.3	84.6	73.2	**65.1**	13
Silver City, NM	73.7	**97.1**	47.5	29.8	66.3	13.8	54.7	71
Smith Mountain Lake, VA	20.2	83.7	43.5	**98.6**	56.4	4.9	51.2	94
Sonora–Twain Harte, CA	49.5	24.3	79.2	39.7	40.0	22.7	42.6	152
Southern Berkshire County, MA	85.1	36.2	10.3	62.9	**95.0**	19.3	51.5	91
Southern Pines–Pinehurst, NC	50.9	36.7	40.5	55.5	**87.6**	45.5	52.8	84
Southport–Brunswick Islands, NC	4.4	35.7	51.4	68.4	6.4	70.2	39.4	167
State College, PA	73.2	51.0	17.8	**90.6**	66.3	48.0	57.8	50
Summerville, SC	15.3	**85.7**	47.5	28.8	17.8	43.5	39.8	165
Table Rock Lake, MO	3.9	**88.2**	20.2	57.0	0.4	26.2	32.7	195
Taos, NM	**86.6**	43.6	23.7	17.9	53.4	42.0	44.5	140
Thomasville, GA	47.5	**99.1**	62.3	23.8	**90.0**	6.9	54.9	69
Toms River–Barnegat Bay, NJ	**91.5**	14.9	25.7	78.3	77.7	69.8	59.7	43
★ Traverse City, MI	60.8	59.0	8.9	79.8	**93.0**	66.3	**61.3**	25
Trinity Peninsula, TX	4.9	**95.6**	64.3	52.5	2.9	0.0	36.7	183
Tryon, NC	6.9	62.4	40.0	**87.2**	15.8	10.3	37.1	180
★ Tucson, AZ	**100.0**	44.1	73.2	8.5	**91.0**	**94.0**	**68.5**	6
Vero Beach, FL	10.8	41.6	75.7	24.8	36.6	63.8	42.2	155
Victorville–Apple Valley, CA	**89.1**	21.3	83.6	14.4	59.4	**96.0**	60.6	31

continued

RETIREMENT PLACE	AMBIANCE	COSTS OF LIVING	CLIMATE	PERSONAL SAFETY	SERVICES	THE ECONOMY	MEAN SCORE	RANK
Virginia Beach, VA	53.9	38.2	52.4	58.0	56.9	82.1	56.9	59
Wenatchee, WA	76.2	25.3	31.6	35.2	80.6	34.6	47.3	121
Western St. Tammany Parish, LA	64.3	42.1	54.9	43.6	74.7	84.1	60.6	33
Whidbey Island, WA	22.7	14.4	78.2	**96.6**	25.7	31.6	44.9	136
★ Wickenburg, AZ	3.4	32.7	80.6	71.8	**85.6**	**99.0**	**62.2**	23
Williamsburg, VA	**87.6**	7.0	31.6	69.4	**94.5**	59.9	58.3	46
Wimberley, TX	7.9	29.8	47.0	50.0	41.5	76.2	42.1	156
Woodstock, VT	83.6	22.3	1.4	**96.1**	28.7	30.1	43.7	146
York Beaches, ME	22.2	38.7	11.3	**89.7**	**92.0**	46.5	50.1	103
Yuma, AZ	74.2	81.7	**95.5**	35.7	24.7	50.4	60.4	37

RETIREMENT REGIONS

If your sights are set on southwestern desert retirement, parts of five states qualify. If you're tending toward mountain living, even more states fill the bill. Considering retirement somewhere near a blue-water ocean coastline? Join the three out of five Americans in twenty-six states who are already there. Rather than focusing on states, why not think of regions?

Here are 18 regions that look, feel, talk, and act differently from one another, yet the places within them share a number of attributes. Few of their boundaries match the political borders you'll find in your road atlas. Most of them embrace parts of more than one state. Some states are apportioned among more than one region.

On the following pages *Retirement Places Rated* describes these regions into which the 203 places geographically and culturally seem to fall.

CALIFORNIA COAST

North County San Diego (5)
Santa Barbara (12)
Laguna Beach–Dana Point (16)
Carmel–Pebble Beach (45)
Morro Bay–Cambria (67)
Mendocino–Fort Bragg (131)

This region is the best of all the retirement areas profiled in *Retirement Places Rated* when one looks at average scores across all six categories.

Its settled coast certainly isn't homogeneous, stretching from the Border Beach on the Mexican boundary to the wine country north of San Francisco. About the only natural features these six California Coast places have in common are a Pacific shoreline and a mild climate that moves from Mediterranean to marine as you move north.

All six places in this region rank high, not just for their mild climates, but also for their available services and long-term prospects for job growth. The locations get middling marks for crime and for ambiance. After home price depreciation through much of the 1990s, the expensive real estate sets this region apart from all the others. Consequently, all six cluster near the bottom in costs of living and how far typical retirement incomes will stretch.

For all that, these locations have been popular for retirement since the end of World War II. One in seven retired Navy officers lives somewhere within San Diego County, as does one in fifty retired physicians. For decades, San Luis Obispo County was one of the most populous areas in the country without a large central city. Much of its current growth comes from attracting older persons.

Nonetheless, because of the high cost of living, a limited supply of water, and restrictions on development, population growth along the California coast has slowed since the last years of the 20th century. Indeed, some experts predict the area will continue to lose more retired persons than it will attract. The living may be easy, but it is not cheap.

DESERT SOUTHWEST

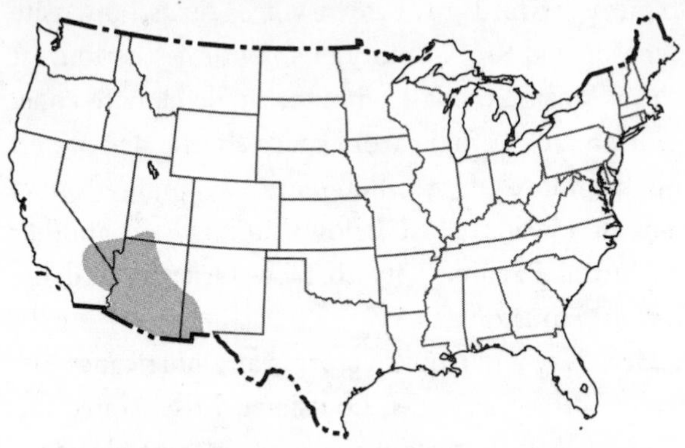

Scottsdale, AZ (2)
Tucson, AZ (6)
Sedona, AZ (13)
Wickenburg, AZ (23)
Mesa, AZ (26)
Victorville–Apple Valley, CA (31)
Palm Springs–Coachella Valley, CA (33)
Yuma, AZ (37)
Lake Havasu City, AZ (41)
Cottonwood–Verde Valley, AZ (48)
Henderson, NV (53)
St. George–Zion, UT (64)
Prescott–Prescott Valley, AZ (65)
Silver City, NM (71)
Bisbee, AZ (75)
Bullhead City, AZ (99)
Kingman, AZ (116)
Payson, AZ (129)
Apache Junction, AZ (151)
Pahrump Valley, NV (181)

Of all the retirement regions, the Desert Southwest has the highest number of places to rank in the Top 30. It generally sits in the southern end of the Great Basin between the country's two highest mountain ranges, the Rockies to the east and the Sierra Nevadas to the west. The two mountain ranges not only add beauty, grandeur, and ruggedness to the region but they also block moist air coming from either the Pacific Ocean or the Gulf of Mexico.

If it's sun you're after, this is the place. One location, Yuma, is officially designated America's sunniest by federal climate record keepers. Hot, bright, cloudless days followed by cool, even chilly, nights are the rule here. This means you can enjoy outdoor activities in the daytime and still get a good night's rest under a blanket or two.

Rapidly growing Arizona is the prototypical Sun Belt state. Tucson, a leading retirement area, has an excellent supply of health care and public transportation facilities. A surprise to some, it also has a high degree of ambiance by *Retirement Places Rated*'s standards. The "Valley of the Sun," taking in greater Phoenix, is home to the world's largest planned retirement development, Sun City, as well as Mesa and Scottsdale, two popular destinations profiled here.

Many parts of the Desert Southwest suffer from high crime rates. Large areas such as Mesa, Tucson, and Palm Springs, and even smaller areas such as Bullhead City and Kingman, all rank near the bottom in that category. The supply of health care facilities varies greatly from location to location. Indeed, residents of the Pahrump Valley in Nevada must drive 50 miles to Las Vegas for specialized care.

Despite its rapid population growth (the counties surrounding the 20 places profiled above together have gained nearly 2.5 million persons since 1999, for example), this is thinly settled land. There is so much space here, with such great distances even between small towns, that people who have lived in thickly populated regions such as the Great Lakes or the Northeast may find it difficult to adjust to the feeling of isolation.

FLORIDA INTERIOR

Lakeland–Winter Haven (14)
Gainesville (31)
Ocala (56)
Leesburg–Mount Dora (72)
Inverness (95)
Sebring–Avon Park (142)
Kissimmee–St. Cloud (187)

Florida has been elevated to its so-called "megastate" niche by a migration unique in American history. In 1950, the state had 2 million people. When the year

2000 figures were tallied, the number topped 16 million, nearly all of the increase coming from people moving in from other states. The state's population exceeded Ohio in 1984, Illinois in 1986, and Pennsylvania in 1987. In 2015, perhaps sooner, the Sunshine State will surpass New York as the third largest behind California and Texas.

If you're determined to find whatever it is you're searching for in retirement, you'll find it somewhere in Florida. Florida is the number one tourist destination in the world. It has nine distinct media markets, two coasts, snow, perpetual sunshine, swamps, islands, new no-down-payment homes for $65,000, and houses you can't afford if you have to ask their price. If there are three factors that account for the numbers of highly rated places here, they are low living costs, climate, and the near-term outlook for employment. Two factors that mar their ratings, however, are unquestionably crime and a slight lack of ambiance—qualities that *Retirement Places Rated* admits are difficult to define.

GULF COAST

Largo, FL (18)
Sarasota, FL (24)
New Port Richey, FL (28)
Pensacola, FL (29)
Western St. Tammany Parish, LA (33)
Fort Myers–Cape Coral, FL (42)
Port Charlotte, FL (55)
Fairhope–Gulf Shores, AL (60)
Naples, FL (63)
Bay St. Louis–Pass Christian, MS (76)
Bradenton, FL (88)
Apalachicola, FL (125)
Panama City, FL (135)
Rockport–Aransas Pass, TX (192)

Extending along a 1,700-mile arc from Naples, Florida, westward to Brownsville, Texas, opposite Mexico on the Rio Grande, this region is the longest reach of American coast within a single climate zone. View it on a clear night from space shuttle height and you'll see most of the illumination coming from a stretch of Florida coast below Tampa Bay, another stretch from Panama City to New Orleans, and the enormous Houston galaxy.

Here is where tropical storms and hurricanes historically batter the Texas, Louisiana, Mississippi, and Alabama coasts, but spare a good stretch of Florida's. In spite of the threat, this area is the fastest-growing part of each of these states.

Except for a poor score for Rockport–Aransas Pass, on an empty stretch above Corpus Christi, each Gulf Coast retirement place ranks among the best in employment growth. Aside from several Florida locations—Fort Myers, Naples, Sarasota—each ranks among the top half in living costs. Many newcomers find summer weather wearyingly hot and regularly stormy, which accounts for the regions modest scores in climate.

HAWAII

Maui (100)
Kauai (150)

Hawaii is the only state in the tropical climate zone, officially defined as anywhere temperatures never fall below 64°F. Orchids grow wild here; the sun shines most of the time; the Pacific trade winds keep the islands temperate; the beaches are superb; and the water is deep and blue.

The cost of living, however, is so high that this is the only state to discourage mainland persons from moving in for retirement. From the Commission on Aging on down to pitchmen on the street selling condominiums to visitors, you're going to hear the discouraging word. Though the islands are relatively inexpensive to visit, they are unaffordable for year-round living for most retired persons. Here Housing and Urban Development, the federal agency subsidizing housing costs, reports the country's highest fair-market rent.

Still, they come. Honolulu, like San Diego and San Antonio, is extremely popular with ex-military. Apropos of its size, it ranks high in services, prospects for employment growth, and leisure living. It also experiences a surprisingly modest level of crime. Maui, Kauai, and the Big Island of Hawaii are now drawing older newcomers at a faster rate than Honolulu.

HEARTLAND

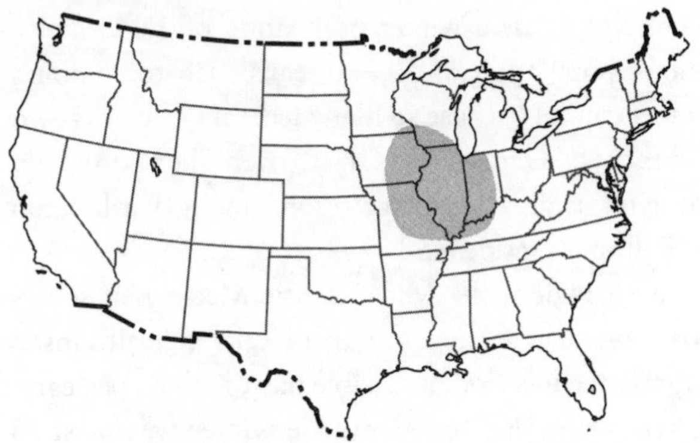

Madison, WI (61)
Iowa City, IA (101)
Columbia, MO (115)
Brown County, IN (198)

Heartland, Middle Earth, Breadbasket—the names sometimes given to the central states—evoke the change of seasons on featureless farmland or an area mostly flown over by persons bound for either coast.

Though farming is important here, industry is more so in certain parts. Though the land seems plain from the air, it is far from being homogeneous. One way to find choice retirement spots is to home in on large universities. Of the four places rated in this region, three are cities where the academic calendar plays a central role in community life. While Brown County in south-central Indiana isn't a college town, it is next door to one of the country's best: Indiana University in Bloomington.

It isn't conjecture that Heartland college towns make up a distinct retirement region of their own. The proportion of persons 65 and over tends to be greater here than it is in the nation as a whole. Large land-grant universities in the Heartland have huge alumni organizations, and many of these alums from the 1940s and 1950s are returning for the benefits of the college town they knew years ago: past friendships, the cultural and recreational amenities, the youthful population, and the human services usually found only in larger cities.

INNER SOUTH

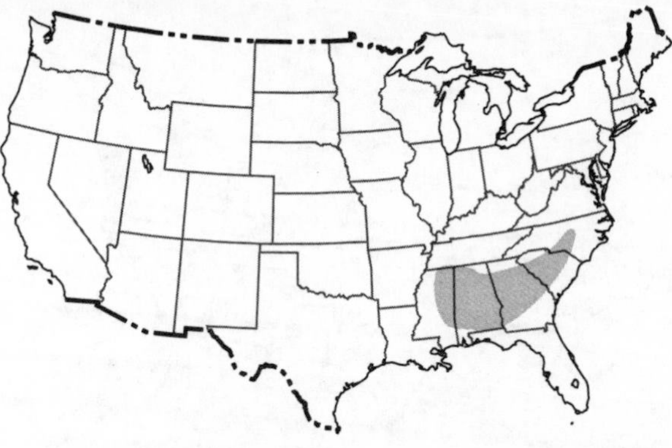

Thomasville, GA (69)
Southern Pines–Pinehurst, NC (84)
Chapel Hill–Carrboro, NC (85)
Hattiesburg, MS (93)
Oxford, MS (95)
Murray–Kentucky Lake, KY (102)
Aiken, SC (109)
Athens, GA (112)
Natchitoches, LA (140)
Eufaula, AL (161)

This region is neither north nor, with the exception of Thomasville, too far south to be thoroughly Dixie. It's mainly in the center of the country's eastern half and includes North Carolina's and Georgia's Piedmont (but not their mountains—they are part of *Retirement Places Rated*'s Southern Highlands region) and most of Kentucky, Mississippi, and Tennessee.

Why is the Inner South such an attractive retirement region? For one thing, the region lies north of more established retirement areas of the Sun Belt. Although the Sun Belt still remains a big drawing card for older adults, the "Retirement Belt" seems to be widening north. People are discovering the benefits of being closer to their former homes in the Midwest or Northeast; the desirability of mild, four-season climates as opposed to the monotony of the semitropical varieties; and the great advantages of low costs and low crime rates compared with many retirement areas farther south.

Furthermore, the gently rolling terrain with its pleasant scenery, the unhurried pace of life that is far less manic than in many parts of Florida, the outdoor recreational options and the weather to enjoy them make the Inner South a winner.

MID-ATLANTIC METRO BELT

East End Long Island, NY (30)
Charlottesville, VA (35)
Fredericksburg–Spotsylvania, VA (38)
Toms River–Barnegat Bay, NJ (43)
Williamsburg, VA (46)
State College, PA (50)
Virginia Beach, VA (59)
Annapolis, MD (107)
Rehoboth Bay–Indian River Bay, DE (111)
Charles Town–Shepherdstown, WV (112)
Chestertown, MD (120)
Northern Neck, VA (144)
Easton–St. Michaels, MD (149)
Lake Placid, NY (154)
Berkeley Springs, WV (172)
Lower Cape May, NJ (176)
Front Royal, VA (179)
Pike County, PA (201)
Ocean City, MD (202)

The area south from New York City to Washington and through the northern Virginia suburbs to Richmond is the most densely settled in America. Many cities in this region—notably Newark, Trenton, Philadelphia, Wilmington, Baltimore, and Washington—have been losing population for years.

In the midst of urban stagnation, however, one can easily overlook the pockets of suburban and rural retirement growth not visible from the Amtrak rails or I-95: the Atlantic beach counties, Chesapeake Bay, the Catskills, and small-scale metro areas such as State College and Charlottesville, home of major state universities.

The 127 miles of New Jersey's sandy Atlantic coastline, particularly from the tip of Cape May north to Toms River, has rebounded after years of decline. One in five residents of Ocean County is over 65, compared with the U.S. average of one in nine.

Farther south, you'll find retirement destinations within hailing distance of Washington and Baltimore on the Delmarva Peninsula and the shores of Chesapeake Bay. Many of the bigger summer resorts resemble Miami Beach rather than the charming, small seaside communities they once were before the opening of the Chesapeake Bay Bridge in 1952. Delaware's Rehoboth Beach, which has a winter population of 2,040 and a summer population of 50,000, calls itself the nation's summer capital because so many federal workers crowd its beaches. Ocean City, just over the border in Maryland, is also a popular resort among Washington and Baltimore residents.

As a region, the Mid-Atlantic Metro Belt scores above average in freedom from crime, health care, continuing education, its visible past, and the performing arts. Its faults, for many, are winter weather and high living costs.

NORTH WOODS

Traverse City, MI (25)
Door Peninsula, WI (118)
Petoskey–Harbor Springs, MI (131)
Eagle River–Woodruff, WI (184)
Oscoda–Huron Shore, MI (189)
Leelanau Peninsula, MI (196)

One region violating the "Law of Thermodemographics" (warm bodies eventually head south to the Sun Belt and stay) has got to be the land that includes the northern counties of Michigan's lower peninsula and the Wisconsin counties in Packer country near Green Bay. Spring, summer, and fall here are lovely seasons but all too short. Winters are long and cold and are the main reason behind the low marks in climate for the above six places.

The area's pull is strong for many vacationers from the big industrial cities of the Great Lakes. Many of these people later decide to winterize their rural lakefront or flatwoods second home and retire for year-round residency.

This is recreation land with a rugged, Paul Bunyan flavor, not only in the summer months, when the population doubles, but also during the fall deer-hunting and winter skiing season. Most of Michigan's 11,000 and Wisconsin's 15,000 lakes are up here. "In some lakes," the *New York Times* reported in a profile of Eagle River and its environs, "the fishermen can see thirty feet down in waters forest green, or black, or blue, depending on the time of day or the perspective, and can retrieve dropped eyeglasses or snagged fishing lures."

In spite of high personal income and property taxes in these two North Woods states, the cost of living is still lower than in most other retirement regions. The crime rate is low, too. Except for small cities such as Sturgeon Bay in Wisconsin and Traverse City and Petoskey in Michigan, though, you won't find much in the way of structured retirement activities or a full range of health care facilities. Nor will you find expanding job prospects. Do expect to drive a good distance for retail shopping; this is rough, beautiful, but sparsely settled, country.

OZARKS & OUACHITAS

Fayetteville, AR (10)
Hot Springs, AR (73)
Norfork Lake, AR (105)
Lake of the Cherokees, OK (159)
Branson, MO (168)
Eureka Springs, AR (177)
Table Rock Lake, MO (195)
Lake of the Ozarks, MO (199)

After the Texas Interior, the Ozarks and Ouachitas retirement region has the lowest average rating for ambiance and for services, but the highest for living costs. Its record for freedom from crime runs from middling to good.

Like the Southern Highlands, the Ozarks and Ouachitas of southern Missouri, northern and western Arkansas, and eastern Oklahoma are a highland area with distinct folkways and geology that are undergoing rapid changes. In both areas, country craft galleries and bluegrass music festivals abound, and the mountain roads that wind through small towns also wind through some of the nation's prettiest countryside. Here, an automobile is a virtual necessity. Many Ozark and Ouachita natives can trace their family names all the way back to Carolina and Virginia mountain roots.

When the public utilities built hydroelectric dams, they produced a series of large impounded lakes in hardwood forests, which in turn produced resorts and a steady migration of retired people from Des Moines, Omaha, Tulsa, Oklahoma City, Memphis, Kansas City, St. Louis, and especially Chicago.

Lately, this region has been waking up to the problems that come with growth. Concerns about the loss of a special way of life are increasingly voiced; some locals say it may have already passed from the scene, never to be revived, despite local folk culture institutes and craft schools. The areas outside the biggest cities—Fayetteville and Fort Smith, Arkansas, and Springfield and Joplin, Missouri—aren't densely populated, yet some of the lakes are having pollution problems, and some of the better-known resorts are acquiring a tacky patina of liquor stores, fast-food outlets, tourist attractions, and New Age crystal shops.

PACIFIC NORTHWEST

Florence, OR (1)
Medford–Ashland, OR (7)
Bellingham, WA (11)
Port Angeles–Sequim, WA (44)
Grants Pass, OR (57)
Bend, OR (98)

Anacortes, WA (104)
Port Townsend, WA (106)
Brookings–Gold Beach, OR (108)
San Juan Islands, WA (117)
Wenatchee, WA (121)
Newport–Lincoln City, OR (122)
Whidbey Island, WA (136)
Chewelah, WA (194)
Palmer–Wasilla, AK (203)

In the 1970s, no other state made so clear its desire to discourage immigration as did Oregon when its popular governor, Tom McCall, urged tourists to give the state a try. "But for heaven's sake," he quickly added, "don't come to live here." This awareness of the harm that rapid population growth can bring to beautiful, pristine land is commonly felt elsewhere in the Pacific Northwest.

Nevertheless, the near collapse of the lumber industry in Oregon and Washington in the early 1980s caused local planners to behave like their counterparts in other states and compete for industrial development and population growth.

Certain rural areas are being pitched as retirement havens—ironic, because older adults from the Great Lakes, the distant Northeast, and even sun-baked Southern California have been coming to this area for years to enjoy the clear air, quiet, and uncrowded space.

In Washington state, retirement destinations are most often the islands reached by bridge or ferry from downtown Seattle, and places such as Port Angeles, Port Townsend, Sequim, and Bellingham with salt-water frontages. The area, with the tall Cascades and Olympic mountains in view, has a somewhat wet marine climate, low crime rates, and outstanding outdoor recreation endowments.

In Oregon, retired persons settle along the spectacular but damp Pacific Coast and in the forested cities and towns along I-5 between Portland and the California border.

Calvin Beale, a well-known demographer, observed not long ago that the popularity of the Pacific Northwest Cloud Belt just goes to show that "'Sun Belt' is a very imperfect synonym for population growth."

During the 1970s, for example, Bend and the surrounding forested environs in Deschutes County, Oregon, made up one of the fastest-growing places west of Florida. Of more than 3,100 counties in the United States, the counties along Puget Sound in Washington state ranked among the top 10 in rate of growth over the same period.

After 30 years, the growth has slowed considerably, and so has the economy. That last factor, plus relatively high living costs, hurt this region despite good marks in ambiance, services, climate, and crime.

RIO GRANDE COUNTRY

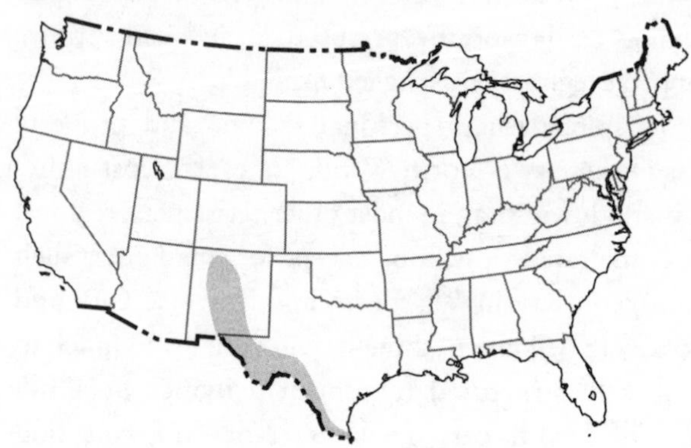

Mission–McAllen–Alamo, TX (19)
Santa Fe, NM (38)
Las Cruces, NM (78)
Rio Rancho, NM (82)
Alpine–Big Bend, TX (92)
Taos, NM (140)
Las Vegas, NM (145)
Ruidoso, NM (148)
Alamogordo, NM (161)
Roswell, NM (190)

The Rio Grande River rises in the Rocky Mountains in southwestern Colorado, flows south through the center of New Mexico west of Santa Fe, continues through Albuquerque and Las Cruces, and serves as a 1,240-mile boundary between Texas and Mexico before emptying into the Gulf of Mexico some 60 miles downriver from Brownsville.

This area has a large ethnic population. Two of every five persons are Mexican-American, and one in ten is Native American. Like the Delta South, too, Rio Grande Country is distinguished by low incomes, large families, poor housing, joblessness, low levels of education, and other social problems.

Along the river's southward progress are a few pockets of phenomenal retirement growth. Not only Albuquerque and suburban Rio Rancho, but also Las Cruces and the settled areas around them have all seen their number of residents over age 65 jump at three or more times the average national rate. Even with the well-publicized growth that most of semiarid New Mexico has experienced, there are still fewer than eight persons per square mile. The desert-mesa vastness is imposing, the distances between towns great, and the loneliness outside city limits a little scary to retired persons hailing from large cities.

The lower valley in southernmost Texas isn't lonely at all. This is the number-one winter tourist destination in all of Texas. Since 1990, Cameron County (Brownsville) and Hidalgo County (Mission–McAllen–Alamo) have together gained 360,000 people, many of them retired Midwesterners who found a climate as mild as Florida's and living costs nearly as low as Mexico's.

ROCKY MOUNTAINS

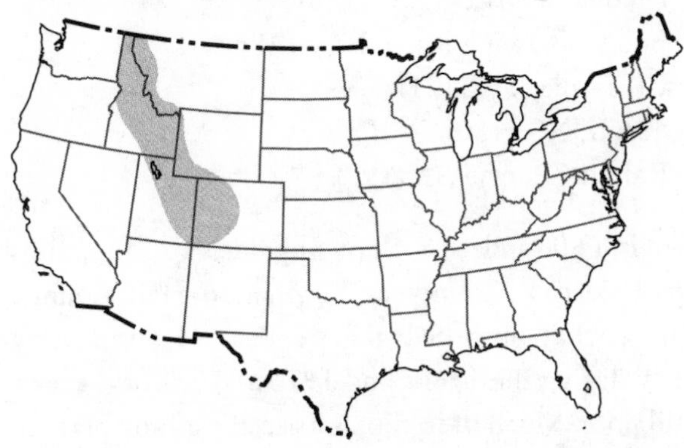

Fort Collins–Loveland, CO (17)
Grand Junction, CO (27)
Flagstaff, AZ (36)
Kalispell–Flathead Valley, MT (40)
Colorado Springs, CO (47)
Bozeman, MT (58)
Durango, CO (79)
Coeur d'Alene, ID (80)
Polson–Mission Valley, MT (123)
Montrose, CO (137)
Delta County, CO (138)
Sandpoint–Lake Pend Oreille, ID (147)
Hamilton–Bitterroot Valley, MT (158)
Cedar City, UT (163)
Ketchum–Sun Valley, ID (164)
Jackson Hole, WY (173)
Park City, UT (174)
Pagosa Springs, CO (185)
McCall, ID (186)
Salida, CO (188)

In spite of the reservations many older adults have about high altitudes and cold winters, the Rockies are emerging from their vacation-only status, becoming an area where older adults are moving for year-round living. With the Desert Southwest, this high, rugged, and beautiful region has the greatest number of places profiled in *Retirement Places Rated.* Alas, just two places here are among the Top 30.

The area is distinguished by middling marks in services, the economy, and costs of living, and a poor one for winter climate. It is above average only in ambiance and freedom from crime.

In Colorado, one can easily distinguish between the eastern slope and western slope areas. Large cities such as Colorado Springs (in a setting that reminds many of Asheville in the North Carolina mountains) and Fort Collins are eastern slope. Grand Junction, near the Utah border, is the population center of the western slope. The two slopes have different political orientations (conservative western slope versus urban Denver–Boulder liberalism) and different growth rates.

In Idaho, where the population rose by more than one-quarter since 1990, retired newcomers head for the city of Coeur d'Alene, within commuting distance of Spokane, Washington, or they settle near metropolitan Boise. In Montana, the spectacular but sparsely settled western counties—particularly Flathead, Lake, Missoula, and Ravalli—are the ones drawing older newcomers.

SOUTH ATLANTIC

Charleston, SC (3)
Melbourne–Palm Bay, FL (4)
Daytona Beach, FL (9)
Savannah, GA (22)
Boca Raton, FL (74)
St. Augustine, FL (97)

Myrtle Beach, SC (112)
Conway, SC (118)
Key West, FL (126)
Hilton Head Island, SC (130)
Beaufort, SC (133)
Beaufort–Bogue Banks, NC (142)
Vero Beach, FL (155)
St. Simons–Jekyll Islands, GA (157)
Edenton, NC (160)
Summerville, SC (165)
Southport–Brunswick Islands, NC (167)
New Bern, NC (170)
Dare Outer Banks, NC (191)

The retirement places along the South Atlantic coast have a special appeal and flavor. Although the coastline is dotted with cities such as Charleston and Savannah, whose history starts centuries ago, it first experienced rapid growth during the 1970s. In the intervening years, in spite of cyclical downturns, the growth has not stopped.

Most of these resort-retirement areas lie in low, marshy land either on the mainland itself or on nearby barrier islands. Palmetto palms, scrub oak, dune grass, and Spanish moss swaying in the sea breezes impart a languid, relaxed mood. Fishing shanties lie scattered near the piers where shrimpers, crabbers, and trawlers moor. Stately planter-style cottages set back from the narrow streets are almost hidden behind tall hedges and are surrounded by massive live oaks. Streets paved with old oyster and clam shells; small gift shops, boutiques, and shops offering seafood, gumbo, and chicory coffee; taverns and inns of all ages and sizes—these are what you'll find in every metro area, town, and village of the coastal islands.

The South Atlantic resorts are less crowded and have lower living costs than most comparable places on the Florida peninsula. Furthermore, their summer months, while sometimes uncomfortable, are less rugged than those farther south. You are likely to find newer buildings and younger people here than in some older retirement havens.

On the minus side, crime rates are high. Of the 19 retirement places in this region, only three—Edenton, Beaufort–Bogue Banks, and Southport—have above-average ratings for personal safety. Health care facilities can be inadequate, and while housing costs are generally low for the region, places such as the Dare Outer Banks are joining Hilton Head and Beaufort as expensive havens. Finally, these low-lying oceanside locations are subject to damage from severe tropical storms.

SOUTHERN HIGHLANDS

Asheville, NC (20)
Brevard, NC (68)
Hendersonville–East Flat Rock, NC (70)
Maryville, TN (83)
Smith Mountain Lake, VA (94)
Pendleton District, SC (124)
Boone–Blowing Rock, NC (128)
Crossville, TN (171)
Tryon, NC (180)
Rabun County, GA (197)

There is a 600-mile stretch of Appalachian Mountains from Frederick County in Virginia to Hall County, Georgia, that absorbed a good deal of antipoverty money during the 1960s and 1970s. Much of the area is still poor. Much of it, too, is as scenic as any place in the nation.

This is a land of peaks and ridges, rushing streams, and thundering waterfalls. In the earliest spring days, the hillsides burst with flowering trees and shrubs: rhododendron, azalea, dogwood, and magnolia. The George Washington, Pisgah, and Chattahoochee national forests stand tall with black walnut, pine, beech, poplar, birch, and oak. The mountain vistas, especially along the Blue Ridge Parkway, show row after spectacular row of parallel mountain ridges. Distant parts of what you see from the road are so inaccessible that it's unlikely humans have regularly hiked more than 10 percent of the topography.

Because the area is bookended, so to speak, by Atlanta in the south and Washington in the north, it isn't at all unusual to encounter former urbanites from these major cities among the retired persons in places such as Rabun County in north Georgia, Asheville and Hendersonville in western North Carolina, and Smith Mountain Lake in Virginia. What is unusual are the "Florida Clubs" formed by retired persons who settle here after a disappointing stint in the Sunshine State.

The Southern Highlands are a major destination for retired persons. Many of the region's communities are ideal for retirement living, offering a wide range of special services for older residents. The Appalachian counties generally combine low costs of living and housing, low crime rates, adequate health care facilities in most places, and some of the country's mildest four-season climates.

TAHOE BASIN & SIERRAS

Santa Rosa (21)
Carson City–Carson Valley, NV (51)
Reno–Sparks, NV (51)
Paradise–Magalia, CA (54)
Grass Valley–Nevada City, CA (134)
Sonora–Twain Harte, CA (152)
Amador County, CA (169)
Oakhurst–Coarsegold, CA (182)
Mariposa, CA (200)

In California, three out of four people live either in the hugely populated Los Angeles basin or in equally populated metropolitan San Francisco–Oakland–San Jose. Everyone else seems to live in a part of the state the Beach Boys seem never to have sung about.

You might call it the Other California. Parts of it—the Mother Lode Country and the area surrounding Lake Tahoe in both California and Nevada—are seeing a growing number of retired newcomers, most of whom are Californians.

Mother Lode Country, the interior marked by the Sierra Mountains, with alpine meadows, blizzard-filled passes, clear lakes, trout streams, and magnificent scenery, was once a hard-worked mining area. Now it is a tourist haven. Donner Lake, a popular summer beach resort, also doubles as a winter ski area. Even in midsummer, this high mountain lake tends to be on the chilly side. Tuolumne County, roughly 100 miles to the south, contains spectacular Yosemite National Park, with all of the opportunities for outstanding outdoor recreation. Although the gold rush is over, these areas continue to attract people with scenery, mountain climate, and open spaces. Places such as Grass Valley, Nevada City, Mariposa, and Twain Harte are seeing higher living costs, especially those associated with owning a home.

TEXAS INTERIOR

Georgetown (61)
Fredericksburg (87)
Kerrville (89)
Marble Falls–Lake LBJ (139)
Cedar Creek Lake (153)
Wimberley (156)
Lake Conroe (165)
Boerne (175)
New Braunfels (178)
Trinity Peninsula (183)

Texas is a state with contrasting retirement regions. The lower Rio Grande Valley is distinctly Hispanic and has winters as mild as Florida's. So do the Gulf Coast beaches, from South Padre Island up to just above Corpus Christi. Then there's an area in the middle of the state encompassing the lovely cedar-scented Hill Country along with greater Austin and greater San Antonio.

According to visitors, Austin, state capital and home of the University of Texas, seems to have the same terrain and natural vegetation as New England. Metropolitan Austin has expanded so quickly that its population is triple what it was 30 years previously. The negative housing-price appreciation due to the slumping Texas economy is long over. Housing costs here are high and rising. Austin is a "books and bureaucrats" city, drawing a good many retired

University of Texas alumni from all over the nation along with Texas government employees. Wimberley, Georgetown, and Marble Falls are each close by.

San Antonio's appeal as a retirement destination, on the other hand, has five causes: Brooks, Kelly, Lackland, and Randolph Air Force bases; and Fort Sam Houston. Many veterans who were posted to them during the 1940s and 1950s have returned for the mild San Antonio winters, low living costs, and pleasant Hispanic atmosphere. Nearby are New Braunfels and Boerne, two suburban retirement destinations.

West of Austin and northwest of San Antonio, the Hill Country towns of Fredericksburg and Kerrville have spic-and-span layouts in their old sections. These are towns settled by Germans who fled their homeland in the mid–19th century. So attractive is this area that much of it is experiencing second-home development by prosperous Texans and Californians.

YANKEE BELT

Lake Winnipesaukee, NH (8)
Hanover, NH (15)
Monadnock Region, NH (49)
Bar Harbor, ME (66)
Northampton–Amherst, MA (77)
Burlington, VT (81)
Camden, ME (85)
Litchfield Hills, CT (89)
Southern Berkshire County, MA (91)
York Beaches, ME (103)
Middle Cape Cod, MA (109)
St. Jay–Northeast Kingdom, VT (127)
Woodstock, VT (146)
Martha's Vineyard, MA (193)

In New England, the preferred retirement destinations aren't in heavily urbanized Connecticut, Massachusetts, or Rhode Island. One big exception is Massachusetts' Barnstable County (Cape Cod), where one in three residents over the past 15 years has been a newcomer and where one in five is now over age 65. To find the most popular retirement spots in New England, however, look in the rural pockets of the north, in Maine, New Hampshire, and Vermont.

In the decades since 1970, Maine's population has jumped 30 percent. By Sun Belt standards, such growth seems paltry. For the Pine Tree State, though, it's been the fastest upsurge since the mid–19th century.

Most retired newcomers choose the rocky Atlantic coast over the hard-going farm areas and rough-cut paper- and lumber-mill towns in Maine's interior. Within the seascape counties—Hancock, Knox, Lincoln, and York—the places that draw retired people are the small lobster ports and summer resort towns off old U.S. Highway 1, places with names like Camden, Bar Harbor, Ellsworth, Wiscasset, and Rockland.

New Hampshire, too, is growing. Indeed, it is growing the most quickly of all the northeastern states—mainly at the expense of Massachusetts, its heavily taxed neighbor. You'll pay no income or sales taxes here. The only other state where this is still possible is Alaska. But you will pay handsomely for real estate along huge Lake Winnipesaukee's shoreline and around Hanover, home of Dartmouth College, and in the environs of North Conway, a resort town.

For all its attraction for disaffected New Yorkers and Pennsylvanians who come to live year-round, Vermont remains the most rural state in America according to the Census Bureau. Two of every three residents here live beyond the built-up limits of cities. Much of the state unmistakably remains a 19th-century Currier & Ives landscape of sugar maples, dairy farms, and steepled white Congregational churches that dominate every green town common. In early October, the brilliant fall foliage draws busloads of weekenders from Boston and New York.

Appendix

RELOCATION RESOURCES

It may be that while *Retirement Places Rated* helped you, there are still some areas where you need more information or want to do your own research. Here are some resources—print and electronic—that will help.

HOW PLACES PRESENT THEMSELVES

There are more than 800 separate Chamber of Commerce organizations promoting the benefits of living and doing business somewhere within the 203 places profiled in this book (see the "Place Finder" later in this Appendix for address and phone listings of the major chambers). That should give you an idea of how competitive the market is for attracting new residents, especially ones with large net worths.

Writing to Chambers of Commerce for their "newcomer's pack" produces a collection of promotional brochures, maps, business statistics, cost-of-living data, and events calendars, and may also trigger mail and telephone calls from real estate brokers. The annual *World Chamber of Commerce Directory* lists the chamber name, address, and telephone number, as well as the name of the chamber's contact person, for over 4,000 locations in the United States. It is available in larger libraries. By far, the most authoritative, clutter-free, noncommercial Internet gateway is www.uschamber.com, the website of the U.S. Chamber of Commerce.

Be aware that some chambers promptly respond to your inquiry with useful materials while others do not respond at all. Frequently, you'll receive more material if you identify yourself as a prospective new resident than you will if you say you're retired.

WHAT REALLY GOES ON IN OTHER PLACES

If you've identified a few likely locations, a short-term subscription to their local newspapers is invaluable (see the "Place Finder" later in this Appendix for address listings). After reading a month's worth, you'll have an excellent idea of consumer prices, political issues, and other matters on the mind of residents.

For the name, address, telephone number, monthly subscription cost, special features, and politics (typically independent) of each of the country's 1,635 daily newspapers, the best source is *Editor & Publisher's International Yearbook*. Good Internet gateways to online newspapers include The Internet Public Library (www.ipl.org) and NewsVoyager (www.newspaperlinks.com)

Note: you'll learn that one or two newspapers arriving in the mail every day quickly becomes overwhelming. A weekend edition is adequate for keeping up with local happenings. Most dailies publish Sunday editions and will fill "Sunday Only" subscriptions. Whether you want a daily or just a Sunday subscription, be sure to tell the circulation department that you want to receive the classified sections and shopping inserts. To save postage, newspapers omit these sections in mail subscriptions.

For similar information on the 6,890 semiweekly and weekly newspapers (often the only publications covering rural areas), *Gale's Directory of Publications* is an alternative source.

VACATIONS CAN LEAD TO MIGRATION

Free, quality travel guides abound. Attracting tourists is a competitive aspect of state government, and more than a few realize that capturing new residents is a happy consequence of strong travel promotion. You'll find that many of the contacts listed below can send you information on local retirement, in addition to a state travel guide, events calendar, and official road map. Each state's tourism office Internet address is found to the right of the toll-free telephone number.

Alabama Bureau of Tourism & Travel
P.O. Box 4927, Montgomery 36103
800/ALABAMA http://touralabama.org/index-FL.htm

Alaska Division of Tourism
P.O. Box 110801, Juneau 99811
800/862-5275 www.dced.state.ak.us/trade/tou/home.htm

Arizona Office of Tourism
1110 W. Washington, Phoenix 85007
800/842-8257 www.arizonaguide.com

Arkansas Department of Parks & Tourism
One Capitol Mall, Little Rock 72201
800/NATURAL www.arkansas.com

California Division of Tourism
P.O. Box 1499, Sacramento 958142
800/TO-CALIF http://gocalif.ca.gov

Colorado Travel & Tourism Authority
P.O. Box 38700, Denver 80238
800/COLORADO www.colorado.com

Connecticut Tourism Division
505 Hudson St., Hartford 06106
800/CT-BOUND www.tourism.state.ct.us

Delaware Tourism Office
99 Kings Highway, Dover 19903
800/441-8846 www.delaware.gov/yahoo/Visitor

Florida Tourism
P.O. Box 1100, Tallahassee 32302
888/7-FLA-USA www.flausa.com

Georgia Tourism Division
P.O. Box 1776, Atlanta 30301
800/VISIT-GA www.georgia.org

Hawaii Visitors & Convention Bureau
P.O. Box 2359, Honolulu 96804
800/353-5846 www.visit.hawaii.org

Idaho Division of Tourism
700 West State St., Boise 83720
800/635-7820 www.visitid.org

Illinois Bureau of Tourism
100 West Randolph, Chicago 60601
800/223-0121 www.enjoyillinois.com

Indiana Department of Tourism
One North Capitol, Indianapolis 46204
800/289-6646 www.ai.org/tourism

Iowa Division of Tourism
200 East Grand Ave., Des Moines 50309
888/472-6035 www.traveliowa.com

Kansas Travel & Tourism
1000 SW Jackson, Topeka 66612
800/2-KANSAS www.travelks.com

Kentucky Department of Travel
500 Mero St., Frankfort 40601
800/225-TRIP www.kytourism.com

Louisiana Office of Tourism
P.O. Box 94291, Baton Rouge 70804
800/334-8626 www.louisianatravel.com

Maine Office of Tourism
189 State St., Augusta 04333
800/533-9595 www.visitmaine.com

Maryland Office of Tourism Development
217 E. Redwood St., Baltimore 21202
800/543-1036 www.mdisfun.org

Massachusetts Office of Travel & Tourism
10 Park Plaza, Boston 02116
800/227-MASS www.massvacation.com

Travel Michigan
P.O. Box 30226, Lansing 48909
888/78-GREAT www.michigan.org

Minnesota Office of Tourism
121 7th Pl. E., St. Paul 55101
800/657-3700 www.exploreminnesota.com

Mississippi Tourism Development Division
P.O. Box 849, Jackson 39205
800/WARMEST www.visitmississippi.org

Missouri Division of Tourism
P.O Box 1055, Jefferson City 65102
800/877-1234 www.missouritourism.org

Montana Travel Promotion Division
301 South Park Ave., Helena 59620
800/VISIT-MT www.visitmt.com

Nebraska Travel & Tourism Division
P.O. Box 94666, Lincoln 68509
800/228-4307 www.visitnebraska.org

Nevada Commission on Tourism
401 North Carson St., Carson City 89701
800/NEVADA-8 www.travelnevada.com

New Hampshire Travel & Tourism
P.O. Box 1856, Concord 03302
800/FUN-IN-NH www.visitnh.gov

New Jersey Division of Travel & Tourism
20 West State St., Trenton 08625
800/JERSEY-7 www.state.nj.us/travel

New Mexico Department of Tourism
491 Old Santa Fe Trail, Santa Fe 87503
800/545-2040 www.newmexico.org

New York State Division of Tourism
One Commerce Plaza, Albany 12245
800/CALL-NYS www.iloveny.state.ny.us

North Carolina Travel & Tourism Division
301 N. Wilmington St., Raleigh 27601
800/VISIT-NC www.visitnc.com

North Dakota Tourism Department
604 E. Boulevard Ave., Bismarck 58505
800/435-5663 www.ndtourism.com

Ohio Division of Travel and Tourism
P.O. Box 1001, Columbus 43266
800/BUCKEYE www.ohiotourism.com

Oklahoma Tourism & Recreation Department
15 N. Robinson, Suite 100, Oklahoma City 73105
800/652-6552 http://tourism.state.ok.us

Oregon Tourism Commission
775 Summer St., NE, Salem 97310
800/547-7842 www.traveloregon.com

Pennsylvania Travel & Tourism Office
453 Forum Building, Harrisburg 17120
800/VISIT-PA www.state.pa.us/papower

Rhode Island Tourism Division
One West Exchange St., Providence 02903
800/556-2484 www.visitrhodeisland.com

South Carolina Tourism Division
1205 Pendleton St., Columbia 29201
803/734-1700 www.discoversouthcarolina.com

South Dakota Department of Tourism
711 East Wells Ave., Pierre 57501
800/SDAKOTA www.travelsd.com

Tennessee Department of Tourist Development
320 Sixth Ave., N., Nashville 37243
800/491-TENN www.state.tn.us/tourdev

Texas Department of Tourist Development
P.O. Box 12728, Austin 78711
800/888-8TEX www.state.tx.us

Utah Travel Council
P.O. Box 147420, Salt Lake City 84114
800/200-1160 www.utah.com

Vermont Department of Tourism and Marketing
6 Baldwin St., Montpelier 05633
800/VERMONT www.travel-vermont.com

Virginia Tourism Corporation
901 E. Byrd St., Richmond 23219
800/VISIT-VA www.virginia.org

Washington, DC Convention and Tourism Corporation
901 7th Ave., NW, DC 20001
800/422-8644 www.washington.org

Washington Tourism Division
P.O. Box 42500, Olympia 98504
800/544-1800 www.tourism.wa.gov

West Virginia Division of Tourism
2101 Washington St., E., Charleston 25305
800/225-5982 www.callwva.com

Wisconsin Department of Tourism
201 W. Washington Ave., Madison 53703
800/432-TRIP www.travelwisconsin.com

Wyoming Division of Tourism
I-25 & College Dr., Cheyenne 82002
800/225-5996 www.wyomingtourism.org

GENERAL LIVING COSTS

For some who live in high-cost areas, the only way to afford retirement is to move away. Living costs vary enormously around the country, but so do household budgeting skills. While it isn't possible to settle anywhere you wish if your retirement income is typical, you can settle in most places in differing degrees of comfort.

Every 3 months, the American Chamber of Commerce Researchers Association (ACCRA) surveys the costs of housing, food, services, transportation, and health care in nearly 300 locations around the United States. While the ACCRA survey is modeled on what a young family of four buys, and hence isn't meant for retirement purposes, it is still useful for making comparisons.

You can order a four-quarter subscription for $140, or the latest quarter's survey for $85 from:

ACCRA
P.O. Box 407
Arlington, VA 22210
703/522-4980

You can also obtain quick living cost comparisons online for $6.95 for two locations and $2.95 for each additional location at ACCRA's website, www.accra.org.

Better yet, save your money. If you're thinking of only one or two destinations, call your local Chamber of Commerce. If it belongs to ACCRA, it can readily give you cost comparisons over the telephone.

STATE RESIDENT INCOME TAX FORMS

After housing prices, the biggest cost difference between places in differing states is taxes. The best way to learn what your income tax will be in a new state is to write for its *resident* (not its *out-of-state*) income tax form and instructions, fill it out, and compare the bottom line with that of your current state income tax return. Even better, download the state's tax form from the Internet and e-mail the director of revenue if you have questions.

Telephone numbers listed below are "taxpayer assistance" lines. To the right of these are Internet addresses. The best Internet gateway is maintained by the Federation of Tax Administrators, a professional association of revenue department officials from each of the states: www.taxadmin.org/fta/link.

Alabama Department of Revenue
50 North Ripley St., Montgomery 36132
800/829-1040 www.ador.state.al.us

Alaska Department of Revenue
P.O. Box 110420, Juneau 99811-0420
907/465-2320 www.revenue.state.ak.us

Arizona Department of Revenue
1600 W. Monroe, Phoenix 85007-2650
602/255-3381 www.revenue.state.az.us

Arkansas Department of Finance and Administration
1509 W. 7th St., Little Rock 72201
501/682-2242 www.state.ar.us/dfa

California State Board of Equalization
Box 942879, Sacramento 94279-0001
800/400-7115 www.boe.ca.gov

California Franchise Tax Board
3321 Power Inn Rd., Sacramento 95826
800/852-5711 www.ftb.ca.gov

Colorado Department of Revenue
1375 Sherman St., Denver 80261-0005
303/238-7378 www.revenue.state.co.us

Connecticut Department of Revenue
25 Sigourney St., Hartford 06106-5032
860/297-5962 www.ct.gov/drs

Delaware Division of Revenue
820 N. French St., Wilmington 19801
302/577-8200 www.state.de.us/revenue

District of Columbia
1350 Pennsylvania Ave., NW, Washington 20004
202/727-2476 www.cfo.dc.gov/main.asp

Florida Department of Revenue
1379 Blountstown Hwy., Tallahassee 32304
850/488-6800 www.state.fl.us/dor

Georgia Department of Revenue
1800 Century Center Blvd., NE, Atlanta 30345
404/417-2300 www2.state.ga.us/Departments/DOR

Hawaii Department of Taxation
P.O. Box 259, Honolulu 96809-0259
808/587-4242 www.state.hi.us/tax

Idaho State Tax Commission
800 Park Blvd., Boise 83712
208/334-7660 www2.state.id.us/tax

Illinois Department of Revenue
101 West Jefferson St., Springfield 62702
217/782-3336 www.revenue.state.il.us

Indiana Department of Revenue
100 North Senate Ave., Indianapolis 46204
317/232-2240 www.state.in.us/dor

Iowa Department of Revenue & Finance
1305 E. Walnut, Des Moines 50319
800/367-3388 www.state.ia.us/tax

Kansas Department of Revenue
915 SW Harrison St., Topeka 66612
785/296-8222 www.ksrevenue.org

Kentucky Revenue Cabinet
200 Fair Oaks Lane, Frankfort 40620
502/564-4581 www.revenue.state.ky.us

Louisiana Department of Revenue
617 North Third St., Baton Rouge 70802
225/219-2448 www.rev.state.la.us

Maine Bureau of Taxation
24 State House Station, Augusta 04333-0024
207/287-2076 www.state.me.us/revenue

Maryland Comptroller of the Treasury
80 Calvert St., Annapolis 21411
410/260-7980 www.comp.state.md.us

Massachusetts Department of Revenue
100 Cambridge St., Boston 02114
617/887-MDOR www.dor.state.ma.us

Michigan Department of Treasury
Michigan Department of Treasury, Lansing 48922
517/373-3200 www.michigan.gov/treasury

Minnesota Department of Revenue
10 River Park Plaza, St. Paul 55146
651/556-6091 www.taxes.state.mn.us

Mississippi State Tax Commission
P.O. Box 1033, Jackson 39215-1033
601/923-7000 www.mstc.state.ms.us

Missouri Department of Revenue
301 West High St., Jefferson City 65105
573/751-3505 http://dor.state.mo.us

Montana Department of Revenue
P.O. Box 5805, Helena 59604-5805
406/444-6900 www.state.mt.us

Nebraska Department of Revenue
P.O. Box 94818, Lincoln 68509-4818
402/471-5729 www.revenue.state.ne.us

Nevada Department of Taxation
1550 E. College Parkway, Carson City 89706
775/687-4820 http://tax.state.nv.us

New Hampshire Department of Revenue
P.O. Box 457, Concord 03302
603/271-2191 www.state.nh.us/revenue

New Jersey Division of Taxation
50 Barrack St., Trenton 08695
609/292-6400 www.state.nj.us/treasury/taxation

New Mexico Department of Taxation and Revenue
P.O. Box 630, Santa Fe 87504
505/827-0700 www.state.nm.us/tax

New York Department of Taxation & Finance
W.A. Harriman Campus, Albany 12227
800/225-5829 www.tax.state.ny.us

North Carolina Department of Revenue
501 North Wilmington St., Raleigh 27640
877/252-4052 www.dor.state.nc.us

North Dakota Office of Tax Commissioner
600 E. Boulevard Ave., Bismarck 58505
701/328-2770 www.state.nd.us/taxdpt

Ohio Department of Taxation
30 E. Broad St., Columbus 43215
800/282-1780 www.state.oh.us/tax

Oklahoma Tax Commission
P.O. Box 26800, Oklahoma City 73126-0800
405/521-3160 www.oktax.state.ok.us

Oregon Department of Revenue
955 Center St., NE, Salem 97301-2555
503/378-4988 www.dor.state.or.us

Pennsylvania Department of Revenue
Revenue Pl., Harrisburg 17129
717/783-1405 www.revenue.state.pa.us/revenue

Rhode Island Division of Taxation
1 Capitol Hill, Providence 02908
401/222-1040 www.tax.state.ri.us

South Carolina Department of Revenue
301 Gervais St., Columbia 29214
803/898-5822 www.sctax.org

South Dakota Department of Revenue
445 E. Capitol Ave., Pierre 57501
800/829-9188 www.state.sd.us/revenue

Tennessee Department of Revenue
500 Deaderick St., Nashville 37242
800/342-1003 www.state.tn.us/revenue

Texas Comptroller of Public Accountants
111 West Sixth St., Austin 78701
512/463-3961 www.cpa.state.tx.us

Utah State Tax Commission
210 North 1950 West, Salt Lake City 84134
801/297-2200 www.tax.utah.gov

Vermont Department of Taxes
109 State St., Montpelier 05601
802/828-2865 www.state.vt.us/tax

Virginia Department of Taxation
P.O. Box 1115, Richmond 23218
804/367-8031 www.tax.state.va.us

Washington State Department of Revenue
P.O. Box 47450, Olympia 98504
800/647-7706 www.dor.wa.gov

West Virginia State Tax Department
P.O. Box 3784, Charleston 25337
800/982-8297 www.state.wv.us/taxdiv

Wisconsin Department of Revenue
2135 Rimrock Rd., Madison 53708
608/266-2772 www.dor.state.wi.us

Wyoming Department of Revenue
122 West 25th St., Cheyenne 82002
307/777-7961 http://revenue.state.wy.us

HOW CLIMATE HITS YOU

Good books about climate's sway over health and personality are few. Here are two, plus a valuable sourcebook that steers you to professional-level articles in the field of bioclimatology:

Gallagher, Winifred, *The Power of Place,* New York, Poseidon Press, 1993. While some psychologists put down relocation as "running away from your problems," many people who purposely move do end up feeling much better. A book about seasonal affective disorders (SAD), bipolar personalities, and a lot about how we thrive and suffer by where we live.

Landsberg, H.E., *Weather and Health,* Garden City, Anchor Books, 1969. Deliberate climate selection can lead to improved physical health. Alas, the perfect climate in the United States may be an illusion. A small classic, now out of print, by an eminent bioclimatologist.

Beware of chamber of commerce blandishments about a place's annual average temperature. A more comprehensive source, for day-by-day climate data, is located in Asheville, North Carolina. Meteorologists at the National Climatic Data Center can take your order for comparative data that the Center publishes for any of thousands of locations in this country.

The Center's best-seller is the annual *Comparative Climatic Data for the United States,* a collection of month-by-month and annual summaries for normal daily maximum and minimum temperature, average and maximum wind speed, percent of possible sunshine, rainfall, snowfall, and morning and afternoon humidity at each of 300 "first order" weather stations in this country. The cost is $3.

If the place you have in mind doesn't have a first order weather station, it may yet be one of 5,000+ locations with a "cooperative" weather station. Their data are *in Climatography of the United States,* Series 20, a two-page publication for each location containing freeze and precipitation probability data; tables of long-term monthly and annual mean maximum, mean minimum, and average temperature; and tables of monthly and annual total precipitation and total snowfall. The cost is $1 for each location.

All orders carry a $5 shipping and handling fee and must be prepaid by check, MasterCard, Visa, or American Express. Call or write:

National Climatic Data Center
Federal Building
Asheville, NC 28801
704/271-4871

There are other sources of valuable climate scuttlebutt. Where is North Carolina's "banana belt," and how hot can it *really* get in Pahrump, Nevada? State climatologists are persons appointed by state government and who are also recognized by the director of the National Climatic Data Center of the National Oceanic and Atmospheric Administration as the chief climatologist of a particular state. Note: as of January, 2004, Montana, Rhode Island, and West Virginia do not have state climatologists. The Internet gateway is www.ncdc.noaa.gov/oa/climate/stateclimatologists.html.

Alabama State Climatologist
National Space Science and Technology Center
320 Sparkman Dr., Huntsville 35805
256/961-7763 www.atmos.uah.edu/aosc

Alaska State Climatologist
University of Alaska
707 A St., Anchorage 99501
907/257-2737
www.uaa.alaska.edu/enri/ascc_web/ascc_home.html

Arizona State Climatologist
Box 870104
Arizona State University, Tempe 85287
480/965-6165 http://geography.asu.edu/azclimate

Arkansas State Climatologist
Dept. of Geography
University of Arkansas, Fayetteville 72701
501/575-3159

California State Climatologist
California Dept. of Water Resources
P.O. Box 219000, Sacramento 95821
916/574-2614

Colorado State Meteorologist
Dept. of Atmospheric Sciences
Colorado State University, Fort Collins 80523
970/491-8545 http://climate.atmos.colostate.edu

Connecticut State Climatologist
Dept. of Natural Resources
University of Connecticut, Storrs 06269
860/486-0135 www.canr.uconn.edu/nrme/cscc

Delaware State Climatologist
Dept. of Geography
University of Delaware, Newark 19716
302/831-2294 www.udel.edu/leathers/stclim.html

Florida State Climatologist
Dept. of Meteorology
Florida State University, Tallahassee 32306
850/644-4581 www.coaps.fsu.edu/climate_center

Georgia State Climatologist
Biological & Agricultural Engineering Dept.
University of Georgia, Athens 30602
706/583-0156 http://climate.engr.uga.edu

Hawaii State Climatologist
Department of Meteorology
University of Hawaii, Manoa, Honolulu 96822
808/587-0264 http://lumahai.soest.hawaii.edu/Hsco/

Idaho State Climatologist
Biological & Agricultural Engineering Dept.
University of Idaho, Moscow 83844
208/885-6184 www.uidaho.edu/~climate

Illinois State Climatologist
Illinois State Water Survey
2204 Griffith Dr., Champaign 61820
217/333-0729
www.sws.uiuc.edu/atmos/statecli/index.htm

Indiana State Climatologist
1150 Lilly Building
Purdue University, West Lafayette 47907
765/494-8105 http://shadow.agry.purdue.edu

Iowa State Climatologist
Iowa Dept. of Agriculture and Land Stewardship
Wallace State Office Bldg., Des Moines 50319
515/281-8981
www.agriculture.state.ia.us/climatology.htm

Kansas State Climatologist
Dept. of Communications
Kansas State University, Manhattan 66506
785/532-7019 www.oznet.ksu.edu/wdl

Kentucky Climate
Dept. of Geography & Geology
Western Kentucky University, Bowling Green 42164
270/745-5983 http://kyclim.wku.edu

Louisiana State Climatologist
Louisiana Office of State Climatology
Louisiana State University, Baton Rouge 70803
225/578-6870 www.losc.lsu.edu

Maine State Climatologist
Climate Change Institute
University of Maine, Orono 04469
207/581-3441 www.umaine.edu/maineclimate

Maryland State Climatologist
Department of Meteorology
University of Maryland, College Park 20742
301/405-7223 http://metosrv2.umd.edu/~climate

Massachusetts State Climatologist
496 Park St., North Reading 01864
781/676-1000

Michigan State Climatologist
Department of Geography
417 Natural Sciences Building
Michigan State University, East Lansing 48824
517/355-0231 http://climate.geo.msu.edu

Minnesota State Climatologist
439 Borlaug Hall
University of Minnesota, St. Paul 55108
651/296-4214 http://climate.umn.edu

Mississippi State Climatologist
Geosciences Dept.
Mississippi State University, Starkville 39762
662/325-3915
www.msstate.edu/Dept/GeoSciences/climate

Missouri State Climatologist
Missouri Climate Center
University of Missouri, Columbia 65211
573/882-8599 www.mcc.missouri.edu

Nebraska State Climatologist
15 L.W. Chase Hall
University of Nebraska, Lincoln 68583
402/472-5206 www.nebraskaclimateoffice.unl.edu

Nevada State Climatologist
322 Mackay Science Hall
University of Nevada, Reno 89557
755/784-1723

New Hampshire State Climatologist
Dept. of Geography
University of New Hampshire, Durham 03824
603/862-3136 www.unh.edu/stateclimatologist

New Jersey State Climatologist
Dept. of Geography
Rutgers University, Piscataway 08854
732/445-4741 http://climate.rutgers.edu/stateclim

New Mexico State Climatologist
Dept. of Agronomy & Horticulture
New Mexico State University, Las Cruces 88003
505/646-2104 http://weather.nmsu.edu

New York State Climatologist
1117 Bradfield Hall
Cornell University, Ithaca 14853
607/255-3034 http://nysc.eas.cornell.edu

North Carolina State Climatologist
Campus Box 7236
North Carolina State University, Raleigh 27695
919/515-3056 www.nc-climate.ncsu.edu

North Dakota State Climatologist
Dept. of Soils Science
North Dakota State University, Fargo 58105
701/231-8576 http://ndawn.ndsu.nodak.edu

Ohio State Climatologist
Dept. of Geography
Ohio State University, Columbus 43210
614/292-0148
www.geography.ohio-state.edu/faculty/rogers/statclim.html

Oklahoma State Climatologist
Sarkey's Energy Center
University of Oklahoma, Norman 73019
405/325-2541 www.ocs.ou.edu

Oregon State Climatologist
Oregon Climate Service
Oregon State University, Corvallis 97331
541/737-5705 www.ocs.orst.edu

Pennsylvania State Climatologist
Dept. of Meteorology
Pennsylvania State University, University Park 16802
814/865-3197
http://pasc.met.psu.edu/PA_Climatologist

South Carolina State Climatologist
Dept. of Natural Resources
2221 Devine St., Columbia 29205
803/734-9110 http://water.dnr.state.sc.us/climate/sco

South Dakota State Climatologist
Agricultural Engineering Dept.
South Dakota State University, Brookings 57007
605/688-5678 http://abe.sdstate.edu/weather

Tennessee State Climatologist
Tennessee Valley Authority
400 West Summit Hill Dr., Knoxville 37902
865/632-4222

Texas State Climatologist
Dept. of Atmospheric Sciences
Texas A & M University, College Station 77843
979/845-5044 www.met.tamu.edu/met/osc/osc.html

Utah State Climatologist
Utah Climate Center
Utah State University, Logan 84322
435/797-2190 http://climate.usu.edu

Vermont State Climatologist
Dept. of Geography
University of Vermont, Burlington 05405
802/656-3060 www.uvm.edu/~ldupigny/sc/index.html

Virginia State Climatologist
Clark Hall
University of Virginia, Charlottesville 22903
804/924-0549 http://wsrv.clas.virginia.edu/~climate

Washington State Climatologist
Climate Impacts Group
University of Washington, Seattle 98195
206/616-5346 www.climate.washington.edu

Wisconsin State Climatologist
University of Wisconsin
1225 West Dayton St., Madison 53706
608/263-2374 www.aos.wisc.edu/~sco

Wyoming State Climatologist
Water Resources Data System
1000 E. University Ave., Laramie 82071
307/766-6659 www.wrds.uwyo.edu/wrds/wsc/wsc.html

FINDING SPECIALIZED HOSPITAL SERVICES

Health care guides are expensive, but they usually sit on reference shelves in major public libraries, in libraries at colleges with health science programs, and also in hospitals. Your doctor's guess is as good as yours when it comes to what's available in distant, unfamiliar locations. The best source for that purpose is the American Hospital Association's annual *Guide to the Health Care Field.*

Organized by state and by city, the guide has data on every hospital in the United States, including address and telephone number, control (public, private, investor-owned, federal, city, state), length of stay (short term, long term), and which ones are certified for Medicare participation and accredited by the joint Commission on Accreditation of Health Care Organizations.

More importantly, the guide details which of 85 specialized facilities are available in each hospital. Cardiac intensive care, physical therapy, hemodialysis, oncology services, psychiatric outpatient service, blood bank, home care, and health promotion, for example, are several important facilities not obtainable everywhere.

Finding Better Hospitals

The federal government's Bureau of Health Standards and Quality tracks several factors for each of America's 5,500 short-term, acute-care hospitals. Three of these factors can help you compare hospitals: (1) death rates for Medicare patients, (2) percent of doctors who are board-certified, and (3) teaching programs.

A nonprofit group publishes these data in *The Consumer Guide to Hospitals* for $19.95, including postage and handling. You can order online at www.checkbook.org or call or write:

Center for the Study of Services
733 15th St. NW
Washington, DC 20005
202/347-7283

The Joint Commission on Accreditation of Healthcare Organizations (JCAHO), the main accrediting body for U.S. hospitals, has also started selling report cards on individual hospitals, nursing homes, ambulatory-care facilities, and other institutions. Each report costs $30 and includes an overall score plus individual scores on areas such as medication and staff qualifications.

JCAHO
875 North Michigan Ave.
Chicago, IL 60611
708/916-5600

Or you can obtain basic status reports—called Quality Checks—on all health care facilities accredited by JCAHO at www.jcaho.org.

Verifying Medical Credentials

It is up to the states to license and regulate professions. Kentucky licenses watchmakers and auctioneers but not psychologists; Maine certifies tree surgeons and movie projectionists but not occupational therapists; Arkansas licenses insect exterminators but not opticians. Fortunately, physicians and dentists must be certified before they can practice in any state.

Check a dentist's background in the *American Dental Directory.* Check a doctor's background in the *Directory of Board-Certified Medical Specialists* and *Directory of Physicians in the United States.* The three sources are updated each year, and are organized by state and by city. What to look for: medical or dental school attended, year graduated (you're not looking for a health care professional who is about to retire), specializations, and board certifications.

Contact hospitals in distant places that interest you for their directory of physicians with admitting privileges. These Dr. Finders, as they're called, can be better sources of information on local M.D.s than any national publications.

Quacks operate everywhere, however, because credentials that look impressive aren't difficult to obtain. One California firm, recently shut down by the Postal Service, furnished a medical degree complete with transcript, diploma, and letters of recommendation to anyone for $28,000. For $5, another firm mailed out "Outstanding Service" citations.

Experts testifying in a recent House of Representatives hearing estimated that 1 out of 50 "doctors" is doing a thriving business with fraudulent credentials, and that three out of five of their patients are over 65.

The Public Citizen Health Research Group can send you a list of doctors disciplined for negligence, substance abuse, or other misconduct by state or federal authorities. The cost is $15 per state. Call or write:

Public Citizen Health Research Group
2000 P St., NW
Washington, DC 20036
202/833-3000

Note that there are big differences in the way states discipline physicians. An M.D. not on the list may never have had disciplinary action brought against him or her yet still be regarded as questionable.

STATE AGING COMMISSIONS

Don't be put off by the bureaucratic titles. State aging offices are gold mines of information on government services, job openings, self-employment opportunities, volunteer activities and programs, and taxes. They also put you in touch with other local public and private organizations for retired persons.

Alabama Department of Senior Services
770 Washington Ave., Montgomery 36130
334/242-5743 www.adss.state.al.us

Alaska Commission on Aging
Box 110693, Juneau 99811-0693
907/465-3250 www.alaskaaging.org

Arizona Aging and Adult Administration
1789 West Jefferson St., Phoenix 85007
602/542-4446 www.de.state.az.us/aaa

Arkansas Office of Aging and Adult Services
P.O. Box 1437, Little Rock 72203
501/682-2441 www.arkansas.gov/dhs/aging

California Department of Aging
1600 K St., Sacramento 95814
916/322-5290 www.aging.state.ca.us

Colorado Aging and Adult Services
1575 Sherman St., Denver 80203
303/866-2800 www.cdhs.state.co.us

Connecticut Division of Elderly Services
25 Sigourney St., Hartford 06106
860/424-5298 www.dss.state.ct.us

Delaware Division of Services for Aging
1901 North DuPont Highway, New Castle 19720
302/577-4791 www.dsaapd.com/index.htm

Florida Department of Elder Services
4040 Esplanade Way, Tallahassee 32399
850/414-2000 http://elderaffairs.state.fl.us

Georgia Division of Aging Services
2 Peachtree St., NE, Atlanta 30303
404/657-5258
www2.state.ga.us/Departments/DHR/aging.html

Hawaii Executive Office on Aging
250 South Hotel St., Honolulu 96813
808/586-0100 www2.state.hi.us/eoa

Idaho Office on Aging
P.O. Box 83720, Boise 83720
208/334-3833 www.idahoaging.com

Illinois Department on Aging
421 East Capitol Ave., Springfield 62701
217/785-3356 www.state.il.us/aging

Indiana Bureau of Aging and In-Home Services
402 West Washington St., Indianapolis 46207
317/232-7123
www.in.gov/fssa/elderly/aging/index.html

Iowa Department of Elder Affairs
200 Tenth St., Des Moines 50309
515/242-3333 www.state.ia.us/elderaffairs

Kansas Department on Aging
503 S. Kansas Ave., Topeka 66603
785/296-4986 www.agingkansas.org/kdoa

Kentucky Office of Aging Services
275 East Main St., Frankfort 40621
502/564-6930 www.chs.state.ky.us/aging

Louisiana Office of Elderly Affairs
412 North 4th St., Baton Rouge 70898
225/342-7100

Maine Bureau of Elder and Adult Services
Statehouse, Station 11, Augusta 04333
207/624-5335 www.state.me.us/dhs/beas

Maryland Department of Aging
301 West Preston St., Baltimore 21201
410/767-1100 www.mdoa.state.md.us

Massachusetts Office of Elder Affairs
1 Ashburton Pl., Boston 02108
617/727-7750 www.800ageinfo.com

Michigan Office of Services to the Aging
P.O. Box 30676, Lansing 48909
517/373-8230 www.miseniors.net

Minnesota Board on Aging
444 Lafayette Rd., St. Paul 55155
651/296-2770 www.mnaging.org

Mississippi Division of Aging and Adult Services
750 North State St., Jackson 39202
601/359-4925 www.mdhs.state.ms.us/aas.html

Missouri Division on Aging
P.O. Box 1337, Jefferson City 65102
573/751-3082 www.dhss.state.mo.us

Montana Senior and Long Term Care Division
P.O. Box 4210, Helena 59620
406/444-4077 www.dphhs.state.mt.us/sltc

Nebraska Division on Aging
1343 M St., Lincoln 68509
402/471-4619 www.hhs.state.ne.us/ags/agsindex.htm

Nevada Division for Aging Services
3416 Goni Rd., Carson City 89706
775/687-4210 http://aging.state.nv.us

New Hampshire Division of Health and Human Services
129 Pleasant St., Concord 03301
603/271-4680 www.dhhs.state.nh.us

New Jersey Division of Senior Affairs
P.O. Box 807, Trenton 08625
609/588-3141
www.state.nj.us./health/senior/sraffair.htm

New Mexico State Agency on Aging
228 East Palace Ave., Santa Fe 87501
505/827-7640 www.nmaging.state.nm.us

New York Office for the Aging
2 Empire State Plaza, Albany 12223
518/474-5731 http://aging.state.ny.us

North Carolina Division of Aging
2101 Mail Service Center, Raleigh 27699
919/733-3983 www.state.nc.us/DHR/DOA/home.htm

North Dakota Aging Services Division
600 South 2nd St., Bismarck 58504
701/328-8910 www.state.nd.us/humanservices/services/adultsaging/index.html

Ohio Department of Aging
50 West Broad St., Columbus 43215
614/466-5500 www.state.oh.us/age

Oklahoma Aging Services Division
312 NE 28th St., Oklahoma City 73125
405/521-2327 www.okdhs.org/aging

Oregon Senior Services Division
500 Summer St. NE, Salem 97310
503/945-5811 www.dhs.state.or.us/seniors

Pennsylvania Department of Aging
555 Walnut St., Harrisburg 17101
717/783-1550 www.aging.state.pa.us

Rhode Island Department of Elderly Affairs
160 Pine St., Providence 02903
401/277-2858 www.health.state.ri.us

South Carolina Office of Senior Services
P.O. Box 8206, Columbia 29202
803/898-2501 www.dhhs.state.sc.us

South Dakota Office of Adult Services
700 Governors Dr., Pierre 57501
605/773-3656 www.state.sd.us/social/ASA/index.htm

Tennessee Commission on Aging
500 Deaderick St., Nashville 37243
615/741-2056 www.state.tn.us/comaging

Texas Department on Aging
701 W. 51st St. MC:W 235, Austin 78751
512/438-3200 www.tdoa.state.tx.us

Utah Division of Aging Services
P.O. Box 45500, Salt Lake City 84145
801/538-3910 www.hsdaas.state.ut.us/SrvAge.htm

Vermont Department of Aging
103 South Main St., Waterbury 05671
802/241-2400 www.dad.state.vt.us

Virginia Department for the Aging
1600 Forest, Richmond 23229
804/662-9333 www.aging.state.va.us

Washington Adult Services Administration
P.O. Box 45050, Olympia 98504
360/493-2500 www.aasa.dshs.wa.gov

West Virginia Bureau of Senior Services
1900 Kanawha Blvd. East, Charleston 25305
304/558-3317 www.state.wv.us/seniorservices

Wisconsin Bureau on Aging
P.O. Box 7851, Madison 53707
608/266-2536 www.dhfs.state.wi.us/Aging

Wyoming Office on Aging
117 Hathaway Building, Cheyenne 82002
307/777-7986 http://wdhfs.state.wy.us/wdh/index.htm

RETIREMENT CONTACTS AND PLACE FINDER

The following listing, organized alphabetically by state, presents the 203 retirement places, cities, towns, and unincorporated areas within their county boundaries. Population figures are in parentheses to the right of each name.

Each place's listing includes contact information for its largest newspaper ("D" indicates daily publication, "C" indicates a community newspaper publishing fewer than 5 days a week), and its Chamber of Commerce (C/C).

ALABAMA

Eufaula (Barbour County)
Eufaula Tribune (C)
514 East Barbour St.
Eufaula, AL 36027
334/687-3506
www.eufaulatribune.com

Eufaula–Barbour County C/C
102 N. Orange Ave.
Eufaula, AL 36072-0697
334/687-6664
www.eufaula-barbourchamber.com
Blue Springs (118)
Clayton (1,436)
Clio (2,187)
Eufaula (13,768)
Louisville (595)

Fairhope–Gulf Shores (Baldwin County)
Mobile Register (D)
P.O. Box 2488
Fairhope, AL 36630
251/219-5400
www.mobileregister.com

Eastern Shore C/C
327 Fairhope Ave.
Fairhope, AL 36532
251/928-6387
www.eschamber.com
Bay Minette (7,804)
Daphne (14,972)
Elberta (510)
Fairhope (12,045)
Foley (6,433)
Gulf Shores (4,029)
Loxley (1,378)
Orange Beach (3,327)
Point Clear (2,125)
Robertsdale (3,126)
Silverhill (602)
Spanish Fort (4,031)
Summerdale (637)

ALASKA

Palmer–Wasilla (Matanuska–Susitna Borough)
Anchorage Daily News (D)
1001 Northway Dr.
Anchorage, AK 99508
907/257-4200
www.adn.com

Greater Palmer C/C
P. O. Box 45
Palmer, AK 99645
907/745-2880
www.palmerchamber.org

Greater Wasilla C/C
415 East Railroad Ave.
Wasilla, AK 99654
907/376-1299
www.wasillachamber.org
Big Lake (1,477)
Butte (2,039)
Chickaloon (145)
Houston (838)
Lazy Mountain (838)
Meadow Lakes (2,374)
Palmer (3,938)
Sutton (308)
Talkeetna (250)
Trapper Creek (296)
Wasilla (5,350)
Willow (285)

ARIZONA

Apache Junction (part of Pinal County)
Independent (C)
850 S. Ironwood Dr.
Apache Junction, AZ 85220
480/982-7799
www.newszap.com/apache

Apache Junction C/C
567 W. Apache Junction Trail
Apache Junction, AZ 85220
480/982-3141, 800/252-3141
www.apachejunctioncoc.com
Apache Junction (19,190)
Superior (3,516)

Bisbee (Cochise County)
The Bisbee Observer (C)
7 Bisbee Rd., Suite L
Bisbee, AZ 85603
520/432-7254
www.thebisbeeobserver.com

The Bisbee C/C
31 Subway St.
Bisbee, AZ 85603
www.bisbeearizona.com
Benson (4,716)
Bisbee (5,985)
Douglas (16,441)
Huachuca City (1,786)
Sierra Vista (38,999)
Tombstone (1,537)
Willcox (3,741)

Bullhead City (part of Mohave County)
Mohave Valley Daily News (D)
2435 Miracle Mile
Bullhead City, AZ 86442
520/763-2505
www.mohavedailynews.com

Bullhead Area C/C
1251 Hwy. 95
Bullhead City, AZ 86429
928/754-4121
www.bullheadchamber.com
Bullhead City (21,951)
Golden Valley (2,619)
Mohave Valley (6,962)

Cottonwood–Verde Valley (part of Yavapai County)
Verde Independent (C)
116 S. Main St.
Cottonwood, AZ 86326
928/634-2241
www.verdevalleynews.com

Cottonwood/Verde Valley C/C
1010 S. Main St.
Cottonwood, AZ 86326
928/634-7593
http://cottonwood.verdevalley.com
Camp Verde (7,552)
Clarkdale (2,719)
Cornville (2,089)
Cottonwood (6,937)
Jerome (436)

Flagstaff (Coconino County)
Arizona Daily Sun (D)
1751 S. Thompson
Flagstaff, AZ 86001
928/774-4545
www.azdailysun.com

Flagstaff Visitor Center and C/C
One E. Route 66
Flagstaff, AZ 86001
928/774-9541
www.flagstaff.az.us
Flagstaff (55,173)
Fredonia (1,062)
Page (6,933)
Williams (2,915)

Kingman (part of Mohave County)
Kingman Daily Miner (D)
3015 Stockton Hill Rd.
Kingman, AZ 86401
928/753-6397
www.kingmandailyminer.com

Kingman Area C/C
120 W. Andy Devine Ave.
Kingman, AZ 86402
928/753-6253
www.kingmanchamber.org
Kingman (17,270)

Lake Havasu City (part of Mohave County)
Today's News-Herald (D)
2225 W. Acoma Blvd.
Lake Havasu City, AZ 86403
928/453-4237
www.havasunews.com

Lake Havasu Area C/C
314 London Bridge Rd.
Lake Havasu City, AZ 86403
928/855-4115
www.havasuchamber.com
Lake Havasu City (39,503)

Mesa (part of Maricopa County)
East Valley Tribune (D)
120 W. First Ave.
Mesa, AZ 85210
480/898-6500
www.aztrib.com

Mesa C/C
120 N. Center St.
Mesa, AZ 85201
480/969-1307
www.mesachamber.org
Mesa (344,764)

Payson (part of Gila County)
Payson Roundup (C)
708 N. Beeline Hwy.
Payson, AZ 85547
928/474-5251
www.paysonroundup.com

Rim Country Regional C/C
100 W. Main St.
Payson, AZ 85547
928/474-4515
www.rimcountrychamber.com
Payson (10,978)

Prescott–Prescott Valley (part of Yavapai County)
The Daily Courier (D)
147 N. Cortez
Prescott, AZ 86301
928/445-3333
www.prescottaz.com

Prescott C/C
117 W. Goodwin
Prescott, AZ 86302
928/445-2000
www.prescott.org

Prescott Valley C/C
3001 N. Main St.
Prescott Valley, AZ 86314
928/772-8857
www.pvchamber.org/chamber.htm
Bagdad (1,858)
Prescott (32,841)
Prescott Valley (16,919)

Scottsdale (part of Maricopa County)
East Valley Tribune (D)
7525 E. Camelback Rd.
Scottsdale, AZ 85251
480/970-2330
www.eastvalleytribune.com

Scottsdale CVB
7343 Scottsdale Mall
Scottsdale, AZ 85251
480/421-1004
www.scottsdalecvb.com
Scottsdale (179,012)

Sedona (part of Coconino and Yavapai counties)
Red Rock News (C)
298 Van Daren St.
Sedona, AZ 86001
928/282-6888
www.redrocknews.com/index.htm

Sedona–Oak Creek Canyon C/C
331 Forest Rd.
Sedona, AZ 86336
928/282-7722
www.sedonachamber.com
Rimrock (500)
Sedona (9,000)
Williams (2,706)

Tucson (Pima County)
Arizona Daily Star/Tucson Citizen (D)
4850 S. Park Ave.
Tucson, AZ 85726
520/573-4398
www.azstarnet.com

Tucson Metropolitan C/C
465 W. St. Mary's Rd.
Tucson, AZ 85701
520/792-1212
www.tucsonchamber.org
Ajo (2,919)
Avra Valley (3,403)
Catalina (4,864)
Flowing Wells (14,013)
Green Valley (13,231)
Marana (5,711)
Oro Valley (17,379)
Picture Rocks (4,026)
Pisinemo (341)
Santa Rosa (493)
Sells (2,750)
South Tucson (5,924)
Three Points (2,175)
Tucson (449,002)
Tucson Estates (2,662)
Valencia West (3,277)

Wickenburg (part of Maricopa County)
Wickenburg Sun (C)
180 N. Washington St.
Wickenburg, AZ 85358
928/684-5454
www.wickenburgsun.com

Wickenburg C/C
216 N. Frontier St.
Wickenburg, AZ 85390
928/684-5479
www.outwickenburgway.com
Wickenburg (5,312)

Yuma (Yuma County)
Yuma Daily Sun (D)
2055 S. Arizona Ave.
Yuma, AZ 85364
928/783-3333
www.yumasun.com

Yuma County C/C
180 W. 1st St.
Yuma, AZ 85364
928/782-2567
www.yumachamber.org
Fortuna Foothills (7,737)
San Luis (9,539)
Somerton (6,271)
Wellton (1,144)
Yuma (60,519)

ARKANSAS

Eureka Springs (Carroll County)
Eureka Springs Times-Echo (C)
Carroll County Newspapers
P.O. Box 232
Berryville, AR 72616
870/423-6636
www.eurekaspringstimesecho.com

Greater Eureka Springs C/C
137-B W. Van Buren
Eureka Springs, AR 72632
479/253-8737
www.eurekaspringschamber.com
- Beaver (109)
- Berryville (4,621)
- Blue Eye town (37)
- Eureka Springs (2,308)
- Green Forest (2,810)
- Oak Grove (389)

Fayetteville (Washington County)
Northwest Arkansas Times (D)
212 N. East Ave.
Fayetteville, AR 72701
479/442-1700
www.nwanews.com/times

Fayetteville C/C
123 W. Mountain St.
Fayetteville, AR 72702
501/521-1710
www.fayettevillear.com
- Elkins (934)
- Elm Springs (981)
- Farmington (2,156)
- Fayetteville (52,360)
- Goshen (705)
- Greenland (899)
- Johnson (1,516)
- Lincoln (1,545)
- Prairie Grove (2,120)
- Springdale (36,928)
- Tontitown (458)
- West Fork (1,919)
- Winslow (382)

Hot Springs (Garland County)
Sentinel-Record (D)
300 Spring St.
Hot Springs, AR 71901
501/623-7711
www.hotsr.com

Greater Hot Springs C/C
659 Ouachita
Hot Springs, AR 71902
501/321-1700
www.hotsprings.dina.org
- Hot Springs (32,462)
- Hot Springs Village (5,259)
- Lake Hamilton (1,331)
- Lonsdale (144)
- Mountain Pine (941)
- Piney (2,500)
- Rockwell (2,514)

Norfork Lake (Baxter County)
Baxter Bulletin (D)
16 W. 6th St.
Mountain Home, AR 72653
870/508-8000
www.baxterbulletin.com

Mountain Home Area C/C
1023 Hwy. 62 E.
Mountain Home, AR 72653
870/425-5111
www.mtnhomechamber.com
- Big Flat (102)
- Cotter (966)
- Gassville (1,386)
- Lakeview (664)
- Mountain Home (11,236)
- Norfork (620)
- Salesville (458)

CALIFORNIA

Amador County (Amador County)
Amador Ledger Dispatch (C)
10776 Argonaut Lane
Jackson, CA 95642
209/223-1767
www.ledger-dispatch.com

Amador County C/C
125 Peek St.
Jackson, CA 95642
209/223-0350
www.amadorcountychamber.com
- Amador City (198)
- Ione (6,849)
- Jackson (3,752)
- Plymouth (843)
- Sutter Creek (2,037)

Carmel–Pebble Beach (part of Monterey County)
Monterey County Herald (D)
8 Upper Ragsdale Dr.
Monterey, CA 93940
831/372-3311
www.montereyherald.com

Monterey Peninsula C/C
380 Alvarado St.
Monterey, CA 93940
831/648-5360
www.mpcc.com
Carmel (4,084)
Carmel Valley (4,407)
Monterey (27,722)
Pacific Grove (15,339)
Seaside (31,406)

Grass Valley–Nevada City (Nevada County)
The Union (D)
464 Sutton Way
Grass Valley, CA 95945
530/273-9561
www.theunion.com

Grass Valley/Nevada County C/C
248 Mill St.
Grass Valley, CA 95945
530/273-4667
www.grassvalleychamber.com

Nevada City C/C
132 Main St.
Nevada City, CA 95959
530/265-2692
www.nevadacitychamber.com
Alta Sierra (5,709)
Glenshire–Devonshire (2,133)
Grass Valley (9,566)
Lake of the Pines (3,890)
Nevada City (3,204)
Penn Valley (1,242)
Truckee (9,994)

Laguna Beach–Dana Point (part of Orange County)
Laguna Coastline Pilot (C)
384 Forest Ave.
Laguna Beach, CA 92651
949/494-4321
www.latimes.com/news/local/coastline

Laguna Beach C/C & VB
357 Glenneyre Ave.
Laguna Beach, CA 92651
949/494-1018
www.lagunabeachchamber.org
Aliso Viejo (7,612)
Dana Point (33,875)
Laguna Beach (24,641)
Laguna Hills (29,414)
Laguna Niguel (51,701)
Mission Viejo (84,689)

Mariposa (Mariposa County)
Mariposa Gazette (C)
5081 Jones St.
Mariposa, CA 95338
209/966-2500

Mariposa County C/C
5158 Hwy. 140
Mariposa, CA 95338
209/966-2456
www.mariposa.org
Bootjack (1,295)
Mariposa (1,152)

Mendocino–Fort Bragg (Mendocino County)
Fort Bragg Advocate News (C)
The Mendocino Beacon (C)
450 N. Franklin St.
P.O. Box 1188
Fort Bragg, CA 95437
707/964-5642
www.advocate-news.com
www.mendocinobeacon.com

Fort Bragg–Mendocino Coast C/C
332 North Main St.
P.O. Box 1141
Fort Bragg, CA 95437
www.mendocinocoast2.com
Fort Bragg (7,029)
Point Arena (475)
Ukiah (15,544)
Willits (5,096)

Morro Bay–Cambria (part of San Luis Obispo County)
San Luis Obispo County Telegram-Tribune (D)
3825 S. Higuera St.
San Luis Obispo, CA 93406
805/781-7800
www.sanluisobispo.com

Morro Bay Visitors Center and C/C
880 Main St.
Morro Bay, CA 93442
805/772-4467
www.morrobay.org

Cambria C/C
767 Main St.
Cambria, CA 93428
805/927-3624
www.cambriachamber.org
Arroyo Grande (14,914)
Baywood–Los Osos (14,377)
Cambria (5,382)
Cayucos (2,960)
Morro Bay (9,955)
Oceano (6,169)
Pismo Beach (8,127)
San Miguel (1,123)

North County San Diego (part of San Diego County)
North County Times (D)
207 E. Pennsylvania Ave.
Escondido, CA 92025
760/745-6611
www.nctimes.com

Vista C/C
201 Washington St.
Vista, CA 92084
760/726-1122
www.vistachamber.org

Oceanside C/C
928 N. Coast Hwy.
Oceanside, CA 92054
760/722-1534
www.oceansidechamber.com
Bonsall (1,881)
Carlsbad (69,069)
Chula Vista (151,963)
Encinitas (57,873)
Escondido (116,184)
Fallbrook (22,095)
Oceanside (145,941)
San Marcos (47,265)
Vista (78,494)

Oakhurst–Coarsegold (Madera County)
Madera Tribune (C)
100 E. Seventh St.
Madera, CA 93638
559/674-2424
www.maderatribune.com

Eastern Madera County C/C
49074 Civic Circle Dr.
Oakhurst, CA 93644
559/683-7766
www.oakhurstchamber.com
Bonadelle Ranchos–Madera (5,705)
Chowchilla (6,740)
Madera (35,648)
Madera Acres (5,245)
Oakhurst (2,602)
Parksdale (1,911)
Parkwood (1,659)
Yosemite Lakes (2,367)

Palm Springs–Coachella Valley (Riverside County)
Desert Sun (D)
750 N. Gene Autry Trail
Palm Springs, CA 92263
760/322-8889
www.thedesertsun.com

Palm Springs C/C
190 W. Amado Rd.
Palm Springs, CA 92262
760/325-1577
www.pschamber.org
Cathedral City (36,327)
Coachella (21,767)
Desert Hot Springs (14,819)
Indian Wells (3,065)
Indio (43,741)
La Quinta (17,987)
Moreno Valley (140,932)
Palm Desert (27,916)
Palm Desert Country (5,626)
Palm Springs (43,347)
Rancho Mirage (10,894)
Sun City (14,930)
Thousand Palms (4,122)

Paradise–Magalia (part of Butte County)
Paradise Post (C)
5399 Clark Rd
Paradise, CA 95969
530/877-4413
www.paradisepost.com

Paradise C/C
5587 Scottwood
Paradise, CA 95969
530/877-9356
www.paradisechamber.com
Magalia (8,987)
Paradise (25,630)

Santa Barbara (Santa Barbara County)
Santa Barbara News-Press (D)
715 Anacapa St.
Santa Barbara, CA 93101
805/564-5200
www.newspress.com

Santa Barbara Region C/C
924 Anacapa St., Suite 1
Santa Barbara, CA 93101
805/965-3023
www.sbchamber.org
Buellton (3,547)
Carpinteria (14,103)
Guadalupe (5,714)
Isla Vista (20,395)
Lompoc (40,925)
Mission Hills (3,112)
Santa Barbara (86,154)
Santa Maria (67,012)
Santa Ynez (4,200)
Solvang (4,933)
Vandenberg Village (5,971)

Santa Rosa (Sonoma County)
Press Democrat (D)
427 Mendocino Ave.
Santa Rosa, CA 95401
707/546-2020
www.pressdemocrat.com

Santa Rosa C/C
637 First St.
Santa Rosa, CA 95404
707/545-1414
www.santarosachamber.com
Bodega Bay (1,127)
Boyes Hot Springs (5,973)
Cloverdale (5,505)
Cotati (6,251)
El Verano (3,498)
Eldridge (1,144)
Forestville (2,443)
Glen Ellen (1,191)
Graton (1,409)
Guerneville (1,966)
Healdsburg (9,674)
Larkfield–Wikiup (6,779)
Monte Rio (1,058)
Occidental (1,300)
Petaluma (48,455)
Rohnert Park (39,477)
Roseland (8,779)
Santa Rosa (121,879)
Sebastopol (7,331)
Sonoma (8,737)
South Santa Rosa (4,128)
Temelec (1,594)
Windsor (13,228)

Sonora–Twain Harte (Tuolumne County)
Union Democrat (C)
84 S. Washington St.
Sonora, CA 95370
209/532-7151
www.uniondemocrat.com

Tuolumne County C/C
222 S. Shepherd St.
Sonora, CA 95370
209/532-4212
www.tcchamber.com
Columbia (1,799)
East Sonora (1,675)
Groveland–Big Oak Flat (2,753)
Jamestown (2,178)
Mi–Wuk Village (1,175)
Mono Vista (2,599)
Phoenix Lake–Cedar Ridge (3,569)
Sonora (4,217)
Soulsbyville (1,732)
Tuolumne City (1,686)
Twain Harte (2,170)

Victorville–Apple Valley (part of San Bernardino County)
Daily Press (D)
13891 Park Ave.
Victorville, CA 92393
760/241-7755
www.vvdailypress.com

Apple Valley C/C
17852 Hwy. 18
Apple Valley, CA 92307
760/242-2753
www.avchamber.org

Victorville C/C
14174 Green Tree Blvd.
Victorville, CA 92392
760/245-6506
www.vvchamber.com
Apple Valley (54,865)
Hesperia (60,635)
Twentynine Palms (14,157)
Upland (67,095)
Victorville (67,089)

COLORADO

Colorado Springs (El Paso County)
Colorado Springs Gazette Telegraph (D)
30 S. Prospect St.
Colorado Springs, CO 80903
719/632-5511
www.gazette.com

Greater Colorado Springs C/C
2 N. Cascade Ave., Suite 110
Colorado Springs, CO 80903
719/635-1551
www.coloradospringschamber.org
Black Forest (8,143)
Calhan (646)
Cascade–Chipita Park (1,479)
Cimarron Hills (11,160)
Colorado Springs (345,127)
Fort Carson (11,309)
Fountain (11,823)
Gleneagle (1,661)
Green Mountain Falls (672)
Manitou Springs (4,835)
Monument (1,125)
Palmer Lake (1,626)
Ramah (102)
Security–Widefield (23,822)
Stratmoor (5,854)
Woodmoor (3,858)

Delta County (Delta County)
Delta County Independent (C)
401 Meeker St.
Delta, CO 81416
970/874-4421
www.deltacountyindependent.com

Delta Area C/C
301 Main St.
Delta, CO 81416
970/874-8616
www.deltacolorado.org
Cedaredge (1,742)
Crawford (257)
Delta (4,235)
Hotchkiss (918)
Orchard City (2,731)
Paonia (1,603)

Durango (La Plata County)
Durango Herald (D)
1275 Main Ave.
Durango, CO 81301
970/247-3504
www.durangoherald.com

Durango Area Chamber Resort Association
111 S. Camino del Rio
Durango, CO 81302
970/247-0312
www.durangobusiness.org
Bayfield (1,576)
Durango (13,923)
Ignacio (791)

Fort Collins–Loveland (Larimer County)
Fort Collins Coloradoan (D)
1212 Riverside Ave.
Fort Collins, CO 80522
970/224-6397
www.coloradoan.com

Fort Collins Area C/C
225 S. Meldrum St.
Fort Collins, CO 80521
970/482-3746
www.fcchamber.org

***Loveland Daily Reporter-Herald* (D)**
201 E. Fifth St.
Loveland, CO 80537
970/669-5050
www.lovelandfyi.com

Loveland C/C
5400 Stone Creek Circle, Suite 200
Loveland, CO 80538
970/667-6311
www.loveland.org
Berthoud (3,904)
Campion (1,692)
Estes Park (3,989)
Fort Collins (104,196)
Loveland (44,923)
Timnath (220)
Wellington (1,362)

Grand Junction (Mesa County)
Daily Sentinel (D)
734 S. Seventh St.
Grand Junction, CO 81501
970/242-5050
www.gjsentinel.com

Grand Junction Area C/C
740 Horizon Dr.
Grand Junction, CO 81506
800/962-2547
www.visitgrandjunction.com
Clifton (12,671)
Collbran (272)
De Beque (275)
Fruita (4,285)
Fruitvale (5,222)
Grand Junction (34,540)
Orchard Mesa (5,977)
Palisade (1,979)
Redlands (9,355)

Montrose (Montrose County)
Montrose Daily Press (D)
535 S. First St.
Montrose, CO 81401
970/249-3444
www.montrosepress.com

Montrose C/C
1519 E. Main St.
Montrose, CO 81401
970/249-5000
www.montrosechamber.com
Olathe (1,483)
Naturita (491)
Nucla (715)
Montrose (11,003)

Pagosa Springs (Archuleta County)
Pagosa Springs Sun (C)
466 Pagosa St.
Pagosa Springs, CO 81147
970/264-2101
www.pagosasun.com

Pagosa Springs Area C/C
402 San Juan St.
Pagosa Springs, CO 81147
970/264-2360
www.pagosaspringschamber.com
Pagosa Springs (1,584)

Salida (Chaffee County)
The Mountain Mail (D)
Salida, CO 81201
719/539-6691
www.themountainmail.com

Heart of the Rockies C/C
406 W. Hwy. 50
Salida, Co 81201
719/539-2068
www.salidachamber.org
Buena Vista (2,213)
Poncha Springs (474)
Salida (5,557)

CONNECTICUT

Litchfield Hills (part of Litchfield County)
Litchfield Enquirer (C)
43 West St.
Litchfield, CT 06759
860/567-8766
www.zwire.com/site/news.cfm?brd=1658

Northwest Connecticut C/C
333 Kennedy Dr., Suite R101
Torrington, CT 06790
860/482-6586
www.northwestchamber.org
Canaan (1,056)
Cornwall (1,485)
Goshen (2,431)
Kent (3,051)
Litchfield (8,593)
Salisbury (4,111)
Sharon (2,965)

DELAWARE

Rehoboth Bay–Indian River Bay (Sussex County)
Cape Gazette (D)
Rehoboth Beach, DE 19971
302/226-2273
www.capegazette.com

Rehoboth Beach–Dewey Beach C/C
501 Rehoboth Ave.
Rehoboth Beach, DE 19971
302/227-8351
www.beach-fun.com
Bethany Beach (345)
Bethel (193)
Blades (929)
Bridgeville (1,327)
Dagsboro (438)
Delmar (1,038)
Dewey Beach (216)
Ellendale (346)
Fenwick Island (198)
Frankford (649)
Georgetown (4,092)
Greenwood (631)
Henlopen Acres (114)
Laurel (3,571)
Lewes (2,505)
Long Neck (886)
Milford (3,943)
Millsboro (1,898)
Millville (226)
Milton (1,561)
Ocean View (658)
Rehoboth Beach (1,319)
Seaford (6,400)
Selbyville (1,516)
Slaughter Beach (124)
South Bethany (158)

FLORIDA

Apalachicola (Franklin County)
Apalachicola Times (C)
82 Market St.
Apalachicola, FL 32320
850/653-8868
www.apalachtimes.com

Apalachicola Bay C/C
99 Market St. #100
Apalachicola, FL 32320
850/653-9419
www.apalachicolabay.org
Apalachicola (2,350)
Carrabelle (1,315)

Boca Raton (part of Palm Beach County)
The News (D)
33 SE Third St.
Boca Raton, FL 33432
561/893-6400
www.bocanews.com

Greater Boca Raton C/C
1800 N. Dixie Hwy.
Boca Raton, FL 33432
561/395-4433
www.bocaratonchamber.com
Boca Raton (68,507)
Boca West (2,847)
Boynton Beach (50,742)
Delray Beach (50,720)
Lake Worth (28,491)
Lantana (8,470)

Bradenton (Manatee County)
Bradenton Herald (D)
102 Manatee Ave. W.
Bradenton, FL 34205
941/748-0411
www.bradenton.com/mld/bradentonherald

Manatee C/C
222 10th St. W.
Bradenton, FL 34206
941/748-3411
www.manateechamber.com
Anna Maria (1,813)
Bayshore Gardens (17,062)
Bradenton (47,219)
Bradenton Beach (1,639)
Cortez (4,509)

Ellenton (2,573)
Holmes Beach (4,871)
Memphis (6,760)
Palmetto (10,052)
Samoset (3,119)
South Bradenton (20,398)
West Bradenton (4,528)
West Samoset (3,819)
Whitfield (3,152)

Daytona Beach (Volusia County)
News-Journal (D)
901 Sixth St.
Daytona Beach, FL 32117
386/252-1511
www.n-jcenter.com

Daytona Beach–Halifax Area C/C
126 E. Orange Ave.
Daytona Beach, FL 32114
386/255-0981
www.daytonachamber.com
Daytona Beach (65,203)
Daytona Beach Shores (3,046)
De Bary (7,176)
De Leon Springs (1,481)
DeLand (18,607)
DeLand Southwest (1,249)
Deltona (50,828)
Edgewater (17,445)
Glencoe (2,282)
Holly Hill (11,512)
Lake Helen (2,508)
New Smyrna Beach (17,995)
North De Land (1,493)
Oak Hill (1,062)
Orange City (5,967)
Ormond Beach (32,266)
Ormond-by-the-Sea (8,157)
Pierson (3,084)
Ponce Inlet (2,200)
Port Orange (41,387)
Samsula–Spruce Creek (3,404)
South Daytona (13,231)
West DeLand (3,389)

Fort Myers–Cape Coral (Lee County)
News-Press (D)
2442 Martin Luther King, Jr. Blvd.
Fort Myers, FL 33901
239/335-0200
www.news-press.com

Greater Fort Myers C/C
2310 Edwards Dr.
Fort Myers, FL 33902
239/332-3624
www.fortmyers.org
Alva (1,036)
Bonita Springs (13,600)
Cape Coral (88,053)
Cypress Lake (10,491)
Estero (3,177)
Forest Island Park (5,988)
Fort Myers (45,917)
Fort Myers Beach (9,284)
Fort Myers Shores (5,460)
Iona (9,565)
Lehigh Acres (13,611)
Lochmoor Waterway (4,091)
McGregor (6,504)
Morse Shores (3,771)
North Fort Myers (30,027)
Page Park–Pine Manor (5,116)
Punta Rassa (1,493)
St. James City (1,904)
San Carlos Park (11,785)
Sanibel (5,584)
Suncoast Estates (4,483)
Tice (3,971)
Villas (9,898)
Whiskey Creek (5,061)

Gainesville (Alachua County)
Gainesville Sun (D)
2700 SW Thirteenth St.
Gainesville, FL 32608
352/378-1411
www.gainesvillesun.com

Gainesville Area C/C
300 E. University Ave.
Gainesville, FL 32601
352/334-7100
www.gainesvillechamber.com
Alachua (5,274)
Archer (1,373)
Gainesville (87,295)
Hawthorne (1,375)
High Springs (3,237)
La Crosse (140)
Micanopy (632)
Newberry (1,834)
Waldo (985)

Inverness (Citrus County)
Citrus County Chronicle (D)
1624 N. Meadowcrest Blvd.
Crystal River, FL 34429
352/563-6363
www.chronicleonline.com

Citrus County C/C
208 W. Main St.
Inverness, FL 34450
352/726-2801
www.citruscountychamber.com
Beverly Hills (6,163)
Citrus Springs (2,213)
Crystal River (4,200)
Floral City (2,609)
Hernando (2,103)
Homosassa (2,113)
Homosassa Springs (6,271)
Inverness (6,786)
Lecanto (1,243)
Sugarmill Woods (4,073)

Key West (Monroe County)
Key West Citizen (D)
3420 Northside Dr.
Key West, FL 33040
305/292-7777
http://keysnews.com

Key West C/C
402 Wall St.
Key West, FL 33040
305/294-2587
www.keywestchamber.org
Islamorada (6,846)
Key Colony Beach (804)
Key West (25,273)
Marathon (10,199)

Kissimmee–St. Cloud (Osceola County)
Osceola News Gazette (C)
108 Church St.
Kissimmee, FL 34741
407/846-7600
www.oscnewsgazette.com

Kissimmee/Osceola County C/C
1425 E. Vine St.
Kissimmee, FL 34744
407/847-3174
www.kissimmeechamber.com
Buena Ventura Lakes (14,148)
Campbell (3,884)
Kissimmee (36,510)
Poinciana Place (3,618)
St. Cloud (14,489)

Lakeland–Winter Haven (Polk County)
The Ledger (D)
300 W. Lime St.
Lakeland, FL 33811
863/802-7323
www.theledger.com

Lakeland Area C/C
35 Lake Morton Dr.
Lakeland, FL 33802
863/688-8551
www.lakelandchamber.com

Winter Haven Area C/C
401 Ave. B NW
Winter Haven, FL 33881
863/293-2138
www.winterhavenfl.com
Auburndale (9,466)
Babson Park (1,125)
Bartow (15,003)
Combee Settlement (5,463)
Crooked Lake Park (1,575)
Crystal Lake (5,300)
Cypress Gardens (9,188)
Davenport (1,625)
Dundee (2,518)
Eagle Lake (1,769)
Fort Meade (5,246)
Frostproof (2,913)
Fussels Corner (3,840)
Gibsonia (5,168)
Haines City (12,352)
Highland City (1,919)
Highland Park (145)
Hillcrest Heights (210)
Inwood (6,824)
Jan Phyl Village (5,308)
Kathleen (2,743)
Lake Alfred (3,711)
Lake Hamilton (1,145)
Lake Wales (9,930)
Lakeland (73,157)
Lakeland Highlands (9,972)
Loughman (1,214)
Medulla (3,977)
Mulberry (3,040)
Polk City (1,640)
Wahneta (4,024)
Waverly (2,071)
Willow Oak (4,017)
Winston (9,118)
Winter Haven (25,484)

Largo (part of Pinellas County)
St. Petersburg Times (D)
490 First Ave. S.
St. Petersburg, FL 33701
727/893-8111
www.sptimes.com

Greater Largo C/C
151 3rd St. NW
Largo, FL 33770
727/584-2321
www.largococ.com
Belleair (3,983)
Belleair Beach (2,012)
Belleair Bluffs (2,158)
Indian Rocks Beach (4,146)
Largo (65,793)

Leesburg–Mount Dora (Lake County)
Daily Commercial (D)
212 E. Main St.
Leesburg, FL 34748
352/365-8200
www.dailycommercial.com

Leesburg Area C/C
103 South 6th St.
Leesburg, FL 34748
352/787-2131
www.leesburgchamber.com
Astatula (1,261)
Astor (1,273)
Bassville Park (2,752)
Clermont (7,073)
Eustis (14,422)

Fruitland Park (2,988)
Groveland (2,350)
Hawthorne (1,804)
Howey-in-the-Hills (904)
Lady Lake (12,315)
Leesburg (16,416)
Mascotte (2,478)
Mid Florida Lakes (2,776)
Minneola (1,900)
Montverde (902)
Mount Dora (8,766)
Mount Plymouth (1,752)
Oakland Park (1,743)
Silver Lake (1,573)
Sunnyside (1,008)
Tavares (8,261)
Umatilla (2,517)
Yalaha (1,168)

Melbourne–Palm Bay (Brevard County)
Florida Today (D)
One Gannett Plaza
Melbourne, FL 32940
321/242-3500
www.floridatoday.com

Melbourne–Palm Bay Area C/C
1005 E. Strawbridge Ave.
Melbourne, FL 32901
321/724-5400
www.melpb-chamber.org
Cape Canaveral (8,377)
Cocoa (18,279)
Cocoa Beach (12,635)
Cocoa West (6,160)
Indialantic (2,930)
Indian Harbour Beach (7,530)
June Park (4,080)
Malabar (2,425)
Melbourne (67,631)
Melbourne Beach (3,172)
Melbourne Village (622)
Merritt Island (32,886)
Micco (8,757)
Mims (9,412)
Palm Bay (74,982)
Palm Shores (414)
Port St. John (8,933)
Rockledge (18,899)
Satellite Beach (10,093)
Sharpes (3,348)
South Patrick Shores (10,249)
Titusville (41,543)
West Melbourne (9,144)

Naples (Collier County)
Naples Daily News (D)
1075 Central Ave.
Naples, FL 34102
239/263-4470
www.naplesnews.com

Naples Area C/C
3620 Tamiami Trail N.
Naples, FL 34103
239/262-6141
www.naples-florida.com
East Naples (22,951)
Everglades (314)
Golden Gate (14,148)
Immokalee (14,120)
Lely (3,014)
Marco (9,493)
Naples (19,777)
Naples Manor (4,574)
Naples Park (8,002)
North Naples (13,422)
Palm River (3,507)

New Port Richey (Pasco County)
Suncoast News (C)
6241 US Hwy. 19
New Port Richey, FL 34652
727/815-1000

West Pasco C/C
5443 Main St.
New Port Richey, FL 34652
727/842-7651
www.westpasco.com
Bayonet Point (21,860)
Beacon Square (6,265)
Dade City (5,867)
Dade City North (3,058)
Elfers (12,356)
Holiday (19,360)
Hudson (7,344)
Jasmine Estates (17,136)
Lacoochee (2,072)
Land O' Lakes (7,892)
New Port Richey (14,797)
New Port Richey East (9,683)
Port Richey (2,634)
St. Leo (688)
San Antonio (875)
Zephyrhills (8,991)

Ocala (Marion County)
Ocala Star-Banner (D)
2121 SW 19th Ave.
Ocala, FL 34474
352/867-4010
www.starbanner.com

Ocala–Marion County C/C
110 E. Silver Springs Blvd.
Ocala, FL 34470
352/629-8051
www.ocalacc.com
Belleview (2,852)
Dunnellon (1,855)
McIntosh (438)
Ocala (44,975)
Reddick (565)
Silver Springs Shores (6,421)

Panama City (Bay County)
News Herald (D)
501 W. 11th St.
Panama City, FL 32402
850/747-5050
www.newsherald.com

Bay County C/C
235 W. 5th St.
Panama City, FL 32402
850/785-5206
www.panamacity.org
Callaway (13,060)
Cedar Grove (1,601)
Hiland Park (3,865)
Laguna Beach (1,876)
Lower Grand Lagoon (3,329)
Lynn Haven (11,722)
Mexico Beach (1,033)
Panama City (35,986)
Panama City Beach (5,214)
Parker (4,880)
Pretty Bayou (3,839)
Springfield (9,312)
Upper Grand Lagoon (7,855)

Pensacola (Escambia County)
Pensacola News-Journal (D)
101 E. Romana St.
Pensacola, FL 32574
850/435-8500
www.pensacolanewsjournal.com

Pensacola Area C/C
117 W. Garden St.
Pensacola, FL 32593
850/438-4081
www.pensacolachamber.com
Bellview (19,386)
Brent (21,624)
Century (1,989)
Ensley (16,362)
Ferry Pass (26,301)
Gonzalez (7,669)
Goulding (4,159)
Molino (1,207)
Myrtle Grove (17,402)
Pensacola (59,162)
Warrington (16,040)
West Pensacola (22,107)

Port Charlotte (Charlotte County)
Sun Herald (D)
23170 Harborview Rd.
Charlotte Harbor, FL 33980
941/629-2805
www.sun-herald.com

Charlotte County C/C
2702 Tamiami Trail
Port Charlotte, FL 33952
941/627-2222
www.charlottecountychamber.org
Charlotte Harbor (3,327)
Charlotte Park (2,225)
Cleveland (2,896)
Grove City (2,374)
Harbour Heights (2,523)
Manasota Key (1,395)
Port Charlotte (41,535)
Punta Gorda (12,552)
Rotonda (3,576)
Solana (1,128)

St. Augustine (St. Johns County)
St. Augustine Record (D)
One News Place
St. Augustine, FL 32086
904/829-6562
www.staugustinerecord.com

St. Augustine/St. Johns County C/C
One Riberia St.
St. Augustine, FL 32084
904/829-5681
www.staugustinechamber.com
Butler Beach (3,377)
Crescent Beach (1,081)
Fruit Cove (5,904)
Hastings (784)
Palm Valley (9,960)
St. Augustine (12,167)
St. Augustine Beach (4,232)
St. Augustine Shores (4,411)
St. Augustine South (4,218)
Sawgrass (2,999)
Villano Beach (1,867)

Sarasota (Sarasota County)
Sarasota Herald-Tribune (D)
801 S. Tamiami Trail
Sarasota, FL 34236
941/953-7755
www.heraldtribune.com

Greater Sarasota C/C
1945 Fruitville Rd.
Sarasota, FL 34236
941/955-8187
www.sarasotachamber.org
Bee Ridge (6,406)
Desoto Lakes (2,807)
Englewood (10,079)
Fruitville (9,808)
Gulf Gate Estates (11,622)
Kensington Park (3,026)
Lake Sarasota (4,117)
Laurel (8,245)
Longboat Key (3,524)
Nokomis (3,448)

North Port (15,233)
North Sarasota (6,702)
Osprey (2,597)
Plantation (1,885)
Ridge Wood Heights (4,851)
Sarasota (50,891)
Sarasota Springs (16,088)
Siesta Key (7,772)
South Gate Ridge (5,924)
South Sarasota (5,298)
South Venice (11,951)
Southgate (7,324)
The Meadows (3,437)
Vamo (3,325)
Venice (17,707)
Venice Gardens (7,701)
Warm Mineral Springs (4,041)

Sebring–Avon Park (Highlands County)
Highlands Today (D)
231 US Hwy. 27 N.
Sebring, FL 33870
863/382-1163
www.highlandstoday.com

***News Sun* (C)**
203 W. Main St.
Avon Park, FL 33825
863/453-5500

Greater Sebring C/C
309 S. Circle
Sebring, FL 33870
863/385-8448
www.sebringflchamber.com

Avon Park C/C
28 E. Main St.
Avon Park, FL 33825
863/453-3350
www.apfla.com
Avon Park (8,101)
Lake Placid (1,279)
Placid Lakes (2,045)
Sebring (8,849)
Sylvan Shores (2,155)

Vero Beach (Indian River County)
Press-Journal (D)
1801 US Hwy. 1
Vero Beach, FL 32960
772/562-2315
www.pressjournal.com

Vero Beach–Indian River County C/C
1216 21st St.
Vero Beach, FL 32960
772/567-3491
www.indianriverchamber.com
Fellsmere (2,263)
Florida Ridge (12,218)
Gifford (6,278)
Indian River Shores (2,383)
Roseland (1,379)
Sebastian (13,014)
South Beach (2,754)
Vero Beach (16,458)
Vero Beach South (16,973)
Wabasso (1,145)

GEORGIA

Athens (Clarke County)
Athens Banner Herald/Daily News (D)
One Press Place
Athens, GA 30601
706/549-0123
www.onlineathens.com

Athens Area C/C
246 W. Hancock Ave.
Athens, GA 30601
706/549-6800
www.athenschamber.net
Athens (45,734)
Gaines School (11,354)
Winterville (1,000)

Rabun County (Rabun County)
Clayton Tribune (C)
120 N. Main St.
Clayton, GA 30525
706/782-3312
www.theclaytontribune.com

Rabun County C/C
232 Hwy. 441
Clayton, GA 30525
706/782-4812
www.gamountains.com
Clayton (1,699)
Dillard (190)
Mountain City (797)
Sky Valley (180)
Tiger (292)

St. Simons–Jekyll Islands (Glynn County)
Brunswick News (D)
3011 Altama Ave.
Brunswick, GA 31521
912/265-3885
www.thebrunswicknews.com

Brunswick–Golden Isles C/C
4 Glynn Ave.
Brunswick, GA 31520
912/265-0620
www.bgicoc.com
Brunswick (15,525)
Country Club Estates (7,500)
Dock Junction (7,094)
St. Simons (12,026)

Savannah (Chatham County)
Savannah Morning News (D)
111 W. Bay St.
Savannah, GA 31401
912/236-9511
www.savannahnow.com

Savannah Area C/C
222 W. Oglethorpe Ave. #100
Savannah, GA 31402
912/944-6400
www.savannahchamber.com
Bloomingdale (2,180)
Garden City (7,591)
Georgetown (5,554)
Isle of Hope–Dutch Island (2,637)
Montgomery (4,327)
Pooler (5,174)
Port Wentworth (3,971)
Savannah (136,262)
Skidaway Island (4,495)
Thunderbolt (2,859)
Tybee Island (2,949)
Vernonburg (139)
Whitemarsh Island (2,824)
Wilmington Island (11,230)

Thomasville (Thomas County)
Times-Enterprise (D)
106 South St.
Thomasville, GA 31792
912/226-2400
www.timesenterprise.com

Thomasville–Thomas County C/C
401 S. Broad St.
Thomasville, GA 31799
912/226-9600
www.thomasvillechamber.com
Barwick (286)
Boston (1,390)
Coolidge (694)
Meigs (1,196)
Ochlocknee (662)
Pavo (479)
Thomasville (17,565)

HAWAII

Kauai (Kauai County)
The Garden Island (D)
3137 Kuhio Hwy.
Lihue, HI 96766
808/245-3681
www.kauaiworld.com

Kaua'i C/C
2970 Kele St., Suite 112
Lihu'e, HI 96766
808/245-7363
www.kauaichamber.org
Anahola (1,181)
Eleele (1,489)
Hanalei (461)
Hanamaulu (3,611)
Hanapepe (1,395)
Kalaheo (3,592)
Kalihiwai (435)
Kapaa (8,149)
Kaumakani (803)
Kekaha (3,506)
Kilauea (1,685)
Koloa (1,791)
Lawai (1,787)
Lihue (5,536)
Omao (1,142)
Pakala Village (565)
Poipu (975)
Princeville (1,244)
Puhi (1,210)
Wailua (2,018)
Wailua Homesteads (3,870)
Waimea (1,840)

Maui (Maui County)
Maui News (D)
100 Mahalani St.
Wailuku, HI 96793
808/244-3981, 800/827-0347
www.mauinews.com

Maui C/C
250 Alamaha, Unit N-16A
Kahului, Maui, HI 96732
808/871-7711
www.mauichamber.com
Haiku–Pauwela (4,509)
Haliimaile (841)
Hana (683)
Kaanapali (579)
Kahului (16,889)
Kapalua (408)
Kaunakakai (2,658)
Kihei (11,107)
Kualapuu (1,661)
Lahaina (9,073)
Lanai City (2,400)
Maalaea (443)
Makawao (5,405)
Maunaloa (405)
Napili–Honokowai (4,332)
Paia (2,091)
Pukalani (5,879)
Waihee–Waiehue (4,004)
Waikapu (729)
Wailea–Makena (3,799)
Wailuku (10,688)

IDAHO

Coeur d'Alene (Kootenai County)
Coeur d'Alene Press (D)
201 N. 2nd St.
Coeur d'Alene, ID 83814
208/664-8176
www.cdapress.com

Coeur d'Alene Area C/C
1621 N. 3rd St.
Coeur d'Alene, ID 83816
208/664-3194
www.coeurdalenechamber.com
Athol (461)
Coeur d'Alene (31,076)
Dalton Gardens (2,388)
Fernan Lake Village (195)
Harrison (236)
Hauser (486)
Hayden (7,951)
Hayden Lake (474)
Huetter (101)
Post Falls (14,303)
Rathdrum (3,409)
Spirit Lake (840)
State Line (35)
Worley (1,201)

Ketchum–Sun Valley (Blaine County)
Idaho Mountain Express (C)
591 First Ave. N.
Ketchum, ID 83340
208/726-8060
www.mtexpress.com/index2.htm

Sun Valley–Ketchum C/C
Box 2420
Sun Valley, ID 83353
208/726-3423, 800/634-3347
www.visitsunvalley.com
Bellevue (1,491)
Hailey (5,423)
Ketchum (2,743)
Sun Valley (1,013)

McCall (Valley County)
Star-News (C)
1000 1st St.
McCall, ID 83638
208/634-2123
www.webdms.com/~starnews

McCall C/C
102 N. 3rd St.
McCall, ID 83638
208/634-7631
www.mccall-idchamber.org
Cascade (1,059)
Donnelly (166)
McCall (2,876)

Sandpoint–Lake Pend Oreille (Bonner County)
Daily Bee (D)
310 Church
Sandpoint, ID 83864
208/263-9534
www.bonnercountydailybee.com

Greater Sandpoint C/C
900 N. 5th Ave.
Sandpoint, ID 83864
208/263-0887, 800/800-2106
www.sandpointchamber.org
Clark Fork (582)
Dover (375)
East Hope (280)
Hope (123)
Kootenai (377)
Oldtown (204)
Ponderay (529)
Priest River (1,783)
Sandpoint (6,748)

INDIANA

Brown County (Brown County)
Brown County Democrat (C)
147 E. Main St.
Nashville, IN 47448
812/988-2221
www.browncountyindiana.com

Brown County CVB
37 W. Main St.
Nashville, IN 47448
812/988-7303
www.browncounty.com
Nashville (935)

IOWA

Iowa City (Johnson County)
Iowa City Press Citizen (D)
1725 N. Dodge St.
Iowa City, IA 52245
319/337-3181
www.press-citizen.com

Iowa City Area C/C
325 E. Washington St.
Iowa City, IA 52244
319/337-9637
www.iowacityarea.com
Coralville (11,789)
Hills (669)
Iowa City (60,923)
Lone Tree (1,021)
North Liberty (4,039)
Oxford (648)
Shueyville (217)
Solon (1,059)
Swisher (729)
Tiffin (557)
University Heights (953)

KENTUCKY

Murray–Kentucky Lake (Calloway County)
Murray Ledger & Times (D)
1001 Whitnell Ave.
Murray, KY 42071
270/753-1916
www.murrayledger.com

Murray–Calloway County C/C
805 N. 12th St.
Murray, KY 42071
270/753-5188
www.murraylink.com
Hazel (472)
Murray (15,316)

LOUISIANA

Natchitoches (Natchitoches Parish)
Natchitoches Times (D)
P.O. Box 904
Natchitoches, LA 71457
www.natchitochestimes.com

Natchitoches C/C
550 2nd St.
Natchitoches, LA 71458
318/352-6894
www.natchitocheschamber.com
Ashland village (287)
Campti (1,059)
Clarence village (501)
Goldonna village (453)
Natchez village (584)
Natchitoches (17,714)
Provencal village (706)
Robeline village (181)

Western St. Tammany Parish (part of St. Tammany Parish)
News-Banner (C)
19290 19th Ave.
Covington, LA 70433
985/892-7980
www.newsbanner.com

St. Tammany-West C/C
201 Holiday Blvd., Suite 108
Covington, LA 70433
985/892-3216
www.sttammanychamber.org
Abita Springs (1,636)
Covington (8,576)
Mandeville (8,677)

MAINE

Bar Harbor (Hancock County)
Bar Harbor Times (C)
76 Cottage St.
Bar Harbor, ME 04609
207/288-3311
www.courierpub.com/barharbortimes

Bar Harbor C/C
93 Cottage St.
Bar Harbor, ME 04609
207/288-5103
www.barharbormaine.com
Amherst (262)
Aurora (93)
Bar Harbor (4,571)
Blue Hill (2,235)
Brooklin (899)
Brooksville (867)
Bucksport (4,925)
Castine (1,224)
Cranberry Isles (214)
Dedham (1,247)
Deer Isle (1,829)
Eastbrook (289)
Ellsworth (6,292)
Franklin (1,166)
Frenchboro (43)
Gouldsboro (2,101)
Great Pond (65)
Hancock (1,902)
Lamoine (1,404)
Mariaville (278)
Mount Desert (1,985)
Orland (1,780)
Osborn (69)
Otis (407)
Penobscot (1,175)
Sedgwick (1,048)
Sorrento (342)
Southwest Harbor (2,096)
Stonington (1,265)
Sullivan (1,208)
Surry (1,077)
Swans Island (399)
Tremont (1,357)
Trenton (1,178)
Verona (526)
Waltham (327)
Winter Harbor (1,145)

Camden (Knox County)
Camden Herald (C)
69 Elm St.
Camden, ME 04843
207/236-8511
www.courierpub.com/camdenherald

Rockport–Camden–Lincolnville C/C
Public Landing
Camden, ME 04843
207/236-4404
www.camdenme.org/index.html
- Appleton (1,191)
- Camden (5,096)
- Cushing (1,178)
- Friendship (1,087)
- Hope (1,138)
- Isle au Haut (53)
- North Haven (343)
- Owls Head (1,645)
- Rockland (7,905)
- Rockport (3,020)
- St. George (2,372)
- South Thomaston (1,325)
- Thomaston (3,313)
- Union (2,020)
- Vinalhaven (1,118)
- Warren (3,379)
- Washington (1,226)

York Beaches (York County)
York County Coast Star (C)
17 Woodbridge Rd.
York, ME 03909
207/985-2961
www.seacoastonline.com/news/yorkstar/index.htm

Greater York Region C/C
One Stonewall Lane
York, ME 03909
207/363-4422
www.gatewaytomaine.org
- Acton (1,769)
- Alfred (2,352)
- Arundel (3,038)
- Berwick (6,226)
- Biddeford (20,788)
- Buxton (7,039)
- Cornish (1,359)
- Dayton (1,536)
- Eliot (5,518)
- Hollis (3,855)
- Kennebunk (8,787)
- Kennebunkport (3,411)
- Kittery (9,156)
- Lebanon (4,491)
- Limerick (1,883)
- Limington (3,080)
- Lyman (3,656)
- Newfield (1,110)
- North Berwick (3,987)
- Ogunquit (974)
- Old Orchard Beach (7,712)
- Parsonsfield (1,613)
- Saco (15,681)
- Sanford (20,801)
- Shapleigh (1,936)
- South Berwick (6,112)
- Waterboro (5,289)
- Wells (8,148)
- York (10,162)

MARYLAND

Annapolis (part of Anne Arundel County)
The Capital (D)
2000 Capital Dr.
Annapolis, MD 21401
410/268-5000
www.hometownannapolis.com

Annapolis & Anne Arundel County C/C
151 West St., Suite 101
Annapolis, MD 21401
410/268-7676
www.annapolischamber.com
- Annapolis (33,234)
- Arden-on-the-Severn (2,427)
- Arnold (20,261)
- Cape St. Claire (7,878)
- Crofton (12,781)
- Crownsville (1,514)
- Herald Harbor (1,707)
- Mayo (2,537)
- Riva (3,438)
- Riviera Beach (11,376)
- Selby-on-the-Bay (3,101)
- Severn (24,499)
- Severna Park (25,879)

Chestertown (Kent County)
Kent County News (C)
217 High St.
Chestertown, MD 21620
410/778-2011

Chestertown & Kent County C/C
122 N. Cross St.
Chestertown, MD 21620
410/810-2968
www.kentchamber.org
- Betterton (357)
- Chestertown (4,644)
- Galena (438)
- Rock Hall (2,077)

Easton–St. Michaels (Talbot County)
Star-Democrat (D)
29088 Airpark Dr.
Easton, MD 21601
410/822-1500
www.zwire.com/site/news.cfm?brd=2101

Talbot County C/C
Easton Plaza Suite 53
Easton, MD 21601
410/822-4653
www.talbotchamber.org
- Easton (10,195)
- Oxford (701)
- St. Michaels (1,262)
- Trappe (1,084)

Ocean City (Worcester County)
Maryland Times-Press (C)
115 E. Carroll St.
Salisbury, MD 21801
410/249-7171
www.delmarvanow.com/oceancity

Ocean City C/C
12320 Ocean Gateway
Ocean City, MD 21842
410/213-0552
www.oceancity.org
Berlin (3,050)
Ocean City (6,766)
Ocean Pines (4,251)
Pocomoke City (4,074)
Snow Hill (2,305)
West Ocean City (1,928)

MASSACHUSETTS

Martha's Vineyard (Dukes County)
Vineyard Gazette (C)
34 S. Summer St.
Edgartown, MA 02539
www.mvgazette.com

Martha's Vineyard C/C
P.O. Box 1698
Vineyard Haven, MA 02568
508/693-0085
www.mvy.com
Aquinnah (353)
Chilmark (889)
Edgartown (3,881)
Gosnold (87)
Oak Bluffs (3,797)
Tisbury (3,833)
West Tisbury (2,591)

Middle Cape Cod (part of Barnstable County)
Cape Cod Times (D)
319 Main St.
Hyannis, MA 02601
508/775-1200
www.capecodonline.com/cctimes

Falmouth–Cape Cod C/C
20 Academy Lane
Falmouth, MA 02541
508/548-8500
www.falmouth-capecod.com
Barnstable (40,949)
Bourne (17,529)
Brewster (9,261)
Chatham (6,930)
Dennis (14,423)
Eastham (4,855)
Falmouth (30,451)
Harwich (11,328)
Mashpee (8,935)
Orleans (6,185)
Sandwich (17,916)
Truro (1,729)
Wellfleet (2,713)
Yarmouth (22,335)

Northampton–Amherst (Hampshire County)
Daily Hampshire Gazette (D)
115 Conz St.
Northampton, MA 01061
413/584-5000
www.gazettenet.com

Greater Northampton C/C
99 Pleasant St.
Northampton, MA 01060
413/584-1900
www.northamptonuncommon.com

Amherst Area C/C
409 Main St.
Amherst, MA 01002
413/253-0700
www.hidden-hills.com/amherstchamber
Amherst (35,468)
Belchertown (11,756)
Chesterfield (1,121)
Cummington (793)
Easthampton (15,744)
Goshen (851)
Granby (5,850)
Hadley (4,367)
Hatfield (3,243)
Huntington (2,126)
Middlefield (448)
Northampton (28,838)
Pelham (1,428)
Plainfield (609)
South Hadley (17,047)
Southampton (4,853)
Ware (9,817)
Westhampton (1,448)
Williamsburg (2,593)
Worthington (1,210)

Southern Berkshire County (part of Berkshire County)
Berkshire Record (C)
21 Elm St.
Great Barrington, MA 01230
413/528-5380

Berkshire Eagle (D)
75 S. Church St.
Pittsfield, MA 01201
413/496-6355
www.berkshireeagle.com

Southern Berkshire C/C
362 Main St.
Great Barrington, MA 01230
413/528-1510
www.greatbarrington.org

Becket (1,481)
Great Barrington (7,656)
Lee (5,743)
Lenox (5,022)
Monterey (801)
New Marlborough (1,240)
Otis (1,071)
Sandisfield (661)
Sheffield (2,967)
Stockbridge (2,339)
Tyringham (369)
Washington (615)
West Stockbridge (1,464)

MICHIGAN

Leelanau Peninsula (Leelanau County)
Leelanau Enterprise Tribune (C)
7200 E. Duck Lake Rd.
Lake Leelanau, MI 49653
231/256-9827
www.leelanaunews.com

Leelanau Peninsula C/C
5046 S. West Bayshore Dr.
Suttons Bay, MI 49652
231/256-9895
www.leelanauchamber.com
Empire (351)
Greilickville (1,165)
Leland (600)
Northport (607)
Suttons Bay (626)

Oscoda–Huron Shore (Iosco County)
Oscoda Press (C)
311 S. State
Oscoda, MI 48754
989/739-2055
www.oscodapress.com

Oscoda–Au Sable C/C
4440 N. US Hwy. 23
Oscoda, MI 48750
989/739-7322, 800/235-4625
www.oscoda.com
Au Sable (1,542)
East Tawas (2,282)
Oscoda (1,061)
Tawas City (1,696)
Whittemore (398)

Petoskey–Harbor Springs (Emmet County)
Petoskey News-Review (D)
319 State St.
Petoskey, MI 49770
231/347-2544
www.petoskeynews.com

Petoskey Regional C/C
401 E. Mitchell St.
Petoskey, MI 49770
231/347-4150
www.petoskey.com

Harbor Springs C/C
368 E. Main St.
Harbor Springs, MI 49740
231/526-7999
www.harborspringschamber.com
Alanson (695)
Harbor Springs (1,516)
Mackinaw City (509)
Pellston (81)
Petoskey (7,241)

Traverse City (Grand Traverse County)
Traverse City Record-Eagle (D)
120 W. Front St.
Traverse City, MI 49685
231/933-1420
www.record-eagle.com

Traverse City Area C/C
202 E. Grandview Parkway
Traverse City, MI 49685
231/947-5075
www.tcchamber.org
Fife Lake (449)
Kingsley (851)
Traverse City (15,040)

MISSISSIPPI

Bay St. Louis–Pass Christian (part of Hancock and Harrison counties)
The Sun Herald (D)
205 DeBuys Rd.
Gulfport, MS 39507
228/896-2168
www.sunherald.com

Hancock County C/C
412 Hwy. 90 #6
Bay Saint Louis, MS 39520
228/467-9048
www.hancockchamber.org

Mississippi Gulf Coast C/C
1401 20th Ave.
Gulfport, MS 39501
228/863-2933
www.mscoastchamber.com
Bay St. Louis (9,433)
Kiln (1,262)
Long Beach (16,756)
Pass Christian (5,957)
Pearlington (1,603)
Waveland (6,571)

Hattiesburg (Forrest County)
Hattiesburg American (D)
825 N. Main St.
Hattiesburg, MS 39401
601/582-4321
www.hattiesburgamerican.com

Area Development Partnership
One Convention Center Plaza
Hattiesburg, MS 39401
601/296-7500
www.theadp.com
Hattiesburg (45,175)
Petal (8,684)

Oxford (Lafayette County)
Oxford Eagle (D)
916 Jackson Ave.
Oxford, MS 38655
662/234-4331
www.oxfordeagle.com

Oxford–Lafayette County C/C
299 W. Jackson
Oxford, MS 38655
662/234-4651
www.oxfordms.com
Abbeville (414)
Oxford (11,714)
Taylor (298)

MISSOURI

Branson (Taney County)
Branson Daily News (D)
120 N. Commercial St.
Branson, MO 65616
417/334-3161
www.bransondailynews.com

Branson/Lakes Area C/C
Box 1897
Branson, MO 65615
417/334-4136
www.explorebranson.com
Branson (5,039)
Forsyth (1,442)
Hollister (4,522)
Merriam Woods (785)
Rockaway Beach (323)
Table Rock (167)
Taneyville (322)

Columbia (Boone County)
Columbia Daily Tribune (D)
101 N. Fourth St.
Columbia, MO 65201
573/815-1600
www.showmenews.com

***Columbia Missourian* (D)**
221 S. 8th St.
Columbia, MO 65201
573/882-5700
www.columbiamissourian.com

Columbia C/C
300 S. Providence Rd.
Columbia, MO 65203
573/874-1132
http://chamber.columbia.mo.us/index.asp
Ashland (1,243)
Centralia (3,242)
Columbia (76,756)
Hallsville (883)
Harrisburg (192)
Hartsburg (147)
Rocheport (287)
Sturgeon (952)

Lake of the Ozarks (Camden County)
Lake Sun Leader (D)
450 N. Hwy. 5
Camdenton, MO 65020
573/346-2132
www.lakesunleader.com

Lake Area C/C
One Willmore Lane
Lake Ozark, MO 65049
573/964-1008
www.lakeareachamber.com

Camdenton C/C
Ryland Center
611 N. Hwy. 5
Camdenton, MO 65020
573/346-2227
www.camdentonchamber.com
Camdenton (3,088)
Climax Springs (107)
Linn Creek (273)
Macks Creek (332)
Osage Beach (3,073)
Stoutland (192)
Sunrise Beach (130)
Village of Four Seasons (912)

Table Rock Lake (Stone County)
Monett Times (D)
505 E. Broadway St.
Monett, MO 65708
417/235-3135
www.monett-times.com

Table Rock Lake–Kimberling City Area C/C
N. Hwy. 13
Kimberling City, MO 65686
800/595-0393
www.tablerocklake.org
Blue Eye (152)
Crane (1,511)
Galena (519)
Hurley (158)
Indian Point (571)
Kimberling City (2,655)
Lakeview (37)
Reeds Spring (544)

MONTANA

Bozeman (Gallatin County)
Bozeman Daily Chronicle (D)
2820 W. College
Bozeman, MT 59718
406/587-4491
www.bozemandailychronicle.com

Bozeman Area C/C
2000 Commerce Way
Bozeman, MT 59715
406/586-5421
www.bozemanchamber.com
Belgrade (6,588)
Bozeman (29,459)
Manhattan (1,421)
Three Forks (1,775)
West Yellowstone (1,201)

Hamilton–Bitterroot Valley (Ravalli County)
Ravalli Republic (D)
232 W. Main St.
Hamilton, MT 59840
406/363-3300
www.ravallinews.com

Bitterroot Valley C/C
105 E. Main St.
Hamilton, MT 59840
406/363-2400
www.bvchamber.com
Darby (851)
Hamilton (4,059)
Pinesdale (983)
Stevensville (1,965)

Kalispell–Flathead Valley (Flathead County)
Daily Inter Lake (D)
727 E. Idaho
Kalispell, MT 59901
406/755-7000
www.dailyinterlake.com

Kalispell Area C/C
15 Depot Park
Kalispell, MT 59901
406/758-2800
www.kalispellchamber.com
Columbia Falls (3,922)
Evergreen (4,109)
Kalispell (15,678)
Whitefish (5,793)

Polson–Mission Valley (Lake County)
Lake County Leader (C)
213 Main St.
Polson, MT 59860
406/883-4343
www.leaderadvertiser.com

Polson Area C/C
#7 3rd Ave. W.
Polson, MT 59860
406/883-5969
www.polsonchamber.com
Arlee (489)
Charlo (358)
Finley Point (395)
Kicking Horse (281)
Pablo (1,298)
Polson (4,316)
Ronan (1,877)
St. Ignatius (913)

NEVADA

Carson City–Carson Valley (Carson City and Douglas County)
Nevada Appeal (D)
580 Mallory Way
Carson City, NV 89701
775/882-2111
www.nevadaappeal.com

Carson City Area C/C
1900 S. Carson St.
Carson City, NV 89701
775/882-1565
www.carsoncitychamber.com
Carson City (47,237)
Gardnerville (2,177)
Gardnerville Ranchos (7,455)
Indian Hills (2,544)
Johnson Lane (2,551)
Kingsbury (2,238)
Minden (1,441)
Stateline (1,379)
Zephyr Cove–Round Hill (1,434)

Henderson (part of Clark County)
Las Vegas Sun/Review Journal (D)
1111 W. Bonanza Rd.
Las Vegas, NV 89125
702/383-0211
www.reviewjournal.com

Henderson C/C
590 S. Boulder Hwy.
Henderson, NV 89015
702/565-8951
www.hendersonchamber.com
Henderson (122,339)

Pahrump Valley (part of Nye County)
Pahrump Valley Times (C)
2160 E. Calvada Blvd.
Pahrump, NV 89048
775/727-5102
www.pahrumpvalleytimes.com

Pahrump Valley C/C
1021 S. Frontage Rd. Hwy. 160
Pahrump, NV 89041
775/727-5800
www.pahrumpchamber.com
Beatty (1,623)
Gabbs (947)
Pahrump (7,424)
Tonopah (3,616)

Reno–Sparks (Washoe County)
Reno Gazette-Journal (D)
955 Kuenzli St.
Reno, NV 89520
775/788-6200
www.rgj.com

Reno–Sparks C/C
1 E. 1st St., Suite 1600
Reno, NV 89501
775/337-3030
www.reno-sparkschamber.org
Incline Village–Crystal Bay (7,119)
New Washoe City (2,875)
Reno (155,499)
Sparks (59,496)
Sun Valley (11,391)
Wadsworth (640)

NEW HAMPSHIRE

Hanover (Grafton County)
Valley News (D)
P.O. Box 877
White River Junction, VT 05001
603/298-8711
www.vnews.com

Hanover Area C/C
216 Nugget Bldg.
47–53 S. Main St.
Hanover, NH 03755
603/643-3115
www.hanoverchamber.org
Alexandria (1,322)
Ashland (2,029)
Bath (811)
Benton (332)
Bethlehem (2,131)
Bridgewater (865)
Bristol (2,555)
Campton (2,466)
Canaan (3,306)
Dorchester (398)
Easton (238)
Ellsworth (87)
Enfield (4,265)
Franconia (850)
Grafton (925)
Groton (364)
Hanover (9,844)
Haverhill (4,189)
Hebron (401)
Holderness (1,740)
Landaff (416)
Lebanon (12,571)
Lincoln (1,222)
Lisbon (1,682)
Littleton (6,036)
Lyman (430)
Lyme (1,579)
Monroe (787)
Orange (260)
Orford (1,205)
Piermont (633)
Plymouth (5,959)
Rumney (1,451)
Sugar Hill (503)
Thornton (1,524)
Warren (827)
Waterville Valley (154)
Wentworth (754)
Woodstock (1,218)

Lake Winnipesaukee (part of Belknap and Carroll counties)
Conway Daily Sun (D)
64 Seavey St.
North Conway, NH 03860
603/356-3456
www.mountwashingtonvalley.com

***The Citizen* (D)**
171 Fair St.
Lanconia, NH 03246
603/524-3800
www4.citizen.com

Greater Laconia–Weirs Beach C/C
11 Veterans Sq.
Laconia, NH 03246
603/524-5531
www.laconia-weirs.org

Wolfeboro C/C
32 Central Ave.
Wolfeboro, NH 03894
603/569-2200, 800/516-5324
www.wolfeboroonline.com/chamber

Alton (3,436)
Barnstead (3,293)
Belmont (6,129)
Center Harbor (1,057)
Gilford (6,045)
Gilmanton (2,809)
Laconia (16,264)
Meredith (5,019)
Moultonborough (3,234)
Ossipee (3,421)
Tamworth (2,629)
Wolfeboro (5,193)

Monadnock Region (Cheshire County)
Transcript (C)
One Phoenix Mill Lane, Suite 100
Peterborough, NH 03458
603/924-3333
www.peterboroughtranscript.com

Jaffrey C/C
7 Main St.
Jaffrey, NH 03431
603/532-4549
www.jaffreychamber.com

Greater Keene C/C
48 Central Sq.
Keene, NH 03431
603/524-5531
www.keenechamber.com
Alstead (1,736)
Chesterfield (3,526)
Dublin (1,497)
Fitzwilliam (2,024)
Gilsum (751)
Harrisville (1,003)
Hinsdale (4,001)
Jaffrey (5,330)
Keene (22,325)
Marlborough (2,006)
Marlow (649)
Nelson (546)
Richmond (950)
Rindge (5,085)
Roxbury (258)
Stoddard (614)
Sullivan (731)
Surry (682)
Swanzey (6,596)
Troy (2,112)
Walpole (3,239)
Westmoreland (1,688)
Winchester (4,182)

NEW JERSEY

Lower Cape May (part of Cape May County)
Star & Wave (C)
600 Park Blvd.
Cape May, NJ 08204
609/399-5411
www.starandwave.com

C/C of Greater Cape May
609 Lafayette St.
Cape May, NJ 08204
609/884-5508
www.capemaychamber.com
Avalon (1,860)
Cape May (4,490)
Cape May Court House (4,426)
Cape May Point (260)
Lower Township (21,931)
North Wildwood (4,988)
Stone Harbor (1,024)
West Wildwood (456)
Wildwood (4,442)
Wildwood Crest (3,597)

Toms River–Barnegat Bay (Ocean County)
Ocean County Observer (D)
8 Robbins St.
Toms River, NJ 08753
732/349-3000
www.injersey.com/observer

Toms River–Ocean County C/C
1200 Hooper Ave.
Toms River, NJ 08753
732/349-0220
www.oc-chamber.com
Barnegat (13,912)
Barnegat Light (700)
Bay Head (1,275)
Beach Haven (1,542)
Beachwood (9,923)
Berkeley (37,319)
Brick (73,323)
Dover (83,776)
Eaglewood (1,546)
Island Heights (1,564)
Jackson (38,244)
Lacey (24,316)
Lakehurst (3,177)
Lakewood (48,658)
Lavallette (2,393)
Leisure Village (4,295)
Leisure Village East (1,989)
Leisure Village West–Pine (10,139)
Little Egg Harbor (14,482)
Long Beach (3,630)
Manchester (37,602)
Mantoloking (411)
Mystic Island (7,400)
New Egypt (2,327)
North Beach Haven (2,413)
Ocean (5,802)
Ocean Acres (5,587)
Ocean Gate (2,178)
Pine Beach (2,056)
Pine Ridge at Crestwood (2,372)
Pleasant Plains (2,577)
Plumsted (6,920)
Point Pleasant (19,050)
Point Pleasant Beach (5,302)
Seaside Heights (2,423)

Seaside Park (1,920)
Ship Bottom (1,394)
Silver Ridge (1,138)
Silverton (9,175)
South Toms River (3,962)
Stafford (15,834)
Surf City (1,456)
Toms River (7,524)
Tuckerton (3,241)
Waretown (1,283)

NEW MEXICO

Alamogordo (Otero County)
Alamogordo Daily News (D)
518 24th St.
Alamogordo, NM 88310
505/437-7120
www.alamogordonews.com

Alamogordo C/C
1301 White Sands Blvd.
Alamogordo, NM 88311
505/437-6120
www.alamogordo.com
Alamogordo (29,036)
Boles Acres (1,409)
Cloudcroft (651)
La Luz (1,625)
Mescalero (1,159)
Tularosa (2,865)

Las Cruces (Dona Ana County)
Sun-News (D)
256 W. Las Cruces Ave.
Las Cruces, NM 88005
505/541-5400
www.lcsun-news.com

Greater Las Cruces C/C
760 W. Picacho
Las Cruces, NM 88004
505/524-1968
www.lascruces.org
Anthony (5,160)
Chaparral (2,962)
Dona Ana (1,202)
Hatch (1,360)
Las Cruces (74,779)
Mesilla (2,040)
Sunland Park (9,265)
University Park (4,520)
White Sands (2,616)

Las Vegas (San Miguel County)
Las Vegas–San Miguel County C/C
701 Grand Ave.
Las Vegas, NM 87701
505/425-8631
www.lasvegasnewmexico.com
Las Vegas (14,223)
Pecos village (1,426)

Rio Rancho (Sandoval County)
Observer (D)
1594 Sara Rd.
Rio Rancho, NM 87124
505/892-8080
www.observer-online.com

Rio Rancho C/C
1781 Rio Rancho Dr.
Rio Rancho, NM 87124
505/892-1533
www.rrchamber.org
Bernalillo (7,450)
Cochiti (434)
Corrales (5,318)
Cuba (957)
Jemez Pueblo (1,301)
Jemez Springs (492)
Pena Blanca (300)
Placitas (1,611)
Rio Rancho (32,505)
San Felipe Pueblo (1,557)
San Ysidro (292)
Santa Ana Pueblo (476)
Santo Domingo Pueblo (2,866)
Zia Pueblo (637)

Roswell (Eddy County)
Roswell Daily Record (D)
2301 N. Main
Roswell, NM 88201
505/622-7710
www.roswell-record.com

Roswell C/C
131 W. Second St.
Roswell, NM 88202
505/623-5695
www.roswellnm.org
Dexter (954)
Hagerman (1,061)
Lake Arthur (363)
Roswell (47,559)

Ruidoso (Lincoln County)
Ruidoso News (C)
104 Park Ave.
Ruidoso, NM 88345
505/257-4001
www.ruidosonews.com

Ruidoso Valley C/C
720 Sudderth Dr.
Ruidoso, NM 88355
505/257-7395, 800/253-2255
www.ruidoso.net
Capitan (1,131)
Carrizozo (1,351)
Corona (274)
Ruidoso (5,714)
Ruidoso Downs (1,148)

Santa Fe (Santa Fe County)
Santa Fe New Mexican (D)
202 E. Marcy St.
Santa Fe, NM 87501
505/983-3303
www.santafenewmexican.com

Santa Fe County C/C
8380 Cerrillos Rd., Suite 302
Santa Fe, NM 87507
505/988-3279
www.santafechamber.com
- Agua Fria (3,717)
- Cuyamungue (329)
- Edgewood (2,880)
- Eldorado at Santa Fe (2,260)
- Jaconita (375)
- La Cienega (1,066)
- Nambe (1,246)
- Pojoaque (1,037)
- Santa Cruz (2,504)
- Santa Fe (66,522)
- Tesuque (1,490)

Silver City (Grant County)
Silver City Daily Press (D)
300 W. Market St.
Silver City, NM 88061
505/388-1576
www.thedailypress.com

Silver City–Grant County C/C
201 N. Hudson Ave.
Silver City, NM 88061
505/538-3785
www.silvercity.org
- Bayard (2,575)
- Central (1,835)
- Hurley (1,479)
- Silver City (12,007)

Taos (Taos County)
Taos News (C)
226 Albright
Taos, NM 87571
505/758-2241
www.taosnews.com

Taos County C/C
1139 Paseo del Pueblo Sur
Taos, NM 87571
505/758-3873, 800/732-8267
www.taoschamber.com
- Chamisal (272)
- Penasco (648)
- Questa (1,951)
- Ranchos De Taos (1,779)
- Red River (423)
- Taos (5,270)
- Taos Pueblo (1,187)
- Vadito (283)

NEW YORK

East End Long Island (part of Suffolk County)
Southampton Press (C)
135 Windmill Lane
Southampton, NY 11968
631/288-4965
www.southamptonpress.com

Southampton C/C
76 Main St.
Southampton, NY 11968
631/283-0402
www.southamptonchamber.com
- Aquebogue (2,060)
- Cutchogue (2,627)
- East Hampton (1,421)
- East Hampton North (2,780)
- East Quogue (4,372)
- Greenport (2,027)
- Greenport West (1,614)
- Hampton Bays (7,893)
- Jamesport (1,532)
- Laurel (1,094)
- Mattituck (3,902)
- Old Field (784)
- Peconic (1,100)
- Remsenburg–Speonk (1,851)
- Riverhead (8,814)
- Sag Harbor (2,151)
- Shelter Island (1,193)
- Shelter Island Heights (1,042)
- Southampton (4,051)
- Southold (5,192)
- Watermill (1,893)
- Westhampton (2,129)
- Westhampton Beach (1,590)

Lake Placid (Essex County)
Lake Placid/Essex County CVB
216 Main St.
Lake Placid, NY 12946
518/523-2445
www.lakeplacid.com
- Chesterfield (2,407)
- Crown Point (2,092)
- Elizabethtown (1,312)
- Essex (709)
- Jay (2,294)
- Keene (1,061)
- Lake Placid village (2,674)
- Lewis (1,198)
- Minerva (802)
- Moriah (4,875)
- Newcomb (482)
- North Elba (8,799)
- North Hudson (265)
- Port Henry village (1,133)
- Schroon (1,773)
- St. Armand (1,319)
- Ticonderoga (5,153)
- Westport (1,353)
- Willsboro (1,909)
- Wilmington (1,132)

NORTH CAROLINA

Asheville (Buncombe County)
Asheville Citizen-Times (D)
14 O'Henry Ave.
Asheville, NC 28801
828/252-5611
www.citizen-times.com

Asheville Area C/C
151 Haywood St
Asheville, NC 28801
828/258-6101
www.ashevillechamber.org
- Asheville (64,067)
- Avery Creek (1,144)
- Bent Creek (1,487)
- Biltmore Forest (1,268)
- Black Mountain (7,572)
- Fairview (1,830)
- Montreat (671)
- Royal Pines (4,418)
- Swannanoa (3,538)
- Weaverville (2,539)
- Woodfin (3,121)

Beaufort–Bogue Banks (part of Carteret County)
Carteret County News-Times (D)
4034 Arendell St.
Morehead City, NC 28557
252/726-7081
www.carteretnewstimes.com

Carteret County C/C
801 Arendell St.
Morehead City, NC 28557
252/726-6350
www.nccoastchamber.com
- Atlantic Beach (2,003)
- Beaufort (3,887)
- Cape Carteret (1,278)
- Cedar Point (707)
- Emerald Isle (2,930)
- Harkers Island (1,759)
- Indian Beach (164)
- Morehead City (6,567)
- Newport (2,887)
- Pine Knoll Shores (1,432)

Boone–Blowing Rock (Watauga County)
The Blowing Rocket (C)
452 Sunset Dr.
Blowing Rock, NC 28605
828/295-7522
www.blowingrocket.com

***The Watauga Democrat* (C)**
474 Industrial Park Dr.
Boone, NC 28607
828/264-3612
www.wataugademocrat.com

Boone Area C/C
208 Howard St.
Boone, NC 28607
828/264-2225
www.boonechamber.com

Blowing Rock C/C
1038 Main St.
Blowing Rock, NC 28605
828/295-7851
www.blowingrock.com
- Beech Mountain (232)
- Blowing Rock (1,237)
- Boone (13,583)
- Seven Devils (92)

Brevard (Transylvania County)
Transylvania Times (C)
100 North Broad St.
Brevard, NC 28712
828/883-8156
www.citcom.net/cgi-bin/headlines.pl

Brevard–Transylvania C/C
35 W. Main St.
Brevard, NC 28712
828/883-3700
www.brevardncchamber.org
- Brevard (5,455)
- Rosman (437)

Chapel Hill–Carrboro (Orange County)
Herald-Sun (D)
2828 Pickett Rd.
Durham, NC 27705
919/419-6500
www.herald-sun.com

Chapel Hill–Carrboro C/C
104 S. Estes Dr.
Chapel Hill, NC 27515
919/967-7075
www.carolinachamber.org
- Carrboro (13,832)
- Chapel Hill (43,039)
- Hillsborough (6,468)

Dare Outer Banks (Dare County)
Outer Banks Sentinel (D)
P.O. 546
Nags Head, NC 27959
252/480-2234
www.obsentinel.womacknewspapers.com

Outer Banks C/C
101 Town Hall Dr.
Kill Devil Hills, NC 27948
252/441-8144
www.outerbankschamber.com
- Kill Devil Hills (4,606)
- Kitty Hawk (2,153)
- Manteo (1,290)

Nags Head (2,206)
Southern Shores (1,732)
Wanchese (1,380)

Edenton (Chowan County)
Roanoke-Chowan News-Herald (C)
801 Parker Ave.
Ahoskie, NC 27910
252/332-2123
www.roanoke-chowannewsherald.com

Edenton–Chowan C/C
116 E. King St.
Edenton, NC 27932
252/482-3400
www.co.chowan.nc.us/commerce.htm
Edenton (5,234)

Hendersonville–East Flat Rock (Henderson County)
Times-News (D)
1717 Four Seasons Blvd.
Hendersonville, NC 28792
828/692-0505
www.hendersonvillenews.com

Greater Hendersonville C/C
330 N. King St.
Hendersonville, NC 28792
828/692-1413
www.hendersonvillechamber.org
Balfour (1,118)
Barker Heights (1,137)
East Flat Rock (3,218)
Etowah (1,997)
Fletcher (3,211)
Hendersonville (7,394)
Laurel Park (1,402)
Mountain Home (1,898)
Valley Hill (1,802)

New Bern (Craven County)
Sun-Journal (D)
3200 Wellons Blvd.
New Bern, NC 28562
252/638-8101
www.newbernsunjournal.com

New Bern Area C/C
316 Tryon Palace Dr.
New Bern, NC 28563
252/637-3111
www.newbernchamber.com
Bridgeton (527)
Cove City (497)
Dover (474)
Havelock (20,437)
James City (4,279)
Neuse Forest (1,110)
New Bern (21,464)
River Bend (2,497)
Trent Woods (4,040)
Vanceboro (995)

Southern Pines–Pinehurst (Moore County)
Southern Pines Pilot (C)
145 W. Pennsylvania Ave.
Southern Pines, NC 28387
910/692-7271
www.thepilot.com

Sandhills Area C/C
10677 Hwy. 15-501 N.
Southern Pines, NC 28387
910/692-3926
www.sandhillschamber.com
Aberdeen (3,180)
Cameron (237)
Carthage (1,040)
Foxfire (354)
Pinebluff (867)
Pinehurst (6,919)
Robbins (1,015)
Seven Lakes (2,049)
Southern Pines (10,168)
Taylortown (619)
Vass (687)
Whispering Pines (1,469)

Southport–Brunswick Islands (Brunswick County)
State Port Pilot (C)
105 S. Howe St.
Southport, NC 28461
910/457-4568
www.stateportpilot.com

Southport–Oak Island C/C
4841 Long Beach Rd. SE
Southport, NC 28461
910/457-6964, 800/457-6964
www.southport-oakisland.com
Bald Head Island (116)
Belville (84)
Boiling Spring Lakes (2,274)
Bolivia (264)
Calabash (1,579)
Caswell Beach (217)
Holden Beach (770)
Leland (2,215)
Long Beach (5,450)
Navassa (507)
Ocean Isle Beach (613)
Sandy Creek (315)
Shallotte (1,381)
Southport (2,581)
Sunset Beach (409)
Varnamtown (461)
Yaupon Beach (809)

Tryon (Polk County)
Tryon Daily Bulletin (D)
106 N. Trade St.
Tryon, NC 28782
828/859-9151
www.tryondailybulletin.com

Polk County C/C
2753 Lynn Rd., Suite A
Tryon, NC 28782
828/859-6236
www.polkchamber.org
Columbus (822)
Saluda (518)
Tryon (1,648)

OKLAHOMA

Lake of the Cherokees (Delaware County)
Grove Sun (C)
P.O. Box 450969
Grove, OK 74344
918/786-2228
www.grovesun.com

Grove Area C/C
9630 Hwy. 59 N., Suite A
Grove, OK 74344
918/786-9079
www.groveok.org
Bernice (385)
Colcord (748)
Grove (5,161)
Jay (2,459)
Kansas (655)
Oaks (469)
West Siloam Springs (628)

OREGON

Bend (Deschutes County)
The Bulletin (D)
1777 SW Chandler Ave.
Bend, OR 97708
541/382-1811
www.bendbulletin.com

Bend C/C
777 NW Wall St.
Bend, OR 97701
541/382-3221
www.bendchamber.org
Bend (31,733)
Deschutes River Woods (2,373)
Redmond (10,618)
Sisters (806)
Terrebonne (1,143)
Three Rivers (1,268)

Brookings–Gold Beach (Curry County)
Curry Coastal Pilot (D)
507 Chetco Ave.
Brookings, OR 97415
541/469-3123
www.currypilot.com

Gold Beach C/C
29692 Ellensburg Ave. #6
Gold Beach, OR 97444
541/247-0923
www.goldbeachchamber.com

Brookings–Harbor C/C
16330 Lower Harbor Rd.
Brookings, OR 97415
541/469-3181, 800/535-9469
www.brookingsor.com
Brookings (5,001)
Gold Beach (1,555)
Harbor (2,143)
Port Orford (1,025)

Florence (part of Lane County)
Siuslaw News (C)
148 Maple St.
Florence, OR 97439
541/997-3441

Florence Area C/C
270 Hwy. 101
Florence, OR 97439
541/997-3128
www.florencechamber.com
Florence (6,214)

Grants Pass (Josephine County)
Grants Pass Daily Courier (D)
409 SE 7th St.
Grants Pass, OR 97526
541/474-3700
www.thedailycourier.com

Grants Pass/Josephine County C/C
1995 NW Vine St.
Grants Pass, OR 97528
541/476-7717, 800/547-5927
www.grantspasschamber.org
Cave Junction (1,183)
Grants Pass (20,894)
Harbeck–Fruitdale (3,982)
Redwood (3,702)

Medford–Ashland (Jackson County)
Mail Tribune (D)
111 N. Fir St.
Medford, OR 97501
541/776-4411
www.mailtribune.com

The Tidings **(D)**
1661 Siskiyou Blvd.
Ashland, OR 97520
541/482-3456
www.dailytidings.com

Chamber of Medford/Jackson County
101 E. 8th St.
Medford, OR 97501
541/779-4847
www.medfordchamber.com

Ashland C/C
110 E. Main St.
Ashland, OR 97520
541/482-3486
www.ashlandchamber.com
Ashland (17,678)
Butte Falls (415)
Central Point (9,740)
Eagle Point (3,588)
Gold Hill (972)
Jacksonville (1,917)
Medford (56,067)
Phoenix (3,703)
Rogue River (2,053)
Shady Cove (2,135)
Talent (3,929)
White City (5,891)

Newport–Lincoln City (Lincoln County)
News-Times (C)
831 NE Avery
Newport, OR 97365
541/265-8571
www.newportnewstimes.com

***News Guard* (C)**
930 SE Hwy. 101
Lincoln City, OR 97367
541/994-2178
www.thenewsguard.com

Lincoln City C/C
4039 NW Logan Rd. & Hwy. 101
Lincoln City, OR 97367
541/994-3070
www.lcchamber.com

Greater Newport C/C
555 SW Coast Hwy.
Newport, OR 97365
541/265-8801, 800/262-7844
www.newportchamber.org
Depoe Bay (1,070)
Lincoln Beach (1,507)
Lincoln City (6,889)
Newport (9,786)
Rose Lodge (1,257)
Siletz (1,144)
Toledo (3,312)
Waldport (1,904)
Yachats (648)

PENNSYLVANIA

Pike County (Pike County)
Pike County Dispatch (C)
105 W. Catharine St.
Milford, PA 18337
570/296-6641
www.pikepa.com/news.html

Pike County C/C
The Callahan House
101 Rt. 209, S.
Milford, PA 18337
570/296-8700
www.pikechamber.com
Matamoras (2,300)
Milford (1,277)

State College (Centre County)
Centre Daily Times (D)
3400 E. College Ave.
State College, PA 16801
814/238-5000
www.centredaily.com

Chamber of Business & Industry of Centre County
200 Innovation Blvd. #201
State College, PA 16803
814/234-1829
www.cbicc.org
Bellefonte (6,231)
Boalsburg (2,206)
Centre Hall (1,187)
Howard (740)
Milesburg (1,154)
Millheim (833)
Park Forest Village (6,703)
Philipsburg (2,966)
Pine Grove Mills (1,129)
Pleasant Gap (1,699)
Port Matilda (657)
Ramblewood (1,104)
Snow Shoe (813)
South Philipsburg (427)
State College (39,400)
Unionville (288)
Zion (1,573)

SOUTH CAROLINA

Aiken (Aiken County)
Aiken Standard (D)
326 Rutland Dr.
Aiken, SC 29801
803/648-2311
www.aikenstandard.com

Aiken C/C
121 Richland Ave., E.
Aiken, SC 29801
803/641-1111
www.aikenchamber.net

- Aiken (22,834)
- Belvedere (6,133)
- Burnettown (518)
- Clearwater (4,731)
- Gloverville (2,753)
- Jackson (1,854)
- Monetta (197)
- New Ellenton (2,599)
- North Augusta (16,355)
- Perry (276)
- Salley (481)
- Wagener (884)
- Windsor (141)

Beaufort (part of Beaufort County)
Beaufort Gazette (D)
1556 Salem Rd.
Beaufort, SC 29901
843/524-3183
www.beaufortgazette.com

Greater Beaufort C/C
1006 Carteret St.
Beaufort, SC 29901
843/986-5400
www.beaufortsc.org

- Beaufort (9,897)
- Port Royal (3,283)

Charleston (part of Charleston County)
Post & Courier (D)
134 Columbus St.
Charleston, SC 29403
843/577-7111
www.charleston.net

Charleston Metro C/C
81 Mary St.
Charleston, SC 29403
843/577-2510
www.charlestonchamber.net

Charleston CVB
375 Meeting St.
Charleston, SC 29403
800/774-0006
www.charlestoncvb.com

- Awendaw (1,202)
- Charleston (96,545)
- Folly Beach (2,213)
- Hollywood (4,233)
- Isle of Palms (4,509)
- Kiawah Island (1,120)
- Lincolnville (890)
- McClellanville (460)
- Meggett (1,301)
- Mount Pleasant (53,096)
- North Charleston (76,979)
- Ravenel (2,211)
- Rockville (135)
- Seabrook Island (1,205)
- Sullivan's Island (1,863)

Conway (part of Horry County)
Horry Independent (D)
2510 Main St.
Conway, SC 29526
843/248-6671
www.horryindependent.com

Conway Area C/C
203 Main St.
Conway, SC 29526
843/248-2273
www.conwayscchamber.com

- Conway (10,115)

Hilton Head Island (part of Beaufort County)
Island Packet (D)
10 Buck Island Rd.
Bluffton, SC 29910
843/706-8100
www.islandpacket.com

Hilton Head Island C/C
One Chamber of Commerce Dr.
Hilton Head Island, SC 29938
843/785-3673
www.hiltonheadisland.org

- Bluffton (901)
- Burton (6,917)
- Hilton Head Island (29,088)
- Laurel Bay (4,972)
- Parris Island (7,172)
- Shell Point (2,885)

Myrtle Beach (part of Horry County)
Sun News (D)
914 Frontage Rd. E.
Myrtle Beach, SC 29578
843/626-8555
www.myrtlebeachonline.com

Myrtle Beach Area C/C
1200 N. Oak St.
P.O. Box 2115
Myrtle Beach, SC 29578
843/626-7444, 800/356-3016
www.mbchamber.com

- Atlantic Beach (418)
- Aynor (474)
- Briarcliffe Acres (555)
- Bucksport (1,022)
- Forestbrook (2,502)
- Garden City (6,305)

Little River (3,470)
Loris (3,074)
Myrtle Beach (25,456)
North Myrtle Beach (9,216)
Red Hill (6,112)
Socastee (10,426)
Surfside Beach (4,118)

Pendleton District (Oconee County)
Daily Journal (D)
210 W. North First St.
Seneca, SC 29678
864/882-2375
www.dailyjm.com

Greater Seneca C/C
236 Main St.
Seneca, SC 29678
864/882-2097
www.senecachamber.com
Salem (197)
Seneca (8,133)
Utica (1,478)
Walhalla (3,982)
West Union (274)
Westminster (4,351)

Summerville (Dorchester County)
Journal-Scene (D)
104 E. Doty Ave.
Summerville, SC 29483
843/873-9424
www.summervillejournalscene.com

Greater Summerville–Dorchester County C/C
402 N. Main St.
Summerville, SC 29483
843/873-2931
www.gsdcchamber.org
Harleyville (626)
Reevesville (206)
Ridgeville (1,539)
St. George (2,105)
Summerville (23,513)

TENNESSEE

Crossville (Cumberland County)
Crossville Chronicle (C)
125 West Ave.
Crossville, TN 38555
931/484-5145
www.crossville-chronicle.com

Greater Cumberland County C/C
34 S. Main St.
Crossville, TN 38555
877/465-3861
www.crossville-chamber.com
Crab Orchard (1,031)
Crossville (9,036)
Fairfield Glade (2,209)
Pleasant Hill (575)

Maryville (Blount County)
Daily Times (D)
307 E. Harper Ave.
Maryville, TN 37804
865/981-1100
www.thedailytimes.com

Blount County C/C
201 S. Washington St.
Maryville, TN 37804
865/983-2241
www.blountchamber.com
Alcoa (7,137)
Eagleton Village (5,169)
Friendsville (950)
Maryville (23,042)
Rockford (746)
Townsend (426)

TEXAS

Alpine–Big Bend (Brewster County)
Alpine Avalanche (C)
118 N. Fifth
Alpine, TX 79831
432/837-3334
www.alpineavalanche.com

Alpine C/C
106 N. 3rd St.
Alpine, TX 79830
432/837-2326
www.alpinetexas.com
Alpine (6,077)

Boerne (Kendall County)
Boerne Star (C)
282 N. Main St.
Boerne, TX 78006
830/249-2441
www.boernestar.com

Greater Boerne Area C/C
126 Rosewood Ave.
Boerne, TX 78006
830/249-8000
www.boerne.org
Boerne (5,778)
Comfort (1,477)

Cedar Creek Lake (Henderson County)
Athens Daily Review (D)
201 S. Prairieville St.
Athens, TX 75751
903/675-5626
www.athensreview.com

Athens C/C
1206 S. Palestine
Athens, TX 75751
903/675-5181
www.athenscc.org
Athens (11,588)
Berryville (838)
Brownsboro (595)
Caney City (192)
Chandler (2,079)
Coffee City (238)
Enchanted Oaks (315)
Eustace (788)
Gun Barrel City (4,005)
Log Cabin (572)
Malakoff (2,183)
Moore Station (285)
Murchison (549)
Payne Springs (667)
Poynor (263)
Seven Points (844)
Star Harbor (398)
Tool (1,925)
Trinidad (1,123)

Fredericksburg (Gillespie County)
Standard-Radio Post (C)
108 E. Main
Fredericksburg, TX 78624
830/997-2155
www.fredericksburgstandard.com

Fredericksburg C/C
302 E. Austin
Fredericksburg, TX 78624
830/997-6523
www.fredericksburg-texas.com
Fredericksburg (8,428)

Georgetown (Williamson County)
Georgetown C/C
100 Stadium Dr.
Georgetown, TX 78627
512/930-3535
www.georgetownchamber.org
Anderson Mill (9,299)
Bartlett (1,014)
Brushy Creek (5,833)
Cedar Park (10,727)
Florence (1,047)
Georgetown (22,393)
Granger (1,450)
Hutto (827)
Jollyville (14,094)
Leander (6,410)
Round Rock (52,479)
Serenada (3,242)
Taylor (14,336)
Thrall (698)
Weir (276)

Kerrville (Kerr County)
Kerrville Daily Times (D)
429 Jefferson St.
Kerrville, TX 78028
830/896-7000
www.dailytimes.com

Kerrville Area C/C
1700 Sidney Baker St.
Kerrville, TX 78028
830/896-1155
www.kerrvilletx.com
Ingram (1,598)
Kerrville (19,986)

Lake Conroe (Montgomery County)
Conroe Courier (D)
100 Avenue A
Conroe, TX 77301
936/756-6671
www.thecourier-online.com

Lake Conroe Area C/C
505 W. Davis
Conroe, TX 77305
936/756-6644
www.conroe.org
Chateau Woods (641)
Conroe (33,748)
Cut and Shoot (1,263)
Magnolia (1,157)
Montgomery (430)
Oak Ridge North (3,128)
Panorama Village (1,951)
Patton Village (1,626)
Pinehurst (3,284)
Porter Heights (1,448)
Roman Forest (1,270)
Shenandoah (1,960)
Splendora (1,038)
Stagecoach (412)
The Woodlands (29,205)
Willis (3,352)
Woodbranch (1,580)
Woodloch (336)

Marble Falls–Lake LBJ (Burnet County)
The Highlander (C)
304 Gateway Loop
Marble Falls, TX 78654
830/693-4367
www.highlandernews.com

Marble Falls–Lake LBJ C/C
801 Hwy. 281
Marble Falls, TX 78654
830/693-4449, 800/759-8178
www.marblefalls.org
Bertram (1,053)
Burnet (4,349)
Cottonwood Shores (686)
Granite Shoals (1,747)
Marble Falls (5,229)
Meadowlakes (1,116)

Mission–McAllen–Alamo (Hidalgo County)
Monitor (D)
1101 Ash St.
McAllen, TX 78501
956/686-4343
www.themonitor.com

McAllen C/C
1200 Ash Ave.
McAllen, TX 78501
956/682-2871
www.mcallenchamber.com

Mission C/C
220 E. Ninth St.
Mission, TX 78572
956/585-2727, 800/580-2700
www.missionchamber.com
Alamo (10,486)
Alton (3,708)
Donna (14,832)
Edcouch (3,292)
Edinburg (37,742)
Elsa (6,250)
Hidalgo (5,424)
La Homa (1,403)
La Joya (2,797)
La Villa (1,643)
Lopezville (2,827)
McAllen (103,352)
Mercedes (14,393)
Mila Doce (2,089)
Mission (37,777)
Palmhurst (459)
Palmview (2,388)
Penitas (1,632)
Pharr (40,425)
Progreso (4,568)
Progreso Lakes (189)
San Juan (16,454)
Scissors (1,513)
Sullivan City (2,371)
Weslaco (26,975)

New Braunfels (Comal County)
New Braunfels Herald-Zeitung (D)
1342 Industrial Dr.
New Braunfels, TX 78130
830/625-9144
www.herald-zeitung.com

New Braunfels C/C
390 S. Seguin St.
New Braunfels, TX 78131
800/572-2626
www.nbcham.org
Canyon Lake (9,975)
Garden Ridge (1,939)
New Braunfels (33,466)

Rockport–Aransas Pass (Aransas County)
The Rockport Pilot (C)
1002 Wharf St.
Rockport, TX 78382
361/729-9900
www.rockportpilot.com

Rockport–Fulton Area C/C
404 Broadway
Rockport, TX 78382
361/729-6445, 800/242-0071
www.rockport-fulton.org
Fulton (946)
Rockport (6,463)

Trinity Peninsula (Trinity County)
Polk County Enterprise (C)
100 Calhoun
Livingston, TX 77351
936/327-4357
www.easttexasnews.com/enterprise1.htm

Trinity Peninsula C/C
Box 549
Trinity, TX 75862
936/594-3856
www.trinitychamber.org
Groveton (1,156)
Trinity (2,746)

Wimberley (Hays County)
Hill Country Sun (C)
6 De Luna Lane
Wimberley, TX 78676
512/847-5162
www.hillcountrysun.com

Wimberley C/C
P.O. Box 12
Wimberley, TX 78676
512/847-2201
www.wimberley.org
Buda (2,193)
Dripping Springs (1,275)
Hays (301)
Kyle (2,943)
Mountain City (465)
Niederwald (199)
San Marcos (34,895)
Uhland (270)
Wimberley (2,403)
Woodcreek (1,212)

UTAH

Cedar City (Iron County)
Cedar City C/C
581 N. Main St.
Cedar City, UT 84720
435/586-4484
www.chambercedarcity.org
- Brian Head (114)
- Cedar City (21,427)
- Enoch (3,824)
- Kanarraville (305)
- Paragonah (464)
- Parowan (2,549)

Park City (Summit County)
The Park Record (C)
1670 Bonanza Dr.
Park City, UT 84060
435/649-9014
www.parkrecord.com

Park City C/C
750 Kearns Blvd.
Park City, UT 84060
435/649-6100
www.parkcityinfo.com
- Coalville (1,262)
- Francis (679)
- Henefer (664)
- Kamas (1,432)
- Oakley (827)
- Park City (6,104)

St. George–Zion (Washington County)
The Spectrum (D)
275 E. St. George Blvd.
St. George, UT 84770
435/674-6200
www.thespectrum.com

Saint George Area C/C
97 E. St. George Blvd.
Saint George, UT 84770
435/628-1658
www.stgeorgechamber.com
- Enterprise (1,110)
- Hildale (2,049)
- Hurricane (5,821)
- Ivins (3,149)
- La Verkin (2,684)
- Leeds (263)
- New Harmony (154)
- Rockville (277)
- Santa Clara (3,857)
- Springdale (324)
- St. George (42,763)
- Toquerville (724)
- Virgin (271)
- Washington (6,121)

VIRGINIA

Charlottesville (Charlottesville city and Albemarle County)
Daily Progress (D)
685 W. Rio Rd.
Charlottesville, VA 22901
804/978-7200
www.dailyprogress.com

Charlottesville Regional C/C
Fifth & E. Market St.
Charlottesville, VA 22902
434/295-3141
www.cvillechamber.org
- Barracks (4,710)
- Charlottesville (40,767)
- Commonwealth (5,538)
- Crozet (2,256)
- Hollymead (2,628)
- Rio (5,133)
- Scottsville (214)
- University Heights (6,900)

Fredericksburg–Spotsylvania (Spotsylvania County)
Free Lance-Star (D)
616 Amelia St.
Fredericksburg, VA 22401
540/374-5000
www.freelancestar.com

Fredericksburg Regional C/C
2300 Fall Hill Ave., Suite 240
Fredericksburg, VA 22401
540/373-9400
www.fredericksburgvirginia.net
- Fredericksburg (22,586)
- Spotsylvania Courthouse (2,694)

Front Royal (Warren County)
Front Royal C/C
414 E. Main St.
Front Royal, VA 22630
540/635-5788
www.frva.com
- Front Royal (13,894)

Northern Neck (Lancaster and Northumberland counties)
Rappahannock Record (C)
27 Main St.
Kilmarnock, VA 22482
804/435-1701
www.rrecord.com

Kilmarnock C/C
Box 1357
Kilmarnock, VA 22483
804/435-1552
www.northernneck.com/kilmarnock
- Irvington (500)
- Kilmarnock (1,198)
- White Stone (385)

Smith Mountain Lake (Bedford County)
Franklin County C/C
261 Franklin St.
Rocky Mount, VA 24151
540/483-9542
www.franklincounty.org
Boones Mill (258)
Ferrum (1,514)
Forest (5,624)
Rocky Mount (4,404)

Virginia Beach (Virginia Beach Independent City)
Daily Press (D)
7505 Warwick Blvd.
Newport News, VA 23607
757/247-4600
www.dailypress.com

Virginia Beach C/C
2101 Parks Ave., Suite 500
Virginia Beach, VA 23451
757/437-4700

Hampton Roads C/C
420 Bank St.
Norfolk, VA 23501
757/622-2312
www.hamptonroadschamber.com
Virginia Beach (430,385)

Williamsburg (Williamsburg Independent City)
Virginia Gazette (D)
216 Ironbound Rd.
Williamsburg, VA 23188
757/220-1736, 800/944-6908
www.vagazette.com

Williamsburg Area CVB
421 N. Boundary St.
Williamsburg, VA 23187
757/253-0192
www.williamsburgcc.com
Williamsburg (12,922)

VERMONT

Burlington (Chittenden County)
Burlington Free Press (D)
191 College St.
Burlington, VT 05402
802/863-3441
www.burlingtonfreepress.com

Lake Champlain C/C
60 Main St., Suite 100
Burlington, VT 05401
802/863-3489
www.vermont.org
Bolton (985)
Burlington (39,466)
Charlotte (3,641)
Colchester (17,167)
Essex (18,896)
Essex Junction village (8,641)
Hinesburg (4,436)
Huntington (1,942)
Jericho (5,063)
Milton (9,906)
Milton village (1,564)
Richmond (4,112)
St. George (707)
Shelburne (6,953)
South Burlington (15,870)
Underhill (3,007)
Westford (2,106)
Williston (8,178)
Winooski (6,469)

St. Jay–Northeast Kingdom (Caledonia County)
Caledonian-Record (D)
190 Federal St.
St. Johnsbury, VT 05819
802/748-8121
www.caledonianrecord.com

Northeast Kingdom C/C
357 Western Ave.
St. Johnsbury, VT 05819
802/748-3678
www.nekchamber.com
Barnet (1,445)
Burke (1,440)
Danville (2,067)
Groton (903)
Hardwick (3,139)
Kirby (408)
Lyndon (5,572)
Lyndonville (1,301)
Newark (416)
Peacham (631)
Ryegate (1,109)
St. Johnsbury (7,523)
Sheffield (541)
Stannard (160)
Sutton (895)
Walden (701)
Waterford (1,282)
West Burke (361)
Wheelock (568)

Woodstock (Windsor County)
Vermont Standard (C)
Rte. 4, Box 88
Woodstock, VT 05091
802/457-1313

White River Junction C/C
P.O. Box 697
White River Junction, VT 05001
802/295-6200

Upper Valley Bi-State Regional C/C
P.O. Box 697
White River Junction, VT 05001
802/295-6200
www.uppervalleychamber.com

Woodstock Area C/C
18 Central St.
Woodstock, VT 05091
802/457-3555
www.vtliving.com/towns/woodstock

- Andover (382)
- Baltimore (204)
- Barnard (850)
- Bethel (1,887)
- Bridgewater (1,015)
- Cavendish (1,500)
- Chester (2,786)
- Hartford (9,391)
- Hartland (3,440)
- Ludlow (2,569)
- Norwich (3,187)
- Perkinsville (152)
- Plymouth (419)
- Pomfret (855)
- Reading (605)
- Rochester (1,208)
- Royalton (2,735)
- Sharon (1,402)
- Springfield (9,375)
- Stockbridge (586)
- Weathersfield (2,740)
- West Windsor (915)
- Weston (488)
- White River Junction (31,011)
- Windsor (3,540)
- Woodstock (3,111)

WASHINGTON

Anacortes (Skagit County)
Anacortes American (C)
901 6th St.
Anacortes, WA 98221
360/293-3122
www.goanacortes.com

Anacortes C/C
819 Commercial
Anacortes, WA 98221
360/293-7911
www.anacortes.org

- Anacortes (13,903)
- Burlington (5,782)
- Concrete (777)
- Hamilton (238)
- La Conner (747)
- Lyman (319)
- Mount Vernon (22,059)
- Sedro–Woolley (7,506)
- Shelter Bay (1,069)
- Snee Oosh (302)
- Swinomish Village (563)

Bellingham (Whatcom County)
Bellingham Herald (D)
1155 N. State St.
Bellingham, WA 98225
360/676-2600
www.bellinghamherald.com

Bellingham–Whatcom C/C
1435 Railroad Ave.
Bellingham, WA 98225
360/734-1330
www.bellingham.com

- Bellingham (61,043)
- Birch Bay (2,656)
- Blaine (3,267)
- Everson (1,880)
- Ferndale (7,102)
- Lynden (7,943)
- Marietta–Alderwood (2,766)
- Nooksack (884)
- Sudden Valley (2,615)
- Sumas (780)

Chewelah (Stevens County)
Chewelah C/C
P.O. Box 94
Chewelah, WA 99109
509/935-8991
www.chewelah.org

- Chewelah (2,189)
- Colville (4,976)
- Kettle Falls (1,537)
- Marcus (118)
- Northport (333)
- Springdale (283)

Port Angeles–Sequim (Clallam County)
Peninsula Daily News (D)
305 W. First St.
Port Angeles, WA 98362
360/452-2345, 800/826-7714
www.peninsuladailynews.com

Sequim–Dungeness Valley C/C
1192 E. Washington
Sequim, WA 98382
360/683-6197
www.cityofsequim.com

Port Angeles C/C
121 E. Railroad Ave.
Port Angeles, WA 98362
360/452-2363, 877/456-8372
www.portangeles.org

- Forks (3,256)
- Neah Bay (916)
- Port Angeles (18,674)
- Port Angeles East (2,672)
- Sequim (4,138)

Port Townsend (Jefferson County)
Port Townsend/Jefferson County Leader (D)
226 Adams St.
Port Townsend, WA 98368
360/385-2900
www.ptleader.com

Port Townsend C/C
2437 E. Sims Way
Port Townsend, WA 98368
360/385-2722
www.ptchamber.org
Hadlock–Irondale (2,742)
Port Townsend (8,727)

San Juan Islands (San Juan County)
Journal of the San Juan Islands (C)
580 Guard St.
Friday Harbor, WA 98250
360/378-5696
www.sanjuanjournal.com

San Juan Island C/C
Box 98
Friday Harbor, WA 98250
360/378-5240
www.sanjuanisland.org
Friday Harbor (1,747)

Wenatchee (Chelan County)
Wenatchee World (D)
P.O. Box 1511
Wenatchee, WA 98807
509/662-2904
www.wenworld.com

Wenatchee C/C
300 S. Columbia
Wenatchee, WA 98807
509/662-2116
www.wenatchee.org
Cashmere (2,771)
Chelan (3,455)
Entiat (561)
Leavenworth (2,091)
South Wenatchee (1,207)
Sunnyslope (1,907)
Wenatchee (23,837)
West Wenatchee (2,220)

Whidbey Island (Island County)
Whidbey News-Times (D)
800 SE Barrington Dr.
Oak Harbor, WA 98277
360/675-6611
www.whidbeynewstimes.com

Central Whidbey C/C
P.O. Box 152
Coupeville, WA 98239
360/678-5434
www.whidbey.com/coup

Greater Oak Harbor C/C
5506 Hwy. 20
Oak Harbor, WA 98277
360/675-3535
www.oakharborchamber.org
Ault Field (3,795)
Clinton (1,564)
Coupeville (1,631)
Freeland (1,278)
Langley (1,033)
Oak Harbor (19,356)

WISCONSIN

Door Peninsula (Door County)
Door County Advocate (D)
233 N. Third Ave.
Sturgeon Bay, WI 54235
920/743-3321
www.doorcountyadvocate.com

Door County C/C
1015 Green Bay Rd.
Sturgeon Bay, WI 54235
920/743-4456, 800/527-3529
www.doorcountyvacations.com
Egg Harbor (200)
Ephraim (247)
Forestville (466)
Sister Bay (765)
Sturgeon Bay (9,348)

Eagle River–Woodruff (Vilas County)
Vilas County News-Review (C)
346 W. Division St.
Eagle River, WI 54521
715/479-4421
www.vilascountynewsreview.com

Vilas County C/C
300 Court St.
Eagle River, WI 54521
715/479-3649
www.vilas.org
Eagle River (1,607)
Lac du Flambeau (1,423)

Madison (Dane County)
Capital Times (D)
1901 Fish Hatchery Rd.
Madison, WI 53708
608/252-6400
www.madison.com/captimes

Greater Madison C/C
615 E. Washington Ave.
Madison, WI 53701
608/256-8348
www.greatermadisonchamber.com

- Belleville (1,575)
- Black Earth (1,341)
- Blue Mounds (578)
- Brooklyn (434)
- Cambridge (988)
- Cottage Grove (2,473)
- Cross Plains (3,058)
- Dane (730)
- De Forest (6,262)
- Deerfield (1,740)
- Fitchburg (17,954)
- Madison (197,630)
- Maple Bluff (1,278)
- Marshall (2,743)
- Mazomanie (1,400)
- McFarland (5,724)
- Middleton (14,369)
- Monona (8,329)
- Mount Horeb (4,699)
- Oregon (6,220)
- Rockdale (234)
- Shorewood Hills (1,578)
- Stoughton (10,621)
- Sun Prairie (17,825)
- Verona (5,993)
- Waunakee (7,717)
- Windsor (2,182)

WEST VIRGINIA

Berkeley Springs (Morgan County)
The Morgan Messenger (C)
P.O. Box 567
Berkeley Springs, WV 25411
507/249-3130
www.morganmessenger.com

Berkeley Springs–Morgan County C/C
127 Fairfax St.
Berkeley Springs, WV 25411
304/258-3738
www.berkeleysprings.com/chamber

- Bath (Berkeley Springs) (652)
- Paw Paw (517)

Charles Town–Shepherdstown (Jefferson County)
Spirit of Jefferson-Advocate (C)
210 N. George St.
Charles Town, WV 25414
304/725-2046

Jefferson County C/C
201 Frontage Rd.
Charles Town, WV 25414
304/725-2055, 800/624-0577
www.jeffersoncounty.com

- Bolivar (1,009)
- Charles Town (3,012)
- Corporation of Ranson (2,890)
- Harpers Ferry (336)
- Shepherdstown (1,147)

WYOMING

Jackson Hole (Teton County)
Jackson Hole News & Guide (D)
1225 Maple Way
Jackson, WY 83001
307/733-2047
www.jacksonholenews.com

Jackson Hole C/C
555 E. Broadway #107B
Jackson, WY 83001
307/733-3316
www.jacksonholechamber.com

- Jackson (5,614)
- Rafter J Ranch (1,092)

INDEX

C

D

E

F

G

H

I

J

K

L

M

O

P

R

S

T

V